Learning UNIX®

Learning UNIX®

James Gardner

A Division of Macmillan Computer Publishing
11711 North College, Carmel, Indiana 46032 USA

Dedicated to all the folks at MKS—keep up the good work.

Trademarks

Publisher:
Richard Swadley

Publishing Manager:
Joseph Wikert

Managing Editor:
Neweleen Trebnik

Acquisitions Editor:
Linda Sanning

Development Editor:
Ella Davis

Production Editor:
Kathy Grider-Carlyle

Copy Editor:
Lori Cates

Cover Design:
Dan Armstrong

Cover Art:
Tim Amrhein

Illustrator:
Dennis Sheehan

Indexer:
Hilary J. Adams

Production Assistance:

Jeff Baker, Claudia Bell, Sandy Grieshop, Denny Hager, Betty Kish, Bob LaRoche, Sarah Leatherman, Laurie A. Lee, Julie Pavey, Howard Peirce, Cindy L. Phipps, Tad Ringo, Lisa A. Wilson

Overview

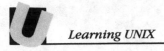

Part IV Appendixes

Contents

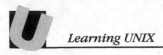

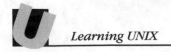
Part II Using the KornShell

Part III Command Manual Pages (Man Pages)

Part IV Appendixes

Foreword

Learning something new can start out being exciting, but it can become tedious if there is no way to experiment, investigate, practice, and eventually use the new information. With the superb combination of text and software that is available in this book, you have the best of all affordable and portable environments to learn and enjoy UNIX. *Learning UNIX*; this book couldn't have a better title!

I have been cheering the development of this book since the beginning of the project. Why? Because I love the UNIX world, and have the greatest respect for the work of Mortice Kern Systems (MKS—the developer of the UNIX tools for MS-DOS that are included with this book). Whenever I have to use a DOS system for any extended period, I install the MKS Toolkit, at least to maintain my sanity, if not for the convenience. It isn't just the MKS software that I like, it is the excellent documentation as well, much of which is the work of Jim Gardner. Now, in this book we see that Mr. Gardner is good at writing more than man pages (the standardized format of the on-line UNIX reference manual); he has brought a clarity to UNIX utilities that comes only from an intimate familiarity and a style that is appealing to anyone.

This book not only complements the many fine UNIX books published by SAMS, but stands on its own with honor.

Unlike MS-DOS, UNIX is more than a program loader. The UNIX utilities are what have made UNIX so popular. Because the utilities are written so that they can be tied together to perform complex tasks, the UNIX environment is synergistic; it is more than the sum of its parts. The best way to reach a level of competence with these tools is to use them separately and together to solve as many problems as you can. Once you become familiar with the UNIX KornShell, you will never want to see an MS-DOS prompt again. Once you begin solving your data and text input, output, and translation problems by using the UNIX utilities rather than writing programs in C (or some other programming language), you will begin to appreciate UNIX as I do.

Read this book; use these tools; and enjoy the flexible, configurable, extensible, and practical world of UNIX.

Ben Smith
Editor of *BYTE Magazine* and author of *UNIX Step-by-Step*
Peterborough, NH, 1991

Introduction

Learning UNIX guides you through a series of hands-on explorations that are geared toward helping you learn to use the UNIX operating system productively...but you don't need a UNIX machine to do the work. This book includes a software package that simulates UNIX software but runs on DOS or PC DOS on an ordinary IBM PC or IBM-compatible computer.

This book provides everything you need to make your DOS machine look and feel like UNIX. There are several benefits to this approach:

- If you are curious about UNIX, you can "test the waters" without having to spend time or money to get a UNIX machine.

- Sites that are planning to migrate to UNIX in whole or in part can prepare people for the transition using their current DOS systems.

- You can mix UNIX work with DOS work. For example, you can use your normal DOS applications in the usual way, but if you have a task that is easier to do with UNIX commands, you can use the UNIX-simulation software to get the job done.

In short, this book's approach gives you the power of UNIX with the availability and familiarity of DOS.

DOS and UNIX Comparisons

If you're already a DOS user, you'll be pleased with this book's constant cross-references between DOS and UNIX. This book shows you how UNIX ideas compare to DOS ideas: where the two systems are similar and where they are different.

1

The differences can be considerable or they can be subtle. This book will explain new concepts carefully and completely, so that you'll have no trouble with the large-scale differences between the systems...and it will guide you around the booby traps that lie in wait for DOS users who are unaware of technical subtleties.

A Level Playing Field

One of the greatest strengths of UNIX is its potential for customization. There are many different ways you can tailor the system to your needs and preferences. When you start using an existing UNIX system it probably won't work exactly the way that the manuals describe, because someone else may have adjusted the system to his or her tastes. This can bewilder newcomers.

You don't have to worry about such complications if you use the software that comes with this book. You won't have to cope with someone else's UNIX customizations, because you'll be on DOS. The software that comes with this book starts everyone with the same initial setup. I will certainly talk about customization and show how you can fine-tune the software to work the way you want; but that comes in later chapters, after you've gained some experience with the system. In this way, you can start your UNIX education on solid ground: a level playing field for everyone.

What This Book Deals With

Learning UNIX looks at the software that the majority of UNIX users work with on a daily basis. Unfortunately, there are important UNIX applications that are outside the scope of this book. For example, I don't discuss standard UNIX compilers or the wealth of other programming tools available on the system. Such software is an important part of UNIX, but only for a limited segment of the user population. This book concentrates on the features of UNIX that everyone can use.

The book therefore begins with several chapters discussing such basics as:

- How to log on and start working with UNIX

- How UNIX files are organized and used

- Popular commands for examining and manipulating files

- The many ways to combine simple commands to perform complex operations

- The vi screen editor, probably the most widely used text editor available under UNIX

The KornShell

After dealing with the fundamentals, you will be ready for the main event: several chapters discussing the *KornShell*. UNIX shells are programs that run other programs. To a large extent, your shell determines the "face" that UNIX presents to you. The shell is responsible for the system's look and feel.

Most UNIX systems provide several different shells, and therefore several different "faces." With a collection of shells to choose from, users can pick the one that best fits their needs and tastes. Because of limited time and space, this book looks at only one shell: the KornShell.

The KornShell is comparatively new, but its popularity is growing rapidly. It is a descendant of the Bourne Shell, one of the first UNIX shells and one that is still a favorite for many people. The chapters on the KornShell will show you the power and versatility of the shell, and suggest ways you can use it to best effect. The KornShell is your key to productivity with UNIX, and this book will make sure that you understand its vast potential.

Through Darkest UNIX, Armed Only with Man Pages

I've said that the purpose of this book is to guide you through a series of hands-on *explorations*. Exploring lets you determine how UNIX software can help *you*, in *your* work. Therefore the first two parts of this book lead you on a series of walks to show you the general lay of the land. The third part of the book provides you with the information you need to strike out on your own and truly explore.

This book provides the information in the form of *reference manual pages*, known in the UNIX world as *man pages*. The man pages tell you everything you need to know about the commands supplied with this package. They go far beyond the scope of the tutorial work in the first part of the book. Typically, the tutorial discusses the most useful or important features of commands, while the man pages give complete details on every feature.

Think of it this way: the tutorial is the guidebook, describing interesting things to investigate on your travels. The man pages are the detailed map, giving directions on how to get exactly where you want to go.

Man pages aren't intended for casual reading. They're intended to provide quick answers to urgent questions. Most give the facts as tersely as possible—the fewer words you have to read, the faster you can find out what you want to know. You may find this terseness intimidating at first, but you'll soon appreciate it. Nothing is more annoying to experienced users than fumbling through pages of verbiage in search of the one fact they need. Since you'll be an experienced user after you've worked through this book, I've written the man pages in a form that's well suited to your future needs.

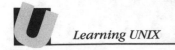

The Role of the MKS Tools

The software supplied with *Learning UNIX* was prepared by Mortice Kern Systems (MKS) for use with this book. This software package is called the *MKS Tools*.

The MKS Tools are derived from MKS Toolkit, a package of UNIX-like commands and utilities available for either DOS or OS/2. Most of the MKS Tools work exactly like their counterparts in MKS Toolkit. A few of the tools have been altered slightly so that they are appropriate in the educational context of this book but are less useful for real applications.

Installing the MKS Tools

Appendix G gives full instructions for installing the MKS Tools on your DOS system. Please read the appendix before starting the main body of this book, and install the software in the manner described.

Typographical Conventions

When the text says that you should enter Ctrl-A, you should hold down the Ctrl key and press the A key. The same applies for entering any other Ctrl sequence.

When the text says that you should enter Alt-A, you should hold down the Alt key and press the A key (while keeping Alt held down). The same applies for entering any other Alt sequence.

UNIX software often uses the notation ^A for Ctrl-A. The same applies for other sequences using the ^ (caret) sequence. For example, the vi screen editor displays ^L for the Ctrl-L character (the ASCII formfeed).

This book often contrasts UNIX commands with DOS commands that do the same sort of thing. To distinguish the two, DOS commands will be written in uppercase while UNIX commands will be written in lowercase. For example, I'll talk about the DOS MORE command and the UNIX more command. This is more than just a convention with UNIX commands; almost all UNIX commands *must* be entered in lowercase. (Of course, DOS lets you enter commands in both upper- and lowercase.)

How to Use This Book

To get the most out of the tutorial part of this book, you should be seated at a DOS system terminal, have MKS Tools installed, and try out the examples as the book discusses them. As an active participant, you'll find you grasp topics more quickly and more thoroughly.

I particularly encourage you to experiment with the commands that this book discusses. If you have a question about how the software behaves, try it out. Some of your best sessions may resemble two-way discussions with the system: you ask a question by trying something out, and the system gives an answer by providing the results of your experiment.

Of course if you're going to experiment, you have to use a bit of caution. Here are some tips:

- Don't experiment with files that you care about. Make copies first, then work with the copies.

- If you want to try a new command, read the man page first...and be sure to read the *whole* man page, not just the first little bit.

- UNIX commands are usually stingy with output. For example, most don't display any messages if they do what you ask them to do successfully; they only issue messages if something goes wrong. As a result, you shouldn't worry if you type in a command and the command displays no output. This usually means that the command worked the way you wanted it to work.

Doing the Exercises

Throughout the book I offer exercises for you to try. You must do some of these exercises at a terminal; others you can think about anytime.

Why are there exercises that aren't directly related to entering commands on a computer? Because UNIX is more than just a collection of useful software. It's a way of doing work, and a way of putting simple pieces together to form a sophisticated whole.

I want to teach you how to see problems the UNIX way. When you've developed this ability, you'll find your productivity with UNIX increases enormously. It may take you a little time to get on the same wavelength as UNIX, but when you do, I think you'll reap the benefits.

A Personal Word

No computing system is perfect, and UNIX has its share of exasperating idiosyn-crasies. When I was first exposed to UNIX ten years ago, I complained about its perverseness to anyone who would listen. UNIX software didn't make sense to me, it wasn't like anything I was familiar with, and it was full of cryptic features that seemed to be far more trouble than they could possibly be worth.

I got over the initial hurdles and reached a point where I could do what I wanted to do on the system; but I still grumbled. Sometimes it seemed like the designers of UNIX had intentionally gone out of their way to make the software obscure.

My work took me to other computing systems. Once in a while I would be attacking a major problem when it occurred to me, "This would be a lot easier to do on UNIX." I found I was searching through system documentation looking for commands that did the same jobs as UNIX commands; and if I couldn't find them, I'd feel cheated. What kind of a computer didn't have software like the `grep`, `diff`, or `find` commands of UNIX? How could anyone use such a system?

The more I worked with other systems, the more fondness I felt for UNIX.

Now I do most of my work on DOS, but I use MKS Toolkit because I want and need features that only UNIX offers. I don't have the patience to work without UNIX tools at my fingertips. Without them, I waste time on trivial details that just slow me down.

No one likes to be slowed down when there's a better way available. Despite its warts and wrinkles, I think UNIX is that better way. By the end of this book, I hope you'll agree with me.

Part I

Finding Your Way Around UNIX

## Chapter 1

Operating Systems

This chapter discusses what an operating system is and what it does for you. In particular, this chapter looks at DOS as an operating system, then compares it with UNIX. The intention is to clarify some general points about operating systems and to address misconceptions that often interfere with understanding what an operating system does and doesn't do.

After talking about operating systems in general, I zero in on UNIX itself. Like any other system in active use, UNIX is evolving to keep pace with the computing industry. I provide some background on the history of UNIX and look at directions for its future. In particular, I discuss POSIX and other efforts to standardize the behavior of UNIX-like systems. Finally, the chapter looks at the *UNIX philosophy*, some of the principles that guided the design of UNIX.

What Is an Operating System?

An *operating system* is software that supervises the ways you can use the resources of a computer. With some computers, the operating system is a single program; with others, it is a collection of programs that interact with each other in a variety of ways.

The operating system is part butler and part security guard. The sections that follow will look at both of these roles.

The Operating System as a Butler

As a butler, an operating system performs *services* that would be too complicated or dangerous for other programs to do for themselves. For example, when a program wants to write output to a file on disk, the program prepares the output, then calls on the operating system to perform the actual write operation. In this way, the operating system looks after all the complications of choosing an area on the disk that can hold the output, transmitting the data, keeping the disk organized, and so on. The program just says "Write this," and the operating system does the rest of the work.

Here are a few other services that operating systems typically provide.

- Executing a program: When you type in a command that you want to execute (like the command to sort the contents of a file), it's the operating system that does all the work of loading the program into memory and starting the program up.

- Keeping track of the time and date: Some types of hardware have a built-in clock, but even in these cases, the operating system sets the clock and reads the clock when a program wants to know the time.

- Performing most operations related to input, output, and disk organization, including maintaining the organization of files on disks, receiving input from a keyboard, and writing output to a display screen.

The Operating System as a Security Guard

As a security guard, the operating system *protects* the users and their data. For example, I just mentioned that the operating system performs all the actual write operations that a program does. In doing so, the operating system makes sure that data written to one file does not get written on top of data belonging to another file. The operating system keeps files from interfering with each other.

If several people can use the computer simultaneously, the operating system also keeps those users from interfering with each other. For example, it makes sure that they cannot read or write to each other's files unless they have permission. It also lets users have their fair share of the computer's resources—each gets a share of the memory, a share of the disk space, a share of the available processing time, and a share of any other facilities the computer has to offer. Some operating systems can deny certain users access to certain facilities. For example, a user may only be allowed to run a small collection of programs.

Operating systems often restrict computer access to authorized users. If you try to talk to such a system, it asks you to identify yourself with a name and a password. If you are not an authorized user, the operating system won't allow you to work on it.

The Layers of an Operating System

Conceptually, an operating system can be divided into three components:

- Utilities
- Shells
- The kernel

I'll discuss each of these in the sections that follow, but first I should warn you that the division between these components may not be clear-cut. Many systems are constructed in ways that hide the distinctions between these components; UNIX stands out as one of the few systems that use these distinctions to give users more flexibility.

Utilities

The *utilities* of an operating system are the standard commands and programs associated with the operating system. For example, the utilities of DOS are the commands that you expect to find on every DOS system: CHKDSK, DISKCOPY, BACKUP, and so on.

Utilities are the most visible part of the operating system. If you're a typical computer user, you use utilities many times a day, for copying or deleting files, for backing up your system, and for many other routine chores. The utilities are responsible for much of a system's look and feel.

At the same time, the utilities are the most changeable components of the operating system. Utilities are just programs; it's easy to write or buy different programs that provide similar services. For example, a computer bulletin board in my town offers nine replacement programs for the standard DOS SORT utility. The bulletin board advertises these programs as faster, more versatile, or easier to use than the SORT command that comes with the operating system. People who want to use one of these alternate SORT commands can get rid of the old SORT (or rename it) and put a new SORT in its place.

Shells

A shell is a program that runs other programs. On DOS, such a program is usually called a *command interpreter*. You're probably familiar with the standard DOS command interpreter COMMAND.COM.

To understand what a shell does, consider all the things that COMMAND.COM does on DOS when you type in a simple command like FORMAT A:

The process of executing this command involves the following steps:

1. The shell prompts you to input a command (frequently with the notation C>).

2. As you type in the command, the shell gives you the chance to correct typing mistakes by backspacing and using other methods.

3. After the Enter key is pressed, the shell analyzes the line to figure out that you want to execute the FORMAT command.

4. The shell must figure out how to execute the FORMAT command. To execute this command on DOS, the shell finds the file named FORMAT.COM and uses the contents of that file as the FORMAT program.

5. After FORMAT is finished, the shell prompts you to enter a new command.

The shell talks with you on behalf of the operating system. It reads the command lines that you type in, figures out what they mean, and does whatever is necessary to carry out those commands.

Often shells offer additional, more sophisticated facilities. For example, some shells have features that let you reduce the amount of typing you do:

- They may let you set up short forms for longer commands.

- They may keep a record of all the commands you've entered recently, and let you edit or re-execute those commands in some simple way.

- They may let you execute a collection of commands that have been stored in a file. In this way, you can set up a file containing any sequence of commands, then execute all the commands in the file with a single command line.

Some operating systems only recognize one shell. On such systems, there is only one piece of software that has the ability to run other programs—you can't use anything else. Operating systems like DOS and UNIX, however, do not tie you down to one shell. They make it possible for you to write or buy a different shell, and to use that shell in place of the standard one. On the local bulletin board I mentioned before, there are four shells offered as alternatives to the standard DOS shell.

The standard DOS shell is called COMMAND.COM, and I'll refer to it a lot in the chapters to come. There are several popular shells in wide use on UNIX systems, including the Bourne Shell, the C Shell, and the KornShell. This book concentrates on the KornShell because it's the standard shell for UNIX System V Version 4, and because I believe it is the most suitable shell for learning and using UNIX.

Built-in Commands

Usually when you execute a program, the shell has to find the file that contains that program, load the program into memory, then start executing the program. This can take a significant amount of time, especially on older computers with slow processors and disks.

To save time, some shells have *built-in commands*: commands that they can execute immediately without finding and reading an appropriate file. The most often used commands are frequently built into the shell to reduce the amount of delay in execution. For example, the familiar DIR, DEL, and TYPE commands of DOS are all built into DOS's COMMAND.COM so that they can be executed as quickly as possible.

The Kernel

The *kernel* is the collection of software that provides the basic capabilities of the operating system. Programs rely on the kernel for services and security. For example, if a program wants to write output it can perform a lot of operations to format the output and prepare it for delivery to the output device. But when this work has been done, the program must call the kernel to do the actual job of taking data from memory and making it appear on the monitor screen or in a disk file.

Most users have no direct contact with the kernel—its operations are as invisible as the wires that run through a wall to feed power to an electric outlet. However, the nature of the kernel affects everything that you do with your computer. The abilities of the kernel are probably the most significant factor in determining what programs can and can't do.

> **The Kernel and the Shell**
>   *Kernel* suggests the heart of a seed or nut, just as the kernel is the heart
> of an operating system.
>   *Shell* suggests the part of a nut that surrounds and hides the kernel.
> The shell is all that you can see until you crack open the nut. In the same
> way, a shell in an operating system stands between the kernel and the
> user; it's the part you can see.

Comparing UNIX and DOS

Now that I've discussed the basic components of operating systems in general,
I've laid the groundwork for comparing UNIX and DOS. At this point, the
comparisons will be made only in general forms. Later chapters will provide more
specific details.

Brief Histories

A brief look at the history of the two systems and the factors that influenced their
developments should help you understand the differences between the current
versions of UNIX and DOS.

UNIX

The first UNIX system was developed by AT&T Bell Laboratories of Murray Hill,
New Jersey, in the late 1960s. It was a research system, constructed to try out new
concepts of operating system design and to provide a handful of expert computer
scientists with a highly productive programming environment. It was not intended to be commercial, nor was it intended to be used outside Bell Labs. UNIX
contrasted with operating systems of that day in several ways:

- It was intended to be used by only a small number of people, unlike
  large commercial systems, which sometimes allowed hundreds of people
  to work simultaneously on the same machine.

- It assumed all its users were experienced professionals.

- It had few security provisions, because all its users were friends working for the same research group.

- It was intended as a system for developing new programs, unlike most other systems of the day, which were designed to run large-scale business programs day in and day out.

These factors made UNIX a programmer's dream. As a result, university Computer Science departments became interested in the system and AT&T made UNIX available to educational institutions for a nominal fee. Throughout the 1970s, UNIX use spread slowly. It proved to be popular in colleges and universities, where students and teachers appreciated the programming power and flexibility it gave them. Because of its popularity with students and because of its programming power, UNIX became the operating system of choice for many of the most enterprising programmers of that time. Graduates fresh out of school wanted to work on UNIX; programmers with adventurous ideas found they could produce programs more easily on UNIX than on other systems. As a result, many ambitious programs started life on UNIX and only later were transported to more mainstream operating systems.

During this time, AT&T upgraded the system often. For example, as more and more people began to use UNIX, security became a more important issue. Consequently, AT&T introduced new security features that brought UNIX more in line with what was available on other systems.

AT&T owns the rights to the UNIX name, but nothing prevents other companies from producing systems that look and act like UNIX. UNIX look-alikes began to appear in the late 1970s. The rise of personal computers in the early 1980s accelerated this trend—it was a boom time for tiny companies started by recent computer science graduates, and UNIX was often the system they wanted.

The majority of UNIX look-alikes were derived directly from versions of AT&T's UNIX code. Manufacturers licensed the code from AT&T, converted it to run on their own machines, and often added extra features to make the products more attractive. Because AT&T retained ownership of the UNIX name, other manufacturers gave their UNIX look-alikes other names—XENIX, AIX, UCOS, and HP/UA to name a few. There was a steady growth in the number of machines for which a UNIX-like operating system was available—some supported directly by AT&T and some supported by other vendors, usually based on AT&T's code. (A few UNIX look-alikes were written from scratch without using AT&T code as a starting point, either because the designers didn't want to pay AT&T licensing fees or because they thought starting from scratch would produce a better product.)

The machines on which UNIX originated were minicomputers, much more powerful than the microcomputers of the same era. Over the years, however, microcomputers have grown in speed and power. The current-generation micros are comparable to the original machines that ran UNIX. Thus, UNIX and UNIX look-alikes are quite at home on the microcomputers of today.

DOS

MS-DOS and PC DOS arrived on the scene in the early 1980s. Because DOS was constructed much later than UNIX, its programmers could build on existing experience with UNIX and borrow many UNIX features. DOS systems also owe much to CP/M, an operating system that ran on some of the earliest microcomputers. (Version 1.0 of DOS is based on CP/M, while later versions incorporate more UNIX-like concepts.)

DOS was designed specifically for IBM personal computers. Originally, these computers might have as little as 128K of memory. As a result, DOS had to be small because size was a major constraint. The designers had to economize, and in the process, many desirable features they might have borrowed from UNIX couldn't be incorporated into the system.

Over the years, PCs grew more powerful, with more memory and speed. Versions of DOS for such systems could be more comprehensive because they weren't as limited by memory and speed considerations. Thus DOS grew up to take advantage of new, more powerful machines.

Even so, DOS hasn't advanced to the current state of UNIX. UNIX began on machines comparable to modern micros; DOS began on much smaller machines. Those limited origins still have their effect on DOS's behavior. In my opinion, UNIX is much better equipped to cope with today's powerful PCs than DOS is.

The Multiuser System Versus the Single-User System

UNIX is a *multiuser* system. The design of UNIX anticipates the fact that several people will use the system, and that each person will have personal files he or she doesn't want to share with the other users. You can picture a multiuser system as an office where users have their own separate desks but also have access to some resources held in common. In an office, common resources might include the photocopier and the water cooler; in a multiuser system, they might include certain directories and the line printer.

DOS, on the other hand, is a *single-user* system. If you start up a standard DOS system, you are automatically given access to every file on the system. (DOS *hidden files* and *read-only* files are a little harder to access than normal files, but only a little. Making a file hidden or read-only can prevent accidents, but it doesn't prevent you from accessing those files if you really want to.)

File security is only one difference between multiuser systems and single-user systems. If you want to start using a multiuser system, you have to identify yourself so that the system knows which user you are. Thus UNIX users go through a *log-in* procedure where they tell the system their names and enter a password to prove they are who they claim to be. With standard DOS, you simply turn on the machine and start working; you don't have to identify yourself, because DOS has no facilities to distinguish among different people who may use the same machine.

Both DOS and UNIX provide facilities that let you customize the system to your personal needs. With standard DOS, however, the customizations affect everything you do with the machine. With UNIX, customizations made by one user need not affect other users. Typically, when you log in to a UNIX system, the system identifies who you are, then looks to see if you've asked to have any personal customizations in effect while you're using the computer. Those customizations stay in effect as long as you're working; if you *log out* and another user logs in, the system cleans away your customizations and checks for any customizations desired by the new user. Each user starts with a completely clean slate, unaffected by others who might use the system.

A multiuser system lets users set up their work sessions according to their tastes, without interfering with other users who share the same machine. A multiuser system makes it possible for you to set up private files that no one else can access, as well as public files that are available to all.

Multitasking Versus Single-Tasking

In the description of multiuser systems, I spoke as if one person uses the machine for a while, then the first person leaves and a new one comes in. But a UNIX system allows several people to use the same system simultaneously. This process is called *multitasking* because the system seems to perform several tasks at the same time.

DOS, on the other hand, is a *single-tasking* system. It can do only one thing at a time. A few special arrangements can make it look like DOS is doing several jobs simultaneously (e.g., the print queue makes it possible for you to start printing something, then go to do other work while material prints out), but these don't approach the versatility of true multitasking.

Software such as Microsoft Windows introduces a form of true multitasking to DOS. In essence, Windows and similar programs act like small operating systems working within DOS itself. They supervise the multitasking process using the technique described in the box titled *How Multitasking Works*.

UNIX's multitasking facilities are very versatile. Not only can several different users work with the system simultaneously, but a single user can actually run several different programs at the same time. It is common for a UNIX user to start a long job running, then work on a shorter job while waiting for the long job to finish. This is one reason why you can be more productive with UNIX than with a single-tasking system; you can do several things at once.

How Multitasking Works

Some types of hardware can indeed do several things at once because they contain multiple processors. The majority of computers, however, has only a single processor and can really only do one thing at a time.

Computers like this can still perform multitasking, because the processor is much faster than the many devices attached to the computer. For example, if a program is waiting for you to type in input, the processor will be (mostly) idle. Even if you are typing quickly, the processor is still idle most of the time. It can handle each input character in such a small fraction of a second that it spends most of its time waiting for you to enter the next character. The same is true when the computer is reading or writing to a disk—the disk is thousands of times faster than a typist, but it is still much slower than the processor itself. So the processor has a lot of idle time.

In a multitasking system, the processor doesn't waste this idle time. If the system is waiting for you to type in a character, it switches to work for someone else for a moment. After it has done some work for that person, it comes back to you to see if you've entered something yet. In other words, the operating system tries to keep the processor as busy as possible by doing a bit of work for one user, a bit for another, and so on. In many cases, the processor is so fast that you can't tell that it is working in this fragmented way.

Note that it is the operating system that tells the processor to switch from one program to another. The processor doesn't do so on its own. In the case of Microsoft Windows and other DOS products that simulate multitasking, Windows itself tells the processor to switch from one program to another. DOS does not run more than one program. It runs the single program Windows, which then goes on to run all the other programs.

Why You Should Investigate UNIX

Now that I've discussed a few of the features of UNIX and how they differ from those of DOS, it should be clearer why UNIX is worth investigating. Here's a quick checklist:

- UNIX makes it possible for you to share a system with other people without interfering with each other.

- Multitasking lets you do several things at once. If you start a long job, you aren't forced to wait until it is finished; you can work on something else in the meantime.

- UNIX is a *mature* system. It has been in use for thirty years, and it's gone through a thorough shakedown period. UNIX has had a lot of time to eliminate bugs and deficiencies. UNIX has also benefited from the rise of UNIX look-alikes—the pressure of competition has forced continuing improvements.

- A great deal of popular software is available on UNIX. Before the rise of personal computers, UNIX stood out as the favorite system for the development of leading-edge programs.

- Many commercial systems are particularly good at one class of jobs, but poor at others. Because UNIX is extremely customizable, you can stream-line it to do the work you do the most.

- You can find UNIX (or a UNIX look-alike) for almost any type of hard-ware. This makes it possible for you to use the same utilities on a wide variety of machines. Most other operating systems are *proprietary*, and only run on machines that come from a single manufacturer. DOS runs on clones as well as true IBM PCs, but it does not run on larger machines or on computers that do not use one of the family of microprocessing chips used in PCs.

With all these advantages going for it, UNIX has become a dominant force in the computing industry. Companies want to hire people with UNIX expertise. Software developers strive to offer their products on UNIX. Certainly, DOS is still more widely used than UNIX, but even DOS is under pressure to become more like UNIX and to offer the same powerful facilities that UNIX does. For all these reasons, I strongly believe that it's worth an investment of your time to see what UNIX can do for you.

The Different "Flavors" of UNIX

I've already mentioned that the market offers many products with the look and feel of UNIX. To help you distinguish among them, the sections that follow give encapsulated descriptions of some prominent UNIX-like products in use today.

AT&T System V

UNIX System V from AT&T is the preeminent UNIX system. As I noted earlier, AT&T owns the UNIX name, and therefore its product is the only one that can actually use the name. UNIX System V is available on many types of hardware and has gone through several revisions since the first System V release (in the mid-1980s).

Berkeley BSD

Berkeley UNIX BSD (short for *Berkeley Software Distribution*) is an interesting anomaly. In the mid-1970s the University of California at Berkeley used AT&T's UNIX extensively, but felt that they could improve on it. With AT&T's permission, they brought out a set of modifications to the AT&T UNIX system, which Berkeley then sold to interested parties (especially colleges and universities).

AT&T's UNIX continued to evolve and so did Berkeley's modifications, often in completely different directions. The systems are still recognizably UNIX, but they differ in utilities, shells, and especially the kernel. Many heated backroom arguments arise over which is "better," AT&T's UNIX or Berkeley's.

But Berkeley's UNIX is still distributed as a set of modifications to AT&T's UNIX. Sites must purchase a UNIX license from AT&T before they can use Berkeley's product. For this reason, AT&T lets Berkeley use the name UNIX, even though the two systems differ in many respects.

Others

Many other vendors offer versions of UNIX (based on some release of AT&T UNIX) or versions of UNIX-like software. These go by such names as XENIX, HP/UX, AIX, Ultrix, and many more.

Most vendors attempt to provide compatibility with true UNIX, plus additional features that will make their products more attractive.

The Promise of Standards

There are many operating systems based on UNIX. While there are strong similarities between these packages, there are also substantial differences. In recent years, various organizations have worked to establish *standards* for all

UNIX-like systems, to ensure a level of uniformity among all the look-alikes. In the sections that follow, you will see the standards that are being written, why they're being written, and how they may affect the future of UNIX.

POSIX

POSIX is the umbrella name for a family of standards being developed under the auspices of the *IEEE* (the *Institute of Electrical and Electronics Engineers*). The following list describes the most important members of this family:

- **POSIX.1** dictates the services to be provided by the kernel.

- **POSIX.2** describes the utilities, and the features that must be offered by any shell.

- **POSIX.3** describes facilities for testing POSIX systems.

- **POSIX.4** specifies the *real-time* computing services that the kernel can offer. (Normally, programs don't need to keep track of time—they just run as fast as possible. However, programs that control moving objects in the real world—robots and other machines—must be able to keep track of time and synchronize their actions with the objects they control. This process can be very difficult and requires a variety of special services from the operational system.)

There are other standards in the family, each describing a separate aspect of the operating system and related software. At the time of this writing, POSIX.1 is finalized and officially adopted, while POSIX.2 is close to completion. Other standards in the family are still under development and will take a few more years before they are finished.

The POSIX.1 standard has been endorsed by the United States Federal Government, as FIPS (Federal Information Processing Systems) Standard 151. The computing purchases of all branches of government must conform to this standard. If any federal agency wants to buy a different type of system, it needs special congressional approval. In all likelihood, the other POSIX standards will also become FIPS standards as they are finalized. Traditionally, many other governments and corporations follow the U.S. government's lead. Thus, with the backing of the U.S. Government and of a large number of companies throughout the computing industry, POSIX will have a dominant effect on the shape of UNIX in years to come.

SVID

POSIX is not the only candidate for the position of "UNIX standard." AT&T created UNIX, and it is not eager to see outside organizations dictate rules for UNIX systems. AT&T has therefore come out with its own UNIX standard, called UNIX *SVID* (System V Interface Definition).

SVID has the advantage of already being finished, because it is primarily a description of the existing UNIX System V. In this respect, it is better off than POSIX, which is still under development. However, SVID only describes the AT&T UNIX System V and does not include several features available on UNIX look-alike systems.

SVID and POSIX currently differ on numerous points. AT&T has said that the SVID standard will be modified to conform to POSIX standards as they are finalized. Therefore, SVID will move toward POSIX in the long run. In the short term, however, SVID will be influential because of AT&T's prominence in the UNIX world.

X/OPEN

X/OPEN is a European standard for UNIX-like systems, closely related to POSIX. X/OPEN has been instrumental in internationalizing UNIX-like software by introducing features to accommodate differences in languages and other local conventions. Internationalization affects such things as:

- The standard character set used in text files—different languages use different alphabets and punctuation characters.

- The order in which characters are sorted—"alphabetical order" varies from country to country.

- The language in which the operating system displays diagnostic messages.

- The way the system writes numeric values—for example, some cultures use a period as a decimal point (as in 3.14159) while others use a comma (3,14159).

- The way monetary values are displayed.

- The formats of dates and times.

POSIX already incorporates many of the facilities originally designed for the X/OPEN standard, just as X/OPEN incorporates POSIX features. These two standards probably will strive to match each other as time goes on.

Portability

You might wonder why it's so valuable to create a standard for UNIX-like systems. One of the most important reasons is that standards ensure *portability*.

Which Is the "Standard" Standard?

If you're confused by having at least three different documents vying to be the "standard" standard for UNIX, you're not the only one. Several large groups are jostling for position in the UNIX market at present, and who gets to write the standard is one issue of contention. In the long run, I believe POSIX will become *the* UNIX standard; but because POSIX is still under development, AT&T and others are trying to use their own standards to affect the way that POSIX unfolds. The balance of power seems to shift from week to week, providing much amusement for the computing industry, even in the off-season for baseball.

Porting is the process of taking a program that runs on one type of computer and getting it to work on another type. This can be a difficult job, especially if the computers have different hardware and different operating systems. On the other hand, if the computers are running the same operating system (or similar operating systems) and the program does not rely on idiosyncrasies of the hardware, porting can be easy.

Standardizing the behavior of UNIX-like operating systems is the first step in simplifying the job of porting. If programmers know that all UNIX-like systems offer a standard set of features, programmers can use those features (and only those features) in the applications they write. By restricting themselves to the features that are guaranteed to be available on all UNIX look-alikes, applications become easier to port.

Portability is important for several reasons:

- If you upgrade to a new computer, you usually want to take all your favorite programs with you to the new machine. This is particularly important for companies that have a lot of programs for bookkeeping, billing, production, and so on. The companies don't want to rewrite all their software just because they bought a new machine. Programs should last longer than hardware.

- Many companies use many different types of computers. For example, big jobs may run on a large computer, while other work is done on PCs. Ideally, you'd like to be able to use the same programs on each computer you own, so that you don't have to learn a lot of different programs and so that you don't get confused as you switch from system to system.

- Any company that writes and sells programs is pleased when it can sell the same program to people on a wide variety of systems.

Porting also applies to data: you can ship data from one machine to another. This process is easy if the systems use the same data formats. Standards can ensure that different systems keep the same kind of data in the same formats, so that you don't have to reformat when data goes from one computer to another.

Familiarity

Familiarity is another benefit of standardization. Learn one UNIX-like system, and you'll be familiar with all such systems. There may still be some variations— almost every software manufacturer adds features to its package, to make the package a better buy than its competitor's package. But for the most part, familiarity with one UNIX-like system carries over to the other UNIX-like systems.

An Introduction to the UNIX Philosophy

As I discussed how different UNIX look-alikes can be, you might have wondered how they can all be recognized as UNIX-like systems. The common thread that draws them all together is the UNIX *philosophy*: the design principles that dictated the original form of UNIX and have continued to influence UNIX-like systems through the years. The sections that follow look at some of these design principles and how they are reflected in UNIX-like systems.

Reducing User Effort

UNIX software goes to great lengths to reduce the amount of effort a user needs to expend to do work. For example, UNIX utilities have been streamlined in many ways to reduce the number of keystrokes required to type in the command line:

- Command names are as short as possible. For example, the UNIX command for copying files is cp, not COPY (as in DOS), and the UNIX command for moving files is mv, not MOVE. (Dropping the vowels from a command name is a favorite UNIX trick.)

- Most command line options are only a single character long.

- Short forms can be used in many parts of the command line. For example, UNIX lets you represent a large collection of file names with a single symbol. I'll talk about this feature in the section on *glob constructs* in Chapter 4.

UNIX commands are as terse as possible, and therefore they can be hard to understand at first glance. The commands often look like just a snarl of characters. Don't be intimidated by this. Reading the commands can be difficult, but when you have learned what the commands do, using them is easy.

The underlying rationale is that you only have to *learn* a command once, but you have to *use* it frequently over a long period of time. UNIX commands may take longer to learn, but they're much faster to use after you've done so; it's a short-term sacrifice for a long-term gain. You probably won't find UNIX very user-friendly when you first start using it. Like most friendships, your esteem for UNIX has to build with time.

Combining Small Tools into Larger Ones

Life would be simple if there were a specific utility for every job you could possibly want to do. If that were true, you'd only have to execute one command for any given job. However, there's a practical limit to how many utilities an operating system can provide, not to mention the limit on the number of utilities that a person can learn how to use.

The number of utilities that an operating system can reasonably provide is therefore relatively small—a few hundred commands at most. But those commands must cover the complete spectrum of jobs that people want to do with their computer. Any operating system's designers must therefore choose a set of utilities that is small but can do all the necessary jobs.

The UNIX approach is to make utilities that are very basic and simple, but can be combined to do more complex jobs. As you'll see in later chapters, UNIX offers a multitude of ways commands can be combined:

- In *pipelines*, where the output of one command is input to the next.

- With *command substitution*, where the output of one command is used to construct a new command line.

- With *command programming constructs*, which allow you to write "programs" with statements that are operating system commands.

All of these combination methods (and more) will be thoroughly covered in later chapters.

Customization

I've already mentioned several times that UNIX lets you customize the system and your work sessions with the system. But why is customization really an advantage?

To give you an idea of the benefits of customization, let's look at a job that many people do frequently: backing up the hard disk on diskettes. If you use the UNIX-like MKS Tools commands on DOS, the command line

```
find c:/ -mtime -7 ¦ tar -cvf a:archive -
```

finds all the files on disk C that you have changed in the past week and backs them up to the disk in drive A. You probably think the line would be difficult to remember, but the beauty of UNIX customization is that you don't *have* to remember it. Instead, you might set up the name backup to be a synonym or *alias* for the command. After you've done that, you can just type the command

```
backup
```

and the system will run the complicated command line for you.

You might be asking why the system doesn't just supply a standard backup command instead of forcing you to set up an alias. The answer is that different people can choose to back up their system in different ways. The preceding command backs up anything that has changed in the last week. But you might want to back up on a daily basis instead of a weekly basis, or you may only want to back up certain files. If the system lets you define your own backup command, you can customize it to suit your work habits. If you have to use some standard backup command, you have less flexibility.

Pipes

In the last section I discussed the command line

```
find c:/ -mtime -7 ¦ tar -cvf a:archive -
```

This line is actually a combination of two commands: the find command locates files that have a certain property, and the tar command writes out a set of files to drive a:. The two commands are joined by the *pipe* symbol (¦, also called the *or-bar*, *stick*, or *vertical bar*). The pipe symbol takes the normal output of one command and submits it as input to another command. In the preceding example, it takes the list of files that find writes out and submits that list as input to tar. The tar command then backs up all the files in the list. This is a typical example of using pipes to combine commands, a very frequent operation on UNIX.

You may already be familiar with *pipes*, because they're also available on DOS. This is an example of the influence that UNIX had on the design of DOS. From experience with UNIX, the DOS designers knew that pipes were useful, so they implemented pipes under DOS.

Chapter Review

An operating system is software that supervises the ways you can use the resources of a computer. It provides services and enforces security. Operating systems have three layers:

- The utilities, a set of commands and programs that can perform standard tasks like printing or copying files

- The shells, programs that let you invoke other programs

- The kernel, the underlying software that supports all the other software that the computer runs

The UNIX operating system was developed for use on minicomputers by AT&T in the late 1960s. It spread slowly, primarily through colleges and universities. Because modern microcomputers are comparable to those old minicomputers, UNIX is well suited to the current generation of micros. DOS, by contrast, started on much smaller machines and has not yet caught up with recent hardware enhancements.

UNIX is a multiuser system, designed to accommodate the needs of many people using the same machine. It is also a multitasking system, so that several people can use the same machine simultaneously.

There are many UNIX look-alikes on the market today, with names like Berkeley UNIX BSD, XENIX, AIX, and so on. The POSIX family of standards and other standards (SVID, X/OPEN) will ensure that these different products stay in step with each other, which will in turn ensure portability of software and data.

UNIX was designed in accordance with several philosophical principles including:

- Giving high priority to reducing user effort

- Providing a collection of simple commands, plus a variety of ways to combine those commands to perform more complex tasks (for example pipes, which take the output from one command and send it as input to another command)

- Allowing users to customize their dealings with the system

Exercises

1. Make a list of the ten most common command lines you type in the course of a day. Analyze this list. Are any of these command lines particularly difficult to type? Are there any sequences of commands that you frequently type in a row?

2. Are there any commands that you find you have to look up in the manual almost every time you use them? If so, what is it about the command that you have to look up?

3. What are the five most time-consuming jobs you have to do with the computer on a regular basis? With any of these jobs, is there anywhere that it would save time to substitute a single command in place of a commonly used sequence of commands?

4. What are the five most common typing mistakes you make when you're typing in a command line? Can you think of a way that operating system software could reduce the probability of you making those mistakes?

## Chapter 2

Getting Started: Hello World

This chapter shows you how to start up the MKS Tools software that comes with this book and how to enter a few simple commands (assuming that you've already installed the software by following the instructions in Appendix G). The goal is to make you feel at home with the software and to discuss several basic principles about UNIX software.

Man Pages: The First Step

In UNIX parlance, the reference manual descriptions for commands are called *man pages* (short for *manual pages*). For example, the description of the cp command is usually called the cp man page, even if this documentation is actually several pages long.

Part III of this book provides man pages for each of the MKS Tools commands in the *Learning UNIX* software package. These man pages are the key to developing a full appreciation of UNIX. They tell you everything you need to know about the commands and how to use them.

Man pages are not light reading. UNIX documentation is usually written as tersely as possible—the fewer words you have to read, the faster you can find answers to your questions. As a UNIX novice, you may find the man pages intimidating at first. Ultimately, however, you'll have to tackle the man pages to find out more about the commands you want to use. Here's a strategy for familiarizing yourself with the man pages, with a minimum of confusion and aggravation:

1. Read the introduction to Part III, titled *How to Read a Man Page*. You can read this any time you want (for example, right now).

2. As you work through the book, keep track of the commands it discusses. (The Chapter Review at the end of each chapter summarizes the commands that the chapter has discussed.) Find the man page for each of these commands and read it.

3. Don't worry if the man page overwhelms you the first time you read it. The man page may be dealing with concepts that haven't yet been covered by the book. By the time you finish everything else, however, you should be able to work through the man pages with a fuller understanding.

4. As you read a man page, write down any questions you may have about what you read. If you can't find answers to your questions in the man page (or in other parts of this book), experiment with the commands to find out what you want to know. If you don't mind writing in books, write down what you find out on the man page itself, so the answer will be there if you want to look it up again.

Logging In

The first step to using a UNIX system is to *log in* to the system. As mentioned in Chapter 1, there are two steps to the log-in process:

- Telling the computer who you are
- Proving your identity by entering your personal password

I'll walk you through this process now. You should be seated at a PC, following along as I discuss each step in order to get practice with the software. Remember, you should already have the software installed on your machine; if not, turn now to Appendix G and follow the installation procedure described there.

Interrogate the System

As you work through UNIX sessions in this chapter and the ones to follow, don't just follow the steps mechanically. Think about what you're doing and "interrogate" the system. You should ask questions that occur to you as you go along. Ask why UNIX requires you to do some things but not others. Ask why the designers chose a particular approach to a problem. Write down these questions and try to find answers, either from this book, from experienced UNIX users, or by experimenting with the software. I promise that you'll learn faster and more comprehensively with this approach (and you'll be less likely to fall asleep at the keyboard).

The Log-in Procedure

To start the MKS Tools, enter the following commands in response to the DOS C> prompt:

```
cd \lu
lu
```

The first command goes to the directory that holds the UNIX simulation software. The second command starts the MKS Tools.

The MKS Tools program issues the message

```
login:
```

This is what you will see when you begin work on a normal UNIX system. In response to this message, enter your *log-in name* (also known as your *userid*). The installation process asked you to choose a log-in name. Type that name now, and press Enter when you're finished.

In a typical log-in procedure, the system would next display

```
Password:
```

asking you to enter your password. But you're a new user, so you don't have a password yet. You'll see how to create a password for yourself later in this chapter.

This is all you have to do to log in to a UNIX system. In a moment, you'll see the system display a $ to prompt you to enter your first command.

What Are You Talking To?

I said that "the system" prompts you to enter your first command. In fact, it's the shell that does the prompting. The log-in procedure automatically starts up the shell program to interact with you: to read the commands you enter, to find the programs that will carry out those commands, and to start those programs running.

Entering a Command

Now that you've logged in successfully, it's time to enter your first UNIX command. Type in the following:

```
echo Hello
```

and press Enter. (Make sure that echo is in lowercase.) You'll see that the system types back

```
Hello
```

on the display screen.

This is all that the UNIX echo command does: it displays everything else that appears on the command line. As another example, try:

```
echo Hello there!
```

You'll see that the system displays

```
Hello there!
```

echo is a simple command, so simple that you may think it's useless. However, future chapters will show that echo has many different uses—you'll be seeing it a lot.

Correcting Typing Mistakes

Before I discuss echo in more detail, I should tell you how to correct any typing mistakes you make as you enter commands to the KornShell.

Backspacing

As you might expect, pressing the *Backspace* key erases the character immediately before the cursor. Try it by typing in

```
echox
```

then backspacing to erase the x.

Every time you press the Backspace key, another character is erased. You can backspace all the way to the beginning of the current line if you want, but you can't backspace any farther.

Erasing an Entire Line

Pressing the Esc key erases the entire line . . . sort of. To see what I mean, type in some nonsense like

```
xxx
```

and then press Esc (don't press Enter first). You'll see the display change to

```
xxx\
```

and then the cursor jumps down to the next line on the screen. What does this mean? It means that the line with the \ on the end of it no longer counts. In effect, it's been erased, even though it still appears on the screen. If you now type a command like

```
echo hi
```

and press Enter, you'll see

```
hi
```

appear on the screen. The KornShell discards the xxx that you typed first, and executes the echo command that you typed afterward.

You might wonder why the shell doesn't make the xxx line disappear on the screen when you erase it with Esc. There are some technical reasons for this related to the origins of UNIX. In those old days, some terminals weren't able to delete lines, particularly typewriter terminals that displayed everything on paper. However, there's also a philosophical reason for not making the line disappear. Suppose you go to a lot of trouble to enter a complicated command line, but decide to delete the line when you're near the end. You'll find it useful to be able to see the original line, so that you can remember what you did right and correct what you did wrong. The shell leaves the original line on the screen so that you don't have to reconstruct it again from memory.

Editing Modes

In Chapter 9, you'll see how editing modes can change the behavior of the Esc key. For the time being, however, Esc is the line-erase key.

Making Errors

What would have happened if you had tried to execute the original

```
xxx
```

line? Try it and see. Type in the line and press Enter. You'll see that the shell displays the following message:

```
xxx: not found
```

This means that the shell could not find any appropriate program named xxx. Because the shell couldn't find the program, it couldn't execute the command.

The Importance of Lowercase

The first time you typed in the echo command, I told you to make sure that echo was in lowercase. The reason is that UNIX systems are *case-sensitive*: they pay attention to the case of all letters in all command lines, whether the letters are used in the command name itself or in other parts of the command line. Try entering

```
ECHO Hello
```

You'll get the message

```
ECHO: not found
```

because ECHO is not the same as echo.

MKS Tools Are Forgiving

Because you are working with the MKS Tools rather than a true UNIX system, you can get away with typing some commands in uppercase. However, there's no reason to do this; lowercase is the natural alphabet for UNIX, and you should get used to it now.

More About *echo*

Now that I've covered the basics of entering UNIX commands, let's go back to the command I started with: echo. As you saw, the command consists of the word echo, followed by the words you want echo to display. These words are called the *arguments* of the command. For example, in

```
echo Hello there!
```

the arguments are Hello and there!.

In most UNIX commands, arguments are separated by *whitespace*. Whitespace is made up of any number of blank characters or tab characters. For example, see what happens if you put extra blank characters between arguments, as in

```
echo   Hello      there!
```

You'll see that echo displays

```
Hello there!
```

the same way it did before. When the shell executes echo, it puts exactly one blank space between each pair of arguments, no matter how much whitespace the original command line contained. This is typical of all UNIX commands: the amount of whitespace you use to separate arguments doesn't affect the behavior of the command.

But, you might be saying, what happens if you really want to put a lot of whitespace between your arguments? You can get this by using double quotation marks, as in

```
echo "Hello      there!"
```

The output of this command is

```
Hello      there!
```

By using double quotation marks, you make one big argument that has a lot of blanks in the middle. When echo displays this argument, it displays the blanks as part of the argument.

You can also use single quotation marks (apostrophes), as in

```
echo 'Hello      there!'
```

The effect is the same in this case. Try it.

echo (and many other UNIX commands) can accept a huge number of arguments. In MKS Tools, the command line for echo can be up to 8192 characters long. For reasons that you'll see later, it's important for UNIX commands to be able to accept very long command lines. In contrast, DOS usually imposes a maximum of 127 characters on any command line.

The DOS ECHO **Command**

You may be aware that DOS has an ECHO command of its own. (Remember that I'm writing DOS commands in uppercase and UNIX ones in lowercase, so ECHO is the DOS command and echo is the UNIX one.) ECHO can display output in the same way that echo does, because DOS borrowed its ECHO command from UNIX. However, there are some differences between the two commands. For example, the DOS version preserves the number of blanks between arguments. The output of

```
ECHO Hello    there!
```

is

```
Hello    there!
```

You'll see other differences between the two commands as you examine more sophisticated features of UNIX.

Choosing Your Password

Now that you've gained some familiarity with entering commands, there's an important administrative job that you should do while you're still at the terminal: you should choose your password.

When you signed on at the beginning of this chapter, you had no password. In the interest of security, you should choose a password as soon as possible so that other people can't sign on under your name. (Even if you aren't concerned about security right now, thinking about it is a worthwhile exercise. If and when you begin working on a real UNIX system, you owe it to yourself and other users to take sensible precautions.)

What sort of password should you choose? Here are a few guidelines:

- A UNIX log-in password can consist of any sequence of zero or more characters. It can contain blanks, punctuation characters, and other characters you might think of as unusual. Uppercase letters aren't the same as lowercase ones, so HELLO and hello are different passwords.

- Don't choose a normal English word. It's easy to find an on-line dictionary, and it's easy for someone to write a program that runs through the dictionary, trying each word until it finds the one you've chosen as your password.

- Don't choose any piece of personal information that someone else might be able to guess. Names of family members or their birthdates are too obvious.

- Don't choose some entirely arbitrary collection of characters. If a password is too difficult to remember, you'll be tempted to write it down somewhere close to your computer, and when a password is written down, it becomes vulnerable to prying eyes.

- If your password has less than six characters, it's relatively easy to guess. It's not hard to write a program that tries every single character, every two-character combination, and so on. However, the longer your password, the longer it takes for a program to try all the combinations. With more than six characters, the process is usually too time-consuming to be worthwhile.

- Try some sort of variation on a simple word or phrase. For example, instead of `hello there`, you could write it backwards (`ereht olleh`) or better, put in punctuation characters, as in `h,el,lo-th,ere` or `he.ll;o#there!`. This sort of thing is usually easy for you to remember, but very difficult for a person or program to guess.

The passwd *Command*

When you've decided on a suitable password, you can use the UNIX `passwd` command to set your chosen password. The `passwd` command also lets you change passwords, so I'll look at both setting a new password and changing an old one.

Start by typing the command

```
passwd
```

and then press Enter.

Usually, the `passwd` command begins by asking you to enter your old password, to prove who you are. This prevents someone from sneaking up to your desk and changing your password while you're not there. However, you don't have a password yet, so `passwd` doesn't ask for your old password.

passwd now asks you to enter the new password you've chosen. Do so and press Enter. You'll notice that the new password doesn't appear on the screen as you type it. This is a security precaution; even if people are watching you as you type, they won't see what your password is.

Because the new password didn't appear on the screen when you entered it, you might have made a typing mistake without knowing it. To avoid confusion, passwd asks you to enter the new password a second time. Do so and press Enter. If you typed the new password the same both times, passwd records that as your new password; if there was some difference between the first time you typed the new password and the second, passwd assumes that you made a typing mistake. Of course, passwd can't tell which time you made the mistake. As a result, it displays the message

```
Passwords do not match. Try again.
```

and asks you to enter the new password again (two times).

> **Your New Password**
>
> The next time you log in, you'll have to type your new password when the log-in procedure asks Password:. When you enter the password, you won't see it appear on the screen. Once again, this is a security precaution, so that people looking over your shoulder can't see your password on the screen.

Logging Out

When you have changed your password, you might decide that you're finished for the time being. To end your session with UNIX, you must *log out*, also called *signing off*.

The steps you have to take in order to log out depend on the shell you are using. With the KornShell of the MKS Tools package, you sign off by typing

```
exit
```

and then pressing Enter.

With different shells and different versions of UNIX, the `exit` command may not work. The following list gives some alternate ways of signing off a UNIX system; these don't work with the MKS Tools, but you can try them on other systems if `exit` doesn't work.

- You can try entering one of the following commands:

```
logout
logoff
log
bye
```

- You can try entering the Ctrl-D character. On many UNIX systems, this stands for *end of file* or *end of input*, and tells the shell that you are finished entering commands. (Because Ctrl-Z often stands for *end of file* on DOS, you can log out from the MKS Tools package by pressing Ctrl-Z, then Enter.)

Chapter Review

Man pages describe UNIX commands in full. Part III of this book provides man pages for every command in the MKS Tools package.

To start working with a UNIX system, you must log in. During the log-in procedure, you tell the system your name and enter a password to prove that you are who you say you are.

The `echo` command simply displays its arguments on the display screen. `echo` puts a single blank character between each argument. If you want additional whitespace, put the arguments (including the whitespace) in single or double quotation marks.

With the KornShell, you can delete single characters by pressing the Backspace key. You can delete the whole line by pressing Esc.

Almost all UNIX commands must be entered in lowercase. If you enter them in uppercase, the system will not recognize the command names.

The `passwd` command lets you change your password. You must enter your old password, then enter your new password two times.

To end a session with UNIX, you must log out, also called *signing off*. With the KornShell, you can log out by entering `exit`.

Exercises

1. Read the man page for the banner command. Log in and use banner to display the word Hello.

2. Use banner to display Hi there with one word per line. Then use banner to display Hi there with the words all on one line. What happens if you use banner to display a string with more than 12 characters? Try it.

3. Log out and log in again. When you log in, intentionally enter a nonsense user name (a name that isn't the name of anyone authorized to use the system). What happens? Why do you think UNIX takes this approach?

## Chapter 3

The UNIX File System: Go Climb a Tree

The DOS method of organizing and handling files was strongly influenced by the example of UNIX. Because of this, the two have much in common. This chapter begins by looking at the things you do most often with files: read them, copy them, move them, and get rid of them.

After discussing the nature of files, this chapter examines the way UNIX organizes files. Like DOS, UNIX organizes files into *directories*. If computer files are similar to the paper file folders you might find in an office, directories are similar to the filing cabinets that hold such file folders.

Files are contained in directories, but these directories might be contained in larger directories, which are contained in even larger directories, and so on. If you want to work with a particular file, the system has to know which sequence of directories it must search in order to find the file you want. A *path name* is a way of specifying a file by giving a sequence of directories and the file's name. UNIX and DOS path names often look very similar; the most obvious difference is that DOS separates the parts of a path name with backslash (\) characters, while UNIX uses slash (/) characters.

Full path names aren't the only way to refer to files. UNIX also lets you cd to a directory (just as in DOS) and then refer to files under that directory with *relative path names*. This chapter will examine the concept of *current directories* on DOS and UNIX, and I'll show how they can save you some typing.

The discussion of directories shows how to create directories with mkdir and how to get rid of them with rmdir (similar to the DOS MKDIR and RMDIR commands). The chapter also discusses principles of copying files to directories and moving files in and out of directories.

UNIX users have established well-used conventions for naming certain files and directories. For example, various types of information files are usually stored under a directory named /etc. I'll give an overview of these conventions, as a "map" for most of the UNIX file systems you're likely to encounter.

After I have shown how similar the UNIX and DOS file systems are, this chapter will look at some of the ways in which they differ. One of the most important differences is the concept of *file permissions*, restricting the ways people can use files. The chmod utility is the basic UNIX command for changing the permissions associated with a file; chmod is similar to the DOS ATTRIB command, but chmod has a wider range of uses.

Another important difference between UNIX and DOS is the way they handle multiple devices. On DOS, you're probably familiar with the concept of disk drives labelled A:, B:, C: and so on. UNIX doesn't have special device names like this. Instead, UNIX devices have names that look exactly like the names of disk files.

For example, a DOS system might refer to a line printer with a special device name like PRN or LPT1. A UNIX system might create a *special file* for a line printer named /dev/lp. This looks like a normal disk file, but if you write data to the /dev/lp file, it has the effect of writing output to the printer. UNIX systems use a similar approach for floppy disk drives, tape drives, and so on. All of this will be explained in more detail later in this chapter.

Working with Files

The installation procedure that created your userid also created some sample files for you to work with. In this chapter, you'll be working with the following files:

sonnet   Contains Shakespeare's Sonnet 18.

nursery   Contains various nursery rhymes.

These two files are *text files*, containing lines of ordinary text. In Chapter 6 I'll show you how to create text files of your own using the vi text editor.

The other type of file used on UNIX (and DOS) is the *binary file*. On UNIX, any file that isn't a text file is a binary file. Binary files can contain any kind of data, not just text. For example, software packages commonly use binary files to hold such information as:

- Spreadsheets and graphics
- Databases
- Executable programs
- Numeric data

Look Ma, No Suffixes!

If you're familiar with DOS, you'll notice that the files `sonnet` and `nursery` don't have suffixes (also called *file name extensions* on DOS). This is an important distinction between DOS and UNIX. On DOS, most files have suffixes; on UNIX, suffixes are much less common. You can create UNIX file names with suffixes—for example, the files could have been called `sonnet.txt` and `nursery.txt` to show that they contain text, or `sonnet.pm` and `nursery.pm` to show that they contain poems. However, most UNIX users believe in minimizing their typing, so they avoid suffixes unless there is a strong reason to use them.

Of course, it's not absolutely necessary to use binary files to hold such information. You could, for example, store numeric data as strings of digits held in a text file. However, numbers stored in binary form almost always take up less disk space than numbers stored as text digits, so binary files are usually more efficient.

Files created by word processors are usually binary files. These files contain text, but they also contain other types of data describing how the text should be formatted (type font, paragraphing, margin settings, and so on). Because of these special formatting *control characters*, most word processor programs find it more practical to use binary files than text files.

File Formats on Other Operating Systems

Some other operating systems have many other file formats besides binary and text. For example, an operating system might have one file format for executable programs, several formats for databases, several different types of text files, and so on. The operating system itself provides services that read and write these different file formats.

In UNIX, the operating system only provides services for binary and text formats. A program that wants to write to a database, for example, does all the formatting first and then calls the binary input/output routines to write the database as a binary file.

In other words, the UNIX operating system doesn't do any special formatting; programs that want special formatting have to do it themselves. On other systems, the operating system (instead of the programs) may do the formatting. This reduces the amount of work that programs have to do, but it also reduces the amount of control they can exercise over their data. Programs don't have a choice—they *must* use the "official" formats recognized by the operating system.

Reading Files: The more Command

You're ready to start working with files, so you should log in to the MKS Tools software, following the procedures described in the previous chapter. When you're logged in, enter the following command:

```
more sonnet
```

You'll see that this displays a sonnet on your screen, as shown in Listing 3.1. What you see are the contents of the text file `sonnet`.

Listing 3.1.   Contents of `sonnet`.

```
                    Sonnet XVIII
                 William Shakespeare

Shall I compare thee to a summer's day?
Thou art more lovely and more temperate.
Rough winds do shake the darling buds of May,
And summer's lease hath all too short a date.
Sometime too hot the eye of heaven shines,
And often is his gold complexion dimmed;
And every fair from fair sometime declines,
By chance, or nature's changing course, untrimmed:
But thy eternal summer shall not fade
Nor lose possession of that fair thou ow'st,
Nor shall Death brag thou wand'rest in his shade
When in eternal lines to time thou grow'st.
    So long as men can breathe or eyes can see,
    So long lives this, and this gives life to thee.
```

The UNIX `more` command is comparable to the DOS TYPE command. They both display the contents of a file on the terminal screen. In general, a command of the form

```
more filename
```

displays the contents of any text file named *filename*.

> **The Word "Print"**
>
> If you're a DOS user, the word "print" may suggest the action of producing output on paper. However, UNIX software often uses the word "print" to describe the process of displaying text on the terminal screen. For example, it would be normal to say that `more` "prints" the contents of a file. Most UNIX systems have facilities for producing hard copy output, but UNIX is geared toward helping people work productively without paper.
>
> In deference to DOS users, this book normally uses the word "display" to describe the action of making text appear on the terminal screen. However, we'll use "print" now and then, just to remind you of the UNIX terminology.

Displaying Long Files

Now enter the command

```
more nursery
```

This displays the contents of the text file called `nursery`. This file is quite long. Unless you have a huge monitor, the file is too long to fit on the screen.

You'll see that `more` displays the first 24 lines of the file on your screen and then displays the message

```
--More--
```

at the bottom of the screen. On most monitors, `more` highlights this message in some way, usually displaying it in *reverse video* (dark letters on a light background).

After `more` has displayed the `--More--` message, it waits for you to read what is displayed on the screen. When you are ready to see more, you have a choice:

- If you press Enter, `more` displays the next line of the file. Pressing Enter repeatedly displays the file line by line.

- If you press the space bar, `more` displays the next 24 lines in the file. Pressing the space bar after each screen displays the file screen by screen.

- If you enter **q**, `more` quits. You can do this if you've already read enough of the file to find out what you want. If you don't press **q**, `more` quits after it displays the last line in the file.

You can mix the preceding approaches if you like. For example, you can use the space bar to read through the file screen by screen until you find text in which you're particularly interested. You can then use Enter to read through this text line by line. When you reach the end of the text you wanted to see, you can use q to quit.

The DOS MORE Command

DOS users may be familiar with the DOS MORE command. It's almost the same as the UNIX version, except that you use it in conjunction with TYPE, as in

```
TYPE FILE ¦ MORE
```

or with the < construct, as in

```
MORE <FILE
```

Both the DOS and UNIX versions of the command can display output in a screen-by-screen fashion. The difference is that the UNIX more lets you quit with q and lets you display all or part of the file line by line by pressing Enter.

Multiple Files

You can also use more to display several files in a row. For example, enter the command

```
more sonnet nursery
```

more displays the contents of sonnet first, then pauses and displays the message

```
(Next file nursery)--More--
```

This indicates that it's ready to display the next file, and that the name of the file is nursery. You can use the space bar to display the first screenful of nursery, the Enter key to display nursery line by line, or **q** to quit.

Now try displaying the files in the opposite order, by entering the command

```
more nursery sonnet
```

When more pauses at the end of the first screenful of nursery, enter **n**. This stands for *next*, and tells more to skip ahead to the next file. You'll see that more displays the message

```
(Next file sonnet)--More--
```

telling you that it's ready to display `sonnet`.

You can use `more` to display the contents of any number of files. Using **n**, you can skip from one file to the next whenever you choose. You can skip backward too: enter **p** (for *previous*) and `more` goes back and displays the previous file. You can use numbers to go back and forth inside a file. For example, **-2** goes back two screenfuls, while **+1** skips ahead one screen.

The *cat* Command

The `more` command is the most convenient method for reading a file, because it pauses after each screenful of text. It's similar to the DOS MORE command. But UNIX has a less sophisticated command named `cat`.

`cat` simply writes the contents of one or more files to the screen, without pausing when the screen fills up. Enter the command

```
cat nursery sonnet
```

and you'll see the contents of both files zip past on the screen. (This is similar to the behavior of the DOS TYPE command.)

`cat` has its uses, as you'll see in later chapters. However, if you just want to see what's in a text file, you'll find that `more` is the most suitable command for that purpose.

Finding Out What Files You Have

On a DOS system, you'd use the `DIR` command to display a list of files in a directory. On UNIX, the comparable command is `ls`, short for *list*. Enter the command

```
ls
```

and you'll see a list of names, sorted down columns in alphabetical order:

```
browse.v     data    edit.v    profile.ksh   sh-histo   source
comics.lst   doc.v   nursery   program.v     sonnet
```

These are the names of the sample files that were created when you created your `userid`. Among them you should see the `sonnet` and `nursery` files that you've worked with in this chapter.

You've probably noticed that the output of ls is substantially different from the output of DIR, even though the two commands do approximately the same thing. Let's examine the differences:

- The output of ls is in lowercase, while the output of DIR is mostly in uppercase. I've mentioned before that lowercase is the preferred UNIX style.

- The output of ls is sorted in alphabetical order, while the output of DIR is not.

- DIR displays information on its entries, including the size of files, and their creation date and time. ls only displays the names. However, I'll show you later in this chapter how to use options with the ls command to obtain all the information shown by DIR.

Copying Files

DOS users are familiar with the DOS COPY command for copying files. The comparable UNIX command is named cp (in keeping with the UNIX tendency to drop vowels and put all names in lowercase). In most respects, cp works much like COPY. For example, try the command

```
cp nursery poems
```

This copies the existing nursery file into a new file named poems. You can display the contents of the new file with

```
more poems
```

The old nursery file is still around, as you can see if you try the command

```
more nursery
```

cp doesn't delete the old file. It just makes a new one.

> **Silent Running**
>
> When the DOS COPY command copies a file, it usually displays a message of the form 1 File(s) copied. When cp copies a file, you'll notice it prints no output. This is in keeping with the UNIX philosophy of keeping output to a minimum. Many UNIX utilities only print messages if something goes wrong; if they're successful in doing what they intend to do, they see no need to brag.

You can also use cp to copy into an existing file. Enter the following command:

```
cp sonnet poems
```

If you now try

```
more poems
```

you will see that poems has the same contents as the sonnet file. The cp command *overwrites* the previous contents of the poems file with the contents of sonnet.

Removing Files

You don't really need the poems file that you created in a previous section—it's just a copy of one of your other files. On DOS, you get rid of files using the DEL command (short for *delete*); on UNIX, you use rm, short for *remove*. For example, enter the command:

```
rm poems
```

This gets rid of the poems file. To see that the file is gone, enter the command

```
more poems
```

You'll see that the more command prints out a message saying that it can't *open* the input file poems. This means that it can't find the file: you just removed it using rm. You can also use the ls command to see that the poems file is gone.

rm can remove several files at a time. To see how this works, enter the following commands

```
cp sonnet junk1
cp sonnet junk2
```

These cp commands create files named junk1 and junk2. Don't worry about these files—you're going to remove them right away. Enter the rm command

```
rm junk1 junk2
```

and both files disappear. (You can use ls to see that they're actually gone.)

Contrast the behavior of rm with the DOS DEL command. DEL ignores everything but the first argument. On a DOS system, a command like

```
DEL junk1 junk2
```

49

deletes junk1 but not junk2, something that certainly confused me the first time I encountered it.

Moving Files

The UNIX mv command *moves* a file. In one respect, this is similar to the DOS RENAME command. For example, enter the command

```
mv sonnet sonnet18
```

This moves the file sonnet to the new name sonnet18. Enter

```
more sonnet
```

and more will tell you that sonnet can no longer be found. Enter

```
more sonnet18
```

and you'll see that sonnet18 now has the contents of the old sonnet file. In effect, you've renamed the file. To put things back the way they were, enter

```
mv sonnet18 sonnet
```

which changes the file's name back to sonnet.

A little later on, I'll show that mv can do more tricks than just renaming files. However, I can't discuss these tricks until I talk about directories later in this chapter.

Rules for UNIX File Names

According to the POSIX standard, a UNIX file name can contain any of the characters in Table 3.1. This is called the *portable character set* for file names. Many UNIX-like systems let you use other characters too, but the characters in the table are the only ones you can be sure are accepted by every UNIX system.

There are no restrictions on the way these characters can be used. For example, DOS only lets you have one dot (.) in a file name, but UNIX lets you use several. DOS does not let you have names that begin with a dot, but this is perfectly valid on UNIX. For example, the following names are valid in UNIX, but not on DOS:

```
.profile   ellipsis...   please.read.me
```

Table 3.1.   Portable character set for UNIX file names (according to the POSIX standard).

```
abcdefghijklmnopqrstuvwxyz
ABCDEFGHIJKLMNOPQRSTUVWXYZ
0123456789
. (dot)
_ (underscore)
- (dash)
```

The POSIX standard allows names to be up to 14 characters long. (DOS allows a maximum of eight characters, plus a three-character suffix.) Many UNIX-like systems allow names to be much longer than 14 characters, but 14 is the maximum if you want your file name to be valid on every UNIX system.

In file names the uppercase characters are different from the lowercase characters. For example, FILE is not the same name as file. They are two distinct files, with no connection to one another. Of course, having two names that are so similar is bound to be confusing, so it's a good idea to avoid names that only differ in the case of their letters. Most people stick to lowercase letters most of the time.

More About File Suffixes

Earlier, I mentioned that you can use suffixes on UNIX file names if you want. However, there are differences in the ways that DOS and UNIX handle suffixes.

The DOS file system treats a suffix as a special part of the name, and makes sure that the suffix has three characters at most. In the output of DIR, the suffix is shown as a separate part of the name. Internally, DOS stores the suffix and the rest of the name as separate parts of the file name.

On UNIX, the suffix is usually not special, and the dot is just another character in a name. You can use suffixes if they help you organize and identify your files, but that's up to you—the file system doesn't treat suffixes specially. For example, there's no limit to the length of a suffix. You can also have several things that look like suffixes, as in report.doc.1. Some utilities give special treatment to file names that begin with a dot; but that's a feature of particular programs, not the operating system itself.

DOS treats the dot as a special character that separates the first part of a file name from the suffix. On UNIX, the dot is just another character, with no special meaning or treatment.

> **MKS Tools Note:** The DOS file system does not distinguish between upper- and lowercase letters in file names. Therefore, the MKS Tools software cannot make the distinction either. This is one of the few ways in which the package differs from a real UNIX system.

Files and Directories

If you're a DOS user, you are almost certainly familiar with the concept of *directories*. In both DOS and UNIX, a directory contains files in the same way that an office filing cabinet contains file folders. Directories let you organize your files: you can use directories to group together files that have similar types or purposes, making it faster and easier to find the files you want. Directories give *structure* to a file system, in the same way that a chain of command gives structure to an organization.

When a file system uses directories, the structure of the file system is usually compared to a *tree*. The files of the system are like the leaves and the directories are like the branches. Each leaf attaches to a single branch; each branch can support several leaves, and can also support several smaller branches.

In the same way, every file in a UNIX file system belongs to some directory. Each directory can contain several files, and can also contain several other directories, called *subdirectories*. Subdirectories can have subdirectories of their own, in the same way that branches can have branches of their own. Figure 3.1 shows a simple tree-like file structure on a UNIX system.

The Root Directory

At the top of Figure 3.1 there is a directory with the simple name / (the slash character). This directory is called the *root directory*, and it is present in every UNIX file system. As the name suggests, the root directory is the base of the file system tree. Every file in the file system is either contained in the root directory or in some subdirectory of the root.

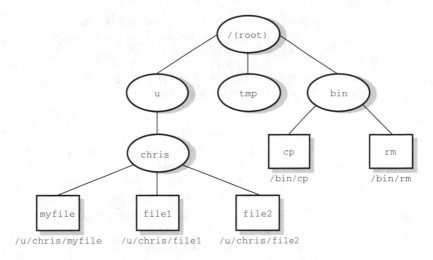

Figure 3.1.   This is a simple UNIX file structure. Ovals represent directories, and squares represent files. The path name of each file is given below the square that represents the file.

Path Names

Figure 3.1 also shows the *path names* of the files it depicts. A path name is a way to specify a file that you want to work with. A full path name describes a path through the file system tree, beginning at the root and ending at the file you want. For example, consider the full path name

```
/u/chris/myfile
```

This full path name consists of several *components*:

1. The first component is the / at the beginning of the name. This indicates that the path should begin at the root.

2. The second component is u. The system looks for u in the root directory and finds that u is a directory. The path therefore leads to the u directory.

3. The next component is chris. (The / between u and chris is just there to separate the components.) The system looks for chris in the u directory and finds that chris is also a directory. The path therefore leads to the chris directory.

53

4. The final component is `myfile`. (Again, the / between `chris` and `myfile` is just a separator.) The system looks for `myfile` in the `chris` directory. This is the end of the path.

As you can see, a path name is like a map that takes you through a series of directories until you reach the directory or file you want.

> **Terminology Note:** Except for the root, every directory is a subdirectory of some other directory. Therefore, it's superfluous to use the word *subdirectory*, and in most cases you simply call everything a directory. I only use the word subdirectory when I want to stress the relationship between a subdirectory and the directory that contains it.

The last component of a path name is often called the *basename*. For example, the basename of

```
/u/chris/myfile
```

is `myfile`. The basename of

```
/u/chris
```

is `chris`.

The collection of components that precede the basename is often called the *dirname*. For example, the dirname of

```
/u/chris/myfile
```

is `/u/chris`, and the dirname of

```
/u/chris
```

is just `/u`. UNIX documentation frequently uses the terms *basename* and *dirname*.

Slash Versus Backslash

You'll notice that UNIX uses the slash (/) character to separate the components of a path name. If you're a DOS user, you're probably aware that DOS uses the backslash (\) for the same purpose. Make sure that you don't get the two mixed up. You can't use the backslash as a separator on UNIX, because UNIX uses the backslash for other purposes. You're almost certain to get confusing results if you use the backslash to separate path name components on a UNIX system.

The Current Directory

Enter the command

```
ls
```

As you've already seen, the `ls` command lists the contents of a directory...but which directory? It lists the contents of the *current directory*, also called your *working directory*.

If you're familiar with DOS, you probably know what a current directory is, but in case you don't, I'll explain the concept from the start.

Figure 3.1 showed how you could specify files with path names, giving a "map" of the path from the root to the desired file. But this can mean a lot of typing. For example, suppose that you're working with a collection of files under the directory /u/chris:

```
/u/chris/file1
/u/chris/file2
/u/chris/file3
    ...
```

It's a lot of extra work to type **/u/chris** in front of every file name. Ideally, you'd like to tell the operating system "Every file I mention is going to be under /u/chris unless I say otherwise." That way you can simply type the names

```
file1
file2
file3
 ...
```

For this reason, both UNIX and DOS use the concept of a current directory. You can specify any directory in the file system as your current directory; then if you give a file name without telling what directory the file is in, the system looks for the file in the current directory.

You've already used this concept without thinking about it. When I talked about the `cp` command at the beginning of the chapter, you used the command

```
cp sonnet poems
```

In this command, sonnet and poems are file names, but not full path names. The system therefore assumes that sonnet and poems are in your current directory.

Determining Your Current Directory

How can you tell what your current directory is? The pwd (print working directory) command displays the name of your current directory. Enter the command

```
pwd
```

and you'll see that the system displays a directory name, such as

```
c:/lu/u/jim
```

Of course, you'll see your own login name instead of jim. On a true UNIX system, you wouldn't see C:, because this kind of device name comes from DOS, not UNIX. This directory name has several components. The last component (the basename) should be your userid. The other components (the dirname) are determined by the way you installed the MKS Tools software on your system.

When you log in, the system automatically sets your current directory to this directory, called your *home directory*. Your home directory is your personal directory. Typically, people use the home directory to keep personal files of various sorts. In Chapter 9, I'll show how you can use files in your home directory to customize the behavior of the system. Right now, the only files in your home directory are the sample files that were set up when you created your userid during installation.

The cd Command

The cd command lets you change your current directory. It is almost exactly like the DOS CD command. For example, enter the command

```
cd /
```

Entering this command sets your current directory to /, the root of the file system. If you now enter

```
ls
```

the command lists the contents of the root directory. Now enter

```
cd lu
ls
```

The `cd lu` line sets your current directory to a directory named `lu` under the root directory. This is where the MKS Tools software is stored if you use the standard installation as described in Appendix G. The `ls` command displays the contents of the `/lu` directory. The output will be

```
bin etc lnibat tmp u
```

Enter

```
cd etc
```

and you go to a directory named `etc` under `lu`. Typing

```
ls
```

now shows you the contents of `/lu/etc`, a set of information files used for system administration and other jobs. You will see

```
issue italic.fnt large.fnt libib passwd small.fnt
```

You can get back to your home directory simply by typing

```
cd
```

A `cd` command without any argument sets your current directory to your home directory. Enter

```
pwd
```

and the system shows you that you're back in your home directory.

Here's one more useful trick when using `cd`. Enter

```
cd
cd /
```

to set your current directory to the root, then enter

```
cd -
```

57

(the final character is a dash or minus sign). You'll see that the system displays the name of your home directory, showing that you're back in that directory again. The reason is that `cd -` goes back to the previous current directory. Enter

```
cd -
```

again, and you'll see that you've gone back to the root. Enter

```
cd -
```

one last time, and you'll see that you're back in your home directory. `cd -` can switch back and forth between directories, a helpful thing to remember if you happen to be doing a job that deals with files in two directories.

    Note: The `cd -` command only works when you're using the KornShell as your shell. If you're using some other shell, `cd -` may not work.

DOS CD Versus UNIX cd

  The biggest difference between the DOS `CD` and the UNIX `cd` is that

```
cd
```

goes to your home directory on UNIX, while

```
CD
```

displays the name of your current directory on DOS. This means that `CD` without arguments on DOS is like `pwd` on UNIX.

The . and .. Notations

On UNIX (and on DOS), the notation . (just a dot character) stands for the current directory, and the notation .. stands for the directory that contains the current directory. For example, enter

```
cd
pwd
cd ..
pwd
```

You'll see that the first `cd` command moves you to your home directory, and the second `cd` command moves you from your home directory to the directory that contains your home directory (probably a directory named /u). Now enter the commands

```
cd .
pwd
```

You'll see that you're still in the same directory. The command

```
cd .
```

has no effect—it changes the current directory to ., which stands for the current directory.

The .. directory is often called the *parent directory* of the current directory. The parent directory contains the current directory.

Use cd to return to your home directory, and then enter

```
cd ../..
```

Ask yourself what directory you should be in now. Use

```
pwd
```

to see if you were right. Finally, enter

```
cd
```

to return to your home directory.

Working with Directories

Now that I've discussed the basics of directories, let's look at a few operations that you can perform on directories.

Listing the Contents of a Directory

You've already seen that the ls command can list the contents of your current directory. You can also list the contents of a different directory, just by specifying the directory name. For example,

```
ls /
```

lists the contents of the root directory.

```
ls /lu
```

lists the contents of `lu` under the root directory.

Creating Directories

The `mkdir` command creates new directories. It is comparable to the DOS `MKDIR` (or `MD`) command. For example, enter

```
cd
```

to make sure you're in your home directory, then enter the command

```
mkdir newdir
```

This creates a directory named `newdir` under your home directory. If you enter the command

```
ls
```

you'll see that `newdir` is now listed in the contents of the current directory.
    Enter the command

```
ls newdir
```

to list the contents of the new directory. You'll see that `ls` simply returns without printing anything out. The `newdir` directory doesn't contain anything yet, so there are no names for `ls` to display.

Distinguishing Files and Directories

You'll notice that directory names can look a lot like file names; for example, there's no visual difference between a file name like `sonnet` and a directory name like `newdir`. In fact, you could create a directory named `sonnet` if there wasn't already a file with that name. (If you try to create a directory named `sonnet`, the system will tell you that the current directory already contains something named `sonnet`.)

So how can you tell whether a particular name is a file or a directory? One solution is to use `ls -p` instead of just `ls`. `-p` is an `option` that tells `ls` to mark each directory name with a `/` character. You'll learn more about options for `ls` in Chapter 4.

Copying and Moving into Directories

To put something into the `newdir` directory, enter

```
cd
```

to go to your home directory, use the command

```
cp nursery newdir
```

This copies the `nursery` file into `newdir`. If you now enter

```
ls newdir
```

you'll see that the output is

```
nursery
```

The general rule is that if the last argument in a `cp` command is the name of a directory, the other arguments should be files to be copied into that directory. `cp` will then make copies of those files and store them in that directory, using the same basenames as the original files.

The same principle applies to moving files. Enter the command

```
mv sonnet newdir
```

This moves the `sonnet` file into `newdir`. Enter the commands

```
ls
ls newdir
```

and you'll see that `sonnet` is no longer in your home directory. `mv` moved it into `newdir`.

Relative Path Names

You've moved `sonnet` into `newdir`. Now you'll want to move it back. Do this with the command

```
mv newdir/sonnet .
```

How does this work?

- First of all, look at the name `newdir/sonnet`. This is similar to the path names you've seen, but it doesn't have the / at the beginning. It's a *relative path name*, telling where a file is relative to the current directory. In this case, the file is in `newdir` under the current directory, and the file's name is `sonnet`.

- The second argument is the dot character (`.`). As mentioned previously, this is shorthand for the name of the current directory.

As a result, the preceding command moves `sonnet` out of `newdir` and into the current directory. Use the commands

```
ls
ls newdir
```

to see that `sonnet` is back in your home directory and no longer in `newdir`.

As another example, ask yourself what command you'd need to display the contents of the `nursery` file in the `newdir` directory. The answer is

```
more newdir/nursery
```

Try this command to see that it works.

Finally, ask yourself what command you'd need to remove the copy of `nursery` from `newdir`. Enter this command, then use the `ls` command to verify that you were right.

Relative Path Names Versus Absolute Path Names

The general rule is this: if a path name starts with a slash (`/`), it is an absolute path name, beginning at the root. If it does not start with a slash, it is a relative path name, beginning at the current directory.

Removing Directories

The `rmdir` command removes a directory. The `rmdir` command is comparable to the DOS `RMDIR` command. For example, enter

```
rmdir newdir
```

This should remove the `newdir` directory.

If you didn't get rid of the `newdir/nursery` file as I suggested in the last section, you will find that `rmdir` doesn't work on this directory. Before you can remove a directory with `rmdir`, you have to remove all the files and subdirectories under that directory. Remove the `newdir/nursery` file and try again.

You Can't Saw Off a Branch When You're Sitting On It

You cannot use `rmdir` to remove a directory if you have used `cd` to make that directory your current directory. You must use `cd` to switch to a different directory first, then you can use `rmdir`.

Common Directories

Over the years, UNIX users have developed *conventions* for the use of directories on UNIX systems. You can think of these conventions as rules of thumb that people have found useful in the past; they aren't mandatory, but they're almost universally observed. You might compare them to the mapmaking convention of putting North at the top of the map—you can do things differently if you want, but it's likely to lead to confusion.

Most UNIX systems have the following directories under the root directory:

`/bin`   Holds many of the utilities and other programs that can be executed on the system. `bin` stands for *binary*, and utilities are almost always binary files.

`/dev`   Holds *device files* (discussed later in this chapter).

`/etc`   Holds various information files that are used for system administration and other purposes. For example, the file `/etc/passwd` typically holds the names of all authorized users, their passwords (encrypted so that no one can read them), and other kinds of personal information.

`/tmp`   Can hold *temporary* files for people or programs. For example, the UNIX `sort` program for sorting the contents of files sometimes needs disk space to hold the partly sorted contents of a file temporarily. If so, `sort` creates a file under `/tmp` and uses this file to hold partly sorted data. When `sort` has finished its work, it removes the working file from `/tmp`. As another example, suppose you're about to start working on an important data file and are afraid you'll make a mistake. You could use the command

```
cp data /tmp/just_in_case
```

to save a copy of the file in /tmp with the name just_in_case. Then if you do make a mistake that ruins the file, you can copy back the original from /tmp. After you've made your changes successfully, you can get rid of the copy under /tmp. Many large UNIX sites automatically clean out /tmp on a regular basis by deleting any file that's been in /tmp for more than a day.

/u   Holds the home directories of system users. For technical reasons, there's a limit to the number of files and directories that can be stored under one directory. Therefore on UNIX systems with a large number of users, it's possible that the home directories won't all fit under /u and additional directories will be necessary. You might also see directories named /usr, /u1, /u2, and so on containing the home directories of additional users. (The convention of using /u for user directories is not universal. Some sites prefer different names.)

Organization of the MKS Tools

The MKS Tools package associated with this book uses an organization that is similar to that of a UNIX system. If you followed the standard installation procedure from Appendix G, everything associated with this package is stored in the directory /lu under the root directory on your hard disk. The /lu directory has subdirectories /lu/bin to hold the software, /lu/etc to hold information files, /lu/tmp for temporary files, and /lu/u to hold the home directories of system users.

Organizing Your Home Directory

Many people find it convenient to organize their home directories in a way that parallels the root directory. They use mkdir to create the following subdirectories under their home directory:

bin   Holds the user's own executable programs

etc   Holds various information files

tmp   Holds temporary working files

You will also find it convenient to create a directory for every project (or group of projects) you work on. For example, suppose you prepare quarterly reports for your company, and each report consists of a financial analysis and personnel ratings. You might create a directory structure like the one shown in Figure 3.2.

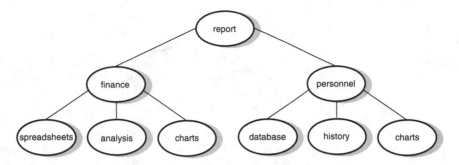

Figure 3.2.   One possible structure for a directory containing all the information for a quarterly report.

In this structure, you make a new directory for each quarter. The directory for a quarter has two subdirectories, `finance` and `personnel`. The `finance` directory might contain separate subdirectories for:

- Spreadsheets

- Analysis documents

- Charts

The `personnel` directory might contain separate subdirectories for:

- Personnel databases

- Personnel history documents

- Charts

This isn't the only possible method of organization. For example, instead of having one directory for finance charts and another for personnel charts, you may find it useful to have a single directory for charts, as shown in Figure 3.3.

There is no definitive way you can use directories to organize your files. The most important principle is to make sure that you do use directories. Without directories, you get what is called a *flat filing system*, comparable to spreading all your file folders out on a desk rather than putting them in some kind of order inside a filing cabinet. Directories make it easier to find files and to show the interrelationships between files.

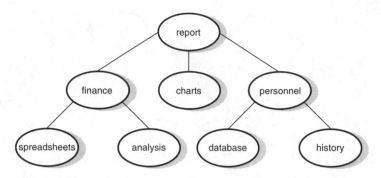

Figure 3.3.   Another possible structure for a directory containing all the information for a quarterly report. Both financial and personnel reports make use of the charts in the `charts` directory.

File Characteristics

The UNIX file system records various kinds of information about each file, called the *characteristics* of the file. File characteristics include the following:

- The size of the file

- The date and time that the contents of the file were last changed

- Who is permitted to use the file, and how they are permitted to use it

The sections that follow explore these characteristics in more detail.

File Permissions

Because DOS was designed as a single-user system, it has a simplistic approach toward file permissions:

- You can *hide* a file so that it doesn't appear in the output of DIR. This makes it a little harder for other users to find the file, but it doesn't prevent them from reading or writing the file when they find it. (A skilled user can easily write a program to find hidden files.)

- In later versions of DOS, you can mark a file as *read-only* using the ATTRIB command, so that you can read the file but not write to it. This prevents you from overwriting the file by accident, but it doesn't provide any security against other users. Anyone else using the system can use ATTRIB to make the file writable again, then overwrite the contents.

UNIX, on the other hand, was designed as a multiuser system and therefore has a broader approach to file permissions. Its approach is not as comprehensive as many other commercial systems—remember that UNIX was originally constructed for use by a handful of professionals all working for the same company, so they did not devote themselves to building in an extensive security system. Still, the UNIX file permission system is quite adequate to meet the needs of most computing sites.

A UNIX file has three sets of permissions: those that apply to the file's *owner*; those that apply to the file's *group*; and those that apply to everyone else on the system.

The Limitations of DOS

The sections to come will examine the file permissions available on UNIX. Unfortunately, these cannot be simulated well on a DOS system, because of DOS's limited permission capabilities. Thus the MKS Tools software cannot let you try out the full range of UNIX permissions. I will discuss the software's limitations after I give some background about UNIX permissions.

The Owner of a File

Every user on a UNIX system has an assigned identification number, called a `userid number`. This is automatically assigned when you are authorized to use the system. When you create a file, UNIX records your `userid` as one of the file's characteristics. From that point on, you are considered the file's *owner*. There are ways you can transfer ownership to someone else, and there are special cases in which you can create a file without becoming the owner, but in general, you are the owner of every file you create.

The *owner permissions* of a file apply to the owner only. For example, you can set the permissions of a file you own so that you are the only one who can read the file or write to it. I'll show how to do this in a later section.

UNIX Groups

The system administrator of a UNIX system can create *groups* on the system. A group is a collection of users who are affiliated in some way. For example, the administrator might create a separate group for each project that uses the machine, or a group for each department in the company.

One person can belong to several groups. One of these is considered your *primary group*; the rest are *secondary groups*. The system administrator decides which groups you can belong to and which one is your primary group.

When you create a file, UNIX records your primary group as one of the file's characteristics. From that point on, the file belongs to your primary group. There are ways to change which group a file belongs to, but this book won't look at those.

The *group permissions* of a file apply to everyone belonging to the same group (whether the group is their primary group or one of their secondary ones). For example, you can set up a file so that everyone in the group can read it but outsiders can't. I'll show how to do this in a later section.

Other Permissions

The *other permissions* of a file apply to everybody on the system who is not the file's owner or in the file's group (in other words, the outsiders). For example, you can set up a file so that everyone on the system can read it. I'll show how to do this after you look at the types of permissions that you can put on a file.

Types of File Permissions

There are three types of file permissions. Each is represented by a code letter:

r   Lets you read the file.

w   Lets you write to the file.

x   Lets you execute the file; for example, if a file contains an executable program, you need x permission to be able to execute the program.

These types of permissions can be separately assigned (or not assigned) to the file's owner, its group, and to all others. They are always written in this order: rwx.

For example, suppose you are working on a file that will be part of a larger project. As the owner of the file, you might give yourself read and write permission on the file, and give read permission to other workers in your group and to everyone else on the system. You would write this set-up as

```
rw-r--r--
```

The first three characters rw- stand for the owner's permissions: read and write, but not execute. (It is traditional to put a dash (-) in place of permissions that have not been given.) The next three characters stand for group permissions: r-- means read permission but not permission to write or execute. The final three characters stand for other permissions: again, r-- means read permission but not write or execute permission.

As another example, consider

```
rwxrwxr--
```

In this case, both the owner and the owner's primary group have `rwx` permission (read, write, and execute), while others only have `r--` permission (read only).

```
rwxr-x--x
```

says that the owner has full permissions, the group has permission to read and execute, and others only have permission to execute.

```
r--------
```

says that only the owner has permission to read (but *not* to write or execute), and no one else can use the file for any purpose.

Types of Directory Permissions

A similar system of permissions applies to directories. You use the same codes, but they have slightly different meanings:

r   Lets you read the names of files and subdirectories contained by the directory. You can only read their names; to read the contents of a file, you need read permission on the file itself.

w   Lets you create new files and subdirectories under the directory.

x   Lets you search through the directory. This is a weaker permission than `r`; it only lets you determine if a particular file or subdirectory exists. If you have x but not `r`, you can try to access a file or subdirectory if you know its name, but you can't browse through the directory to find what names the directory contains.

Listing File Characteristics

A form of the `ls` command can list the characteristics of a file or directory. For example, enter the command

```
ls -l sonnet
```

(where `-l` is a dash character followed by the lowercase letter l). The command displays output of the form:

```
-rwxrwxrwa 1 jim      0        707 Feb 17 15:52 sonnet
```

The output you see won't be exactly like the previous line. In place of jim, you'll see your login name, and in place of Feb 17 15:52 you'll see the date and time that you last changed the sonnet file, but the rest should be similar. Examine this output piece by piece:

-	The first character is a dash for files, or the letter d for directories.
rwxrwxrwx	Permissions for the file; in this case, the owner, the group, and all others have full permissions on the file. (See the sidebar for possible differences in this part of the output.)
1	Stands for the number of *links* to the file. The concept of links is beyond the scope of this book. On DOS, this number will always be 1.
jim	Stands for the userid of the file's owner. This is taken from a file of information that UNIX stores under the /etc directory. With MKS Tools, this file is /lu/etc/passwd, and the first person named in that file is assumed to own every file on the system.
0	Stands for the file's group. This too is taken from a file of information that UNIX stores under the /etc directory. The MKS Tools just use 0 for this, because DOS doesn't have groups.
707	Stands for the size of the file, expressed as a number of bytes. (One byte equals one character in a text file.)
Feb 17 15:52	For a file, this is the date and time that the file was last changed; for a directory, it's the date and time that the directory was created.
sonnet	The name of the file or directory.

In other words, ls -l tells you exactly the same sort of information that the DOS DIR command does.

You don't have to specify the name of a file. If you enter

```
ls -l
```

you'll get the same sort of information about every file and subdirectory under the current directory.

As another example, enter the commands

```
mkdir junkdir
ls -l
```

This creates a directory named junkdir, then uses ls -l to display the characteristics of the current directory again. You'll see that everything is the same as before, except that there is now a line for junkdir. This line begins with d to show that it is describing a directory. Get rid of junkdir with

```
rmdir junkdir
```

before you go on to the next section.

DOS Variations in Permissions

The version of ls that comes with the MKS Tools software is based on ls from MKS Toolkit. Because DOS does not have the concept of group or other permissions, this ls uses the permissions part of its output to display information on DOS file characteristics. In particular, you may see the letter a somewhere, standing for the DOS *archive bit*; this bit is on if the file has changed since the last time it was backed up. You may also see the letter h, indicating a hidden file, or the letter s, indicating a system file.

None of these letters appears on a true UNIX system. UNIX does not have such concepts. They are only present because this version of ls tries to give DOS information in the UNIX format.

The chmod *Command*

The chmod command sets the permissions for a file or directory. The general form of the command is

```
chmod perms name
```

where *perms* indicates the permissions that you want and *name* is the name of the file or directory whose permissions you want to set.

The *perms* argument can take many forms, but the most useful form is this:

1. First, use one or more letters telling which permissions you want to set. You can use u for the owner, g for group, o for other, or a for all.

2. Next, use a + if you want to turn permissions on or a - if you want to turn permissions off.

3. Finally, use one or more letters telling which permissions you want to turn on or off. The standard letters are r, w, and x.

As an example, enter the following command:

```
chmod a-w sonnet
```

This changes the permissions for the sonnet file. In a-w, here's what each part means:

- a   says that you want to change permissions for all users: the owner, the group, and others.

- -   says you want to turn permissions off.

- w   says that you want to turn off write permissions.

        Enter the following

```
ls -l sonnet
```

and you'll see that the permissions are now

```
r-xr-xr-x
```

Write permission has been turned off for each type of user. Remember that you might see an a somewhere in the permissions because of the DOS archive bit, and that the first character on the line will be - because sonnet is an ordinary file.
    Now enter

```
chmod a+w sonnet
ls -l sonnet
```

and you'll see that write permission has been turned back on again for each type of user. The + turns permissions on, while the - turns them off.

        Next is a list of some more examples. As noted before, DOS can't simulate some UNIX permissions properly, so you shouldn't try to enter these examples. These examples just provide more illustrations of how chmod might work on a true UNIX system.

```
chmod o-rwx file     # UNIX only -- don't try to enter this
```

turns off all permissions for other users.

```
chmod ug+x file      # UNIX only -- don't try to enter this
```

turns on execute permission for the owner and the group.

```
chmod a-rwx file    # UNIX only -- don't try to enter this
chmod u+rwx file    # UNIX only -- don't try to enter this
chmod g+r file      # UNIX only -- don't try to enter this
```

turns off all permissions for all users, then turns on full permissions for the owner and read permission for the group. As a result, outsiders cannot do anything with the file, the group can only read it, and the owner has full permissions.

Device Files: All the World's a File

On DOS, there are two ways to refer to specific devices:

- Disk drives are typically referred to by letters, followed by colons, as in A:, B:, C:, and so on.

- Devices attached to *communications ports* are typically referred to by names. For example, the printer can be referred to by the name PRN. (DOS communication ports are plug-in connections, typically found on the back of the machine where you can connect printers, modems, and other devices.)

On UNIX, however, all devices are referred to as if they were files in the file system. Typically, special devices are set up as if they are files under the directory /dev (a directory dev for devices under the root). For example, /dev/lp might represent a line printer. Copying a file to this, as in cp file /dev/lp has the effect of printing the file on the line printer. Other files and directories under /dev might represent tape drives, terminals, or other devices attached to the UNIX system.

Devices with the MKS Tools

Because it simulates UNIX on DOS, the MKS Tools software finds it convenient to use DOS's lettered disk drive system rather than using /dev. Thus you may refer to different disk drives by letter. For example, A:file refers to a file named file, under the root directory of disk A:.

The names of files under /dev are set up by the system administrator as part of the *configuration* of the UNIX system. Different types of UNIX and UNIX look-alikes have different procedures for setting up these files. This process can be very complicated. If you are trying to configure a UNIX or UNIX look-alike system, you must follow the configuration instructions that come with the system.

Device Drivers

When you perform I/O (input and/or output) on a file under /dev, the operating system sees that you want to work with a special device and does whatever work is necessary to make it possible to read or write to that device. As much as possible, the system tries to make it look like the device is just another file in the file system. To do this, the system makes use of a *device driver*, software that handles actual I/O with the device. Different devices require different device driver programs; writing device driver programs is far beyond the scope of this book.

The Null Device

Many UNIX systems contain a special file under /dev called /dev/null. This is not present with MKS Tools, but it is common enough on UNIX that it should be discussed.

Any data written to /dev/null simply disappears forever. You may wonder why you would ever find this desirable. The answer is that some programs produce output that you want to disregard; in such instances, you can simply send the output to /dev/null. When /dev/null is used this way, it is sometimes called a *bit bucket* or *sink*. Similarly, if you try to read from /dev/null, you are immediately told that you've reached the end of the file. Thus, /dev/null is called a *null file* or *empty file*.

The /dev/null file is sometimes called a *bit bucket* or a *sink*. Data that comes in never comes out. In future chapters, I'll show examples where /dev/null comes in handy.

Chapter Review

A text file contains only readable text. You can read the contents of a text file one screen at a time by using the more command. more lets you read several files in a row, and go back and forth between different files.

A binary file can contain any kind of data. I have not yet discussed commands for reading the contents of binary files.

Files on UNIX have an owner and a group. A set of owner permissions, group permissions, and other permissions is associated with each file. r permission lets someone read a file; w lets someone write to the file; and x lets someone execute the file. You can change permissions with the chmod command.

The cp command can copy files into other files, as in

```
cp file1 file2
```

or it can copy several files into a directory, as in

```
cp file1 file2 file3 dir
```

You can use the `mv` command in similar ways to move a file to a new name or to move several files into another directory.

The `rm` command can get rid of one or more files.

The `cd` command changes your current directory and the `pwd` command displays the name of your current directory. The notation `.` stands for the current directory, while `..` stands for the directory containing the current directory.

The `ls` command can list the contents of a directory. If you do not specify a directory name, `ls` lists the contents of the current directory. When used in the form `ls -l`, the command lists additional information about the files and subdirectories of a directory including:

- Permissions

- Owner and group

- The size of a file, expressed as several bytes

- The date and time a file was last changed or a directory was created

The root directory is the base of the UNIX file system. Absolute path names refer to a file or directory by describing a path through a sequence of directories, from the root to the file or directory desired. Relative path names describe the same sort of path, but begin at the current directory instead of the root. An absolute path name begins with the / character, while a relative path name does not. You can use an absolute path name anywhere that a relative path name is valid, and vice versa.

By convention, UNIX systems use the directory /etc to hold various kinds of information files, /dev to hold device files, /bin to hold standard executable programs, /tmp to hold temporary working files, and /u to hold the home directories of users. Many people find it helpful to use the same sort of organization for their home directories.

Special devices such as printers or tape drives are represented as files in the UNIX file system, usually under the /dev directory. Reading or writing to a device file has the effect of reading or writing to the device. /dev/null is a special device, called a null device; data written to /dev/null simply disappears.

Table 3.2 summarizes several UNIX commands, what they do, and their DOS counterparts.

Table 3.2.	**UNIX commands and their DOS counterparts.**	

UNIX	DOS	Purpose
cat	TYPE	Display file contents
cd	CD	Change current directory
chmod	ATTRIB	Change file characteristics
cp	COPY	Copy files
ls	DIR	List directory contents
mkdir	MKDIR	Create directories
more	MORE	Display file contents, with pagination
mv	RENAME	Rename (move) files
pwd	CD	Print working directory name
rm	DEL	Get rid of files
rmdir	RMDIR	Get rid of directories

Exercises

1. You may have noticed there is no man page for the more command. This is because more is traditionally considered a version of another command named pg. Read the pg man page.

2. Use the pg command to display the contents of the sonnet and nursery files. What differences do you see between the way that pg works and the way that more does?

3. What are the advantages of having three commands that display the contents of a file (more, cat, pg)? Are there any disadvantages? If so, what are they?

4. cd to the /lu directory. Using an absolute path name with the ls command, list the contents of your home directory. Do the same thing again, only this time use a relative path name. cd back to your home directory when you're done.

5. Suppose a new user named Chris wants to use your system. Create a new home directory for chris under the /lu/u directory. (If your system already has a user named chris, pick a different name.) Copy the sonnet and nursery files into the new directory for chris.

6. Set up the following subdirectories under the chris directory: bin, tmp, stuff. Move the sonnet and nursery files from the chris home directory to the stuff subdirectory.

7. Now suppose that Chris is leaving to live in Tahiti. Get rid of the chris directory created in the previous exercises.

8. Under your home directory, copy the nursery file into a new file named no_read. Use the chmod command to make this file read-only.

9. Using rm, try to delete no_read. What happens? Can you still delete the file? Read the rm man page if you need help.

10. Read about the -i option of the rm command in the rm man page. Enter the commands

```
cp sonnet nursery /lu/tmp
rm -i /lu/tmp/sonnet /lu/tmp/nursery
```

and reply to rm's questions so that you delete /lu/tmp/sonnet but not /lu/tmp/nursery.

## Chapter 4

Basic Tools: Five Ways to List a Directory

Chapter 3 showed how the ls command can list the contents of a directory, and how ls -l lists additional information about files and directories.

This chapter examines five different ways to do the same sort of job. This might sound odd or redundant, but there are several reasons why it makes sense:

- It shows there are several ways to do the same task—there is no uniquely "right" answer.

- Each approach uses a different format for displaying the information. Each of these formats has its strengths and weaknesses. When you know how to produce information in a variety of formats, you have more freedom to choose within a particular context.

- Most importantly, the different approaches illustrate several of the ways you can combine UNIX commands to produce results.

The first technique you'll look at is the use of *command options*. As you probably know from working with DOS, options modify the behavior of commands. In particular, you'll look at various options that you can use with the ls command, to change the information that ls outputs and the format of that output.

The second technique uses *glob constructs*, also called *wild card constructs* or *file name generation constructs*. UNIX lets you use simple character strings to stand for a collection of file names, in much the same way that some DOS commands use *.* to stand for every file under a directory. The UNIX facilities for file name representation are more extensive than the DOS facilities, and they're carried out in a different way. The way glob constructs are handled has repercussions that I'll discuss in detail.

The third technique uses the UNIX find command. This command searches through a directory to identify files and subdirectories that meet certain criteria. For example, you can use find to display all the files under a directory that have changed in the last week.

The fourth technique uses *redirection* to divert the output of a command like ls into a file. This is convenient when you want to keep the information for later use. Otherwise, the information just sweeps past on the screen and disappears forever.

The fifth technique uses *pipes* in a variety of ways. A pipe takes the output from one command and feeds it as input to another command. Using pipes you can link together several commands into a *pipeline* that performs a complex task with simple components. DOS has pipes too, but DOS utilities don't exploit pipes as effectively as UNIX utilities do.

ls Revisited

I've discussed several forms of the ls command:

```
ls
```

displays the names of the files and subdirectories in the current directory;

```
ls dirname
```

displays the names of the files and subdirectories in the directory given by dirname; and

```
ls -l dirname
```

provides detailed information about the files and subdirectories of dirname, including the size of the files, their permissions, and the date and time the files were last modified.

The Form of UNIX Options

The -l in the last ls form in the previous section is an example of a UNIX *option*. Most UNIX options take the form of a dash – (the minus sign) followed by a single letter or digit. Contrast this with DOS, where command options usually begin with a slash (/) instead of a dash. The option -l is usually pronounced "dash-ell."

In UNIX commands, it matters whether option letters are in uppercase or lowercase. For example, the `ls` command has both an `r` and an `-R` option, with completely unrelated effects.

Options must come immediately after the command name, before any other arguments on the command line. For example, you must write

```
ls -l dirname
```

If you switch the position of `-l` and `dirname`, you'll get incorrect results. Try it and see.

Options of ls

Now it's time to examine several of the more useful options of the `ls` command. Sign on to the MKS Tools software and follow along as I discuss each example.

Changing the Columns

First, enter the command

```
cd /lu/bin
```

to make `/lu/bin` your current directory. This directory contains a lot of files, and that will make it easier to see what I'm talking about.

Enter the command

```
ls
```

As always, `ls` displays the basenames of the files and directories under `/lu/bin`, arranged in columns with names sorted in alphabetical order down the columns. Now try

```
ls -x
```

(with a lowercase x). This gives you the same kind of output, except that names are sorted in alphabetical order across the columns instead of down the columns.

You can use this option to display the contents of any directory. For example, enter

```
ls -x /
```

This displays the contents of the root directory in the new form.

Now enter

```
cd
```

to return to your home directory.

Across or Down?

In some versions of UNIX, the default is for `ls` to sort names down columns, as we've shown. In others, the default is for `ls` to sort names across columns even if you don't specify `-x`. If the default is to sort names across columns, specifying the `-C` (uppercase C) option will sort down columns.

Size Information

Enter the command

```
ls -s /lu
```

This command displays the size of each file and subdirectory under the `/lu` directory. Sizes are given *blocks*, where each block is 512 bytes long. You'll find that measuring file sizes in terms of blocks is more convenient than in the byte counts that DOS uses. The numbers are smaller, so they're easier to compare and understand, just as it's simpler to measure long distances in miles rather than inches.

How Big Is a Block?

With the MKS Tools `ls` command, a block is 512 bytes, or half a kilobyte. On some other systems, blocks are 1024 bytes, or a full kilobyte.

You'll see that subdirectories are shown with a size of zero. This is one way that you can distinguish files from the subdirectories on DOS. Unfortunately, subdirectories don't necessarily have a size of zero on UNIX, so you can't distinguish files from directories using this technique on a true UNIX system.

The first line of output gives the total of the file and subdirectory sizes for the directory. This is just the sum of the other numbers shown. For example, the output of `ls -s /lu` is

```
total 1
  0 bin  0 etc  1 lu.bat  0 tmp  0 u
```

Combining Options

You can specify several options in the same command. For example, enter

```
ls -s -x
```

This displays file and subdirectory sizes in the column format discussed previously.

```
ls -s -x /
```

does the same thing for the root directory.

When you specify several options for a command, UNIX lets you use a short form to save typing. Simply enter the dash followed by all the letters and digits for the options you want. For example, enter

```
ls -sx
```

and you'll see that the output is the same as for

```
ls -s -x
```

When you specify several options, the order of the options usually doesn't matter. For example, all of the following are equivalent:

```
ls -s -x
ls -x -c
ls -xs
ls -sx
```

There are a few commands in which the order of the options does matter, but these are special cases. I'll note them as you encounter them.

Sometimes options can conflict with each other. For example, the -x option asks for a column form of output, while the -l option asks for full information, including permissions, file sizes, and so on. What happens when you use both options? Try it:

```
ls -lx
```

The output is the same as if you had just entered

```
ls -l
```

With -l, ls is obliged to provide full information on files and subdirectories. Because there's too much information to put into multiple columns, ls just ignores the -x.

If two options conflict with each other, a command often chooses one option as the important one and ignores the other. You might think that UNIX commands should give an error message instead of simply ignoring an option, but that would be at odds with the UNIX philosophy. UNIX presumes that users would rather see some kind of output than receive an error message.

File Types

Enter the command

```
ls -p /
```

You'll see that ls puts a slash (/) on the end of each subdirectory name, while it prints each file name without the slash. This is another way that you can use ls to distinguish between files and directories.

The -F option is related to -p. Enter

```
ls -F /
```

and you'll see that the output is similar to the output of ls -p. Directory names end in /. You'll also see that some files have a * at the end of their names. These are files that are *executable*.

On a true UNIX system, files are executable when you have x permission on them. Under DOS, all files are considered executable, so all files are marked with an *.

Information on a Directory Itself

The -d option tells ls that you want information on a directory itself, rather than its contents. For example, enter

```
ls -l /lu/etc
```

and you'll see the usual -l information on the contents of /lu/etc. Enter

```
ls -ld /lu/etc
```

and you'll see the usual `-l` information on `/lu/etc` itself.

Information on Subdirectories

The `-R` (uppercase) option tells `ls` to *walk* through the file system tree, listing the contents of each directory and subdirectory it encounters. (This is comparable to the DOS TREE command.) To see how this works, begin with the commands

```
cd
mkdir testdir
cp sonnet nursery testdir
```

to create a subdirectory named `testdir` under your home directory and to make copies of the `sonnet` and `nursery` files under `testdir`. Next, enter the command

```
ls -R
```

You'll see that `ls` first displays

```
.:
```

and lists the names of the files under the current directory. (Remember that `.` stands for the current directory.) `ls` then prints a blank line followed by

```
./testdir:
```

and the names of the file under `testdir`. If `testdir` contained a subdirectory of its own, `ls` would continue to list the contents of that subdirectory, and so on through the tree of files and subdirectories under your current directory.

You can, of course, combine the `-R` option with other `ls` options. For example, enter

```
ls -Rl
```

This combines the `-R` and `-l` options to print full information on the files under the current directory, then under subdirectories of the current directory, and so on.

Other ls *Options*

The ls command accepts many other options. I won't discuss them in this part of the book—while the other options are useful in specialized cases, most people will never need them. For full details, see the ls man page later in this book.

Note that many of the options described in the man page are only useful on a true UNIX system. For example, the -u option tells ls to display files in the order in which they were last accessed for either reading or writing. DOS does not keep track of the time of last access, so there's no way that the MKS Tools version of ls can implement -u correctly.

File Names That Begin with a Dot

By default, most UNIX versions of ls do not list files or directories with names that begin with the dot character. Such names are used for *initialization files* and other work files, as I'll discuss in later chapters. By specifying the -a option, you can tell ls to list these initialization files along with the ones it usually lists.

On DOS, file names cannot begin with a dot. Thus, the only difference between ls and ls -a on DOS is that ls -a displays . (standing for the current directory) and .. (standing for the parent directory of the current directory) as well as all the other files and directories.

Glob Constructs

If you're like most DOS users, you've probably used commands like

```
COPY A:*.* C:
```

to copy everything from diskette A: to your hard disk C:. The construct A:*.* stands for all the files on A:. This kind of short form lets you work with a group of files, without having to type in the names of all the files.

Like many features of DOS, *.* and similar constructs originated on UNIX. UNIX calls these constructs *glob constructs*, *wild card constructs* or *filename generation constructs*. You can use these constructs in place of path names, or as part of path names, to reduce the amount of typing you have to do.

> **What Does Glob Mean?**
> At one time, there was a UNIX program named `glob` that converted glob constructs into file names. I've heard a few speculations as to why people called it `glob`, but none of them sounds convincing. Unearthing the truth of this UNIX legend is a job for a better historian than I.

The ? Glob Construct

The simplest UNIX glob construct is the question mark (?). This stands for any single character that can appear in a file name, except the slash (/) separating path name components. For example, enter the command

```
more ?onnet
```

When the shell sees the ? glob character, it tries to *expand* the argument that contains the character. This means that the shell makes a list of the names of all existing files with names that look like a character followed by `onnet`. In this case, there is only one such file: `sonnet`. Therefore, the shell changes the previous command into

```
more sonnet
```

then executes the command.

Now, let's make the situation a little more complex. Enter the command

```
cp nursery bonnet
```

to make a new copy of the `nursery` file called `bonnet`. Now see what happens if you enter the command

```
more ?onnet
```

Again, the shell expands `?onnet` into a list of all file names that have the appropriate form. Now that you have two files with names that are in the right form, the preceding command becomes

```
more bonnet sonnet
```

When the ?onnet construct has been replaced with the list of file names, the shell executes the command. (The list is always sorted in alphabetical order.)

As another example of the same thing, enter the command

```
echo ?onnet
```

You'll see that the output is

```
bonnet sonnet
```

Once again, the shell expanded the ?onnet construct into a list of file names, changing the original command into

```
echo bonnet sonnet
```

Thus echo's output gives the list of names.

Here are a few more examples of the use of ? as a glob construct:

```
more ??????
```

displays the contents of all files in the current directory with names that have exactly six characters.

```
ls -l ???????
```

lists file information on all files with names that have exactly seven characters.

```
echo /lu/etc/??????
```

displays the names of all files under /lu/etc with names that have exactly six characters.

As a final example, enter the command

```
echo ?
```

When the shell sees the ? argument, it tries to expand that argument into a list of matching file names. But the argument stands for a file with a name that is only one character long, and if you've been following this tutorial as you've gone along, your current directory won't contain any such files. This means that the ? can't be expanded into an appropriate file name list. As a result, the argument just stays as ? and echo displays

```
?
```

If an argument can't be expanded into an appropriate list of file names, the shell leaves that argument as it is.

When Glob Expansion Happens

Under UNIX, the shell expands any arguments that contain glob constructs and then executes the expanded command line. Under DOS, glob constructs are expanded by each individual program rather than by the shell. Some programs have not been written to deal with glob constructs, so the usual glob constructs don't work.

As a result, glob constructs work with any UNIX command or program, because they're expanded by the shell before the command or program is executed. On DOS, glob constructs only work with specially written commands.

The * Glob Construct

The asterisk (*) is a glob construct that expands to any string of zero or more characters. For example, issue the command

```
echo *t
```

When the shell sees the * in the argument *t, it expands the argument into a list of all files in the current directory with names consisting of any string of characters, followed by a t. In other words, the above echo command displays the names of all files in the current directory with names ending in t. Similarly,

```
echo s*
```

displays the names of all files whose names begin with s.

The * is commonly pronounced "star" when it is used in glob constructs. For example, *t is usually pronounced "star-tee."

Enter the commands

```
cp sonnet sonnet18
echo sonnet*
```

You'll see that the output is

```
sonnet sonnet18
```

The * matches zero or more characters; thus sonnet* matches both sonnet and sonnet18.

You'll recall that this chapter is devoted to different ways to list the contents of a directory. You've probably guessed how glob constructs let you do this. Enter the command

```
echo *
```

Because the * can stand for any string of characters, the shell expands * into a list of all the files in the directory. Similarly,

```
echo /lu/etc/*
```

displays the names of all files in the /lu/etc directory.

Note the difference between this kind of list and the kind produced by the ls command (without options). The list produced by echo consists of all the file names on a single line, with a single space between each name. The list produced by ls is arranged into columns.

As a final example of the use of *, enter the command

```
cp * testdir
```

which copies all the files under the current directory into the testdir directory you created a few sections ago. The shell replaces the * with a list of all the appropriate names in the directory. Note that testdir will be one of these names, because * expands to names of both files and directories. When cp tries to copy testdir into itself, it will output an error message, but don't worry about it.

To get rid of everything under testdir, enter the command

```
rm testdir/*
```

This removes every file under testdir. You should be able to figure out how the command works.

Differences Between * and ? in UNIX and DOS

The * character means almost the same thing in DOS as it does in
UNIX; it stands for an arbitrary string of characters. In DOS, however, *
does not match the dot character. Thus the DOS command to copy
everything in the current directory into `testdir` would be

```
COPY *.* TESTDIR
```

while it would be only

```
cp * testdir
```

under UNIX. You need to write *.* on DOS, because of the difference in
the way the two treat the dot character. Similarly, a DOS command like
`DIR *T.*` will not list all the file names that end in T because the .*
stands for zero or more characters in the suffix, *after* the T.

The same principles apply with the ? character. On DOS, ? never
matches the dot character.

The [ ] Constructs

The ? and * glob constructs are recognized by both DOS and UNIX. UNIX,
however, has additional glob constructs that DOS does not recognize.

Matching a Set of Characters

The first glob construct that is unique to UNIX is written as a set of characters
inside square brackets, as in

```
[abc]
```

This construct can match any one of the characters inside the brackets. For
example,

```
[abc]def
```

could be expanded to any or all of

```
adef   bdef   cdef
```

It will not match names like `abdef` or `bcdef` because `[abc]` only matches a single character.

Remember that the shell only expands glob constructs to produce file names of existing files. Enter the command

```
echo [abc]onnet
```

and you'll see that the output is only

```
bonnet
```

The argument `[abc]onnet` could also be expanded to `aonnet` or `connet`, but your current directory doesn't contain anything that has these names. The only appropriate file is `bonnet`, so this is the only name created by the expansion. Enter the commands

```
cp sonnet connet
echo [abc]onnet
```

and you'll see that the output is now

```
bonnet connet
```

All glob constructs are expanded by checking for existing files with names of the appropriate form.

You can put *ranges* of characters inside the square brackets by specifying the first character in the range, a dash –, and the last character in the range. For example,

```
[a-z]
```

stands for all the lowercase characters. Enter the command

```
echo [a-z]onnet
```

and you'll see that the output is

```
bonnet connet sonnet
```

This is the set of all files with names that have the appropriate form. Note that [a-z]onnet is not the same as *onnet. *onnet also includes files that start with a digit, with uppercase letters, and with other characters valid in file names (- and .).

The square brackets can contain several ranges. For example,

```
[a-zA-Z0-9]
```

stands for the lowercase letters, the uppercase letters, and the digits. (Remember that UNIX file names can contain both upper- and lowercase letters.)

A Special Case

If you want a dash sign in the list of characters inside square brackets, you have to put it at the beginning or the end of the list. For example, [-az] matches a dash, the letter a or the letter z. You would not get the same effect if you wrote [a-z], because the construct looks like a range of characters.

Matching Anything Not in a Set of Characters

If the first character inside the square brackets is an exclamation point (!), the construct matches any single character that is *not* inside the brackets. For example,

```
[!abc]
```

matches any character except a, b, or c. Enter the command

```
echo [!abc]onnet
```

and you'll see that the output is

```
sonnet
```

93

The construct [!abc]onnet expands to a list of all file names ending in onnet, except those that begin with a, b, or c. Similarly, enter

```
echo [!n-z]onnet
```

and you'll see that the output is

```
bonnet connet
```

The [!n-z] stands for any character outside the range n through z.

Combining Glob Constructs

You can combine glob constructs if you like. For example, enter the command

```
echo [n-z]*
```

The output is the list of all names that begin with any character from n through z.

Quotation Marks and Glob Constructs

Enter the following command:

```
echo You are my lucky *
```

You'll see that the final * is expanded into a list of the files and directories under your current directory. This probably doesn't surprise you, but it does raise the question of how you would output an actual * character using the echo command.

The answer is to enclose the character in single or double quotation marks. For example, you can enter any of

```
echo "You are my lucky *"
echo 'You are my lucky *'
echo You are my lucky "*"
echo "You are" 'my lucky *'
```

and get the output

```
You are my lucky *
```

As long as the * is inside an argument that is quoted, the shell doesn't try to expand it into a file list.

The same goes for other glob constructs, of course. For example, enter

```
echo Put on your old grey ?onnet
echo "Put on your old grey ?onnet"
```

and you'll see that expansion happens in the first command but not the second.

Unbalanced Quotation Marks

If you're putting arguments into quotation marks, there's a chance that you might leave off a quotation mark by mistake. For example, enter

```
echo 'Hello
```

without putting in the closing single quotation mark. When you press Enter, you'll see

```
>
```

appear on the screen. Here's what is happening. You didn't put in a single quotation mark to close off the string, so the shell is still gathering input for the string. It prompts you with > rather than the usual command prompt to show you that it expects a continuation of the previous line. Enter a single quotation mark (') to finish off the string, then press Enter. You'll see that echo displays the string Hello, plus a blank line. The blank line shows that the argument for echo went to another line.

If the shell prompts you for input with >, remember that this means the shell is looking for a continuation of the previous line. This frequently means that you forgot a quotation mark in the previous line.

The Backslash and Glob Constructs

Quotation marks around an argument tell the shell to ignore any special meaning that a glob construct has. You can do the same thing by putting a backslash (\) in front of the construct's special characters. For example, enter

```
echo \*
```

and you'll see that the command simply displays

```
*
```

In UNIX, the backslash is called the *escape character*. When you put it in front of any special character, it turns off the special meaning of that character.

The backslash only turns off the special meaning of the character immediately following it. For example, enter

```
echo \* *
```

The output is a * followed by the names of everything in your current directory. Because of the backslash, the shell does not expand the first *; however, the second * has no backslash, so it is expanded normally.

The *find* Command

Continuing with the discussion of different ways to display the contents of a directory, I'm going to turn to a UNIX utility I haven't yet discussed: the find command. This has no relationship to the DOS FIND command. The UNIX find command has some features in common with the DOS TREE command, but it is more versatile than TREE.

The UNIX find command *finds* the names of files and directories that meet a specified set of criteria. To get an idea of find's output, enter the command

```
find /lu -print
```

This displays the names of all files and directories under the /lu directory, including those in subdirectories, sub-subdirectories, and so on. Names are grouped by directory and subdirectory. The first name in the list is /lu, the name of the directory itself.

The general form of a simple find command is

```
find dir -print
```

where *dir* is the name of the directory containing the files and subdirectories you want to list. For example, enter

```
find . -print
```

and you'll see the contents of the current directory (.).

Enter the command

```
ls
```

and contrast the output of ls with the output of find. The ls command only displays the basenames of files and directories; find displays absolute path names (if the directory is given with an absolute path name, as in /lu) or relative path names (if the directory is given with a relative path name, as in ., the current directory). Thus

```
ls /lu
```

displays

```
bin etc lu.bat tmp usr
```

but

```
find /lu -print
```

displays

```
/lu
/lu/bin
/lu/bin/banner.exe
```

and a list of all the other files and directories under /lu.

Complex UNIX Options

The examples of find commands that you've looked at so far all end with -print. This argument looks like a UNIX option because it starts with a dash (-). However, it is longer than other options discussed so far. As you've seen, the options of most UNIX commands are only one character long (not counting the dash).

-print is an example of a more complex kind of UNIX command option. Like other options, it starts with a dash, but the option name itself can be longer than one character.

The find command has many examples of complex UNIX options. In the subsections to follow, you'll see some of the options of find and how you can use them productively.

The -print **Option**

The -print option tells find to display the names that it finds under the given directory. With some versions of UNIX you have to remember to specify -print; otherwise, find won't display anything. With MKS Tools, find automatically displays its results, whether you specify -print or not. I'll always include the -print option in the examples to remind you that it is necessary with some versions of UNIX; however, if you want to save some typing, you can omit it for the purposes of these exercises.

The Type of Files

The -type option tells find what kind of thing you want it to find. (Note that this option has no connection with the DOS TYPE command.) For example, enter the command

```
find . -type d -print
```

find displays the names of all directories under your current directory, but does not display the names of any files. Enter

```
find . -type f -print
```

and find displays the names of all files, but not directories. Contrast this with

```
find . -print
```

which displays all the file names plus the names of the directories . and testdir. The -type option tells find to select only certain types of names to print.

Notice the form of the options:

```
-type d
-type f
```

This is one of several standard forms for complex UNIX options: the option name
(-type), followed by whitespace, followed by another argument. The argument
d stands for directories and f stands for files.

> **Whitespace Separation**
>
> With most versions of UNIX, you can put one or more whitespace
> characters between a complex option like -type and the value that
> follows it. However, a few older versions require exactly one space as
> separation.

You'll see many other options with a similar form:

```
-name value
```

where *name* is the name of the option itself, and *value* is some value that provides
additional information. You'll see another example of this in the next section.

> **Interrupting Commands**
>
> Some of the find examples suggested in this section and those that
> follow can take a good deal of time to execute. The time required
> depends on factors such as the type of machine you have and the num-
> ber of files on your hard disk.
>
> If you discover that a particular example takes longer to finish than you
> want to wait, you can *interrupt* the command by pressing Ctrl-C. This is
> one standard technique for interrupting programs on UNIX systems. The
> Del (or Delete) key is also widely used as an interrupt on UNIX systems,
> but that won't work on DOS.
>
> If you interrupt a command with Ctrl-C, the command might not stop
> right away. Several commands are designed to ignore interruptions until
> they reach a convenient time to quit.
>
> You shouldn't interrupt a command if the output of the command is
> important for subsequent exercises. However, if the output is just being
> displayed on the screen, you can usually skip looking at the output
> without missing much.

Change Times

The `-ctime` option tells `find` to display the names of files that have been *changed* in a certain number of days. For example, enter

```
find . -ctime 0 -print
```

`find` displays the names of all files under your current directory that have been changed in the past zero days (in other words, those that have been changed today). This will probably include files like `bonnet` and `connet` (which you just created recently), but will not include files that you haven't touched recently.

Now enter

```
find . -ctime 1 -print
```

This displays the names of all files under your current directory that were changed one day ago but haven't been changed since. (Of course, there would not be any such files if you didn't touch any files yesterday, and if you're scrupulous about setting the date and time on your system to reflect the real date and time.) Similarly,

```
find . -ctime 2 -print
```

displays the names of all files under your current directory that were changed two days ago but haven't been changed since. In general, the option

```
-ctime n
```

tells `find` to look for files that were changed *n* days ago but haven't been changed since.

A file is considered to have changed if its contents have been changed. If you just read the file, without changing the contents, the file itself does not change. For example, a command like

```
cp bonnet connet
```

does not change `bonnet`, because it just reads the contents of the file; however, it does change `connet` because it copies data into the file.

Now suppose you want to find the names of all the files that have been changed in the past week (because you want to back them up). Consider (but don't enter) the command

```
find / -ctime 7 -print
```

(You can enter the command if you want, but it might take a long time to finish.) The command looks under the root directory for all files that were changed exactly seven days ago. The option `-ctime 7` does not, for example, display files that were changed today.

To get around this problem, you need some way to specify change times of seven days or less. Do this with the option

```
-ctime -8
```

The `-8` stands for *less than eight days*, which is the same as *seven days or less*. Thus if you enter

```
find / -ctime -8 -print
```

the command displays the name of every file that has changed in the past week. You can enter this command now to see how it works, but be warned that it will search your entire hard disk—the process might take several minutes, depending on how fast your machine is and how many files you have. You might prefer to try a faster command like

```
find . -ctime -8 -print
```

which only searches your current directory rather than the entire disk.

You can also use an option of the form `-ctime +n` to find files that last changed more than n days ago. For example,

```
find . -ctime+7 -print
```

finds files that were changed more than a week ago.

Other Time Options

The `-atime` option works in the same way as `-ctime`, but it looks at *access times* rather than change times. A file is accessed whenever you try to read or write it. DOS doesn't keep track of access times, so the MKS Tools version of `find` treats `-atime` and `-ctime` as equivalent.

The `-mtime` option works in the same way, but it looks at *modification times* rather than change times. A file is modified whenever you change its characteristics (in other words, its permissions). Again, DOS doesn't keep track of modification times, so the MKS Tools version of `find` treats `-mtime` and `-ctime` as equivalent.

Comparing Change Times

The -newer option can serve much the same purpose as -ctime. The option has the form

```
-newer file
```

where *file* is the name of a file (an absolute or relative path name). This option tells find to compare all the files in a directory to the given *file* and to display those files that are newer (those with contents that have been changed more recently than the contents of *file*). For example, enter the command

```
find . -newer nursery -print
```

This displays all the files in the current directory with contents that have been changed more recently than the contents of the nursery file. The list should include all the files you've created while working through this chapter.

Name Forms

The -name option lets you use find to display a collection of file and directory names that have a given form. The option has the format

```
-name "form"
```

where *form* describes the form of a name using glob constructs. For example, enter the commands

```
cp sonnet testdir
find . -name "?onnet" -print
```

find tells you all the files and directories under the current directory with names of the given form. This includes the copy of sonnet that the cp command puts into testdir.

Note that the *form* must be put inside double or single quotation marks. You should be able to figure out why. If you entered the command

```
find . -name ?onnet -print
```

the shell would immediately expand ?onnet into a list of matching names. (Remember that the shell expands any argument that contains a glob construct, unless the argument is enclosed in single or double quotation marks.) The expansion would create

```
find . -name bonnet connet sonnet -print
```

which is not a valid form for `find`.

If you put quotation marks around *form*, the shell doesn't expand the glob constructs. The whole *form* is passed without change to the `find` command, and `find` can use that *form* to identify matching file names. If you omit the quotation marks, the shell expands the glob constructs immediately, before invoking `find`; the `find` command itself never sees the glob constructs.

Here are a few more examples of the `-name` option that you might find useful:

```
find / -name "*.bak" -print
```

searches the entire file system for files and directories with names that end with the suffix `.bak`. Files with this suffix are created by some programs as back-up copies of other files.

```
find / -name "*.tmp" -print
```

searches the entire file system for files and directories with names ending with the suffix `.tmp`. Files with this suffix are often temporary working files that can be deleted.

```
find . -name "*.doc" -print
```

searches the current directory for files and directories with names ending with the suffix `.doc`. Files with this suffix often contain documents produced by a word processing program.

Negating an Option

You can reverse the meaning of any `find` option by putting an exclamation mark (`!`) in front of it. For example,

```
find . ! -name "?onnet" -print
```

displays the names of all files and directories with names that do *not* end with `onnet`.

```
find / ! -ctime -365 -print
```

displays the names of all files and directories that have not changed in the last 365 days. You might use this command to identify files that are no longer in active use and that might be candidates for deletion.

```
find . ! -newer connet -print
```

displays the names of all files and directories under the current directory that are not newer than `connet`.

Combining Options

A `find` command can contain several options. In this case, `find` only displays the names of files and directories that satisfy all the criteria. For example,

```
find . -type d -newer sonnet -print
```

displays the names of all directories that are newer than the `sonnet` file.

Redirection

Commands like `ls` and `find` can produce a great deal of output, especially when you turn them loose on large directories. You might already have had the experience of watching the output from one of these commands disappear off the top of the screen before you could read it.

This section looks at a way to save a directory listing so that you can read it later. The approach does not use new commands, but it uses old commands in a slightly different way.

I/O Streams

UNIX programs perform input and output on *streams*. You might picture a stream as a door between the program and the kernel of the operating system. If the program wants to read input, it asks the kernel to deliver some input through the door; if the program wants to write output, it sends data out the door and the operating system does whatever else is necessary to deliver that data to its intended destination.

The streams used by a program are numbered. In effect, each door has its own number. These numbers are called *file descriptors*. File descriptors help the program distinguish between one door and another. For example, a command like

```
cp sonnet new
```

would have one stream (door) for the sonnet file and another for the new file. The cp program would tell the kernel to bring in data through the sonnet door and send out the same data through the new door. cp would use file descriptor numbers to tell the kernel which door was which.

In order to use a stream, the program has to *open* the stream; this is like opening a door. More precisely, the program must ask the kernel to open the stream, just as you might get a butler or a security guard to open a door for you. The kernel opens the stream and assigns a file descriptor number to the stream; this is like painting a number on the door, so that you have a way to refer to the door and distinguish it from all others.

To see how this works, let's go back to the cp command shown previously. cp says to the kernel "Open a stream that lets me read from the file sonnet," and "Open a stream that lets me write to the file new." The kernel does whatever work is necessary to create the two streams, and gives cp a file descriptor number for each door. The file descriptor numbers let cp identify the two doors later on when it starts reading and writing.

Notice that cp tells the kernel whether it wants to read or write on a stream. This lets the kernel check whether you have appropriate read or write permissions on the associated file. It also offers a bit of insurance against programming errors; if a program says it only wants to read a particular stream but later tries to write on that stream, the program might have an error and the kernel might have to kill the program to prevent trouble.

Standard Streams

When you ask the shell to execute a program, the shell automatically opens three streams for the program:

- The *standard input* stream, which always has the file descriptor number 0. This is set up so that the program can only read from the stream, not write to it.

- The *standard output* stream, which always has file descriptor 1. This is set up so that the program can only write to the stream, not read from it.

- The *standard error* stream, which always has file descriptor 2. This is set up so that the program can only write to the stream, not read from it.

The program can use these streams as soon as it starts executing. If it wants to use another stream, it has to ask the kernel to open a new stream and wait until the kernel has set up the stream appropriately.

105

Standard Output

Normally, when the shell sets up a standard output stream for a program, the stream is attached to the monitor screen. As a result, if the program writes data to the standard output, the data shows up on the monitor screen. Commands like ls, echo, and find display their information by writing to the standard output.

You can tell the shell to attach the standard output stream to a file rather than the terminal screen. For example, enter the command

```
ls >info
```

You won't see any output on the screen from this command. The >info notation is an instruction to the shell. DOS users will be familiar with this redirection construct, because you can use the same notation on DOS. The notation says that you want the shell to attach the standard output of this ls command to a file named info instead of to the monitor screen. When ls produces its information, it just sends the information out the standard output door as usual; however, the kernel delivers the information to a new file called info instead of to the monitor. Enter

```
more info
```

to display the contents of info, and you'll see that it contains the output that ls usually displays on the screen.

This gives you a new way to display the contents of a directory: save the output of ls or find in a file, then display the file with more. For example, enter

```
find . -type f -print >out
more out
```

In the first instruction, you *redirect* the standard output of find into a file named out. In the second instruction, you read the contents of out with more. Note that this technique avoids the problem of information disappearing from the screen faster than you can read it. All the information is saved in a file, and then you can read the file bit by bit, using more.

Redirection Order

A redirection argument can appear anywhere on the command line, provided that it comes after the command name itself. For example, the following are equivalent:

```
find . -type f -print >out
find . -type f >out -print
find . -type >out f -print
find . >out -type f -print
find >out . -type f -print
```

In most cases, however, you'll find that it's a good policy to put the redirection at the end of the command—it makes the command easier to read.

Appending to the Standard Output

Now enter these commands:

```
ls -l >out
more out
```

This saves the output of ls in the out file you just created, then uses more to read the file.

With the >out notation, the output of ls *overwrites* (replaces) the previous contents of out. Sometimes, however, you want output to add to what is already in a file rather than overwriting the current contents. To do this, use >> rather than >. For example, enter

```
find . -type f -print >>out
more out
```

The `>>out` construct *appends* the output of `find` to the existing contents of `out`. The `more` command will show you that `out` contains the output of the previous `ls` command, followed by the output of the `find` command.

Here's a practical example of redirection in action. Suppose you want a list of all files in the file system with names ending with the `.bak` or `.tmp` suffixes. You can get this list with the commands

```
find / -name "*.bak" -print >out
find / -name "*.tmp" -print >>out
more out
```

The first `find` command uses `>out`, so it overwrites the current contents of `out`. The second `find` command uses `>>out`, so it appends new data to the current contents of `out`. Finally, `more` displays the result.

You can use this kind of redirection as a way to put text into a file. Enter the commands

```
echo "Mary had a little lamb" >out
echo "Its fleece was white as snow" >>out
echo "And everywhere that Mary went" >>out
echo "The lamb was sure to go." >>out
more out
```

and you'll see that the contents of `out` are

```
Mary had a little lamb
Its fleece was white as snow
And everywhere that Mary went
The lamb was sure to go.
```

The first `echo` command uses `>out` to overwrite the previous contents of `out`. The subsequent commands use `>>out` to add to the contents.

Redirection Is Handled by the Shell

It's important to remember that redirection is handled by the shell, not by the command itself. The shell sets up the standard output, standard input, and standard error streams for a command, then starts the command running. If the command line contains any redirection constructs like >out, the shell uses them to set up the standard streams, then throws the constructs away. The command itself doesn't know that it's been redirected.

For example, if you enter

```
find . -type f -print >out
```

the shell sets up the standard output for the command to go to out, then executes the command as if it were

```
find . -type f -print
```

The command itself doesn't know that its output has been redirected.

Standard Input

The standard input stream is usually associated with the keyboard. As it happens, you haven't examined many commands that take input from the keyboard, but there is one: the cat command discussed in Chapter 3 reads from the standard input if you don't give it an input file. For example, enter

```
cat >out
This is an example of input.
It goes into the "out" file.
^Z
```

where ^Z is the Ctrl-Z character (not a ^ followed by Z). On DOS, Ctrl-Z stands for *end of file*, or in this case, *end of input*. UNIX uses the Ctrl-D character for the same purpose, but because MKS Tools is a simulation of UNIX on DOS, you have to use the DOS Ctrl-Z.

The previous `cat` command reads the standard input and writes to the standard output; because the standard output is redirected to `out`, the text that you typed in is copied to `out`. You can see this for yourself by entering

```
more out
```

which displays

```
This is an example of input.
It goes into the "out" file.
```

As an example of redirecting the standard input, enter the command

```
cat <out
```

The <out construct tells the shell that `cat`'s standard input should be the `out` file. Because the command line doesn't redirect the standard output, the output goes to the screen. In other words, the preceding command displays the contents of `out`.

`more` is another command that reads the standard input if you don't specify an input file. For example, enter

```
more <nursery
```

and you'll see that `more` uses the `nursery` file as its input. The preceding command has exactly the same effect as

```
more nursery
```

but the different forms are processed differently. In the first form, the shell sets up `nursery` as the standard input for `more`; it then invokes `more` without any arguments. Because `more` doesn't have any arguments, it reads from the standard input, which is the `nursery` file. In the second form, the name `nursery` is passed as an argument to `more` and `more` reads that file.

You'll see more examples of redirecting the standard input in future chapters, after I've discussed other commands that make use of input.

Standard Error

Programs use the standard error stream when they want to write out a diagnostic message. By default, the shell associates the standard error stream with the terminal screen.

You might wonder why UNIX separates the standard output from the standard error—they're both output streams, and (by default) they both display information on the screen. To see why it's a good idea to separate the two, enter the command

```
find testdi -type f -print >out
```

Notice that I asked you to type `testdi`, not `testdir`. This is a simple typing error, the sort of mistake that's easy to make. You'll see that `find` displays a message saying that it can't find `testdi`.

`find` displayed this message on the standard error, and the message appeared on your screen. If `find` had written the message on the standard output, the message would have gone into `out`, because the standard output was redirected to `out`. As a result, you wouldn't see the error message; if you didn't notice the typing mistake, you might think that the `find` command did its job properly, even though an error took place. By writing important messages on the standard error rather than the standard output, a program can make sure that you see the message, even if the standard output has been redirected.

There is a way to redirect the standard error if you really want to. For example, if you're a programmer, you know that you frequently get a lot of errors the first time you compile some new source code. In this case, you might want to redirect those error messages into a file so that you can read them at your leisure, rather than have them flash by on the screen. You can redirect the standard error with a construct of the form

```
2>file
```

where *file* is the name of the file where you want the program to write the errors. Remember that 2 is the file descriptor number for the standard error, so `2>`*file* redirects the standard error. For example, enter

```
find testdi -type f -print >out 2>errout
```

111

This command contains the typing error you made before. The command redirects the standard output into out and redirects the standard error into a file called errout. Enter the command

```
more errout
```

and you'll see that it contains the error message produced by find.

Pipes

In the last section, you looked at a way of saving a directory listing in a file. By displaying that file, you can display the directory contents (or more precisely, what the contents were at the time that the listing was obtained).

One advantage of saving directory listings in files is that long listings don't disappear off the top of the screen. In this final section, you'll look at another way to get around this problem: *pipes*.

Pipelines

A *pipe* connects the standard output of one command with the standard input of another command. In other words, the output of one command is *piped into* another command as input.

To connect two commands with this kind of pipe, just put the or-bar character (¦) between the two commands. For example,

```
find . -type f -print ¦ more
```

tells the shell to create a pipe between the two commands

```
find . -type f -print
more
```

You'll recall that if `more` is called without arguments, it reads its input from the standard input. This means that the information produced by `find` is piped as input into `more`, and then `more` displays that information. By piping information into `more`, you don't have to worry about lines disappearing off the top of the screen before you have a chance to see them.

You can use the same approach with `ls`. For example, enter

```
ls -l ¦ more
```

This pipes the output of `ls -l` into `more` to make the output easier to read.

Machines and Bins

In order to understand the distinction between pipes and redirection, some people find it helpful to picture commands as machines that take input and produce output, and to picture files as bins that can feed input into a machine or take output from a machine. Using output redirection in a set of commands such as

```
find . -type f -print > out
more out
```

is like saving the output of the `find` machine in a bin named `out`, then wheeling the bin over to a new machine named `more` and running the contents of the `out` bin through the `more` machine. In contrast, using pipes such as

```
find . -type f -print ¦ more out
```

is like hooking up the `find` machine to the `more` machine so that whatever comes out of `find` immediately goes into `more`.

Thus output redirection with > always sends the output to a file (a bin), and piping with ¦ always sends the output to another command (a machine).

A sequence of commands linked together by pipes is called a *pipeline*. You can put any number of commands into a pipeline, and you'll see some examples of this in later chapters. For now, the most important use of pipes is using `more` to paginate the output of other commands.

DOS Pipes Versus UNIX Pipes

As experienced DOS users probably know, DOS also lets you create pipelines. However, there is a difference between the ways that DOS and UNIX handle pipes.

On DOS, the system executes the first command in the pipeline and saves its output in a temporary file. After the first command is finished, the system executes the next command in the pipeline, passing the temporary file as input, and saving its output in another temporary file. After this second command is finished, the next command in the pipeline is executed, and so on until all the commands are finished. The temporary files created during this process are deleted when they are no longer needed. With this approach, the system only executes one command at a time.

On UNIX, the system executes all the commands simultaneously. Data is not stored in temporary holding files; it is piped directly from the memory of one executing command into the memory of another. This means that you can get faster results, because you don't have to wait for one command to finish before the next command starts working.

Chapter Review

Table 4.1 shows the `ls` command options discussed in this chapter. For a complete option list, see the `ls` man page.

Table 4.1. Options for the `ls` command.

Option	Meaning
-a	List all files, including names starting with dot
-C	Multicolumn output, sorted down columns
-d	Give information only on directory itself
-F	Mark directories with /, executables with *
-l	Give complete information
-p	Mark directories with /
-R	List information on directories, subdirectories, sub-subdirectories, etc.
-s	Display size in blocks
-x	Multicolumn output, sorted across rows

Table 4.2 shows the glob constructs that can be used in arguments for UNIX commands. If an argument contains a glob construct, the shell expands the argument by checking for any appropriate file or directory names with a form that matches the form of the argument. If there are matching names, the shell replaces the argument with a list of all matching names, sorted in alphabetical order. If there are no matching names, the shell leaves the argument alone. The shell does not perform file name expansion on arguments enclosed in single or double quotation marks, and it ignores the special meaning of any character preceded by a backslash (\).

Table 4.2.   UNIX glob constructs.

Construct	Meaning
?	Matches any single character
*	Matches any sequence of zero or more characters
[...]	Matches any single character inside the brackets
[!...]	Matches any single character not inside the brackets

The find command displays the names of all files and subdirectories under a directory that meet specified criteria. The criteria are specified by complex options. Options for find include those given in Table 4.3.

Table 4.3.   Options for find.

Option	Meaning
-print	Displays results
-atime *n*	Finds files accessed *n* days ago
-ctime *n*	Finds files changed *n* days ago
-ctime *-n*	Finds files changed less than *n* days ago
-mtime *n*	Finds files whose characteristics were modified *n* days ago
-name *"form"*	Finds files with names matching *form*
-newer *file*	Finds files newer than *file*
-type d	Displays only directories
-type f	Displays only files

UNIX programs perform I/O using streams. A stream is like a door through which a program can obtain input or send output. Each stream has an associated file descriptor number to distinguish it from other streams.

115

When the shell invokes a program, it sets up three streams for it:

- The standard input (file descriptor 0)
- The standard output (file descriptor 1)
- The standard error (file descriptor 2)

By putting redirection constructs on a command line, you can tell the shell to redirect one or more of a program's standard streams so that the stream is associated with a file instead of the keyboard or the monitor screen. Table 4.4 shows the possible redirection constructs. These constructs can appear anywhere on the command line, as long as they come after the command name itself; however, a command line is usually easier to read if you put redirection constructs at the end.

Table 4.4.   Redirection constructs.

Construct	Meaning
`>file`	Send standard output to `file`, overwriting current contents
`>>file`	Append standard output to `file`
`<file`	Read from `file` as standard input
`2>file`	Send standard error to `file`

If you are entering input from the keyboard, you enter a special character to indicate the end of the input. On DOS and on MKS Tools, the character is Ctrl-Z; on UNIX, the character is usually Ctrl-D, but this can be changed by customization.

A pipe takes the standard output of one command and feeds it in as the standard input of another command. Pipes are indicated by putting the or-bar (¦) between commands. A sequence of commands joined by pipes is called a pipeline. The `more` command is very popular as the last command in a pipeline, because it makes it easier to read large amounts of output.

Exercises

1. Read the man page for the `ls` command. Use the appropriate option of `ls` to display the contents of your home directory in reverse alphabetical order.

2. Read the man page for the head command. Use head to display the first five lines of sonnet. Then use head to display the first ten lines of nursery. Why is head useful when UNIX already offers so many other ways to display the contents of a file?

3. The ls -s command tells you file sizes in terms of blocks. The du command does much the same thing. Read the man page for du and find out the sizes of your home directory and the /lu directory.

4. The df command determines the amount of free space on a device. Read the man page for df and find the amount of free space on your hard drive.

5. Use banner to display big-letter versions of all file names ending in onnet under your current directory.

6. Enter the command

```
echo "It's time!"
```

This shows that you can put a single quotation mark (used as an apostrophe in this example) inside double quotation marks. Use banner to display the words DON'T PANIC in large, friendly letters (one word per line).

7. The KornShell lets you enter two separate commands on the same line by separating them with a semicolon (;). For example,

```
ls ; ls /lu
```

has two ls commands, one displaying the current directory and one displaying /lu. Use echo to display the string Faster; ever faster. (Hint: you'll need quotation marks to overcome the special meaning of the ;.)

8. Find the names of all files under /lu that have the .exe suffix. What do these files hold?

9. Create a file containing the names of all the files under your home directory.

10. The cal command creates a calendar—see the cal man page. Using cal, create a file that contains calendars of the next three months.

11. cd to the /lu/bin directory. Using ls and banner, display the file names in this directory with large letters.

12. Using find and banner, display the file names in the /lu/bin directory with large letters. What's the difference between this and the output of the previous exercise?

## Chapter 5

Popular Tools

T his chapter examines a few of the most popular commands on UNIX. You'll find that the commands are straightforward and simple to use. However, you can combine them with other commands, through pipes and redirection, to perform very sophisticated operations.

The grep command scans one or more text files to see if they contain specified strings. At its simplest, you specify a string like abc, and grep displays all lines that contain the string. However, grep also has a sophisticated *pattern-matching* ability that lets you specify more complex searching jobs. For example, you can ask grep to look for lines that begin with the letter A and end with the letter Z. You'll see just how useful this can be in the examples, and in later chapters of this book.

The diff command compares two text files and displays the differences between the two. This is particularly useful when you have two closely related files to compare, such as two different versions of the same report. diff can quickly summarize how the two versions differ.

The wc command displays the number of lines, words, and characters in a text file.

The sort command lets you sort the contents of text files according to selected criteria. In some respects, it is similar to the DOS SORT command, but the UNIX sort is more versatile.

The tar command is one of several commands that can be used to back up and restore files on a UNIX system. The facilities of tar are also convenient when you are shipping files from one system to another.

The lp command can print hard copy versions of text files. Some UNIX and UNIX look-alike systems call this command lpr.

Searching for Strings: *grep*

The grep command searches through one or more files and displays lines that contain matches for a specified string. For example, enter

```
grep Mary nursery
```

This searches through nursery and displays all the lines that contain the string Mary. It is important to enter the arguments in the right order:

```
grep string file
```

The string you want to find must be given before the file you want to search.

The Origin of the Name grep

As you'll see shortly, grep can display lines that match *regular expressions*. Thus the command could be called Global Regular Expression Print, or grep for short.

To be technically correct, the name actually comes from a command from a UNIX text editor, which is written g/re/p, where g stands for *global*, re is a regular expression, and p stands for *print*. However, the effect is the same.

You can use grep to search through several files. For example, enter

```
grep the sonnet nursery
```

This searches through sonnet and nursery and displays all the lines that contain the string the. Notice that the string might be part of longer words like thee or breathe.

You may find that the output of the last grep command is too large to fit on the screen. To avoid losing information off the top of the screen, you can always pipe the output through more. To do this, enter the line

```
grep the sonnet nursery ¦ more
```

This pipes the output of grep through the more command, so that you can read through the output screen by screen.

You can use grep to search for strings that contain blanks. However, you must enclose the search string in quotation marks. For example, enter

```
grep "The lamb" nursery
```

and grep displays all lines in nursery that contain The lamb.

Clarifying with Quotation Marks

grep command lines can be confusing to look at, because it's difficult to distinguish the string argument from the files. Some people make it a policy to enclose the string argument in quotation marks, even when it's not necessary. For example, in the command

```
grep "the" sonnet nursery
```

the quotation marks around the string the make it stand out from the file names that follow it.

Case Sensitivity

Normally, grep pays attention to the case of letters when it looks for strings. For example, enter

```
grep "the" sonnet nursery
grep "The" sonnet nursery
```

You'll notice that the two commands display different collections of lines. The first looks for the (entirely in lowercase), while the second looks for The (with the first letter in uppercase).

From time to time, you may want grep to ignore the case of letters. To do this, specify the option -i before the string argument. For example, enter

```
grep -i "the" sonnet nursery ¦ more
```

In this case, grep displays lines that contain either the or The, as well as any other combination of upper- and lowercase letters.

Remember that the option -i comes before the string argument. In UNIX commands, options come before arguments.

Regular Expressions

grep searches for strings that meet specified criteria. So far, you've only used it to look for strings that exactly match the string given on the command line. However, you can specify more sophisticated searching criteria by using *regular expressions*.

A regular expression is a string that describes a pattern of characters. Regular expressions can contain special characters, sometimes called *metacharacters*. Regular expressions can also contain normal characters, in other words, letters and digits. The next sections discuss the most common metacharacters and how you can use them in grep commands.

Note: This chapter describes a collection of the most useful regular expressions. However, there are many others that I don't touch on here. For a complete description of all recognized regular expressions, see Appendix C.

The Beginning of a Line

The caret (^) is a metacharacter that stands for the beginning of a line. For example, enter

```
grep "^Mary" nursery
```

The argument in quotation marks is a regular expression made up of the metacharacter ^ (the beginning of the line) followed by the normal characters Mary. The regular expression therefore tells grep to look for lines where Mary occurs at the beginning of the line. Enter

```
grep "Mary" nursery
```

to see the contrast. If you omit the ^, grep displays lines that contain Mary anywhere in the line.

As another example, enter the two commands

```
ls -l >out
grep "^d" out
```

The `ls` command obtains information about the current directory and redirects that information into `out`. Then the `grep` command looks for all lines that begin with the letter `d`. Lines that begin with `d` provide information about directories. As a result, the `grep` command extracts only the information about directories and displays that information on the screen. You can use the same principle to obtain information on ordinary files only. Enter

```
grep "^-" out
```

and the `grep` command only displays the lines that begin with `-`. These lines describe files.

Regular Expressions Never Match More Than One Line
   `grep` always searches one line at a time. You cannot tell `grep` to find a string that starts on one line and ends on another.

The End of a Line

The dollar sign ($) is a metacharacter that stands for the end of a line. For example, enter

```
grep "lamb$" nursery
```

to display all lines that contain `lamb`, followed by the end of the line. `grep` therefore displays all lines that end in `lamb`.
Enter

```
grep "lamb" nursery
```

to see the contrast. This displays lines that contain `lamb` anywhere in the line.

Metacharacters Aren't Always Special

The $ has its special meaning only when it appears at the end of a regular expression. For example, consider $1.00 as a regular expression. Here, it's clear that $ can't stand for the end of the line; you can't follow the end of a line with additional characters. As a result, `grep` knows that you're looking for a real dollar sign followed by a string that matches 1.00.

The same principle holds for ^. If you want it to stand for the beginning of the line, it has to appear in an appropriate place in the regular expression (usually at the beginning). Otherwise, `grep` assumes that you're looking for a real caret character.

Matching an Arbitrary Character

The dot (.) is a metacharacter that will match any other character. For example, enter

```
grep ".he" nursery
```

This searches through `nursery` for lines that contain any character followed by he. You'll see lines that contain words like the, The, She, and so on. With some lines, you may have to look closely to see where the matching string is. For example, in the line

```
And everywhere that Mary went
```

the matching string is whe inside everywhere. In the line

```
And sat down beside her
```

the matching string is ' he': the space and the he at the beginning of her.

> **Dot and ?**
>
> Because . can stand for any character, it serves the same purpose as the ? glob construct. However, it can be misleading to draw too many comparisons between regular expressions and glob constructs. Regular expressions are used when you want to locate strings in text files; glob constructs are used when you want to generate a list of file names in a command line.

It is often useful to combine the dot metacharacter with other metacharacters. For example, enter

```
grep "^.he" nursery
```

This displays all lines that have a string matching .he at the beginning of the line. These lines begin with The, There, and She.

Be careful to remember the special meaning for the dot. For example, consider the command

```
grep ".$" nursery
```

At first glance, you might think that this displays all lines ending in a period. However, enter the command and you'll see this isn't so. The regular expression .$ stands for any character followed by the end of the line; in other words, it stands for the last character on the line. As a result, grep finds a match on every line of the file, except for lines that don't contain any characters at all.

You'll learn how to display all lines that end in a period later in this chapter.

Character Repetitions

The asterisk (*) is a metacharacter that stands for zero or more repetitions of the preceding character. For example, enter

```
grep "uf*e" nursery
```

125

You'll see that the output is

```
Little boy blue
Little Miss Muffet
Sat on a tuffet
And frightened Miss Muffet away.
```

The regular expression uf*e stands for a u, followed by zero or more f characters, followed by an e. In

```
Little boy blue
```

there are zero f characters between the u and the e. In the other lines, there are two.

---

*—Glob Versus Regular Expressions

In regular expressions, * always refers to the preceding character. For example, a* matches a, aa, aaa, and so on. as well as a zero number of as.

In glob constructs, * stands for any string of zero or more characters and has nothing to do with the preceding character. For example, a* as a glob construct expands to all files whose names start with a, including files named abc, apple, aardvark.doc, and so on. The glob construct * is most similar to the regular expression .*.

The * is most often used in the .* construct, which stands for any string of zero or more characters. For example, enter

```
grep "W.*e" nursery
```

This looks for any line that contains a W followed by any number of characters, followed by an e. In the output, you'll see the lines

```
Wee Willie Winkie
Who could travel much faster than light
Who ate a bad apple and died
```

The .* always matches the longest possible string of characters. For example, in

```
Wee Willie Winkie
```

the `W.*e` expression matches the whole line, even though `We`, `Wee`, `Willie`, `Wee Willie`, and so on are all strings that start with *W* and end in *e*. Matching the whole line doesn't make any difference when you're using regular `grep`, because `grep` always prints the whole line anyway. It can make a difference when you use regular expressions with other UNIX software (e.g., the `vi` text editor, which is discussed in Chapter 6).

As another example of `.*`, enter

```
grep "^A.*r$" nursery
```

This regular expression may look cryptic at first, but you should find it simple if you take it apart piece by piece:

- `^A`   An uppercase letter A at the beginning of the line

- `.*`   followed by any sequence of zero or more characters

- `r$`   and having a lowercase r at the end of the line

The regular expression therefore stands for any line that begins with A, ends with r, and has zero or more characters in between. This matches the lines

```
Along came a spider
And sat down beside her
```

Character Sets

In the last chapter, you saw that you could make a glob construct that stood for a set of characters by enclosing the characters in square brackets. The same trick works in regular expressions. Enter

```
grep "[Tt]he" nursery
```

and you'll see all lines that contain either `The` or `the`. Enter

```
grep "[TS]he" nursery
```

and you'll see all lines that contain either `The` or `She`.

When you use character sets like this, it's important to enclose the regular expression in single or double quotation marks. Otherwise, the shell will assume that the character set is a glob construct and expand it.

Character sets in regular expressions can contain ranges, just like the ranges in the corresponding glob construct. For example, enter

```
grep "[a-z]he" nursery
```

This displays lines that contain any lowercase character followed by he.

If the first character after the opening bracket is a caret (^), the construct stands for any character that is not inside the character set. For example, enter

```
grep "[^a-z]he" nursery
```

This displays lines that contain any character that is not a lowercase letter, followed by he. These lines include such matches as The, She, and ' he' (where he follows a blank character). Note that ^ doesn't mean *the beginning of a line* when it appears inside brackets in this way.

! Versus ^

[!a-z] is the glob construct that matches any character that is not a lowercase letter. [^a-z] is the regular expression that does the same thing. Notice that the glob construct uses the exclamation mark (!), while the regular expression uses ^. (I've never heard a good explanation why the two are different. It's just one of those UNIX idiosyncrasies you have to get used to.)

Metacharacters and the Backslash

How would you display all the lines that end in a period? I've already mentioned that

```
grep ".$" nursery
```

doesn't work, because the dot is a metacharacter.

The answer is to use the backslash (\) character. You've already seen that you can tell the shell to ignore the special meaning of a glob character by putting a backslash in front of the character. The same trick works for metacharacters in regular expressions. Enter

```
grep "\.$" nursery
```

and grep displays only the lines that end with a period.

Summary of Regular Expressions

Table 5.1 shows the regular expressions that we've discussed so far, and Table 5.2 reviews the glob constructs. These tables should help you compare and contrast the two.

Table 5.1.   Regular expressions.

Construct	Meaning
^	Beginning of a line
$	End of a line
.	Matches any character
*	Zero or more repetitions of the previous regular expression
[. . .]	Matches any character listed inside the brackets
[^ . . .]	Matches any character not listed inside the brackets

Table 5.2.   Glob constructs.

Construct	Meaning
?	Matches any character
*	Matches any string of zero or more characters
[. . .]	Matches any character listed inside the brackets
[! . . .]	Matches any character not listed inside the brackets

Using grep *in Pipes*

If you don't specify a file for grep to search, grep searches the standard input. This makes it possible to use grep in pipes, to extract information from other commands. For example, enter the command

```
ls -l ¦ grep "^d"
```

This executes ls -l to obtain information about the current directory, then pipes that information through grep. grep displays all the lines that begin with d, the ones that provide information about directories. Similarly,

```
ls -l | grep "^-"
```

only displays information about the files under the current directory.

You'll recall that the -p option of ls marks directories by putting a slash (/) at the end of their names. Enter

```
ls -p / | grep "/$"
```

This executes ls -p on the root directory, then pipes the result through a grep command that only displays lines that end with a slash. As a result, the preceding command displays the names of all the directories under your root directory. If the list is too long to fit on your display screen, you could enter

```
ls -p / | grep "/$" | more
```

to pipe the information through more. Remember that there is no limit to the number of commands you can connect in a pipeline.

With a bit of imagination, you should be able to figure out many ways you can use grep in a pipeline to select only the information you want to see. For example, how would you obtain a list of all the files under the root directory that were changed in the month of April? You can use ls -l to obtain the change dates of all the files under the directory, then use grep to display all the output lines that contain the string Apr:

```
ls -l / | grep "Apr"
```

You can, of course, use a similar command for any other month of the year. (Note: the preceding grep command just displays any line that contains the string Apr. Remember that the output of ls -l displays many other pieces of information besides the change date. If any of these other pieces of information contains the string Apr, grep displays the line, even if the file didn't actually change in April. Such coincidences happen only rarely, but you should be aware of the possibility.)

Extended Regular Expressions

According to draft 10 of the POSIX.2 standard, grep also accepts *extended regular expressions* in addition to the basic regular expressions discussed in previous sections. Extended regular expressions make it possible for you to make more sophisticated searches; for example, with an extended regular expression, you can search for several different strings at once.

The *-E* Option

If you want to use an extended regular expression with `grep`, you must specify the `-E` option. This tells `grep` that you are going to use an extended regular expression rather than a basic one.

The `-E` option for `grep` is a feature of the proposed POSIX.2 standard; it is not currently recognized by SVID or older versions of UNIX. Those older versions of UNIX used a separate command named `egrep` to search using extended regular expressions. For example, where POSIX.2 would say

```
grep -E "regexp" file
```

older versions of UNIX would say

```
egrep "regexp" file
```

Because AT&T is committed to conforming to POSIX at some time in the future, the MKS Tools only have a `grep` command, instead of having separate `grep` and `egrep` commands that do almost the same thing. Be warned, however, that if you use an older version of UNIX, you may need to use `egrep` instead of `grep -E`.

Multiple Choice

In extended regular expressions, the or-bar (¦) is a metacharacter that separates several possible choices. For example, enter

```
grep -E "Little¦Wee" nursery
```

The `-E` tells `grep` that you're using an extended regular expression. The expression `Little¦Wee` matches either `Little` or `Wee`. You'll see that the output is

```
Little boy blue
Little Miss Muffet
Little Jack Horner
Wee Willie Winkie
```

The or-bar indicates a multiple choice: either/or. In this context, it has nothing to do with pipes. In fact, you need to enclose the regular expression in single or double quotation marks to ensure that the or-bar isn't interpreted as a pipe symbol.

131

You can write several alternatives separated with or-bars. For example, enter

```
grep -E "sheep¦cow¦lamb" nursery
```

and grep displays lines that contain any of the three specified animals.

The Beginning and End of a Word

In extended regular expressions, the construct \< (a backslash followed by an opening angle bracket) stands for the beginning of a word. For example, enter

```
grep -E "\<he" nursery
```

and grep displays all lines from the nursery file containing words that begin with he (such as the word her).

Similarly, the construct \> (a backslash followed by a closing angle bracket) stands for the end of a word. For example, enter

```
grep -E "he\>" nursery
```

and grep displays all lines from the nursery file containing words that end with he (such as the word the).

Of course, you can combine the two. "\<he\>" matches he if and only if he is a complete word. For example, enter the command

```
grep -E "\<he\>" nursery
```

The command searches through nursery to see if there are any lines that contain the word he (in lowercase). There are no such lines, so grep does not display output. Now enter,

```
grep -E -i "\<he\>" nursery
```

The -i option tells grep to ignore the case of the letters, so grep looks for the words he, He, HE, and hE. This time grep finds the line

```
He stuck in his thumb
```

Remember that you can combine options if you like, so you can write

```
grep -Ei "\<he\>" nursery
```

if you want to save yourself some typing.

Why Do You Need the Backslash?
  You might be wondering why grep wants you to enter \> and \< instead of just > and <. The answer should be clear if you look at an example. If you just wrote

```
grep -E <he nursery
```

the <he looks like a redirection construct. Even if you put it inside quotation marks, as in

```
grep -E "<he" nursery
```

there's still the possibility of confusion. By using a backslash, you turn off the meaning of < and > as redirection constructs. If you omit the backslash, grep looks for the characters themselves. For example, <he stands for a < character followed by he.

Fast Searches

Earlier, we mentioned the egrep command and how earlier versions of UNIX used this separate command for extended regular expression searches. Such systems also had a third command named fgrep, which worked like grep and egrep but didn't use regular expressions. For example,

```
fgrep "^abc" file
```

looks for the ^ character followed by abc; it wouldn't recognize ^ as a special character meaning the beginning of a line. Because fgrep didn't need to worry about the meanings for special characters, it usually worked faster than either grep or egrep.

To get the same effect, POSIX.2 supplies a -F option for grep. For example, enter

```
grep -F "^Mary" nursery
```

to search for a ^ character followed by Mary. The nursery file doesn't contain that string of characters, so grep doesn't display output.

Fast searches with grep -F are good if you don't want to use any metacharacters or if you just want to search for a string without doing anything fancy. Remember that if you use an older UNIX system, you'll have to use fgrep instead of grep -F.

Backwards Compatibility
To keep old-timers happy, POSIX.2 actually has fgrep and egrep commands that work like grep -F and grep -E. However, MKS Tools only has grep, so it doesn't take up disk space with three commands that do almost the same thing.

Comparing Files: *diff*

The diff command compares two text files to see how they differ. In order to understand how diff works, you need to do a little setup by executing the following commands:

```
echo "Roses are red" >2line
echo "Violets are blue" >>2line
cp 2line 3line
echo "Some poems rhyme, but this one doesn't." >>3line
```

Notice that the second and third echo commands use >> to append text to existing files. To see what you've created, enter the commands

```
more 2line
more 3line
```

Notice that 2line contains

```
Roses are red
Violets are blue
```

and 3line contains

```
Roses are red
Violets are blue
Some poems rhyme, but this one doesn't.
```

Comparing the Two Files

You're now ready to use `diff` to compare the two files you've just created. Enter the command

```
diff 2line 3line
```

and you'll get the output

```
2a3
> Some poems rhyme, but this one doesn't.
```

In essence, the output of `diff` tells what you would need to do if you wanted to change the first file into the second file; in this case, it tells how to change `2line` into `3line`. The output

```
2a3
```

says that after line 2 of `2line`, you'd have to *append* line 3 of `3line`. (The a in `2a3` stands for *append*.) The output also shows you what line 3 of `3line` is:

```
> Some poems rhyme, but this one doesn't.
```

Notice that this line begins with a > character. In `diff` output, lines from the first file (in this case `2line`) are always marked with <, and lines from the second file (in this case `3line`) are always marked with >.

To summarize the output of the command, `diff` tells you that you'd have to add a line, and it shows you what line you'd have to add.

The Format of `diff` Output

You may wonder why `diff`'s output has such an unusual format. The answer is that this format is much like the instructions you would give to a UNIX text editor named `ed` in order to change `out1` into `out2`. The `ed` editor isn't used very much these days—most people prefer to use `vi`, as described in Chapter 6 of this book—but it's too late to change `diff` now.

Deleted Lines

Now try the command in reverse. Enter

```
diff 3line 2line
```

You'll get the output

```
3d2
< Some poems rhyme, but this one doesn't
```

Again, `diff` tells what you would need to do to change the first file into the second file. In this case, it tells what you'd have to do to change `3line` into `2line`. The 3d2 says that you would need to *delete* line 3 from the first file (the d stands for *delete*); the 2 in 3d2 says that line 2 in `2line` is the last line before the one deleted.

Notice that the line from `3line` (Some poems...) is marked with a < character. As mentioned earlier, `diff` always uses < to mark lines from the first file being compared (in this case, `3line`) and uses > to mark lines from the second file (in this case `2line`).

Comparison Conventions

As you can see, the order in which the files appear on the command line has a strong influence on `diff`'s output. When you said

```
diff 2line 3line
```

`diff` reported that you had to add lines to `2line` to get `3line`. When you said

```
diff 3line 2line
```

`diff` reported that you had to delete lines from `3line` to get `2line`.

Many people find it helpful to adopt the policy of always comparing files in the order

```
diff old new
```

where `old` is the older file of the two and `new` is the newer. By being consistent, you can save yourself a great deal of confusion. However, this is just a useful policy, not a hard and fast rule.

Changed Lines

Now let's make a change in `2line` and try the comparison again. First, enter the command

```
echo "Peonies are pink" >>2line
```

Make sure you use `>>` in the above command. This adds another line to `2line`, so that `2line` now contains

```
Roses are red
Violets are blue
Peonies are pink
```

Now enter the command

```
diff 2line 3line
```

You'll see that the output is

```
3c3
< Peonies are pink
---
> Some poems rhyme, but this one doesn't.
```

This time the output starts with the line 3c3. `diff` is saying that if you want to change the first file (`2line`) into the second file (`3line`), you need to *change* line 3 of `2line` into line 3 of `3line`. The c in 3c3 stands for *change*. As the above output shows, `diff` also tells you how the lines are different: the line marked with `<` is what was in the first file (`2line`), and the line marked with `>` is what was in the second file (`3line`). `diff` uses `---` to separate the line from `2line` from the line from `3line`.

Now, try one more experiment. Enter the following commands

```
cp 2line 4line
echo "THE END" >>4line
```

Be sure to use `>>` so that the line is appended to `4line`. After executing the above command, the contents of `4line` will be

```
Roses are red
Violets are blue
Peonies are pink
THE END
```

Now enter the command

```
diff 3line 4line
```

This time the output is

```
3c3,4
< Some poems rhyme, but this one doesn't
---
> Peonies are pink
> THE END
```

The first line says that line 3 in 3line changes into a *range* of lines in 4line. The range is written 3,4, which stands for lines 3 through 4. (As another example, a range of the form 5,10 stands for lines 5 through 10, inclusive.) Again, diff shows you what lines were in the first file (marked with <) and what lines were in the comparable position in the second file (marked with >); the two groups of lines are separated with ---.

Now, try one more experiment. Enter the commands

```
cat 3line 3line >6line
cat 4line 4line >8line
```

The first cat command creates a new file named 6line which contains two copies of 3line; the second cat command creates a new file named 8line that contains two copies of 4line. The contents of 6line are given in Listing 5.1, and the contents of 8line are given in Listing 5.2.

Listing 5.1.   Contents of 6line.

```
Roses are red
Violets are blue
Some poems rhyme, but this one doesn't
Roses are red
Violets are blue
Some poems rhyme, but this one doesn't
```

Listing 5.2.   Contents of 8line.

```
Roses are red
Violets are blue
Peonies are pink
THE END
Roses are red
Violets are blue
Peonies are pink
THE END
```

Now enter the following command

```
diff 6line 8line
```

to compare the two files. The output is given in Listing 5.3.

Listing 5.3.   Results of Comparing 6line and 8line.

```
3c3,4
< Some poems rhyme, but this one doesn't
---
> Peonies are pink
> THE END
6c7,8
< Some poems rhyme, but this one doesn't
---
> Peonies are pink
> THE END
```

You'll notice that this output reports two changes. The first begins with the heading 3c3,4. This says that to change 6line into 8line, you have to change line 3 from 6line into lines 3 and 4 from 8line; the output from diff also shows the lines in question. After that comes another set of changes, beginning with the heading 6c7,8. This says that to change 6line into 8line, you also have to change line 6 from 6line into lines 7 and 8 from 8line. Again, the output shows the lines in question.

This example demonstrates that diff may report several groups of differences between the same two files. Each group begins with a heading that tells whether the difference is an addition, a deletion, or a change.

Summary of diff Output

To review what I've discussed, suppose you enter the command

```
diff old new
```

to compare two files named `old` and `new`. The output of `diff` will divide into separate pieces. Pieces can have one of three forms:

```
XaY,Z
> new lines
```

says that `new` contains lines that are not in `old`. The number X gives a line number in `old`; the new lines were added after this line. The new lines are numbers Y through Z in `new`. The new lines are marked with the > character. If there is only one new line, you'll only see XaY.

```
X,YdZ
< old lines
```

says that `old` contains lines that are not in `new`. Lines numbered X through Y in `old` were deleted in order to get `new`. Line Z in `new` is the last line before the ones that were deleted. The old lines are marked with the < character. If there is only one old line, you'll see only XdZ.

```
W,XcY,Z
< old lines
---
> new lines
```

says that `old` contains lines W through X in the same location where `new` contains lines Y through Z. The old lines are marked with < while the new lines are marked with >. If there is only one old line, you'll only see one line number before the c. Similarly, if there is only one new line, you'll only see one line number after the c.

If there are no differences between the files being compared, `diff` issues no output. It simply returns, without displaying anything. To see this, enter the commands

```
cp 4line fourline
diff 4line fourline
```

There are no differences between 4line and fourline, so you will see no output. As is often the case with UNIX commands, diff only displays output if there is something significant to say.

Cleaning Up

In order to clean up unneeded files, I recommend that you enter the command

```
rm [23468]line fourline
```

This removes all files created during this discussion of diff.

The Size of Text Files

The wc command offers a quick way to determine the size of a text file. Enter the command

```
wc sonnet
```

You'll see that the command displays the following.

```
17      118     690     sonnet
```

The first number is the number of *lines* in the file, the second is the number of words, and the third is the number of bytes (characters). The name of the file is given at the end of the line.

You can use wc on a list of files, as in

```
wc sonnet nursery
```

For each file, wc displays a count of lines, words, and bytes, in that order.

If you do not specify any files, wc displays information about the standard input. For example, enter

```
wc <sonnet
```

This displays a count of lines, words, and bytes in `sonnet`. You'll notice that it doesn't display the name of the file. Because the shell takes care of redirection before calling `wc`, `wc` doesn't know the name of the file it is examining. `wc` only knows that it is reading the standard input.

The `-l` option tells `wc` to display only a line count. For example,

```
wc -l nursery
```

only displays the number of lines in `nursery`. This feature is particularly useful in pipelines. For example, enter

```
find . -type f -print ¦ wc -l
```

The `find` command produces a list of all files under the current directory, and the `wc` command displays the number of lines in this list. As a result, the preceding command displays the number of files under the current directory.

The `-w` option tells `wc` to display only a word count and the `-c` option tells `wc` to display only a byte (character) count. For more information, see the `wc` man page.

Sorting Text Files

The `sort` command lets you sort the contents of a text file. `sort` offers you the choice of sorting according to several different criteria: alphabetical order, numeric order, time/date order, and so on.

Throughout this section, you'll use a file named `comics.1st`, located under your home directory. This file was created at the time you installed your userid. The file contains information about a collection of comic books—Listing 5.4 shows a few representative records. Currently the records are in random order. You'll be sorting this information in several ways as you go along.

Listing 5.4. Contents of the `comics.1st` file.

```
Detective Comics:572:Mar:1987:$1.75
Demon:2:Feb:1987:$1.00
Ex-Mutants:1:Sep:1986:$2.60
Justice League of America:259:Feb:1987:$1.00
```

Sorting Prerequisites

In order for the sort command to sort a file properly, the file must meet the following conditions:

- The file must be a text file.

- The file must contain one *record* per line. This means that each line of the file must be a separate record; you can't have records that extend over several lines and you can't put several records on the same line.

- Each record must be made up of zero or more *fields*. A field is just a piece of information. The different fields of the record must all be separated by the same character. For example, you can separate fields with blanks, with commas, with colons, or with any other suitable character.

Looking at the comics.1st file, you can see that the file satisfies these criteria. The file is a text file, and each line describes a different comic book. Each line contains several pieces of information (fields), and the fields are separated from each other with colon (:) characters.

Simple Sorting

The simplest sort command is just

```
sort comics.1st
```

Enter this command. You'll see that sort displays the sorted result on the standard output; Listing 5.5 shows the beginning of this output.

Listing 5.5.   Beginning of sorted comics list.

```
Batman:566:Sep:1986:$1.00
Border Worlds:1:Jul:1986:$2.80
Boris the Bear:1:Sep:1986:$1.50
Boris the Bear:3:Dec:1986:$2.30
```

The sort command does not change the contents of the input file. If you use more to display comics.1st, you'll see that the file is still in random order.

You can write the sorted result into a file with normal redirection. For example, enter

```
sort comics.lst >out
more out
```

You'll see that `out` contains the same data as `comics.lst`, only it is sorted. When you use `sort` in this way, the output file must not be the same as the input file. For example, you could not use `>comics.lst` to write the sorted output back into the original file. If you want to overwrite a file with its sorted contents, use the `-o` option; this option is described in the `sort` man page.

By default, `sort` sorts according to all the information in the record, analyzed character by character. If two records begin with the same character, `sort` looks at the second character to see which character should come first; if the second characters are also the same, `sort` looks at the third characters, and so on.

Merging Files

The `sort` command lets you *merge* the contents of several sorted or unsorted files. The result is sorted, and it contains all the records from all the input files. For example,

```
sort sonnet nursery >out
```

merges the contents of the given files, sorts everything, and writes the combined result into `out`. (The preceding command is not very useful—who wants to sort lines of poetry? However, the command does demonstrate the principle.)

Sorting Keys

Suppose now that you want to sort according to some different piece of information in the record. For example, suppose that you want to sort according to date of publication. You do this using *sorting keys* (frequently shortened to *sort keys*).

A sorting key tells `sort` to look at one or more specific fields in a record, instead of looking at each record as a whole. A sorting key also tells what kind of information is stored in a particular field (such as a word, a number, or a month) and how that information should be sorted (in ascending or descending order).

A sorting key can refer to one or more fields. Fields are specified by number. The first field in a record is field 1, the field after the first separator character is field 2, and so on. In the comic book list, the name is field 1, the issue number is field 2, the month is field 3, and the year is field 4.

A single sort command can have several sorting keys. The most important sorting key is given first; less important sorting keys follow. As an example, you'll sort by year, then by month within the year. Therefore the first sorting key should refer to the year field, and the second to the month field.

A sorting key has two halves. The first half tells the number of the field where the key begins. For the first sorting key (referring to the year), you will start with 4 (because the year is field 4). After the number comes a letter indicating the type of data in the field and how the data should be sorted. Possible letters include:

d	The field contains upper- and/or lowercase letters, and/or digits. The field should be sorted in *dictionary* order, ignoring all other characters (except whitespace characters). Uppercase letters will always precede lowercase ones, thus ZITHER will precede apple because uppercase letters come first.
f	When sorting the field, upper- and lowercase versions of the same letter should be considered equivalent.
M	The field contains the name of a month. With this method of comparison, sort only looks at the first three characters of the month and ignores the case of letters. Thus, January, JAN, and jan are all equal.
n	The field contains an *integer* (a positive or negative number that doesn't have a fractional part or an exponent). Some versions of sort may allow fractions, but not MKS Tools.

Putting an r after any of these letters tells sort to sort in reverse order, from highest to lowest rather than from lowest to highest. For example, Mr means to sort in the order December, November, October, and so on.

For the sorting key based on the year, you use n. Thus, the first half of the sorting key is 4n.

The second half of a sorting key tells where the sorting field ends. It consists of the number of the field after the field in the sorting key. In the example, this is 5, because the field after the year field is field 5. If you omit the second half of a sorting key, sort assumes that the key extends to the end of the record.

The two halves of the sorting key are separated with a comma, and the whole key is preceded by -k to indicate that it is a sorting key. Thus the full sorting key for the year field is

```
-k 4n,5
```

-k is POSIX.2

The -k format for a sorting key is dictated by the POSIX.2 standard. There are older forms in which you can specify sorting keys, but these are deprecated by POSIX and may become obsolete at some point in the future.

The M code is an extension to the POSIX.2 standard, but it is found in most UNIX and UNIX look-alike versions of sort.

The second sorting key refers to the month field. This key will have the form

```
-k 3M,4
```

because the month field is field 3, and the field after the month field is field 4.

The Separator Character

A sort command that uses sorting keys needs to know which character is used to separate fields within a record. You give sort this information by specifying the option -t followed by the character used to separate fields. For the comics.lst file, the option is -t:.

Putting the sort keys and the -t option together, you get the command

```
sort -t: -k 4n,5 -k 3M,4 comics.lst >out
```

Notice that the name of the file you want to sort comes after all the other options, including the sorting keys. The beginning of the resulting out file is shown in Listing 5.6.

> **Listing 5.6.   Beginning of comics lists sorted by year and month.**
>
> ```
> Howard the Duck:29:Jan:1979:$0.35
> Moonshadow:2:May:1985:$1.75
> Moonshadow:3:Jul:1985:$1.75
> Bozz Chronicles:2:Feb:1986:$1.75
> ```

As an exercise in the use of sorting keys, try to sort the comics list according to price. Then try to sort the comics list in reverse order according to date of publication.

Archiving Tools: *tar*

The `tar` command is often used for *backing up* disk files to tapes or diskettes. More precisely, `tar` can create and manipulate *archives*. An archive is a single file that contains the complete contents of a set of other files. An archive can contain whole directories; it keeps a record of the directory structure (i.e., which file belongs to which subdirectory) so that you can use `tar` to restore the directories just as they were at the time they were backed up. The name `tar` was derived from `tape archive`, but you can store archives on any medium, including hard drives and floppy disks.

Creating Archives

The most common command form for creating an archive file is

```
tar -cvf outfile directory
```

where `outfile` is the name you want to give to the archive file and `directory` is the name of a directory with the contents you want to back up. For example, put a formatted blank diskette in drive A: and enter the command

```
tar -cvf a:archive .
```

In this case, the command backs up the current directory (.) and stores the resulting archive in a file named `archive` on the diskette in A:. The archive will contain all the information needed to recreate everything in your current

147

directory, including everything in all subdirectories. The archive also records file and directory characteristics (in other words, permissions) so that you can restore characteristics if and when you restore the directory contents.

The preceding command line contains several options. Look at each of these in turn:

`-c`	Tells `tar` to *create* an archive.
`-v`	Tells `tar` to be *verbose*. This option isn't necessary, but when you use it, `tar` displays information about everything it is doing as it creates the archive. This lets you keep track of `tar`'s progress.
`-f a:archive`	Gives the name of the archive file. If you don't specify this option, the archive is written to the standard output.

The preceding options are the only ones that you'll normally need when you create the archive file.

In some cases, you may only want to back up specific files, rather than an entire directory. You can do this in several ways. The most straightforward way is to list the files on the command line, as in

```
tar -cvf a:archive file file file ...
```

Notice that the name of the archive file must come immediately after the `-f` option. The files that you want to back up come afterward. Of course, you can use glob constructs to generate the list of file names. For example

```
/ tar -cvf a:archive *.doc
```

backs up every file with the `.doc` suffix.

`tar` can also read the list of files you want to back up from the standard input. If you want to do this, put a dash (–) in place of the directory name. I'll give some examples of this next, but they're simply for you to think about; don't try to enter them.

```
tar -cvf a:archive -
```

says that you want to type the file names in from the standard input. When you have issued this command, you can begin typing the names (because the standard input is associated with the keyboard). You can type any number of names per line, provided that you separate the names on a line with at least one space. To indicate the end of the list of names, enter a line that consists only of the character Ctrl-Z (then press Enter).

The technique of reading names from the standard input lends itself to use with redirection and pipes. For example, consider the following:

```
find / -ctime -7 >weeklist
tar -cvf a:archive - <weeklist
```

This uses `find` to identify any files that have changed in the last seven days. The output of `find` is redirected into a file named `weeklist`. The `tar` command has the correct format to read the list of files from the standard input, but because of redirection, `weeklist` is used as the standard input. As a result, `tar` backs up all the files that have changed in the last seven days. You can use this approach for weekly backups. You can combine the two previous commands into a single command line using pipes, as in

```
find / -ctime -7 | tar -cvf a:archive -
```

This is similar to the previous example, but it uses a pipe to connect the `find` and `tar` commands. The standard output of `find` is the list of names; the pipe feeds this list of names to `tar` as its standard input. You may think this example is complicated, but it's exactly like the previous one, except that it doesn't use `weeklist` as an intermediary holding file for the list of names.

Backup Drives and UNIX

  With a true UNIX or UNIX look-alike system, you would normally *mount* a tape or diskette drive to do a backup. The mount operation lets you associate a directory in the normal file system with the contents of a tape or diskette, by making use of a special device file for the tape or diskette drive. Such procedures vary from system to system and are outside the scope of this book.

 The examples in this section avoid such complications by using standard DOS notation (drive `A:`, drive `B:`, and so on). This notation works with the MKS Tools and illustrates most of the points you'll see on a true UNIX or UNIX look-alike system.

Examining Archives

Another form of the `tar` command lets you read the contents of an existing archive file. Enter the command

```
tar -tf a:archive
```

This produces a list of all the files currently contained in the archive. With large archives, you may want to use

```
tar -tf a:archive | more
```

By piping the output through `more`, you can read the output screen by screen. You'll notice that this form of the command has two options:

`-t`	Tells `tar` you want to see a *table of contents*.
`-f a:archive`	States the name of the archive file, as in the previous form of the command.

To obtain more details on the contents of the archive, enter

```
tar -tvf a:archive
```

The addition of the `-v` option produces more verbose output. In this case, each line of output is similar to the information produced by `ls -l`.

Extracting from Archives

Another form of the `tar` command lets you extract files from an archive file. Put the disk containing your `tar` archive into disk A: and enter the commands

```
rm sonnet
tar -xvf a:archive ./sonnet
```

This gets rid of the existing copy of `sonnet`, then extracts the backed up copy from the archive. The `-x` option stands for *extract*. As before, `-v` asks `tar` to display what it is doing, and `-f a:archive` gives the name of the archive. The name at the end of the line tells which file you want to extract.

You can extract several files at a time. The general form would be

```
tar -xvf a:archive file file file ...
```

where the `file` arguments name the files that you want to extract. As you might expect, you can use glob constructs in the usual way to generate the list of files. If you do not put any file names on the end of the command, `tar` extracts everything from the archive.

Files extracted from an archive normally overwrite any files of the same name that already exist. For example, `tar -xvf a:archive sonnet` will overwrite `sonnet` if it already exists. If you want to control this process, you can add the `-w` option to the command line. For example, enter

```
tar -xvwf a:archive ./sonnet ./nursery
```

You'll see that `tar` checks with you before extracting each file. Enter a y if you want `tar` to go ahead with the operation and an n if you want `tar` to skip the operation. At the moment, it doesn't matter whether you answer yes or no, because the archived versions of the files are the same as the ones in the current directory. You have to be more careful if the archived versions are different from the existing ones; then you must decide whether you want to keep the existing ones as they are or restore the archived versions (thereby overwriting the previous contents of the existing files).

Other Backup Software

There are several other commands found on UNIX and UNIX look-alikes that can be used for backup and restore operations. The best known of these is `cpio`, found in MKS Toolkit and on all AT&T UNIX systems after Version 7. The POSIX.2 standard offers `pax`, an archiver utility that can work with `tar` archives and `cpio` files.

The principles underlying `cpio` and `pax` are similar to those of `tar`, although the command line options are different. Due to space limitations, `cpio` or `pax` could not be included with the MKS Tools that accompany this book.

Printing Hard Copy

According to the POSIX.2 standard, UNIX systems should offer an `lp` command that sends text output to the printer. The simplest form of this command is

```
lp file
```

where `file` is a text file. Due to space limitations on the disks, this command is not part of the MKS Tools that come with this book.

Many UNIX and UNIX look-alike systems do not have an `lp` command. The most common alternative is named `lpr`. You can use `lpr` to print files with a command line of the form

```
lpr file
```

You might wonder what the difference is between `lp` and `lpr`. Different versions of the commands take different options; they may also work differently internally. To see how the commands work with any particular UNIX or UNIX look-alike system, read the manuals that come with that system.

Both `lp` and `lpr` print the standard input if there is no `file` specified. This means that you can use them at the end of a pipeline, as in

```
ls -l ¦ lp
```

This pipes the output of the `ls` command into `lp`, which then prints the output on a line printer (or some other hard copy device). Remember that you can't use this technique with the MKS Tools, because there is no `lp` command.

Printing with MKS Tools

There are (at least) two ways you can print the files that you create with MKS Tools commands. First, you can quit your MKS Tools session and print the file with the normal DOS PRINT command (or whatever command you normally use to print DOS text files). Second, you can use the command

```
cat file >PRN
```

inside an MKS Tools session. `cat` copies the contents of the text `file` to the DOS PRN device. Copying data to PRN has the effect of sending the data to the printer, if you have a printer attached directly to your system.

Note that the `cat` approach only sends the text of the file. If your printer requires special control characters as well as normal text, you may not get the sort of output you expect. For example, most laser printers require formatting instructions as well as the text you want to print; if you simply send the output of `cat` (sometimes called *catting a file*) into PRN, you may not get any output.

Chapter Review

The grep command can search through a set of files and display all lines that match a given string. The general form of the command is

```
grep options string file file file ...
```

Possible options are given in Table 5.3. It is a good idea to enclose string in single or double quotation marks. If there are no files given on the command line, grep examines the standard input.

Table 5.3.   Options for grep.

Option	Meaning
-E	Use extended regular expressions
-F	Do not use regular expressions
-i	Ignore the case of letters when comparing

The string argument for grep can be a regular expression. A regular expression is a string used to match a pattern of characters in a file. Regular expressions can contain metacharacters, which give special criteria for pattern matching. Table 5.4 summarizes the metacharacters discussed in this chapter; those marked with *[Ext]* are extended regular expressions and are only special when you specify the -E option for grep. Appendix C gives a complete description of all recognized metacharacters.

Table 5.4.   Regular expression metacharacters.

Construct	Meaning
^	Beginning of a line
$	End of a line
.	Matches any character
*	Zero or more repetitions of the previous regular expression
[...]	Matches any character listed inside the brackets
[^...]	Matches any character not listed inside the brackets
¦	Separates multiple choices *[Ext]*
\<	The beginning of a word *[Ext]*
\>	The end of a word *[Ext]*

The `fgrep` command searches for strings inside files, but does not recognize regular expressions. The `egrep` command searches for strings inside files, but always uses extended regular expressions.

The `diff` command compares two files to see how they differ. The format of the command is typically

```
diff old new
```

The output shows the changes necessary to change the `old` file into `new`. Output may show that lines were appended, deleted, or changed.

The `wc` command counts the number of lines, words, and bytes (characters) in a text file. Table 5.5 shows possible options for `wc`. You can use `wc` in pipelines to count such things as the number of files under a directory.

Table 5.5.   Options for `wc`.

Option	Meaning
-l	Show line count only
-w	Show word count only
-c	Show byte (character) count only

The `sort` command can sort the contents of a text file according to a variety of criteria. The file must consist of one record per line, and each record must be divided into fields with a specified separator character. The general format of a `sort` command line is

```
sort options file file file ...
```

Output is written to the standard output; you can use redirection to save the sorted output in a file. The `-t` option tells what character you are using to separate fields.

Sorting keys (or sort keys) indicate which field(s) should be considered for the purpose of sorting. They also tell what the fields contain. A sorting key has the general form

```
-k start,end
```

where `start` is the number of the first field to be considered and `end` is the number of the second field. The `start` number can be followed by characters from Table 5.6.

Table 5.6. Codes that can be used in sorting keys.

Code	Meaning
d	Sort in dictionary order
M	Sort in month order
n	Sort in numeric order
r	Sort in reverse order

The `tar` command can be used to back up and restore files. `tar` manipulates archives, files that can contain the contents of many files and directories. To create an archive, use

```
tar -cvf archive name name ...
```

where `archive` is the name of the archive file you want to create and the `names` are names of files or directories with contents you want to save in the archive. If you specify – in place of the list of names, `tar` will read names from the standard input; you can use redirection to supply this list of names from a file, or use pipes to supply the list of names from another command's output. To list the contents of an existing archive, use

```
tar -tf archive
```

To extract files from an archive, use

```
tar -xvf archive name name ...
```

The `lp` command is a POSIX.2 command for producing hard copy output. Many UNIX and UNIX look-alike systems have an `lpr` command to perform the same function.

Exercises

1. Search all the files under your current directory and find all occurrences of the string ex. (Hint: use a glob construct to generate the list of file names.)

2. Search all the files under your current directory and find all occurrences of the string ex at the beginning of a line.

3. The *level* of a directory X is the number of directories between X and the root. For example, a directory /u/chris/dir has a level of 2, because /u and /chris come between /dir and the root. Display the names of all directories on your hard drive with a level greater than 2. (Hint: pipe the output of find / -type d through grep.)

4. Enter the following commands:

```
du >out1
du >out2
diff out1 out2
```

Explain the diff output. (Note: du was discussed in the Exercises for Chapter 4.)

5. Use a single command line to count the number of files in the /lu directory. (Hint: use find and wc, with pipes.)

6. Use a single command line to produce a file that contains a sorted list of all the files in your home directory and its subdirectories.

7. Sort the comics.1st file according to title and price. Pipe the output through more so you can read it.

8. Read the man page for the pr command. This command can format text files in a nice, readable form for printing on a line printer. Format the sonnet file into a file named nice and examine the results with more.

9. Repeat the previous exercise, but use pipes instead of using nice to hold the formatted version of sonnet.

10. Skim through the man page for bc. bc is a desk calculator program that lets you perform extensive arithmetic operations. Use bc to find the average of the numbers 34, 82, and 192. (While this exercise seems quite arbitrary, it will actually require you to learn many of the fundamentals of using the bc program.)

## Chapter 6

Text Files—Veni, Vidi, *vi*

This chapter deals with the `vi` text editor, a program for creating and editing text files. The `vi` text editor lets you enter text, change text in a variety of ways, and save that text in files.

The *vi* Text Editor

There are many text editors available on UNIX and UNIX look-alike systems, but the most popular is almost certainly `vi`. `vi` is a *screen editor*; this means that when you start editing a file, the display screen shows the current contents of the file. As you enter editing commands, the commands usually do not appear on the screen; instead, the text displayed on the screen changes to reflect the changes you have made.

This contrasts sharply with *line editors* like the `EDLIN` editor of DOS. With a line editor, you do not see the text of your file unless you explicitly enter a command asking to see it. For the most part, the display screen shows the commands that you type in, not the text.

`vi` was one of the earliest screen editors created; at the time `vi` was designed, line editors were far more common. Now, the balance has shifted in the other direction, and today, most widely used editors (such as WordPerfect and Microsoft Word) are screen editors.

How to Pronounce vi

Many UNIX purists claim that the proper pronunciation of vi is *vee-eye* (pronouncing each letter separately). Others claim that UNIX purists should have better things to do with their time, and pronounce it *veye* or *vie* (a single syllable). In keeping with the UNIX philosophy, I suggest you customize the pronunciation to suit your own tastes.

Contrasting vi With Word Processors

If you're a DOS user, you're probably familiar with one or more of the popular DOS word processors (such as WordPerfect or Microsoft Word). Before I discuss how vi actually works, it's worthwhile to take a moment to contrast the text editor vi with word processors.

The most popular word processors are primarily concerned with the production of documents. They are designed to work with different types of printers, and to give you the ability to use special typefaces, font sizes, and other tricks of the printing trade.

vi is primarily concerned with creating text files, especially text files that will be used by other programs. For example, vi has several features aimed at helping programmers prepare source code files that can be run through compilers to produce executable programs. It is seldom used to produce documents directly. On UNIX systems, vi is often used to create text files that can be run through the troff text-formatting program to produce actual documents.

If you're expecting vi to be similar to word processors, you'll be disappointed. vi is missing several features offered by most word processors, particularly the features aimed at producing hard copy documents. But by the same token, word processors often have difficulty doing the things that vi does well. You'll find, for example, that word processors typically put special characters (characters that are aimed at formatting the files for output to a printer) into files. Such characters aren't useful in straight text files; most of the time the characters are just gobbledygook that confuses other programs that try to read the files.

The proper approach is to recognize the strengths of both types of programs. Use a word processor when you want to produce a document. Use vi when you want to produce a text file for use by another UNIX program.

On-Line Files for Learning *vi*

Much of the rest of this chapter works through files that you'll find under your home directory. Each of these files is designed as an on-line exercise for using vi. You use vi to read through the files, and as you go, the files suggest exercises you can do while using vi.

> **Quitting** vi
> As you work through the exercises, you can quit at any time by pressing Esc and then typing
>
>> :q!
>
> This tells vi to quit immediately, without saving any changes to the exercise file. If you were using vi to edit a file, you would almost never use this command; you would normally save your work before quitting. However, these are just exercises and there's no benefit to saving the work.

browse.v—Browsing Through Text

The first vi exercise file is named browse.v. In order to work through the exercises in the file, enter the command

```
vi browse.v
```

The file tells how to read files using vi. I recommend that you enter the preceding command now and work through the exercise file. The rest of this section essentially repeats what you will see in the file; if you don't want to work through the file, you can read the book instead. However, I think you'll learn about vi faster if you actively work through the file rather than passively reading the book. (Of course, having the text of the exercise files in the book is useful for reference and for study when you aren't at your computer.)

```
This file is the "vi" Browser's Guide. In it, we will
describe how to move backwards and forwards through a file
while using "vi".

**********************************************************
*******     Part I: Moving Around in a File     *******
**********************************************************

When reading files with "vi", you must keep track of the
position of the cursor. The cursor is a small line or box
that indicates a particular position on the display screen.
On some systems, the cursor blinks; on others, it does not.

Because you have just started using "vi", the cursor
marks the first non-blank character on the first line
of the screen. When you start a "vi" session by reading
in a file, the cursor always appears at the first non-blank
character of the file.

Now press the Enter key. You will see that the cursor
moves down to the first non-blank character of the next
line. Keep pressing Enter. See where it puts the cursor
on each line. When you get to the bottom of the screen,
keep pressing Enter. New lines will appear one at a
time. Keep pressing Enter until this line is the top
one on the screen. Then stop and read some more.

Press the "-" key (the minus sign). You will see that
the cursor moves up to the first non-blank character of
the previous line. In other words, entering a minus is
the opposite of pressing Enter.

Keep pressing "-" until the cursor gets to the top line
of the screen, then press it once more. You will see
the whole screen move down to make room for an old line
at the top. Thus, Enter and "-" let you go backward and
forward through the file. Just those two keys will let
you read everything in this file. If you ever find that
you've read everything on the screen and have no other
instructions, just keep pressing Enter to read more of
the file. If you want to review something that is no
longer on the screen, back up with "-".
```

Positioning the Cursor on the Screen

If you just use Enter and "-" to move the cursor, you move very slowly. Here are three commands for moving the cursor faster:

(a)Typing **L** (for *Low*) moves the cursor to the bottom line of the screen.

(b)Typing **H** (for *High*) moves the cursor to the top line of the screen.

(c)Typing **M** (for *Middle*) moves the cursor to the middle line of the screen.

Try all of these. It's important that you use uppercase for "L", "H", and "M". The case of letters is important in "vi".

Moving the Cursor Up and Down

Now, hold down the Ctrl key and press the D key (this is called typing Ctrl-D, sometimes shortened to ^D). You will see several new lines appear at the bottom of the screen. Ctrl-D moves **D**own half a screen.

Type Ctrl-D once more, then type Ctrl-U (hold down Ctrl and press U). You will see that Ctrl-D moves the cursor **D**own half a screen, and Ctrl-U moves it **U**p. Using Ctrl D and Ctrl-U to move forward and backward through a file is less work than using Enter and -; you don't need to type as many keystrokes.

Ctrl-D and Ctrl-U move quickly, moving half a screen at a time. Ctrl-F (for **F**orward) and Ctrl-B (for **B**ackward) move almost a full screen at a time. Right now, type Ctrl-F, and then Ctrl-B.

Ctrl-F (probably) took you forward off this screen and Ctrl-B brought you back. Ctrl-F and Ctrl-B are good for moving very quickly through files. They aren't particularly good for going through this "vi" file, however—they move too far in one jump and you'll

lose what is on the screen. But remember them for later
work.

For practice, use Ctrl-U or Ctrl-B to go back to the
beginning of the file, then use Ctrl-D or Ctrl-F to
come back to this point in the file. You shouldn't have
trouble finding this spot again, because it comes right
before the *Part II* heading.

```
**********************************************************
*******   Part II: Horizontal Cursor Movement   *******
**********************************************************
```

In the last section, you moved the cursor up and down. In
this section, you'll move the cursor back and forth on the
line. Just keep pressing Enter or Ctrl-D to see new
material.

The cursor is likely to be on the first non-blank
character of some line. Press the **l** (lowercase ell).
The cursor will move one character to the right.

Pressing "l" repeatedly keeps moving the cursor to the
right, until you get to the end of the line. Then it
stops because it can't go any farther.

Now press **h**. You should see the cursor move to the
left. By pressing "h" repeatedly, you can move the
cursor to the left margin.

Vertical Line Movement

Between "h" and "l" on a standard keyboard are "j" and "k".
Pressing "j" moves the cursor down one line. Pressing "k"
moves the cursor up one line.

"k" and "j" move up and down like "-" and Enter.
However, when you press "j" or "k", the cursor stays in
the same column on the screen; when you press "-" or
Enter, the cursor goes to the first non-blank character
of the line. Check this out for yourself.

Moving to the Start or End of the Line

Moving the cursor back and forth on a line can take a long
time if you are using "h" and "l". Try this instead. Move
the cursor to the beginning of a line and enter the **$** character.
You will see the cursor jump to the end of the same line.

Press the **0** (zero) key, and the cursor jumps to the
beginning of the line. Thus "$" and "0" give you a
quick way to jump to the end or the beginning of a
line.

Word Movement

Now move the cursor to the beginning of this very line, and
type **w** (lowercase). You will see that the cursor jumps from
the "N" in *Now* to the "m" of *move*. "w" stands for "word",
and the "w" command jumps to the start of the next
word...more or less.

Keep typing **w** and you will see that the cursor usually
jumps from one word to the next, but occasionally stops
at things normally not thought of as words. For
example, it will stop at the comma after *line*. This is
because "vi" defines a "word" as a sequence of
alphabetic/numeric characters or a sequence of non-
alphabetic/numeric characters (not including blanks).
As a result, "vi" regards punctuation characters as
"words". You'll get used to this quickly.

Keep pressing **w**, and you'll see the cursor jump from
the last word on one line to the first word of the
next. Pressing **w** sends the cursor to the beginning of
the next word, even if that means going to the next
line.

Now press **b** (lowercase). You will see that the cursor
jumps backward to the beginning of a word. If the
cursor is already at the beginning of a word, it will
jump back to the start of the previous word. However,
if you use the arrow keys to move the cursor to the

middle of a word, pressing **b** goes to the start of the
word that contains the cursor. Try it.

```
************************************************************
*******            Part III: Searching            *******
************************************************************
```

You now know how to move the cursor up and down on the
screen and back and forth on the line. In this part of the
guide, I'll discuss another way to move through text:
searching.

When you begin looking at a file, "vi" puts the cursor
at the file's first line, but often what you want to
look at is in the middle of the file. You can use Ctrl-D
to work your way down through the file...but this can
take time. If you know what sort of material you are
looking for, it is often faster to use the *search*
facility. The search facility tells "vi" to search
through the file from the current cursor position to
the next occurrence of a particular word or phrase.

Searching Forward

To see how it works, start by pressing Ctrl-D or Enter until
this entire paragraph is on the screen. Move the cursor to
the beginning of this line and type a slash (/). Be careful
not to confuse this with the backslash (\).

When you type the slash, you will see the cursor move
down to the bottom of the screen. Now type the word
hello, then press Enter. You will see the cursor jump
to the beginning of the word *hello* above. When you type
a word or phrase after a slash, "vi" searches forward
for the next occurrence of that string of characters.
The cursor is placed on the first character of the
string that is found.

Now, move the cursor to the beginning of this line and
type a slash followed by Enter. You will see that "vi"
finds this occurrence of *hello*. If you just type a
slash without anything after it, "vi" looks for the
most recent word or phrase you searched for.

Searching Backward

Move the cursor to this line and type a question mark (?)
followed by the word "hello", then press Enter. You will see
that "vi" moves the cursor backward to the previous
occurrence of *hello*. When you type a word or phrase after a
question mark, "vi" searches backward for that string of
characters. As you might guess, if you just type a question
mark followed by Enter, "vi" searches backward for the most
recent thing you searched for. Try it.

Case Sensitivity

When you type in characters after a slash or question mark,
you should make sure you enter them in the correct case. For
example, ask "vi" to search for "hello", but type the word
in uppercase. You will see that "vi" prints the message
"Pattern not found" at the bottom of the screen. As it turns
out, this file does not contain the word *hello* in uppercase,
although it has the word many times in lowercase.

Patterns and Regular Expressions

In a vi command, anything after a slash or question mark is called a
pattern. The patterns of vi are the same as the regular expressions used
by grep.

Regular Expressions in "vi"

In order to make searching more useful, "vi" lets you use
regular expressions, just like the ones used by "grep". For
example, the caret character (^) stands for the beginning of
a line. Move the cursor to this line and type

/^line

"vi" will look for the word *line* occurring at the beginning of a
line (which is this one).

The end of a line is represented by the dollar sign
($). Move the cursor to this line and type

/line$

You will see that "vi" will search forward for a line
that ends in the word *line* (the previous line).

Inside patterns, the dot (.) stands for any character.
For example, move the cursor to the beginning of this
line and type

/t.e

You will see that the cursor moves to the word *the*. Type /
over and over, and the cursor will keep jumping forward to
any sequence of three letters that starts with "t" and ends
in "e". Were you surprised that the cursor jumped into the
middle of the word *letters*? "vi" finds character strings,
even when they are in the middle of larger words.

Whenever you enter a pattern, remember that the dot has
a special meaning. It may look like the end of a
sentence, but don't be fooled. For example, move the
cursor to the beginning of this paragraph and type

/end of a sentence.

The cursor moves to the string *end of a sentence*, in the
previous paragraph. The dot in the pattern matches the comma
in the actual string. This is a mistake that beginners
frequently make.

Inside patterns, a dot followed by a star (*) stands
for any sequence of zero or more characters. For
example, move the cursor to this line and type

/^Y.*s$

You will find the next line that begins with the letter Y, ends
with the letter *s*, and has any number of characters in between.

```
Wrap-around Searches

By default, all searches in "vi" wrap around from the bottom
of the file to the top. For example, consider a string
consisting of two percent signs (%%). This line is the only
place in this file where that string occurs. Now move the
cursor to this line and search forward for the two percent
signs. The search starts by going down to the bottom of the
file. Because "vi" won't find the string by then, "vi" goes
back to the top of the file and keeps searching, eventually
finding the string on the preceding line.

Similarly, if you use question marks to search backward
through a file, the search will wrap around from the
top of the file to the bottom, if necessary.

************************************************************
*******          Part IV: Moving to a Line        ********
************************************************************

I had to save this last part until the end because it tells
you a quick way to go to the end of a file. Just type G
(uppercase) and the cursor goes to the last line of the
file. If you type a number before the "G", the cursor moves
to that line in the file. For example, "1G" goes to the
first line of the file. Try going to the first line of the
file, then coming back here to the end.

Remember, to quit "vi" now, type :q! and press Enter.
```

edit.v—Editing Text

The second vi exercise file is named edit.v. In order to work through the exercises in the file, enter the commands

```
cp edit.v myedit.v
vi myedit.v
```

This makes a copy of the `edit.v` file, then uses `vi` to read the copy. I suggest looking at the copy rather than the real thing, just in case you make mistakes or someone else wants to try.

The exercise file tells how to create and edit files using `vi`. As in the last section, I recommend that you enter the preceding command now and work through the exercise file. The rest of this section essentially repeats what you will see in the file.

```
The "browse.v" file explained how to read through a
file using "vi". Unless the text suggests a different
way to move through the file, just read through this file
by pressing Enter or Ctrl-D.


*******************************************************
*******         Part I: Entering Text         *******
*******************************************************


The most commonly used command for entering text is "a"
(standing for append or add). The steps for using "a" are
simple:

1.Determine where you want to add text and move the
cursor to the character immediately before that point.

2.Type the letter a. This switches you to Insert Mode,
where anything you type is added to the text showing on the
screen.

3.Type in your text (as many lines as you want).

4.Press the Esc key. This tells "vi" that you are
finished entering text at this location. In other words, you
leave Insert Mode and enter Command Mode. Anything that you
type now will be regarded as a command. Up until now, you've
been reading through this file in Command Mode. For example,
Ctrl-D is regarded as a command to move forward in the file.

To see how the "a" command works, move the cursor until all
four of the preceding steps are on the screen, then move the
cursor to the beginning of the next line. Type a, then
hello, then press Esc.

You should have seen the word "hello" appear on the
screen as you typed. You did not see the "a" for
append—that was a command to "vi", not text to display
```

on the screen. You might also have noticed that the cursor changed from a line to a block; "vi" doesn't do this on all systems, but it does on some machines. For people who have such machines, the block indicates when you are in Insert Mode.

Creating several lines of text is just as easy as creating one line. Type an **a**, type your text lines, then press Esc. For example, try entering the first few lines of *Mary Had A Little Lamb* immediately after this line.

Correcting Mistakes

Did you have any trouble? Perhaps you made a typing mistake. If you make mistakes while typing in text, they're easy to correct. Press the Backspace key until you have backed up over the error. After you have done this, you can type over the old characters to correct them. Try it. Move the cursor to the next blank line, then type an **a** to enter Insert Mode. Type **hello**, backspace back to the "h", and type **hi!**. Then press Esc.

Notice that before you pressed Esc, the line looked like *hi!lo*—the old letters from the end of *hello* were still visible. After you pressed Esc, the *lo* disappeared. Backing over characters with the Backspace key removes the text, even if it doesn't erase the characters from the screen. The characters are only erased when you type over them or when you press Esc.

If you're like many writers, you may change your mind partway through a line and want to get rid of the whole thing. If you are in Insert Mode and you want to get rid of everything on the line you have just typed in, enter an at-sign (@). You will see the cursor jump back to the first character you inserted on the current line. You can then type over the old line. (Note that this does not work outside of Insert Mode.)

Adding Text in the Middle of a Line

So far, I've just been talking about adding new lines. You can add text to an existing line too. For example, move the cursor to the end of the next line, type an **a**, enter the word **hello**, and press Esc. When you moved the cursor to the end of the line, it sat on the last character. When you pressed "a", it moved to the next position on the line. You could then type in your new text.

You can add text in the middle of a line too. For example, this line contains the word *math*. Can you add text to change it to *mathematics*? Try it. If you try to do it and find that the text is being added in the wrong place, you started with the cursor in the wrong place. Backspace over what you have typed in, press Esc, and move the cursor so you can try again.

The Insert Command

There are several other commands you can use for entering text. The "i" (*insert*) command lets you insert text in front of the current cursor position. For example, move the cursor to the beginning of this line. Type an **i**, then **hello**, then press Esc. You will see the text inserted in front of the cursor.

The Open Command

The "o" (*open*) command creates a blank line after the line that contains the cursor and lets you append text there. For example, move the cursor anywhere on the next line, then type an **o**, then **hello**, then Esc. You will see that a blank line opens up when you type the "o", and anything you type next is added to that line. Note that all the rest of the text in the file shifts down to make room for the new line.

The Write Command

When you use commands like "a", "i", and "o", you add text to the material shown on the screen. Before you quit "vi", however, you should *save* these changes in a file. To do this, you can use the "write" command.

Using Enter or Ctrl-D, make sure that the entire next paragraph is on the screen. Now, type a colon (:). You will see the cursor move to the bottom line of the screen and display the colon there. Next, type a w (for *write*), then a space, then a file name like **junk**. If you make any typing mistakes while you do this, you can correct them in the usual way, using the Backspace key. When you have the command correct, it should look something like

:w junk

at the bottom of the screen. When it looks like this, press Enter.

You will see that "vi" pauses for a few moments, then prints information on the bottom of the screen: the name of the file and how much text was written out. The "w" command writes the text you have entered into the file called "junk". This saves the text so you can use it later. After you have written your text into a file, it is safe to quit "vi" by typing **:q** and pressing Enter. (**Don't do this now!**)

Limited Writing Capabilities

   The vi that comes with the MKS Tools will only write out a maximum of 100 lines. The vi that comes with the full MKS Toolkit can write much larger files.

Quitting Without Writing

If you try to quit with ":q" before writing out your text with ":w", "vi" will check to see if you've made changes since the last time you wrote out the file. If you have, "vi" won't let you quit. This is a safety measure—if you do not use ":w" to write out your text before you quit "vi", all the changes you have made since the last write will be lost. Thus "vi" stops you from quitting if you haven't saved your recent changes.

If you really want to quit without saving your changes, type **:q!** and press Enter. You've probably used this while working through this guide. ":q!" is just an emphatic ":q". When you are actually working with "vi", you should probably use ":q" instead of ":q!". Leaving off the "!" gets you that safety feature I just talked about.

If you want to quit now, use ":q!". Otherwise, go on to
the next section.

```
********************************************************
*******         Part II: Simple Editing        *******
********************************************************
```

I've shown you how to add new text to a file. Now I'm going
to show you how to change the text that the file already
contains.

Deleting Lines

Look at deleting text first. The command to delete a line of
text is "dd". Try it. Move the cursor to the next line and
type **dd**.

TWINKLE, TWINKLE, LITTLE STAR

You should see the line disappear on the screen. The other
lines on the screen close in to fill the gap.

To delete more than one line, type a number followed by
dd. This deletes the given number of lines, beginning
at the line that contains the cursor. Try **4dd** to delete
the next four lines.

TWINKLE, TWINKLE, LITTLE STAR
HOW I WONDER WHAT YOU ARE
UP ABOVE THE WORLD SO HIGH
LIKE A TEA TRAY IN THE SKY

Again, the lines disappear on the screen and the remaining
lines close in.

The Undo Command

Now, type a **u**. You should see the lines reappear. "u" stands
for *undo*, and it reverses the effect of commands like "dd".
This is a very useful command to remember. If you delete
something by mistake, you can get it back again if you
immediately type **u** for *undo*. However, you can only undo the
most recent command that changed text. If you type **u** and **u**
again, the second "u" will "undo the undo", so you'll go
back to the way things were before the first undo. Try it.

Deleting Blocks of Text

Another way to delete text is to type **d** followed by a command that moves the cursor. This deletes everything from the beginning cursor position to where the cursor ends up. For example, move the cursor to the "*" in the next line, then type **d$**.

*   AND AWAY WE GO!

You see that all the text from the "*" to the end of the line disappears. "$" moves the cursor to the end of the line, so "d$" deletes to the end of the line.

Move the cursor to the beginning of the word *BACON* in the line above this one and type **dw**. You will see the word disappear. Remember that "w" moves the cursor forward one word, so "dw" deletes everything from the cursor to the beginning of the next word. What will "db" do? Try it on a word in this line.

You can even use searches after "d". Type a / or a **?** to begin the search, then the pattern you want to search for, then a closing / or **?** (whichever you started with). When you're done, press Enter. "vi" will search forward or backward for a string that matches the desired pattern and delete everything from the cursor to the matching string. Move the cursor to the beginning of the next line and type

d/hello/

As you see, this deletes everything up to the *hello*.

Deleting a Single Character

If you want to delete a single character, move the cursor on top of the character and type a lowercase **x**. Use this to get rid of the double quotation marks around "x" in this sentence.

Changing Lines

The "cc" command changes a line. To see how it works, begin by getting this whole paragraph on the screen. Move the cursor to any part of the next line and type **cc**.

THE WALRUS AND THE CARPENTER WERE WALKING HAND IN HAND.

You will see the whole line disappear. The cursor can also change into a block. You are now in Insert Mode, and anything you type will be displayed on the screen. Type **hello**, press Enter, and type **hello again**. You will see the two new lines replace the one old one. To get out of Insert Mode, press Esc.

If you type a number followed by **cc**, "vi" will get rid of that number of lines and let you type in new text to replace them. For example, move the cursor to the first of the new lines you entered in the last paragraph and type **2cc**. "vi" replaces the two lines with a single blank line. Just press Esc and that blank line will stay there in place of the two old lines.

Changing Blocks of Text

A "c" followed by a command to move the cursor lets you change everything from the starting position of the cursor to its final position. To see how this works, begin by getting this whole paragraph on the screen. Move the cursor to the first letter of the word *BACON* on this line and type **cw**.

You will see that "vi" puts a "$" sign on the last letter of the word. This marks the end of the material that the command will change. The cursor will still be at the beginning of the word. Now type **VEGETABLE** and press Esc. You see that the characters that you type print over the characters that were there until you get to the "$" sign. Then the rest of the line moves over to make room for the extra characters that you add to the line.

Whenever you change text with a "c" command, you can enter as much or as little new text as you want. For example, you could have replaced "BACON" with many lines of text if you liked. The rest of the text would have moved to make room for the new text you entered.

Replacing a Single Character

If you want to change a single character in your text, move the cursor to that character, type **r** (for *replace*) and then type the new character. You do not have to type Esc. The new character will replace the old one.

More About Undo

The "u" command undoes "c" and "r" commands as well as "d". For example, move the cursor to the "X" on this line and type **rY** to change the "X" to a "Y". If you now type **u**, you will see the "Y" change to an "X". Keep pressing **u**, and the character will flip-flop back and forth between "X" and "Y".

```
********************************************************
*******        Part III: Moving Text Around    *******
********************************************************
```

One common editing job is moving text from one part of a file to another. For example, you may want to move a sentence or paragraph from one section of a report to another. You may want to move whole sections around. You may also want to copy chunks of text and then modify them. For example, I made the heading for this part of the exercise file by making a copy of the heading for Part II and editing the title that was inside the stars. And, of course, I made the heading for Part II by copying the heading for Part I and editing that. There are repetitious aspects of most word processing jobs, and you can save yourself some typing by using the copy-and-edit process.

The Yank Command

There are two commands involved in the copy-and-edit process. The first is the "y" command, also called *yank*. The yank command makes a copy of a block of text. It works like "c" and "d"—you move the cursor to the beginning of the block you want to copy, then type **y** plus a cursor movement command that moves to the end of the block you want to copy. For example, here's a line of text:

LITTLE BOY BLUE, COME BLOW YOUR HORN

Move the cursor to the beginning of the line and type **y$**. This makes a copy of the text from the cursor position to the end of the line. Not much happens when you make the copy—you may hear the disk do some writing and the screen may blink once, but that's about it. The text you just copied stays where it is.

The Paste Command

Now move the cursor to the empty line following this line

and type **p**. "p" stands for *put* or *paste*, and it puts copied text back into the file you're editing. The text is written down immediately after the cursor. Any text that was already there moves to make room for the next text. Now move the cursor to the beginning of the next blank line and type **p** again.

As you can see, typing **p** pastes down the same line of text again. You can paste the same text any number of times. However, if you use "y" to copy/yank some new text, "p" will paste the new text instead of the old.

More on Yank and Paste

If you want to yank an entire line, put the cursor anywhere on the line and type **yy**. (You have already seen that "cc" changes a line and "dd" deletes one.) If you want to yank several lines, type the number and then **yy**. For example, move the cursor to the beginning of this paragraph and type **8yy**. This yanks the eight lines of this paragraph. Move the cursor to the next blank line and type **p**. This pastes in the whole paragraph.

Up to this point, you have been yanking text by going to the beginning of what you want to copy and typing **y** followed by a cursor movement command that went to the end of what you want to copy. "vi" lets you do the opposite too. For example, move the cursor to the end of this paragraph and type **yH**. You will see the cursor jump to the first line of the screen (which is what it does when you type **H** for *high*). You have just yanked everything to the top of the screen. Go to the blank line after this paragraph and type **p** to paste in what you just yanked.

Cutting

The yank process is similar to the copy operation in a number of word processors. You might be wondering if there is an operation similar to the cut operation in word processors (which deletes text but saves the text so that you can paste it in later).

The answer is that the "d" command automatically saves whatever you delete so that you can paste it in later. For example, use "dd" to delete the next line of poetry:

RUB A DUB DUB, THREE MEN IN A TUB

Now move the cursor to the end of this line and type **p**. You'll see that the line you just deleted comes back again when you paste it in. In short, "d" deletes something but saves it for later pasting; "y" copies text without deleting it.

Sentences

Now suppose you want to copy a particular sentence. To do this, put the cursor at the beginning or end of the sentence, then type **y** followed by a cursor movement command that goes to the end or beginning of the sentence. What kind of cursor movement command would this be? Well, you could enter a search command that looked for the first or last word of the sentence, but that's a bit clumsy...and what happens if that word is somewhere in the middle of the sentence too?

To deal with problems like this, "vi" has a command that moves the cursor to the beginning of a sentence.

This is the "(" command. For example, move the cursor
to the "X" in this line and type the (. You will see
the cursor move back to the beginning of the sentence.
Move the cursor to the beginning of this line and type
(. You will see the cursor jump back one line to the
beginning of the sentence. So yanking a sentence is
easy. Move to the end of this very sentence and type
y(. The cursor will jump back to the first word of the
sentence. Now move the cursor to the next blank line
and type **p** to see what you've yanked.

You will see that the word *Move* is on one line and the
rest of the sentence is on the next line. This is
because the yanking process copies the *line break* after
"Move". If you want to make things prettier, move the
cursor to the word *Move* and type **J**. "J" stands for
join, and it joins two lines in the way you just saw.
The cursor can go anywhere on the first line; when you
type "J", "vi" joins the next line onto the end of the
current line.

By the way, I should point out what happens if you type
the **(** command when the cursor is already at the
beginning of a sentence. Move the cursor to the "X" in
this line and type (. The cursor jumps to the beginning
of the sentence. Type **(** again, and the cursor jumps to
the beginning of the previous sentence. This shows that
you can use "(" to go backward sentence by sentence.

```
*************************************************************
*******  Part IV: Contextual Cursor Movement  *******
*************************************************************
```

The "(" command is one example of *contextual cursor
movement*. It moves the cursor to a position that is
important in the context of your text. There are several
others.

")" goes to the beginning of the next sentence. Move
the cursor to the beginning of the previous line and
type **)** to see what happens. Now type it again.

"{" (the opening brace) goes back to the beginning of a paragraph. Move the cursor to the end of the preceding paragraph and type { to see what happens. Now what do you think will happen if you type }? Try it and find out.

The "(",")","{", and "}" commands all use technical definitions for what a "sentence" and/or "paragraph" look like. These definitions are given in the man page for "vi". Once in a while, you and "vi" may disagree on what constitutes a sentence, but most of the time, "vi" knows what it's doing.

```
**********************************************************
*******        Part V: Editing Options        *******
**********************************************************
```

"vi" has many options that change the way the editor behaves during an editing session. The "vi" man page contains a complete list of these options. In this exercise file, I'll only discuss a few that can be immediately useful.

You must be in Command Mode to set options (i.e. not appending text). To set an option, begin by typing a colon (:). You will see the cursor move to the bottom of the screen. Then type

:set *option*

I'll talk about option names in a moment. You can correct typing mistakes by backspacing. When you have typed everything correctly, press Enter.

Ignoring Case in Searches

One commonly used option is "ignorecase". If you type

:set ignorecase

"vi" will not pay attention to the case of letters when searching. For example, type in the preceding "set" command, then move to the beginning of this paragraph and type **/for** (followed by Enter). You will see that the cursor moves to the *For* at the beginning of the previous sentence, even though the "F" is uppercase. Now type / followed by Enter. This time, you see that the search finds the word *for* with the "f" in lowercase. Many people prefer *caseless* searches over *case-sensitive* ones. If you want to go back to case sensitive searches, type

:set noignorecase

Setting Tab Positions

By default, "vi" sets tab stops every eight spaces. For example, if you begin a paragraph by typing a tab, the tab moves the cursor over eight spaces. If you are entering a program using tabs for indentation, each level of indentation will be eight spaces. Move the cursor to the next blank line, type an **a** to append text, then a tab and **Hello!** to see how much space is created for the tab. Press the Esc key to leave Insert Mode.

Many people feel eight spaces is too big for a tab stop. For example, when I took typing classes, I was told the "proper" indentation was five spaces. You can set tab stops of five spaces with

:set tabstop=5

When you press Enter, keep your eye on the *Hello!* line you entered a few lines back. You should see the word jump backward from column 8 to column 5. All tab stops in the file are changed with the one command. (Note: You are changing how "vi" displays tabs, but you are not changing the contents of the file. The file just contains a tab character.) Similar commands can set tab stops to any number of spaces.

```
************************************************************
*******       Part VI: Editing Several Files     *******
************************************************************
```

In a typical "vi" session, you may want to edit several files. When you have finished editing one file, you must

first write out the text. If you do not save the text you
have been editing, any editing you have done will be lost
when you quit "vi". If you started your "vi" session with
the command

vi filename

you can save your text in that file just by typing

:w

and pressing Enter. You can try this now.

If you want to save your text in a new file, you can
type

:w newfile

where "newfile" is the new file name. Try this now. Type

:w myjunk

and press Enter. When "vi" has finished writing the file,
you will see that it prints the name of the file and some
information about the file's size.

If you want to save your text in a file that already
exists but was not the file you were originally
editing, you have to type

:w! file

The exclamation point indicates that you know the write
operation will overwrite the old contents of the file and
that you want this to happen. (Don't try this unless you
have some files you don't mind writing over.)

After you have written out your changes, you can start
editing a different file by typing

:edit newfile

and pressing Enter. This will clear out the text you have
been editing and set things up so you can edit the new file.

If the file already exists, its current contents will be read in.

Now here's a trick I can't demonstrate in this guide, but it's something to remember when you want to edit several files. If you start "vi" with a command line of the form

vi *file1 file2 file3 ...*

you can edit several files one after the other. After you have finished editing a file and have written it out (with ":w"), you can start editing the next file by typing

:next

or just

:n

It may be particularly useful to use wild card characters on the "vi" command line, as in

vi *.v

This will be expanded to a list of all the files under the current directory that have the ".v" extension (the "vi" exercise files).

Time to Experiment

I now recommend that you experiment with vi, creating small files of your own and editing them. After you are familiar with the parts of the editor that this guide has discussed, begin reading bits of the complete description of vi in the man pages. vi has a great number of features. Some of them may be useful in the work you do, while others are not. Just remember that vi has something for everyone.

doc.v—Documentation Tips

The third vi exercise file is named doc.v. In order to work through the exercises in the file, enter the command

```
cp doc.v mydoc.v
vi mydoc.v
```

The cp command creates a copy of the doc.v file and the vi command lets you look at that file. It's better to work with a copy instead of the real thing, in case you make a mistake or someone else wants to try.

The exercise file contains several tips for people who might use vi in creating documents. As in the last section, I recommend that you enter the preceding command now and work through the exercise file. The rest of this section essentially repeats what you will see in the file.

```
The "browse.v" file explained how to read through a
file using "vi". Unless the text suggests a different
way to move through the file, just read through this file
by pressing Enter or Ctrl-D.


**********************************************************
*******          Part I: General Tips         *******
**********************************************************


The wrapmargin Option

When you are typing in lines of text in paragraph form, your
job is easier if you don't have to remember to press Enter
when you reach the end of a line. Try entering the following
command.

:set wrapmargin=8

Now go to the next blank line, type a to begin appending
text, and start typing out the contents of this paragraph,
beginning with When you. Don't press Enter when you start
copying the second line. Keep on going. Press Esc to leave
Insert Mode after a few lines.

You should see that the word easier automatically jumps
down to a new line. The option "wrapmargin=8" says that
if you end a word within eight spaces of the right
```

margin of the screen, the next word should wrap around to begin on the next line. You do not have to press Enter. With this kind of wrap-around margin, you can just keep on typing words. The only time you need to press Enter will probably be at the end of paragraphs.

Abbreviations

"vi" lets you define abbreviations for commonly used words and phrases. This uses the ":ab" (*abbreviate*) command. As an example, try typing

:ab xyz XYZ Widgets Inc. International

and then press Enter. This says that "xyz" will be an abbreviation for "XYZ Widgets Inc. International". To see how it works, move the cursor to the next blank line, press **a** to begin appending text, and type

xyz welcomes you!

You will see that as soon as you type the space after "xyz", the abbreviation is expanded into the associated phrase. Now move the cursor to the next blank line, press **a** to begin appending text, and type

This is the XYZ factory.

This time, you'll see that "XYZ" is not expanded into the abbreviation. The abbreviation feature pays attention to the case of letters. Now move the cursor to the next blank line, press **a** to begin appending text, and type

xyzwill not expand.

When you type this, you will see that the "xyz" is not expanded because it is part of another "word". "vi" only expands abbreviations when they are not part of other words.

If you want to get rid of an abbreviation that has been set, use the ":una" (*unabbreviate*) command. For example, type

```
:una xyz
```

This tells "vi" to forget about the "xyz" abbreviation.

Command Files for "vi"

An abbreviation only lasts for the duration of a "vi" session. If you set up an abbreviation now, it will be remembered as long as you stay in "vi", but will be forgotten when you leave "vi". This means that you have to set up common abbreviations every time you start "vi". This would be a lot of work if you did it by hand, but you can simplify things quite a bit by setting up a *command file*.

A command file contains several commands that can be executed as if they were typed in a "vi" session. For example, you might use "vi" to create a file with the contents

```
set wrapmargin=8
set tabstop=5
ab mks Mortice Kern Systems Inc.
ab aa another abbreviation
ab bb another abbreviation
   ...and so on...
```

setting all the options you want to use and all the abbreviations you commonly need. The file can only contain instructions that normally start with a colon (:) in "vi", and you omit the colons in the command file. You can execute all the instructions in the command file inside "vi" with the instruction

```
:so filename
```

where *filename* is the name of your command file. "so" stands for *source*, and it tells "vi" that the given file should be taken as the source of several commands.

As a matter of fact, you can execute the commands in a command file when you first start "vi". You do this by starting "vi" with the command line

```
vi -c "so cmdfile" editfile
```

where *cmdfile* is the name of your command file and *editfile*
is the name of the file you want to edit. After I've
discussed aliases in Chapter 7, you might want to set up a
KornShell alias for

```
vi -c "so cmdfile"
```

```
**********************************************************
*******         Part II: Combining Files       *******
**********************************************************
```

Occasionally, you may want to combine several files into a
single document. For example, you may have a table of data
stored in one file and want to add the table to another
file. To demonstrate how this can be done, move the cursor
to the next blank line and type

:r sonnet

You should see the contents of the file read in after
the line that holds the cursor. "r" stands for *read*,
and it reads in the text of a file. This text is added
to the current file after the line indicated by the
cursor.

The same sort of command can be used to combine the
chapters of a document into a single file. For example,
consider the following commands (but don't enter them):

```
:r chapter1
G
:r chapter2
G
:r chapter3
```

These will read in chapters that are stored in separate
files. Notice that you had to add "G" commands to go to
the end of the file after each "r" operation, so that the
next input file would be added to the end of the text.

It's a good idea to store large documents in several
smaller files and only combine them when you are ready
to create the finished product. The smaller the file,
the faster "vi" can read and write the text. Small
files are also more convenient for you to edit, because
it takes less time to find the text you want to change.

```
**********************************************************
*******          Part III: Sorting Data          *******
**********************************************************
```

In many types of reports, it is convenient to be able to
sort a few lines of text (for a table of information). As an
example, consider the following lines.

```
a    -- append after cursor
o    -- open an input line
dd   -- delete a line
cc   -- change a line
w    -- move forward a word
b    -- move backward a word
x    -- delete a letter
u    -- undo
```

I entered these descriptions of "vi" commands in the order I
thought of them, but it would be nice to sort them into
alphabetical order. To do this, you can send the preceding
lines through the "sort" command.

First, you have to find out the line numbers of the
lines you want to sort. To do this, move the cursor to
the first line of the preceding table and press Ctrl-G.
"vi" displays the name of the file and a notation of
the form "line N of M", where "N" is the line number of
the current line and "M" is the total number of lines
in the file. Note the line number (it should be 200, or
a number close to that). Move the cursor to the last
line of the table and press Ctrl-G again. You should
find out the line number is 207. Now type

```
:200,207!sort
```

and press Enter. This asks "vi" to send lines 200 to 207
through the "sort" command. The lines will be replaced with
the output of the sort command, namely the sorted lines. Go
back and check the list, and you will see that it is now
sorted.

The same technique can be used to send lines through
other commands if you like. However, "sort" is probably
used in this context more often than any other command.

If you do not specify a range of lines for a command,
the command will just be executed. Its output will be
displayed on the screen, but it will not replace any of
the text of the file. For example, write out this file
and then try the command

:!wc doc.v

Because "wc" prints the number of lines, words, and
characters in a text file, this command gives you a quick
word count for your document.

```
**********************************************************
*******        Part IV: Formatting by Hand       *******
**********************************************************
```

Most UNIX systems do not have word processors; the most
common way to create documents on UNIX is to use a text
formatting program named "troff", discussed in Chapter 10.
Using "troff" is definitely recommended for long documents,
but for short documents such as letters, you can often format
text "by hand," using "vi" to create a text file that can
be printed directly on a printer.

Page Breaks

The Ctrl-L character is called the *formfeed*. You can use it
to separate pages. However, there's a catch. On a UNIX
system, you can't just append a Ctrl-L character to your
text, since Ctrl-L is a special instruction that works
even when you're in Insert Mode. This instruction tells "vi"

to *redraw* the screen; it's needed because there are a variety of ways in which the text that is displayed on your screen can get messed up by output written by other processes. (It's too complicated to explain how this might happen, but take my word for it, once in a while you have to tell "vi" that some other program messed up your screen and you want "vi" to clean things up again.)

However, you can still add a Ctrl-L character to your text; you just have to be a little more clever about it. To see what you have to do, move the cursor to the next blank line and press **a** to begin appending text. First press Ctrl-V, then press Ctrl-L. The Ctrl-V tells "vi" to append the next character you enter, even if that character usually has a special meaning. After you do this, you should see that the screen displays ^**L**, standing for Ctrl-L. By inserting these formfeed characters, you can break a document into pages.

On a normal line printer, an 8 1/2 by 11-inch sheet of paper holds a maximum of 66 lines. For the purpose of formatting, 54 lines fit nicely on a page, with an inch of space at the top and the bottom for margins. Thus you should consider inserting formfeeds every 54 lines (give or take one or two).

If you indent a paragraph with a tab character, the amount of indentation is determined by the tab stops set for the printer on which the document is printed. If you indent a paragraph with spaces, the amount of indentation does not depend on the printer setting.

Indentation

The ">" command can indent several lines in a uniform way. For example, try typing

`:1,306>`

and press Enter. This indents the first 306 lines of this file. You can get rid of the indentation by typing

`:1,306<`

```
and pressing Enter. As an instruction to try later, you can
indent the entire file with

:1,$>

When you are giving a range of lines to a command, "$" is a
special symbol that stands for the last line of the file.
The reason I suggest you try this later is that the cursor
will move to the last indented line (the end of the file),
which would cause you to lose your place in this file.

After you have formatted a document, write it out to a
file (with :w). On a true UNIX system, you could then
print the file using the "lp" or "lpr" commands. On
DOS, you can quit the MKS Tools and use "PRINT".
```

program.v—Topics of Interest to Programmers

The final vi exercise file is named program.v. In order to work through the exercises in the file, enter the command

```
cp program.v myprog.v
vi myprog.v
```

As before, working with a copy of the file makes sure that accidents don't damage the original file.

This exercise file is intended for those who will use vi to enter program source code. Because vi originated on UNIX, the editor contains several features primarily aimed at programming in the C language. However, these same features are applicable to many other languages, particularly structured ones like Pascal, Modula-2, and Ada.

Even if you do not intend to program on UNIX, you'll find useful information by reading through this file. The examples may look a little odd if you aren't used to looking at programs, but the vi features are still applicable to other work.

As in the last section, I recommend that you enter the preceding command now and work through the exercise file. The rest of this section essentially repeats what you will see in the file.

The "browse.v" file explained how to read through a
file using "vi". Unless the text suggests a different
way to move through the file, just read through this file
by pressing Enter or Ctrl-D.

```
**********************************************************
******         Part I: Indentation Control      ******
**********************************************************
```

The source code for a program differs from ordinary text in
several ways. One of the most important of these is the way
source code uses indentation. Indentation shows the logical
structure of the program: the way statements are grouped
into blocks.

The autoindent Option

Issue the command

:set autoindent

(Don't forget to press Enter after you have typed this.) The
command turns on a "vi" option that controls indentation
when you enter source code. To see how it works, copy
(append) the next two lines into the blank line that follows
them.

```
  if (a > b) max = a;
    else max = b;
```

(Make sure you add the blank space at the beginning of the
first line, either with several spaces or by pressing the
Tab key.) You will notice that when you press Enter after
typing the first line, the cursor goes to the next line and
automatically indents the same distance as the previous
line.

The "autoindent" option automatically indents each line
the same distance as the previous one. This can save
quite a bit of work getting the indentation right,
especially when you have several levels of indentation.

When you are entering code with "autoindent" in effect,
typing Ctrl-T gives you another level of indentation,
and typing Ctrl-D takes one away. For example, copy
(append) the next four lines into the blank line that
follows them.

To indent the next line, type Ctrl-T at the start of the line.
    The next line will be indented this same distance.
        On the next line, type Ctrl-D at the start of the line.
Notice how Ctrl-D moves the cursor back one level of indent.

I should point out that you type Ctrl-T and Ctrl-D while you
are in Insert Mode.

The amount of indentation provided by Ctrl-T is one
"shiftwidth". Like tab stops, shiftwidths are set
every eight spaces by default. A command like

:set shiftwidth=5

can change the shiftwidth for a "vi" session.

Try using the "autoindent" option when you are entering
source code. It makes correct indentation easier. It
can even help you avoid bugs—correct indentation
often makes it easier to notice certain types of syntax
errors.

Shift Commands

The "<<" and ">>" commands can also help you indent source
code. By default, ">>" shifts a line right one shiftwidth;
"<<" shifts a line left one shiftwidth. For example, move
the cursor to the beginning of this line and press > twice.
You will see the line move right. If you now press < twice,
the line will move back again.

You can shift several lines by typing the number followed by
>> or <<. For example, move the cursor to the first line of
this paragraph and type "**5>>**". You will shift all five lines
in the paragraph. What command will move the paragraph back?
Try it to make sure.

Two Different Shift Commands

In doc.v, I discussed shift commands that started with a colon, as in

:1,200>

There's no significant difference between this kind of shift and >>. If you use the :> form, you can specify a range of lines. If you use the >> form, you can specify the number of lines. Use whichever form is more convenient to whatever job you're trying to do.

```
*****************************************************
*******    Part II: Special Search Commands    *******
*****************************************************


The characters "(", "[", "{", and "<" can all be called
opening brackets. When the cursor is resting on one of these
characters, pressing % moves the cursor from the opening
bracket forward to the corresponding closing bracket—")",
"]", "}", or ">", keeping in mind the usual rules for
nesting brackets. For example, move the cursor to the first
"(" in

if ( cos(a[i]) > sin(b[i]+c[i]) )
{
    printf("cos and sin equal!");
}

and press %. You will see that the cursor jumps to the
parenthesis at the end of the line. This is the closing
parenthesis that matches the opening one.

Similarly, if the cursor is on one of the closing
bracket characters, pressing % moves the cursor
backward to the corresponding opening bracket
character. For example, move the cursor to the closing
brace after the preceding "printf" line and press %.

Not only does "%" help you move forward and backward
through a program in long jumps, it lets you check the
nesting of parentheses in source code. For example, if
you put the cursor on the first "{" at the beginning of
a C function, pressing % should move you to the "}"
```

that (you think) ends the function. If it doesn't,
you've made a typing mistake somewhere.

```
*********************************************************
*******      Part III: Large-Scale Changes      *******
*********************************************************
```

If the name of a data object or function has to be changed
in a program for some reason, it becomes necessary to change
every occurrence of that name. This would be a tedious
process using the "vi" features I have discussed up to this
point, because you would have to search through each source
file for the name and then type in the new name wherever the
old one was found. To avoid much of this work, "vi" offers
the **substitute** command.

The Substitute Command

The usual form of the **substitute** command is

:s/*pattern*/*replacement*/

where *pattern* is a regular expression and *replacement* is any
string. For example, move the rest of this paragraph onto
the screen, then move the cursor to THIS line and type

:s/THIS/this/

As soon as you type the colon, you see the cursor move
to the bottom of the screen. Type the rest of the
command and press Enter. You will see *THIS* turn into
this. The command puts the given *replacement* string in
the place of the first string that matches the given
pattern.

What happens if a line has more than one string that
matches the pattern? This line contains the word *the*
several times. If you move the cursor to the line and
type

:s/the/XXX/

what happens? "vi" only replaces the first matching string.
The position of the cursor in the line does not matter.

If you want to change every occurrence of a string on a
line, type a **g** (standing for *global*) after the last
slash. For example, move the cursor to this line and
type

:s/h/H/g

You will see both "h" characters change. Notice that
"global" only refers to a single line in this context,
not to the whole file.

Now how does the "s" command help you make large-scale
changes? In addition to applying "s" to a single line,
you can apply it to a *range* of lines. For example, type
the following command and press Enter.

:1,205s/^/!/

What happens? The "1,205" in front of the "s" indicates
that the command should be applied to the lines from 1
through 205 (everything up to the 205th line in the
file). The "s" command itself says that the beginning
of the line "^" should be replaced by an exclamation
mark. So (as you have probably seen by now), "vi" puts
an exclamation mark at the beginning of every line up
to number 205. To get rid of the exclamation marks,
type

:1,205s/^!//

(which says "Change every '!' at the beginning of a line
into *nothing*").

Line Numbers

In the preceding instructions, I made use of line numbers to
refer to lines. How do you know what number a line has? If
you just want to know the number of one line, move the
cursor to that line and press Ctrl-G. For example, find out
what the line number of this line is. For another approach,
type

:set number

and press Enter. As you can now see, this displays the number of every line in the file. If you want the numbers to go away, type

:set nonumber

It's up to you whether or not you want to keep the numbers.

Line Ranges

There are several special symbols that can be used when specifying a range of lines. The "." stands for the line that currently holds the cursor. For example, move the cursor to this line and type

:1,.s/$/???/

This adds "???" to the end of every line from the start of the file to the line containing the cursor. Move the cursor down to this line and type

:1,.s/???$//

This removes the question marks. Notice that the command worked, even though the last few lines before the cursor did not end in "???". When you issue a "substitute" command with a range, it is all right if some of the lines in the range do not contain the pattern you are replacing.

When specifying a range of lines, "$" stands for the last line in the file. Try this command

:1,$s/the/THE/g

What does it do? It changes every *the* in the file to uppercase (including words like *there* where "the" is part of the word). Now, just to put things back the way they were, type **u** to undo the change you just made. This demonstrates that the "u" command can undo changes made by ":s" as well as those made by "c" and "d".

It should be obvious now how to make a global change in a file. For example, here's a small piece of program source code to change.

```
int bubble()
{
    extern int array[30];
    int i, j, temp;
    for (i = 0; i < 30; i++)
        for (j = 29; j > i; j—)
            if (array[j] < array[j-1])
            {
                temp = array[j];
                array[j] = array[j-1];
                array[j-1] = temp;
            }
    return array[0];
}
```

Now, use an "s" command to change every occurrence of *array* into *list*. Make sure you get the line range correctly—use Ctrl-G to find out the line numbers of the first and last lines if you no longer have the line numbers shown on your screen. You can also use

:set number

to make the line numbers reappear on your screen.

Now check the sample source code to make sure that you changed every occurrence of *array* into *list*. The command you should have used to do this was

:266,279s/array/list/g

If you forgot the "g" on the end, the lines that contain *array* twice will still have references to *array*. Without the "g", the "s" command only changes the first occurrence of the given pattern.

Confirmation of Substitution

What would you do if you wanted to change the variable "i" into a "k?" You can't just use an instruction like

:266,279s/i/k/g

because that changes the letter "i" into "k", even when the letter appears in words like *int* and *list*. The solution is to add a "c" (for *check*) on the end of the "s" command. When you do this, "vi" checks with you before making every substitution. Before each possible change, "vi" prints the line at the bottom of your screen and puts a "^" under the string that is eligible to be changed. If you want the change to happen, press **y** followed by Enter. If you do not want the change to happen, press **n** followed by Enter. To see how this works, try

:266,279s/i/k/gc

and only change those occurrences of "i" that are related to the variable "i".

Using ":s" is much faster (and less error-prone) than trying to change every occurrence of a symbol by hand. Remember the "c" option if you think there's a chance that the name you are trying to change might be part of a larger symbol.

```
**********************************************************
*******        Part IV: Executing Commands        *******
**********************************************************
```

Suppose you have just finished creating a source code file using "vi" and you are ready to compile it. You can write out the file, quit "vi", and then compile it if you want...but everybody knows that there are likely to be errors the first time you compile a new file. To fix these compilation errors, you'll have to use "vi" again to edit the source code.

To avoid the time and effort of quitting "vi" to
compile, then going back into "vi" to fix errors, you
can invoke the compile command directly from "vi". A
step-by-step description of how you can do this
follows; however, you can't do it right now because
you're looking at this exercise file, and not at a
program's source code.

(a)First, write out your source code to a file by saying

:w *filename*

You don't have to specify the file name if you've already
written to the file once before, or if you originally read
the text in from the file.

(b)Type a colon (:), followed by an exclamation mark (!),
followed by the command you would normally use to compile
that file. On a true UNIX system, this might be

:!cc filename

because "cc" is the usual command for compiling C code
under UNIX. This won't work on MKS Tools, because the
software doesn't include a C compiler. Press Enter when you
have typed the line. "cc" compiles the program, and displays
any diagnostic messages in the usual way.

(c)After the compilation is finished, you automatically
return to "vi", where you can correct any errors that might
have been detected.

The ability to execute commands from inside "vi" has
other benefits. For example, enter

:!more sonnet

This shows that you can use "more" if you want to look up
information in some other file. If you were really
programming, you might want to check another source code
file for the name of a function or variable.

A Glimpse of *vi*'s Cousins

UNIX systems offer several other editors in addition to vi. I don't have the space here to provide a complete introduction to these programs, but I'll provide brief overviews in case you ever find the programs necessary.

The sed *Editor*

The sed editor is a *non-interactive* editor, sometimes called a *stream editor*. At the same time that you call sed to edit a file, you specify the editing commands that sed should perform on that file. In other words, you don't interact with the program—you specify all your commands up front. As an analogy, using an interactive program is like shopping in a store where you can decide what you want to buy as you go along; using a non-interactive program is like shopping through a mail-order catalogue, where you write a complete list of everything you want, then send off your list and wait to have the order filled.

The advantage of sed is the same as the advantage of shopping through a mail-order catalogue: lower overhead. The sed editor doesn't need any facilities for interacting with a user, so it can be smaller and faster than comparable interactive editors. Interactive editors like vi, on the other hand, require extra memory and execution time because they have to interact with the user, just as normal retail stores require extra staff because they need clerks to provide personal help for customers.

Obviously, you can only use sed when you know exactly what you want to do. Here are some cases when sed comes in handy:

- When you want to make the same simple changes in a large number of files. With an interactive editor, you would have to read in a file, make the changes, read in the next file, make the changes, and so on. With sed, you just give sed the list of files you want to change and a set of changes you want performed on each file. By using sed, you don't have to do a lot of work by hand, and you don't have to worry about the mistakes that inevitably happen when you do a lot of typing.

- When there's a particular editing job that you expect to perform frequently. For example, suppose a particular program produces output every day, and every day you have to modify that output slightly in order to include it in a report. You can save time by creating a file of sed commands that automatically do the editing for you. Then, instead of making the changes by hand every day, you can have sed do all the work for you. Again, you save time and you avoid mistakes; if you always use the same sed commands, you ensure consistency from day to day.

The commands of sed are not very different from the commands you use in vi. For example, the basic command for making a substitution is

```
s/pattern/replacement/
```

where pattern is a regular expression and replacement is what you want to substitute in place of the first string that matches the regular expression. For more information on sed, see the man page in this book.

> **Making *sed* Scripts**
> I've said that you write up instructions for sed before you actually call the editor. One way to do this is to create a text file containing the instructions you want sed to perform. Such a text file is called a sed *script*. How do you create a sed script? With vi, of course. vi is the natural way to create any text file.

The ed *Line Editor*

The ed editor is an interactive line editor with many of the same features as vi. It is an older editor, and many people believe vi makes ed obsolete because vi contains almost all of ed's commands.

ed is primarily of interest because of its connection with diff. diff's output resembles ed's input. ed is not included as part of the software that accompanies this book.

Chapter Review

vi is a screen editor, primarily intended to create text files. Table 6.1 lists the vi commands discussed in this chapter. For a full discussion of vi and its commands, see the vi man page.

Table 6.1. `vi` commands discussed in this chapter.

Command	Meaning
	Movement Commands
Ctrl-B	Go backward a full screen
Ctrl-D	Go down half a screen
Ctrl-F	Go forward a full screen
Ctrl-U	Go up half a screen
Enter	Go down a line
$	Go to the end of the line
%	Jump to the balancing bracket
(	Go to the beginning of the previous sentence
)	Go to the beginning of the next sentence
–	Go up a line
/string	Search forward for `string`
/	Search forward for the previous string
?string	Search backward for `string`
?	Search backward for the previous string
{	Go to the start of the previous paragraph
}	Go to the beginning of the next paragraph
0	Go to the beginning of the line
b	Move backward one word
G	Go to a specific line
h	Go left one character
H	(*High*) go to the top of the screen
j	Go down one line
k	Go up one line
l	Go right one character
L	(*Low*) go to the bottom of the screen
M	(*Middle*) go to the middle of the screen
w	Move forward one word
	Editing Commands
a	Append text (enters Insert Mode)
c	Change text (enters Insert Mode)

Command	Meaning
cc	Change line (enters Insert Mode)
d	Delete text
dd	Delete line
i	Insert text (enters Insert Mode)
J	Join two lines into one
o	Open a new line (enters Insert Mode)
p	Paste
r	Replace a single character
u	Undo
x	Delete a single character
y	Yank
yy	Yank line
<<	Shift left
>>	Shift right
:!command	Execute command
:<	Shift left
:>	Shift right
:ab	Create abbreviation
:edit file	Edit new file
:n	Edit next file
:next	Edit next file
:q	Quit if you've already saved text
:q!	Quit immediately, without saving
:r file	Read file
:s/X/Y/	Substitute Y for the first X on the line
:s/X/Y/c	Confirm before substituting
:s/X/Y/g	Substitute Y for every X on the line
:so file	Get vi commands from file
:una	Get rid of abbreviation
:w	Write file
:w!	Overwrite file
Ctrl-G	Find out line number

`vi` has several options that let you control its behavior. Table 6.2 lists the options discussed in this chapter. Again, the `vi` man page provides the complete list.

Table 6.2. `vi` options.

Option	Meaning
`:set autoindent`	New lines automatically match the indentation of the previous line
`:set ignorecase`	Ignore the case of letters when matching
`:set noignorecase`	Pay attention to the case of letters when matching
`:set nonumber`	Do not show line numbers
`:set number`	Show line numbers
`:set shiftwidth=n`	Shift actions should shift by n columns
`:set tabstop=n`	Set tabs every n columns
`:set wrapmargin=n`	Wrap around if within n columns of the end of the line

Several other editors are available under UNIX. `sed` is a non-interactive editor with speed as its great virtue. `ed` is an older editor that is mainly of interest because of its connection with `diff`.

Exercises

1. Use `vi` to edit the file `profile.ksh`. Change the line that begins with PATH so that it reads

   `PATH=".;c:/lu/bin"`

   (This exercise is very important—it sets up a definition that will become important in later chapters.) If you installed the MKS Tools under a non-standard directory, change the line to refer to that directory instead of `c:/lu`. For example, if you installed the package under `c:/lux`, the line should read

   `PATH=".;c:/lux/bin"`

2. Starting with the command line

   `vi *onnet`

use vi to edit all the onnet files so that the last two lines are not indented (they should line up with the rest of the poem).

3. Using vi, change all the colon (:) characters in comics.lst into semi-colons. Sort the result according to month and year. (Note: if the sort command line refers to the semicolon character, you must put the character in quotation marks, as demonstrated in the exercises at the end of Chapter 4.)

4. Create a file containing the names of all files under your home directory, sorted in alphabetical order. Read this file into vi. Delete all the directory names. For all remaining lines of the form

   filename

   edit the line to read

   cat *filename* >>junk

   (Editing a list of files with vi is a simple way to produce *shell scripts*, as you'll see in Chapter 8.)

Part II

Using the KornShell

## Chapter 7

The KornShell

The KornShell was developed by David Korn of AT&T laboratories. It is a descendant of the Bourne Shell, one of the first UNIX shells to gain wide popularity. The KornShell incorporates many of the features of the C Shell, another popular UNIX shell.

Every time you log into the MKS Tools that accompany this book, you use the KornShell. The KornShell reads the commands you type in and executes them.

From time to time I've discussed what the shell does for you. For example, the shell expands glob constructs into the names of appropriate files and directories. However, I have concentrated primarily on commands rather than the shell itself.

This chapter introduces several of the most basic features and capabilities of the KornShell:

- *Command substitution*—the ability to use the output of one command as part of the command line for another command.

- *Aliases*—the ability to define short forms for frequently used commands, to save you time and help you avoid typing mistakes.

- *Shell options*—the ability to let you change the default behavior of the shell.

- *Command history*—the ability to keep a record of the commands you have entered most recently. Such a record preserves an exact history of what you do during your session with the KornShell. You can tell the shell to reexecute any command from the command history, thereby saving you the trouble of typing the command again.

- *Command editing*—the ability to edit and reexecute commands stored in your command history. For example, if you make a typing mistake while entering a command, you don't have to type in the command all over again; you can just correct the mistake in the command and resubmit it.

- *Variables*—the ability to save information and pass that information on to commands, as well as using the information to construct command lines.

Information about the KornShell is provided by the sh man page and by the man pages of commands listed in the *See Also* section of the sh man page.

Note: On a system that has both the Bourne Shell and the KornShell, the Bourne Shell is called sh and the KornShell is called ksh.

Command Substitution

A pipe lets you use the output of one command as the input to another command. *Command substitution* is similar, but it lets you use the output of one command as part of the command line that invokes another command.

An example will make this situation easier to understand. To set this up, it's useful to create some junk files, so enter the following commands:

```
cp sonnet junk1
cp sonnet junk2
cp sonnet testdir/junk1
cp sonnet testdir/junk2
```

This creates two junk files under your home directory, and two more under testdir.

Now suppose that time passes, and a month from now you notice that you have some file names that start with junk. You don't remember what these files contain, but they're taking up disk space and you want to know if you can get rid of them. To do this, you have to look at their contents.

You could examine their contents with the instruction

```
more junk1 junk2 testdir/junk1 testdir/junk2
```

but there are two problems to doing this. First, it's a lot of typing. Second, I'm assuming that you've forgotten why you created the files, so you've probably forgotten how many files you created and what names you gave them.

You already know how to get a list of all files with names beginning with junk. The basic command to do this is

```
find . -name "junk*" -print
```

Enter this command and you'll see that it displays the names of all the junk files you created. You may also find that you have other junk files left over from previous exercises.

Now that you know the names of the files, you could enter a more command to look at them all. However, there's an easier way. Whenever the shell finds a command line containing a construct of the form

```
$(command)
```

the shell executes the *command*, then replaces the $(*command*) with the output of the command. For example, enter

```
more $(find . -name "junk*" -print)
```

The shell executes this command in two stages. First, it executes the find command inside the parentheses in order to get a list of file names; then the shell executes the more command, using those file names as arguments. You'll find that you can use more to look at each junk file in turn.

Note that you can execute the preceding command without knowing how many junk files you have. The find command will find all the appropriate files, and then more will display those files one by one. You don't have to remember how many files there were, or what their names were.

It's important to distinguish between the command we've just discussed

```
more $(find . -name "junk*" -print)
```

and a command like

```
find . -name "junk*" ¦ more
```

The second form pipes the output of find into more, and more displays the list of file names that find generates. The first form, however, displays the contents of the same files, not just the file names. Therefore, the first command (the one with command substitution) lets you examine the files to see if you want to keep them; the second command (with the pipe) simply tells you the file names.

You can use the same trick with the series of files with names ending with `onnet` (created several chapters ago). How can you find out what these files are and what they contain? Enter the command

```
more $(find . -name "*onnet" -print)
```

The form of the command is almost the same. You just change the options of the `find` command so that it finds a different set of files.

You can use similar constructs in many different contexts. For example, ask yourself how to get rid of the junk files you created at the beginning of this section. You should be able to figure out an easy way to do so. Enter the command

```
rm $(find . -name "junk*" -print)
```

The `find` command creates a list of names. The shell substitutes this list of names into the `rm` command, then executes the `rm` command to remove the files.

As you can see, the `find` command is well suited for use in command substitution. `cat` also lends itself to this purpose. As an artificial example, enter the following commands

```
find . -newer sonnet -print >out
ls -l $(cat out)
```

The first command obtains a list of all files newer than `sonnet` and stores this list in `out`. The second command uses `cat` in a command substitution. The result is that the `ls` command lists information on all the files newer than `out`. You could get the same results with

```
ls -l $(find . -newer sonnet -print)
```

but you may find there are times when it's useful to put the name list into a file rather than calling `find` in a direct command substitution.

One such time might be when you want to edit the list of files before you do the second command. For example, here's a situation for you to consider (but don't enter any of the commands). Suppose that your hard disk contains several old files. You intend to back up most of these files, then clear them off your disk.

To start this process, you want a list of all files that have been around a long time.

```
find / ! -ctime -365 -print >out
```

finds all files that haven't changed in the past year and writes the list into `out`.

Now, you may want to get rid of most of the files listed in `out`, but not all of them. You can therefore read `out` into `vi` and read through the list for files you don't want to delete. Using vi you can remove such files from the list, so that the list only contains the names of files that you want to delete.

After you've written out the edited list, the file out contains the names of all the files you want to back up and then remove. To back them up, you might use a command along the lines of

```
tar -cvf a:archive $(cat out)
```

The cat command just outputs the file list contained in out. The shell replaces the $(cat out) with the actual file list, then calls tar. As a result, tar backs up all the files in the list. To get rid of the files after they've been backed up, you can use

```
rm $(cat out)
```

As these examples show, command substitution can save you a good deal of typing. Not only does this save time, but it also eliminates some possible errors. It's easy to make typing mistakes or to overlook files when you are trying to remember all the files you want to work with. By having commands like find generate file lists for you, you know that the lists are going to be right.

An Alternate Format for Command Substitution

The command substitution examples have used the format $(command), as in

```
rm $(cat out)
```

for command substitution. You can get the same effect by enclosing command in grave accents, as in

```
rm `cat out`
```

This format has been in use for several years, but the POSIX.2 standard *deprecates* the form. This means that the form is considered obsolete and should not be used. I only mention it here because you may see it used in old UNIX applications.

Aliases

An *alias* is a personalized name that stands for all or part of a command. Typically, you set up your own personal aliases for commands that you intend to use frequently. Here are some reasons for setting up aliases:

- Simply to reduce the amount of typing you have to do. For example, you can set up a short, easy-to-type alias that stands for a much longer command.

- To create easy-to-remember names that stand for hard-to-remember commands.

You'll see examples of these in the sections to come.

Creating an Alias

Begin by setting up a simple alias. Enter the command

```
alias p="more"
```

This is an example of the `alias` command. It says that when you issue a command named p, you want the shell to replace the p with the string `more`. This process is called *alias substitution*. For example, enter

```
p sonnet
```

The shell substitutes `more` in place of the p, then executes the command. As a result, the preceding command is equivalent to

```
more sonnet
```

This example only saves you a few characters, but for some people that's useful. Here's another example that shows the power of aliases more clearly. Enter the two commands

```
alias findnew="find / -ctime -7 -print"
findnew
```

The `alias` command tells the shell that the name `findnew` stands for the `find` command given inside the double quotation marks. You can then enter `findnew` as if it were a command; the shell replaces the alias with the associated `find` command and executes the command. This alias saves you typing, and also saves you the trouble of remembering the format of a complex command.

You can use an alias name any time you could use the string associated with the alias. For example, enter

```
findnew >out
```

The shell changes this to

```
find / -ctime -7 -print >out
```

and then executes the command. You can also use aliases in a pipeline, as in

```
findold ¦ more
```

DOS-Like Aliases

If you're a DOS user, you may prefer to set up aliases that let you use DOS command names. For example, enter the commands

```
alias del="rm"
alias dir="ls -l"
```

After you have set up these aliases, you can use del to get rid of files, and dir to display the contents of directories. Notice that you set up dir to be equivalent to ls -l. For example, you can enter

```
dir /lu/etc
```

and the effect is the same as

```
ls -l /lu/etc
```

I chose to put the -l option into the alias because the output of the DOS DIR command is more like ls -l than the plain ls command. If you prefer, you can enter

```
alias dir="ls"
```

or

```
alias dir="ls -x"
```

so that the name dir is associated with one of the other forms of the ls command.

The Position of Aliases

Aliases only work when they're at the beginning of a command. For example, suppose you've set up the alias `dir` as in the previous paragraph. The shell only performs alias substitution when the alias appears in a place that a command can begin. For example, you can say

```
mkdir dir
```

to create a directory named `dir`. The shell won't replace `dir` because it's not at the beginning of a command.

Note that I say *the beginning of a command*, not *the beginning of a line*. You can use an alias in a pipeline or command substitution if it is appropriate. For example, enter

```
ls -l ¦ p
```

This uses the p alias that you created earlier. The preceding line is equivalent to

```
ls -l ¦ more
```

The General Form of the alias Command

The general form of the `alias` command is

```
alias name="string"
```

where *name* is a name you choose and *string* is all or part of a command. Remember that *string* must be the first part of a command, because the alias can only be used in a place where it's valid for a command to begin.

Built-in Aliases

If you just enter

```
alias
```

without any arguments, the shell displays all the aliases that are currently defined. This includes the aliases you've created in the past few sections. It also includes some aliases you won't recognize. These are *built-in aliases*.

Built-in aliases are automatically defined for you by the shell when you first log in. I'll be discussing the purpose of some of these built-in aliases in later sections. If you're eager to find out about them now, you can check the man pages for information.

> **How Long Do Aliases Last?**
>
> Aliases are created through the KornShell and, therefore, they always disappear when you log out. There is no such thing as a *permanent* alias. However, there is a way to tell the KornShell to set up aliases automatically for you every time you log in. This is discussed in Chapter 9.

Getting Rid of Aliases

Normally, an alias lasts from the time you define it until the time you log out. If you want to get rid of an alias before you log out, use the `unalias` command. For example, enter

```
unalias dir
dir /lu/etc
```

You'll see that you get the message

```
dir: not found
```

The `unalias` command tells the shell to forget about a particular alias. After that, the shell doesn't recognize the alias any longer.

The general form of the `unalias` command is

```
unalias name name ...
```

where the *names* given on the command line are existing alias names that you want the shell to forget.

Shell Options

The KornShell lets you set various options to control its behavior. To do this, you use the `set` command. In this section you'll see a few simple options that you can set. As I discuss more KornShell features in later sections, I'll discuss other options that pertain to those features.

Glob Constructs

If you call the `set` command with the `-f` option, the shell will stop expanding glob constructs. For example, enter

```
set -f
echo *
```

If the shell were expanding glob constructs, it would expand the `*` in the `echo` command into a list of all the files and subdirectories under the current directory. However, `set -f` tells the shell not to expand glob constructs. As a result, the `echo` command simply displays the `*` character.

Now enter the commands

```
set +f
echo *
```

As you might guess, the `+f` option is the opposite of the `-f` option. It tells the shell to go back to expanding glob constructs. This time, the `echo` command displays the names of all the files and subdirectories under the current directory.

> **Plus and Minus Signs**
> In general, if `set -option` sets an option, `set +option` reverses the option setting. This works for any valid option.

Showing Expansions

The `-x` option (also called the `xtrace` option) tells the shell to display each command line after expansions have been performed and before the command is actually executed. For example, enter

```
set -x
p sonnet
```

You'll see that the shell displays the line

```
+ more sonnet
```

before it calls more to display the contents of the sonnet file. This shows you the command that the shell is actually executing—the shell has replaced the alias p with its associated string more. The + at the beginning of the line is added to make the command stand out from other information that's displayed on the screen.

Now enter

```
p *onnet
```

and you'll see that the shell displays

```
+ more bonnet connet sonnet
```

The shell replaced the alias p with the command name more and expanded the glob construct *onnet into the three file names. Once again, the shell shows you the actual command it is executing.

You may find that you like turning on the xtrace every time you log in. If you're confused about how the shell deals with complicated commands, xtrace helps clarify what's going on. For example, enter the command

```
ls -l $(find . -ctime -3 -print)
```

You'll see that the shell prints out two lines. The first is

```
+ find . -ctime -3 -print
```

This shows that the shell begins by executing the find command inside the parentheses. (This command finds the names of all files under the current directory that have changed in the last three days.) The second line that the shell prints out begins with

```
+ ls -l
```

followed by the list of file names obtained by the find command. These two lines show the two-stage process that the shell uses in order to execute the original command line: first the find command, then the ls using the file names obtained by find.

I suggest that you work with the -x option through the next few sections. If you decide you don't want to use the option, you can get rid of it with

```
set +x
```

The Duration of Options

Options only stay in effect until you log out. For example, if you use

```
set -x
```

in your current session, it will last until you log out (or until you change the option with set +x). The next time you log in, the option will not be in effect. In Chapter 9, I'll show how you can set things up so that your favorite options are turned on automatically every time you log in. For the time being, you'll just have to remember to set up the options by hand if you want to use them.

Command History

Enter the command

```
history
```

You'll see that it displays a list of the most recent commands that you've entered during this session. (If you have set -x in effect, you'll see that the history command is an alias and expands into a cryptic-looking command that begins with fc. Ignore this for the time being.)

As you enter commands, the KornShell keeps records of those commands. These records are called your *command history*. On UNIX, your command history is stored in a file named .sh_history. DOS won't accept file names that begin with a dot, so the MKS Tools version of the KornShell stores your command history in a file named sh_histo. The file that contains your command history is called your *history file*.

The command history is useful in itself for providing a record of what you've done during your session with the computer. On the simplest level, suppose you enter a command and, due to a typing mistake, it doesn't do what you expect it to do. By the time you find out something went wrong, the command you entered may have disappeared from the top of the screen, especially if the incorrect command wrote a lot of text to the screen. However, you can still use `history` to display your command history and see what you actually typed. This can often help you correct the error.

You might also check your command history if you recently executed a complicated command and want to execute the same command or a similar one. For example, many people find it hard to remember the `tar` command for backing up a directory. They usually have to look up the command to make sure they've got the right arguments in the right order. If you're backing up several directories, you may have to look up the `tar` command in the manual the first time; however, the next time you want to do the same backup operation (or a similar one), you can just check your command history to see what you did the last time (within the same session). This means you don't have to keep going back to the manual to see what you did.

> **Note:** If you really do have this problem with `tar`, the simplest solution is to create an alias. For example, if you're using the MKS Tools you might define
>
>   alias backup="tar -cvf a:archive"
>
> as your standard command for backing up a directory. When you have this alias, you can just say
>
>   backup name
>
> to back up a directory or file named *name*. That way you don't have to look up the command at all; you can just use the alias. There are also more sophisticated solutions to this problem using shell functions or shell scripts. (You'll see these in later chapters.)

The output of `history` only shows the last 16 commands entered. The shell history file (`.sh_history` on UNIX, `sh_histo` on DOS) holds a much larger number of commands, but there's no point in showing all the commands if most of them just disappear off the top of your screen.

Reexecuting Commands with the r Command

Enter the command

```
history
```

again. You'll notice that the output of history shows a number beside each command. These numbers reflect how many commands you've entered since you logged in. The first command is number 1, the next is number 2, and so on. As I noted before, the history command only shows the 16 most recent commands, so if you've been working for a while, the numbers beside the commands can be quite large.

In the last section I mentioned that you could consult the history file if you wanted to retype a complicated command and needed to check the format of that command. But why should you have to go to the trouble of typing the command again when the system already has a copy of the command stored in the history file?

In fact, you don't have to retype such commands. You can simply tell the shell to read a command from the history file and reexecute that command. To see how this works, enter the two commands

```
ls -l
r
```

The r command reexecutes a command from the shell history file. When you issue an r command without arguments, it runs the most recent command you executed. In the preceding example, it runs ls -l again.

Here's an example that's a bit more realistic. Enter

```
find / -ctime -3 -print
```

Suppose you issue the find command to display several files but discover that the number of files is larger than you expected and that the output runs off the top of the screen. You'd like to rerun the command, only this time you'd like to pipe the output through more so you can read it screen by screen. You can rerun the command and pipe the output through more by entering

```
r | more
```

The r command is equivalent to reexecuting the original find command, and the addition of ¦ more pipes the result of the find command into more.

The *r* Command is an Alias for *fc*

If you are running with set -x, you'll notice that the r command is an alias for another command that begins with the name fc. The fc command is a multipurpose command for working with the history file. The trouble is that fc can be a complicated command, and many people have trouble remembering how to use it.

The designer of the KornShell solved this problem by creating several built-in aliases that were easier to use than fc itself. The r command is one of these; history is another. Enter the command

    alias

and you'll see that several of the built-in aliases are forms of the fc command. If you're interested in fc itself, see the man pages.

Reexecuting Other Commands by Number

You can use the r command to reexecute any command in the command history. For example, enter the commands

```
ls -l /lu/etc
history
```

The history command displays the numbers of all the recent commands. You can reexecute any command in the history file by entering

```
r number
```

where *number* is the number of the command, as shown in the output of history. Try this. Reexecute the ls -l command by entering r followed by the number of the command, as shown by history.

Reexecuting Other Commands by Name

There's an even easier way to reexecute commands with the r command. Enter the following command.

```
r ls
```

This version of the r command tells the shell to reexecute the most recent command that began with ls. In this case, it will be the command

```
ls -l /lu/etc
```

that you executed in the last section.

You don't even have to type in the full name of the command. For example, enter

```
r l
```

and you get the same effect. The shell looks for the most recent command with a name beginning with l and executes the command. Once again, it will be the ls command.

Substitutions in Reexecuted Commands

Enter the commands

```
set -x
ls /lu/etc
```

The ls command displays the contents of /lu/etc. Now enter

```
r etc=bin
```

You'll see that the shell displays the contents of /lu/bin instead of /lu/etc. The output -x shows that the shell has run the command

```
ls /lu/bin
```

You should have no trouble guessing why the command has changed. The argument

```
etc=bin
```

tells the shell to change the first occurrence of the string etc into bin. By default, r runs the most recent command, so it runs ls /lu/etc but changes the etc to bin. As another example, enter the commands

```
ls /lu/etc
cd /lu
r etc=bin ls
```

Again, you'll see that the r command runs ls /lu/bin. The ls on the end of the r command says to reexecute the most recent ls command, and etc=bin says to change etc to bin before running the command.

This example shows that you can make simple substitutions in commands before reexecuting them with r. The general form is

```
r old=new indicator
```

The *indicator* indicates which command you want to run. This can either be a number (indicating that you want to execute the command that has that number) or it can be a string (indicating that you want to execute the most recent command that begins with that string). The *old=new* says that you want to replace the first occurrence of the string *old* with the string *new*. In the example, *old* was etc and *new* was bin.

You can do the same thing again, in reverse. Enter

```
r bin=etc ls
```

and the shell reexecutes the ls command you just executed, except that it changes bin back to etc. You'll see that the effect is the same as

```
ls /lu/etc
```

Typically, you use this kind of substitution when you want to execute a command that is nearly the same as a previous one. For example, enter

```
cd
```

to go back to your home directory. Then enter

```
cp sonnet testdir
r so=bo
```

The first command copies sonnet to testdir; the second copies bonnet. You save a small amount of typing by using r for the second command rather than another cp. Obviously, the longer the original command, the more typing you save by using a short substitution.

> **Substitutions Only Work for the First Occurrence**
>
> An *old=new* substitution only substitutes the first occurrence of *old*. You have to be careful about this. For example, suppose you want to rename file1 to f1 and file2 to f2. You might try this with
>
> ```
> mv file1 f1
> r 1=2
> ```
>
> However, the result of the r command is
>
> ```
> mv file2 f1
> ```
>
> because the shell only changes the first 1 to a 2. In this instance, it would certainly be more useful for r to replace *every* occurrence of *old* with *new*...but the UNIX convention is to replace only the first occurrence (such as in vi s commands).

Command Editing

Command editing is a natural outgrowth of the action that was discussed in the previous section: obtaining a command from the history file, changing the command slightly, then reexecuting the command. With command editing, however, you have much more freedom to modify commands. In fact, you have most of the same editing features that vi has.

Activating Command Editing

To start up command editing, enter the command

```
set -o vi
```

This tells the shell that you want to be able to edit commands as if you were using vi.

Using Command Editing

As I've discussed, your history file records the commands you have entered most recently. Command editing is much like using vi to edit the history file, except that you only get to see one line at a time.

When the shell prompts you to enter a command, you are in Insert Mode. Press the Esc key. As with vi, this switches from Insert Mode to Command Mode. Pressing k moves back through the history file. The first time you press the key, you should see

```
set -o vi
```

This is the command that you just entered. Press k again and you'll see other commands that you entered recently.

Go back to the command

```
ls /lu/etc
```

that you entered a few sections ago. You're now going to edit this into

```
ls /lu/bin
```

You'll notice that the cursor is on the first character of the line. By entering w (for *move forward a word*) several times, you can move across until you get to the first character of etc. Now, you want to change the word etc into bin. Do this using standard vi commands. First you enter cw to say you want to change a word; then you enter bin as the new word. Press Enter when you're done, and the shell executes the command.

With command editing, you can't use the vi commands that begin with a colon (:). For example, you can't use :s. However, you can use most of the other vi commands with this form of command editing. For example, 0 goes to the beginning of the line and $ goes to the end. You can use c for changing text, d for deleting it, and a for adding to it. The j and k keys let you move from one command line to another.

After you've edited a command into the form you want, you can press Enter to execute the command. It doesn't matter whether you're in Insert Mode or Command Mode, and the cursor doesn't have to be at the end of the command line.

You should practice using command editing for a while until you're comfortable with it. Command editing is so useful that the designers of DOS copied it from UNIX. The standard DOS shell, COMMAND.COM, has command editing facilities, and many alternative DOS shells also have these facilities.

Why is the ability to reuse previous commands useful? Because most people use the same commands over and over again. For example, I'm writing this book with a word processor. From time to time I have to check the commands I'm talking about, so I quit the word processor to try out the commands. When I'm finished, I want to go back to the word processor to continue writing. Rather than writing out the command to invoke the word processor again, I just use command editing to go back through my history file to find the last time I invoked the word processor. I can find the command much more quickly than I can retype it, and I don't have to stop and remember the name of the file I was editing.

I use command editing all the time and I strongly recommend that you try it out for yourself. If you haven't used the facility on DOS, it may take a while for you to learn how to exploit its potential. Invest the time now; you'll save a good deal of time and trouble later.

Variables

Experienced DOS users are familiar with the concept of *environment variables*. In DOS, an environment variable is a piece of information with a name and a value. Any DOS program can consult the environment variables that are currently defined.

For example, the login procedure for the DOS MKS Toolkit defines an environment variable named HOME. The value of this variable is the name of your home directory. Any program that wants to determine the name of your home directory can ask DOS to look up the value of HOME.

UNIX also has variables that can be used in this way. However, DOS and UNIX variables differ in at least one important respect:

- In DOS, environment variables are stored in a single *table*. Every program has access to every variable in the table. If a program creates a new variable, it gets added to the table, and all other programs can use the new variable. If a program changes the value of a variable, all subsequent programs that consult the table will see the changed value.

- In UNIX, each program has its own separate table of variables. If a program creates a new variable or changes the value of an existing variable, it only affects the program's own table. It doesn't affect the variable table of any other program.

The variable table of a UNIX program is created by whatever invokes the program. For example, when you tell the shell to run a program, the shell loads the program into memory and creates a variable table for that program. The shell decides what to put into the table. To do this, the shell looks at its own variable table and decides which of those variables should be passed on to the program. When the shell passes some of its variables to a new program, we say that the shell *exports* those variables to the new program.

After the new program starts executing, it can change the value of its variables or add new variables to its table. These changes only affect the program's own table; normally, such changes do not affect the shell's table or the table of any other program. However, a program can explicitly ask the operating system to export selected variables back to the shell, in which case the shell's variable table is affected.

Variables Exported by the Shell

The KornShell works with many variables. You can create variables of your own, as you'll see in a later section; in addition, the shell automatically creates several variables by default when you first log in. The sh man page gives a complete list of these variables. In the sections to come, you'll only see some of the most basic variables.

Displaying Your Shell Variables

You can display the shell's list of variables at any time by entering the command

```
set
```

without any arguments. If you do, you'll probably see a lot of variables you don't recognize right now. These are set up automatically for you when the shell starts up. For more information on any of these variables, see the sh man page.

History Variables

The value of the HISTFILE variable is the name of your command history file. By default, this is .sh_history on UNIX, sh_histo on DOS.

The value of the HISTSIZE variable is the maximum number of commands that the shell should record in the history file. By default, this is 127. If you exceed this number of commands, the shell begins to discard old commands. For example, when the shell records command 128, it throws away its information about command 1.

You can use the set command as described in the sidebar *Displaying Your Shell Variables* to verify that HISTFILE and HISTSIZE have these values.

Your Home Directory

The value of the HOME variable is the name of your home directory. This is set at the time that you log in.

Working Directories

The value of the PWD variable is the name of your current working directory. The shell automatically changes this every time you issue a cd command.

The value of the OLDPWD variable is the name of your previous working directory. Whenever you issue a cd command to change directories, the shell uses OLDPWD to record the name of the directory you're leaving. When you issue the command

```
cd -
```

to switch back to your previous working directory, the shell uses OLDPWD to determine the name of that directory.

Using Variables in Commands

If you want to use the value of a variable in a command, write a dollar sign ($) followed by the name of the variable. For example, enter the command

```
echo $HOME
```

This displays the value of the HOME variable, which is the name of your home directory. This is the same name that you'll see if you enter the pwd command right after logging in. The process of replacing a $name construct with the value of the variable name is called *variable expansion*.

Enter the command

```
cd /
```

This makes the root directory your current directory. If you enter the commands

```
echo $PWD
```

you'll see the output is

```
c:/
```

because PWD holds the name of your current directory, and your current directory is the root directory. Now enter

```
more $HOME/sonnet
```

This displays the sonnet file from your home directory. When the shell processes this command, it expands $HOME into the name of your home directory, so that the argument of more is the absolute path name of the sonnet file.

You can use $HOME to refer to your home directory, no matter what your current directory is. Constructs like this simplify the job of writing shell programs, as you'll see in Chapter 8.

Creating Your Own Variables

You can create your own variables with a command of the form

```
name='string'
```

This is called an *assignment*; it assigns a value to a variable. For example, enter the command

```
TD='testdir'
```

This creates a variable named TD with a value equal to the string testdir. You can use this variable in commands. For example, enter the following:

```
echo $TD
ls -l $HOME/$TD
cd
ls -l $TD
```

The echo command simply echoes the string testdir. The first ls command displays the contents of the testdir directory under your home directory. The cd command returns to your home directory, and the last ls command displays the contents of testdir again. Of course, you could save more typing by defining

```
TD='$HOME/testdir'
```

This way, TD contains the full pathname of testdir, and you don't have to add things to the name when you change directories.

> **Variable Names**
> The first character of a variable name must be an upper- or lowercase letter, or the underscore character (_). The rest of the name (if any) can consist of upper- or lowercase letters, underscores, and/or the digits 0 through 9.
> The case of letters is significant. For example, VAR, Var and var are all distinct variables.

Changing the Value of a Variable

You can change the value of a variable with another assignment. For example, enter

```
TD='sonnet'
```

This changes the value of TD to sonnet. Enter the command

```
ls -l $TD
```

and you'll see that it displays information about the file sonnet rather than the directory testdir.

You can change the value of built-in shell variables such as HOME and HISTSIZE. For example,

```
HISTSIZE=200
```

tells the shell that you want it to keep up to 200 history commands in your history file rather than the default value of 127.

Getting Rid of Variables

You can get rid of any variable using the unset command.

```
unset name
```

gets rid of the variable that has the given name. For example, enter

```
unset TD
```

This gets rid of the TD variable. Enter

```
set
```

and you'll see that TD is no longer in the list of defined variables. Also, enter

```
echo $TD
```

You'll see that the command just outputs a blank line. Because TD is no longer defined, $TD has no meaning and there's nothing for echo to display. Technically speaking, $TD is expanded into the *null string*, a string that has no characters. If a variable does not currently exist, its value is always taken to be the null string.

Arithmetic with Variables

Enter the following commands:

```
i=1
j=$i+1
echo $j
```

You'll see that echo displays the string 1+1. Even though the assignments look like they're doing arithmetic, they're really just assigning strings of characters to variables. In

```
j=$i+1
```

the shell changes $i to the value of i, namely 1. Thus the variable j is assigned the string 1+1, and that's what the echo command displays.

If you want to perform true arithmetic with variables, you can do so using the let command. The command has the form

```
let variable=expression
```

where *variable* is the name of a new or existing variable, and *expression* is an arithmetic expression. For example, enter the commands

233

```
i=1
let j=$i+1
echo $j
```

This time the echo command displays 2. The let command evaluated the expression 1+1 and assigned the result to j.

You can also use let to change the value of i itself. For example, enter

```
i=1
let i=$i+1
echo $i
```

Again, the echo command displays 2. The let command works like this. First, the shell expands $i and replaces it with the value of i. Thus the command turns into

```
let i=1+1
```

As a result, i is assigned a new value of 2. The echo command shows you that the new value of i is 2.

Table 7.1 shows operations that can be used in expressions in a let command. In keeping with standard mathematical practice, all negation operations are evaluated first, then all *, /, and/or % operations (from left to right in the order they appear), then all + and − operations (from left to right in the order they appear). I've grouped Table 7.1 to show this.

Table 7.1. Operations in a `let` Command.

Operation	Meaning
-A	Negative A
A*B	A times B
A/B	A divided by B
A%B	Remainder from A divided by B
A+B	A plus B
A-B	A minus B

As an example of the order of operations, enter

```
let i=5+2*3
echo $i
```

The echo command displays the value 11, because the multiplication in the let command takes place before the addition. If you want to change the order in which the expression is evaluated, put parentheses around the operations you want let to evaluate first. For example, enter

```
let i=(5+2)*3
echo $i
```

This time the echo command displays the value 21 because the addition takes place first.

Integers Only

The let command does not let you perform arithmetic with numbers that have fractional parts. You can only use whole numbers (integers).

Exporting Variables

I mentioned earlier that the shell can export variables to the programs that it invokes. However, the shell doesn't do so automatically. You have to tell it which variables it can export.

The export command tells the shell which variables it should export. It has the form

```
export name name name ...
```

where each *name* is the name of a variable. For example, enter

```
export HOME PWD
```

This says that the shell should export HOME and PWD to every command it invokes from now on.

When you issue an export command for a set of variables, we say that those variables are *marked for export*. They will be exported to every subsequent command that the shell executes. Remember, a program can't use a variable unless the shell exports that variable. Therefore, you must mark for export any variable that programs might want to use. We'll see examples of how this works in later chapters.

The command

```
set -a
```

tells the shell that it should export every variable that you define from now on. This means that when you create a new variable, the shell automatically marks it for export. Note that this only works for variables after you issue the `set` command. If you want to export a variable that existed before you issued the `set` command, you have to use the `export` command.

Quotation Marks and the KornShell

In previous chapters, you've seen how you can enclose arguments in quotation marks (single or double). Quotation marks enclose an argument when the argument contains whitespace. Quotation marks also tell the shell not to expand glob constructs that occur inside the quotation marks. In this section, you'll see the effects of quotation marks on other shell constructs.

The shell does not perform command substitutions, alias substitutions, or variable expansions inside single quotation marks. For example, enter

```
i=1
echo '$i'
```

and you'll see that the output is $i. The variable is not expanded because the $i construct appears inside single quotation marks. Enter

```
echo '$(ls)'
```

and you'll see that command substitution doesn't take place either. Finally, enter

```
alias p=more
p sonnet
'p' sonnet
```

You'll see that the p alias works when it isn't inside single quotation marks. However, when p is quoted, the shell doesn't perform alias substitution; instead, it just tries to execute a command named p. There is no such command, so you get the message

```
p: not found
```

Now, let's try the same sequence of commands with double quotation marks instead of single quotation marks. Enter

```
echo "$i"
echo "$(ls)"
"p" sonnet
```

Despite the double quotation marks, the shell expands the variable $i and the command substitution $(ls). However, it doesn't recognize the alias p, so double quotation marks still turn off alias substitution.

In a sense then, double quotation marks are *weaker* than single quotation marks. With single quotation marks, the shell ignores all special constructs inside the quotation marks. With double quotation marks, the shell ignores glob constructs and aliases, but still performs command substitution and variable expansion.

There's one other special case to note. Enter the two commands

```
echo $(ls)
echo "$(ls)"
```

With the first command, the names under the current directory are displayed on one long line (which the shell *folds* several times so that the long line fits on the screen). With the second command, the names are displayed with one name per line.

Why does this happen? The output of the ls command normally shows one name per line when ls is used in command substitution. However, when the command substitution takes place in the unquoted form, the shell processes the output from ls, changing each line break into a single space. This long line is then given to echo as input. However, when $(ls) appears in double quotation marks, the shell doesn't process the line breaks. It leaves them as they are, so echo displays the line breaks as well as the names.

Line Breaks

In a UNIX text file, lines are separated by special characters called *new-line* characters. Most UNIX systems use the ASCII linefeed character as their new-line character, although this isn't necessary. The POSIX.1 standard lets you customize your system to use a different character as the new-line if you want.

In a DOS text file, lines are usually separated by a pair of characters: the ASCII carriage return and the ASCII linefeed. Thus DOS text files usually have two characters between each pair of lines, while UNIX text files only have one.

Chapter Review

When a construct of the form

```
$(command)
```

appears in a command line, the shell performs command substitution. It executes the given *command* and puts the standard output of the *command* into the command line in place of the original $(*command*) construct.

An alias is a personalized name that stands for all or part of a command. To create an alias, use

```
alias name="string"
```

where *name* is the name of the alias you want to create. When the shell sees an alias at the beginning of a command, it replaces the alias *name* with its associated *string*. This process is called alias substitution. The command

```
alias
```

displays all aliases currently defined, and the command

```
unalias name name ...
```

gets rid of the aliases that have the given names.

Shell options are set with the set command. Table 7.2 shows the shell options discussed in this chapter. Options turned on with a minus sign (-) are turned off with a plus sign (+) in the same position.

Table 7.2. Shell options discussed in this chapter.

Option	Meaning
set -a	Export all variables defined in the future
set -f	Do not expand glob constructs
set +f	Expand glob constructs
set -o vi	Permit cditing of commands with vi commands
set -x	Show all expansions and substitutions performed on commands (xtrace)
set +x	Turn off set -x

The `history` command displays a list of the most recent commands that you have executed with the shell. This list is called your command history and is stored in a history file.

The `r` command reexecutes a command from the history file. Table 7.3 shows various forms of the `r` command.

Table 7.3.   Forms of the r command.

Form	Meaning
`r`	Executes the most recent command
`r number`	Executes the command with the given `number`
`r string`	Executes the last command to begin with `string`
`r old=new X`	Replaces the first occurrence of `old` with `new` in command X, then reexecutes the command

Command editing lets you edit and execute command lines from the history file in the same way that you edit text with `vi`. Most of the common `vi` operations can be used. When you press Enter, the (edited) command is executed. In order to activate command editing, enter the command

```
set -o vi
```

When you use command editing, pressing Esc switches from Insert Mode to Command Mode. Pressing `k` after that will move back through the history file, one line at a time.

UNIX lets you define variables for use by the shell. To create or change the value of a variable, use

```
name=value
```

where *name* is an appropriate variable name and *value* is a string. Each UNIX program keeps its own table of variables, so changes in the table of one program do not usually change the table of any other program.

Table 7.4 lists some of the variables that are automatically created and maintained by the KornShell. A complete list is given in the `sh` man page.

239

Table 7.4. Shell variables discussed in this chapter.

Variable	Meaning
HISTFILE	The name of your history file
HISTSIZE	The maximum number of entries in your history file
HOME	The name of your home directory
OLDPWD	The name of your previous working directory
PWD	The name of your current directory

When the shell finds the construct

```
$name
```

in a command line, it expands the construct by replacing it with the value of the variable *name*. If there is no such variable, the shell replaces the construct with nothing (in other words, the null string, a string that contains no characters).

You can do arithmetic with variables using the `let` command. The general form of the command is

```
let name=expression
```

where *name* is a name for a new or existing variable and *expression* is an arithmetic expression.

The command

```
export name name ...
```

tells the shell to mark the specified variables for export. The names and values of these variables will be passed on to every subsequent command that the shell invokes.

The command

```
unset name name ...
```

gets rid of the specified variables.

When an argument is enclosed in single quotation marks, the shell does not attempt glob expansion, alias substitution, command substitution, or variable expansion on any part of the argument. When an argument is enclosed in double quotation marks, the shell does not attempt glob expansion or alias substitution, but does attempt command substitution and variable expansion on appropriate constructs within the double quotation marks.

Exercises

1. Create an alias named h5 that prints out the first five lines of any text file. (Hint: use the head command, discussed in the exercises at the end of Chapter 4.)

2. Create an alias named wcl that prints out the number of lines in a text file.

3. Create an alias named rmi that works the same as rm except that it uses the -i option to query you about every file you ask to delete.

4. Consider the following commands:

```
ls >out1
r 1=2 l
```

What is the effect of the r command?

5. When set -o vi is not in effect, pressing Esc gets rid of the current input line so that you can retype the line from scratch. However, when set -o vi is in effect, Esc has a different meaning. (What is it?) When set -o vi is in effect, what can you type to get rid of the current input line? Read Appendix F (*KornShell Editing Features*) to see other alternatives.

6. The env command displays all the environment variables currently defined—see the env man page. What is the difference between this and the set command with no arguments? (See the Glossary for a definition of environment variables.) Try it and see.

7. What is the difference between

```
let x= 4
```

and

```
let x=" 4"
```

Try it and see.

8. Make sure that set -o vi is in effect. Type the following without pressing Enter:

```
more so
```

Now press Esc and *. What happens? Read Appendix F for an explanation of this feature and others related to it. Will this feature help reduce typing errors for you?

## Chapter 8

An Introduction to KornShell Programming

This chapter demonstrates how you can write programs for the KornShell to execute. Shell programs have many features in common with programs written in more conventional programming languages like BASIC, Pascal, and C; however, the "statements" of shell programs are commands like cp, find, and so on.

If you're an experienced DOS user, you may already be familiar with this type of programming—writing a DOS batch file (e.g., with a .bat suffix) is a form of shell programming. However, you'll find that the KornShell's programming capabilities are much more extensive than DOS batch programming.

The chapter begins with an examination of *shell scripts*. A shell script is a file containing a sequence of commands that you want the shell to execute. The first sections discuss very simple scripts; later sections show more sophisticated features that can be used inside scripts, including the following:

- The ability to pass *arguments* to shell scripts and shell functions

- *Control structures* that can be used in shell scripts and shell functions; these include such constructs as if-else and for loops

- The ability to define *shell functions*, comparable to subprograms in a programming language

Shell Scripts

A *shell script* is a file that contains input for the shell. You've already seen what kind of input the shell takes:

- Utilities that you want to execute (such as cp, more, find)

- Commands that set options for the shell (such as set)

- Commands that create or manipulate variables (such as assignments or let)

- Combined utilities (such as ones using pipes or command substitution)

- Other special instructions (such as using alias to create aliases or r to reexecute a previous command)

A shell script can contain the same kind of instructions that you have been typing from the keyboard. In addition, it can contain more specialized instructions that control the behavior of the script. You'll learn about such instructions later in the chapter.

Creating a Shell Script

The easiest way to create a shell script is to use vi. It's best to start with something simple, so enter the command

```
vi simple
```

This command says that you want to edit a file named simple. Because there currently is no file with that name, vi knows you want to create a new file. Use the a command to enter the following text:

```
echo Hello there!
echo "How are you?"
```

Write out the file (using :w) and quit vi.

Needless to say, this shell script consists of only two echo commands. When you execute the script, the shell will read its input from the script file and execute these commands.

Making a Shell Script Executable

Before you can execute the script, you have to make the file executable. In Chapter 3, I discussed how to do this: enter the command

```
chmod +x simple
```

This assigns execute permission to the `simple` file. If you use the preceding `chmod` command, anyone can execute the file. You could also use commands like

```
chmod -x simple
chmod u+x simple
```

if you wanted to be the only one who could execute the file. The first `chmod` command turns off execute permission for you, for those in your group, and for all other users on the system. The second `chmod` command turns execute permission back on, but only for you.

> **Executability on DOS**
>
> Several future sections ask you to create a shell script with vi and then to execute the shell script. On a true UNIX system, you would have to use chmod to make the scripts executable. On DOS, all files are considered to be executable, so you can skip using chmod.

Executing Shell Scripts

There are several ways to execute a shell script. The sections that follow examine some of these and discuss how the various approaches differ from one another.

Executing the Command Directly

The easiest way to execute a shell script is simply to enter the name of the script. Enter

```
simple.
```

(Notice that you need to put a dot on the end of the file name—this is explained in the *simple.* Versus *simple* sidebar.) After you enter the command, you'll see

```
Hello there!
How are you?
```

displayed on the monitor screen. The shell has executed the `echo` commands inside `simple`, and you see the result on the screen.

If you find that the `simple.` command doesn't work, you may have missed doing Exercise 1 in Chapter 6. Use vi to read in the file `profile.ksh` from your home directory and edit the PATH line so that it reads

```
PATH=".;c:/lu/bin"
```

When you have edited the file, write it back out, then log out and log in again. Now when you execute

```
simple.
```

it should work. In Chapter 9 you'll see why the PATH line in profile.ksh is important, and I'll discuss a number of points related to the format of PATH.

---

simple. Versus simple

You'll notice that you had to enter the name of the file as simple. with a dot on the end. This is a property of the DOS simulation of the KornShell. Remember that DOS usually expects file names to have a suffix; however, the simple file doesn't have a suffix. More precisely, it has a *null suffix*, a suffix that doesn't contain any characters. To show that there is no suffix, you have to add the dot on DOS and type simple..

On a true UNIX system, you would only have to type simple (with no dot). UNIX doesn't require a suffix, so there's no need to worry about null suffixes. On UNIX you type the shell script's name exactly as it is; on DOS you have to add a dot if the shell script's name doesn't have a suffix.

If you find the dot on the end of the name to be ugly or hard to remember, you can always create an alias. For example, if you enter

```
Alias simple="simple."
```

you can then execute the script under the name simple instead of simple..

As another example of executing a command file directly, enter the following commands:

```
cp simple testdir
testdir/simple.
```

The cp command creates a copy of simple under the testdir directory. The second line executes the copy of the shell script. (Notice that you need a dot on the end of the file name.)

Executing the Command with a Subshell

You can also execute a shell script with the sh command. As mentioned in earlier chapters, sh is the name of the KornShell. Enter

```
sh simple.
```

and you'll see

```
Hello there!
How are you?
```

displayed on the screen again. Enter

```
sh testdir/simple.
```

and you execute the shell script from the testdir directory.

Now what really happens when you execute a shell script with this form of the command? The shell you are using sees the sh command and recognizes that you want to execute a command named sh. The shell therefore goes looking for a file that contains a program named sh. The name simple. is just an argument for the sh command.

But it so happens that sh is the name of the KornShell program. This means that the sh command line starts a new copy of the KornShell. This new copy of the KornShell looks for arguments on its command line. It finds simple. and executes the contents of the file. When it reaches the end of the simple file, the new KornShell has no more input to process, so it quits. After the new KornShell quits, the old KornShell comes back to start taking input again.

You might picture the process like this: Imagine that the KornShell is a butler who is always by your side to carry out your wishes. You ask the butler to do a job. Your butler rings a bell to summon another butler and tells that butler to do the job. The second butler does the job and reports back to the first butler. The first butler dismisses the second butler, then reports back to you and waits for new instructions.

Technically, your KornShell starts a *subshell* to execute the shell script. The subshell is entirely separate from the original shell, just as the second butler is entirely separate from the first.

You may be bothered by this indirect method of executing a shell script—why start up a new copy of the shell when you're already running an old copy? There are some simple reasons:

- When you invoke the sh command, you can specify *options*. The options for the subshell don't have to be the same as your original shell—it's like hiring a subcontractor with more specialized skills than the primary contractor. For a list of sh command line options, see the sh man page.

- You may want to execute the shell script in a *clean* environment. After all, you may have changed your shell session by defining variables or aliases, or by using set. When you create a subshell, the subshell can start again from scratch. The subshell inherits all variables marked for export in the original shell, but it doesn't inherit anything else. This can be an advantage.

- You may want to protect your original shell session from things that the shell script does. For example, suppose a shell script uses let and other commands to change the values of variables. If you already have variables of the same name defined in your current shell session, you may not want the script to change your variables. By using a subshell, you create a separate environment, making it difficult for the shell script to interfere with your original shell session.

The Dot Command

Enter the command

```
. simple.
```

This is an example of the *dot* command. The name of the command is just a dot character, and the argument is the name of the shell script you want to execute.

In a sense, the dot command is the opposite of the sh command. Instead of executing the shell script in a subshell, the script is executed by your current shell so that all the commands in the script affect the current shell. For example, if the script contains set commands or commands that change the value of variables, the commands affect the current shell.

In general, the only time you use the dot command is when you want the script to change options and/or variables in the current shell. In most other cases, you'll find it's better to execute the script directly or with a subshell.

What's the Difference?

You've now seen three ways to execute shell scripts: directly, in a subshell, and with the dot command. What's the difference?

The difference is related to the concept of *execution environments*. An execution environment is the collection of variables, aliases, options, and so on that are in effect when a command or shell script is executed. Here's what happens to the execution environment in each of the three ways of executing a script:

- If the script is executing under a subshell, the script gets an absolutely clean environment, running under an entirely separate shell. It is possible to specify options that will affect the behavior of this shell; for example, you can tell the shell to reinitialize itself as if you just logged in again.

- If the script is executed with the dot command, the script operates in the same environment as the shell itself, and can affect the shell's variables, aliases, options, and so on.

- If the script is executed directly, the shell creates a separate environment for the script. This is similar to running the script under a subshell, because the script's environment is separate from the shell's and cannot affect the original shell environment. However, it is not exactly like using a subshell because you can't specify options for the shell on the command line and the environment inherits some information from the original shell.

Explaining the exact differences between the subshell environment and the separate environment set up for a script executed directly would require more technical background than the average reader would like to handle. Just remember that using a subshell means a separate copy of the shell, while executing directly just means a separate environment (but the same copy of the shell).

Shell Scripts and Other Constructs

You can execute a shell script anywhere you can execute a normal command. For example, enter

```
simple. | wc
```

This pipes the standard output of `simple` through the `wc` command. The output of `wc` is the number of lines, words, and bytes in the standard output of the shell script. You could also say

```
simple. | more
```

to pipe the output of `simple` through `more`, although there isn't much point to this because `simple` doesn't produce much output.

The preceding examples show that you can use shell scripts in pipes. You can also use scripts in command substitutions. Enter

```
echo $(simple.)
```

and you'll see that the system displays

```
Hello there! How are you?
```

The `$(simple.)` construct tells the shell to execute the command and collect its standard output. The standard output is substituted into the `echo` command to produce

```
echo Hello there! How are you?
```

This explains why the output you see on your screen is all on one line.

You can create aliases for shell scripts. For example, enter

```
alias sim="simple."
sim
```

and you'll see that the `sim` line runs the `simple` shell script.

Comments

If a line in a KornShell script contains a number sign (#) symbol, the shell simply ignores everything after the #. This lets you place *comments* inside your shell scripts, which are explanations of what the script does or what a particular statement does. For example, use `vi` to edit the `simple` file, to change the contents into

```
# This script just prints out two lines of messages
echo Hello there!   # The rest of this line is ignored
echo "How are you?"
```

Now execute `simple` in any of the ways discussed in previous sections. You'll see that `simple` behaves the same way it did before you edited the file. The comments have no effect on the script's behavior; they just provide information that helps you understand what the script does.

Comments make shell scripts more readable. I strongly recommend that you put a comment at the beginning of each script to explain what that script does. This will help other people who read the script and will also help you—a week or a month after writing a script, you may not remember what the script does. A comment helps clarify what the script is for.

You may also want to add comments to explain particularly complicated commands or command sequences. An explanation in plain English can be more comprehensible than a cryptic UNIX command.

Positional Parameters

As you've just seen, you can use shell scripts in the same way you might use an ordinary UNIX command like `cp` or `echo`. You can also pass arguments to shell scripts in the same way that you pass arguments to an ordinary command.

To see how this works, use `vi` to create a file named `easy` that contains the following:

```
# This script displays three lines of output
echo $1 $3 $2
echo "$1" "$3" "$2"
echo '$1' '$3' '$2'
```

When you have done so, quit `vi`, then enter

```
alias easy="easy."
```

With this alias, you can execute the script with `easy` instead of `easy.`, so you don't have to keep remembering that extra dot. Now enter

```
easy Hello there friends!
```

You'll see that the output is

```
Hello friends! there
Hello friends! there
$1 $3 $2
```

To understand this output, examine the first line of the shell script:

```
echo $1 $3 $2
```

The constructs $1, $3, and $2 are called *positional parameters*. A *parameter* is a name or symbol that stands for a command line argument. Inside a shell script, $1 stands for the first argument given on the command line that invokes the script, $2 stands for the second argument, and $3 stands for the third argument. Because the command line for the script was `easy Hello there friends!`, $1 stands for `Hello`, $2 stands for `there`, and $3 stands for `friends!` The order of the parameters given to the `echo` command explains the order in which `echo` displays the words `Hello`, `there`, and `friends!`.

The second `echo` command in the shell script is similar. In

```
echo "$1" "$3" "$2"
```

251

the parameters are again *expanded*, which means that they're replaced with the arguments in the corresponding positions on the command line. As discussed in Chapter 7, double quotation marks are "weak" and don't prevent variable expansion in a command line. This example shows that double quotation marks don't prevent the expansion of parameters either.

The final echo command in the shell script is

```
echo '$1' '$3' '$2'
```

The output of this command is simply

```
$1 $3 $2
```

The single quotation mark characters are "strong" quotation marks. When the shell executes a shell script, it does not expand parameter constructs that are enclosed in single quotation marks.

Now enter the command

```
easy "Hi there" "How are you?" "Fine"
```

You'll see that the output is

```
Hi there Fine How are you?
Hi there Fine How are you?
$1 $3 $2
```

This shows that the first argument on the command line is Hi there. The argument has two words, but the double quotation marks serve to group the words into a single argument.

As another example, enter

```
easy Hello there!
```

The output is

```
Hello there!
Hello there!
$1 $3 $2
```

In this case, there are only two arguments. When the shell sees the parameter $3 inside the shell script, the shell realizes there is no corresponding argument. Therefore, the shell expands $3 into a *null string* (a string that contains no characters). The shell script therefore becomes

```
echo Hello  there!
echo "Hello" "" "there!"
echo '$1' '$3 '$2'
```

In the first `echo` command, replacing $3 with a null string means that `echo` has only two arguments. Because `echo` puts a single blank between each of its arguments, the output is only `Hello there!` In the second `echo` command, there are three arguments; `""` is a null string. This means that the second `echo` command outputs `Hello` followed by a space, the null string (no characters) followed by a space, and finally `there!` As you can see in the output, the result is an extra space between `Hello` and `there!`

Now enter

```
easy A B C D
```

This time the output is

```
A C B
A C B
$1 $3 $2
```

The original command line contained four arguments. However, the shell script only contains references to the first three arguments, $1, $2, and $3. You can specify as many arguments as you want on the command line; if the script doesn't happen to use some of those arguments, those arguments are simply ignored. You could also write a shell script that only uses arguments $2, $3, and $4, for example. You can ignore any or all arguments if you want.

Here's one last example to test your understanding of the way the shell works. Enter the following commands

```
easy *
easy "*"
```

Are you surprised by what you see? Here's how the two commands work and the output you'll see.

- In the first `easy` command, the shell sees the * glob construct and expands it immediately. The shell then executes the `easy` script. The first three arguments to the script will be the first three files in the expansion of *. Other file names in the expansion of * aren't used. Therefore you'll see the usual sort of three-argument output from `easy`, but the arguments will be the first three file names under your current directory.

- In the second easy command preceding, the shell doesn't expand the *
immediately because it's enclosed in quotation marks. Instead, the shell
believes that the first (and only) argument of the script is the * character.
When the shell expands the contents of the shell script, the result is

```
echo *
echo "*" "" ""
echo '$1' '$3' '$2'
```

The first echo command displays all file and directory names under the
current directory. The second echo just displays the * character; the
shell doesn't expand * because it's enclosed in quotation marks. The
final echo command is the same as usual.

Positional Parameter $0

The positional parameter $0 (zero) stands for the name of the shell
script command itself. For example, in

```
easy A B C
```

$0 stands for easy., because that's the real name, not the alias of the
script. If you specify a longer path name to invoke the script, as in

```
./easy. A B C
```

$0 stands for the path name you give.

The preceding examples show the dramatic difference that quotation marks
can make inside shell scripts and on the command lines that invoke shell scripts. In
the first example, you see a few file names; in the second example, you see all the file
names under the current directory, plus the * character. Obviously, you have to be
careful whenever you use quotation marks, inside or outside a script.

Special Parameters

The KornShell lets you use several special parameters inside shell scripts. To see
how some of these work, use vi to create a file named special with the following
contents:

```
# This script demonstrates special parameters.
easy. "$@"
easy. "$*"
```

Notice that this script makes use of the `easy` script you created earlier. This shows that you can call one script inside another script. Next use `vi` to change the existing `easy` script to:

```
echo $1 $3 $2
echo This script has $# arguments
```

Entering an @

In `vi`, the @ character normally tells `vi` to delete everything you typed on the current line. To put @ in a file, enter Ctrl-V @.

The following list examines each of the special parameters used in these shell scripts:

`$#`   Expands to the number of arguments passed to the script.

`$@`   Expands to a list of all arguments, each as a separate argument in the list. This means that $@ is equivalent to $1 $2 $3 ...

`$*`   Expands to a single argument that is a list of all the arguments passed to the shell script. This means that "$*" is equivalent to the single argument $1 $2 $3 ....

You'll understand the difference between $@ and $* after you see an example. When you have created the `special` file, exit `vi` and enter the command

```
special. A B C
```

Listing 8.1 shows the output from this command.

Listing 8.1.   Output from the `special` script.

```
A C B
This script has 3 arguments.
A B C
This script has 1 arguments.
```

The first two lines of output come from the first easy command:

```
easy. "$@"
```

The "$@" construct expands into a list of the arguments to the `special` script; each item in the list is a separate argument. Therefore, the preceding line becomes

```
easy. "A" "B" "C"
```

The results of the command are

```
A C B
This script has 3 arguments
```

The $# construct inside easy changes into the number of arguments.
Now, consider the second easy command in the special script:

```
easy. "$*"
```

The "$*" construct expands into a single argument made up of all the arguments
passed to special. Therefore the preceding line becomes

```
easy. "A B C"
```

Because there is only one argument this time, $1 inside the easy script is "A B C"
and $2 and $3 are null strings. The results of the command are

```
A B C
This script has 1 arguments.
```

Check the definition of the easy script to make sure you understand how this
output was produced.

The shift *Command*

The shift command lets you adjust the list of arguments that a shell script
receives. The easiest way to understand how the command works is to look at an
example. Use vi to create a file named shifty that contains the following:

```
# This script demonstrates the shift command.
# You must specify at least six arguments.
echo "$*"
shift 3
echo "$*"
shift 2
echo "$*"
shift 1
echo "$*"
```

After you have created the file, exit `vi` and enter the following command:

```
shifty. A B C D E F
```

The output from this command is:

```
A B C D E F
D E F
F
```

(with a blank line after the F).

Looking at the output, you should be able to figure out what the `shift` command does. Each `echo` command in the `shifty` script prints out all the arguments to the script. The first `echo` command prints A B C D E F, as you probably would expect. After the `shift` command, however, the output is only D E F.

The `shift` command gets rid of the specified number of arguments from the beginning of the argument list. Therefore,

```
shift 3
```

gets rid of the first three arguments. Because you started with A B C D E F, the `shift` command reduces the argument list to D E F. The command

```
shift 2
```

gets rid of two more arguments, leaving only F. Finally,

```
shift 1
```

gets rid of the last argument. The final `echo` command therefore outputs a blank line.

The `shift` command gets its name because it shifts the parameter numbers of all the arguments. For example, if the original argument list is

```
A B C D E F
```

then A is $1, B is $2, and so on. In particular, D is $4. After

```
shift 3
```

the argument D is $1. As you can see, the argument has shifted from $4 to $1. The other remaining arguments also shift their positions accordingly.

Now enter the command

```
shifty. a
```

This time, you'll see that the first `shift` command gets an error. The error occurs because you tried to `shift` three arguments but there was only one argument in the argument list. You'll get the same sort of error if you enter the command

```
shifty. a b c d e
```

The `shift 3` and `shift 2` commands get rid of all the arguments. Therefore the final `shift 1` command has nothing left to shift.

Redirection with Shell Scripts

Here's a simple example that shows how you can use redirection with shell scripts. Create a file named `sm` that contains the following line:

```
sort $@ ¦ more
```

This shell script simply takes all the command line arguments and uses them to create a `sort` command. The sorted output is then piped through `more` to make it easier to read. For example, enter

```
sm. -t: -k 4n,5 -k 3M,4 comics.1st
```

You'll see that it sorts the `comics.1st` file according to year and month, as discussed in Chapter 5. This is because the command inside the shell script expands to

```
sort -t: -k 4n,5 -k 3M,4 comics.1st ¦ more
```

once the `$@` construct is expanded to all the arguments on the `sm` command line. Now enter

```
sm. -t: -k 4n,5 -k 3M,4 < comics.1st
```

This is almost the same as the last time, except that `comics.1st` is provided as input by redirection rather than by specifying it as an argument.

What happens this time? The `sort` command has a number of options like `-t:` and the `-k` options, but it doesn't have any input file. Therefore it reads the standard input. Because of the `comics.1st` on the command line, the standard input is read from `comics.1st`; therefore, you once again see the `comics.1st` file sorted according to year and month.

Control Structures

Control structures let you make more ambitious shell scripts. For example, there is a control structure that lets you test a condition and take different actions depending on the result. This lets you write "smarter" shell scripts that can take different possibilities into account and act accordingly.

Command Status Values

Before discussing control structures themselves, it's important to understand the idea of *command status values*.

When a command finishes execution, it reports back to the shell; this lets the shell know that the command is done and that it's time to execute a new command. When a command reports back to the shell, the command has the opportunity to give the shell a status report. Most UNIX commands limit their status reports to "I succeeded" or "I failed." Commands can fail for many reasons; for example, a command might fail because you made a typing mistake on the command line, or because you didn't have appropriate permissions to perform a particular action, or because it didn't have the right number of arguments to work with.

The status report that a command presents to the shell is really just a single integer number. This number is called the command's *status value* or *return value*. As a loose rule of thumb, commands use a status value of 0 (zero) to report success and a status value of 1 to report failure. However, there are several commands that don't follow this rule; to find out the status values used by a particular command, see the *Diagnostics* section of the man page for that command.

Some commands use a wider range of status values. For example, `diff` returns the following values:

0   If the files that `diff` compares are identical

1   If the files that `diff` compares are different

2   If `diff` fails for some reason (like a typing mistake on the command line)

By looking at the status value, the shell can determine the results of a command after the command has finished executing. For example, you can tell the shell to take one action if a command succeeded and a different action if the command failed. The next section describes the shell instructions that make this possible.

The if *Construct*

The if construct has the form

```
if condition
then commands
fi
```

where condition is a command and commands is a list of commands.

When the shell sees this construct, it begins by executing the condition command. If the status value of this command is zero, the shell executes the list of commands; otherwise, the shell skips past the commands and executes whatever comes after the fi line. (Note that fi is if backwards.)

For example, enter the following

```
if diff sonnet bonnet
then echo No difference
fi
```

(You should type these commands directly to the shell; don't put them in a shell script file.) When the shell executes the if construct, it begins by executing the diff command. Because the files sonnet and bonnet are identical, diff returns a status of zero. Because of this status, the shell executes the echo command that comes after then, and you'll see the output

```
No difference
```

As contrast, enter the following

```
if diff sonnet nursery >junk
then echo No difference
fi
```

Again, the shell begins by executing the diff command. This time the files are not identical and the status value is 1. Because the status is not zero, the shell skips the command that follows then. As a result, you won't see any output. (Note that the >junk construct on the diff command redirected the normal diff output so that it didn't clutter up the screen. On a true UNIX system, you could redirect into the null file /dev/null, but that doesn't work with MKS Tools.)

Entering if Constructs

When you typed in the lines

```
if diff sonnet bonnet
then echo No difference
fi
```

you probably noticed that the shell prompted for the then line with > instead of the shell's usual input prompt. This shows that the shell isn't expecting you to enter a new command; instead, it's expecting you to enter a continuation of the previous line. You'll keep on getting the > prompt until you enter fi.

The shell doesn't take any action until you enter the fi to finish the if construct. For example, the shell doesn't try to execute the diff command. An if construct is considered to be a single instruction, even though it can contain several commands. The shell won't do anything until you've typed in the entire construct.

As noted earlier in this section, you can put several commands in the then part of an if construct. For example, enter the following:

```
if diff bonnet sonnet
then
    echo No difference
    more sonnet
fi
```

This if construct has two statements in its then part: an echo command and a more command.

DOS IF

DOS has an IF command that can be used in batch files for much the same purpose as the UNIX if construct. However, the DOS IF can only execute a single command if a condition is met, unlike the UNIX if, which can execute any number of commands. In addition, the DOS IF is limited in the kinds of conditions it can test.

Indentation Style

The last example put the `echo` and `more` commands on separate lines, and indented them from the left margin. Indenting these statements serves several purposes:

- It makes the keywords `then` and `fi` stand out more clearly, because they are flush with the left margin and because they are the only words on their lines.

- It emphasizes that the `echo` and the `more` commands are grouped together: the shell either executes both commands or neither of them.

Some people prefer to put the *condition* of an `if` construct on its own line too, as in

```
if
    diff bonnet sonnet
then
    echo No difference
    more sonnet
fi
```

With this style, only the keywords are flush with the left margin. In this way, the keywords stand out more clearly.

These techniques of indentation are all part of *programming style*. A good programming style arranges commands to make them more readable and to emphasize the underlying logic of the statements. The indentation in the preceding code section shows that the `if` construct is broken into two chunks: the first chunk (from `if` to `then`) is the *condition* part, and the second chunk (from `then` to `fi`) tells what to do if the condition is met.

Good programming style can actually help you avoid errors. For example, indenting commands makes it harder to forget the `fi` required to mark the end of the `if` construct. When you see

```
if
    condition
then
    command
    command
```

it's easier to remember that you need some kind of marker to indicate the end of the construct; you need something special to *cancel the indentation*.

You should work to develop a good programming style. A clear and consistent style makes your shell scripts easier to understand when you're writing them and when you're reading them later on.

The *else* Clause

`if` constructs can have the form

```
if condition
then commands
else commands
fi
```

If the `condition` command returns a status value of zero, the shell executes the `commands` that follow the keyword `then`. However, if the `condition` command returns any other status value, the shell executes the commands that follow the keyword `else`. For example, use `vi` to create a file named `dif` that has the contents shown in Listing 8.2.

Listing 8.2. The `dif` shell script (first draft).

```
# This script finds the difference between two files.
# Differences are displayed with the more command.
# Uses "junk" as a temporary working file.
if
    diff $1 $2 >junk
then
    echo No difference
else
    more junk
fi
rm junk
```

This shell script uses `diff` to compare two files whose names are given as arguments to the script. The set of differences are written into a file named `junk`; again you could use `/dev/null` on a true UNIX system. If the two files are identical, the shell executes the `echo` command that follows `then`; otherwise, the shell executes the `more` command that follows `else`. After the `fi` that marks the end of the `if` construct, the script removes the `junk` file.

After you have created the `dif` file, leave `vi` and enter the command

```
alias dif= "dif."
```

so you don't have to worry about the trailing dot. Then enter

```
dif bonnet sonnet
dif sonnet nursery
```

You'll see that dif works very much like the usual diff command. However, when two files are identical, dif displays the message No difference (unlike the usual diff command, which does not display any output if the files are identical). In addition, dif displays diff's output with more, so that you can look at the differences a screenful at a time rather than everything sliding by too fast to read.

Improving *dif*

In some ways, dif is superior to the normal diff command, because it displays a message if the files are identical, and because it uses more to show its output. dif certainly has its weaknesses too—for example, you can specify several options with the command diff, but not with dif. However, this weakness in dif is easily overcome. Use vi to edit dif and change the diff command, as shown in Listing 8.3.

Listing 8.3.   The dif shell script (second draft).

```
# This script finds the difference between two files.
# Differences are displayed with the more command.
# Uses "junk" as a temporary working file.
# You may specify any options you like for the diff command.
if
    diff $@ >junk
then
    echo No difference
else
    more junk
fi
rm junk
```

This version of the command does not single out $1 and $2 as the only arguments to pass to diff. The special parameter $@ expands into all the arguments specified on the shell script's command line. For example, enter

```
dif. -b -C 4 sonnet bonnet
```

As you might guess, -b and -C 4 are possible options for diff. You can read about them in the diff man page if you want, but their meaning isn't really relevant to this example. The important thing to notice is that the diff command inside the shell script receives all the arguments that you specified on the dif command line, in the same order that the arguments were specified. With the preceding command line for dif, the diff command inside the script becomes

```
diff -b -C 4 sonnet bonnet >junk
```

The revised `dif` script is a reasonable substitute for the `diff` command in many instances. There are still times that you might want to use the real `diff` command, such as if you want to pipe the output to another command rather than just reading it on the display screen. However, you may find that most of the time you prefer using `dif` to `diff`.

This is one of the virtues of using shell scripts. With scripts, you can write your own versions of basic UNIX commands that are just as easy to use as the original commands but are better suited to your personal preferences.

The *elif* Clause

It's time now to return to other forms of the `if` construct. `if` constructs can also have the form

```
if condition1
then commands1
elif condition2
then commands2
elif condition3
then commands3
    ...
else commands
fi
```

`elif` is short for *else if*. If the `condition1` command returns a status value of zero, then the shell executes `commands1`. Otherwise, the shell goes on to execute the `condition2` command. If that returns a status value of zero, the shell executes `commands2`. Otherwise, the shell goes on to execute the `condition3` command, and so on. If none of the `condition` commands returns a status value of zero, the shell executes the `commands` after the `else` keyword.

As an example of this, use `vi` to create a file named `dif3` containing the shell script given in Listing 8.4. You pass this script three file names as arguments. The script compares the files and tells you if any pair of files is identical.

When you have created the `dif3` file, leave `vi` and enter the following commands

```
dif3. bonnet sonnet nursery
dif3. bonnet nursery sonnet
dif3. bonnet nursery comics.lst
```

In each case, the script should tell you if any pair of files is identical.

Listing 8.4.   The `dif3` shell script.

```
# This script takes three file names as arguments
# and determines if any pair of the files is identical.
if
    diff $1 $2 >junk
then
    echo $1 and $2 are identical
elif
    diff $2 $3 >junk
then
    echo $2 and $3 are identical
elif
    diff $1 $3 >junk
then
    echo $1 and $3 are identical
else
    echo No files match
fi
rm junk
```

Notice that the script contains three `diff` commands, to compare each possible pair of files. If a `diff` command finds a match, the following `echo` command displays an appropriate message and the shell proceeds to the end of the `if` construct. If a `diff` command finds that two files are not identical, the shell goes down to the next `elif` clause to compare another pair of files. If no files are identical, the shell goes to the `else` clause and executes the `echo` command to display `No files match`.

The script redirects all `diff` output into a file named `junk` and removes `junk` when all comparisons have been made. This is because the script is only interested in finding out if files are identical; if files are different, the script doesn't really care what those differences are.

The test *Command*

The `test` command returns a status value that indicates whether or not a particular condition is true. For example, the command

```
test -f name
```

returns a status of zero if *name* is the name of an existing file and returns a status of 1 otherwise. Table 8.1 shows many other uses of the test command.

Table 8.1.   Uses of the test command.

Command	Meaning

Testing path names:

test -d *name*	Is *name* a directory?
test -f *name*	Is *name* an ordinary file?
test -r *name*	Can you read *name*?
test -w *name*	Can you write to *name*?

Testing the age of files:

test *file1* -ot *file2*	Is *file1* older than *file2*?
test *file1* -nt *file2*	Is *file1* newer than *file2*?

Comparing two integers A and B:

test *A* -eq *B*	Is *A* equal to *B*?
test *A* -ne *B*	Is *A* not equal to *B*?
test *A* -gt *B*	Is *A* greater than *B*?
test *A* -lt *B*	Is *A* less than *B*?
test *A* -ge *B*	Is *A* greater than or equal to *B*?
test *A* -le *B*	Is *A* less than or equal to *B*?

Comparing two strings *str1* and *str2*:

test *str1* = *str2*	Is *str1* equal to *str2*?
test *str1* != *str2*	Is *str1* not equal to *str2*?

Testing a string to be null:

test *string*	Does *string* contain any characters?

267

test commands are obviously useful in if constructs. As an example, use vi to create a file named list that contains the text shown in Listing 8.5.

Listing 8.5.   The list shell script.

```
# This script displays information about files,
# directories, or other arguments.
if
    test -f $1
then
    more $1
elif
    test -d $1
then
    ls $1
else
    echo $1
fi
```

This script is designed to be called with a single argument. If the argument is a file name, the script uses more to display the contents of the file. If the argument is a directory name, the script uses ls to display the contents of that directory. Otherwise, the script merely echoes the argument. Notice that this example shows you can use positional parameters in test commands (you can use positional parameters anywhere in any script).

When you have created the list file, quit vi and enter the following commands:

```
list. sonnet
list. testdir
list. $HOME
```

You'll see that in all cases list provides information about the contents of the argument. You might use list as a general purpose utility for displaying information about things: list gives useful information about files, directories, and other arguments.

> **Reversing Tests**
>
> By putting an exclamation mark (!) as the first argument of a `test` command, you can reverse the sense of a test. For example,
>
> ```
> test -d name
> ```
>
> returns a status of 0 if *name* is a directory and returns a status of 1 otherwise.
>
> ```
> test ! -d name
> ```
>
> returns a status of 0 if *name* is not a directory and returns a status of 1 otherwise.

The [] *Structure*

The KornShell offers an alternate format for executing `test` commands. Instead of putting the word `test` at the beginning, omit the word and put the rest of the command in square brackets. With this technique, you can rewrite the `list` script, as shown in Listing 8.6.

Listing 8.6. The `list` Script with [].

```
# This script displays information about files,
# directories, or other arguments.
if [ -f $1 ]
then
     more $1
elif [ -d $2 ]
then
     ls $1
else
     echo $1
fi
```

This format is slightly more compact than the `test` format, but doesn't really offer any other advantage. Some people prefer it, but the examples in this book will continue to use `test`.

The for *Loop*

The for loop is another control structure often used in shell scripts. Like loop structures in normal programming languages, the shell's for loop repeats a set of commands several times until a given condition is met. The format of the for loop is

```
for name in list
do commands
done
```

where *name* is a name that can be used as a variable name, *list* is a list of arguments, and *commands* is a list of commands. The shell begins executing the loop by assigning the first argument in *list* to the variable *name*. The shell then executes all the *commands*. When the last command has finished, the shell goes back to the top of the loop, assigns the next argument in *list* to *name*, and executes the commands again. The shell keeps repeating this process until it has executed the commands once for each argument in *list*.

You'll understand this more easily with an example. Enter the following as a command (not as a shell script):

```
for file in ?onnet
do
    echo $file
done
```

In this case, *name* is file and the *list* is created by the glob construct ?onnet. This will be a list of all the files in the current directory with names ending in onnet. The *list* will therefore be

```
bonnet connet sonnet
```

To execute the for loop, the shell begins by assigning the name bonnet to the variable file. It then executes the echo command; the construct $file expands to bonnet, so the echo command displays this name. The result of the for loop is that it displays the names of all the files with names ending in onnet, one name per line.

The preceding for loop isn't very useful; you could do almost the same thing in several different ways:

```
echo ?onnet
find . -name "?onnet"
ls ¦ grep "^.onnet$"
```

(Ask yourself how these three approaches differ. Enter the commands to see if you were right.) Listing 8.7 gives an example of a for loop that does a job that isn't as easy to do with other commands.

Listing 8.7. Counting the number of lines in files.

```
total=0
for file in ?onnet
do
    let j="$(wc -l <$file)"
    let total=$total+$j
done
echo $total
```

The commands in Listing 8.7 count the total number of lines in the onnet files. To understand how this works, you have to look at

```
let j="$(wc -l <$file)"
```

The $file construct expands to the name of one of the onnet files each time through the for loop. The command substitution uses wc -l to count the number of lines in the file given by $file. This results in a number that is assigned to the variable j. The next line is

```
let total=$total+$j
```

which adds the value of j to the current value of total. Just before the for loop, you set total to zero, so the total variable represents a running total of the number of lines in all the files examined so far. After the end of the loop, the command

```
echo $total
```

displays the final total of lines.

To expand on the previous example, use vi to create a file named linecnt that contains the text given in Listing 8.8.

This script is almost exactly the same as the previous example, except that it uses the $@ in the for statement. This stands for all the argument names given on the linecnt command line. Quit vi and enter the command

```
linecnt. sonnet nursery
```

You'll see that the script prints out the total number of lines in the two files sonnet and nursery. In general, you can give the linecnt script any number of file names and it will display the total number of lines in the entire set of files.

Listing 8.8.   The `linecnt` shell script.

```
# This script counts the total number of lines in
# a set of files.
#
total=0
for file in $@
do
    let j="$(wc -l <$file)"
    let total=$total+$j
done
echo $total
```

Niceties in the `let` Command

You may wonder why the command

```
let j="$(wc -l <$file)"
```

has this form. You can't just say

```
let j=wc -l $file
```

because wc will output the name of the file as well as the number of lines, and you can't assign a name to a numeric variable. However, wc doesn't display a file name if it is counting the number of lines in the standard input. Thus you might write

```
let j=$(wc -l <$file)
```

to get rid of the file name. But there's one more problem: the output of wc begins with blank spaces and you can't have blanks immediately after the = in a let statement. You can get around this problem by enclosing the command substitution in double quotation marks:

```
let j="$(wc -l <$file)"
```

This expands into a line of the form

```
let j="    integer"
```

where *integer* is the number of lines in the file. There are no blanks after the = and the let command works properly.

There are many ways you can produce a list of files for `linecnt`. For example,

```
linecnt. $(find . -type f -print)
```

uses command substitution to produce the list of files whose lines you want to count. The `find` command obtains the names of all files under the current directory, and the `linecnt` command counts all their lines. As another example:

```
linecnt. s*
```

produces a line count for all the files whose names begin with `s`.

Local Variables

The `linecnt` script creates variables named `total` and `j`. If the script is executing in a subshell, these variables will exist in the subshell but not in the original shell that invoked the script. Remember that the subshell's environment is separate from the original shell's environment, and the subshell variables are not shared by the original shell.

Variables like `total` and `j` are said to be *local* to the subshell and are called *local variables*. You can only use them inside the shell script itself. They cannot be used outside the script and they cannot affect anything outside the script.

On the other hand, if you execute a script with the period command, the script executes inside the original shell environment. When the script creates a variable, the variable is created in the original shell. In this case, the variables aren't local because they are considered part of the original shell's environment.

Combining Control Structures

You can combine several control structures at once. For example, enter the following:

```
for file in $(find . -name "?onnet" -print)
do
    if
        test $file -nt nursery
    then
        echo $file
        more $file
```

```
        fi
 done
```

This uses `find` to produce a list of all names ending in `onnet` under the current directory. The `for` loop repeats the `if` construct for each one of those names. The `if` construct tests to see if each file is newer than `nursery`; if so, it displays the file name with an `echo` command and displays the file contents with `more`.

Notice that I used several levels of indentation to make it easier to understand the different sections of the command. As shell input becomes more complicated, indentation becomes more important if you want to be able to make sense out of what you are writing.

Other Control Structures

The shell offers several other control structures that you may find useful for writing shell scripts. The following list gives an overview of these structures; the `sh` man page gives full descriptions.

- The `while` loop repeats a set of commands while a given condition is true.

- The `until` loop repeats a set of commands until a given condition becomes true.

- The `case` construct lets you break a given situation up into cases and take a different set of actions in each case.

- The `select` construct can be used inside shell scripts to prompt a user for a reply and to take different actions depending on the reply. This is useful if you want to set up scripts that offer users a *menu* of possible actions.

- The `time` construct lets you time how long it takes the shell to execute a given command or pipeline.

Shell Functions

A *shell function* is similar to a subprogram in a programming language like Pascal or C. A shell function is a collection of shell commands that can be executed together as a single command, in much the same way that shell scripts let you execute a collection of commands with a single command line. Shell functions can be executed inside shell scripts or in normal interactive sessions.

Shell functions are well suited to jobs you perform frequently. As with shell scripts, aliases, and other features, you can use functions to reduce the amount of typing you have to do, and to make it unnecessary to remember complicated commands or command sequences.

Before you can use a shell function, you must *define* the function. The definition of a shell function looks like this:

```
function name
{
    commands
}
```

where *name* is the name you choose to give the function and *commands* are the commands that make up the function. Notice that the *commands* are enclosed in *braces*. The part inside the braces is called the *body* of the function.

> **Function Names**
> Function names have the same form as variable names. They can contain uppercase characters, lowercase characters, digits, and the underscore (_) character. The first character cannot be a digit.

As a simple example of a function, enter the following:

```
function cdl
{
    cd $1
    ls
}
```

This defines a function named cdl. After you type in the function definition, nothing special happens—the shell just prompts you for a new command. When you type in a function definition, the shell just stores the definition until you actually use the function. I'll show you how to use the cdl function in a moment. Right now, notice that the statements in the body of the function look much like statements in a shell script. In particular, you see the $1 construct. This stands for the first argument of the function, just as it stands for the first argument of a shell script when it appears in a shell script.

To use the function, you just enter the function name followed by any arguments to the function. For example, enter

```
cdl /
```

When the shell tries to execute this line, it goes back to the definition of the cd1 function and executes the commands in the body of the function. As you might guess, it substitutes the appropriate function argument in place of each positional parameter. Thus the shell executes

```
cd /
ls
```

when it executes the function. In this way, cd1 uses cd to go to a new directory, then uses ls to list the contents of the directory. I find that I use this function a lot when I'm working with UNIX. When I cd to a new directory, I almost always want to list the contents of that directory before I do anything else; by using cd1, I can cd and list the contents with a single command. Now enter

```
cd1 -
```

and you'll go back to your previous directory. Again, cd1 lists the contents of that directory as well.

Shell functions can use control structures such as if constructs and for loops. A shell function can call other functions and shell scripts.

Shell Functions Versus Shell Scripts

Anything you can do with a shell script you can do with a shell function, and vice versa. However, there are a few differences between the two.

Shell functions are always executed within the shell's own execution environment. This means that instructions within a function can affect the shell's variables, options, and so on; shell scripts can't affect the shell's environment unless you execute them with the dot command.

Also, the shell saves shell functions directly in memory. This means that functions can be executed faster than shell scripts. The shell can execute a function immediately, but to execute a script, the shell has to search for the appropriate file containing the script, the read in the file.

As a general rule of thumb, then, shell functions are good for things that you do a lot, where small savings in time can add up to something significant. Shell scripts are good for jobs that you do less often; they are also good for very lengthy sets of instructions, since shell functions occupy memory inside the computer, and the more memory you use to store a function, the less memory you have for other purposes.

The *return* Command

Earlier sections explained that normal UNIX commands return status values. Shell scripts and shell functions can also return status values, using the `return` command. The command has the form

```
return expression
```

where *expression* is the same sort of expression that you use with `let` commands. When the shell encounters a `return` command inside a shell function or shell script, it evaluates the expression and immediately returns the result as the status value of the function or script. Notice that the `return` command tells the shell to return immediately, even if there are more commands left in the function or script.

As an example of `return`, use `vi` to edit the `dif` shell script created in an earlier section, so that the contents are as shown in Listing 8.9.

Listing 8.9. The `dif` shell script (third draft).

```
# This script finds the difference between two files.
# Differences are displayed with the more command.
# Uses "junk" as a temporary working file.
# You may specify any options you like for the diff command.
if
    diff $@ >junk
then
    echo No difference
    rm junk
    return 0
else
    more junk
    rm junk
    return 1
fi
```

In this version, I have introduced two `return` statements. The script returns a status value of 0 if there are no differences and returns a status value of 1 if differences are found. In this way, `dif` sets its status values in much the same way that `diff` does.

Notice that the `then` and `else` clauses both contain `rm` commands before the `return` command. The script has to get rid of the `junk` file before executing a `return` command; after you execute a `return` command the script is finished, so you have to make sure that all the necessary work is done before you `return`.

Just for the sake of interest, Listing 8.10 shows another way you could rewrite `dif`. Inside the `if` construct, the script assigns an appropriate status value to the variable `stat` but doesn't actually return. After the end of the `if` construct, the script executes an `rm` command to remove the `junk` file and then executes `return` to return the value of `stat`. In this way, you don't have to put an `rm` command in each part of the `if` construct; you put it after the end of the construct and then return.

Listing 8.10.   The `dif` shell script (third draft).

```
# This script finds the difference between two files.
# Differences are displayed with the more command.
# Uses "junk" as a temporary working file.
# You may specify any options you like for the diff command.
if
    diff $@ >junk
then
    echo No difference
    stat=0
else
    more junk
    stat=1
fi
rm junk
return $stat
```

Chapter Review

A shell script is a text file that contains shell instructions. In order to execute a shell script on a UNIX system, you must have execute permission on the file.

There are three ways to execute a shell script. You can execute a command whose command name is the name of the script file, as in

```
scriptname
```

You can execute the script in a subshell by using a `sh` command and specifying the name of the script file as an argument, as in

```
sh scriptname
```

Finally, you can execute the script with the dot command, as in

```
. scriptname
```

When you use the dot command, the script is executed in your current shell's environment; this means that commands in the script can affect your current shell, by setting options, creating variables or aliases, and so on. If you execute the script directly or in a subshell, the script is executed in a separate environment and it cannot affect your current shell's environment.

If a line of input to the shell contains a number sign (#), the rest of the line is ignored. This lets you put comments into shell input (such as in shell scripts or shell functions).

You can pass arguments to shell scripts and shell functions. Inside the script or function, the symbol $1 stands for the first argument value, the symbol $2 stands for the second argument value, and so on. The symbols $1, $2, and so on are called *positional parameters*. The shell also recognizes several special parameters, shown in Table 8.2. Parameters are not expanded if they are enclosed in single quotation marks, but they are expanded if they appear in double quotation marks.

Table 8.2. Special parameters discussed in this chapter.

Parameter	Meaning
$#	The number of arguments passed to the script or function.
$@	A list of all arguments, each a separate argument.
$*	A list of all arguments, as a single argument.

The shift command gets rid of arguments in the list of arguments passed to a shell script or function. For example,

```
shift 2
```

gets rid of the first two arguments in the list, so that the third argument becomes $1.

When a command finishes execution, it returns a status value (or return value) to the shell. A status value of zero usually indicates that the command succeeded and a higher status value indicates that the command failed. However, some commands use their status values in different ways.

The most general form of an if construct is

```
if condition1
then commands1
elif condition2
then commands2
elif condition3
then commands3
    ...
else commands
fi
```

In this construct, all conditions are commands. If `condition1` returns a status value of zero, the shell executes `commands1`. Otherwise, the shell executes `condition2`. If this returns a status of zero, the shell executes `commands2`, and so on. If none of the `condition` commands returns a value of zero, the shell executes the commands following the `else`. You can omit the `elif` or `else` clauses if you don't need them.

The `test` command lets you test a variety of conditions about path names, the age of files, numbers, and strings. It is often used in `if` constructs. The following command forms are equivalent:

```
test expression
[ expression ]
```

Table 8.1 lists many uses of the `test` command.

The `for` loop has the form

```
for name in list
do commands
done
```

The shell executes the `commands` once for each item in the `list`. Each time it executes the `commands`, it assigns one of the items in the `list` to the variable `name`.

A shell function is like a subprogram in a programming language. The definition of a shell function has the form:

```
function name
{
    commands
}
```

When a command line begins with the name of the shell function, the shell executes the `commands` specified in the definition of the function. You can pass arguments to the function and refer to the values of those arguments using positional parameters.

Inside shell scripts and shell functions, you can use the statement

```
return expression
```

to return a status value to the shell. As soon as the shell encounters a `return` statement, it evaluates the *expression* and immediately quits the shell script or shell function that contains the `return` statement.

Exercises

1. Create a file containing the names of all the files under your home directory and its subdirectories. Use `vi` to edit this file into a shell script that performs `ls -l` on each of these file names. Run the shell script.

2. Create a shell script named `finds` that takes exactly the same kind of arguments as `find`. The difference between `finds` and `find` should be that the output of `finds` is sorted in alphabetical order.

3. Create a shell script named `last` that just displays its last argument, no matter how many arguments it is passed. For example,

```
last A B C D
```

displays D.

```
last A
```

displays A. (Hint: $# tells how many arguments there are.)

4. Create a shell script named `run` that takes a command line as its argument. The script runs the command line as it is specified, except that the standard error for the command is redirected to a file named `err`.

5. Rewrite the `last` shell script (which was written in an earlier exercise) as a shell function.

6. Suppose that the shell variable `re` contains a regular expression. Write a shell function named `gp` with arguments that are text file names and that searches for the value of `re` in all those files. For example, if you assign

```
re = "^T.*e$"
```

the `gp` function should search for lines that begin with T and end in e.

7. Suppose your favorite word processor is named wpr and you invoke this word processor with a command line of the form

```
wpr filename
```

You can only specify one file name on the wpr command line, so you can only edit one file at a time. However, you want to be able to edit a list of files, such as a list produced by the glob construct *.doc. Write a shell function that accepts a list of file names as its arguments and that invokes the wpr word processor on each file name in the list. (As soon as you quit using wpr to edit one file, the function will start wpr again to edit the next file.)

## Chapter 9

Customization

As mentioned in earlier sections, UNIX can be customized to a greater extent than almost any other operating system. This chapter examines some approaches to customization, primarily with the KornShell but also with vi.

The key to customizing the KornShell is to create a *profile file*. Typically, a profile file is a shell script containing instructions that set shell options, create aliases, define shell functions, and do any other work that you'd like to automatically do each time you log in.

The chapter also examines the role that certain shell variables play in customization. In particular, you'll see how to change the string that the shell uses to prompt you for input. You'll also see how to use the UNIX PATH variable (analogous to the DOS PATH command) to tell the shell where to find the programs you want to run. The which and whence commands can help you find out where the shell finds particular programs if you become confused.

Next, the chapter examines the *passwd file*. This file contains information about all the authorized users of a UNIX system, and provides such information as the name of your home directory and the shell that you've chosen to use.

Finally, the chapter looks at *initialization files*: files that contain commands to set up sessions with software packages like vi. With an initialization file, you can automatically set up options for your vi sessions, without having to type in a lot of commands every time you start the editor.

Profile Files

Over the past few chapters you've seen several useful options that control the behavior of the shell. Among these are

```
set -a
```

which marks all subsequently created variables for export,

```
set -o vi
```

which lets you edit commands with `vi` editing facilities, and

```
set -x
```

which shows you the expansions of all commands that the shell executes. You've also seen how aliases and shell functions can save you time and trouble as you work with the shell.

One drawback to the way you've used the shell so far is that your entire environment disappears whenever you log out. This means that every time you log in, you have to remember to set up the options that you want, any aliases you'd like to use, and so on. This is more than just an annoyance; if you want to set up a lot of things when you log in, you have to do a lot of typing, and the more typing you do, the more likely it is that you'll make a mistake.

If you think a little, you should be able to come up with a solution to this problem. The easiest approach is to write a shell script that sets all your options, creates any aliases and shell functions that you want, and does any other work you'd like to do before you start using the shell. Each time you log in, you could execute the shell script to do all your set-up work. Note that you'd have to execute the script with the period command so that the instructions affect your original shell environment; otherwise the script executes in a separate environment and does not affect the shell environment.

In fact, the KornShell makes this process even easier. Whenever you log in to the shell, the shell automatically tries to execute a *profile file* before it does anything else. For most people, a profile file is a shell script that sets options, creates aliases, and so on. After you've created that profile file, the shell automatically executes the instructions in the file each time you log in. In this way, your session is automatically customized according to your tastes whenever you start up.

Types of Profile Files

There are two types of profile files:

- A *global* profile file sets up the environment for everyone using your UNIX system.

- A *personal* profile file sets up the environment for a single user.

On a true UNIX system, the global profile file is stored in the file

```
/etc/profile
```

With MKS Tools, there is no global profile file, but you can create one if you want, under the name

```
/lu/etc/profile.ksh
```

On a true UNIX system, your personal profile file should be named

```
.profile
```

under your home directory. With the MKS Tools, your personal profile file should be named

```
profile.ksh
```

under your home directory. Table 9.1 summarizes these names.

Table 9.1.   Profile file names.

Name	Description
/etc/profile	Global profile on true UNIX
/lu/etc/profile.ksh	Global profile for MKS Tools
$HOME/.profile	Personal profile on true UNIX
$HOME/profile.ksh	Personal profile for MKS Tools

When you log in, the KornShell executes the instructions in the global profile file first (if there is one). Then the shell looks to see if you have a personal profile file. If so, the shell executes that file too. On most UNIX systems, the global profile file sets up some *default* options, aliases, and so on. You can then use your personal profile file to change those defaults or to add to the environment.

The Global Profile File

The MKS Tools package does not supply a global profile file; each home directory is created with its own local profile file. If you want to create a global profile file, use `vi` to create the file and write the result to `/lu/etc/profile.ksh`.

Your Personal Profile File

If you look at the file `profile.ksh` under your home directory, you'll see that it contains the following:

```
PATH= ".;c:/lu/bin"
export PATH
```

This is an extremely simple profile—it just sets a single variable named PATH and marks that variable for export. Later in this chapter you'll see what the PATH variable is used for.

It's time now to create a more sophisticated profile file. For the purposes of this book, please use `vi` to edit `profile.ksh` under your home directory, so that it contains the shell commands given in Listing 9.1. This suggested profile file contains a more sophisticated setting for PATH than your old profile file. It also sets the three options mentioned earlier, creates the alias p for the `more` command, and defines the shell function `cdl` discussed in the last chapter. Make sure that you put in all the quotation marks shown.

Listing 9.1.   Suggested personal profile file (first draft).

```
# Sample profile file
PATH="c:/lu/bin;."
export PATH
set -a
set -o vi
set -x
alias p="more"
function cdl
{
    cd $1
    ls -x
}
```

After you've created the `profile.ksh` file, log out and log in again. During the log-in process, the shell automatically finds your personal profile file and executes its contents. To see that this has actually happened, enter the command

```
p profile.ksh
```

This should display the contents of `profile.ksh`, because your profile has set up p as an alias for `more`. The shell should also display

```
+ more profile.ksh
```

Because the profile file `set` the `-x` option, the shell displays the expansion of each command before executing it.

Future sections will suggest additions and changes to this personal profile—the file is the key to automatic customization of all your interactions with the shell. You should also think about what you would like to see in your profile file:

- What aliases will make your life easier? Consider an alias for every lengthy command that you type frequently.

- What shell functions would you find convenient to have available? Consider a shell function for any series of commands that you tend to type frequently.

- What variables would you like to define or change? Consider a variable for any piece of information you want to remember.

- What actions do you commonly perform when you first log in? For example, I usually list the contents of my home directory whenever I start a session, so I've put that command directly into my profile file.

Shell Variables and Customization

Shell variables play a major role in customizing UNIX sessions. The sections that follow discuss some of the most useful of these.

Changing Your Prompt

The PS1 variable controls what the shell uses to prompt for input. For example, enter the command

```
echo $PS1 test
```

and you'll see that the command displays

```
$   test
```

There are two blank spaces between the $ and the word test. This is because the value of PS1 is actually "$ " (with a blank after the dollar sign). This is what the shell has used to prompt for commands since you started these exercises. The value of PS1 is called your *command prompt string*. The echo command displays the value of PS1 (ending in a blank), then another blank and the word test, because echo always puts a single blank between output arguments.

To change your command prompt string, you just have to change the value of the PS1 variable. For example, enter

```
PS1="What now? "
```

After you press Enter, you'll see that the shell prompts you for your next command by saying

```
What now?
```

Notice that there's a blank after the question mark—a little bit of whitespace makes it easier to distinguish the prompt from the commands you enter. If the command prompt string contains an exclamation mark (!) character, the shell replaces the character with the number of the command in the shell history file. For example, enter

```
PS1="now-!% "
```

and you'll get prompts of the form

```
now-1%
now-2%
  . . .
```

You'll probably see different numbers than the ones shown previously—the numbers are based on your shell history, and everyone has a different shell history.

Many people find that this kind of prompt makes it easier to use the r command to reexecute previous commands. The prompt shows you the number of each command, so you don't have to look up the appropriate number by typing history.

Putting the Current Directory in Your Prompt

You'll recall that the value of the PWD variable is the name of your current working directory. Many people find that it's useful to have this directory name as part of their prompt; this reminds you what your current directory is, no matter where you cd to. You can put the current directory name into your prompt by making PWD part of your command prompt string. Enter

```
PS1='$PWD-!% '
```

It's important to enclose the string in single quotation marks as shown previously. If you only use double quotation marks, the shell immediately expands the $PWD into the name of your current working directory, and then assigns the result to PS1. This means that you'll always see the name of your working directory at the time that you assigned the string to PS1. However, if you enclose the prompt string in single quotation marks, the shell doesn't try to expand anything inside the quotation marks immediately. PS1 is assigned the value

```
$PWD-!%
```

Whenever the shell displays a prompt, it expands the $PWD into the name of the current directory. To see this in action, enter the commands

```
cd testdir
cd ..
```

You'll see that the prompt changes as your current directory changes.

Choosing a Prompt

You may want to experiment now with various prompt formats until you get one that you like. When you do, you can add an appropriate

    PS1=*prompt*

line to your personal profile file so that the shell will use this prompt every time you log in.

The Secondary Prompt

You'll recall that when you enter a multiline construct like a for loop or a function definition, the shell uses a > to prompt for input. This is called the *secondary prompt string*, and it can be changed as easily as you changed your command prompt string.

    The variable that controls the secondary prompt is named PS2. For example, enter

```
PS2="More> "
if
    diff sonnet bonnet
then
    echo No difference
fi
```

You'll see that the shell uses the string "More> " to prompt for the internal lines of the if construct. When you reach the fi that ends the construct, the shell executes the construct, then goes back to prompting with your command prompt string.

If you want to go back to the default secondary prompt, you can enter the command

```
PS2="> "
```

Notice that there's a space after the > character; this puts a little gap between the > prompt and whatever you type in, making it easier for you to read what's on the screen.

Search Paths

One of the major purposes of the shell is to read the commands you want to execute and then to execute those commands. Some commands (such as `set`) are built into the shell, but most are not. When a command is not built into the shell, the shell must find a file containing the command and execute that command. This file may be a normal program (in a binary file), or it may be a shell script (in a text file). Both these types of files are called executable files, or *executables*.

When you issue a command, the shell has to find the appropriate executable for that command. To do so, the shell looks through a sequence of directories and sees if any of the directories contains a file with a name that matches the command name. If you're an experienced DOS user, you know how DOS lets you use the PATH command to tell the shell which directories to examine. The UNIX approach is similar. However, less-experienced DOS users may not be familiar with PATH and related concepts, so this section will deal with the subject from scratch.

A *search path* is a list of directories. On true UNIX systems, the names in this list are separated by colon (:) characters. With the MKS Tools, the names in the list should be separated by semicolon (;) characters. The MKS Tools can't use colons because these might be confused with DOS device names (such as C:).

When you log in, the shell sets up a default search path and assigns this to the shell variable PATH. To see what your current search path is, enter

```
echo $PATH
```

The value of PATH is sometimes called your list of *search rules*.

When you enter a command, the shell first checks to see if the command name is an alias, the name of a shell function, or one of the built-in commands of the shell. If not, the shell checks under the first directory in your search path to see if that directory contains a file matching the command name. If the directory contains such a file, and if the file is executable, the shell executes the contents of the file. Otherwise, the shell checks the next directory in the search path for a matching file that is executable. The shell goes through the directories in the order specified until it finds a match or it gets to the end of the list.

On true UNIX and UNIX look-alike systems, a file only matches the command name if the names are identical. For example, if you have asked to execute the `diff` command, the shell looks for a file named `diff` under one of the directories in the search path. The case of letters is important; for example, a file named `DIFF` or `Diff` doesn't match the command name `diff`.

With the MKS Tools, the differences of the DOS system force some changes. The following list gives the rules for matching file names and command names:

- The case of letters isn't important. `diff` is the same command as `DIFF`, `Diff`, and so on.

- If a command name has a suffix, the shell looks for a file with the same basename and suffix. For example, if the command name is `xyz.abc`, the shell looks for a file named `xyz.abc`.

- If a command name has a null suffix, the shell looks for a file with the same name and with no suffix. This is why the previous chapter executed the `simple` file by specifying the `simple.` command. You had to specify a null suffix (just the `.`) to tell the KornShell to look for a file without a suffix.

- If the command name doesn't have a suffix, the shell looks for a file with the same basename and with any one of the suffixes

```
.com      .exe      .bat      .ksh
```

For example, if the command name is `xyz`, the shell looks for `xyz.com`, `xyz.exe`, `xyz.bat`, or `xyz.ksh` (in that order).

To see this in action, use `vi` to create three shell scripts. The first should be written into the file `/lu/bin/showpath.ksh` and should contain the command

```
echo Hello! /lu/bin/showpath.ksh
```

The second should be written into the file `showpath.ksh` under your home directory, and should contain the command

```
echo Hello! showpath.ksh
```

The third should be written into the file `testdir/showpath.ksh` under your home directory, and should contain the command

```
echo Hello! testdir/showpath.ksh
```

Obviously, each of these three scripts is designed simply to tell the name of the file that contains the script.

When you've created the file, enter the command

```
PATH="/lu/bin;$HOME;$HOME/testdir"
```

(It's very important to use double quotation marks as shown above.) This setting for PATH says that you want the shell to look for commands in the /lu/bin first, then in your home directory, and then in the directory testdir under your home directory. Now enter the command

```
showpath
```

You'll see that the output is

```
Hello! /lu/bin/showpath.ksh
```

The shell looked for showpath under the /lu/bin directory first and found a matching file. (Remember that when a command name doesn't have a suffix, the shell accepts a file name made out of the command name with the suffix .ksh.) The shell therefore executed the shell script from /lu/bin/showpath.ksh.

It's important to stress that there are three shell scripts that could be executed as the showpath command: the one in /lu/bin, the one under your home directory, and the one in testdir. The shell executes the first one it finds as it goes through your search rules, and it ignores the presence of the other two candidates.

Now enter the commands

```
rm /lu/bin/showpath.ksh
showpath
```

The rm gets rid of the showpath.ksh under the /lu/bin directory. Now when you execute the showpath command, the output is

```
Hello! showpath.ksh
```

In accordance with your search rules, the shell looked under the /lu/bin directory, but couldn't find any matching files. It therefore looked under the next directory in the search path, namely your home directory. It found a matching file and executed it. The output shows that the shell executed the showpath.ksh file under your home directory.

Now, enter the commands

```
PATH="/lu/bin;$HOME/testdir;$HOME"
showpath
```

(Make sure you put in the quotation marks when you assign the value to PATH.) The assignment to PATH changes the order of directories in the search path. Now, the output of the showpath command is

```
Hello! testdir/showpath.ksh
```

because the shell executes the testdir version of the script. The shell finds the testdir version of showpath before it finds the version in your home directory, so that's the one that the shell executes.

PATH in Your Profile File

The best way to specify your search path is to add an appropriate line to your profile file, setting your PATH variable to your desired search rules. In this way, you don't have to set PATH manually and risk the possibility of making a typing mistake.

The whence *Command*

As the previous section shows, it's possible to have several different versions of the same command. Your PATH variable determines which version the shell will execute.

The showpath scripts were written to make it easy for you to tell which version was executing. With other commands, the situation can be more confusing. Therefore the KornShell offers the whence command that can clarify the situation. Enter

```
whence showpath
```

and the KornShell tells you the name of the file it would execute if you issued a showpath command. Using whence, you can see how your search rules affect which command version gets executed.

The whence command can give information on other types of commands. For example, enter

```
whence p set cdl
```

whence tells you that p is an alias (set up in your profile file), set is a built-in command, and cdl is a shell function.

The /lu/bin Directory

If you experiment with setting your own search rules, make sure that the directory /lu/bin is always somewhere in the search path. This is the directory where the MKS Tools package stores all the common commands like cp, rm, more, and so on. If you leave out /lu/bin, the shell won't find any of the everyday UNIX commands and you won't be able to do much work.

Search Paths and the Current Directory

Experienced DOS users know that the DOS COMMAND.COM command interpreter always searches for executables under your current directory before it searches through any of the directories in your search path. It does this regardless of whether you explicitly specify your current directory in the search path.

With UNIX shells, the situation is different. A UNIX shell only searches the directories given in your search path. If you want the shell to search your current directory, you have to put the directory into your path.

You'll recall that the dot . character stands for the current directory. For example, enter

```
PATH= "/lu/bin;."
```

(Make sure you put in the quotation marks.) This setting for PATH says that you want the shell to search /lu/bin first, then your current directory. Note that the . stands for whatever is your current directory at the time that you enter the command. Enter the commands

```
cd $HOME
showpath
cd testdir
showpath
cd
```

When you are in your home directory, the shell executes `showpath` from your home directory; when you are in `testdir`, the shell executes `showpath` from `testdir`.

As a short form, the KornShell lets you omit the dot from the search path. For example, you can write either

```
PATH= "/lu/bin;."
PATH= "/lu/bin;"
```

and get the same effect. Similarly you can write either

```
PATH="/lu/bin;.;$HOME/testdir"
PATH="/lu/bin;;$HOME/testdir"
```

to say that the shell should search `/lu/bin`, then the current directory (whatever that is at the time), then `testdir` under your home directory. I think omitting the dot is confusing, but it is a very common practice in some circles, so you should be prepared for it.

What Your Search Path Should Be

Until you get more experience with UNIX, you probably shouldn't try to set your own search path, by hand or in your profile file. During the log-in process, the system sets a default PATH that will let the shell find all the standard UNIX commands.

When you start writing your own commands (programs and shell scripts), you'll have to change your PATH so that the shell can find those commands. The most common technique is to create a directory named `bin` under your home directory and to store all your personal executables under that directory. You would then change your profile to create a PATH that had your `bin` directory as the first directory in the list. In this way, the shell always starts by seeing if you have a personal version of a command in your `bin` directory; if you don't, the shell then goes on to check other directories.

The first directories in your search path should be the ones where standard commands like `cp` and `rm` are found. For MKS Tools, this is `/lu/bin`. Most UNIX users prefer to put the current directory `.` (dot) as the last in the list, or else omit `.` altogether.

Always remember to mark PATH for export. Other software may need to search for commands too.

The *passwd* File

On every UNIX and UNIX look-alike system, there is a file named /etc/passwd that holds information about all the authorized users of the system. With the MKS Tools, the file is named /lu/etc/passwd, but it serves the same purpose.

Enter the command

```
more /lu/etc/passwd
```

and you'll see what the file looks like. There is one line for each authorized user.

> **You're the One...**
> In most cases, your user ID will be the only one in the passwd file, because the MKS Tools are geared toward one student at a time. However, there are ways to obtain passwd files for several users at once, as explained in Appendix G.

Each line in the passwd file is divided into fields. The fields are separated by colon : characters on a true UNIX system, and by semicolons on DOS. Each line contains the following fields:

- A *user name* (log-in id)—the rest of the line provides information about that user.

- An *encrypted password*—this is a version of the password you enter when you log in. However, the password has been *encrypted*. This means that it has been put into a special code so that people reading the password file cannot figure out what your true password is. The encryption technique is sometimes called a *one-way scheme*. Such a scheme makes it easy for the computer to encrypt the password, but very difficult for someone to decrypt the result. On true UNIX systems, the encrypted password is always 13 characters long, but UNIX look-alikes may differ.

- Your *user number*—on a true UNIX system, each user is assigned a number as well as a log-in name. With the MKS Tools, this number is always 0.

- Your *group number*—on a true UNIX system, this number would indicate your primary group. With the MKS Tools, this number is always 0.

- A *comments field*—this can contain anything, but most sites use the field to give a user's full name. With the MKS Tools, the comment field contains Learning UNIX. This field is also called the GECOS or GCOS field.

- The name of your home directory—this is how the log-in procedure finds out the name of your home directory. It assigns this directory name to the HOME variable.

- A command line for invoking your shell—previous chapters have mentioned that different users can have different shells. When you log in, the log-in procedure checks your entry in the passwd file to find out which shell you want to use. The log-in procedure then uses the command line from passwd to invoke your chosen shell.

Various commands let you change parts of your passwd entry for the purpose of customization. For example, you've already seen how the passwd command lets you change your password.

vi Initialization Files

The shell's profile file is an example of an *initialization file*. Whenever you invoke a new copy of the shell (either when you log in or when you start a subshell with sh -L), the shell executes the commands in your profile file as if you were typing those commands as input. In this way, the profile file *initializes* your shell session, by creating aliases, setting options, defining functions, and so on.

Several other UNIX programs accept initialization files too. For example, you can create an initialization file for vi. Such a file would have the same form as the command files discussed in Chapter 6: a sequence of vi commands that would normally begin with the colon : character. Chapter 6 showed that you could use command lines of the form

```
vi -c "so cmdfile" editfile
```

With this command line form, vi executes the commands from *cmdfile* first, then reads in *editfile* so that you can begin editing it.

In order to see how initialization files work, use vi to create two command files. First, create a file named viab that contains

```
ab xyz XYZ Widgets Inc. International
```

This instruction says that xyz is an abbreviation for XYZ Widgets Inc. International. Next create a file named ex.rc that contains

```
set tabstop=4
```

This instruction sets tab stops every four columns. When you have created the two files, quit `vi`.

Now, enter the command

```
vi
```

to start editing a new file. When the MKS Tools version of `vi` begins executing, it automatically looks for a file named `ex.rc`. First it looks under your current directory, then it looks under your home directory. If it finds such a file, it executes the commands in the file before it does anything else. To see how this works, enter `a` to begin appending text, then enter a tab and the string `xyz!`.

You'll see that `vi` displays four blank spaces in place of the tab. Your `ex.rc` file contained the instruction to set tabs every four columns. `vi` automatically executed this instruction when it started up, so your tabs are automatically set every four columns.

The Name of the `vi` Initialization File

On a true UNIX or UNIX look-alike system, the name of the `vi` initialization file is `.exrc`, not `ex.rc`. However, DOS does not allow file names that begin with a dot, so the MKS Tools have to use `ex.rc`.

Now press Esc, and quit `vi` by typing

```
:q!
```

This just quits without saving the text. Now enter the command

```
vi -c "so viab"
```

This starts `vi` again, but this time it specifies that `vi` should read `viab` as a command file. Press `a` to begin entering text again, then enter a tab and the string `xyz!`.

Once again, you'll see that `vi` displays four blank spaces in place of the tab. This is because `vi` has read your `ex.rc` file again. However, you'll also see that the string `xyz` changes into `XYZ Widgets Inc. International`. The `-c "so viab"` option told `vi` to read initialization commands from `viab` as well as the `ex.rc` file. In this way, you've specified two initialization files, not just one.

Quit `vi` by pressing Esc and typing

```
:q!
```

```
alias vix = 'vi -c "so viab"'
```

This sets up an alias that automatically specifies the `viab` initialization file. Notice that you must put double quotation marks around `so viab`, and single quotation marks around everything after the = sign. After you have set this alias, a command like

```
vix connet
```

lets you edit the `connet` file. Whenever you want, you can use the abbreviation `xyz` as you edit `connet`.

This kind of setup can be very useful. You can create any number of abbreviations in the `viab` file. When you start an editing job where those abbreviations might come in handy, you can use the `vix` alias to set up those abbreviations automatically. In other editing jobs, however, where the presence of the abbreviations would just be confusing, you can use the `vi` command directly; this doesn't use `viab` as a command file, so you don't have to worry about the abbreviations.

Note that both `vix` and `vi` itself read the `ex.rc` file. Thus you can use `ex.rc` to set up options and initializations that you would like every time you use `vi`. For example, your `ex.rc` can set tab stops, set your `wrapmargin`, and so on.

Other Initialization Files

Several other UNIX commands accept initialization files. For example, electronic mail packages often accept initialization files named `.mailrc` and the RCS revision control system (discussed in the next chapter) uses `.rcsrc`. The `rc` at the end of such names could be taken as a short form for *reconfigure*, because the initialization files let you reconfigure the way the software behaves.

Discussing software packages like `mail` is outside the scope of this book. The important point to remember is that initialization files are used by many software packages, to let you customize the way that the software behaves.

Chapter Review

A profile file is typically a shell script containing shell instructions. Whenever the shell starts up, it looks for your profile file and executes the instructions in that file. This means that you can use your profile file to set options, create aliases, define shell functions, and do any other work you would like to do every time you log in.

Profile files often set variables that control the behavior of the shell. Table 9.2 summarizes the shell variables discussed in this chapter.

Table 9.2.   Shell variables discussed in this chapter.

Variable	Meaning
PS1	Command prompt string
PS2	Secondary prompt
PATH	Search path

If the PS1 string contains the ! character, the shell replaces that character with the command number each time the shell prompts you to enter a command.

A search path is a list of directories. When you enter a command that is not a built-in command, shell function, or alias, the shell searches through the directories in your search path, looking for an executable file whose name matches the command name. If and when the shell finds a matching file, it executes that file in order to carry out the command.

The whence command provides information about command names. It can identify aliases, shell functions, and built-in commands. It can also tell you the file that will be executed to carry out a normal command.

Unlike DOS, a UNIX shell will not search the current directory unless its name appears in the search path. This means that you must put . as one of the directory names in the search path if you want the shell to look for commands in the current directory.

The file /etc/passwd (/lu/etc/passwd with the MKS Tools) contains a line for each authorized user of a UNIX system. This line provides such information as the name of the user's home directory and the user's chosen shell. Thus, the file controls some of the most basic facets of your use of the system.

The profile file is an example of an initialization file. An initialization file supplies instructions that a particular command carries out whenever that command begins execution. `vi` accepts an initialization file named `.exrc` (`ex.rc` with the MKS Tools). This file should be a `vi` command file, containing `vi` instructions that you would normally enter beginning with a colon `:`. One good use of `vi` command files is to create a series of abbreviations that you can use when creating files.

Exercises

1. Change your profile file so that it uses `banner` to say `Good Morning!` every time you log in. When you've made this change, log out and log in again to make sure you've done it correctly. Then edit your profile file to get rid of this silly instruction.

2. Change the definition of `PATH` in your profile file so that the shell only searches the `/lu/bin` directory, then your home directory, then the current directory.

3. Make a copy of `/lu/etc/passwd` named `/lu/etc/oldpass`. Use `vi` to edit `/lu/etc/passwd` to change your home directory to `/lu`. Log out and log in again to see if the change worked. Then copy `/lu/etc/oldpass` back to `/lu/etc/passwd` so that things go back to the way they were.

Specialized Topics

This chapter surveys several topics that, although they are important for understanding the current state of UNIX, didn't fit into previous chapters. There are no exercises in this chapter, and no instructions for you to try on your machine. The MKS Tools do not support the software discussed in this chapter, either because of the limitations of the DOS system or the limited amount of space on the disks that accompany *Learning UNIX*. Unlike the rest of the book, this chapter is not a how-to guide; instead, it's an armchair travelogue, intended to provide further glimpses of the UNIX world.

The travelogue starts with a quick tour of some of the useful software packages commonly associated with UNIX:

- *Revision control* software lets you keep a complete history of the changes that take place in a file. For example, I used a revision control package to keep track of the various drafts of this book, as the text went through copyediting, technical editing, proofreading, and all the other stages of preparation. This let me see what changes were made along the way, and also gave me a chance to recover older drafts of the book when that became necessary.

- The awk programming language is a cross between a programming language like C and a non-interactive text editor like sed. It is particularly good for *rapid prototyping*: the quick production of programs to solve an immediate need or to test aspects of software design.

- The make program automatically keeps a collection of related files in synch with each other. It was originally created to help programmers make and remake programs, but it can be used in almost any situation where a set of files must be kept up-to-date with each other.

- The troff program lets you create formatted documents for hard copy or display on the terminal screen.

After looking at these software packages, the chapter turns to a few facts about running UNIX systems. The job of being a UNIX system administrator is worthy of a complete book, all on its own, and it's impossible to do more here than sketch some of the simplest principles. However, in the future some readers may find themselves in charge of a microcomputer that runs UNIX, and such people may be grateful for any sort of help.

Finally, the chapter turns its attention to a feature that can't be simulated on DOS, but one that gives UNIX much of its appeal: its ability to run several programs simultaneously. In particular, you'll learn about *foreground* and *background* jobs and how you can use them productively.

A Taste of Popular UNIX Software

As mentioned in Chapter 1, some of the most inventive and popular software of the past two decades was created on UNIX systems. The sections that follow offer a taste of what's available on UNIX systems today. The list is highly selective and doesn't begin to cover many important software packages; nevertheless, it should give you a head start on a few programs you may want to learn more about.

Revision Control

Computer files are seldom fixed—they change with time. Documents are edited and revised. Spreadsheets receive new data and expand to fit more sophisticated needs. Software packages are updated as new releases are issued. More than 40 percent of the files on my personal computer have changed in the past year, and I suspect that percentage is low compared to those of many other users.

A *revision control* software package lets you keep track of the changes in your files. In effect, it keeps a *history* of all the revisions you make. This has several useful aspects:

- It provides a record of what changes were made and the reasons for them. This is particularly important if several people are working on the same project. Suppose, for example, that Clark and Lois are working together on a report. If Clark makes several changes to Chapter 1 of the report, Lois can use the revision control software to identify the changes that Clark made and keep up-to-date on what's happening. Clark can also remind himself what he did, in case he forgets later on.

- You can recover earlier versions of a file. For example, suppose that Clark and Lois create a report and take the document to their boss, Perry. Perry tells them to make some revisions, but when they present him with a new draft, he decides he liked the first one better. (We've all had bosses like that!) With revision control software, Clark and Lois can immediately go back to the previous version—the package can restore any earlier version of the file in almost no time.

- You can avoid interfering with each other. For example, suppose both Clark and Lois decide they want to change Chapter 1 of the report at the same time. (Remember, several people can use the same UNIX system simultaneously.) If Clark is the first one to start editing the report, the revision control software will prevent Lois from starting too; it will tell her that Clark is already at work on the file. This warning system prevents people from getting in each other's way and working at cross purposes.

There are several popular revision control software packages on UNIX, but the two most prominent are RCS (Revision Control System) and SCCS (Source Code Control System). The two work in different ways.

With RCS, every file on the system has an associated *history file*. The history file has a complete copy of the most recent version of the file. It also has a record of the changes between the most recent version and the second most recent, the changes between the second most recent and the third, and so on back to the original version. Because changes tend to be minor from one version to the next, the history file doesn't take up nearly as much disk space as storing complete copies of all versions would. However, the history of changes is enough to let you reconstruct any version of the file—you can start with the current version of the file and work backwards through the changes to reproduce any earlier version. Usually, history files are only a little larger than the current version of the file, but they provide information on all versions.

SCCS also uses history files, but the information is stored in an entirely different way. The history file is modeled after the original version of the associated file. At points where the original file has changed, there are records showing what changes were made. As more and more changes are made, more and more change records are embedded into the history file at the locations where the changes are made.

In summary then, an RCS history file starts with one complete copy of the associated file, then has a list of all the changes made from the previous file, a list of all changes made from the one before that, and so on. An SCCS history file is one big file, with entries scattered throughout the file showing how versions of the file differ at those locations.

The awk *Programming Language*

awk was developed by **A**ho, **W**einberger, and **K**ernighan of AT&T Bell Laboratories. As a programming language, it is closely related to the C programming language—many statements in awk look the same as statements in C, so awk is a good stepping stone toward C. awk is found on most UNIX systems, and is a good program to turn to when you want to perform single actions on text files quickly.

awk is also a good first language for people who would like to learn how to program. It's simple, and you can write useful programs soon after you start learning the language. (With many other languages, you have to learn a great deal of background before you can understand the simplest programs.) This short section can't do justice to awk's versatility, but it can give an overview of how awk works.

All awk programs perform operations on text input. The general form of an awk program is

```
criterion { actions }
criterion { actions }
criterion { actions }
criterion { actions }
    ...
```

awk reads a specified data file line by line. After awk reads a line of input, it checks to see if that line meets one or more of the specified *criteria*. If so, awk executes the *actions* associated with the matching *criteria*. After awk has finished checking the line against all the given *criteria*, it reads the next line and does the same thing all over again.

Here's a simple example of an awk program:

```
/^abc/  { print }
/^def/  { print "Hello!" }
```

This program has two statements. The criteria of the statements are both regular expressions, of the sort accepted by vi, grep, and other commands. The first statement says that if a line begins with the string abc, awk should print the line. The second statement says that if a line begins with the string def, awk should print Hello!. When you use this awk program, you specify a data file; awk then reads through the data file line by line, checking each line against the specified criteria, and taking appropriate action for lines that meet the criteria.

There is a great deal more to the awk programming language, but this gives you the general idea. Because of its extreme simplicity, I often turn to awk when I want to whip off a program quickly. awk automatically takes care of tedious details that other programming languages make you deal with from scratch.

The make *Program*

People who program on UNIX like to break their programs into a lot of small files. As a rule, they use a separate file for each subprogram, and they try to keep each subprogram short (usually no more than 50 lines of text, unless there's a very good reason for going longer). This means that a single program can be produced from a huge number of smaller files; more than 100 files is not an unusual amount for large software packages.

Typically, the programmer creates many *source files*, containing instructions in a programming language like C or Pascal. Next these source files are sent through a compiler program to produce *object files*. An object file is a translation of the original source file into a format that is close to the internal language of the machine. The object files are often gathered together into an *object library*, which is a single file containing all the separate object files. Object libraries usually take up less disk space and can be easier to work with than a lot of little object files. Finally, separate object files and object libraries must be *linked* together to form a single, unified program.

This means that a programmer has many files to keep track of: source files, object files, object libraries, and final programs. If the programmer changes one of the source files, it's necessary to remake the corresponding object file, the object library, and the final program. This is a lot of work, and if you're changing a lot of source files, it's easy to forget to update some of the corresponding object files. The problem is multiplied if several people are working on the program; a change made by one worker can affect a file belonging to another worker, and keeping track of which files have to be updated can get very confusing.

make avoids this confusion. To use make, you create a *makefile*, which shows the interdependencies between the files that make up a program. For example, object files depend on source files, object libraries depend on object files, and the final program depends on its object libraries. When you run make, it checks the *change times* of all these files to determine which files need to be updated. For example, if the change time on a source file is more recent than its corresponding object file, the object file must be updated to stay in synch with the source. But make also realizes that a change in the object file necessitates updating the object library, which necessitates updating the final program.

The makefile doesn't just show interdependencies; it also tells how to update any file that needs to be updated. Thus make uses the information in the makefile and automatically updates every part of the program that needs updating. Programmers don't have to keep track of what work needs to be done; make figures out what needs to be done and does it for you.

The troff *Text Formatter*

The troff text formatting program is frequently used for producing documents on UNIX and UNIX look-alike systems. It is quite different from word processors like WordPerfect or Microsoft Word—troff has more in common with programming languages than it does with conventional word processors.

The input to troff is a text file containing the text of the document, interspersed with instructions for formatting that text. Formatting instructions are also given in text format. For example

```
.sp lv
```

is a formatting instruction that tells troff to space down one vertical line. There are similar instructions for all the usual text formatting operations: changing font, indenting lines, adding headers and footers to the page, and so on.

When you want to create a document with troff, you process this kind of input with the troff program itself. You don't actually interact with troff; you prepare the input file ahead of time (with a text editor such as vi), then simply submit the file to be processed by troff. Thus, you can start the formatting process, then go off and do other work while the job is running.

troff formatting instructions are very basic. For example, there is no single instruction to start a paragraph—you might have to issue several instructions to do the job. For example, you might have to put an instruction that spaces down from the previous paragraph, and another instruction to indent the next output line by an appropriate amount. Obviously, this situation has drawbacks; you have to do a lot of typing to get a simple effect (such as starting a paragraph), and there's always the possibility you'll forget one of the instructions and mess up the document.

For this reason, troff lets you create *macros*, which are combinations of several simple instructions. For example, you can create a "start paragraph" macro, a "put this in italics" macro, and so on. Most UNIX systems have several standard macro packages already provided for you, so you don't have to create macros of your own. The most popular macro packages are named mm, me, and ms, names derived from the command line option that lets you specify what macro package you want to use.

In recent years, another text-formatting program called TeX (pronounced *Teck*) has been increasingly popular on UNIX systems. TeX works in the same way as troff, although the format of the input is different. One popular macro package for TeX is called LaTeX (pronounced *Lay-Teck*).

Basic System Administration

Historically, UNIX systems have offered few software tools for system administration. In the absence of such tools, each manufacturer of UNIX or a UNIX look-alike system has created its own software packages to do these jobs.

This situation complicates any discussion of UNIX system administration. For example, consider the process of making backup copies of UNIX files. Many UNIX and UNIX look-alike systems offer their own backup software, and each of these software packages is different. This book can't examine all the different packages, so it can only discuss techniques that work on all UNIX and UNIX look-alike systems. Such techniques are probably inferior to the specialized software offered by individual manufacturers; therefore, if you find yourself in charge of a UNIX machine, you are strongly advised to read the system administration documentation and to seek out any special commands especially designed for your specific system.

The Superuser

On every UNIX and UNIX look-alike system, one user ID is designated as the *superuser*. The superuser has user number zero, and often has the user name `root`. However, this can vary from system to system.

The superuser can do anything on the system. The kernel never checks the superuser's permissions, so the superuser can access any file. The superuser can also control any of the programs running on the system, and can terminate those programs if necessary.

Various system administration jobs can only be performed by the superuser. For example, the superuser is the only user who can create new device files, in order to make new devices available to other users. In addition, the superuser is often the only user who can create new userids or new groups.

In order to use the superuser's powers, you must log in as the superuser. To do so, you must know the superuser's password, which is set up at the time that UNIX is installed on the machine. The superuser can change the password with the usual `passwd` command.

At large UNIX sites, several people may be told the superuser password. Because the superuser can do anything on the system, you don't want too many people knowing the password, because that can cause security problems. On the other hand, it's risky for only one person to know the password; if something happens to that person, many system administration jobs (like backups) can come to a halt.

Backups

If a system doesn't offer its own backup software, the `tar` command is often used as an alternative. Usually, system backups must be run by the superuser, because the superuser is the only person who has permission to access every file on the system.

Chapter 5 showed how you can use the `tar` command to write directories to a diskette. To make backups, you use the same principle. However, there's a catch. You must make sure that the backup medium (whether it's a diskette or tape) has enough space to hold all the data you want to back up. Ideally, of course, you want your backup software to be smart: if it fills up one diskette, it should ask you to put in another diskette, then continue writing to the new diskette. However, `tar` doesn't work that way. If it runs out of space on a diskette, it just gives up.

If you have a lot of data to back up and you want to use `tar`, you're forced to do the backups in chunks. Make a list of all the files you want to back up, then break this list into subsets, where each subset is small enough to fit on a diskette. Run `tar` for each of these subsets, using an empty diskette each time.

Alternatives to `tar`

The `cpio` and `pax` commands are alternatives to `tar`. They work on the same basic principle—they can save many directories and files in a single file archive. If you find a UNIX or UNIX look-alike that doesn't have `tar`, look for `cpio` or `pax` instead.

The `tar` command is often used to transfer sets of files from one machine to another. For example, software packages are often distributed as `tar` archives. If you want to transfer several files to another system, you might put copies of all those files together in one directory, then use `tar` to save that directory on diskette. Take the diskette to the destination system, and use `tar` to extract the files from the diskette.

Background and Foreground Modes

Chapter 1 mentioned that UNIX can run several programs simultaneously. This is one of the system's greatest strengths: it lets you do several things at once. Pipelines are one example of this capability. The programs in the pipeline start simultaneously. As soon as the first program begins producing output, the output is piped to the second program so it can start working too, and so on all through the pipeline. By running several programs simultaneously, you can get results faster and more easily than if you ran them one at a time.

There are many kinds of jobs that take a long time to complete and don't produce output directly on the screen. For example, most of the stages of writing programs—compiling, linking, and so on—fit into this category. With many operating systems, you type in a command line, then sit around waiting for the job to finish. This can take minutes or even hours if the job is big enough.

On UNIX, you don't have to sit and wait. Instead, you can tell the system to run such jobs in the *background* while you do other work at the keyboard. It works like this:

- When you issue a command, you can put an ampersand (&) at the end of the command line. This tells the shell that you want the command to run in the background.

- The shell starts the command running, then immediately prompts you for another command. The first command keeps running, but you can do other work in the meantime. For example, a programmer can start compiling one file, then immediately go on to edit additional files. The job that is running on its own is called a *background job*; the jobs that you are doing at the terminal are called *foreground jobs*.

- If the background job produces output, the output appears on your screen as it is produced. Because this can get in the way of other work, you usually redirect the output of the background job.

- When the background job finishes, it may notify the shell that it's done. The shell then displays a message telling you that the job has been completed.

You can have any number of jobs running in the background. For example, you might use

```
cc file1 >out1 2>err1 &
cc file2 >out2 2>err2 &
cc file3 >out3 2>err3 &
cc file4 >out4 2>err4 &
```

to start compiling four files in the background. (cc is the usual UNIX command for compiling C programs.) Notice that the command lines redirect both the standard output (into the out files) and the standard error (into the err files), so that this output doesn't get lost and doesn't get in the way of what you're doing in the foreground.

The ps command tells you what programs you currently have running, both in the foreground and the background. Each program is identified by a number, called the program's *process ID*. This number is used to identify programs for various purposes. In particular, the kill command lets you terminate a background job if there's some good reason to do so (such as, you suddenly realize you made a mistake); to kill the correct job, you have to specify that job's process ID, as reported by ps.

None of these commands can really be simulated on DOS, because DOS can only run one job at a time. This overview has been provided to let you know about the possibility of running jobs in the background on UNIX. When you start using a real UNIX or UNIX look-alike system, read the man pages for ps and kill to see how they work.

Chapter Review

Revision control software keeps track of all the changes that have been made to a file. It helps you identify what changes have been made from one version to the next, lets you recover previous versions of a file, and can prevent people from interfering with each other as they work on the same project.

The awk programming language is a simple language well suited to being a novice's first programming language. An awk program takes the form

```
criterion { actions }
criterion { actions }
criterion { actions }
criterion { actions }
   . . .
```

When you apply such a program to a data file, awk reads through the data file line by line. If a line meets one or more of the specified *criteria*, awk executes the *actions* associated with those *criteria*. awk then reads the next line, checks the *criteria*, and so on.

The make program helps keep a collection of files in synch with each other. It does so by consulting a makefile, which states all the interdependencies of the files in question. The makefile also tells make how to update any file that needs updating.

The troff program takes text files as input and produces formatted documents. troff input consists of the words of the document interspersed with formatting instructions. Macro packages make it easier to produce documents, by combining basic formatting instructions into more sophisticated actions.

Most UNIX systems offer their own system administration software, and there is little uniformity in the way that different systems approach system administration tasks. One common facet of system administration is the use of a user ID called the *superuser*. The kernel lets the superuser access any file on the system and control all executing processes.

While individual systems can offer their own backup software, many sites use `tar`, `cpio`, or `pax` for backing up files. These commands can also be used to create archives, convenient for transferring several files or directories to other systems.

Programs can run in two modes on a UNIX system. In foreground mode, the process can interact with the terminal in the normal way. In background mode, the process is cut off from the terminal to some extent, executing on its own without interacting with the user. Background mode is ideal for commands that take a long time to do the work and that do not need to interact with you, such as compiling programs.

Part III

Command Manual Pages
(Man Pages)

Introduction to Man Pages

The documentation describing UNIX commands is made up of *man pages*, which is short for *reference manual pages*. This section of the book contains man pages for the MKS Tools package. Before I get to the actual man pages, however, I'll discuss the format of the pages and how to understand them.

How to Read a Man Page

UNIX documentation is traditionally divided into several numbered sections:

1. Section 1 describes the standard utility commands (`cp`, `vi`, and so on).

2. Section 2 describes the basic services provided by the kernel. These man pages are organized according to *system calls* that programmers can use in their programs. A system call looks like a subprogram written in the C programming language. For example, the kernel provides facilities that let a program open a file. The `open` system call is presented as a C subprogram that programs can use when they want to open files.

3. Section 3 describes additional subprograms that programmers can use when they are writing programs. For example, this section would contain an explanation of the C programming language's `fopen` subprogram. `fopen` stands for *file open*; the `fopen` subprogram calls `open` to open a file, then does some additional work to prepare the file for use by the C program. Writing programs with Section 3 subprograms is like building a house with prefabricated parts—you still use the same basic materials (the system calls), but someone else has already put them together to make your job faster and easier.

4. Section 4 describes the formats of files used by various utilities. For example, Section 4 would show what a `tar` archive looks like inside.

5. Section 5 provides supplementary information on various topics. For example, several of the appendixes to this book are based on Section 5 documentation from the MKS Toolkit package.

Within each section, topics are in alphabetical order. Additional sections may be added for such topics as system administration procedures, communication features, games, and so on. Section 3 is often divided into subsections, one for each programming language. For example, subprograms for the C programming language would be in Section 3C, while subprograms for the FORTRAN programming language would be in Section 3F.

It's common to refer to man pages by name and section. For example, the description of the `tar` utility in Section 1 would be `tar(1)`. The description of the `tar` archive file format in Section 4 would be `tar(4)`.

The rest of this chapter describes the parts of a Section 1 man page as used in this book. The format of this book's man pages is similar to the format of man pages for any UNIX or UNIX look-alike system; when you can find your way through a *Learning UNIX* man page, standard UNIX documentation should look familiar to you.

Section 1 Only

Learning UNIX only offers Section 1 man pages. This book doesn't deal with programming, so there's no point in providing Sections 2 or 3. Section 4 information tends to vary from one UNIX system to another, because different manufacturers use different file formats with their software. Finally, the appendixes provide as much Section 5 information as you'll need to use the MKS Tools productively.

Parts of a Man Page

Man pages are divided into parts, with each part providing a different kind of information. The following sections describe the various parts of a man page for a utility command.

The Synopsis Section

Every Section 1 man page begins with a Synopsis section that gives a quick summary of the command's format. For example, here is the synopsis of the `ls` command.

```
ls [-1abcCdfFgilmnopqrRstux] [pathname ...]
```

The synopsis takes the general form of a command line; it shows what you can type, and the order in which the arguments should appear. The parts that are enclosed in square brackets are optional; you can omit them if you choose. Parts that are not enclosed in square brackets must be present for the command to be correct. (Note that the square brackets are just markers to make the synopsis easier to read. You shouldn't enter these square brackets when you type in an actual command.)

The synopsis begins with the name of the command itself. After the command name comes a list of options, if the command accepts any. UNIX options generally consist of a minus sign (-) followed by a single character, usually an upper- or lowercase letter. For example, -l and -x are two of the valid options for ls.

Unless otherwise stated, the order of options is not important. If you are going to specify several of this type of option for the same command, you can put all the option characters after the same dash; for example,

```
ls -l -x
ls -x -l
ls -xl
ls -lx
```

are all equivalent.

Because you can put a group of options together in one string, the synopsis usually puts them together. In the ls synopsis, for example, the options are given as

```
-1abcCdfFgilmnopqrRstux
```

This means that the valid options are -1, -a, -b, and so on.

Some commands have options of the form

```
-name value
```

where *name* is the name of the option and *value* is some value for the option. For example, the banner command synopsis is

```
banner [-f fontfile] [-c char] [-w n] [text ...]
```

This synopsis shows several options of this form. For example, consider

```
-w n
```

319

This option controls how many characters wide the output of banner will be. In this case, the *name* of the option is w and the value is *n*. Notice that *n* is written in italics. In a command synopsis, arguments written in italics are *placeholders* for information that you should supply when you enter the command. In this case, *n* stands for an integer that specifies the actual output width. When you type in a banner command and choose to specify a -w option, you would put a number in place of *n*, as in

```
banner -w 72 "Hello"
```

> **Note:** Whenever a synopsis contains a *placeholder* in italics, the rest of the man page will tell you what kind of value you should use to fill the placeholder.

Some commands contain options of the form

```
-xvalue
```

where there is no space between the letter of the option and its value. For example, the synopsis of the sort command contains an entry of the form

```
-tx
```

This is similar to the previous option type, except that there is no space between the argument *name* and its *value*. In this example, the name is -t and the value is represented by a placeholder *x*. As the rest of the sort man page explains, this placeholder stands for a single character. If you want to use the -t option for sort, you would type -t immediately followed by another character, as in

```
sort -t:
```

The banner synopsis ends with

```
[text ...]
```

As the italics suggest, this is another placeholder. The . . . indicates that you may enter a list of *text* strings, as in

```
banner Each of these is a text argument
```

The list supplied in the preceding command consists of the arguments

```
Each
of
these
is
a
text
argument
```

There are a few arguments that are used frequently:

```
[file ...]
```

stands for a list of file names.

```
[pathname ...]
```

stands for a list of path names (which can be either file names or directory names). It is common to use glob constructs to create lists of file names or pathnames; for more information on glob constructs, see Chapter 4.

The synopsis shows the order in which command line arguments should be specified. Typically, options must come immediately after the command name, and other arguments come after the options. If a command has a special format that does not follow this order, the synopsis will show the order you must use.

The Description Section

The *Description* section describes what the command does and how you can use the command productively. It usually starts by explaining the command line synopsis, and telling what happens if you omit any of the optional arguments.

For complex utilities like the KornShell and vi, the *Description* section may be divided into subsections, each dealing with a particular aspect of using the utility.

The Options Section

The *Options* section lists the options accepted by the utility and what each of these options means. The options are often described in a table format to make it faster for you to pick out the options you want to use.

If a utility only takes a few options, there may not be a separate *Options* section. Instead, the options are discussed in the *Description* section.

321

The Examples Section

Some man pages have an *Examples* section, giving examples of how the utility can be used. The man page tries to give a mix of simple examples that show how the utility works on a basic level, plus more complex examples that show how the utility can perform sophisticated tasks.

The Diagnostics Section

The *Diagnostics* section shows the status values that the utility returns; status values are discussed in Chapter 8. The *Diagnostics* section may also show some of the error and warning messages that the utility can display. Usually, the man pages only show messages that might be difficult to understand; the man pages often omit messages that are self-explanatory.

The Files Section

The *Files* section lists any *supplementary* files to which the utility may refer. Supplementary files are files that are not specified on the command line. Such files usually provide information that the command needs. For example, the *Files* section of the `passwd` man page mentions the `/etc/passwd` file because that is where a UNIX system stores password information.

The *Files* section may also mention temporary files that the command creates as it does its work. For example, the *Files* section of the `sort` command shows that `sort` may create temporary files with names of the form `/etc/stm*` to hold partly sorted data.

The Limits Section

The *Limits* section lists any limits on the operation of the utility. For example, the *Limits* section of the `diff` command mentions that `diff` cannot handle files with lines longer than 1024 characters. Limits of this sort are inevitable when writing software, but MKS does its best to set the limits high enough that they will not get in your way.

Some limits may depend on how much other work you are doing with the computer. For example, the amount of memory available to any DOS program depends on how many other programs you are already executing (Terminate-and-Stay-Resident programs, the shell, and so on). Such limits are seldom described in the *Limits* section because they are dictated by factors outside the utility's control.

The Portability Section

The *Portability* section lists other systems where the utility command is available. This information is important because of the many "flavors" of UNIX currently in use.

As discussed in Chapter 1, there are many differences between UNIX and UNIX look-alikes, and utilities that are standard on one version may not be found on another version.

Most of the commands provided with MKS Tools are based on Draft 10 of the proposed POSIX.2 standard. Because the standard has not been finalized, MKS cannot claim conformance with the standard; however, MKS has taken great care to agree with the standard to the maximum amount possible on a non-UNIX system. Because the MKS Tools are based on the MKS Toolkit, the *Portability* section always mentions the MKS Toolkit. There are versions of the Toolkit available for DOS and for OS/2.

The Portability section may also mention the X/OPEN standard. The X/OPEN corporation is a consortium of companies that leads in UNIX systems sales. Current members include Apollo Computer, AT&T, Bull, DEC, Fujitsu, Hewlett-Packard, Hitachi, IBM, ICL, NCR, NEC, Nokia Data, Olivetti, Phillips, Prime Computer, Siemens, Sun Microsystems, and Unisys. X/OPEN has produced a Common Applications Environment standard to ensure portability and connectivity of applications, and to allow users to move between systems without retraining. The X/OPEN specification is committed to conformance with POSIX, and defines a commercially viable operating environment.

Finally, the *Portability* section often discusses ways the MKS Tools version of a utility differs from other commonly available versions of the same utility.

The See Also Section

The *See Also* section refers to other man pages that may contain information relevant to the man page you have just read. For example, the man page for `alias` refers to the man page for `sh`, because aliases are handled by the shell. The man page for `alias` also refers to `unalias`, the command that can get rid of the aliases you create with `alias`.

The Warning Section

If a man page has a *Warning* section, the section contains important advice for using the command. In MKS Tools documentation, the *Warning* section is often aimed at those who are already familiar with UNIX; it tells how the MKS Tools may differ from the utilities on a true UNIX system.

The Notes Section

The *Notes* section offers additional notes about using the software. The *Notes* section serves approximately the same purpose as the *Warning* section: it provides important information that you shouldn't overlook. However, the *Notes* section usually addresses issues that are less serious than those covered by *Warnings*.

Command Manual Pages

alias—Display or Create Command Alias

Synopsis

```
alias [-tx] [name[=value] ...]
```

Description

alias displays or creates command *aliases*. alias is built into the KornShell.

How Aliases Work

When you type in a command line, the shell checks to see if the first word of the line is a shell keyword (like cd, set, and so on). If it isn't, the shell checks to see if the word appears in the list of currently defined aliases. If it does, the shell replaces the alias with its associated string value. The result is a new command line that might begin with a shell function name, a built-in command, or an external command.

When an alias has been replaced, the shell checks the command line again. If the new command line starts with an alias, this alias will also be replaced. After this second replacement, the shell does not check for aliases. Thus, alias replacement happens a maximum of two times per command line.

Typically, you use aliases to simplify the job of entering a command. For example, you might set up a short alias to stand for a command that you type in a lot (to save typing) or for a command that is complicated and hard to type (so that you only have to remember the alias, not the full command).

Generally, the shell only checks to see if the first word on the line is an alias. However, if the substituted value ends with a blank, the next word of the command line is also checked for aliases. This means that you can have aliases for things in the middle of a command line (such as file names or options) as well as for the part of the command line that comes at the beginning.

The Form of the *alias* Command

If alias is called without arguments, it displays all the currently defined aliases and their associated values.

If alias is called with arguments of the form

```
name=value
```

it creates an alias for each *name* with the given string *value*. From this point on, when the shell sees a command line that begins with *name*, it will replace *name* with *value*.

If alias is called with parameters of the form *name* without any value assignment, *name* and its associated *value* are displayed.

Options

The -x option marks each alias *name* on the command line for *export*. If -x is specified without any names on the command line, alias displays all exported aliases. Only exported aliases are understood in a *subshell* (a child process of the shell).

If you use the -t option, each *name* specified on the command line becomes a *tracked* alias. A tracked alias is assigned its full path name the first time that the alias is used. Whenever you use the alias after this, the shell can find the appropriate command immediately using the full path name, without doing the usual search through the directories in PATH. If you change PATH, the shell will reexamine the tracked alias the next time you use it, and assign a new value to the alias based on the new PATH. The same type of reexamination happens if you execute the shell command cd. Invoking alias with the -t option but without any specified names displays all currently defined tracked aliases.

If you issue the command

```
set -h
```

each command that you use in the shell automatically becomes a tracked alias.

There are several aliases built into the shell. These are described in Table 1.

Table 1. Aliases built into the KornShell.

Alias	Value
echo	print -
false	let 0
functions	typeset -f
hash	alias -t
history	fc -l
integer	typeset -i
nohup	'nohup '
pwd	print - $PWD
r	fc -e -
true	:
type	whence -v

Any of these aliases can be removed or changed. See the relevant manual pages for details.

Examples

The command

```
alias
```

simply displays all currently defined aliases.

```
alias rm="rm -i"
```

defines rm as an alias. From this point on, when you issue an rm command, it automatically turns into rm -i and asks you to confirm each file being removed.

```
alias ls="ls -x"  p= "more"
```

defines two aliases: ls stands for ls -x, and p stands for more.

Diagnostics

Possible exit status values are:

0   Successful completion.

1   Failure because of an invalid command line option.

If you ask alias to determine the values of a set of names, the exit status is the number of those names that are not currently defined as aliases.

Possible error messages include:

`Cannot assign value to tracked alias "name"`	A tracked alias may not be given a new value. If you really want to create an alias with that name, you must unalias the existing name, then issue a new alias command.

Portability

KornShell. POSIX.2. MKS Toolkit. On UNIX, alias is a built-in command of the KornShell, but not of the Bourne Shell.

See Also

```
cd, echo, fc, let, set, sh, true, typeset, unalias, whence
```

banner—Display Text in Large Type

Synopsis

```
banner [-f fontfile] [-c char] [-w n] [text ...]
```

Description

If text arguments are specified, banner writes the arguments on the standard output in large letters according to a default font. If no such arguments are present, text is read from the standard input. Listing 1 shows a typical example of banner output.

Listing 1.   A typical use of banner.

```
banner hello
XXX                     XXX       XXX
 XX                     XX        XX
 XX         XXXXX       XX        XX          XXXX
 XX XXX   XX    X       XX        XX        XX   XX
 XXX XX   XXXXXXX       XX        XX        XX   XX
 XX XX  XX             XX        XX        XX   XX
XXX   XXX  XXXXX        XXXX      XXXX       XXXX
```

Options

By default, banner does not check the output line length or truncate the output to fit the line. If you specify the -w *n* option, the output width is limited to *n* characters at the most.

Output characters are normally formed from the X character. You can use the -c option to use any other single character in the output. The character used to make the large letters is called the *fill character*.

If you specify the -f option, banner obtains the output font from the specified *fontfile* instead of using the default font. To create your own fontfile, follow the fontfile examples mentioned in the following *Files* section.

Diagnostics

Possible exit status values are:

0   Successful completion.

1   Failure because of an unknown command line option, inability to open or missing font file, invalid font file format, missing fill character, or missing width.

Files

/etc/small.fnt   Optional small font file.

/etc/italic.fnt   Optional italic font file.

Portability

X/Open Portability Guide. All UNIX systems. MKS Toolkit.

329

bc—Arbitrary-Precision Arithmetic Calculation Language

Synopsis

```
bc [-l] [-i] [file ...]
```

Description

bc is a programming language that can perform arithmetic calculations to arbitrary precision. It can be used interactively, by entering instructions from the terminal. It can also run programs taken from files.

If *file* arguments are specified on the command line, they should be text files containing bc instructions. bc will execute the instructions from those files, in the order that they appear on the command line. Then bc will execute instructions from the standard input. bc terminates when it executes a quit instruction or reaches the end-of-file character on standard input.

The *bc* Language

bc is a simple but complete programming language with a syntax reminiscent of the C programming language. This version of bc is a superset of the standard language available on most systems. It has several additional features intended to make the language more flexible and useful. Features that are unique to this implementation are noted in the text.

Input consists of a series of instructions that assign values to variables or make calculations. You can also define subprograms called *functions*; functions perform a sequence of instructions to calculate a single value.

bc displays the result of any line that calculates a value but does not assign the value to a variable. For example, the instruction

```
2+2
```

displays

```
4
```

bc saves the last value displayed in a special variable denoted by the dot character (.).

Numbers

Numbers consist of an optional minus sign (-) followed by a sequence of zero or more digits, followed by an optional decimal point (.), followed by a sequence of zero or more digits. Digits can be the usual 0 through 9, plus the hexadecimal digits A through F. These uppercase letters represent the values from 10 through 15. They must be uppercase.

A number must have at least one digit, either before or after the decimal point. If not, bc interprets the decimal point as the special variable (.) mentioned in the previous section.

A number can be arbitrarily long and can contain spaces. Here are some valid numbers with an input base of 10:

```
0    0.    .0    -3.14159    +09.    -12    1 000 000
```

Here are some valid numbers with an input base of 16:

```
0    FF    FF.3    -10.444    A1
```

See the following *Bases* section for more information on input bases.

You can break up numbers using spaces but not commas. For example, you can write 1000000 or 1 000 000, but not 1,000,000.

Identifiers

Identifiers consist of any number of letters, digits, or the underscore (_) character; the first character must be a lowercase letter. Spaces are not allowed inside identifiers. (Note: some versions of bc only let you use identifiers that are a single character long.)

Identifiers are used as names for *variables*, *functions*, or *arrays*:

- A *variable* holds a single numeric value. Variables that are *local* to a function are declared using the auto statement, described in the *Functions* section. All other variables are *global* and can be used inside any function or outside all functions. You do not have to declare global variables. Variables are created as required, with an initial value of zero. Remember that there is also the special dot variable (.), which contains the last value displayed. Single numeric values and variables are sometimes called *scalars*.

- A *function* is a name for a sequence of instructions that calculate a single value. Function names are always followed by a list of zero or more values enclosed in parentheses, as in my_func(3.14159). Functions are discussed in more detail in the *Functions* section.

- An *array* is a list of values. Values in the list are called the *elements* of the array. These elements are numbered; the first element in the array is always numbered 0 (zero). The number of an element is called the *subscript* or *index* of the element. Subscripts always appear in square brackets after the array name. For example, a[0] refers to element zero in the array a (the first element in the array). If a subscript value is given as a floating point number, bc discards the fractional part to make the subscript into an integer. For example, all of the following expressions refer to the same element.

```
a[3]    a[3.2]    a[3.999]
```

The valid array subscripts range from 0 to 32767 inclusive. In bc (unlike many other programming languages), you don't need to declare the size of an array. Elements are created dynamically as required, with an initial value of zero.

Because function names are always followed by parentheses and array names are always followed by square brackets, bc can distinguish among all three types of names. Therefore you can have variables, functions, and arrays with the same name. For example, sample can be a variable, while sample() is a function and sample[] is an array.

Built-in Variables

bc has several built-in variables that are used to control various aspects of the interpreter. These are described in the sections that follow.

Scale

The *scale* value is the number of digits to be retained after the decimal point in arithmetic operations. For example, if the scale is 3, at least three digits after the decimal point will be retained in each calculation. This would mean that

```
5 / 3
```

would have the value

```
1.666
```

If you specify the -l option on the bc command line, the scale starts with the value 20; otherwise it starts with the value 0.

The variable scale holds the current scale value. To change scales, assign a new value to scale, as in

```
scale = 5
```

Because `scale` is just a regular `bc` variable, it can be used in any `bc` expression.

The number of decimal places in the result of a calculation is affected by the scale but also by the number of decimal places in the operands of the calculation. Details are given in the *Operations* section that follows.

There is also a function called `scale()`, which can determine the scale of any expression. For example,

```
scale(1.1234)
```

returns a result of 4, which is the scale of the number 1.1234. The result of the `scale()` function is always an integer.

Bases

`bc` lets you specify numbers in different bases besides decimal, including octal (base 8) and hexadecimal (base 16). `bc` lets you input numbers in one base and output them in a different base, simplifying the job of converting from one base to another. It does this using the built-in variables `ibase` and `obase`.

`ibase` is the base for input numbers. It has an initial value of 10 (normal decimal numbers). To use a different base for inputting numbers, assign an integer to `ibase`, as in

```
ibase = 8
```

This says that all future numbers will be input in base 8 (octal). The largest input base accepted is 16.

When the base is greater than 10, use the uppercase letters as digits. For example, base 16 will use the digits 0 through 9, and A through F. The digits larger than 9 are allowed in any number, regardless of the setting of `ibase`, but they are usually inappropriate if the base is smaller than the digit. There is one useful exception: the constant A always has the value 10 no matter what `ibase` is set to, so

```
ibase = A
```

always sets the input base to 10, no matter what the current input base is.

`obase` is a variable that controls the base in which numbers are output. It has an initial value of 10 (normal decimal numbers). To change output bases, assign an appropriate integer to `obase`.

If the output base is 16 or less, `bc` displays numbers with normal digits and hexadecimal digits (if needed). The output base can also be greater than 16, in which case each "digit" is printed as a decimal value, and digits are separated by a space. For example, if `obase` is 1000, the decimal number 123456789 is printed as

```
123 456 789
```

Here, the "digits" are decimal values from 0 through 999. As a result, all output values are broken up into one or more "chunks," with three decimal digits per chunk. Using output bases that are large powers of 10, you can break your output into columns; for example, many people find that 100000 makes a good output base because numbers are grouped into chunks of five digits each.

Long numbers are output with a maximum of 70 characters per line. If a number is longer than this, bc puts a backslash (\) at the end of the line, indicating that the number is continued on the next line.

Internally, bc performs all calculations in decimal, regardless of the input and output bases. The number of places after the decimal point is therefore dictated by the scale when numbers are expressed in decimal form. For example, if the scale is 5, bc does calculations with five base 10 digits after the decimal point. If the result of a calculation is displayed in some other base, you might get less than five digits of accuracy in the new base because of the conversion from base 10 to the new base.

Arithmetic Operations

bc can perform a large number of arithmetic operations. In accordance with the usual arithmetic conventions, some operations are calculated before others; for example, multiplications take place before additions, unless you use parentheses to change the order of calculation. Operations that take place first are said to have a higher *precedence* than operations that take place later.

Operations also have an *associativity*. The associativity dictates the order of evaluation when you have a sequence of operations with equal precedence. Some operations are evaluated left to right while others are evaluated right to left. Table 2 shows the operators of bc from highest precedence to lowest.

Table 2. bc operators from highest precedence to lowest.

Operator	Associativity
( )	Left to right
unary -, !, ++, --	Right to left
^	Right to left
*, /, %	Left to right
+, -	Left to right
=, +=, -=, *=, /=, ^=	Right to left
==, <=, >=, !=, <, >	Left to right
&&	Left to right
||	Left to right

If you're familiar with the C programming language, you should notice that bc's order of precedence is not the same as C's. In C, the assignment operators have the lowest precedence.

Next I describe what each operation does. In the descriptions, *A* and *B* can be numbers, variables, array elements, or other expressions. *V* must be either a variable or an array element.

(A)	An expression in parentheses is evaluated before any other operations are performed.
-A	Is the negation of the expression *A*.
!A	Is the logical complement of the expression. This means that if *A* is zero, *!A* is 1. If *A* is not zero, *!A* is 0. This operator may not be found in other versions of bc.
++V	Adds 1 to the value of *V*. The result of the expression is the new value of *V*.
- - V	Subtracts 1 from the value of *V*. The result of the expression is the new value of *V*.
V++	Adds 1 to the value of *V*, but the result of the expression is the old value of *V*.
V- -	Subtracts 1 from the value of *V*, but the result of the expression is the old value of *V*.
A^B	Calculates *A* to the power *B*. *B* must be an integer. If you let *a* be the scale of *A* and *B* be the absolute value of *B*, the scale of *A^B* is `min(a * b, max(scale,a))`. Where `min` calculates the minimum of a set of numbers and `max` calculates the maximum.
A*B	Calculates *A* multiplied by *B*. If you let *a* and *b* be the scales of the two expressions, the scale of the result is the expression `min(a+b,max(scale,a,b))`.
A/B	Calculates *A* divided by *B*. The scale of the result is the value of `scale`.
A%B	Calculates the remainder from the division of *A* by *B*. This is calculated in two steps. First, bc calculates *A/B* to the current scale. It then obtains the remainder through the formula *A-(A/B)*B* calculated to the scale `max(scale + scale(B), scale(A))`.

A+B	Adds *A* to *B*. The scale of the result is the maximum of the two scales of the operands.
A-B	Calculates *A* minus *B*. The scale of the result is the maximum of the two scales of the operands.

The operators in the next group are all *assignment* operators. They assign values to objects. An assignment operation has a value: the value that is being assigned. Therefore, you can write operations such as

```
a=1+(b=2)
```

In this operation, the value of the expression inside parentheses is 2 because that is the value assigned to b. Therefore, a is assigned the value 3.

The recognized assignment operators are:

V=B	Assigns the value of *B* to *V*.
V^=B	Is equivalent to *V=V^B*.
V=B*	Is equivalent to *V=V*B*.
V/=B	Is equivalent to *V=V/B*.
V%=B	Is equivalent to *V=V%B*.
V+=B	Is equivalent to *V=V+B*.
V-=B	Is equivalent to *V=V-B*.

The following expressions are called *relations*, and their values can be either true or false. In some versions of bc, you can only use relations in the conditional parts of if, while, or for statements; however, this version of bc lets you use relations in any expression.

Relations work in exactly the same way as their counterparts in the C language. This means that the result of a relation is a number: 1 if the relation is true and 0 if the relation is false. For example, consider

```
V = (A > B)
```

If A is greater than B, the relation is true and therefore V is assigned a value of 1. If A is not greater than B, the relation is false and V is assigned a value of 0. The following list shows all the relations recognized by bc.

A==B	Is true if and only if *A* equals *B*.
A<=B	Is true if and only if *A* is less than or equal to *B*.
A>=B	Is true if and only if *A* is greater than or equal to *B*.
A!=B	Is true if and only if *A* is not equal to *B*.

A<B	Is true if and only if *A* is less than *B*.
A>B	Is true if and only if *A* is greater than *B*.
A&&B	Is true if and only if *A* is true (non-zero) and *B* is true. If A is not true, the expression *B* is never evaluated because bc can already tell the relation is false. This operator is an extension to the POSIX.2 standard.
A¦¦B	Is true if either *A* or *B* is true (or both). If *A* is true, the expression *B* is never evaluated, because bc can already tell the relation is true. This operator is an extension to the POSIX.2 standard.

Comments and White Space

A *comment* has the form

```
/* Any string */
```

Comments can extend over more than one line of text. When bc sees /* at the start of a comment, it discards everything up to the next */ and replaces the whole comment with a single blank.

As an extension to the POSIX.2 standard, this version of bc provides an additional comment convention using the # symbol. All text from a # to the end of the line is treated as a single blank, as in

```
2+2 # this is a comment
```

bc is *free format*. This means that you can insert blanks or horizontal tab characters anywhere you like to improve the readability of the code. Instructions are assumed to end at the end of the line. If you have an instruction that is so long you need to continue it on a new line, use a backslash (\) as the last character of the first line and continue on the second, as in

```
a = 2\
 + 3
```

The \ indicates that the instruction continues on the next line, so the preceding is equivalent to

```
a = 2 + 3
```

Instructions

A bc instruction can be an expression, an assignment, a function definition, or a statement. If an instruction is not an assignment, bc displays the result of the instruction after the calculation has been carried out. For example, if you enter

```
3.14 * 23
```

bc displays the result of the calculation. However, with

```
a = 3.14 * 23
```

bc does not display anything because the expression is an assignment. If you want to display the value of an assignment expression, put parentheses around the expression. For example,

```
(a=2)
```

displays the result 2.

Here are the instruction forms recognized by bc:

expression	Calculates the value of the *expression*.
"*string*"	Is a string constant. When bc sees a statement of this form, it displays the contents of the string. For example, the instruction "Hello world!" tells bc to display Hello world!. bc doesn't output a new-line character after the string. This lets you issue such commands as foo = 15 "The value of foo is "; foo. With these commands, bc displays The value of foo is 15.
statement ; *statement* ...	Is a sequence of statements on the same line. In bc, a semicolon (;) and a new-line character have the same effect: they both indicate the end of a statement. bc executes the given statements in order from left to right.
{*statement*}	Is a brace-bracketed statement. Brace brackets are used to group sequences of statements together, as in

338

```
{
statement
statement
  ...
}
```

As shown, brace brackets can group a series of
statements that are split over several lines. Braces
are usually used with control statements such as
if and while.

`print` *expression, expression, ...*

Displays the results of the argument expressions.
Normally bc displays the value of each expression or string it encounters. This can make it
difficult to format your output in programs. For
this reason, the MKS bc has a `print` statement to
give you more control over how things are
displayed. `print` displays all of its arguments on
a single line. It places a single space between
adjacent numbers, but not between numbers and
strings. A `print` statement with no arguments
displays a new-line. If the last argument is null,
subsequent output will continue on the same
line. Here are some examples of how to use
print:

```
/* basic print statement */
print "The square of ", 2, "is ",2*2 The square
of 2 is 4
/* insert a space between adjacent numbers */
print 1,2,3
1 2 3
/* note - no spaces because of null strings */
print 1,"",2,"",3
123
/* just print a blank line */ print
/* two statements with output on same line */
print 1,2,3,"" ; print 4, 5, 6
1 2 3 4 5 6
```

void *expression*

void throws away or *voids* the result of the evaluation of the *expression* instead of displaying it. This is useful when using ++ and - - operators, or when you want to use a function but don't want to display the return value. For example void sample++ increments sample but does not print the result. The void statement is not found in other versions of *bc*.

if *(relation) statement*

Tests whether the given *relation* is true. If so, bc executes the *statement*. Otherwise, bc skips over the *statement* and goes to the next instruction. For example,
if ((a%2)==0) "a is even"
displays a is even if a has an even value.

if (*relation*) *statement1* else *statement2*

Is similar to the simple if statement. It executes statement1 if relation is true. Otherwise it executes statement2. It can be used as follows:
if ((a%2)==0) "a is even" else "a is odd"
Note that there is no statement separator between a is even and the else keyword. Here is another example:
```
if (a<10) {
    "a "
    "is "; "less than 10 "
    a
} else {
    "a is"
    " greater than or equal to 10 "
    a
}
```
The braces must be on the same line as the if and the else keywords. This is because a new-line or a semicolon immediately after the conditional part of the statement tells bc that the body of the conditional is the null statement. One common source of errors in bc programs is typing the

statement body portion of an if statement on a separate line. If you specify -i on the bc command line, bc displays a warning when an if statement has a null body.

The else form of if is an extension to the POSIX.2 standard. while (*relation*) *statement* repeatedly executes the given statement while relation is true. For example,

```
i = 1
a = 0
while (i <= 10) {
    a += i
    ++i
}
```

adds the integers from 1 through 10 and stores the result in a.

If the relation is not true when bc encounters a while loop, bc will not execute *statement* at all.

for (*initexp* ; *relation* ; *endexp*)

is equivalent to
```
initexp
while (relation) {
    statement
    endexp
}
```
where *initexp* and *endexp* are expressions and *relation* is a relation. For example,
```
a = 0
for (i = 1; i <= 10; ++i) a += i
```
is equivalent to the while example given earlier. C programmers should note that all three items inside the parentheses must be specified; unlike C, bc doesn't let you omit any of these expressions.

break

Can only be used inside a while or for loop. break terminates the loop.

sh *command*

Lets you send a line to the shell for execution, as in sh more myfile.

This command passes everything from the first non-blank character until the end of the line to the command interpreter for execution. The preceding command would use more to display the contents of myfile.sh. It is an extension to the POSIX.2 standard.

quit   Terminates bc. In other implementations of bc, the interpreter exits as soon as it reads this word. This version of bc treats quit as a real statement, so you can use it in loops, functions, and so on.

Several other types of statements are only relevant in function definitions. These are described in the *Functions* section.

Functions

A function is a *subprogram* that calculates a result based on *argument* values. For example, the following function converts a temperature given in Fahrenheit into the equivalent temperature in Celsius.

```
define f_to_c(f) {
    return ( (f-32) * 5 / 9 )
}
```

This defines a function named f_to_c that takes a single argument called f. The *body* of the function is enclosed in braces. Note that the opening brace must be on the same line as the define keyword. The function body consists of a sequence of statements that calculate the *result* of the function. An expression of the form

```
return (expression)
```

returns the value of expression as the result of the function. The parentheses around the expression are compulsory according to the POSIX.2 standard, but optional in this version of bc.

To make use of a subprogram, you create a *function call*. A function call has the form

```
name(expression,expression,...)
```

where name is the name of the function, and the expressions are argument values for the function. A function call can be used anywhere you can use any other expression. The value of the function call is the result value of the function, as calculated using the given *expressions* as argument values. For example, with the function f_to_c() defined previously, f_to_c(41) has the value 5 (because 41° Fahrenheit is equivalent to 5° Celsius).

The general form of a function definition is

```
define name(parameter,parameter,...) {
    auto local, local, ...
    statement
    statement
        ...
}
```

The *parameters* on the first line can be variable names or array names. Array names are indicated by putting square brackets after them. For example, if addvec is a function that adds two vectors, the function definition might start with

```
define addvec(a[],b[]) {
```

Parameter names do not conflict with arrays or variables of the same name. For example, you can have a parameter named a inside a function and a variable named a outside; the two are separate entities. Assigning a value to the variable will not change the parameter, and assigning a value to the parameter will not change the variable.

All parameters are passed *by value*. This means that a copy is made of the argument value and the copy is assigned to the formal parameter. This also applies to arrays. If you pass an array to a function, a copy is made of the whole array, so any changes made to the array parameter don't affect the original array. If you want to change the original array, don't pass it as an argument; simply refer to the array by name inside the function.

You might create a function that does not need any arguments. In this case, the define line will not have any parameters inside the parentheses, as in

```
define f() {
```

Local Variables

The auto statement declares one or more *local* variables. When a variable or array name appears in an auto statement, the current values of those items are saved away and the items are initialized to zero. For the duration of the function, the items have their new values. When the function terminates, the old values of the items are restored.

For example, `addarr` in Listing 2 is a function that adds the elements in an array. The argument `l` stands for the number of elements in the array. The function uses two local names: a variable named `i` and a variable named `s`. These variables are local to the function `addarr` and are unrelated to any objects of the same name outside the function (or in other functions).

Listing 2. A function that sums the elements of an array.

```
define addarr(a[],l) {
    auto i, s
    for (i=0; i < l; ++i) s += a[i]
    return (s)
}
```

Objects that are named in an `auto` statement are called *autos*. Autos are initialized to zero each time the function is called. In `addarr`, the sum `s` is set to zero each time the preceding function is called.

Listing 3 shows that you can also have local arrays that are specified by placing square brackets after the array name in the `auto` statement. This defines a local array called `local_array`. Local arrays start out with no elements in them.

Listing 3. A function with `local_array`.

```
define func_with_local_array() {
    auto local_array[];
    for(i=0; i<100; i++) local_array[i] = i*2
}
```

If a function refers to an object that is not a parameter and is not declared `auto`, the object is assumed to be *global*. Global objects can be referred to by other functions or by statements that are outside functions. In Listing 4, the `sum_c` function references a global array named `c` that is the element-by-element sum of two other arrays. If `c` did not exist before you called `sum_c`, `bc` creates the array when it is referenced. After the program has called `sum_c`, statements in the program or in functions can refer to `c`.

Listing 4.   Reference to a global array

```
define sum_c(a[],b[],l) {
    auto i
    for (i=0; i < l; ++i) c[i] = a[i] + b[i]
}
```

Functions usually require a `return` statement. This has the form

```
return (expression)
```

The `expression` is evaluated and used as the result of the function. The expression must have a single numeric value; it cannot be an array.

A `return` statement terminates a function, even if there are more statements left in the function. Listing 5 shows a function that returns the absolute value of its argument. If `i` is less than zero, the function takes the first `return`; otherwise, it takes the second.

Listing 5.   Absolute value function.

```
define abs(i) {
    if (i < 0) return (-i)
    return (i)
}
```

A function can also terminate by executing the last statement in the function. If so, the result of the function is zero. The function `sum_c` in Listing 4 is an example of a function that doesn't have a `return` statement. The function doesn't need a `return` statement, because its work is to calculate the global array `c`, not to calculate a single value. If you want to return from a function but not return a value, you can use

```
return ()
```

or simply

```
return
```

If there are no parameters to the `return` statement, a default value of zero will be returned.

345

Built-in Functions

bc has several built-in functions that perform various operations. These functions are similar to user-defined functions but you don't have to define them yourself—they are already set up for you. The recognized functions are:

length(*expression*)
: Calculates the total number of decimal digits in the value of *expression*. This includes digits both before and after the decimal point. The result of length is an integer. For example, length(123.456) returns 6.

scale(*expression*)
: Returns the scale of the value of *expression*. For example, scale(123.456) returns 3, because there are three digits after the decimal point. The result of scale is always an integer. Subtracting the scale of a number from the length of a number lets you determine the number of digits before the decimal point.

sqrt(*expression*)
: Calculates the square root of the value of *expression*. The result is truncated in the least significant decimal place (not rounded). The scale of the result is the scale of the value of *expression* or the value of scale, whichever is larger.

The following functions can be used if you specify -l on the bc command line. (The -l option is discussed in the *Options* section.) If you do not specify -l, the function names will not be recognized. Note that there are two names for each function: a full name, and a single-character name for compatibility with the POSIX.2 standard. The full names are the same as the equivalent functions in the standard C math library.

atan(*expression*) or a(*expression*)
: Calculates the arctangent of *expression*, returning an angle in radians.

cos(*expression*) or c(*expression*)
: Calculates the cosine of *expression*, where this is taken to be an angle in radians.

exp(*expression*) or e(*expression*)
: Calculates the exponential of *expression* (i.e., the value e raised to the power of *expression*).

jn(*integer*,*expression*) or j(*integer*,*expression*)
: Calculates the Bessel function of *expression*, with order *integer*.

log(*expression*) or l(*expression*)
: Calculates the natural logarithm of *expression*.

sin(*expression*) or s(*expression*)
: Calculates the sine of *expression*, where this is taken to be an angle in radians.

Options

The -l option loads a library of standard mathematical functions before processing any other input. This library also sets the *scale* to 20.

The -i option puts bc into *interactive mode*. In this mode, bc displays a prompt when it is waiting for input. In addition, errors are handled somewhat differently. Normally, when bc encounters an error while processing a file, it prints an error message and exits. In interactive mode, bc prints the message, then returns to the interactive mode to allow debugging. -i is unique to this version of bc.

Examples

Listing 6 shows a simple function that calculates the sales tax on a purchase. The amount of the purchase is given by purchase, and the amount of the sales tax (in percent) is given by tax. For example,

```
sales_tax(23.99,6)
```

calculates six percent tax on a purchase of $23.99. The function temporarily sets the scale value to 2 so that the monetary figures will have two figures after the decimal point. Remember that bc truncates calculations instead of rounding, so some accuracy might be lost. It is better to use one more digit than needed and perform the rounding at the end.

Listing 6.   Function to calculate sales tax.

```
define sales_tax(purchase,tax) {
    auto old_scale;
    old_scale = scale
    scale = 2
    tax = purchase*(tax/100)
    scale = old_scale
    return (tax)
}
```

Division resets the scale of a number to the value of scale. Listing 7 shows how you can use this to extract the integer portion of a number.

Listing 7. Extracting the integer part of a number.

```
define integer_part(x) {
    # a local to save the value of scale
    auto old_scale;

    # save the old scale, and set scale to 0
    old_scale = scale; scale=0

    # divide by 1 to truncate the number. Truncate means scale is 0
    x /= 1

    # restore the old scale
    scale=old_scale
    return (x)
}
```

Using the integer_part function, Listing 8 shows how to define a function to return the fractional part of a number.

Listing 8. Obtaining the fractional part of a number.

```
define fractional_part(x) {
    return (x - integer_part(x))
}
```

Listing 9 shows a function that lets you set the scale of a number to a specified number of decimal places.

Listing 9. Setting the scale of a number.

```
define set_scale(x, s) {
    auto os;
    os = scale
    scale = s
    x /= 1
    scale = os
    return (x)
}
```

Listing 10 shows how the `set_scale()` function can be used in a function that will round a number to two decimal places. This is a useful function if you want to work with monetary values.

Listing 10. Rounding a number to two decimal places.

```
define round(num) {
    auto temp;
    if(scale(num) < 2) return (set_scale(num, 2))
    temp = (num - set_scale(num, 2)) * 1000
    if(temp > 5) num += 0.01
    return (set_scale(num,2))
}
```

A *recursive* function calls itself. Listing 11 shows a recursive function that calculates the factorial of its argument. (The factorial of a positive integer is the product of the integer with all the positive integers that are smaller. For example, `fact(3)` returns `3*2*1`, or 6.)

Listing 11. Recursive factorial function.

```
define fact (x) {
    if(x < 1) return 1
    return (x*fact(x-1))
}
```

Listing 12 shows a non-recursive way to write the same function.

Listing 12. Non-recursive factorial function.

```
define fact (x) {
    auto result
    result = 1;
    while(x>1) result *= x--
    return (result)
}
```

Listing 13 shows another recursive function. This one calculates the nth element of the Fibonacci sequence.

Listing 13.   Recursive Fibonacci function.

```
define fib(n) {
    if(n < 3) {
        return (1)
    } else {
        return (fib(n-1)+fib(n-2))
    }
}
```

Listing 14 defines functions that convert radians to degrees and vice versa.

Listing 14.   Radian/degree conversion.

```
define rad_to_deg(n) {
    auto pi
    pi = 4 * atan(1)
    return (n * 180/pi)
}
define deg_to_rad(n) {
    auto pi
    pi = 4 * atan(1)
    return (n * pi/180)
}
```

Diagnostics

Possible exit status values are:

0   Successful completion.

1   Failure due to any of the following errors:

Break statement found outside of a loop

Parser stack overflow

Syntax error

End-of-file in comment

End-of-file in string

Numerical constant is too long

String is too long

Unknown option

Empty evaluation stack

Can't pass scalar to array

Can't pass array to scalar

Invalid array index

Built-in variable can't be used as a parameter or auto variable

'Name' is not a function

Invalid value for built-in variable

Shell command failed to execute

Division by 0

Invalid value for exponentiation operator

Attempt to take square root of negative number

Out of memory

Portability

POSIX.2. All UNIX systems. MKS Toolkit.

Notes

Unlike the C language (which uses lexical scoping rules), bc uses dynamic scoping. This is most easily explained by examining the example in Listing 15.

Listing 15.   Scoping example.

```
a=10
define f1() {
      auto a;
      a = 13;
      return (f2())
}
define f2() {
      return (a)
}

f1()
13
f2()
10
```

If you call f1(), bc displays the number 13 instead of the number 10. This is because f1() hides away the old (global) value of a (which is 10) and then sets a to 13. When f2() refers to a, it sees the variable that was dynamically created by f1() and so it prints 13. When f1() returns, it restores the old value of a. When f2() is called directly instead of through f1(), it sees the global value for a and prints 10. The corresponding C code would print 10 in both cases. Whenever possible, you should avoid situations where dynamic scoping makes a difference, since it can be confusing and it can foster bad habits that won't work if you ever try to program in C.

bc stores numbers as strings and converts them into numbers each time they are used. This is important because the value of a constant number can change depending on the setting of the ibase variable. For example, consider the instructions in Listing 16. When the base is set to 10, ten() returns the decimal value 10. However, when the input base is changed to 16, the function returns the decimal value 16. This can be a source of confusing errors in bc programs.

Listing 16.   Example of number storage.

```
define ten() {
      return (10)
}

ten()
10
ibase=16
ten()
16
```

352

The library of functions loaded using the `-l` option is stored in the file `/lib/lib.b` under your root directory. This is a simple text file that you can examine and change to add new functions as desired.

---

break—Exit From the Shell Loop

Synopsis

```
break [number]
```

Description

`break` exits from a `for`, `select`, `until`, or `while` loop. It is built into the shell.
If *number* is given, `break` exits from the given number of enclosing loops. The default value of *number* is 1.

Diagnostics

Possible exit status values are:

0 Successful completion.

1 There is no `for`, `while`, `until`, or `select` command currently active.

Portability

POSIX.2. X/Open Portability Guide. MKS Toolkit. `break` is a built-in command of the Bourne Shell and KornShell on UNIX systems.

See Also

```
continue, sh
```

cal—Display a Calendar for a Month or Year

Synopsis

```
cal [month] [year]
```

Description

cal displays a simple calendar on the standard output.

With no arguments, cal displays a calendar for the current month of the current year.

If there is one argument and it is numeric, it is interpreted as a year (such as 1992). If there is one argument and it is not numeric, it is interpreted as the name of a month, possibly abbreviated (such as apr).

When two arguments are given, the first is assumed to be the *month* (either a number from 1 to 12 or a month name) and the second is the *year*.

Diagnostics

Possible exit status values are:

0   Successful completion.

1   Failure due to an invalid command line argument, an invalid date, or a year outside the range of 1 A.D. to 9999 A.D.

Portability

X/Open Portability Guide. All UNIX systems. MKS Toolkit.

Note

Year numbers less than 100 refer to the early years A.D., not the current century. September 1752, the month when most of Europe switched from the Julian calendar to the Gregorian calendar, is handled correctly.

cat—Concatenate and Display Text Files

Synopsis

```
cat [usvte] [file ...]
```

Description

cat is most often used to display or concatenate files. It copies each *file* argument to the standard output. If you do not specify any files on the command line, cat reads the standard input.

Options

Normally, cat buffers its output (which means that output is only written to the terminal when cat has accumulated several lines to display). The -u option tells cat to display output as soon as it is produced.

Normally, cat produces an error message if one of the specified files does not exist or cannot be read. Specifying the -s option prevents such error messages.

Unprintable characters are shown if the -v flag is specified. If the top bit in a byte is on, cat outputs the character without that bit but preceded by the two characters M-. Other unprintable characters are displayed with ^ followed by the character representing the control character (for example, ^A for Ctrl-A).

If -e is specified in addition to -v, cat indicates the end of each line with a $ character. When -e is in effect, tabs are represented as ^I if -t is given and as white space if -t is not given.

Diagnostics

Possible exit status values are:

0   Successful completion.

1   Failure due to an invalid command line argument, inability to open the input file, inability to write to the standard output, or the input file being the same as the output file. (This version of cat does not check to see if the input and the output are the same file.)

Portability

POSIX.2. X/Open Portability Guide. All UNIX systems. MKS Toolkit. Berkeley UNIX systems have a cat command, but the command has different options.

See Also

```
cp, more, mv, pg
```

cd, chdir—Change Working Directory

Synopsis

```
cd [directory]

cd old new

chdir [directory]

chdir old new
```

Description

The command

```
cd directory
```

changes the working directory to *directory*. If *directory* is an absolute path name (one that begins with /), cd goes to that directory. If *directory* is a relative path name, cd takes it to be relative to the current working directory.

In the KornShell, if the variable CDPATH is defined, the built-in cd command searches for relative path names under each of the directories defined in CDPATH. If the directory is found outside the current working directory, cd displays the name of the new working directory.

The value of CDPATH should be a list of directory names separated by colons on UNIX, and by semicolons on DOS. To specify the current directory in CDPATH, use a null string. For example, if the value of CDPATH begins with a separator character, cd searches the current directory first; if the value of CDPATH ends with a separator character, cd searches the current directory last. To see how CDPATH works, consider

```
CDPATH= "/dir1; /dir2;"
cd mydir
```

The cd command looks for mydir under /dir1, then under /dir2, then under the current directory.

In the KornShell, the special command

```
cd -
```

changes the working directory to the previous working directory by exchanging the values of the variables PWD and OLDPWD. Repeating this command switches back and forth between the two directories.

If you call cd without arguments, cd sets the working directory to the value of the HOME environment variable, if this variable exists. If there is no HOME variable, the current directory is not changed.

The form

```
cd old new
```

is specific to the KornShell. The KornShell keeps the name of the current directory in the variable PWD. The preceding cd command scans the current value of PWD and replaces the first occurrence of the string *old* with the string *new*. cd displays the resulting value of PWD and makes it the new working directory.

In the KornShell, chdir is a synonym for cd.

Diagnostics

Possible exit status values are:

0   Successful completion.

1   Failure because of an invalid command line option, no HOME directory, no previous directory, a search for *directory* failed, or an old/new substitution failed.

Possible error messages include:

`"directory" bad directory`	The target directory could not be located. The working directory is not changed.
`Restricted`	You are using the restricted version of the KornShell (e.g., by specifying the -r, option for sh). The cd command is not allowed under the restricted shell.

357

`No HOME directory`	You have not assigned a value to the HOME environment variable. Thus when you just say cd to return to your home directory, the command can't figure out which directory is your home directory.
`No previous directory`	You tried the command cd - to return to your previous directory. However, there was no record of what your previous directory was.
`Pattern "old" not found in "dir"`	You tried a command of the form cd *old new*.
	However, the name of the current directory *dir* does not contain any string matching the regular expression *old*.

Portability

POSIX.2. X/Open Portability Guide. MKS Toolkit. The first form of the command is found on all UNIX systems. All forms are built into the KornShell.

See Also

```
sh
```

Note

Unlike the command of the same name under the DOS command.com, cd can change the current disk as well as the current directory.

---

chmod—Change Access Permissions of a File or Directory

Synopsis

```
chmod [-fR] mode pathname ...
```

Description

chmod changes the access permissions or *modes* of the specified files or directories. Modes determine who can read, change or execute a file.

Options

The -R option can be used when a directory is specified on the command line. chmod will give all subdirectories and files under that directory the attributes specified for the directory itself.

The -f option forces chmod to return a successful status and no error messages, even if errors are encountered. This is useful if you're using -R to change a lot of files but you don't really care if chmod changes everything, provided that it changes a particular subset of the files.

Modes

The *mode* value on the command line can be specified in symbolic form or as an octal value.

A symbolic *mode* has the form

```
[who] op permission [op permission ...]
```

The *who* value can be any combination of the following:

u	Sets user (individual) permissions.
g	Sets group permissions.
o	Sets other permissions.
a	Sets all permissions; this is the default.

On DOS, there are no group or other permissions. Therefore, they always match the individual permissions.

The *op* part of a symbolic mode is an operator telling whether permissions should be turned on or off. The possible values are:

+	Turns on a permission.
-	Turns off a permission.
=	Turns on the specified permissions and turns off all others.

The *permission* part of a symbolic mode is any combination of the following:

r	Read permission. If this is turned off, you will not be able to read the file. On DOS, all files are always readable, so this permission is ignored.

w	Write permission. If this is turned off, you will not be able to write to the file.
x	Execute permission. If this is turned off, you will not be able to execute the file. On DOS, all files are considered to be executable, so this permission is ignored.
h	Hidden attribute. This is only recognized under DOS.
a	Archive bit. This is only recognized under DOS.
s	On UNIX, this stands for *setuid or setgid on execution* permission; discussion of this concept is outside the scope of this book. On DOS, this stands for a system file.
t	On UNIX, this stands for the "sticky" bit; discussion of this concept is outside the scope of this book. On DOS, it refers to the archive bit (so it is equivalent to a).

Multiple symbolic modes can be specified, separated by commas.

Absolute modes are supported for conformance to UNIX versions of chmod. Absolute modes are octal numbers specifying the complete list of attributes for the files; attributes are specified by ORing together these bits:

```
4000    Hidden file; setuid bit
2000    System file; setgid bit
1000    Archive bit; sticky bit
0400    Individual read
0200    Individual write
0100    Individual execute (or list directory)
0040    Group read
0020    Group write
0010    Group execute
0004    Other read
0002    Other write
0001    Other execute
```

The first three bits are shown with their meanings on DOS. These bits have different meanings on UNIX. This version of chmod tries to handle options in a way that parallels the UNIX approach. In the following list, each line shows a group of calls that are all equivalent.

```
chmod 0000    chmod o=s
chmod 2000    chmod g=s    chmod =s
chmod 4000    chmod u=s    chmod =h
chmod 6000    chmod a=s    chmod ug=s    chmod =hs
```

Note that +s is equivalent to 2000 on DOS; on UNIX, +s is equivalent to 6000. All of these equivalences are intended to support commands ported to DOS from UNIX. Such ported commands will not do the same thing that they do on UNIX (because DOS does not have the same file attributes as UNIX), but the commands will work in a consistent manner.

To make a DOS file read-only, all three write permission bits must be turned off. If any of the three is on, DOS considers the file to be writable.

On DOS, the ls command indicates the mode settings of files. The DOS DIR command does not show these attributes.

Examples

```
chmod -w nowrite
```

makes a file named nowrite read-only.

```
chmod +hrs sysfile
```

sets the hidden, read-only, and system attributes for a file named sysfile.

```
chmod a=rwx file
```

turns on read, write, and execute permissions, and turns off the hidden, archive, and system attributes. This is equivalent to

```
chmod 0777 file
```

Diagnostics

Possible exit status values are:

0   Successful completion.

1   Failure because chmod couldn't access a specified file, couldn't change the modes on a specified file, couldn't read the directory containing the directory entry to change, or encountered a fatal error when using the -R option.

2   Failure because the command line was missing the *mode* argument, or had an invalid *mode* argument, or had too few arguments.

Possible error messages include:

`Fatal error during "-R" option`	The -R option was specified but some file or directory in the directory structure was inaccessible. This can happen because of permissions or because a removable unit has been removed.
`Read directory "name"`	You do not have read permissions on the specified directory.

Portability

POSIX.2. X/Open Portability Guide. MKS Toolkit. Different systems interpret some mode bits in different ways.

See Also

```
ls
```

continue—Skip to Next Iteration of Enclosing Loop

Synopsis

```
continue [number]
```

Description

continue skips to the next iteration of an enclosing for, select, until, or while loop. It is built into the shell.

If *number* appears on the command line, execution continues at the loop-control of the *number*th enclosing loop (when loops are nested inside other loops). The default value of *number* is 1.

Diagnostics

Possible exit status values are:

0   Successful completion.

1   There is no for, while, until, or select command currently active.

Portability

POSIX.2. X/Open Portability Guide. MKS Toolkit. continue is a built-in command of the Bourne Shell and KornShell on UNIX systems.

See Also

break, sh

cp —Copy Files

Synopsis

```
cp [-cfimp] file1 file2

cp [-cfimp] file ... directory

cp -R [-cfimp] dir1 dir2

cp -r [-cfimp] dir1 dir2
```

Description

cp copies files (called the *sources*) to a *target* named by the last argument on its command line.

If the target is an existing file, it is overwritten. If it does not exist, it is created.

If there are more than two path names, the last path name (the target) must be a directory. If the target is a directory, the sources are copied into that directory with names given by the final component of the source path name. For example,

```
cp file1 file2 file3 dir
```

would create `dir/file1`, `dir/file2`, and `dir/file3`.

Options

If the target file already exists and does not have write permission, `cp` normally asks whether to overwrite the target or continue with the next copy. If you specify the `-f` (force) option, `cp` will overwrite such files immediately, without asking the question. The `-i` (interactive) flag always asks the question before overwriting an existing file, whether or not the file is read-only.

The `-m` flag sets the modify and access time of each destination file to that of the corresponding source file. Normally, the modification time of the destination file is set to the present.

The `-p` option also preserves the modify and access times. In addition, it preserves the file mode, owner, and group owner, if possible.

Problems can arise when copying files to diskettes. You might expect that

```
cp *.c a:
```

copies all `.c` files to drive A:. If, however, the diskette in drive A: fills up before all files are copied, it becomes difficult to construct a wild card to copy only the remaining files to the next diskette. If you specify the `-c` (change) flag, `cp` will prompt you to change the diskette if there is insufficient room to complete a copy operation. Note that the parent directories must already exist on the new target diskette.

The `-R` option lets you clone an entire directory. It copies all the files and subdirectories of *dir1* into *dir2*. The `-r` option does almost the same thing. The difference is that `-R` is careful to duplicate all special files (e.g., device files), where `-r` makes no special allowance for special files. Since DOS doesn't have special files, there is no difference between `-R` and `-r` in the MKS Tools.

Diagnostics

Possible exit status values are:

0   Successful completion.

1   Failure because an argument had a trailing / but was not the name of a directory, a file could not be found, an input file could not be

opened for reading, an output file could not be created or opened for output, a read error occurred on an input file or a write error occurred on an output file, the input and output files were the same file, a fatal error was encountered when using -r or -R. Possible fatal -r or -R errors include:

The inability to access a file

The inability to chmod a target file

The inability to read a directory

The inability to create a directory

A target that is not a directory

The source and destination directories being the same

2   Failure because of:

An invalid command line option

Too few arguments on the command line

A target that should be a directory but isn't

No space left on the target device

Out of memory to hold the data to be copied

The inability to create a directory to hold a target file.

Possible error messages include:

cannot allocate target string	cp has no space to hold the name of the target file. Try to free up some memory to give cp more space.
copying directory "*name*" as plain file	You did not specify -r or -R, but one of the names you asked to copy was the name of a directory. cp will create a file corresponding to the original directory, but this file will probably be useless.
read only?	You are attempting to copy a file, but there is already a file with the target name and the file is read-only. If you really want to write over the existing file, enter **y** and press Enter. If you do not want to write over the existing file, enter **n** and press Enter.

source "*name*" and target "*name*" are identical	The source and the target are actually the same file (e.g., because of links, on UNIX systems). In this case, cp does nothing.
unreadable directory "*name*"	cp cannot read the specified directory (e.g., because you do not have appropriate permissions).

Portability

POSIX.2. X/Open Portability Guide. All UNIX systems. MKS Toolkit. The -c and -m flags are specific to MKS Tools and are not found on UNIX systems.

On DOS, if the target of cp is a device, the device is put into binary mode for the duration of the copy.

See Also

cat, mv, rm

date—Set and Display Date and Time

Synopsis

```
date [-uc] [+format] [[yy[mm[dd]]]hhmm[.ss]]
```

Description

date can display the operating system's idea of the current date and time, or set it to a new value. The default format of the date is given by the following example:

```
Wed Feb 26 14:01:43 EST 1992
```

Options

The -u option displays or sets the date and time according to Greenwich Mean Time (also called Coordinated Universal Time). When displaying the date, -u uses GMT as the time zone. The -c option is exactly the same as -u, except that it uses CUT as the time zone.

If the argument to date does not begin with +, the date and time are set from values in that argument in the following way: *yy* is the optional last two digits of the year, *mm* is the optional number of the month (01-12), *dd* is the optional day of the month, *hh* is the hour in 24-hour format, *mm* is the minutes, and . *ss* is the optional seconds. Note that you must specify the hours and the minutes; other arguments are optional.

If the argument to date begins with a + character, it is treated as a format to use when displaying the date. All characters of the *format*, excluding the + character, are written directly to the standard output, with the exception of *placeholders* consisting of a % character immediately followed by another character. Placeholders are described in the *Placeholders* section. The *format* should be enclosed in single or double quotation marks if it contains blanks or other special characters.

date outputs a new-line character after the *format* string is exhausted.

Placeholders

The % character introduces a placeholder, similar to those in the printf function of the C programming language. The following special formats are recognized.

%%	Displays the % character literally.
%a	Displays the three-letter abbreviation for the day of the week (for example, Sun).
%A	Displays the full name of the day (for example, Sunday).
%b	Displays the three-letter abbreviation for the month name (for example, Feb).
%B	Displays the full month name (for example, February).
%c	Displays the local representation of the date and time (see %D and %T).
%d	Displays the two-digit day of the month as a number.
%D	Displays the date in the form *mm/dd/yy*.
%E	Displays the day of the month in a two-character, right-justified, blank-filled field.
%h	Displays the three-letter abbreviation for the month (for example, Jun).
%H	Displays the two-digit hour (00 to 23).
%I	Displays the hour in the 12-hour clock representation (01 to 12).
%j	Displays the numeric day of the year (001 to 366).
%m	Displays the month number (01 to 12).
%M	Displays the minutes (00 to 59).

%p	Displays the local equivalent of AM or PM.
%r	Displays the time in AM/PM notation (for example, 11:53:29 AM).
%S	Displays the seconds (00 to 59).
%T	Displays the time in 24-hour notation (for example, 14:53:29).
%U	Displays the week number in the year, with Sunday being the first day of the week (00 to 52).
%w	Displays the number for the day of the week, with Sunday being 0.
%W	Displays the week number in the year, with Monday being the first day of the week (00 to 52).
%x	Displays the local date representation (see %D).
%X	Displays the local time representation (see %T).
%y	Displays the two-digit year (e.g., 92).
%Y	Displays the full year (e.g., 1992).
%Z	Displays the time zone name (for example, EDT).

Examples

Assume that it is Thursday, January 10, 1991, 6:55 PM, Eastern Standard Time. Listing 17 displays a variety of date commands and the resulting output. Output is indented to distinguish it from the date commands.

Listing 17. Samples of date output.

```
date
    Thu Jan 10 18:55:00 EST 1991
date '+%A, %B %d'
    Thursday, January 10
date '+%a, %b %d'
    Thu, Jan 10
date '+The time is %T'
    The time is 18:55:00
```

Diagnostics

Possible exit status values are:

    0   Successful completion.

    2   Failure due to an invalid command line option, too many arguments on the command line, a bad date conversion, a formatted date that was too long, or no permission to set the date.

Possible error messages include:

`No permission to set date`	The system denies you the right to set the date.
`Bad format character x`	A `format` string contained something of the form %x, but it wasn't a recognized placeholder.
`Bad date conversion in "string"`	The date and/or time specified on the command line has an invalid format (for example, the hour might be greater than 24).

Portability

AT&T System V. X/Open Portability Guide. All UNIX systems. MKS Toolkit.

Note

On machines that have a time-of-day clock with battery backup, using `date` will not necessarily change this real-time clock. You may have to use a special command that is unique to your system.

---

df—Display Amount of Free Space Remaining on Disk

Synopsis

```
df [ [device] [directory] ] ...
```

Description

df shows the amount of free space left on a disk device, and the total amount of space that the device has (both used and unused). Space is measured in units of 512 byte disk sectors. A device is specified either by name, or by naming any directory on that device. If no argument is given, space is reported for the device containing the current working directory.

Diagnostics

Possible exit status values are:

0   Successful completion.

1   Failure because of an invalid command line option, inability to access *directory*, inability to access *device*, *directory* is not a directory, or *device* is not a device.

Portability

AT&T System SVID. X/Open Portability Guide. All UNIX systems. MKS Toolkit.

See Also

```
du, ls
```

---

diff—Compare Two Text Files and Show Differences

Synopsis

```
diff [-bBefhHimnrstw] [-c[n]] [-C [n]] [-Difname] path1 path2
```

Description

diff attempts to determine the minimal set of changes needed to convert one file into another.

If either (but only one) pathname is -, diff uses the standard input for that file. If one of *path1* or *path2* is a directory, the file name of the other file is used in the specified directory. For example,

```
diff dir1/filex dir2
```

compares `dir1/filex` and `dir2/filex`.

If both names are directories, files with the same file names under the two directories will be compared. However, files in subdirectories are not compared unless the `-r` option is specified.

Output consists of descriptions of the changes in a style reminiscent of the `ed` text editor. Each set of differences begins with a line indicating the type of difference. These lines have the form

```
a1,b1 code a2,b2
```

This indicates that lines *a1* through *b1* in *path1* are different from lines *a2* through *b2* in *path2*. The *code* tells the nature of the difference. Possible codes are a (for append), d (for delete), and c (for change). For example, if lines 3-5 in *path1* have been replaced with lines 3-10 in *path2*, the set of differences would begin with the line

```
3,5c3,10
```

After the line giving the type of change, deleted or added lines are displayed. Lines from *path1* have the < prefix. Lines from *path2* have the > prefix.

Options

Options that control the output or style of file comparison are:

-b
For the purpose of comparing lines from *path1* and *path2*, trailing blanks and tabs are ignored. Adjacent groups of blanks and tabs elsewhere in input lines are considered equivalent.

-B
Checks to see whether files are text files before comparing them. If files are not printable ASCII text, they will be taken to be binary files. If the files are different, `diff` displays a message to this effect, but does not show the differences. If this option is not used and non-text files are compared, `diff` will attempt to display differences; this usually results in nonsense on the screen.

-c[*n*]
With each difference, *n* lines of context before and after each change are shown. The default value for *n* is 3. Lines removed from `path1` are marked with -, while lines added to *path2* are marked with +. Lines changed in both files are marked with !.

-C*n*	Equivalent to -c*n*.
ifname	Under this option, the output of diff is the appropriate input to the C preprocessor to generate *path2* when *ifname* is defined, and *path1* when *ifname* is not defined.
-e	Writes out a script of commands for the ed text editor, which will convert *path1* to *path2*. Output is printed to the standard output.
-f	Produces a script similar to the one produced under -e, but the line numbers are not adjusted to reflect earlier editing changes. Instead, they correspond to the line numbers in *path1*.
-h	Uses a fast algorithm instead of the normal diff algorithm. This algorithm is able to handle arbitrarily large files. However, it is not particularly good at finding a minimal set of differences in files with many differences.
-H	Uses the -h algorithm only if the normal algorithm runs out of memory.
-i	Ignores the case of letters when doing the comparison.
-m	Produces the new file with extra formatter request lines interspersed to show which lines were added (those with vertical bars in the right margin) and deleted (indicated by a * in the right margin). These are nroff/troff requests.
-n	The differences are displayed in a form that is usable by MKS RCS, the Revision Control System.
-r	Can be used when two directory names are specified on the command line. diff compares corresponding files under the directories, and recursively compares corresponding files under corresponding subdirectories under the directories.
-t	Expands tabs into spaces before doing the comparison. Tab stops are set every eight columns (columns 1, 9, 17, and so on).
-w	Ignores white space when making the comparison.

Diagnostics

Possible exit status values are:

0	No differences between the files compared.
1	The files were successfully compared and found to be different.

2   Failure due to an invalid command line argument, inability to open one of the input files, out of memory, or a read error on one of the input files.

Possible error messages include:

`Binary files` *filename* `and` *filename* `differ`	The two specified files are binary files. `diff` has compared the two files and found that they are not identical. With binary files, `diff` does not try to report the differences.
`File "`*filename*`": no such file or directory`	The specified *filename* does not exist. *filename* was either typed explicitly, or generated by `diff` from the directory of one file argument and the basename of the other.
`Common subdirectories:` *name* `and` *name*	This message appears when `diff` is comparing the contents of directories but `-r` is not specified. When `diff` discovers two subdirectories with the same name, it reports that the directories exist, but it does not try to compare the contents of the two directories.
`Insufficient memory (try diff -h)`	`diff` ran out of memory for generating the data structures used in the file differencing algorithm (see the *Limits* section). The `-h` option of `diff` will handle any size file without running out of memory.
`Internal error--cannot create temporary file`	`diff` could not create a working file. You should ensure that you either have a writable directory `/tmp` or that the environment contains a variable `TMPDIR`, which names a directory where temporary files can be stored. Also be sure that there is sufficient file space in this directory.
`Missing #ifdef symbol after -D`	No conditional label was given on the command line after the `-D` option.
`Only one file may be "-"`	Of the two input files normally found on the command line of `diff`, only one is allowed to be the standard input.

373

`Too many lines in "filename"`	diff was asked to work with a file that contains more than the maximum number of lines (see the *Limits* section). This limitation does not apply to the `-h` option, and on DOS you are unlikely to get this message because of other memory limitations.

Limits

The longest input line is 1024 bytes. Files are limited to 32000 lines, except when `-h` is specified.

Memory to compute differences is limited to 64K. This memory limit will normally further restrict the number of lines (except with `-h`).

Portability

POSIX.2. X/Open Portability Guide. All UNIX systems. MKS Toolkit. The `-H`, `-m`, and `-n` options are specific to this implementation. The `-c` and `-D` options are only available on Berkeley systems.

See Also

Hunt, J.W. and M.D. McIlroy. "An Algorithm for Differential File Comparison." `Computing Science Technical Report` 41. Bell Telephone Laboratories.

. (dot)—Execute Shell File in Current Environment

Synopsis

```
. file [argument ...]
```

Description

. (dot) executes a KornShell script in the current environment and then returns. The command is built into the shell.

Normally the shell executes a command file in a subshell so that changes to the environment by commands like cd, set, trap, and so on are local to the command file. The . (dot) command circumvents this feature.

The variable PATH is used to find the file you want to execute. If you try to use dot to execute a file under the current directory, but your search rules don't look at the current directory, the shell won't find the file. If you have this problem, you can use

```
. ./file
```

This explicitly indicates that the shell file you want to run is in the current directory.

If the command line contains an argument list *argument* ..., the positional parameters are set to this list before execution.

Diagnostics

Possible exit status values are:

1   Returned if the path search fails or *file* is unreadable.

Otherwise, the exit status is the exit status of the last command executed from the script.

Portability

POSIX.2. X/Open Portability Guide. MKS Toolkit. On DOS, .ksh is added as a suffix to *file* if *file* doesn't already have a suffix. To execute a DOS file that has no suffix, add a dot, as in

```
. file.
```

Dot (.) is a built-in command of the Bourne Shell and the KornShell on UNIX systems.

See Also

```
cd, set, trap, sh
```

du—Summarize Disk Space Usage by Directory

Synopsis

```
du [-arstx] [directory ...]
```

375

Description

du reports the amount of disk space used in the directories named on the command line. If no directories are named, du reports disk space used in the current directory. Disk space is measured in disk sectors, which are 512 bytes long.

Options

Normally, du reports disk usage in all the subdirectories of the directories under examination. The -s (summary) option suppresses the subdirectory display.

The -t option displays the total amount of space used by all the directories examined.

The -a option shows the sizes of all files under all the directories.

The -x option only reports on the disk usage of files contained on the same device as the specified directory. This has no effect on DOS, since DOS files are always on the same device as the directory that contains the files. On UNIX, files and directories may be on different devices because of links.

Unreadable directories or other errors will be ignored unless the -r option is given.

Diagnostics

Possible exit status values are:

0   Successful completion.

1   Failure because of an invalid command line option, inability to access a directory, inability to read a directory, or inability to access file information.

Portability

AT&T SVID. X/Open Portability Guide. All UNIX systems. MKS Toolkit.

See Also

```
df, ls
```

Note

The disk space usage is computed in units of disk sectors (512 bytes). The actual disk space used by files and directories may be more, because some systems allocate space in units of some multiple of a sector. On versions of DOS before 3.1, this allocation unit is usually eight sectors for disks of size 20M or greater; on DOS 3.1, it is four sectors. On UNIX System V, it is usually two sectors, while on Version 7 UNIX, it is one sector.

echo—Echo Command Arguments

Synopsis

```
echo [argument ...]
```

Description

echo writes its arguments to the standard output. You can represent special characters in the arguments by using the substitutes shown in Table 3. These substitutes are called *escape sequences* and are based on the escape sequences of the C programming language. For example,

```
echo "This is broken\nover two lines"
```

displays

```
This is broken
over two lines
```

because the \n escape sequence is replaced by a new-line character.

Table 3.   Escape sequences.

Escape Sequence	Meaning
\b	Backspace
\f	Formfeed
\n	New-line (linefeed on UNIX, carriage return and linefeed on DOS)
\r	Carriage return
\t	Horizontal tab
\ooo	Three octal digits

The final argument on the command line is followed by a new-line unless \c is found somewhere in the arguments.

Arguments are subject to standard argument expansions. For example, in

```
echo *
```

377

the * undergoes the usual wild card expansion and is replaced by the name of all files under the directory. As a result, the command displays all the file names under the directory.

As always, arguments may be enclosed in double or single quotation marks. See the sh man page for more about quoting.

Examples

```
echo *.[ch]
```

displays the names of all files with names ending in .c or .h, typically C source and header files. The names will be displayed on a single line.

echo is also convenient for passing small amounts of input to other filters.

```
echo 'this is\nreal handy' ¦ banner
```

passes two lines to the banner program.

Diagnostics

echo always returns the status value:

0   Successful completion.

Portability

POSIX.2. X/Open Portability Guide. AT&T SVID. MKS Toolkit. On older UNIX systems, the escape sequences are not available. The -n option is equivalent to \c embedded in an argument.

On UNIX systems using the C Shell, echo is built-in and follows the older UNIX echo syntax.

DOS COMMAND.COM includes a command of the same name but with a somewhat different function.

See Also

```
sh
```

env—Print Environment, Set Environment for Process

Synopsis

```
env [-] [variable=value ...] [command argument ...]
```

Description

If env is called with no arguments, it displays the value of the environment variables that it received from its parent (presumably the shell).

Arguments of the form

```
variable=value
```

let you add new variables or change the value of existing variables of the environment. If the first argument is -, the environment inherited by env is not used.

If the command line includes a *command*, env calls *command* with the arguments that appear on the command line. The accumulated environment is passed to this command. The command is executed directly as a program found in the search PATH, and is not interpreted by the shell.

Examples

Compare the output of the following two examples that illustrate the use of env:

```
env foo=bar PATH=xxxx env
env - foo=bar PATH=xxxx env
```

Diagnostics

Possible exit status values are:

0   Successful completion.

1   Failure due to an invalid command line argument, insufficient memory, or a name that is too long.

Possible error messages include:

`Too many environment variables` The maximum number of environment variables that can be specified in a single env command is 512.

Portability

POSIX.2. X/Open Portability Guide. AT&T SVID. MKS Toolkit. `printenv` on Berkeley UNIX systems has similar functionality.

See Also

```
sh
```

eval—Execute Arguments as if Typed to Shell

Synopsis

```
eval [argument ...]
```

Description

The shell evaluates each argument as it would for any command. `eval` then concatenates the resulting strings, separated by the first character of the environment variable IFS. The shell reevaluates this string and executes it in the current environment. `eval` is built into the shell.

Example

The command:

```
for a in 1 2 3
do
     eval x$a=fred
done
```

sets variables x1, x2, and x3 to `fred` (since $a expands to the value of the variable a each time through the loop). After the `for` loop is finished, entering the command

```
echo $x1 $x2 $x3
```

produces

```
fred fred fred
```

since $x1, $x2, and $x3 will expand to the value of the variables x1, x2, and x3.

Diagnostics

Possible exit status values are:

0   No arguments were specified or the specified arguments were empty strings.

Otherwise, the exit status of eval is the exit status of the command that eval executes.

Portability

POSIX.2. X/Open Portability Guide. MKS Toolkit. eval is a built-in command of the Bourne Shell and the KornShell on UNIX.

See Also

```
exec, sh
```

---

exec—Execute a Command in Place of the Current Shell

Synopsis

```
exec [command_line]
```

Description

The argument to exec is a *command line* for another command. exec executes this command without creating a new process. Some people picture this action as *overlaying* the *command* on top of the currently executing shell. Thus when the command exits, control returns to the parent of the shell. For example,

```
exec echo Bye-bye!
```

381

replaces your shell with the echo command. When echo is finished, you will be logged off unless you were in a subshell—the original shell is gone, so your session is over.

Input and output redirections are valid in the *command*. Input and output descriptors of the shell can be modified by giving only input and output redirections in the command. For example

```
exec 2>errors
```

redirects the standard error stream to errors in all subsequent commands executed by the shell. You can picture this as replacing your original shell with a shell that has its standard error stream redirected.

If no *command* is specified, exec simply returns a successful exit status. exec is built into the shell.

Diagnostics

Possible exit status values are:

0 Successful completion, or no *command* specified.

1 The *command_line* could not be executed because the command could not be found in the current PATH. If the given *command_line* is found but cannot be executed, the shell itself exits with a status of 1.

Portability

POSIX.2. X/Open Portability Guide. MKS Toolkit. exec is a built-in command of the Bourne Shell and the KornShell on UNIX.

See Also

```
sh
```

exit—Exit from the Shell

Synopsis

```
exit [expression]
```

Description

exit terminates the shell. The command is built into the shell. If exit is issued from a subshell, it terminates the subshell; otherwise it terminates the original shell, logging you off.

Diagnostics

The shell returns the value of the arithmetic *expression* to the parent process as the exit status of the shell. If *expression* is omitted, the shell returns the exit status of the last command executed.

Portability

POSIX.2. X/Open Portability Guide. MKS Toolkit. exit is a built-in command of the Bourne Shell and the KornShell on UNIX systems. However, the Bourne Shell only accepts a number, while the KornShell accepts any valid expression.

See Also

```
return, sh
```

fc—Display, Edit, and Reenter Previous Commands

Synopsis

```
fc [-e editor] [-lnr] [first] [last]

fc -s [old=new] [specifier]
```

Description

fc displays, edits, and reenters commands that have been input to an interactive shell. fc stands for *fix commands*.

The environment variable HISTSIZE controls how many commands the shell keeps in its history. If HISTSIZE is defined and has a numeric value *N*, the shell keeps the *N* most recent commands in its history file. If the variable HISTSIZE is not defined, 128 commands are accessible.

Commands are stored in a *history file*. If the HISTFILE environment variable is defined as the name of a writable file, the shell uses this as the history file. Otherwise, the history file is $HOME/sh_history, if HOME is defined and the file is writable. If the HOME variable is not defined or the file is not writable, the shell does not keep a history file.

Note that any invocation of the shell shares its history with all shells that have the same history file. This means that the contents of the history file will contain all the commands executed under different invocations of the shell. Logging in to the shell clears the existing contents of the history file when it begins execution.

Normally, the shell will not keep a history of commands executed from a profile file or the ENV file. By default, however, the shell begins recording commands in the history file if it encounters a function definition in either of these set-up files. This means that the HISTSIZE and HISTFILE variables must be set up appropriately before the first function definition. If you do not want the history file to begin at this time, use

```
set -o nolog
```

For further information, see sh and set.

The first form of fc shown in the synopsis puts you into an editor and lets you edit a range of commands. When you leave the editor, the edited commands are input to the shell. If you specify the -e *editor* option, the specified editor is used to edit the commands.

If you do not specify the -e option, fc looks for an environment variable named FCEDIT. If this variable is defined, its value is taken to be the path name of the editor you want to use; fc therefore invokes that editor. If you do not have FCEDIT defined, fc uses $ROOTDIR/bin/ed (the ed editor, not discussed in this book).

The *first* and *last* arguments let you specify one or more commands that you want to edit and reexecute by specifying a range of commands. There are several ways to specify a command for *first* and/or *last*.

1. If one of these arguments is an unsigned number, fc edits the command with that number.

2. If one of these arguments is a negative number -*n*, fc edits the command that came *n* commands before the current command.

3. If one of these arguments is a string, fc edits the most recent command beginning with that string.

The default value of *last* is *first*. If neither *first* or *last* is given, the default command range is the previous command entered to the shell.

Options

- `-e`   Specifies an editor, as explained earlier.

- `-l`   Simply displays the specified range of commands, rather than editing them or reentering them. With this option, the default command range is the 16 most recently entered commands.

- `-n`   Suppresses command numbers when commands are displayed or edited.

- `-r`   Reverses the order of the commands in the command range.

- `-s`   Reenters exactly one command without going through an editor. If a command *specifier* is given, the command to reenter is selected as described previously. Otherwise, `fc` uses the last command entered.

    `fc` can perform a simple substitution on the command before reentry by using a parameter of the form *old=new*. The first occurrence of string *old* is replaced with the string *new*.

Diagnostics

Possible exit status values are:

0   If `-l` was specified, the 0 indicates successful completion.

1   Failure because of an invalid command line option or argument, missing history file, or inability to find the desired line in the history file.

If `fc` executes one or more commands, the exit status of `fc` is the exit status of the last executed command.

Possible error messages include:

`Cannot create temporary file`   `fc` must create a temporary file to do some operations. This message is printed if `fc` cannot create the temporary file (for example, because the disk is full or because `/tmp` doesn't exist).

`No command matches string`   You asked to edit a command beginning with a particular *string*, but there was no such command in the history file.

Out of space on temporary file   fc cannot increase the size of its working file. This suggests that the disk is full.

Files

/tmp   Used to store temporary files. The ROOTDIR environment variable is used to find /tmp. The TMPDIR environment variable can be used to dictate a different directory to store temporary files.

Portability

MKS Toolkit. This is a command built into the KornShell on UNIX, but it is not built into the Bourne Shell. On UNIX, the KornShell does not truncate the history file at log in.

See Also

```
alias, print, read, sh, vi
```

Note

This command is built into the shell. r is a built-in alias for fc -s. history is a built-in alias for fc -l.

---

find—Find Files Within File Tree

Synopsis

```
find directory ... expression
```

Description

find walks through a directory structure, finding files that match a set of criteria. Each directory, file, and special file is *passed through* the expression given. If the -exec or -ok option is used, the expression has the side effect of invoking some command on the file found. In this version of `find`, an expression with no side effects automatically displays the name of any file that meets the requirements of the expression; on a stock UNIX system, you must specify the `-print` option if you want to display the file names.

Options

The expression is built from a set of options; juxtaposition of two options implies a logical AND. The `-a` and `-o` options are also used between options for logical AND and logical OR operations. You can precede an expression with a `!`, which negates the expression. You can group options with parentheses. All options, numbers, arguments, parentheses, and the terminal semicolon on the `-exec` option, must be delimited by whitespace.

Each *number* argument noted next is a decimal number, optionally preceded by a plus or minus sign. If a number is given without a sign, `find` tests for equality; a plus sign implies *greater than* and a minus sign implies *less than*.

`-print`	Displays the current file name. It is always true.
`-name` *pattern*	The current file name must match the pattern given or the expression fails. The pattern may compare glob constructs, and is compared to the final component of the name of the file. It matches as many trailing path name components as specified in *pattern*.
`-perm` *mask*	The permissions on the file must exactly match the ones given in *mask*. The mask is given in octal. On DOS file systems, the only useful permissions are `0777` (read-write for all) and `0555` (read-only for all). In this form, only the bottom nine bits of the file mode are used; an exact match is required.
	If the mask is preceded by a dash (`-`), 12 bits of the file mode are permitted. In this form, an exact match is not required; `find` only ensures that all the bits given in the mask are turned on. That is, `(mask&mode)==mask`.
	`-perm` may also be followed by a symbolic mode. For more information on symbolic modes, see the man page for `chmod`.
`-type` c	The type of the file must match the type given by the character c. Table 4 gives possible values of the character. On DOS, only directories and regular files exist.

Table 4.	File types for `find`.
Code	**Type**
b	Block-special
c	Char-special
d	Directory
f	Regular file
n	Network file
p	FIFO (named pipe)

`-links` *number*	There are *number* links to the file. DOS does not have links.
`-user` *name*	The owner of the file is *name*. *Name* can also be a userid number. The *name* on DOS must be the name of user 0 (zero), which owns all files.
`-nouser`	The file is not owned by any user with a name in `/etc/passwd`.
`-group` *name*	The group owner is *name*. The same conditions apply as for `-user`.
`-nogroup`	The file is not owned by any group with a name in `/etc/group`.
`-size` *number*	The size of the file is *number* blocks long, where a block is 512 bytes.
`-atime` *number*	The file was last accessed *number* days ago.
`-mtime` *number*	The file was last modified *number* days ago.
`-ctime` *number*	The file was last changed *number* days ago.
`-exec` *command*;	All arguments after `-exec` are taken until `find` reaches an argument consisting only of the semicolon. Any argument that is exactly `{}` (i.e., the two brace characters) is replaced by the current file name. The resulting command string is then executed. A return status of zero from this command is treated as success; a non-zero return status is treated as failure.
`-ok` *command*;	This is similar to `-exec`, but before `find` executes the command, it displays the command to make sure that you really want to go ahead. The

command string is executed only if you type in y
(for *yes*). If you type in n (for *no*), find treats the
situation as if the command was executed but
failed.

-newer *file*	Compares the modification date on this file to that on the file given. The expression is true if this file is more recently modified than *file*.
-depth	Processes directories after their contents. If present, this option is always true.
-prune	Stops traversing lower into the tree at this point. If present, this option is always true.
-xdev	Does not cross device boundaries from the root of the tree traversal. If present, this option is always true.
-none	Indicates that some action has been taken; thus the default -print action will not be invoked. If present, this option is always true.

Examples

Here is an extreme example:

```
find . "(" -name "tmp.*" -o -name "*.tmp" ")" -perm 0555 -exec
rm "{}" ";"
```

On DOS, this finds all read-only files that have tmp in either part of their names,
and deletes all such files. Various parts of this expression are quoted because of
the command-line file name expansion facility.

Diagnostics

Possible exit status values are:

0   Successful completion.

1   Failure due to an invalid command line argument, not enough
    arguments on the command line, a missing option, an argument list
    that isn't terminated properly, insufficient memory, an invalid
    character specified after -type, inability to obtain information on a
    file for -newer, permissions for -perm that do not match, inability to
    open a file for the -cpio option, an unknown user or group name,
    inability to access the PATH variable, inability to execute a command
    specified for -exec or -ok, a syntax error, or a stack overflow caused
    by an expression that is too complex.

Possible error messages include:

`bad number specification in "string"`	You specified an option that takes a numeric value (for example `-atime`, `-ctime`), but did not specify a valid number after the option.
`cannot stat file "name" for -newer`	You used a `-newer` option to compare one file to another. However, `find` could not obtain a modification time for the specified file. Typically, this happens because the file does not exist or you do not have appropriate permissions to obtain this information.

Portability

POSIX.2. X/Open Portability Guide. All UNIX systems. MKS Toolkit. Obviously, many of the options are of dubious portability to DOS, but MKS has tried to supply approximations. The `-depth` option is unique to this implementation. On DOS, `-mtime`, `-ctime`, and `-atime` are always the same.

Stock UNIX systems do not have a default action of `-print`; hence, they do not need the `-none` option. The `-a` operator is undocumented on stock UNIX systems.

grep, egrep, fgrep—Match Patterns in a File

Synopsis

```
egrep [-bcilnsvx][-e pattern][-f patternfile][pattern][file ...]

fgrep [-bcilnsvx][-e pattern][-f patternfile][pattern][file ...]

grep[-bcilnsvxEF][-e pattern][-f patternfile][pattern][file ...]
```

Description

fgrep searches files for one or more *pattern* arguments. It does not use regular expressions; instead, it does direct string comparison to find matching lines of text in the input.

egrep works in a similar way but uses extended regular expression matching, as described in Appendix C. This means that regular expression metacharacters in *pattern* will normally have their special meanings. If you want to "turn off" the special meaning of a metacharacter, put a backslash (\) in front of the character. In general, it is simpler to use fgrep when you don't need special pattern matching.

grep is a combination of fgrep and egrep. If you specify the -F option, grep behaves like fgrep. If you specify the -E option, it behaves like egrep. If you don't specify -E or -F, grep behaves like egrep but matches basic regular expressions instead of extended ones. For more information on basic and extended regular expressions, see Appendix C.

If one of the grep commands finds a line that matches a *pattern*, it displays the entire line. If the command line gives more than one input file, the command labels each output line with the name of the file in which the line appeared.

Options

All three commands accept similar options. Multiple patterns can be specified either through the -e option or by reading from a file using the -f option. The -e option also provides a means of defining a pattern that begins with - (dash). If neither of these options is specified, the first non-option argument is taken as a single search pattern.

The following options can alter the usual behavior of the grep family.

-b	Precedes each matched line with its file block number.
-c	Displays only a count of the number of lines that were matched and not the lines themselves.
-e *pattern*	Searches for lines matching the regular expression *pattern*. To search for several different patterns, use several -e options.
-f *patternfile*	Reads the file *patternfile* and searches for regular expressions given in the file. The *patternfile* should contain one regular expression per line; the command will print lines that match any or all of the regular expressions.
-i	Ignores the case of the letters being matched.
-l	Lists only the file names that contain the matching lines.

-n	Precedes each matched line with its file line number.
-s	Suppresses the display of any error messages.
-v	Complements the sense of the match; i.e., displays all lines not matching a pattern.
-x	Requires a string to match an entire line.

Examples

To display every line mentioning a classical element:

```
grep -E "earth¦air¦fire¦water" astro.log
```

Diagnostics

Possible exit status values are:

0   The command found at least one match for *pattern*.

1   The command found no matches for *pattern*.

2   Failure because an -e option was missing a *pattern*, an -f option was missing a *patternfile*, an input file could not be opened, the program ran out of memory for input or to hold a pattern, the program could not open a *patternfile*, a regular expression was invalid, a command line option was invalid, or the command line had too few arguments. If the program fails to open one input file, it tries to go on to look at any remaining input files, but it will return 2 even if it succeeds in finding matches in other input files.

Possible error messages include:

`out of space for pattern "string"`	grep did not have enough memory available to store the code needed to work with the given pattern (regular expression). The usual cause is that the pattern is very complex. Make the pattern simpler, or try to free up more memory so that grep has more space to work with.

Limits

The longest input record (line) is restricted to 1024 bytes. Longer lines are treated as two or more records.

Portability

POSIX.2. X/Open Portability Guide. All UNIX systems. MKS Toolkit.

See Also

find, Appendix C

---

head—Display Beginning of File

Synopsis

```
head [-n number] [-l] [-c] [-b] [-m] [-k] [file ...]

head [-number] [file ...]
```

Description

By default, head displays the first few lines of one or more files. The number of lines displayed is equal to the *number* value of the -n option. If no -n option is specified, 10 lines are displayed.

The second form of head is supported but is considered obsolete. It simply displays the given number of lines.

Options

-b	Displays the specified number of 512-byte blocks, rather than lines.
-c	Displays the specified number of characters, rather than lines.
-k	Displays the specified number of K (1024 bytes), rather than lines.
-l	Displays the specified number of lines. This is the default.
-m	Displays the specified number of megabytes, rather than lines.

393

Diagnostics

Possible exit status values are:

0   Successful completion.

1   Failure because of an unknown command line option, a missing or invalid *number* in an -n option, inability to open an input file, a read error on the standard input, or a write error on the standard output.

Possible error messages include:

```
Badly formed line/character
         count "string"
```
In an option of the form -n *number* or -*number*, the *number* was not a valid number.

Portability

POSIX.2. X/Open Portability Guide. MKS Toolkit. This program is a Berkeley idea and a frequent add-on to UNIX systems.

See Also

```
cat, pg, sed, tail
```

history—Display Command History

Synopsis

```
history [-nr] [first] [last]
```

Description

history displays commands that you executed previously. These commands make up your *command history*. history is built into the shell.

By specifying values for *first* and *last,* you can display a specified range of commands rather than the 16 most recent. For example,

```
history 1 10
```

displays commands 1 through 10. Commands are numbered consecutively, beginning with the first command after logging in. Therefore command 1 is the first command you executed this session, command 2 is the one after that, and so on.

Your command history is stored in the file given by the variable HISTFILE; by default, this is sh_histo on DOS, sh_history on UNIX. The number of commands kept in the file is given by the variable HISTSIZE. If HISTSIZE is not defined, the default is 128.

history is an alias defined with

```
alias history='fc -l'
```

For further information, see the manual page for fc.

Options

By default, history displays the 16 most recent commands, from the earliest to the most recent. -r displays commands in reverse order, from the most recent to the earliest.

By default, commands are numbered beginning at 1 (for the first command you execute during this KornShell session). -n displays the commands but not the command numbers.

Diagnostics

Possible exit status values are:

0   Successful completion.

1   Failure because of an invalid command line option or argument, a missing history file, or the inability to find the desired command in the history file.

Portability

POSIX.2. X/Open Portability Guide. All UNIX systems. MKS Toolkit.

See Also

```
alias, fc, sh
```

395

let—Evaluate Arithmetic Expressions

Synopsis

```
let expression ...

((expression))
```

Description

`let` evaluates each arithmetic `expression` from left to right, using long integer arithmetic with no checks for overflow. The command is built into the shell.

`let` does not generate output; it simply sets an exit status. The exit status is 0 if the last `expression` has a non-zero value, and 1 otherwise.

```
((expression))
```

is an alternate notation for

```
let "expression"
```

The double parenthesis version lets you avoid quotation marks and enhances readability.

Expressions consist of named variables, numeric constants, and operators. Variables are shell variables—see Chapter 7 for details. Numeric constants have the form

```
[base#]number
```

where `base` is a decimal integer between 2 and 36 inclusive, and `number` is any non-negative number expressed in the given base. For example, 8#12 stands for 12 base 8 (which is 10 base 10). For digits greater than 10, use the lowercase letters a through z. For example, 20#a stands for a base 20 (which is 10 base 10). The default base is 10. Undefined variables evaluate to zero.

Table 5 lists operators in decreasing order of precedence. Operators sharing a line in the table have the same precedence, and are called a *precedence group*. Evaluation within a precedence group is from left to right, except for the assignment operator, which evaluates from right to left. For example, + and - operators are in the same precedence group, so additions and subtractions are performed in the order they appear in an expression.

Table 5.   Summary of operators for `let`.

Operators	Meaning
	Unary Operators
-	Unary minus
!	Logical negation
	Arithmetic Binary Operators
* / %	Multiplication, division, and remainder
+ -	Addition, subtraction
	Relational Operators
< >	Less than, greater than
<= >=	Less than or equal, greater than or equal
== !=	Equal to, not equal to
	Assignment Operator
=	Assignment

Example

The commands

```
let a=7 'b=4*2' c=b+1
echo $a $b $c
```

produce the output

```
7 8 9
```

because $a expands to the value of variable a, $b expands to the value of b, and $c expands to the value of c. See Chapter 7 for more about variables.

Diagnostics

Possible exit status values are:

0   The last argument evaluated to a non-zero value.

1   The last argument evaluated to a zero value, or the expression contained a syntax error or tried to divide by zero.

Portability

MKS Toolkit. `let` is a command built in to the KornShell on UNIX, and is not a Bourne Shell command.

See Also

```
sh
```

ls—List File and Directory Names and Attributes

Synopsis

```
ls [-1abcCdfFgilmnopqrRstux] [pathname ...]
```

Description

`ls` is the command most often used on UNIX to list files and directories. If the *pathname* is a file, `ls` displays information on the file according to the requested options. If *pathname* is a directory, `ls` displays information on the files and subdirectories therein.

Options

If no options are specified, `ls` displays only the file name(s). If output is being sent to a pipe or a file, `ls` writes one name per line; if output is being sent to the terminal, `ls` uses `-C` (multicolumn) format.

The information displayed is at least the name; more information can be requested with various options. The many options are briefly described next. Those marked [UNIX] are only meaningful on UNIX systems, not DOS.

`-1`	Use single-column output on terminal.
`-a`	List all entries, including those starting with dot (`.`).
`-b`	Display non-printable characters in octal, as in `\`*ooo*.
`-C`	Put output into sorted columns, with output going down the columns.
`-c`	Sort according to the last time the file's attributes were modified [UNIX].

-d   Give information on a directory itself instead of its contents.

-F   Put a / at the end of each directory name and a * at the end of every executable file.

-f   Force argument to be a directory [UNIX].

-g   Do not display userid of owner [UNIX].

-i   Display inode number(s) along with file name(s) [UNIX]. (Explaining what inodes are is outside the scope of this book.)

-l   Display permissions, links, owner, group, size, time, name; see *Long Output Format*.

-m   Display the list of names in one long line, with commas separating names.

-n   Display userid and group id numbers [UNIX].

-o   Do not display group id numbers [UNIX].

-p   Put a / at the end of the directory name.

-q   Display non-printable characters as ?.

-R   List subdirectories recursively.

-r   Sort in reverse of usual order; can be combined with other options that sort the list.

-s   Display size in blocks (after the inode number but before other information).

-t   Sort by time. This is normally the time of the last modification; however, with -c it will be the time of the last change, and with -u it will be the time of the last access.

-u   Sort by last access time [UNIX].

-x   Put output into sorted columns, with output going across the rows.

Long Output Format

The output from ls -l summarizes all the most important information about the file on one line. Here is a sample and what it means:

```
-rw-rw-rw- 1 root  dir 104 Dec 25 19:32 file
```

The first character is - for files, and d for directories.

The next nine characters are in three groups of three; they describe the permissions on the file. The first group of three describes owner permissions; the second describes group permissions; the third describes other (or *world*) permissions. On DOS, there is no support for group permissions and other permissions, so these are the same as the owner. Table 6 gives characters that may appear.

399

Table 6. Possible Permission Characters.	
Character	**Meaning**
r	Permission to read file
w	Permission to write on file
x	Permission to execute file
a	Archive bit is on (file has not been backed up)
s	System file
h	Hidden file

On DOS, most of the permissions shown will be artificial, with no real meaning. Some permissions can be set with the chmod command.

After the permissions comes a number telling the number of links to a file. Because DOS does not support links, this will always be 1 when you use the MKS Tools.

Next comes the name of the owner of the file or directory. Because DOS does not support the concept of ownership, this will always be the name of the first user in the passwd file when you use the MKS Tools.

Next comes the name of the group that owns the file or directory. Because DOS does not support the concept of groups, this will always be group 0 (zero) when you use the MKS Tools.

Next comes the size of the file, expressed in bytes.

After this comes a date and time. For a directory, this is the time that the directory was created. For a file, it is normally the time that the file was last modified; however, with -c it is the time of the last change, and with -u it is the time of last access.

The last item on the line is the name of the file or directory.

Diagnostics

Possible exit status values are:

0   Successful completion.

1   Failure because of an invalid command line option, out of memory, inability to find a file's information, too many directories specified on the command line, or file/directory not found.

Possible error messages include:

```
File or directory "name"    The requested file or directory does
   is not found             not exist.
```

Cannot allocate memory for sorting	In order to sort its output, ls needs to use a certain amount of memory; this message says that there was not enough memory for the sorting operation.
Too many directory entries in "*dir*"	The maximum number of entries allowed in a directory is 2048.

Portability

POSIX.2. X/Open Portability Guide. All UNIX systems. MKS Toolkit. Because DOS doesn't keep track of much file structure information, the options -cfginou have no effect. On DOS, files and directories marked with the *hidden* attribute are treated like UNIX file names beginning with . (dot).

Note

On DOS, all files are considered executable. Thus the -F option shows a lot of * characters.

mkdir—Create a New Directory

Synopsis

```
mkdir [-p]  [-m mode] directory ...
```

Description

mkdir creates a new directory for each named *directory* argument.

Options

-m	Lets you specify permissions for the directories. The *mode* argument can have the same value as the *mode* for chmod. See the manual page for chmod for more details.
-p	Creates intermediate directory components that don't already exist. For example, if one of the *directory* arguments is dir/subdir/subsub and subdir doesn't exist already, it will be created. Directories are created with the *mode* u+wx, which gives full permissions to the owner.

401

Diagnostics

Possible exit status values are:

0   Successful completion.

1   Failure because of a missing *mode* after `-m`, an invalid *mode*, an invalid command line option, a missing *directory* name, or the inability to create the directory.

Possible error messages include:

`Path not found`	The parent directory of the named *directory* does not exist.
`Access denied`	The requested *directory* already exists or is otherwise inaccessible.
`Cannot create directory`	Some other error occurred during the creation of the directory.

Portability

POSIX.2. X/Open Portability Guide. All UNIX systems. MKS Toolkit.

A command of the same name is built into `COMMAND.COM`, which is supplied with DOS. This MKS command is provided as an alternative because it accepts multiple names and UNIX-style file names.

See Also

```
rm, rmdir
```

---

more, *pg*—Interactively View Files on a Screen

Synopsis

```
more [-n] [+n] [-p prompt] [-acefnst] [+/pattern/] [file ...]

pg [-n] [+n] [-p prompt] [-acefnst] [+/pattern/] [file ...]
```

Description

more is equivalent to

```
pg -ens -p "--More--" options file ...
```

For complete information, see pg.

Portability

POSIX.2a. MKS Toolkit. All UNIX systems.

See Also

```
cat, pg
```

mv—Rename and Move Files and Directories

Synopsis

```
mv [-fi] file1 file2

mv [-fi] file ... directory

mv -R [-fi] directory1 directory2
```

Description

mv can rename files or move them to a different directory. If you specify more than one file, the target must be a directory. mv moves the files into that directory and gives them names that match the final components of the source path names. For example,

```
mv file1 file2 dir
```

moves file1 to dir/file1 and moves file2 to dir/file2.
When a single source *file* is specified and the target is not a directory, the source is moved to the new name.

403

Options

If a destination file exists and does not have write permission, mv normally asks
if it is all right to overwrite the existing file. If you answer y or yes, the destination
is deleted and the source is moved. The -f (*force*) flag suppresses the question;
in other words, it automatically behaves as if you answered yes. The -i (interactive) flag always asks the question before overwriting an existing file, whether or
not the file is read-only.

The -R (*recursive*) flag copies a directory and all its contents (files, subdirectories,
files in subdirectories, and so on). For example,

```
mv -R dir1 dir2
```

moves the entire contents of dir1 to dir2/dir1. Any directories that need to be
created will be created in the process.

Diagnostics

Possible exit status values are:

0   Successful completion.

1   Failure because an argument had a trailing / but was not the name
     of a directory, a file could not be found, an input file could not be
     opened for reading, or an output file could not be created or
     opened for output. Other possible reasons for failure include: a read
     error occurred on an input file or a write error occurred on an
     output file, the input and output files were the same file, the input
     file was on a different file system than the output, the input file
     could not be unlinked, the input file could not be renamed, or a
     fatal error was encountered when using the -R option.

Possible fatal -R errors include:

The inability to access a file

The inability to read a directory

The inability to remove a directory

The inability to create a directory

A target that is not a directory

The source and destination directories being the same.

2   Failure because of an invalid command line option, too few arguments on the command line, a target should be a directory but isn't,
     no space left on target device, out of memory to hold the data to be
     copied, or the inability to create a directory to hold a target file.

Possible error messages include:

`Cannot allocate target string`	mv has no space to hold the name of the target file. Try to free up some memory to give mv more space.
`read only?`	You are attempting to move a file, but there is already a file with the target name and the file is read-only. If you really want to write over the existing file, enter **y** and press Enter. If you do not want to write over the existing file, enter **n** and press Enter.
`source "`*name*`" and target "`*name*`" are identical`	The source and the target are actually the same file (for example, because of links, on UNIX systems). In this case, mv will do nothing.
`unreadable directory "`*name*`"`	mv cannot read the specified directory, for example because you do not have appropriate permissions.

Portability

POSIX.2. X/Open Portability Guide. All UNIX systems. MKS Toolkit.

While you can move files around easily under DOS, it is not so easy to move a DOS directory. You can rename a directory, but you cannot move it to another directory. Renaming directories is allowed only under DOS 3.0 and later versions.

See Also

`cp, rm`

passwd—Change User Log-in Password

Synopsis

`passwd [`*username*`]`

Description

passwd changes your log-in password. The superuser (user number 0 in /etc/passwd) can also change other users' passwords. If *username* is given, passwd changes the password for that user.

If you (or the specified *username*) already have a password, passwd asks you to enter the old password. passwd then prompts you to enter a new password, then prompts you to enter the same new password to verify that you typed it correctly.

If you are the superuser, passwd prevents you from choosing a password with less than six characters.

Some versions of UNIX have facilities that do not let you change a password too soon after the last time you changed it (to prevent you from changing your password, then changing right back to the old one).

Diagnostics

Possible exit status values are:

0   Successful completion.

1   Failure because of an unknown command line option, an invalid number of arguments, an error opening or writing to a temporary working file, an error opening or writing to the password file, or an error message, such as the ones that follow.

Possible error messages include:

`Sorry.`	When passwd asked you to enter the current (old) password, you did not do so correctly.
`Passwords do not match.` `    Try again.`	The new password and the verification copy do not match. passwd asks you to enter both again.
`Password is too easily broken.` `    Try again.`	As the superuser, you tried to use too simple a password. Try something longer.
`$LOGNAME is not a user in` `    /etc/passwd`	The current setting of the LOGNAME environment variable is not one of the user names in the /etc/passwd file. In other words, you are not one of the recognized users and passwd cannot determine what your

	password should be. (This problem happens only on DOS where you are free to choose any value for LOGNAME. On UNIX, security measures ensure that the system can always identify you.)
`No permission to change user's password`	You tried to change the given user's password but you were not the superuser (user number 0 in /etc/passwd).
`Too many tries. Try again later.`	If you make too many mistakes trying to change the password, passwd simply quits. This is intended to slow down unauthorized users who are trying to guess your password.
`Password may not be changed for number weeks`	You are required to change your password when it becomes too old, on the theory that it's been around long enough for some one to guess. In this situation, people sometimes try to change their old password to something new, then immediately change back to the old one again. To prevent this, passwd will not let you change your password again until a certain amount of time has passed.

Files

`/etc/passwd` File where passwords are stored. This is found under $ROOTDIR if the ROOTDIR environment variable exists.

Portability

AT&T UNIX SVID. X/Open Portability Guide. All UNIX systems. MKS Toolkit. With the MKS Toolkit, the encrypted password is binary-compatible with the encryption scheme used on both UNIX System V.2 and 4.2 BSD systems.

See Also

log-in

Warning

For this command to work properly within a network, you should lock the /etc/passwd file while you are updating it.

pg, more—Interactively View Files on a Screen

Synopsis

pg [-*n*] [+*n*] [-p *prompt*] [-acefnst] [+/*pattern*/] [*file* ...]

more [-*n*] [+*n*] [-p *prompt*] [-acefnst] [+/*pattern*/] [*file* ...]

Description

pg makes it easy for you to read text files or output piped from another command, a screenful at a time. pg displays the contents of each *file* named on the command line. If you haven't specified any file names on the command line, pg displays the standard input. To specify the standard input explicitly, use - in place of a file name.

more is essentially the same as pg, with some small cosmetic differences. Basically, more is pg with a few more options set by default. The *Options* section that follows notes these extra defaults. Because the two commands are so similar, the rest of this manual page just talks about pg, with the understanding that everything I say applies to more as well.

Options

The following command line options control the way you read files with pg and more:

-n   Sets the window size (in other words, the number of lines displayed in each interaction) to *n* lines. When this option is not present, the default window size is one line shorter than the number of lines on the screen. Also see the w command in the *Commands* section.

-p *prompt*	Displays a prompt at the end of each screenful of text. The -p option sets this prompt to the string *prompt*. The default prompt is : for pg and --More-- for more. If the *prompt* string contains the characters %d, as in "[Page %d]", the command will replace those characters with the current page number as it displays each file.
-a	Forces pg to work in *ANSI mode*. This means of display can be more portable to non-PC-compatibles.
-c	Clears the screen before printing each new screenful of text.
-e	Eliminates the (EOF): prompt at the end of each file. This is the default for more but not for pg.
-f	Normally, lines longer than the screen width are *folded* into multiple lines. -f tells pg not to fold lines in this way. This can be useful for files containing device-specific escape sequences.
-n	Normally, when you enter a command while reading a file, you must press Enter at the end of the command. However, if you specify -n on the command line, you won't have to press Enter for most commands; pg will execute the command immediately upon receipt of the command character. This option is set by default for more.
-s	Displays all interactive command prompts in a form that stands out on the screen (most often in reverse video). This option is set by default for more.
-t	Normally, pg lets you go backward and forward when you are reading a file. However, with some types of input files (for example, pipes), there's no direct way to go back to an earlier part of the text. To make going back possible, pg stores the input from such sources in a temporary file. Inside this temporary file, you can go backward and forward, even if you couldn't do so in the original source.
-t	Tells pg not to save such input in temporary files. This saves time and disk space. However, it means that you cannot go back and read text that has disappeared from the screen.
+n	Starts printing at line n of the first file. The default is to start printing at line 1.
+/*pattern*/	Starts printing at the line containing the first occurrence of the regular expression *pattern*. Regular expressions are summarized in Appendix C.

Commands

Depending on the options that are specified on the command line, pg pauses at several points as you read through a file. It pauses between windows (screenfuls) of text, at the end of each file, and before starting any file other than the first. At these pauses, pg lets you enter commands to dictate what pg does next.

Typically, you will just press Enter when pg pauses. This tells pg to display the next screenful of text. If you want a different action, you can type in one of the commands described in this section.

When more pauses, entering a space displays the next screenful of text. Pressing Enter only displays a single line.

You can precede these commands with an optional sign (+ or -), followed by an optional numeric address. Addresses are measured in *screenfuls*. Normally, an address without a sign refers to an *absolute* position (counting from the beginning of the file). An address with a sign is a *relative* position, relative to the current position in the file. Thus 1 is an absolute line number, referring to the first screenful of text in the file. -1 is a relative position referring to the screenful of text immediately before the current screen, and +1 is the screenful of text immediately after the current one.

As you type in commands, you can make corrections with the standard *erase* and *kill* characters. The complete set of interactive commands is:

h	Displays a summary of the interactive commands.
q	Quits pg immediately.
Q	Same as q.
!*command*	Executes the string *command* as if it were typed to the default shell. You must press Enter at the end of the line, whether or not you specified the -n option on the pg command line.
d	Displays a half-screenful of text. The address is measured in half-screenfuls and defaults to the next half screenful.
Ctrl-D	Same as d.
l	With no address, l displays the next line of the file. With an address, l displays a screenful starting at the position addressed, with distances measured in lines rather than screenfuls.
$	Displays the last screenful of text in the file.
.	Redisplays the most recent screenful of text (redraws the screen).
Ctrl-L	Same as . (dot).
s *file*	Saves the entire contents of the file you are looking at in *file*. You must press Enter at the end of the line,

	whether or not you specified the -n option on the pg command line.
n	If no address is specified, this starts displaying the next file. If an address *n* is specified, it must be an unsigned number, and pg displays the *n*th next file, counting from the current file.
p	If no address is specified, this starts displaying the previous file. If an address *n* is specified, it must be an unsigned number, and pg displays the *n*th previous file, counting from the current file.
w	If an address is specified, w sets the window size to that (unsigned) value. In any case, it displays the next screenful of (the new) window size lines.
/pattern/[tmb]	Searches forward within the current file for the first occurrence of a line matching the regular expression *pattern*. An optional character on the end controls where the matching line is displayed on the screen. The letter t is the default and displays the line at the top of the screen. m displays it in the middle of the screen. b displays it at the bottom of the screen. When no letter is present, pg uses the last letter entered (or t if no letter has been entered). You must press Enter at the end of the line, whether or not you specified the -n option on the pg command line.
?pattern?[tmb]	Same as the previous example, but searches backward instead of forward.
^pattern^[tmb]	Same as ?pattern?[tmb].

Examples

The following interactive commands illustrate pg's flexibility. Suppose that you entered the command

```
pg -n *.c
```

and that there are a large number of files with the .c suffix in the current directory.

```
1
```

redisplays the first screenful of the current file.

```
-4
```

goes back four screens in the current file and displays a screenful of text.

```
p
```

displays the first screenful of the previous file.

```
10w
```

sets the window size to 10 lines.

```
/Fred/m
```

finds the first line containing `Fred` after the current position in the file, and displays a screenful of text with that line in the middle of the screen.

Diagnostics

Possible exit status values are:

0   Successful completion.

1   Failure because of an unknown command line option, insufficient memory, inability to create a temporary file, inability to access the terminal, or a missing *prompt* after a -p option.

Portability

POSIX.2. X/Open Portability Guide. MKS Toolkit. pg is available on UNIX System V, while more is available on Berkeley UNIX systems.

On DOS, the character erase is Backspace and the line kill is Esc.

On DOS, if the ansi.sys driver (or its equivalent) is loaded, pg automatically uses ANSI-compatible escape sequences. Otherwise, BIOS calls are used to write characters and attributes on the screen. The -a option forces ANSI mode.

Files

/tmp/pg*   Temporary files to allow backward reading. The /tmp directory is found using the ROOTDIR environment variable. You can specify a different temporary directory using the TMPDIR environment variable. For more information, see Appendix E.

See Also

```
alias, head, sh, tail, vi
```

pr—Print and Format Files

Synopsis

```
pr [+n] [-n] [-h header] [-adFmprtW] [-ecn] [-icn]
[-ncn] [-wn] [-on] [-ln] [-sc] [file ...]
```

Description

pr displays the given files on its standard output in a paginated form. pr uses the standard input if no files are given on the command line, or if - appears in place of a file name.

Each file is formatted into pages. Each page has a header containing the file name and its last modified date, and the current page and line number. Note that pr only formats the pages and displays them on standard output; if you want to get hard copy, you must use an lp or lpr command to send pr's output to the printer.

By default, output is placed in columns of equal width separated by at least one space. If there is more than one column, each line is truncated to fit the column. pr can order items either down the columns or across the page. It can also use multiple columns to represent different files.

Options

+n	Starts printing with the *n*th page of each file; in other words, it skips the first *n*-1 pages. The default for *n* is 1.
-n	Prints *n* columns of output.
-a	Orders input lines across the page when they are output. If -a is not specified, pr orders items down columns (vertically instead of horizontally).
-d	Double-spaces output.
-ecn	Expands tabs on input. If given, *c* is taken to be the character indicating a tab; the default is the ASCII horizontal tab character. Tabs are set every *n* positions; the default for *n* is 8. This option is always on, and is used to change the character and settings. Every occurrence of the input tab character is turned into a sequence of spaces.
-F	Folds lines if they are wider than the column width. Each separate part of the line is treated as a separate line. If you do not use -F or -s, pr simply truncates (chops off) lines that are too wide for the column.

413

-h *header*	Uses the *header* string on each succeeding page header. This option can be specified between files; however, if you also specify -m, only the final -h option has an effect. If you do not specify -h, pr creates a header that contains the name of the current input file.
-i*cn*	Replaces white space with tabs on output. If given, *c* is taken to be the character indicating a tab; the default is the ASCII horizontal tab character. Tabs are set every *n* positions; the default for *n* is 8. If this tab character differs from the input tab character and the input contains this tab character, the output is likely to be messy.
-l*n*	Sets the number of lines per page of output. The default is 66. The actual number of lines printed per page is this number less five lines for the headers and two for the trailers. If you specify both -t and -l, all lines of the page are used.
-m	Outputs each file in its own column down the page. -m overrides the -a option, and forces the -*n* option to the number of files given.
-n*cn*	Numbers the lines of each file. Each number is *n* characters wide; the default for *n* is 5. Each line number is separated from the rest of the line by the character *c*; the default is the ASCII horizontal tab character. If *c* is the same as the input tab character, pr follows the line number with the number of spaces needed to reach the next tab stop. These spaces can in turn be replaced by the output tab character if you specify -i. For multicolumn output, pr adds line numbers to each column. If you specify both -m and -n, pr only puts line numbers in the first column.
-o *n*	Offsets each line of output by *n* character positions.
-p	Pauses between pages if output is going to a terminal device. pr sounds the terminal's bell, then waits for you to press Enter.
-r	Does not print any error messages that might arise when opening files.
-s*c*	Normally each column is padded with spaces or truncated to the exact column width. With -s, each column is printed at its correct length and separated from the next column with the character *c*. The default for *c* is

the ASCII horizontal tab character. The given character *c* is never replaced by the output tab character.

-*t*   Does not print headers or trailers. The full length of the page is used for file output.

-w*n*   Sets the width of the page to *n*. The default is 72. The width is ignored for output using the -s option. It is also ignored for single-column output, unless you specify the -F option.

-W   Normally, lines are truncated at the column width if you don't use -s. -W folds lines instead; each separate part of the line is treated as a separate line.

Diagnostics

Possible exit status values are:

0   Successful completion.

1   Failure because of a syntax error, insufficient memory, insufficient line width, or a write error on the standard output.

Possible error messages include:

```
Missing header
```
You specified -h but did not supply a *header* string after the -h.

```
Width is insufficient
```
The line is not wide enough to hold the given number of columns with the given column width; or a column is not wide enough to hold the minimum amount of data.

Files

/dev/tty   pr writes prompts to this on UNIX (which means that prompts appear on your terminal).

CON: pr writes prompts to this on DOS (which means that prompts should appear on your terminal).

Portability

POSIX.2. X/Open Portability Guide. MKS Toolkit. This version of pr is compatible with UNIX System V, which differs substantially from previous UNIX prs.

See Also

cat

print—Output Arguments from the Shell

Synopsis

```
print [-nprsR] [-u[descriptor]] [argument ...]
```

Description

If print is called without options or with only the - option, the command outputs each *argument* to the standard output using the same escape conventions as echo. In this form, print and echo have the same functionality; see the echo man page. print is built into the KornShell.

Options

The difference between print and echo is that print takes several options.

If you specify the -n option, print does not automatically add a new-line to the end of the output.

With the -r and -R options, print ignores escape sequences. Also, with -R, print treats all subsequent command line options (except -n) as arguments rather than as options.

The -p option sends output to a co-process. This is not useful on DOS, because DOS does not have co-processes.

If you specify the -s option, print appends its output to the command history file rather than sending the output to the standard output. Similarly, if you use -u[*descriptor*], print writes its output to the file corresponding to the file *descriptor*. The default file descriptor is 1. File descriptors are single digits between 0 and 9.

Diagnostics

Possible exit status values are:

0   Successful completion.

1   Failure because of an invalid command line option, an invalid *descriptor* specified with -u, or a non-existent co-process.

Possible error messages include:

`Cannot print on file descriptor ...`	You tried to print on a file descriptor that was not opened for writing.
`History not available`	You specified the -s option to write into a history file, but at present you are not using a history file.

Portability

MKS Toolkit. print is a built-in command of the KornShell on UNIX, but not of the Bourne Shell.

See Also

echo, fc, read, sh

*pwd—*Display Working Directory

Synopsis

pwd

Description

pwd writes the path name of the current working directory to the standard output.

Diagnostics

Possible exit status values are:

0   Successful completion.

1   pwd cannot determine the current working directory.

Portability

POSIX.2. X/Open Portability Guide. All UNIX systems. MKS Toolkit.
On DOS, the CD command in COMMAND.COM has a similar function. On DOS, the output of PWD includes the current drive specification.

See Also

```
sh
```

Note

pwd exists both as a command built into the shell and as a separate command. In the shell, pwd is defined as:

```
alias pwd='print - $PWD'
```

r—Edit and Reexecute Previous Command

Synopsis

```
r [old=new] [specifier]
```

Description

The r command reexecutes a command that you ran previously, possibly editing the command first. Commands are obtained from your *command history* file; see the man pages for fc and sh for more details.

The *specifier* argument tells which command you want to reexecute. It can have any of the following forms:

- An unsigned number: r runs the command that has that number.

- A negative number -*n*: r runs the command that came *n* commands before the current one.

- A character string: r runs the most recent command line beginning with that string.

If you do not give a *specifier*, r runs the most recent command.

The *old=new* feature lets you edit a command before running it. *old* and *new* must be character strings. r replaces the first occurrence of *old* with *new* and then reexecutes the command.

Examples

```
r sh
```

Runs the most recent command beginning with the characters sh. The sh could be the whole command name, or it could be part of a longer command name (for example, shift).

```
cp file1 /dir
r 1=2
r 2=3
```

This is equivalent to

```
cp file1 /dir
cp file2 /dir
cp file3 /dir
```

Compare this with

```
cp file1 /dir/file1
r 1=2
```

which is equivalent to

```
cp file1 /dir/file1
cp file2 /dir/file1
```

Because r only replaces the first occurrence of the *old* string 1, the second 1 does not change. This shows that you have to be careful when you use the substitution feature.

r is an alias built into the shell. It is defined as

```
alias r='fc -s'
```

Diagnostics

Possible exit status values are:

0   Successful completion.

1   Failure because of an invalid command line option or argument, missing history file, or inability to find the desired command in the history file.

Portability

POSIX.2. X/Open Portability Guide. All UNIX systems. MKS Toolkit.

See Also

```
alias, fc, sh
```

---

read—Input a Line to the Shell

Synopsis

```
read [-prs] [-u[descriptor]] [variable?prompt] [variable ...]
```

Description

When read is called without options, it reads one line from the standard input, breaks the line into fields, and assigns the fields to each *variable* in the order they appear on the command line.

To determine where to break the line into fields, read uses the built-in variable IFS (which stands for *Input Field Separator*). When read encounters any of the characters in IFS, it interprets that character as separating the end of one field from the beginning of the next. The default value of IFS is a blank character and a tab, indicating that fields are separated by blanks and/or tabs.

If read finds two IFS characters in a row, it usually assumes there is an empty field between the two characters. For example, if IFS is :, the input a::b has three fields: a, an empty field, and b. However, if IFS contains spaces and/or tabs, a sequence of multiple spaces and/or tabs is considered to be a single field separator. For example, "a   b" is considered to have two fields, even though there are several spaces between the a and the b.

The *n*th `variable` in the command line is assigned the nth field read in. If there are more input fields than there are variables, the last variable is assigned all of the unassigned fields. If there are more variables than fields, the extra variables are assigned the null string (" ").

When no variables appear on the command line, `read` assigns the input to an environment variable named `REPLY`.

Options

If you specify the `-r` option, input is read in *raw mode*. This means that escape sequences are ignored. For example, a backslash (\) is simply part of the input, not a line continuation character.

If you specify the `-p` option, input is read from a co-process. This is meaningless on DOS because DOS doesn't have co-processes.

If you specify the `-s` option, `read` adds its input to the command history file as well as assigning the input to the variables.

If you specify `-u[`*descriptor*`]`, `read` takes its input from the file associated with the single digit file *descriptor*, rather than from the standard input. The default file descriptor is 0.

The first `variable` parameter may take the form

```
variable?prompt
```

If so, `read` outputs the string *prompt* to prompt for input, provided that the shell is interactive. The *prompt* is sent to the file *descriptor* if it is open for write and is a terminal device. If you do not specify `-u`*descriptor*, `read` writes the prompt to the standard error.

Example

Listing 18 shows a short sequence of commands that provide a list of users from the `/etc/passwd` file.

Listing 18.   Listing the system's users.

```
IFS=';'
while read name junk
do
      echo $name
done </etc/passwd
```

Diagnostics

Possible exit status values are:

0   Successful completion.

1   Failure due to an invalid command line argument, end-of-file on input, an invalid `variable`, an incorrect `descriptor` specified after -u, or a missing co-process.

Possible error messages include:

`Cannot read on file` `descriptor ..."`	You tried to read a file descriptor that was not opened for reading.

Portability

POSIX.2. X/Open Portability Guide. MKS Toolkit. `read` is a built-in command of the Bourne Shell and the KornShell on UNIX. The Bourne Shell does not implement parameters of the form `variable?prompt`, or any options.

See Also

`continue`, `fc`, `print`, `sh`

Note

This command is built into the shell.

---

return—Return from Shell Function or Shell

Synopsis

`return [expression]`

Description

`return` returns from a shell function. It is built into the shell. The exit status is the value of `expression`. The default value of `expression` is the exit status of the last command executed.

Diagnostics

Possible exit status values are:

1   Returned when the `return` command is not part of a function.

Otherwise, the current function will return the value of *expression*. If no *expression* is given, the exit status will be the exit status of the last command executed.

Portability

POSIX.2. X/Open Portability Guide. MKS Toolkit. `return` is a built-in command of the Bourne Shell and KornShell on UNIX.

See Also

```
exit, sh
```

rm—Remove Files

Synopsis

```
rm [-firR] file ...
```

Description

`rm` removes (deletes) the files named on the command line.

Options

If you specify `-r`, names on the command line may be directories as well as files. If so, `rm` removes all files and subdirectories under the given directories. The option `-R` is exactly equivalent to `-r`.

Normally, if you ask `rm` to remove a read-only file, `rm` asks if you are sure you want to delete the file. Type **y** or **yes** if you really want the file deleted. The `-f` option tells `rm` to delete read-only files immediately, without asking for confirmation. `-f` also suppresses error messages for files that do not exist.

The `-i` (interactive) option displays the name of every file that might be deleted and prompts you for confirmation. Enter **y** or **yes** if you really want to delete the file. Enter **n** or **no** if you want to keep the file.

423

Diagnostics

Possible exit status values are:

0   Successful completion.

1   Failure because of an invalid command line option, no `file` names specified, inability to remove a file, an attempt to remove a directory without specifying `-r`, or a fatal error during an operation when `-r` is specified (either the inability to find file information or the inability to read a directory).

Portability

POSIX.2. X/Open Portability Guide. All UNIX systems. MKS Toolkit.

See Also

```
cp, mv, rmdir
```

rmdir—Remove Directory

Synopsis

```
rmdir [-p] directory ...
```

Description

`rmdir` removes (deletes) each requested `directory`. `rmdir` only works on directories that are entirely empty (containing no files or subdirectories).

If `-p` is specified, `rmdir` removes all intermediate component directories. For example

```
rmdir -p abc/def/ghi
```

is equivalent to

```
rmdir abc/def/ghi
rmdir abc/def
rmdir abc
```

Diagnostics

Possible exit status values are:

0   Successful completion.

1   Failure because *directory* is not a directory, or because it still contains files or subdirectories.

2   Failure because of an invalid command line option, or no *directory* names specified.

Possible error messages include:

`Non-empty directory`	A directory contains files or subdirectories. Use `rm -r` to remove the directory.
`No such directory`	The requested *directory* does not exist or is otherwise inaccessible.
`Current directory illegal`	Indicates that you should use `cd` to change to another directory before removing the current directory.

Portability

POSIX.2. X/Open Portability Guide. All UNIX systems. MKS Toolkit. A command of the same name is built into the `command.com` shell supplied with DOS. However, the MKS version accepts multiple directory names and UNIX-style file names.

See Also

```
mkdir, rm
```

sed—Stream Editor (Non-interactive)

Synopsis

```
sed [-En] [script] [-e script] [-f scriptfile] [file ...]
```

Description

sed edits text files. More precisely, sed reads a set of editing commands from *script* and applies those commands to each *file* named on the command line. If the command line does not specify any files, the editing commands in *script* are applied to the standard input. A script is simply a list of one or more sed commands. For example, in

```
sed "s/Athletics/Blue Jays/g" file
```

the script is the instruction

```
s/Athletics/Blue Jays/g
```

which is performed on the given file.

Commands in a sed script are similar to commands of the interactive text editor ed, but sed commands view the input text as a stream of characters rather than a directly addressable file.

Options

If -E is specified, sed uses extended regular expressions. Otherwise, it uses basic regular expressions. For more information, see Appendix C.

Each input line is read into a special area known as the *pattern buffer*. A second area, called the *hold buffer*, is used by certain sed commands [gGhHx]. By default, the final contents of the pattern buffer are written to the standard output after each pass through the script. The -n option prevents this automatic write; with -n, sed only produces output through explicit commands in the *script* [acilnpPr].

There are three mutually exclusive ways to specify the script:

- If the -f option appears on the command line, the script is read from the file named *scriptfile*. Only one such file is allowed.

- If the -e option appears on the command line, the string argument after the -e is used as the sed *script*. By specifying several -e options, you can create a script that contains several commands.

- If neither -e nor -f appears on the command line, the first argument (after -E and/or -n) is used as the script.

Addresses

As in ed, sed commands may begin with zero, one, or two addresses. Zero-address commands reference every input line. One-address commands select only those lines matching that address. Two-address commands select those input line ranges commencing with a match on the first address up to an input line matching the second address, inclusive. Permissible addressing constructions are:

n	Refers to the *n*th input line.
$	Refers to the last input line.
/regexp/	Selects an input line that matches the specified regular expression *regexp*. If you do not want to use slash (/) characters around the regular expression, you can use a different pair of characters but you must put a backslash (\) around the first one. For example, if you want to use % characters to enclose the regular expression, write \%*regexp*%.

Commands

Each line of a script contains up to two addresses, a single letter command, possible command modifiers, and a terminating new-line character. The new-line is optional in script strings that are typed directly on the command line.

The following list shows the commands and the maximum number of addresses they can take. You can give a command fewer than the number of addresses specified, but not more. Addresses appear before the command name; for example, the b command is shown as

```
a,bb label
```

This shows that b can take a range of addresses *a*, *b*, and is followed by another argument written as *label*.

aa\	The append command copies subsequent text lines from the script to the standard output. sed outputs the text after all other script operations are completed for the line and just before the next record is read. If you want to append several lines of input text, put a \ on the end of every line but the last. The first line without a \ character is taken as the end of the input text. The \ characters on the ends of lines are not considered to be part of the text.
a,bb label	The branch command branches to the given label. Labels are created with the : command.
a,bc\	The change command changes the addressed lines by deleting the contents of the pattern buffer (input line) and writing new text on the standard output. The new text lines are input in the same way as for a\.

When two addresses are specified, sed delays text output until the final line in the range of addresses; otherwise, the behavior would probably surprise many users. sed skips the rest of the script for each addressed line.

a,*b*d	The delete command deletes the contents of the pattern buffer (input line). The script is restarted with the next input line.
a,*b*D	This is identical to the d command except that sed only deletes the pattern buffer up to and including the first new-line. sed then starts the script again from the beginning and applies it to the text left in the pattern buffer.
a,*b*g	sed copies the text in the hold buffer into the pattern buffer, overwriting the pattern buffer's original contents.
a,*b*G	sed appends the text in the hold buffer to the end of the pattern buffer.
a,*b*h	This copies the text in the pattern buffer into the hold buffer, overwriting the hold buffer's original contents.
a,*b*H	This appends the text in the pattern buffer onto the end of the hold buffer.
*a*i\	The insert command is identical to the a\ command, except that sed outputs the text immediately.
a,*b*l	The list command prints the pattern buffer (input line) onto the standard output in a way that makes non-printable characters visible.
a,*b*n	After copying the pattern buffer to the standard output, sed reads the next line of input into the pattern buffer.
a,*b*N	sed appends the next line of input to the end of the pattern buffer.
a,*b*p	The print command places the text in the pattern buffer onto the standard output. This form of output is not disabled by the -n option. If you do not use -n, p prints the pattern buffer twice.
a,*b*P	This operates like the p command, except that it prints the text in the pattern buffer only up to and including the first new-line character.

*a*q   The quit command quits `sed`. The rest of the script is
                          skipped, and no more input lines are read. Outstand-
                          ing operations (for example, `a\`) are still honored.

a,*b*r *file*   The read command reads text from `file` and places
                          this text onto the standard output after all other script
                          commands have been processed. The timing of this
                          operation is analogous to the `a` command.

a,*b*s/*regexp*/*substitution*/[g*p*n][*wfile*]

                          The substitute command puts the string
                          substitution in place of the first occurrence of text
                          matching the regular expression *regexp*. If *regexp*
                          contains the sequence `\n`, the sequence matches an
                          embedded new-line in the pattern buffer (for ex-
                          ample, one resulting from an `N` command). The `s`
                          command can be followed by a combination of the
                          following:

                          p   This executes the print (p) command only if a
                                 successful substitution occurs.

                          g   Puts *substitution* in place of all occur-
                                 rences matching *regexp*, instead of just the
                                 first.

                          n   Puts *substitution* in place of only the *n*th
                                 occurrence matching *regexp*.

                          wfile If a substitution occurs, the contents of the
                                 pattern buffer (after substitution) are written
                                 to the end of the specified *file*.

a,*b*t *label*   The test command branches to the indicated *label* if
                          any successful substitution has occurred since reading
                          the last input line or executing the last `t` command.

a,*b*w *file*   The write command writes the text in the pattern
                          buffer to the end of *file*.

a,*b*x   The exchange command switches the text in the hold
                          buffer with the text in the pattern buffer.

a,*b*y/*set1*/*set2*/   This construction transliterates any input character
                          occurring in *set1* to the corresponding element of
                          set2. The sets must be the same length. For example,

                          ```
                          y/abcdefghijklmnopqrstuvwxyz/
                          ABCDEFGHIJKLMNOPQRSTUVWXYZ/
                          ```

                          changes lowercase letters to their uppercase counter-
                          parts.

429

`a,b{`	This command groups all commands until the next matching } command, so that the entire group is executed only if the { command is selected by its address(es).
`: label`	This command has no action. It serves only as a placeholder for the *label* that may be the destination of a b or t command.
`a,b!cmd`	The negation command executes the specified *cmd* only if the addresses do not select the ! command.
`#`	Any empty script line is treated as a comment. A script line beginning with the # character is also treated as a comment, except for the first line in a script. If the first line in a script is #n, it is equivalent to specifying -n on the command line.
`a=`	This writes the decimal value of the current line number onto the standard output.

Examples

Here is a filter to switch political allegiance:

```
sed 's/democrat\(ic\)*/republican/g'
```

Diagnostics

Possible exit status values are:

0	Successful completion.
1	Failure because of any of the following:

Missing script

Too many script arguments

Too few arguments

Unknown option

Cannot use both -f and -e options

Can't open script file

Must have at least one (non-comment) command

Label not found in script

Unknown command

Cannot nest ! command

\ must terminate command

End-of-file in command

Command needs a label

Badly formed file name

Cannot open file

Insufficient memory to compile command

Bad regular expression delimiter

No remembered regular expression

Regular expression error

Insufficient memory for buffers

y command must be followed by a printable character as separator

Non-matching { and } commands

Garbage after command

Too many addresses for command

New-line or end-of-file found in pattern

Possible error messages include:

`badly formed file name` `for "command" command`	The given command required a file name, but its operand did not have the syntax of a file name.
`cannot nest "!" command`	A ! command cannot contain a ! command of its own.
`"command" command needs` `a label`	The specified command required a label, but you did not supply one.
`must have at least one` `(non-comment) command`	The input to sed must contain at least one active command (i.e., a command that is not a comment).
`no remembered regular` `expression`	You issued a command that tried to use a remembered regular expression, such as s//abc. However, there is no remembered regular expression yet. To correct this, change the command to use an explicit regular expression.

Portability

POSIX.2. X/Open Portability Guide. All UNIX systems. MKS Toolkit. The -E option is unique to this version of sed.

See Also

```
diff, grep, vi
```

set—Set Shell Flags and Positional Parameters

Synopsis

```
set [±aefhkmnpstuvx-] [±o[ flag]] [parameter ...]
```

Description

If set is called without arguments, it displays the names and values of all the environment variables. Otherwise, set changes the values or the characteristics of shell variables or options.

Options

Arguments of the form -option set each shell flag specified as an option. Similarly, arguments of the form +option turn off each of the shell flags specified as an option.

Shell flags are also turned on with command line arguments of the form -o flag and turned off with command line arguments of the form +o flag. The command set -o lists the shell flags that are currently set. If a *parameter* list is given, the positional parameters are set to the ones specified.

The positional parameters and all the shell flags except -s may be set on the shell command line at invocation.

The following list summarizes shell flags. The manual page for sh gives further information on many of these flags.

-a   All subsequently defined variables are set for export.

-e   If the shell is non-interactive, this tells the shell to execute the ERR trap and then exit. This flag is disabled when reading profiles.

-f	This disables file name generation.
-h	All commands used from now on become *tracked aliases*. See the alias manual page for an explanation of tracked aliases.
-k	Tells the shell that assignment parameters can be placed anywhere on the command line and will still be included in the environment of the command.
-m	Each background job is run in a separate process group and is reported on when completed.
-n	If the shell is non-interactive, commands are read but not executed.
-p	Resets PATH variable to a default value, disables processing of $HOME/.profile ($HOME/profile.ksh on DOS), and uses the file /etc/suid_profile (/etc/suid_pro.ksh on DOS) instead of the file in the ENV variable.
-s	Sorts the positional parameters.
-t	Exits after reading and executing one command.
-u	Tells the shell to give an error message if an unset parameter is used in a substitution.
-v	Shell input lines are printed as they are read.
-x	Commands and their arguments are printed as they are executed.
-	Turns off the -v and -x flags. Also, parameters that follow this option do not set shell flags, but are assigned to be positional parameters (see the manual page for sh).
—	Parameters that follow this option do not set shell flags, but are assigned to positional parameters.

The following options can be turned on with -o or turned off with +o.

allexport	Same as the -a option.
errexit	Same as the -e option.
bgnice	Background jobs run at a lower priority.
ignoreeof	Shell does not exit on end-of-file.
keyword	Same as the -k option.
markdirs	Trailing / added to file name-generated directories.
monitor	Same as the -m option.
noclobber	When set, the output redirection operator > will not overwrite an existing file. Use the alternate operator >¦ to force an overwrite.

433

noexec	Same as the -n option.
noglob	Same as the -f option.
nolog	When set, function definitions are not recorded in the history file.
nounset	Same as the -u option.
protected	Same as the -p option.
verbose	Same as the -v option.
trackall	Same as the -h option.
vi	Specifies vi style in-line editor for command entry.
xtrace	Same as the -x option.

See Appendix F for a description of the effect of setting the vi option.

Diagnostics

Possible exit status values are:

0   Successful completion.

1   Failure due to an invalid command line argument.

Portability

POSIX.2. X/Open Portability Guide. MKS Toolkit. set is a built-in command of the Bourne Shell and KornShell on UNIX. Several shell flags are extensions only in the KornShell: noglob, ignoreeof, trackall, monitor, bgnice, and markdirs.

The -m and -o bgnice options are not useful on DOS. Under DOS, the value of the ROOTDIR environment variable determines where to find the /etc directory.

See Also

alias, export, sh, trap, typeset

Note

This command is built into the shell.

sh—Invoke the KornShell (Command Interpreter)

Synopsis

```
sh [-c cmdstring] [-o optname] [-aefhikmnprstuvx] [-L[-0
executable]] [-R address] argument ...

rsh [-c cmdstring] [-o optname] [-aefhikmnprstuvx] [-L[-0
executable]] [-R address] argument ...
```

Description

This manual page for the KornShell is divided into the following subsections:

- *Options and Invocation*
- *Command Syntax*
- *Command Execution*
- *Quoting*
- *Directory Substitution*
- *Parameter Substitution*
- *Arithmetic Substituion*
- *Command Substitution*
- *File Descriptors and Redirection*
- *File Name Generation*
- *Variables*
- *Shell Execution Environments*
- *Built-In Commands*

Subsections dealing with substituting or interpreting input are arranged in the order in which the shell performs those substitutions and interpretations.

Much of the functionality of the shell is provided through built-in commands like cd and alias. The man pages for such commands may describe additional features of the shell that are not described in this man page.

Options and Invocation

This implementation of the KornShell is a sophisticated command interpreter that accepts all the input accepted by the Bourne Shell; as well as many new kinds of input. It can serve as a replacement for the standard DOS command interpreter, `COMMAND.COM`.

Normally you invoke the shell by logging in. You can also invoke the shell by typing an explicit `sh` command.

Some people find it useful to copy the `sh.exe` file into a file named `rsh.exe`. If you invoke the shell under the name `rsh`, the shell operates in *restricted* mode. This mode is described in connection with `-r` in a later paragraph.

If the shell is invoked with the `-L` option, it is a *log-in shell*. (You also get a log-in shell if you invoke the shell with a name that begins with the `-` character, but that is beyond the scope of this book.) A log-in shell begins by executing the file

```
/etc/profile       on UNIX
/etc/profile.ksh   on DOS
```

It then executes

```
$HOME/.profile      on UNIX
$HOME/profile.ksh   on DOS
```

using the `.` command (see the manual page for `dot`). If there is no profile file under $HOME, the shell searches the current directory for

```
.profile      on UNIX
profile.ksh   on DOS
```

and executes this file with the `.` command, if it exists. The KornShell does not issue an error message if any of these files cannot be found.

You can use the preceding profile files to customize your session with the KornShell. For example, your profile files can set options, create aliases, or define functions and variables.

If there is at least one argument on the `sh` command line, `sh` takes the first argument as the name of a shell script to execute. (The exception to this is when `-s` is used. See the following list.) Any additional arguments are assigned to the positional parameters. These usually serve as arguments to the shell script. See the *Parameter Substitution* section for information about positional parameters, and see the `set` man page for information about changing these parameters.

If `sh` finds the ENV environment variable set when it begins execution, `sh` executes the file named by this variable (see the *Variables* section).

The shell understands the following options on the command line:

-c *cmdstring*   Executes *cmdstring* as if it were an input line to the shell, and then exits. This is used by programs (such as editors) that want to call the shell for a single command.

-i   Invokes an *interactive shell*, as opposed to running a shell script. With -i, the shell catches and ignores interrupts (Ctrl-Break). Without -i, an interrupt terminates the shell. For shells that read from the terminal, -i is the default.

-r   Invokes a *restricted shell*. (As noted earlier, you can also invoke a restricted shell by using the name rsh.) In a restricted shell, you cannot do the following: use the cd command; change the values of the variables ENV, PATH, or SHELL; use > or >> to redirect output; or specify command names that contain /. These restrictions do not apply during execution of your *profile* files.

-s   Normally, if there is at least one *argument* to the shell, the first such *argument* is the name of a file to execute. With the -s option, the shell reads a line from the standard input and all arguments are assigned to the positional parameters.

-L   Makes the shell a *log-in shell*, as described previously.

-R *address*   Applies under only DOS. It lets the shell's code space be relocated so that programs the shell invokes have an additional 64K space for execution. If *address* is zero, the code is placed at the highest part of normal DOS memory. As the shell completes each command, code within the shell's data area checksums the code in high memory. If that checksum fails, the code is reloaded from the original disk file holding the shell program. At start-up time the shell opens this file; thus at reload time it simply reads from the appropriate location in the open file. This means that you should only use -R with the shell running off a hard disk.

If *address* is non-zero, it is assumed to be a hex segment address. Rather than being located at high DOS memory, the text is placed at this given address. sh assumes that this memory exists and is not part of any DOS memory chain. *sh* checksums the memory but does not reload on checksum failure. This is useful if you have a 64K memory area discontiguous from normal DOS memory, or a 386 protected mode program that causes the area to page to high memory.

-0 *file* The -0 (zero) option applies only under DOS. This option is only useful in conjunction with -R; -0 must come before -R on the command line. -R may require you to reload the text area from disk. Normally, the shell can determine the name of the file used to load the shell; however in some cases (such as DOS release 2) that information is not available. With -0 *file*, you can give the name of the file that contains the shell program.

In addition to the preceding options, any valid option to the set command (including -o) can be used on the sh command line. See the man page for set for details.

Command Syntax

The shell supports a sophisticated programming language that gives you complete control over the execution and combination of individual commands. When the shell scans its input, it always treats the following characters specially:

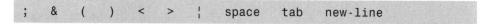

```
;    &    (    )    <    >    ¦    space    tab    new-line
```

If you want to use any of these characters inside an actual argument, the argument must be quoted (so that the shell doesn't use the special meanings of the characters). See the *Quoting* section for more information.

A *simple command* is a list of arguments separated by characters in the IFS environment variable. They are called *internal field separator* characters. The default internal field separator characters are blanks and tabs.

An unquoted argument beginning with an unescaped # introduces a *comment*, and the shell discards all input up to but not including the next new-line.

A *reserved word command* starts with a reserved word (for example if, while, and so on). Reserved word commands provide flow of control operations for the shell. These are described later in this section.

A *command* can be any of the following:

```
command:
     simple command
     reserved word command
     command ¦ command
     command ¦¦ command
     (command)
     command && command
     command & command
     command &
     command ; command
     command ;
```

Table 7 gives the order of precedence of the preceding operators. Highest priority operators are listed first. Operators on the same line have equal priority.

Table 7.   Priority of command forms.

Operators	
( )	
¦	
¦	
&&	¦¦
&	;

The meanings of these operators follow:

(command)	Executes *command* in a subshell. In this way, *command* executes in a completely separate execution environment where its sections will not affect the original shell.
¦	When two commands are connected by the ¦ operator, the shell creates a pipe between them. This means that the standard output of the first command becomes the standard input of the second command. A series of commands connected by pipes is called a *pipeline*.

&&   This is the logical AND operator. The second command is executed if and only if the first command returns a true (zero) exit status.

¦¦   This is the logical OR operator. The second command is executed if and only if the first command returns a false (non-zero) exit status.

&   When the & operator appears after a command, the shell executes the command asynchronously. This means that the shell just starts the command running and then immediately goes on to take new input before the command finishes execution. On systems such as DOS where asynchronous execution is not possible, & is effectively equivalent to ;.

;   This is the sequential execution operator. The second command is executed only after the first command has finished.

new-line   Commands are normally separated by new-line characters. The shell executes each line as a separate command.

The shell contains a rich set of *reserved word commands* that provide flow of control and let you create compound commands. In the following list, a *command* can also be a set of commands separated by new-lines. Square brackets indicate optional portions of commands, and are never part of the command syntax.

!   This is the logical NOT command. When its operand is false (non-zero), this command returns true (zero). When its operand is true (zero), this command returns false (non-zero).

{ *command*;}   Like *(command)* except that the command executes in the same environment rather than under a subshell. { and } are simply reserved words to the shell. To make it possible for the shell to recognize these symbols, you must put a blank or new-line after the {, and a semicolon or new-line before the }.

```
case word in
[pattern[¦pattern] ... command;;]
[pattern[¦pattern] ... command;;]
...
esac
```
The *case* statement is similar to the *switch* statement of the C programming language or the *case* statement of Pascal. If the given word matches any one of the patterns (separated by or-bar characters), sh executes the corresponding command. The patterns should follow the rules given in

the *File Name Generation* section except that the period
(.) and slash (/) are not treated specially. Patterns are
matched in the order they are given, so more inclusive
patterns should be mentioned later. You must use the
double semicolon (; ;) to delimit *command* and introduce
the next *pattern*.

```
for variable [in word word ...]
do commands
done
```
Sets *variable* to each *word*
argument in turn, and ex-
ecutes the set of *commands*
once for each setting of *variable*.

If the in *word* part is omitted, sh sets *variable* to each
positional parameter. You can divert the flow of control
within the loop with break or continue statements.

```
function variable {
        commands
}

variable() {
        commands
}
```
Either of these defines a *function* named
variable whose body consists of the list of
commands. When you actually call the function,
sh saves the current positional parameters. The
function's command line arguments then
replace these parameters until the function
finishes. sh also saves the current ERR and EXIT
traps and any flags manipulated with the set
command; these are restored when the function finishes.
The function terminates either by falling off the end of the
function body, or by reaching a return statement. If the
function uses typeset to declare any variables in the
function body, the variables are local to the function. To
call a function, simply use a command starting with the
function name followed by a list of arguments; this looks
exactly like any other command except that the command
name is the name of the function.

```
if command
then command
elif command
then command
    ...
else command
fi
```
In the if statement, if the first *command* succeeds
(returns a zero exit status), sh executes the *command*
following then. Otherwise, sh executes the *command*
following the elif (which is short for *else if*); if that
succeeds, sh executes the *command* following the next
then. There may be any number of elif-then pairs. If
none of the elif *commands* succeed, sh executes the
command following the else (if any).

441

```
select variable [in word ...]
do commands
done
```
The select statement can handle menu-like interactions with a user. Its syntax is like the `for` statement. Each *word* is printed on the standard error file, one per line, with an accompanying number. If the `in` *word* part is omitted, `sh` displays the positional parameters. `sh` then displays the value of the variable `PS3` to prompt the user to enter a numerical reply. If the reply is an empty line, `sh` displays the menu again. Otherwise, `sh` assigns the input line to the variable `REPLY`, sets *variable* to the *word* selected, then executes the *commands*. (Normally these *commands* contain an `if` or `case` statement to test the value of *word*.) `sh` does this over and over until the loop is terminated by interrupt, end-of-file, or an explicit `break` statement in *commands*.

```
time pipeline
```
This lets you time the execution of a complete *pipeline* with a single command. A *pipeline* is a series of commands connected by ¦ (pipe) operators. Because `time` is a shell keyword, you cannot create an `alias` or `function` named `time`. Times are given in minutes and seconds (usually fractions of seconds).

```
until command1
do commands
done
```
Executes *command1* and tests its exit status for success (zero) or failure (non-zero). If the control `command` succeeds, the loop terminates; otherwise, `sh` executes `commands`, then goes back to execute and test *command1* again. `break` and `continue` commands in the `commands` can affect the operation of the loop.

```
while command1
do commands
done
```
Works similarly to `until`. However, the loop terminates whenever the loop control `command1` is unsuccessful (non-zero exit status).

Many shell reserved words are recognized only when they are the first token of a command. This lets you pass these reserved words as arguments to commands executed from the shell. The following keywords can be passed in this way:

```
! { } case do done elif else esac fi for
function if select then time until while
```

Command Execution

Before executing a *simple command*, the shell processes the command line, performing expansions, assignments, and redirections.

The first step in this process is examining the command line and dividing it into a series of *tokens*. You can think of a token as a complete "chunk" of information: a path name, an option, a quoted string, or anything else that is complete and separate from the other things on the command line. Tokens can be either *operators* or *words*. Operators are either control operators (as described in the preceding *Command Syntax* section), or redirection operators (described in the *File Descriptors and Redirection* section). A word is any token which is not an operator.

After breaking the command line into tokens, the shell expands words in the following order:

1. `sh` performs directory substitution (described in the *Directory Substitution* section).

2. `sh` performs parameter substitution, command substitution, or arithmetic substitution as appropriate, in the order that the words appear on the command line. The result of each expansion is called a *field* of the command.

3. `sh` scans each field produced in Step 2 for unquoted characters from the `IFS` environment variable and further subdivides the field into one or more new fields.

4. `sh` performs path name expansion on each field from Step 3 (see the *File Name Generation* section).

5. `sh` removes all quotes and escape characters that were present in the original word unless the quotes/escapes were themselves quoted or escaped.

The first field of the expanded result is the command name. It is possible that there will be no such field, in which case the original command may have been a variable assignment or a redirection. After expansion, the shell handles all redirection constructs; if a command name was found, the shell performs the redirection in a subshell environment (see the *Shell Execution Environments* section).

When a simple command does contain a command name, variable assignments in the command affect the execution of that command only.

After the shell has expanded all appropriate arguments in a simple command, it examines the command name (if any). It checks this name against currently defined functions; if there is a match, the shell executes the appropriate function. Otherwise, it checks the name to see if it is a *built-in command*; if so, `sh` executes the command directly.

If the command is not a function or a built-in command, the shell looks for a program file or script file that contains an executable version of that command. The KornShell uses the following procedure to locate the file that contains the command:

- If the command name typed to the shell has / characters in its name, the command is taken to be a full path name (absolute or relative). The shell tries to execute the contents of that file.

- Otherwise, the shell starts a *path search*. To do this, the shell obtains the value of the PATH variable. The value should be a list of directory names. sh searches under each directory for a file with a name matching the command name. sh executes the first matching file found.

Extra rules apply on DOS. If the command name does not contain a dot and a suffix, the shell looks for a file that has the given name plus any of the following suffixes:

.com	This is a DOS memory image file, used mostly for older software.
.exe	This is the standard DOS executable file format.
.bat	On DOS, any such file is passed to COMMAND.COM and executed as a standard DOS batch file.
.ksh	This is a KornShell script. Such scripts are executed in a subshell of the current shell.

If the command name has a dot in it, the shell searches under PATH directories for files that have the name exactly as given. If the suffix after the dot is not one of the suffixes listed previously, the shell executes the file as if it contains a KornShell script.

Command names can be marked as *tracked aliases*. For tracked aliases to be useful, the command name should have no slashes or dots in the basename. The first time you execute a command with a tracked alias, the shell does a normal PATH search. If the search is successful, the shell remembers the file that it finds. The next time you execute a command with the same name, the KornShell immediately executes the file found on the last PATH search; there is no new search. This speeds up the time that it takes the shell to find the appropriate file.

The set -h command tells the shell that all commands should be treated as tracked aliases. See alias and set for more information.

Quoting

To let you override the special meaning of certain words or special characters, the shell provides several quoting mechanisms. In general, you can turn off the special meaning of any character by putting a backslash (\) in front of the character. This is called *escaping* the character.

For example, you can tell the shell to disregard the special meaning of the new-line character by putting a backslash at the end of a line. The shell ignores the escaped new-line, and joins the next line of input to the end of the current line. In this way, you can enter long lines in a convenient and readable fashion.

Escaping characters by putting a backslash in front of them is the most direct way of telling the shell to disregard special meanings. However, it can be awkward and confusing if you have several characters to escape.

As an alternative, you can put arguments in various types of quotation marks. Different quotation mark characters have different "strengths." The apostrophe (single quotation mark) characters are the strongest. When a command line argument is enclosed in apostrophes, the shell disregards the special meanings of everything inside the apostrophes. For example,

```
echo '*'
```

just displays the * character.

Double quotation mark characters are weaker. Inside double quotation marks, the shell performs command substitutions of the form

```
$(command)
    or
'command'
```

The shell does not perform such substitutions when they appear inside apostrophes, or single quotation marks. In addition, the shell performs parameter substitutions of the form

```
$parameter
```

when they are inside double quotation marks, but not when they're inside apostrophes.

Internal field separator characters are ignored inside quoted arguments, whether they're quoted with double quotation marks or apostrophes. This means that a quoted argument is considered a single entity, even if it contains IFS characters.

Quoting can override the special meanings of reserved words and aliases. For example, in

```
"time" program
```

the quotation marks around time tell the shell not to interpret time as a normal shell keyword. Instead, sh does a normal command search for a command named time.

Directory Substitution

When a word begins with an unquoted tilde (~), sh tries to perform *directory substitution* on the word. sh obtains all the characters from the ~ to the first / (or \ on DOS) and uses this as a *user name*. sh looks for this *name* in the *name* fields of /etc/passwd, the file that contains information on all the system's users. If sh finds a matching name, it replaces ~*name* with the name of the user's *home directory*, as given in the matching /etc/passwd entry.

For example, if you specify a file name as

```
~jsmith/file
```

sh would look up jsmith's home directory and put that directory name in place of the ~jsmith construct.

If you just specify a ~ without an accompanying name, sh replaces the ~ with the current value of your HOME variable (see *Variables*). For example,

```
echo ~
```

displays the name of your home directory. Similarly, sh replaces the construct ~+ with the value of the PWD variable (the name of your current directory), and replaces ~- with the value of OLDPWD (the name of your previous directory).

Parameter Substitution

The shell acts as a general-purpose *parameter expander*. A *parameter* is just a piece of text that the shell recognizes and replaces with other text before executing the command line. For example, you can think of an alias as a specialized kind of parameter. When sh replaces a macro with its associated value, people say that the shell *expands* the parameter.

The simplest way to use a parameter in a command line is to enter a dollar sign ($) followed by the name of the parameter. For example, if you enter the command

```
echo $x
```

sh will replace $x with the value of the parameter x and will then display the result (because echo displays its arguments). Other ways to expand parameters are shown later in this section.

Some parameters are built into the shell. Here is a list of them:

$#   Expands to the number of positional parameters.

$@   Expands to the complete list of positional parameters, each as a separate argument in the command line being processed. This means that

    "$@"

    is equivalent to

    "$1" "$2 ..."

$*   Expands to the complete list of positional parameters, all put together as a single argument, with parameters separated by the first character of the value of IFS (see

Variables). For example, if the first character of IFS is a blank,

```
"$*"
```

is equivalent to

```
"$1 $2 ..."
```

$d   A single digit *d* expands to the *d*th positional parameter. For example, $1 expands to the first positional parameter. If there is no such parameter, $*d* expands to a null string. As a special case, $0 (zero) expands to the name of the shell function or shell script.

$-   (dash)   Expands to all options that are in effect from previous calls to the set command or from options on the sh command line.

$?   Expands to the exit status of the last command executed.

$$ Expands to the current process number of this shell.

$!   Expands to the process number of the last asynchronous command.

The preceding constructs are called *parameters* of the shell. They include the positional parameters, but are not restricted to the positional parameters.

I have already mentioned that you can expand a parameter by putting a $ in front of the parameter name. Here are more sophisticated ways to expand macros.

${*parameter*}

Expands any parameter.

${*number*}

Expands to the positional parameter with the given number. (Remember that if you just enter $*d* to refer to the *d*th positional parameter, *d* can only be a single digit; with braces, *number* can be greater than 9.) Because braces mark the beginning and end of the name, a letter or digit can immediately follow the expansion.

${*variable*[*arithmetic expression*]}

Expands to the value of an element in an array named *variable*. The *arithmetic expression* gives the subscript of the array.

${*variable*[*]}

Expands to all the elements in the array *variable*, separated by the first character of the value of IFS.

${#*parameter*}

Expands to the number of characters in the value of the given *parameter*.

${#*}, ${#@}

Expands to the number of positional parameters.

${#*variable*[*]}

    Expands to the number of elements in the array named *variable*. Elements that do not have assigned values do not count. For example, if you have only assigned values to elements 0 and 4 of an array, the number of elements is 2. Elements 1 through 3 do not count.

${*parameter*:-*word*}

    Expands *parameter* if it is defined and has a non-empty value; otherwise, the preceding construct expands to *word*. This means that you can use *word* as a default value if the parameter isn't defined.

${*parameter*-*word*}

    Is exactly the same as the previous form, except that the value of the *parameter* can be null.

${*variable*:=*word*}

    Expands word with parameter expansion and assigns the result to *variable*, provided that *variable* is not defined or has an empty value. The result is the expansion of variable whether or not word was expanded.

${*variable*=*word*}

    Is exactly the same as the previous form, except that the *variable* must be undefined (not just null) in order for *word* to be expanded.

${*parameter*:?*word*}

    Expands to the value of *parameter*, provided that it is defined and non-empty. If *parameter* isn't defined or is null, sh expands and displays *word* as a message. If *word* is empty, sh displays a default message. Once a non-interactive shell has displayed a message, the shell terminates.

${*parameter*?*word*}

    Is exactly the same as the previous form, except that *parameter* may be null.

${*parameter*:+*word*}

    Expands to *word*, provided that *parameter* is defined and non-empty.

${*parameter*+*word*}

    Expands to *word*, provided that *parameter* is defined.

${*parameter*#*pattern*}

    The shell attempts to match *pattern* against the value of the specified *parameter*. The *pattern* is the same as a case *pattern*. sh searches for the shortest prefix of the value of *parameter* that matches *pattern*. If sh finds no match, the whole construct expands to the value of *parameter*; otherwise, the portion of the value that matched *pattern* is deleted from the expansion.

${*parameter*##*pattern*}

    Is exactly the same as the previous form, except that sh deletes the longest part that matches *pattern* if it finds such a match.

${*parameter%pattern*}

Is the same as ${*parameter#pattern*}, except that sh searches for *pattern* beginning at the end of *parameter* and moving backward.

${*parameter%%pattern*}

Is the same as ${*parameter##pattern*}, except that sh searches for *pattern* beginning at the end of *parameter* and moving backward.

Arithmetic Substitution

If a command contains

```
$[arithmetic expression]
```

the sequence is replaced with the value of `arithmetic expression`. Arithmetic expressions may consist of expanded variables, numeric constants, and operators. Numeric constants may have the form

```
[base#]number
```

where the optional `base` is a decimal integer between 2 and 36 inclusive, and `number` is any non-negative number in the given base. For example, 8#12 represents the number 12 in base 8 (which is the number 10 in base 10). Digits greater than 9 may be given by upper- or lowercase letters. For example, c stands for the digit 12 in any base that is high enough to allow such a digit.

If an arithmetic expression contains a variable that has no value (an undefined variable), it is treated as if it had the value zero.

In Table 8, operators are listed in decreasing order of precedence. Operators sharing a heading have the same precedence, and are called a *precedence group*. Operators within the same precedence group are evaluated from left to right, except for assignment operators which are evaluated from right to left.

Table 8. Arithmetic Expression Operators in Precedence Order.

Operator	Performs
Unary Operators	
-	Unary minus
!	Logical negation
+ ~	Identity, bitwise negation
Multiplicative Operators	
* / %	Multiplication, division, remainder

continues

Operator	Performs
	Additive Operators
+ -	Addition, subtraction
	Bitwise Shift Operators
<< >>	Bitwise shift right, bitwise shift left
	Relational Operators
< >	Less than, greater than
<= >=	Less than or equal, greater than or equal
== !=	Equal to, not equal to
	Bitwise AND Operator
&	Bitwise AND
	Bitwise Exclusive OR Operator
^	Bitwise exclusive OR
	Bitwise Inclusive OR Operator
|	Bitwise inclusive OR
	Assignment Operator
=	Assignment

Table 8. continued

An arithmetic expression may be used without the enclosing $[and] in assignments to integer variables (see the `typeset` man page), as an argument to the following built-in commands:

```
break   continue   exit   let   return   shift
```

and when used as arguments in `test` comparisons (`-eq`, `-ge`, `-gt`, `-le`, `-lt`, and `-ne`); see the `test` man page for details.

Command Substitution

In *command substitution,* sh uses the expansion of the standard output of one command in the command line for a second command. There are two syntaxes.

The first syntax surrounds a command with grave accents (`` ` ``), as in

```
ls -l `cat list`
```

To process this command line, the KornShell first executes the cat command and collects its standard output. The shell then breaks this output into arguments and puts the result into the command line of the ls command. The preceding command therefore lists the attributes of all files whose names are contained in the file list.

This syntax is easy to type, but it is not useful if you want to put one command substitution inside another (called *nesting* command substitutions). A more useful syntax is

```
$(command)
```

as in

```
vi $(fgrep -l function $(find . -name '*.c' -print))
```

This command uses find to search the current directory and its subdirectories to find all files with names ending in .c. It then uses fgrep to search each of these files to identify those that contain the string function. Finally, it calls vi to edit each of the identified files.

There is an historical inconsistency in the command substitution syntax that uses grave accents. A backslash \ within such a construct is interpreted differently depending on its context. Backslashes are interpreted literally unless they precede a dollar sign ($), grave accent (`` ` ``), or another backslash; in these cases, the leading backslash becomes an escape character to force the literal interpretation of the $, `` ` ``, or \. As a result, the command

```
echo '\$x'
```

issued in response to the KornShell prompt produces the output

```
\$x
```

while the same command nested in a grave accent command substitution

```
echo `echo '\$x'`
```

produces the output

```
$x
```

This convoluted behavior is one reason why I strongly recommend that you avoid the grave accent syntax entirely and only use the $(*command*) form.

sh performs command substitutions as if a new copy of the shell is invoked to execute the command. This affects the behavior of $- (standing for the list of options passed to the shell). If a command substitution contains $-, the expansion of $- will not include the -i option, because the command is being executed by a non-interactive shell.

File Descriptors and Redirection

The shell sometimes refers to files using *file descriptors*. A file descriptor is just a number. Various operations (for example, exec) can associate a file descriptor with a particular file.

Some file descriptors are set up at the time the shell starts up. These are the standard input/output streams:

- Standard input (file descriptor 0)

- Standard output (file descriptor 1)

- Standard error (file descriptor 2)

Commands running under the shell can use these descriptors and streams too. When a command runs under the shell, the streams are normally associated with your terminal. However, you can *redirect* these file descriptors to associate them with other files (so that I/O on the stream takes place on the associated file instead of the terminal). In fact, the shell lets you redirect the I/O streams associated with file descriptors 0 through 9, using the following command line constructs:

digit<*file*	Tells the shell to use *file* for input on the file descriptor with the number *digit*. If you omit digit, as in <*file*, the default is 0; this redirects the standard input.
digit>*file*	Tells the shell to use *file* for output on the file descriptor whose number is *digit*. If *digit* is omitted, as in >*file*, the default is 1; this redirects the standard output. Output written to the file overwrites the current contents of the file (if any). The shell creates the file if it doesn't already exist. If the file already exists and you set -0 noclobber, the redirection will fail.

digit >¦ *file*	Is the same as *digit* > *file*, but the redirection succeeds even if the file exists and you set to noclobber.
digit>>*file*	Is the same as *digit*>*file* except that output is appended to the current contents of the file (if any).
digit<<[-]*name*	This notation, known as a *here document*, lets you specify input to a command from the terminal (or from the body of a shell script). The shell reads input from the standard input and feeds that as input to file descriptor *digit* until it finds a line that exactly matches the given *name*. If you omit *digit*, the default is the standard input. For example, to process the command

cat <<done >out

the shell reads input from the terminal until you enter a line that consists of the word done. This input is passed as the standard input to the cat command, which then copies the text to the file out.

If any character of *name* is quoted or escaped, sh does not perform substitutions on the input; otherwise, it performs variable and command substitutions, respecting the usual quoting and escape conventions. If you put - before name, sh deletes all leading tabs in the *here document*.

digit<>*file*	Tells the shell to use *file* for input and output with the file descriptor *digit*. If *digit* is omitted, as in <> *file*, the default is zero; this redirects the standard input. Output written to the file overwrites the current contents of the file (if any). The shell creates the file if it doesn't already exist.
*digit*1<&*digit2*	The input file descriptor *digit1* becomes a duplicate of file descriptor *digit2*. If you omit *digit1*, the default is the standard input (file descriptor 0). For example, <&4 makes the standard input a duplicate of file descriptor 4. In this case, entering input on 4 has the effect of entering the same input on the standard input.
*digit*1>&*digit2*	The output file descriptor *digit1* becomes a duplicate of file descriptor *digit2*. If you omit *digit1*, the default is the standard output (file

descriptor 1). For example, >&2 makes the standard output a duplicate of file descriptor 2 (the standard error). In this case, writing output on the standard output has the effect of writing the same output on the standard error.

digit<&-   Closes input descriptor *digit*. If you omit *digit*, it closes the standard input.

digit>&-   Closes output descriptor *digit*. If you omit *digit*, it closes the standard output.

Normally, redirection only applies to the command where the redirection construct appears. Shell reserved word statements can be redirected, which can have the effect of redirecting several commands simultaneously.

In some cases, the order of redirection specifications is important. However, these specifications can be freely intermixed with other command arguments. Because the shell takes care of the redirection, the redirection constructs are not passed as arguments to the command itself.

File Name Generation

The *, ?, and [characters are called *glob characters* or *wild-card characters*. If an unquoted argument contains one or more glob characters, the shell processes the argument for *File Name Generation*. The glob characters are part of *glob constructs* that represent file and directory names. In some sense, these constructs are similar to regular expressions, although they are used in very different contexts. The special constructions that can appear in glob constructs follow.

?   Matches exactly one character of a file name, except for the separator character / and a . at the beginning of a file name. (On DOS, it does not match the separator character \ either.) Unlike a similar notation used by some standard DOS programs, ? only matches an actual file name character and does not match nonexistent characters at the end of the file name. ? is analogous to the metacharacter . in regular expressions.

*   Matches zero or more characters in a file name, subject to the same restrictions as ?. * is analogous to the regular expression .*. Unlike the standard DOS wild card syntax, *x.c is a valid pattern.

[*chars*]   Defines a *class* of characters; the glob construct matches any single character in the class. A class can contain a range of characters by writing the first character in the range, a dash -, and the last

character. For example, [A-Za-z] stands for all the uppercase and lowercase letters. If you want a literal - character in the class, put it as the first or last character inside the brackets. If the first character inside the brackets is !, the construct matches any single character that is not in the class.

Some sample glob constructs are:

`[!a-f]*.c`	Matches all .c files beginning with something other than the letters a through f.
`/???/?.?`	Matches all files that are under the root directory in a directory that has a three-letter name, and that have a basename containing one character followed by a . followed by another single character.
`*/*.[chyl]`	Matches all .c, .h, .y, and .l files in a subdirectory of the current directory.
`~mks/*.ksh`	Matches all shell scripts in the home directory of user mks (see the *Directory Substitution* section for the use of ~).

If no files match the pattern, sh leaves the argument untouched. If the set option -f or -o noglob is in effect, the shell does not perform file name generation.

Variables

The shell maintains variables and can expand them where they are used in command lines. See the section on *Parameter Substitution* for details.

A variable must begin with an upper- or lowercase letter or the underscore (_). Subsequent characters in the name, if any, can be upper- or lowercase letters, underscores, and/or digits 0 through 9. You can assign a value to a variable with

```
variable=value
```

You can implicitly declare a variable as an array by using an expression in square brackets when assigning a value, as in

```
variable[arithmetic expression]=value
```

This kind of expression is called a *subscript*, and the variable is called a *subscripted array variable*. A subscripted array variable can be used anywhere an ordinary variable is allowed. Check the man pages of typeset, export, and readonly for details about the attributes of shell variables, and how shell variables can be exported to child processes.

Here are variables that the shell either sets or understands:

_ — The _ (underscore) variable expands to the last argument from the previously executed command. For every command that is executed as a child of the shell, sh sets this variable to the full path name of the executable file and passes this value through the environment to that child process. When processing the MAILPATH variable, this variable holds the value of the corresponding mail file.

CDPATH — A list of directories for the cd command to search. Directory names are separated with colons on UNIX, semicolons on DOS. See the cd man page for details.

COLUMNS — The maximum width of the edit window in the KornShell's vi editing mode. It is also used by several other commands to define the width of the terminal output device.

EDITOR — If the value in this variable ends with vi, the shell enables the corresponding editing mode (see set).

ENV — If this variable is set, sh performs parameter substitution on its value and uses the result as the name of an initialization file. This file is executed with the . command (see the man page for dot). This facility lets you define functions, aliases, and other non-exported items during shell setup.

FCEDIT — The fc command uses this variable for the default editor in editing commands. If this variable is not set, the default is /bin/ed.

HISTFILE — When the shell starts, the value of this variable overrides the default history file. See the *Files* section.

HISTSIZE — If this variable contains a valid number when the shell starts, it overrides the default of 127 for the number of commands that the shell will keep in the history list.

HOME — The default directory for the cd command.

IFS — Each character in the value of this variable is called an *internal field separator* character. Any of these characters can separate arguments in unquoted command substitutions

`'cmd'`
`$(cmd)`

or in parameter substitutions. In addition, the shell uses these characters to separate values put into variables with the read command. Lastly, the first character in the value of IFS separates the positional parameters in $* expansion.

LINES
If this variable has a numeric value, it limits the number of output lines used by the select statement in printing its menu.

MAIL
If the value of this variable is a file name and MAILPATH is not set, the KornShell tells you when new mail arrives in the specified file. The shell assumes that new mail has arrived if the file modification time changes.

MAILCHECK
The number of seconds of elapsed time that must pass before checking for mail; if not set, the default value is 600 seconds. When using the MAIL or MAILPATH variables, the KornShell checks for mail before issuing a prompt.

MAILPATH
When this variable is set, it overrides the MAIL variable. The value of MAILPATH is a set of names of mailbox files separated by colons on UNIX, semicolons on DOS. If any name is followed by ?*message*, sh displays the message if the corresponding file changes. sh performs parameter and command substitution in *message* and the variable _ (temporarily) expands to the name of the mailbox file. If no ?*message* is present, the default message is you have mail in $_.

OLDPWD
The cd command stores the previous directory name in this variable.

PATH
Lists directories that make up the *search path* for executable commands. Directories in this list are separated by colons on UNIX, and by semicolons on DOS. sh searches each directory in the order specified in the list until it finds a matching executable file. If you want the shell to search the current directory, put a null string in the list of directories (for example, starting the list with a colon on UNIX, or a semicolon on DOS, tells the shell to search the current directory first).

PS1
Contains the primary prompt string, used when the shell is interactive. The default value is "$ ". The shell expands parameters before the prompt is printed. A single ! in the prompt string is replaced by the

<table>
<tbody>
</tbody>
</table>

	command number from the history list (see `fc`); for a real exclamation mark in the prompt, use `!!`.
PS2	Contains the secondary prompt, used when completing the input of such things as *reserved word commands*, quoted strings, and here documents. The default value of this variable is `"> "`.
PS3	Contains the prompt string used in connection with the `select` keyword. The default value is `"#? "`.
PS4	Contains the prefix for commands displayed because of `set -x`. The default value is +.
PWD	The name of the current working directory. When the shell starts, the current directory name is assigned to PWD unless the variable already has a value.
RANDOM	Expands to a random integer. Assigning a value to RANDOM sets a new seed for the random number generator.
REPLY	The `select` statement (see *Command Syntax*) sets this variable to the user input. The `read` command also sets this variable if no variable is specified.
SECONDS	The value of this variable grows by 1 for each elapsed second of real time. Any value assigned to this variable sets the SECONDS counter to that value; initially the shell sets the value to 0.
SHELL	Should contain the full path name of the current shell. It is not set by the shell, but is used by various other commands to invoke the shell.
TMOUT	If this variable is set, it contains the number of seconds before user input will time out. If user input has not been received within this length of time, the shell will terminate.
VISUAL	Overrides the EDITOR variable in setting `vi` editing mode.

Shell Execution Environments

A shell *execution environment* is the set of conditions affecting most commands executed within the shell:

- Open files

- The current working directory

- The file creation mask (beyond the scope of this book)

- The traps currently set (see the `trap` man page)

- The shell parameters (see `set` and `export`)

- The shell functions currently defined

- Options set with `set`

A *subshell environment* starts as a duplicate of the shell environment, except that traps caught by the subshell are set to default values. Changes made to a subshell environment do not affect the shell environment.

Command substitutions, commands within parentheses, as in (*command*), and commands to be run asynchronously with *command*&, all run in subshell environments. Each command in a pipeline *command* | *command* also runs in a subshell environment.

Most shell scripts and utilities also run in a separate environment which does not affect the original shell environment; the exceptions are certain built-in utilities like `cd` and `dot`, which explicitly alter the shell environment. The environment of a shell utility is set up by the shell to include the following:

- Open files, subject to redirection

- Current working directory

- File creation mask

- Traps; traps caught by the shell are set to default values and traps ignored by the shell are ignored by the utility

- Variables defined inside the shell and having the `export` attribute

Built-In Commands

Table 9 shows the commands that are built into the shell to increase performance of shell scripts or to access the shell's internal data structures and variables. See the specific manual pages for details on these commands. These built-in commands are designed to have semantics that are indistinguishable from external commands.

Table 9.   Commands built into the shell.

:	.	[	alias	break	cd
continue	eval	exec	exit	export	fc
let	print	read	readonly	return	set
shift	test	times	trap	typeset	ulimit
unalias	unset	whence			

The following built-in commands do nothing under DOS, because DOS does not have the functionality to support the commands:

newgrp	umask	wait

In the interest of compatibility with UNIX, the DOS version of the KornShell recognizes such do-nothing commands, but they have no effect.

As well as built-in commands, the shell has a set of predefined aliases, which are shown in Table 10.

Table 10. Predefined aliases in the KornShell.

chdir	echo	false	functions	hash	history	integer
nohup	pwd	r	true	type		

See the `alias` man page for details.

Examples

Software distributed over computer networks such as Usenet is often distributed in a form known as *Shell Archives*. In essence, a shell archive is a shell script containing the data of one or more files, plus commands to reconstruct the data files and check that the data was transmitted correctly. Listing 19 shows a sample shell archive.

Listing 19.   Sample shell archive.

```
# This is a shell archive.
# It contains the one file "frag.ksh"
# To extract contents, type
# sh file
#
if  [ -f frag.ksh ]
then echo frag.ksh exists: will not overwrite
else
    echo extracting frag.ksh
    sed 's/^X//' >frag.ksh <<_EOF_
X# This is frag.ksh
X# Not very interesting, really.
Xecho frag.ksh here!
```

```
_EOF_
    if [ "`sum frag.ksh¦awk '{print $1}'`" != "52575" ]
    then  echo frag.ksh damaged in transit
    fi
fi
```

Listing 20 is a simple script to produce as much of the Fibonacci sequence as can be calculated in integers.

Listing 20.   Script to produce the Fibonacci sequence.

```
# Print out Fibonacci sequence; start sequence
# with first two positional parameters:
# default 1 1
typeset -i x=${1:-1} y=${2:-1} z
while     [ x -gt 0 ]    # until overflow
do
    echo $x
    let z=y+x x=y y=z
done
```

Listing 21 implements the basename utility as a shell function.

Listing 21.   The basename utility as a shell function.

```
function basename {
    case $# in
    1)   ;;
    2)   eval set \e${1%$2} ;;
    *)   echo Usage: $0 pathname '[suffix]'
         return 1 ;;
    esac
    echo ${1##*/}
    return 0
}
```

Diagnostics

Possible exit status values are:

1   Returned if the shell is invoked with an invalid option. Also returned if the shell is invoked to run a shell script and the command to run the script has a command syntax error, a redirection error, or a variable expansion error.

Otherwise, the exit status of the shell defaults to the exit status of the last command executed by the shell. You can override this default by using the `exit` or `return` commands. The default exit status of a line that contains a pipeline is the exit status of the last command in the pipeline.

Most diagnostics are self-explanatory. See the separate man pages for diagnostics from built-in commands.

`Ambiguous redirection`	A redirection construct was not properly formatted.
`Argument too long`	Any single argument to a command is limited in length (see the *Limits* section). Command and parameter substitution can exceed this limit.
`Coprocess not implemented`	On DOS, you attempted to use an operation or option that depends on coprocesses. DOS does not support coprocesses (an explanation of how coprocessors work is outside the scope of this book).
`ENV variable expands to >1 word`	The ENV variable should name a single file that is executed to set up the shell's environment. To find out the current value of ENV, you can use the command `echo $ENV`.
`File "file" already exists`	You are attempting to redirect output into an existing file, but you have turned on the `noclobber` option. If you really want to redirect output into an existing file, use the construct `>¦filename`, or turn off the option with `set +o noclobber`.

`File descriptor number already redirected`	You attempted to redirect a file descriptor that was already being redirected. You can only redirect a file descriptor once.
`Hangup`	The shell received a *hangup* signal. This signal typically arises when a communication line is disconnected, for example, when a phone connection is cut off.
`Word too long`	See the *Limits* section for information on maximum argument length.
`In base#number: base must be in [2,36]`	In a number of the form base#number, the value of the base was larger than 36 or less than 2. The only valid range for bases is from 2 through 36.
`Invalid subscript`	A shell array was indexed with a subscript that was outside the defined bounds. This usually means the value was negative.
`Insufficient memory ...`	Because 8086- and 80286-based versions of the shell run in the small memory model, its data area is limited to 64K. The preceding message appears if allocated data within the shell outgrows this limit. Possible causes include too many bytes of shell variables, too many functions, too complex an expression tree, and so on. If it is impossible to free any memory (for example, via unset), you should leave the shell or reboot the machine.
	Note that the amount of memory available for the shell's use can be limited by terminate-and-stay resident programs loaded after the shell is invoked. Such programs will limit the amount of memory available for the shell's growth.
`Insufficient memory to reload shell text image`	With the -R option, this error indicates that the shell text image was corrupted, but DOS didn't have enough available memory to reload it.

`Illegal instruction`	The shell received an *illegal instruction* signal. This signal typically occurs when a process tries to execute something that is not a valid machine instruction recognized by the hardware.
`Misplaced subscript "`*name*`"`	The subscript for an array was missing or invalid.
`Misplaced token "`*string*`"`	In an instruction or expression, the shell found a symbol, name, number, or operator that didn't belong. The *string* shows the token that was out of place.
Name `is not an identifier`	You attempted an operation with *Name* as if it were an identifier (for example, you tried an expression like $*Name*). However, *Name* is not a currently defined identifier.
Name`: readonly variable`	The given *Name* is a read-only variable, and cannot be removed or changed.
Name`: no expansion of unset variable`	The shell is operating with `set -u`, and you used an unset variable in a substitution. For more information, see `set`.
`No file descriptor available for redirection`	When a file descriptor is redirected, the old value is remembered by the shell by duplicating it to yet another file descriptor. The total number of file descriptors is limited by the system (set by the `FILES=` value in `config.sys`), hence the shell can run out while it looks like your command is using far fewer than the maximum number of descriptors.
`!Pipe for coprocess`	The shell cannot create a pipe for a coprocess. This may mean that your session or the system as a whole has already set up its maximum number of pipes.
`Prompt too long—reset to default`	You tried to assign too long a string to one of the PS variables. When `sh` found that the string was too long, it set the variable to its default value. The maximum length depends on the amount of space used by other shell variables.

`...: restricted`	If the shell has been invoked as a restricted shell, certain things are disallowed, for example the `cd` command, setting `PATH`, and output redirection.
`!Temporary file error using here document`	`sh` tried to create a temporary file holding the contents of a `<<word here` document. However, the temporary file could not be created. This may indicate a lack of space on the disk where temporary files are created.
`Word after ... expanded to more than one argument`	In a context where only one argument was expected, a construct expanded to more than one argument.

Files

`.sh_history`	Default history storage file on UNIX.
`sh_history`	Default history storage file on DOS.
`.profile`	Profile for log-in shell on UNIX.
`profile.ksh`	Profile for log-in shell on DOS.
`/etc/profile`	System-wide profile for log-in shells on UNIX.
`/etc/profile.ksh`	System-wide profile for log-in shells on DOS.
`/etc/suid_profile`	Profile used under the protected option and when effective and real userids are different on UNIX.
`/etc/suid_profile.ksh`	Profile used under the protected option of `set` on DOS.
`/tmp/sh*`	Temporary files for here documents, command substitution, history reexecution, and so on. You can override the default directory `$ROOTDIR/tmp` by setting the shell variable `TMPDIR` to the name of some other directory.
	`sh` finds the `/etc` and `/tmp` directories using the `ROOTDIR` environment variable if it exists.

Limits

The size of the command line passed between the shell and the utilities it runs is dependent on the operating system. On DOS, this limit is 8192 bytes. Because the shell has no way of knowing the type of command it is calling, it also writes the standard DOS command line. A single command argument is restricted to 1024 bytes.

The number of files that can be open simultaneously under DOS currently defaults to eight. Specifying

```
files=n
```

in `config.sys` (a reasonable value of *n* is 20) is strongly recommended because shell users are likely to be heavy users of open files (for example, for pipes).

The maximum length of an executable file name, including subdirectories and extensions, is 256 bytes.

Portability

POSIX.2. X/Open Portability Guide. MKS Toolkit. Upwardly compatible with the Bourne shell on UNIX.

DOS imposes several functional limitations. There is no multitasking, and therefore no coprocesses, no background tasks, and no job control. The & operator is effectively equivalent to ;. There is no bg command. The commands `set -o bgnice`, `set -o monitor`, `newgrp`, `umask`, and `wait` have no effect.

See Also

```
alias, break, cd, continue, dot, echo, eval, exec, exit, export, fc, let,
print, ps, pwd, read, return, set, shift, test, times, trap, true, typeset,
ulimit, unalias, unset, whence
```

---

shift—Shift Positional Parameters

Synopsis

```
shift [expression]
```

Description

shift renames the positional parameters. It is built into the shell.

If n is the value of the given arithmetic *expression*, the *i+n*th positional parameter becomes the *i*th positional parameter. You can think of this as getting rid of the first *n* parameters and shifting everything that's left to fill the resulting gap.

If you omit *expression*, the default value of *n* is 1. The value of *expression* must be between one and the number of positional parameters ($#), inclusive.

Example

The commands

```
set a b c d
shift 2
echo $*
```

produce

```
c d
```

Diagnostics

Possible exit status values are:

0   Successful completion.

1   Failure because the *expression* had a negative value or was greater than the number of positional parameters.

Possible error messages include:

count cannot be negative	You tried to pass a negative argument to shift; the argument must be positive (or zero).
too few positional parameters to shift by *number*	The number you specified was greater than the number of remaining positional parameters.

Portability

POSIX.2. X/Open Portability Guide. MKS Toolkit. shift is a built-in command of the Bourne Shell and the KornShell on UNIX. Note that the optional *expression* is an extension in the KornShell.

See Also

```
set, sh
```

sort—Sort/Merge Utility

Synopsis

```
sort [-cmu] [-o outfile] [-yn] [-zn] [-dfiMnrb] [-tx]
[-k startpos,endpos] [file ...]
```

Description

The `sort` command provides a full sort and merge facility. `sort` operates on input files containing records that are separated by the new-line character.

Options

The following options select particular operations:

-c   Simply checks the input files to ensure that they are correctly ordered according to the key position and sort ordering options specified. With -c, `sort` does not modify the input files or produce output. `sort` displays a message if the files are not correctly sorted.

-m   Assumes that each input file is already ordered correctly according to the other options on the command line. `sort` merges these presorted files into a single sorted output stream.

           With neither -c nor -m, `sort` sorts the concatenation of all input files and outputs the sorted result on the standard output.

Options that control the operation of `sort` are:

-o *outfile*   Writes output into *outfile*. *outfile* can be one of the input files, in which case `sort` makes a copy of the input data to allow the (potential) overwriting of the input file. If this option is not specified, `sort` writes output onto the standard output.

-t*c*	Indicates that input fields are separated with the character *c*. When no -t option is specified, fields are separated by any number of white space (blank or tab) characters.
-u	Ensures that output records are unique. If two or more input records have equal sort keys, only one record is written to the output. When -u is used with -c, sort displays a diagnostic message if the input records have any duplicates.
-y[*n*]	Restricts the amount of memory available for sorting to *n*K of memory (where a K of memory is enough to hold 1024 characters). If you omit *n*, sort chooses a reasonable maximum amount of memory for sorting, dependent upon system configuration. sort needs at least enough memory to hold five records simultaneously. If you try to request less, sort takes the amount it needs anyway. When the amount of data in the input files surpasses the amount of memory available, sort automatically does a polyphase merge (external sorting) algorithm that is, of necessity, much slower than internal sorting. Using -y can therefore improve sorting performance for medium to large input files.
-z*n*	Indicates that the longest input record (including the new-line character) is *n* characters in length. By default, record length is limited to 400 characters.

The following options control the way sort compares records; this determines the order in which the records are sorted. If the command line contains one of these order options without an accompanying sorting key, the option affects all comparisons; otherwise, it just affects the comparisons done on the associated sorting key. For more on sorting keys, see the *Sorting Keys* section.

-b	Skips any leading whitespace (blank or tab) in any field (or key specification) before making comparisons.
-d	Makes comparisons using *dictionary* ordering—sort only looks at upper- and lowercase letters and numbers (alphanumerics) when doing the comparison.
-f	Converts uppercase letters into lowercase letters for the purpose of the comparison.
-i	Ignores all non-ASCII and control characters for comparison purposes.
-M	Assumes the field contains a month name for comparison purposes. sort ignores any leading whitespace. If the field starts with the first three letters of a month name in upper-

or lowercase, sort makes comparisons in month order. If a field is not a recognizable month name, it is considered to come before January.

-n   Assumes the field contains a number. sort skips any leading whitespace. The number can contain an optional leading + or - sign, and can have an integer and/or functional part, separated by a decimal point.

-r   Reverses the order of all comparisons: output is written from largest to smallest rather than smallest to largest.

Sorting Keys

By default, sort examines entire input records to determine ordering. By specifying *sorting keys*, you can tell sort to restrict its attention to one or more parts of each record.

On the sort command line, you specify a sorting key by telling where the key starts and/or ends in the input record. The start of a sorting key can be indicated with

```
-k m[.n][options]
```

where *m* and the optional *n* are positive integers. You can choose the *options* from the set bdfiMnr to specify the way comparisons are done for just that sorting key. If no *options* are specified for the key, the global ordering options are used.

The number *m* specifies which field in the input record contains the start of the sorting key. The first field is number 1, the next is 2, and so on. Fields are separated by the character given with the -t option; without -t, fields are separated by whitespace. The number *n* specifies which character in the mth field is the start of the sorting key. If you do not specify n, the sorting key starts at the first character of the mth field. In this form of the -k option, the key begins at the specified position and extends to the end of the line.

You can also specify an ending position for a key, with

```
-k m[.n][options],p[.q][options]
```

where *p* and *q* are positive integers. indicating that the sorting key ends with the pth character of the qth field. If you do not specify q, the sorting key ends at the last character of the pth field. If the end of a sorting key is not a valid position after the beginning key position, the sorting key extends to the end of the input record.

Multiple sort key positions can be specified by using several -k options. In this case, the second sorting key is only used for records where the first sorting keys are equal. The third sorting key is only used when the first two are equal, and so on. If all key positions compare equally, the entire record is used to determine ordering.

When you specify -u to determine the uniqueness of output records, sort only looks at the sorting keys, not the whole record. Therefore, records are considered to be duplicates if they have equal sorting keys, even if other fields are not identical. (Of course, if no sorting keys are specified, the whole record is considered to be the sorting key.)

Examples

Suppose an input file has lines consisting of the day of the month, white space, and the month, as in:

```
30 December
23     MAY
25 June
10     June
```

You can sort this file into chronological order with:

```
sort -k 2M -k 1n
```

Suppose you have two *dictionary* files (text files with one word per line and each file sorted in dictionary order). You can merge the two dictionaries with:

```
sort -m -dfi dict1 dict2 >newdict
```

Diagnostics

Possible exit status values are:

0   Successful completion. Also returned if you specify -c and the file is in correctly sorted order.

1   Returned if you specify -c and the file is not correctly sorted. Also returned to indicate failure because of a non-unique key in a record if -u is specified, inability to open the output file, error in writing to the output file, inability to create a temporary file or temporary file name, or an error writing to the temporary file.

2   Failure because of a missing key description after -k, more than one -o option, a missing *file* name after -o, a missing character after -t, more than one character after -t, a missing *number* with -y or -z, an *endpos* coming before a *startpos*, a badly formed sort key, an invalid command line option, too many key field positions specified, or insufficient memory.

The following are some of the more likely error messages that can appear:

`Missing key definition after -k`	You specified `-k`, but did not specify a key definition after the `-k`.
`Non-unique key in record: ...`	With the `-u` and `-c` options, `sort` found a non-unique record.
`Not ordered properly at: ...`	With the `-c` option, `sort` found the input was not correctly sorted.
`Line too long - truncated`	An input line was longer than the default (400 characters) or the number specified with the `-z` option. `sort` truncated this line by discarding characters from the end of the line until it was short enough.
`No new-line at end of file`	`sort` adds a new-line character to any file that doesn't already end in one.
`Insufficient memory for ...`	This error normally occurs when very large numbers are specified for `-y` or `-z` options and there is not enough memory available for `sort` to satisfy the request.
`Write error (no space) on output`	Some error occurred in writing the standard output. Barring write-protected diskettes and the like, this normally occurs when there is insufficient disk space to hold all of the intermediate data.
`Temporary file error (no space) for ...`	Insufficient space was available for a temporary file. Make sure that you have a directory named `/tmp`, and that this directory has space to create files. The directory for temporary files can be changed using the `ROOTDIR` and `TMPDIR` environment variables (see Appendix E).
`Tempfile error on ...`	`sort` could not create the named temporary (intermediate) file. Make sure that you have a directory named `/tmp`, and that this directory has space to create files. The directory for temporary files can be changed using the `ROOTDIR` and `TMPDIR` environment variables; see Appendix E.
`Tempnam() error`	`sort` could not generate a name for a temporary working file. This should almost never happen.

Files

/tmp/stm* Temporary files used for merging and -o option. The /tmp directory is located using the ROOTDIR environment variable. You can specify a different directory for tempo rary files using the TMPDIR environment variable. For further information, see Appendix E.

Portability

POSIX.2. X/Open Portability Guide. MKS Toolkit. Available on all UNIX systems, with only UNIX System V.2 or later having the full functionality described here.

Notes

Previous versions of sort used sorting keys of the form

```
+m.n[options] -p.q[options]
```

instead of the -k form. This form numbered the first fields of the record as zero, the next as 1, and so on. This old format is still supported, but the POSIX.2 standard regards it as obsolete. Therefore, you should use the -k format.

tail—Display the Last Lines of a File

Synopsis

```
tail [+Number] [-number] [lbc] [-f] [file]
```

Description

When tail is called without options, it displays the last 10 lines of a file. This is useful for looking at the most recent entries in log files and any file where new information is added on the end.

Options

An argument of the form +*number* skips that number of lines, then displays the rest of the file. For example, +100 will print from line 101 to the end of the file.

An argument of the form -*number* prints that number of lines from the end of the file. For example, -20 prints the last 20 lines in the file.

Both +*number* and -*number* may be followed by l, b, or c, to specify units of lines, blocks, or characters respectively. The default unit is lines.

The -f or *follow* option monitors a file as it grows. After displaying the end of the file, tail sleeps for two seconds, then prints any new data at the end of the file. This is useful on UNIX, where you can run tail while another program writes to files; it is not useful on DOS, unless you have software like Microsoft Windows which lets you run several programs simultaneously.

Diagnostics

Possible exit status values are:

0   Successful completion.

1   Failure because of an unknown command line option, insufficient memory for buffering, a write error on the standard output, a badly formed line or character count, a missing number after an option, or an error reopening a file descriptor.

Possible error messages include:

`Badly formed line/ character count "string"`	In an option of the form +*number* or -*number*, the *number* was not a valid number.
`Re-opening file descriptor "number"`	-f was used to follow a file as it grew. tail closed the file associated with the given file descriptor *number* then tried to open it two seconds later. At this point, tail found it could not reopen the file for reading, and therefore could not follow the file any longer.

Portability

POSIX.2. X/Open Portability Guide. All UNIX systems. MKS Toolkit.

See Also

```
cat, head, pg
```

tar—USTAR-Compatible Tape Archiver

Synopsis

```
tar -c[#sbfvwlzU] [tapefile] [blocksize] file ...
tar -r[#sbfvwlzU] [tapefile] [blocksize] file ...
tar -t[#sbfvzU] [tapefile] [blocksize] [file ...]
tar -u[#sbfvwlzU] [tapefile] [blocksize] file ...
tar -x[#sbfvwpmozU] [tapefile] [blocksize] [file ...]
```

Description

tar manipulates *archives*. An archive is a single file that contains the complete contents of a set of other files. An archive preserves the directory hierarchy that contained the original files. The name tar was derived from **t**ape **ar**chiver; however, archives can be used with any medium, including floppy disks.

This version of tar writes and reads the original tar format from UNIX as well as the USTAR format defined by the POSIX (IEEE P1003.1) standards group.

Options

The five forms of the command shown in the synopsis represent the main functions of tar as follows:

-c   Create. With -c, tar writes each named file into a newly-created archive. Directories recursively include all components. Under the USTAR (-U) option, tar records directories and other special files in the tape archive. Otherwise, it ignores such files. If - appears in place of any file name, tar reads the standard input for a list of files one per line. This lets other commands generate lists of files for tar to archive.

-r   Replace. With -r, tar writes the named files to the end of the archive. You can put more than one copy of a file into an archive using this method. For this form of the command to be used with a tape, it must be possible to backspace the tape.

-t   Table of contents. With -t, tar writes the names of all the files in the archive, one per line. If you specify one or more files on the command line, tar only displays those file names. Under the verbose (-v) option, tar displays more

information about each tape archive member, in a format
similar to that produced by ls -l.

-u   Update. Works like the -r form of the command, except
        that files are added to the end of the archive only if they are
        not already there, or if they have been modified since the
        original copy was put into the archive.

-x   Extract. With -x, tar extracts each named file and puts the
        data into a file of the same name. If no files are named on
        the command line, tar extracts all files in the archive. tar
        restores all file system attributes, as controlled by other
        options.

You must specify one of the preceding basic functions as the first character
of an option string. You can add other characters to the option string as described
later. Unlike other UNIX commands, tar requires that its options be given as a
single string; for example, you can write -tv, but you cannot separate them as in
-t -v. You can omit the leading dash if you want. Other possible options in the
option string are:

b   Sets the number of 512-byte blocks used for archive
        read/write operations to *blocksize*. You must specify a
        blocksize argument, and you may not specify *blocksize*
        if b is not in the option string. When reading from the tape
        archive, tar automatically determines the blocking factor
        by trying to read the largest legal blocking factor and using
        the actual number read to be the *blocksize*. For UNIX
        compatibility, the largest valid blocksize is 20 blocks; in
        USTAR mode, it is 60 blocks.

f   Uses the file *tapefile* for the archive rather than the
        default (described later). You must specify the *tapefile*
        argument, and you may not specify *tapefile* if f is not in
        the option string. The *tapefile* argument must precede
        the *blocksize* argument if both are present. If *tapefile* is
        the - character, tar uses the standard input for reading
        and uses the standard output for writing archives.

#s   The default archive file name used by tar is /dev/mt/0m.
        This option is the least general way to override this default.
        The file name generated by this option has the form
        /dev/mt/#s. The # can be any digit between 0 and 7
        (including 0 and 7); this selects the tape unit. The density
        selector s can be l (low), m (medium), or h (high).

l   Complains if all links are not resolved when adding files to
        the tape archive.

m   Does not restore the modification time stamp on an
        extracted file. This option can only be specified on extract-

ing operations. If m is not in the option string, tar restores the time stamp from information contained in the archive.

o   If you specify o when the tar archive is created, tar does not record the owner and modes of directories in the archive. If this is specified when extracting from an existing archive, tar does not restore any owner or group information in the archive. The default is to record this information when creating an archive, and to restore it when extracting from the archive.

p   Restores the three high-order file attribute bits, exactly as in the archive. This can only be used when extracting. On DOS, the high-order file attribute bits indicate *system*, *archive*, and *hidden* attributes. On UNIX systems, they indicate the setuserid, setgroupid, and saved-text attributes. In order to use p on UNIX, you must have appropriate privileges; tar restores the modes exactly as in the archive and ignores the UMASK. (On DOS, every extracted file has the archive attribute turned on.)

U   When creating a new tape archive with the -c option, -U must be specified to force the USTAR format. The default format used when creating a new archive is the original UNIX tar format. When -c is not specified, tar can deduce whether or not the tape archive is in USTAR format by reading it, so U can be used to suppress a warning about USTAR format.

v   Uses a more verbose mode of operation in which tar displays each file name, along with the appropriate action key letter, as the archive is processed. With the -t form of the command, this option gives more detail about each archive member being listed.

w   Confirms each operation, such as replacing or extracting. tar displays the operation and the file involved. You can then confirm whether or not you want the operation to take place. Typing in an answer that begins with y tells tar to do the operation; anything else tells tar to go on to the next operation.

Example

To identify all files that have been changed in the last week (seven days), and to archive them to a file on diskette, you might type:

```
find directory -mtime -7 -print | tar -cvf a:archive -
```

Diagnostics

Possible exit status values are:

0   Successful completion.

1   Failure because of an invalid option, invalid command line arguments, out of memory, compression error, failure on extraction, or failure on creation.

Limits

Path names in the archive are normally restricted to a maximum length of 100 bytes. However, in USTAR mode, path names can be up to 255 bytes long.

Portability

All UNIX systems. MKS Toolkit. -U is an extension to provide POSIX USTAR format compatibility. -p is a common extension on BSD UNIX systems, but it is not available on AT&T UNIX System V systems.

Notes

This version of tar does not currently support the u (update) command for existing archives.

The file permission modes of UNIX are not the same as those of DOS. In particular, the archive, hidden, and system attributes of a DOS file mean something else on UNIX.

---

test—Test for Condition

Synopsis

```
test expression

[ expression ]
```

Description

test checks for various properties of files, strings and integers. It produces no output (except error messages) but it returns the result of the test as the exit status. See the *Diagnostics* section for more information.

The command line is a Boolean expression. The simplest expression is a *string*; a string is considered true if the string is non-empty (i.e. it contains one or more characters). More complex expressions are composed of operators and operands, each of which is surrounded by whitespace. Different operators take different numbers and types of operands. Operators that take a *file* operand will fail (without error) if the file does not exist. *expression* can be:

-b *file*	True if the *file* is a block special file.
-c *file*	True if the *file* is a character special file (e.g. a device file).
-d *file*	True if the *file* is a directory.
-f *file*	True if the *file* is an ordinary file.
-g *file*	True if the setgid attribute of the *file* is on; explaining this is beyond the scope of this book.
-k *file*	True if the save text attribute under UNIX (or the system attribute under DOS) of the *file* is on.
-n *string*	True if the length of *string* is non-zero.
-p *file*	True if the *file* is a FIFO (named pipe).
-r *file*	True if the *file* is readable.
-s *file*	True if the size of the *file* is non-zero.
-t [*fd*]	True if the numeric file descriptor *fd* is associated with a terminal; if *fd* is omitted it defaults to 1 (the standard output).
-u *file*	True if the setuid attribute of the *file* is on; explaining this is beyond the scope of this book.
-w *file*	True if the *file* is writable.
-x *file*	True if the *file* is executable.
-z *string*	True if the length of the *string* is zero.
-L *file*	True if *file* is a symbolic link.
string=*string*	True if the strings are identical.
string!=*string*	True if the strings are not identical.
number -eq *number*	True if the numbers are equal. Within the KornShell (only), either *number* can be an

	arbitrary `let` arithmetic expression; the same applies for the other five numerical comparisons that follow.
number `-ge` *number*	True if the first *number* is greater than or equal to the second.
number `-gt` *number*	True if the first *number* is greater than the second.
number `-le` *number*	True if the first *number* is less than or equal to the second.
number `-lt` *number*	True if the first *number* is less than the second.
number `-ne` *number*	True if the first *number* is not equal to the second.
file1 `-nt` *file2*	True if *file1* is newer than *file2*.
file 1 `-ot` *file2*	True if *file1* is older than *file2*.
file1 `-ef` *file2*	True if *file1* has the same device and inode number as *file2*.
expr `-a` *expr*	Logical AND; true if both *exprs* are true.
expr `-o` *expr*	Logical OR; true if either *expr* is true.
`!` *expr*	Logical negation; true if *expr* is false.
`(`*expr*`)`	True if *expr* is true; this is used for grouping other operations and expressions.

The precedence of the operators in descending order is:

> unary operators
>
> comparison operators
>
> logical AND
>
> logical OR

The second form of the test command

```
[ expression ]
```

is synonymous with the first.

Examples

The following command reports on whether the first positional parameter contains a directory or a file:

```
if [ -f $1 ]
then
    echo $1 is a file
elif [ -d $1 ]
then
    echo $1 is a directory
else
    echo $1 neither file nor directory
fi
```

This example illustrates the use of test, and is not intended to be an efficient method.

Diagnostics

Possible exit status values are:

0   The *expression* was true.

1   The *expression* was false.

2   The *expression* was badly formed.

Portability

POSIX.2. X/Open Portability Guide. All UNIX systems. MKS Toolkit. The following file attributes do not apply to the DOS file system: -b, -c, -g, -p, -u, -x, -L, and -ef.

See Also

```
expr, find, let, ls, sh
```

Note

test is built into the shell and is also implemented as a separate utility. In the KornShell, test can compare variables; however, if the variable is null, the expression may be invalid for test. For example,

```
NULL=
test $NULL = "so"
```

will not work, because the KornShell will expand this to

```
test = "so"
```

which is not a valid expression for `test`. You can get around this by adding some value to the front of both strings, as in:

```
test x$NULL = x"so"
```

---

trap—Intercept Abnormal Conditions and Interrupts

Synopsis

```
trap ['handler'] [traptype ...]
```

Description

`trap` intercepts certain kinds of exception conditions. The command is built into the KornShell.

The *handler* argument is a list of one or more commands. Because it usually contains more than one word, it must be quoted to serve as a single argument. It is scanned when you issue the `trap` command. If an appropriate exception condition occurs, the shell scans the command list again and executes the commands. A missing argument or an argument of - (dash) resets the default trap condition. A null argument (' ') causes the trap condition to be ignored.

If the *traptype* argument is the word ERR, the shell invokes the trap *handler* upon any command having a non-zero exit status. This trap is not triggered inside functions.

If *traptype* is 0 or the word EXIT, the shell invokes the trap handler when the shell terminates. Within a function, the trap is invoked when the function exits.

Any other *traptype* argument should be a number corresponding to a signal number. On DOS, the valid signal numbers are 2 (SIGINT), 14 (SIGALRM) and 10 (SIGSTOP). SIGINT is sent by Ctrl-Break or Ctrl-C. SIGALRM is sent when the TMOUT variable expires. SIGSTOP is sent when a program run under the shell exits through a terminate-and-stay resident program. The words INT, ALRM, and STOP can be used instead of the signal numbers.

If a signal is being ignored at the time that you enter the shell, it continues to be ignored without regard to any traps.

If there are no arguments at all, `trap` prints a list of all the traps and their commands.

Examples

```
trap 'rm -f /tmp/xyz$$; exit' ERR EXIT
trap 'read REPLY?"ABORT??"
    case $REPLY in
    y)   exit 1
    esac'      2
```

On error or exit, this example deletes a temporary file created during command execution. Upon an interrupt signal (Ctrl-C under DOS), the example asks whether to abort, and exits if the answer is y.

Diagnostics

Possible exit status values are:

0   Successful completion.

1   Failure due to an invalid command line argument, an invalid signal name or *number*.

Possible error messages include:

"*name*" Not a valid trap name   You specified an unrecognized trap name. This error usually happens because of a typing mistake on the command line.

Portability

POSIX.2. X/Open Portability Guide. MKS Toolkit. A built-in function of the Bourne Shell and KornShell on UNIX.

See Also

```
sh
```

483

true—Do Nothing, Successfully

Synopsis

```
: [argument ...]

true [argument ...]
```

Description

The : (colon) command simply yields an exit status of zero (success). This can be surprisingly useful, such as when you are evaluating shell expressions for their side effects. This command is built into the KornShell.

true is a built-in alias for the colon command. It is defined with

```
alias true=':'
```

Diagnostics

Because this command always succeeds, the only possible exit status is:

0   Successful completion.

Examples

```
: ${VAR:="default value"}
```

sets VAR to a default value if and only if it is not already set. This is because the := construct inside the parameter expansion assigns the value to VAR if VAR doesn't have a value. The result of the parameter expansion is the value of VAR, and this is an argument to :. As usual, : just ignores this argument and returns a zero exit status. For more details, see the *Parameter Substitution* section of the sh man page.

Portability

POSIX.2. X/Open Portability Guide. All UNIX systems. MKS Toolkit.

See Also

```
alias, sh
```

---

typeset—Assign Attributes and Values to Variables

Synopsis

```
typeset [±f[tux]] name name ...

typeset [±lprtuxH] [±iLRZ[number]] [variable[=value] ...]
```

Description

If no options are specified, typeset displays a list of all variables and their attributes. typeset is built into the KornShell.

Options

When only arguments of the form +*option* are specified, typeset displays a list of the variables that have all the specified attributes set.

If all parameters are of the form -*option,* typeset displays a list of all the variables having all the specified attributes set, and also displays their values.

When you specify the f option, typeset applies to functions. Otherwise, it applies to variables. For functions, the only applicable options are the ones shown in the *Synopsis* section.

If the command line contains at least one *variable,* typeset changes the attributes of each *variable.* Parameters of the form -*option* turn on the associated attributes, and parameters of the form +*option* turn off the associated attributes. Parameters of the form *variable=value* turn on the associated attributes and also assign *value* to *variable.*

When a function invokes typeset, the shell creates a new instance of each *variable.* After the function terminates, the shell restores each *variable* to the value and attributes it had before the function was called.

Here is a summary of the possible attribute options:

-l   Converts uppercase characters to lowercase characters in any value assigned to a *variable.* If -u is currently turned on, this option turns it off.

-p	Writes output to the coprocess. This is not useful on DOS, because DOS does not have coprocesses.
-r	Makes each *variable* read-only.
-t	Tags each *variable*. Tags are user-definable, and have no meaning to the shell. For functions, this turns on the xtrace option. See the man set page for a discussion of xtrace.
-u	Converts lowercase characters to uppercase characters in any value assigned to a *variable*. If -l is currently turned on, this option turns it off.
	When used with -f, -u indicates that the functions named in the command line are not yet defined. The attributes specified by the typeset command are applied to the functions when they are defined.
-x	Sets each variable for automatic export. See the man page for export.
-H	Performs UNIX to host-name file mapping. On DOS, slashes are mapped to backslashes.
-i[*number*]	Marks each variable as having an integer value, thus making arithmetic faster. If *number* is given and it is non-zero, the output base of each *variable* is *number*.

The following options justify the values assigned to each *variable* within a field. The width of the field is *number* if it is defined and non-zero; otherwise, the width of *variable* is the width of the first value assigned to *variable*.

-L[*number*]	Left-justifies the values assigned to each *variable* by removing any leading blanks. If -Z is turned on, leading zeros are also removed. Then blanks are added on the end or the end of the value is truncated as necessary. If -R is currently turned on, this option turns it off.
-R[*number*]	Right-justifies the values assigned to each *variable* by adding leading blanks or by truncating the end of the value as necessary. If -L is currently turned on, this option turns it off.
-Z[*number*]	Right-justifies values assigned to each *variable*. If the first non-blank character of value is a digit, leading zeros are used. Also see the -L option.

Diagnostics

Possible exit status values are:

   0   Successful completion.

   1   Failure due to an invalid command line argument.

If the command is used to display the values of variables, the exit status value is the number of names that are invalid.

Possible error messages include:

`Base number not in [2,36]`	You used the `-i` option to specify a base for an integer, but the base was not in the range 2 through 36. All bases must be in this range.
`name: Not a function`	You tried to declare the given *name* as a function, but the name already referred to something that was not a function (for example, a variable).
`Subscripts illegal with integers`	You tried to subscript a variable that was a simple integer. Subscripts can only be applied to array variables.

Portability

POSIX.2. MKS Toolkit. `typeset` is a built-in command of the KornShell on UNIX, but it is not a Bourne Shell command.

See Also

```
export, sh
```

unalias—Remove Aliases

Synopsis

```
unalias name ...
```

487

Description

unalias removes each alias *name*. It is built into the KornShell.

Diagnostics

Possible exit status values are:

0   Successful completion.

Otherwise, unalias returns the number of specified *names* that are not currently defined as aliases.

Possible error messages include:

name is not an alias   You tried to unalias a name that was not a
currently defined alias.

Portability

POSIX.2. MKS Toolkit. On UNIX, unalias is built into the KornShell but not the
Bourne Shell.

See Also

```
alias, sh
```

---

unset—Remove Shell Variable or Function

Synopsis

```
unset [-f] name...
```

Description

unset removes the value and attributes of each variable *name*. This command is
built into the shell.

unset cannot remove names that have been set read-only, or the internal
variables PS1, PS2, PS3, IFS, _, PATH, MAIL, MAILPATH, MAILCHECK.

Options

If you specify -f, unset removes the value and attributes of each function *name*.

Diagnostics

Possible exit status values are:

0   Successful completion.

1   Failure due to an invalid command line argument.

Otherwise, unset returns the number of specified *names* that are invalid, not currently set, or read-only.

Possible error messages include:

"*name*" : permanent variable   The given *name* cannot be deleted; for example, it may have been marked read-only.

Portability

POSIX.2. X/Open Portability Guide. MKS Toolkit. unset is a built-in command of the Bourne and Korn shells on UNIX System V.

See Also

```
sh
```

vi, ex—Display-Oriented Interactive Text Editor

Synopsis

```
vi [-sevR] [-t tag] [-w size] [-c command]
```

Description

vi is actually two text editors in one:

- vi is a screen editor, which uses the full screen to show the text you are editing. If you type an editing command, you see the results of the command but the command itself doesn't appear on the screen.

- vi is also a line editor, in which commands and text are displayed on the screen together. The editor only shows you the text you are editing if you explicitly ask it to do so.

Usually, people call the screen editor vi and the line editor ex. Each editor has a different set of commands, and each has its own strengths. Most people find that the screen editor is easier to use, but the line editor lets you perform more sophisticated operations.

To give you the best of both worlds, vi has a way for you to issue an ex command in the middle of a vi session. This makes it harder to remember that you are working with two separate editors, but the distinction is important: ex commands are independent from vi and vice versa.

There are two ways to start an ex session:

- You can invoke the command under the name ex;

- You can invoke it under the name vi, but specify the -e option.

Similarly, there are two ways to start a vi session:

- You can invoke the command under the name vi (without specifying -e);

- You can invoke it under the name ex, but specify the -v option.

Options

-c *command*	Executes the given *command* before it displays any text on the screen. The command should be an ex command without a leading :, and should be enclosed in quotes if the *command* contains whitespace.
-R	Sets the readonly variable, telling vi not to write on the file.
-s	Turns on *quiet mode*. This tells the editor not to print file information messages, so you can use ex as a filter.
-t	Lets you search for a tag in the same way as the ex tag command (described later).
-w *size*	Sets the option variable window to the number *size*. For more information, see the *Option Variables* section later in this man page.

Editor Fundamentals

vi and ex work on ASCII text files. If a file contains the ASCII null character (value 0 or \0), the character is turned into the ASCII value 0x7F. Files may not contain characters with values greater than 127 (hex 0x7F, octal 0177. The new-line character (\n, or 012, or 0x0A) is interpreted as a line delimiter. Each line is limited to a maximum length of 1024 bytes, including the new-line. If any lines are greater than 1024 bytes, they are chopped at that length. If the last line in the file does not end in a new-line, the editor adds a new-line. In all these abnormal cases, the editor marks the file as modified and displays a message.

In vi, you are in either *Insert Mode* or *Command Mode*. In Command Mode, every character you type is immediately interpreted as a command. In Insert Mode, every character you type is added to the text that you are editing.

The *current position pointer* indicates a text position that you are currently editing or that you've just edited. In ex, the current position pointer is just the line number of the line being edited. In vi, the pointer uses this line number plus the position of the cursor within the line. The line indicated by the current position pointer is always on the screen.

There are two display conventions that you should note:

1. When a file is shorter than the screen can hold, vi puts the true contents of the file at the top of the screen. vi then puts a single ~ character in the first column of all the screen lines after the last line in the file. These ~ lines are just padding; they are not part of the file. The same convention is used for other situations where the last line of the file is shown somewhere in the middle of the screen.

2. If the last line on the screen is too long to fit on the screen, vi puts an @ character in place of the line. This shows that there is a line there, but vi doesn't have room to display the whole line.

~ and @ lines are not actually part of the file; they are just used to show special situations.

vi commands can be divided into several categories.

- *Scrolling commands* adjust the position of text on the screen. The current position pointer changes only if the current line scrolls off the screen. For example, Ctrl-E scrolls the text on the screen up one line. The cursor continues to point to the same text that it was pointing to, unless you move the text off the screen.

- *Movement commands* move the cursor in the file. For example, the character j moves the cursor down one line; the screen only scrolls if it's necessary. There are two types of movement commands: *absolute* movements and *context-dependent* movements. An absolute movement moves the cursor, regardless of the nature of the surrounding text. For example, j always moves the cursor down one line. A context-dependent movement moves the cursor based on the nature of the text; for example, w moves the cursor to the beginning of the next word, so it must look at the text to determine where the next word begins.

- *Text insertion* commands let you add new text to the existing text.

- *Manipulation* commands let you change the text that is already in the file.

vi *Command Summary*

vi scrolling and movement commands can be preceded by a decimal integer that serves as a *count*. The count means different things with different commands. If you type a count, it will not be displayed anywhere on the screen.

Scrolling

Ctrl-E
Scrolls a new line onto the bottom of the screen. vi doesn't change the current position pointer unless the current line scrolls off the top of the screen; then it sets the pointer to the top line. A count scrolls forward the given number of lines.

Ctrl-Y
Scrolls a new line onto the top of the screen. vi doesn't change the current position pointer unless the current line scrolls off the bottom of the screen; then it sets the pointer to the bottom line. A count scrolls backward the given number of lines.

Ctrl-D
Scrolls a half-screen onto the bottom of the screen. The current position pointer moves forward the same amount in the text, which means that the cursor stays in the same relative position on the screen. If you give a count, the screen scrolls forward by that number of lines; this number is used for all future Ctrl-D and Ctrl-U commands (until you give a new count). The default scrolling amount is half the screen, or 12 lines.

Ctrl-U
Scrolls a half-screen onto the top of the screen. The current position pointer moves backward the same amount in the text, which means that the cursor stays in the same relative position on the screen. A count works the same way as Ctrl-D.

Ctrl-F
Scrolls forward by a page (in other words, a screen), less two lines. vi places the cursor on the top line of the screen. If you specify a count, vi scrolls forward that number of pages.

Ctrl-B
Scrolls back by a page, less two lines. vi places the cursor on the bottom line of the screen. If you specify a count, vi scrolls backward that number of pages.

z	Redraws the screen. If the z is followed by Enter or Ctrl-M, vi places the current line at the top of the screen. If it is followed by ., vi places the current line in the middle of the screen. If it is followed by -, vi places the current line at the bottom of the screen. If a count is given, vi first sets the current position pointer to that absolute line number; then it positions the screen according to the character following the z.

Absolute Movement

All the following movement commands can be preceded by a count to repeat the movement that many times.

j, », Ctrl-N, Ctrl-J	Moves the cursor to the next line at the same column on the screen. Scrolls the screen one line if needed.
+, Ctrl-M	Moves the cursor to the first non-space character on the next line. Scrolls the screen one line if needed.
k, ¡, Ctrl-P	Moves the cursor to the previous line at the same column on the screen. Scrolls the screen up one line if needed.
-	Moves the cursor to the first non-space character on the previous line. Scrolls the screen up one line if needed.
Backspace, ←, h, Ctrl-H	Moves the cursor one position to the left.
«, l, Space	Moves the cursor one position to the right.
¦	Moves the cursor to the column number specified as a count. The first column of the screen is number 1.
^	Moves the cursor to the first non-blank character of the current line.
0 (zero)	Moves the cursor to the first character of the current line.
$	Moves the cursor to the last character of the current line.
G	Moves to the absolute line number specified as the count. As a special case, a count of zero or no count moves the cursor to the last line of the file.

m	Records the current position pointer under a *mark name*. A mark name is a single lower-case letter, given immediately after the m. For example, the command ma records the current location of the current position pointer under the name a.
`	The grave accent character followed by a mark name moves the cursor to the position that has been associated with that name. You have to assign a mark name to the position with the m command before you can use ` to go to that position. A grave accent followed by another grave accent moves the cursor to the *previous context*. The previous context is typically the last place you made a change. More precisely, the previous context is set whenever you move the cursor in a non-relative manner.
'	The apostrophe works almost the same as the grave accent character, except that it sets the cursor to the first non-blank character on the marked line.

Movement By Context

w	Moves forward to the start of the next word. The start of a word is defined as the first non-blank character following a sequence of alphanumeric characters or a sequence of non-alphanumeric characters, starting at the character under the cursor. Blank characters for this purpose are the space, the tab, and the new-line character.
W	Moves forward to the start of the next *full word*. The start of a full word is defined as the first non-blank character after the first whitespace that follows the cursor position.
e	Moves the cursor forward to the end of a word, as defined for w.
E	Moves the cursor forward to the end of a full word, as defined for w.
b	Moves back a word. To do this, vi starts at the character before the cursor, then backs over blank characters. It finally backs over a word as defined for w. The cursor stays on the first character of the word.

B   Moves back a full word. To do this, `vi` starts at the charac-
            ter before the cursor, then backs over blank characters. It
            finally backs over a full word as defined under `W`. The
            cursor stays on the first character of the word.

(Moves back to the beginning of the previous sentence. A
            sentence is bounded by a closing punctuation mark `.`, `!` or
            `?`, followed by any number of closing quotation marks
            (such as `"`, `'`, `)`, or `]`) followed by two spaces or the end of
            the line. Paragraph and section boundaries are also sen-
            tence boundaries; see `[[` and `{`.

)   Moves forward to the beginning of the next sentence. See `(`
            for the definition of a sentence.

{   Moves back to the beginning of a paragraph. A paragraph
            begins on a blank line, a section boundary (see `[[`), or a
            `troff` text formatter macro in the `paragraphs` variable;
            `troff` is a popular UNIX text formatter discussed briefly in
            Chapter 10. `vi` checks each pair of characters in the
            `paragraphs` variable to see if it follows a leading period (`.`)
            on each line; if there is a match, the pair is assumed to be a
            text formatter paragraph macro.

}   Moves forward to the beginning of the next paragraph. See
            `{` for the definition of a paragraph.

[[Moves back to the beginning of a section. A section begins
            on lines starting with a formfeed (Ctrl-L), with an open
            brace (`{`), or with a macro in the `sections` variable.

]]   Moves forward to the beginning of the next section. See `[[`
            for the definition of a section.

%   Finds the balancing character to the one under the cursor.
            The character should be one of `[` `{` `(` `<` or `]` `}` `)` `>`. For example,
            if the cursor is on a `(`, pressing `%` moves to the matching `)`.
            Pressing `%` again moves back to the `(`.

H   Places the cursor on the first non-blank character of the top
            line of the screen.

M   Places the cursor on the first non-blank character of the
            middle line of the screen.

L   Places the cursor on the first non-blank character of the
            bottom line of the screen.

f*c*	Searches forward in the line for the single character *c* and positions the cursor on top of it. If you specify a count *n*, the editor searches for the *n*th such character.
F*c*	Same as f*c*, except that the editor searches backward in the line.
t*c*	Searches forward in the line for the character *c* and positions the cursor on the preceding character. If you specify a count *n*, vi searches for the *n*th matching character following and then positions the cursor on the preceding character.
T*c*	Same as t*c*, except that vi searches backwards and positions the cursor after the character being sought.
;	Repeats the most recent t, T, f, or F command.
,	Repeats the most recent t, T, f, or F command in the opposite direction.
/*regexp*	Searches forward in the file for a line matching the regular expression *regexp* and positions the cursor at the first character of the matching string.
?*regexp*	Same as /, but searches backwards in the file.
n	Repeats the most recent / or ?.
N	Repeats the most recent / or ?, but in the opposite direction.
Ctrl-]	Uses the word after the cursor as a tag. See the ex command tag.

Object Manipulators

An object manipulator command works on a block of text. To define the block of text you want to manipulate, put a movement command immediately after the command character for the object manipulator command. vi applies the manipulation command to all text from the current position pointer to wherever the movement command would leave the cursor.

For example, in dL, d is the object manipulator command to delete an object. It is followed by the movement command L, which moves to the bottom line of the screen. vi will therefore delete all text from the current position pointer to the bottom line on the screen.

Normally an object extends up to, but not including, the position of the cursor after the movement command. However, some movements work in a *line* mode; for example, L puts the cursor on the first non-blank character of the last line on the screen. If it is used in an object manipulation command, it includes the entire starting line and the entire ending line. Some other objects include the cursor position; for example, d$ deletes up to and including the last character on a line; by itself the $ would have placed the cursor on the final character.

When vi deletes or changes a block of text because of an object manipulation command, it saves the original block of text in a *buffer*. A buffer is just an area of computer memory that can hold text. There are several ways you can use buffers with object manipulation commands:

- You can use a *named* buffer. A buffer name is a single lowercase letter. To use a named buffer, type a double quotation mark (") followed by the buffer name, followed by the object manipulator command, as in

```
"adL
```

This deletes text from the current line to the bottom line on the screen and puts the deleted text in buffer a. Normally, this sort of operation overwrites the current contents of the buffer. However, if you use the same form but specify the buffer name in uppercase, vi appends the deleted text to the current contents of the buffer. For example,

```
"AdL
```

deletes from the current line to the bottom line on the screen, and adds the deleted text to whatever is already in buffer a.

- If you are deleting material and delete at least one full line, vi uses buffers numbered 1 through 9. The first time a full line or more is deleted, the text is placed in buffer 1. The next time, the old contents of 1 are copied to 2, and the newly deleted text is put into 1. In this way, deleted text *ripples* through the nine numbered buffers. When text ripples out of buffer 9, it is gone for good.

- In all other cases, the original text goes into the *unnamed* buffer. For example, vi uses the unnamed buffer if you delete less than a line of text. The unnamed buffer is like the other buffers, but it doesn't have a name.

Here are some examples of the use of buffers:

dL	Deletes text from the current position to the bottom of the screen. The deleted text goes into buffer 1, and the other numbered buffers ripple to make room for the new text.
"ad/fred/+0	Deletes text from the current line up to and including the first line containing the string fred. The deleted text goes into buffer a.
dw	Deletes the next word, and puts the word into the unnamed buffer.

Repeating the command letter applies the command to an entire line. Therefore dd deletes the current line, and 5dd deletes five lines.

The object manipulator commands follow.

d   Deletes the object.

c   Begins by deleting the object. Then vi enters Insert Mode to let you insert text following the current cursor position. If the object you want to change is less than one line, vi puts a dollar sign ($) on the final character of the object. The input that you enter to replace the object appears directly on top of the current object as you type, until you reach the $. If you keep typing more text, the existing text shifts to make room for what you type.

<   Shifts the object left by the value of the variable shiftwidth. This operator always works on a line basis. In order to make this shift, < gets rid of the correct number of leading blanks and/or tabs on each line.

>   Shifts the object right by the value of the variable shiftwidth. This operator always works on a line basis. In order to make this shift, > adds an appropriate number of blanks and/or tabs.

y   *Yanks* the object to the appropriate buffer; vi only copies the text to the buffer, it does not change the original text. Yanking text to a buffer is the first step in moving or duplicating text.

!   Filters the object through an external command. After you issue the command to move to the end of the object, vi lets you enter a system command that is parsed in the same manner as the ex system command (:!). vi then invokes the given command and sends the entire object to that command. Finally, vi replaces the original object with the output from the command. For example, 1G!Gsort moves to the first line of the file; then !Gsort takes all the text from the first line to the last line and runs it through the sort command. The output of sort then replaces the original text. As a result, the entire contents of the file are sorted on a line-by-line basis.

Object Manipulator Abbreviations

To make things easier, the following shorthand commands automatically imply a particular object. You can put a count and/or buffer name in front of any of these commands.

C	Changes text to the end of the line (c$).
D	Deletes to the end of the line (d$).
s	Substitutes text for a single character (cl).
S	Substitutes text for a single line (cc).
x	Deletes a single character (dl).
X	Deletes the single character before the cursor (dh).
Y	Yanks a line (yy).

Inserting Text

The following commands let you insert new text into existing text. They work by entering Insert Mode, where you can enter new text. When you are finished typing the input text, press Esc to return to Command Mode. The major difference between the following commands is where they put the new text.

a	Appends text after the current cursor position.
i	Inserts text before the current cursor position.
A	Appends text at end of line ($a).
I	Inserts text before the first non-blank character on a line, but after any blanks at the beginning of the line (^i).
o	Opens up a new line after the current line and appends text to it.
O	Opens up a new line before the current line and appends text to it.
r	Replaces the character under the cursor with the next character typed. With a count, this command changes that number of characters following the cursor to the same character. For example, 5rX changes the next five characters to X.
R	Replaces characters on the screen with characters typed, until you press Esc. Each character that you type replaces the character already on the screen. While you enter text, the screen may not correspond exactly to the contents of the file, due to tabs, and so on. The screen is properly updated after you press Esc.

Miscellaneous

p	Appends the contents of a buffer after the cursor. This is sometimes called a *paste* operation. If you specify a "*buffername* (for example, "b or "z) before p, vi appends

the contents of that buffer; otherwise, vi appends the contents of the unnamed buffer. If you created the buffer with an ex command, vi appends the contents of the buffer after the current line. If you created the buffer with a vi command, vi adds the contents after the cursor. As a special case, if you repeat a paste operation with the . command and you use a numbered buffer, vi increments the number of the buffer each time. Thus, "1p..... pastes in the contents of buffers 1 through 6 (i.e., it puts back the last six things you deleted).

P   Same as p except that vi pastes text before the cursor instead of after it.

u   Undoes the last change. If you do this again, you undo the undo (i.e., go back to what the text was before the first undo). Some operations are treated as single changes; for example, u can undo everything done by a global (g) command.

U   Undoes all changes to the current line. As soon as you move off a line or invoke an ex command on the line, vi forgets the original contents of the line and U no longer works on that line.

.   Redoes the most recent command. You can repeat any command that changes the contents of the file. vi remembers the count of the previous command and uses it unless you specify a new count with . .

~   *Toggles* the case of the character under the cursor; lower-case characters change to uppercase and vice versa. After changing the character, vi moves the cursor right by one. If you specify a count *n*, vi changes the case of the next *n* characters.

Ctrl-G   Provides information on the current file; this is equivalent to the ex command file. vi tells you the current line number, the number of lines in the file, and expresses the current position as a percentage of the way through the file.

J   Joins *n* lines together into one long line. The count *n* defaults to 2, which joins the current line to the next line. To join lines, vi removes all whitespace at the end of one line and at the beginning of the next. Then, if the final character of the first line is a period, vi puts two spaces between the two lines. If the first character of the next line

	is an opening parenthesis, vi does not put in any spaces; otherwise, vi puts in one space.
Q	Switches to ex. The editor stops behaving like vi, and begins to prompt for commands the way that ex does.
&	Repeats the most recent ex substitute command. This is equivalent to the ex command &.
:	Lets you execute a single ex command. When you type :, vi puts the cursor on the bottom line of the screen and displays a : to prompt you for input. You can then type one or more ex commands. When you type Esc or Enter, ex executes the line you have entered.
@	Invokes a macro. The character after @ must be a letter from a through z giving the name of a buffer. vi then executes the contents of that buffer as if you typed the same characters as input. The text of a macro can contain an @ calling another macro; however, if you have a macro call itself, vi goes into an infinite loop until it runs out of memory. If vi gets an error while executing a macro, it terminates all currently executing macros. All changes made during a macro call are treated as a unit and can be undone with a single u command.
ZZ	Writes the file out, if it has changed since the last time you wrote out the file. vi then terminates. ZZ is equivalent to the ex command xit.
Ctrl-L	Redraws the screen. You shouldn't need to do this unless a filter ! command writes directly to the screen instead of the standard output.
Ctrl-^	Switches to edit the *alternate file*. If you attempt this and you have not written out the current file since you made a change, vi refuses to switch to the alternate file.

Insert Mode

The object manipulation command c, and the text insertion commands (aAiIoOrR) put vi into Insert Mode. In this mode, most characters typed are inserted in the file. The following characters have special meaning.

Backspace, Ctrl-H	Deletes the last character you typed. vi does not remove the character from the screen, but it is no longer in your file. If you backspace over characters then start typing again, the new text overwrites the

	text you backspaced over. You can backspace to the start of the current line regardless of where you started to insert text. (This is not true of some other versions of vi.)
←	Backs over the last typed character. If you start typing again, the new text is inserted before the characters you backed over.
@	Deletes the current line in input mode. The cursor moves back to the first character that you inserted on this line. vi does not remove the current characters of the line from the screen, but they are no longer in your file. If you have backspaced past the point that you started inserting text, @ deletes back to the start of the current line. You can ask for a different line-delete character using the linedelete variable; this is described in the *Option Variables* section.
Enter, Ctrl-M	Ends the current line and starts a new one.
Ctrl-Q, Ctrl-V	Inserts the next character literally, instead of using its special meaning. For example, if you want your text to contain an Esc character, type Ctrl-V followed by Esc. If you didn't type Ctrl-V first, vi would think that Esc meant you were finished with Insert Mode. If the character after Ctrl-Q or Ctrl-V is an upper- or lowercase letter, vi inserts the control value; for example, Ctrl-VV inserts a Ctrl-V character. You cannot insert a Ctrl-J or the null character in your line. If you try to insert a Ctrl-M, it will disappear the next time you edit your file under DOS.
Ctrl-D	Decrements the *autoindent* for the current line by one level. This is only relevant if you have turned on the variable autoindent. See the *Option Variables* section for more details.
Ctrl-T	Increments the autoindent for the current line by one level. This is only relevant if you have turned on the variable autoindent.
Alt-A, Ctrl-@	If this is the first character typed after entering Insert Mode, vi repeats whatever you entered the last time you were in Insert Mode. After this, vi leaves Insert Mode. vi can insert a maximum of

256 characters in this way. On UNIX, Ctrl-A is the keystroke that performs this operation; however the DOS system won't let programs know when you type Ctrl-A, so this version of `vi` uses Alt-A instead.

Ctrl-W   Backs up by a word. Even though the characters are not removed from the screen, they are no longer in your file.

Break, Esc   Leaves Insert Mode.

ex *Command Mode*

You enter `ex` if you invoke the program with the `vi -e` option or if you issue the `Q` command from `vi`. You can issue a single `ex` command from `vi` using the `:` command.

The general form of an `ex` command is

```
[address-list] [command] [!] [parameters] [count] [flags]
```

Each part is optional, and some parts are not used with some commands. You can enter more than one command on a line by separating the commands with an or-bar (¦). Here is a brief description of each part of a command.

address-list   Gives a line or range of lines that you want the command to affect. For example, the `change` command changes a block of text, so the *address-list* would specify which text you want to change. See *Addresses* for more information.

command   The *command* is a word, which can be abbreviated. In the documentation, characters shown in square brackets are optional. For example, the `ex` *Command Summary* describes the `a[ppend]` command. This notation indicates that the append command can be abbreviated to simply `a`.

!   Some commands take a variant. This is often indicated by putting ! immediately after the *command*.

parameters   The *parameters* specify more information for the command. For example, the `parameters` for a `substitute` command specify the string that you want to replace and what you want to put in instead.

count   The *count* is used for a variety of purposes, similar to the *count* that can be supplied with `vi` commands.

503

flags   These *flags* indicate actions that ex should take after executing the command. A flag can consist of a leading + and - to adjust the value of dot; followed by p, 1, or # to print (display), list, or number a line. Thus

```
.+5 delete 6 ++#
```

goes to the fifth line after the current line, and deletes six lines. It then moves dot (the current line) ahead two lines in the file, then displays the line with its line number.

Addresses

Commands may take zero, one, two, or three addresses:

- With commands that do not apply to a particular line (such as commands that set options), you do not supply an *address-list*.

- If the command only applies to one line, the *address-list* may be a single address.

- If the command applies to a range of lines, you can specify the address in several ways.

      address,address   Specifies the range from the first *address* to the *address* (inclusive).

      address command *count*   Specifies the range of lines beginning at *address* and extending for the next *count* lines.

      %   Is a short form that stands for the entire file.

- There are a few special commands that can take three addresses. In this case, the command takes the form

> *address,address* command *address*

Any or all of the addresses can be omitted. If you omit an address with a command that usually takes an address, ex assumes a default address or range. Possible default addresses are shown as:

    [.,.]   Used for commands that can take a range of lines. This notation indicates that if you do not specify an *address-list*, the command only applies to the current line.

    [1,$]   Used for commands that can take a range of lines. This notation indicates that if you do not specify an *address-list*, the command applies to the entire file.

[.+1] Used for commands that take a single address. This notation indicates that if you do not specify an *address-list*,
the command applies to the line after the current one.

Here is a list of the possible forms in which you can specify an address.

. (dot) Stands for the current line.

n A line number indicates an absolute line in the file; the first
line has absolute line number 1.

$ The dollar sign stands for the last line in the file.

+*n* Stands for the line *n* lines ahead in the file.

+ Stands for the next line.

-*n* Stands for the line *n* lines back in the file.

- Stands for the previous line.

'*x* Stands for the value of the mark x.

/*pat*/ Searches for a string matching the regular expression *pat*,
starting at the line after the current line and moving
forward.

?*pat*? Searches for a string matching the regular expression *pat*,
starting at the line before the current line and moving
backward.

For example,

```
/pattern/+3
++
100
```

are three addresses: the first searches for a pattern and
then goes three lines further; the second indicates two
lines after dot; and the third indicates the 100th line in the
file.

Regular Expressions

A *regular expression* or *pattern* matches a set of characters. A regular expression
may consist of a string of normal characters that exactly match characters in a line.

Regular expressions can also contain special characters, known as
metacharacters. Metacharacters have special meanings; for example, the
metacharacter $ stands for the end of a line, so the regular expression x$ stands for
an x at the end of a line. Some metacharacter constructs consist of several characters.

Because $ is a metacharacter, you need some way to tell ex when you are
referring to a literal dollar sign rather than the character's special *end-of-line*
meaning. To do this, put a backslash (\) character in front; for example, \$1 matches

the string $1. The same principle applies to other metacharacters. Putting a backslash in front of a metacharacter is called *escaping* the metacharacter.

If you turn off the `magic` option, many of the metacharacters are disabled. If you put a backslash in front of a metacharacter that is currently turned off, `ex` uses the special meaning of the metacharacter. In other words, \ temporarily turns off metacharacters that are on, and temporarily turns on metacharacters that are off. See Appendix E for examples of regular expressions.

Here is a list of the metacharacter sequences and their meanings.

^	Matches the start of a line. ^ is not affected by the setting of `magic`: it is always a metacharacter unless it is escaped.
$	Matches the end of a line. $ is not affected by the setting of `magic`: it is always a metacharacter unless it is escaped.
.	Matches any single character.
*	Matches zero or more occurrences of the previous expression.
\<	Matches the start of a *token*. More precisely, it matches the empty string preceding an alphanumeric or underscore that is not preceded by an alphanumeric or underscore. \< is not affected by the setting of `magic`: it is always a metacharacter unless it is escaped.
\>	Matches the end of a token. More precisely, it matches the empty string following an alphanumeric or underscore that is not followed by an alphanumeric or underscore. \> is not affected by the setting of `magic`: it is always a metacharacter unless it is escaped.
[*string*]	The *string* is a list of characters that defines a *class*. This construct matches any of the characters in the class. For example, [aeiouy] matches any of the vowels. You can put a range of characters in a class by specifying the first and last characters of the range, with a - between them. For example, [A-Za-z] matches any upper- or lowercase letter. If the first character of a class is the caret (^), the regular expression matches any character not specified inside the square brackets. Thus, [a-z_][^0-9] matches a single alphabetic character or the underscore, followed by any non-numeric character.
\(...\)	Any set of characters in the pattern can be surrounded by escaped parentheses. See the discussion of the *n* replacement pattern in the following section to find the meaning of this construct.

Replacement Patterns

Replacement patterns are used in substitute commands. The usual form of such a command is

```
s/regexp/repl/
```

where *regexp* is a regular expression and *repl* is a replacement pattern. The command searches for a string that matches the regular expression, and replaces that string with another indicated by *repl*. In most cases, *repl* is just a normal string of characters; however, it can contain other characters with special meanings:

&	Stands for the entire string matched by *regexp*. For example, s/abc/&d/ changes abc to abcd.
~	Stands for the most recent replacement pattern used in an earlier command.
\n	Stands for the string that matches the *n*th occurrence of \(...\) in the regular expression. For example, consider s/\([a-zA-Z]*\)our/\1or/ The \1 represents the string that matched the regular expression \([a-zA-Z]*\). Thus the preceding command might change the word colour to color.
\u	Turns the next character in the replacement to uppercase.
\l	Turns the next character in the replacement to lowercase.
\U	Turns all following characters in the replacement to uppercase.
\L	Turns all following characters in the replacement to lowercase.
\E, \e	Turns off the effects of \U or \L.

ex *Commands*

Here is a list of the ex commands. You can also use these commands in vi, but you must start with the : command to warn vi that you want to execute an ex command.

ab[breviate] *lhs rhs*	Says that the string *lhs* is an abbreviation for *rhs*. If you enter *lhs* surrounded by white space in vi's Insert Mode, the editor automatically changes the input to *rhs*. For example, if you set up ab ls long long string

	every time you type ls as a separate word in Insert Mode, the editor replaces it with long long string. If you do not specify any arguments for ab, it displays the abbreviations that are already defined.
[.] a[ppend][!]	Enters ex Insert Mode. ex places input text after the specified line. To leave Insert Mode, enter a line consisting of the single character period (.). If you specify an address of zero, ex inserts text before the first line of the file. After you leave Insert Mode, dot is the last line typed.
	If you specify !, ex turns autoindent on if it's off and off if it's on. You may not use append from vi; you must be using ex.
ar[gs]	Displays the current list of files being edited. To show you which is the current file, ex puts square brackets around the file name.
cd *path*	Changes your current working directory to *path*.
[.,.] c[hange][!] [*count*]	Deletes the given line range and then enters Insert Mode. If you specify !, ex turns autoindent on if it's off and off if it's on. You may not use change from vi; you must be using ex.
[.,.] co[py] *addr* [*flags*]	Makes a copy of the given line range, and appends the copy after *addr*. If *addr* is zero, ex inserts the copied lines before the first line of the file. Dot is left on the last line of the inserted text.
[.,.] d[elete] [*buffer*] [*count*] [*flags*]	
	Deletes the specified line range. Dot is left on the line following the deleted text.
	buffer can be a letter (A-Za-z). If so, ex saves the deleted lines in the buffer with that name. If the letter is upper-

case, the lines are added to the buffer; if the letter is lowercase, the lines overwrite the contents of the *buffer* with the corresponding uppercase name. If you do not specify a `buffer`, deleted lines go to buffer 1, the old contents of buffer 1 go to buffer 2, and so on up through buffer 9, whose previous contents are lost.

`e[dit] [!] [+command] [file]`   Begins a new editing session on a new `file`; the new file replaces the old file on the screen. Normally, ex won't let you edit a new file if you haven't saved the old file since the last time you changed its contents. If you specify !, the editor starts editing the new file even if you haven't saved the changes in the old one. *command* can be any ex command; if you specify one, ex executes the command as soon as it reads the new file.

`f[ile] [file]`   Changes the current file name to `file` and marks the file [`Not edited`]. If this file exists, you may not overwrite it unless you use ! with the `write` command. If you do not specify a `file` name, ex displays information about the current file.

`[1,$] g[lobal] [!] /pat/ commands`

Checks the given range of lines for strings that match the regular expression *pat*. On lines that contain matches, ex executes the given *commands*. The *commands* may not contain another `global` command or `undo`. An `undo` command after the `global` command undoes the effect of the entire `global` command. In ex mode, you can have multiple lines of *commands* by putting a backslash (\) on the end of each line but the last. If one of the *commands* takes input, put the input in the command list. If the last line of *commands* is input text, you don't have to add a . to mark the end of the input. For example,

```
g/rhino/a\
hippo
```

appends the single line `hippo` after each line containing `rhino`. The total length of a global command list is limited (see the *Limits* section).

[.] i[nsert] [!]   Enters Insert Mode. This is identical to the append, except that `ex` inserts input text before the specified line. You may not use `insert` from `vi`; you must be using `ex`.

[.,.+1] j[oin] [!] [*count*] [*flags*]

Joins together all lines of text within the range. If you specify !, `ex` joins the lines without changing the white space between the lines; otherwise, it joins the lines using the same approach as the `vi` J command.

[.] k x   Is the same as the `mark` command.

[.,.] l[ist] [*count*] [*flags*] Displays the specified line in a visually unambiguous manner. Tabs are printed as ^I, and the end of lines are marked as $. Dot is left at the last line displayed.

map[!] *lhs rhs*   Defines macros for use in `vi`. *lhs* is a string of characters; whenever you type that string exactly, `vi` behaves as if you typed the string *rhs*. If *lhs* is more than one character long, `vi` does not echo or act upon any of the characters until you type a character that isn't in the *lhs* (in which case all the characters up to that point in the *lhs* are executed) or you type the last character of *lhs*. If the remap option is on, *rhs* itself can contain macros. If you specify !, the map only works in `vi` Insert Mode; otherwise it only works in `vi` Command

<table>
<tr><td></td><td>Mode. A map command with no arguments displays all macros currently defined.</td></tr>
<tr><td>[.] ma[rk] x</td><td>Marks the specified line with the name x. x must be a single lowercase letter. When you have marked a line, you can refer to that line in subsequent commands with the address ' x.</td></tr>
<tr><td>[.,.] m[ove] [addr] [flags]</td><td>Copies the specified line range, then deletes it. ex then appends the copied text after the given addr. If addr is zero, ex moves the text to the start of the file. Dot is left at the first line of the moved range.</td></tr>
<tr><td>n[ext] [!] [+command] [file ...]</td><td></td></tr>
</table>

Specifies a *file list*, given by the arguments `file` ... This is a list of files that you want to edit. After ex has made note of the file list, it executes the command

edit [!] [+*command*] *file*

to begin editing the first file in the list. If you do not specify a file list with the next command, it begins editing the next file in the current file list. The current file list is either the list of files given on the vi command line, or a file list set up by a previous next command. The ! and *command* have the same meaning as with edit.

<table>
<tr><td>[.,.] nu[mber] [count] [flags]</td><td>Displays the specified line range with leading line numbers. Dot is left at the last line displayed.</td></tr>
<tr><td>[.,.] # [count] [flags]</td><td>Is the same as number.</td></tr>
<tr><td>[.,.] p[rint] [count] [flags]</td><td>Displays the specified line range. Dot is left at the last line displayed.</td></tr>
<tr><td>[.] pu[t] [buffer]</td><td>Is similar to the p (paste) command of vi. ex pastes lines that have been deleted or yanked back into the file after the given line. If you don't specify a</td></tr>
</table>

511

	buffer name, ex uses the most recently changed buffer.
q[uit] [!]	Exits from vi/ex. If you have modified the current file since the last time you wrote the file, you must use ! or you will not be permitted to exit until you write the file.
[.] r[ead] [*file*]	Reads the contents of *file* and appends the text after the given line number. If the line number is 0, ex reads the contents of the given file and inserts the text at the beginning of the file being edited. If the current file name is not set, you must specify a *file*, and that becomes the current file name. If there already is a current file name, *file* becomes the alternate file name. If *file* begins with !, it is taken as a command; ex executes the command and reads the output via a pipe.
rew[ind] [!]	Goes back to the start of the current file list and starts editing the first file in the list. If you have modified the current file since the last time it was written, you must specify !; otherwise, you will not be able to leave the current file until you have written it out. If autowrite is set, ex writes out the current file automatically if necessary.
se[t] [*parameter-list*]	If called without a parameter list, set displays all the variables with values that have changed since the editing session started. If you specify the parameter all, ex displays all variables and their values. You can use the parameter list to set or display each of many variable values. Each argument in the list is a variable name.
	Some variables are *Boolean*, which means they can be on or off. To turn a Boolean variable on, give the variable's name; to turn it off, type no followed by the name.

Other variables are *non-Boolean*, which means that they can be assigned values. If you specify the name of a non-Boolean variable (without a value), set displays the current value. To display the value of a Boolean variable, use a parameter consisting of the variable name followed by a question mark (?). You can set numeric or string variables with a *parameter* of the form

`name=value`

In a string variable, you must put a backslash in front of spaces. As an example,

`set readonly? noautowrite shell=/ bin/sh`

displays the value of the Boolean `readonly` variable, turns off `autowrite`, and sets `shell` to `/bin/sh`.

`set report report=5`	Displays the value of the `report` variable, and then sets the value to 5. See the *Set Option Variables* section for further details.
`sh[ell]`	Invokes a subshell; on DOS, this is normally `COMMAND.COM`. The editor uses `shell` to find the name of the shell to execute. On DOS, you normally use the `exit` command to return to the editor from `COMMAND.COM`.
`so[urce] file`	Starts executing editor commands from `file`. `file` can contain `source` commands of its own.
`st[op]`	Suspends the editor session and returns to system level. For further information, see the description of the `vi` command Ctrl-Z.
`[.,.] s[ubstitute] [/pat/repl/] [opts] [count] [flags]`	
	For each line in the line range, the editor searches for the regular expression *pat* and replaces matching strings

513

with *repl*. Normally, ex only replaces the first matching string in each line; if *opts* contains g (*global*), it replaces all matching strings. If *opts* contains c (*confirm*), ex first prints the line with caret (^) characters marking the *pat* matching location; you can then type **y** if you want ex to go ahead with the substitution. *pat* does not match strings that start on one line and end on the next; however in ex, the *repl* string can contain a new-line, escaped by a preceding backslash (\). See the section on *Regular Expressions* and *Replacement Patterns* for full information on both *pat* and *repl*. If there is no pat and/or *repl*, ex uses the most recently specified regular expression and/or replacement string.

[.,.] t *addr* [*flags*] Is the same as the copy command.

ta[g] [!] *identifier* Is used in locating C function definitions in C source files. The first step is to create a *tags* file using the ctags command (not included in the MKS Tools of this package). After you do this, you can use the ex tag command to look up a particular function definition and go directly to that definition in the file that contains it.

When you issue a tag command, ex looks up the *identifier* in the files listed in the variable tags. If it finds the identifier in a tags file, the line in the tags file will give the name of the file that contains that function and a regular expression that lets you locate the function inside the file. If the file containing the function is different from the one you are currently editing, ex normally begins editing the new file; however, if you have modified the current file since the last time it was written out, ex doesn't start editing the new file unless the tag command contains !. (If autowrite is on, ex automatically saves the current file and reads in the new file.) After ex reads in the new file, it uses the regular expression from the tags file to find the function in the file.

All characters in tag names are significant unless the variable taglength is non-zero; in this case, ex only uses the given number of characters in the comparison.

una[bbreviate] *lhs*

Deletes the abbreviation *lhs* previously created by abbreviate.

u[ndo]

Undoes the last change or set of changes that modified the current file. global commands and vi macros are both considered as single changes that can be undone. If you issue an undo, and then a second undo, the second undoes the first and you go back to the way things were originally. You cannot undo an edit command, nor can you undo operating system commands or commands that write output to the file system.

unm[ap] [!] *lhs*

Deletes the macro associated with lhs. If you specify !, it applies to Insert Mode macros; otherwise it applies to Command Mode macros.

[1,$] v /*pat*/ *commands*

Is a synonym for the global command with the ! flag; i.e. a global for all non-matching lines.

ve[rsion]

Displays the current version information for vi/ex.

[.] vi[sual] [*flag*]

Switches from ex to vi. If you do not specify a *flag*, vi puts the current line at the top of the screen. If *flag* is ^, the bottom line of the vi screen will be one

	window before the current line in ex. If *flag* is -, the current line will be at the bottom of the screen, and if flag is ., the current line will be in the middle.
vi[sual] [+*command*] [*file*]	In this form, this is the same as the edit command.
[1,$] w[rite] [!] [>>] [*file*]	Writes the given range of lines to *file*. If you specify >>, the lines are appended to the current contents of the file. If the current file name is not set, you must give a *file* name; this name becomes the current file name. If there already is a current file name, *file* becomes the alternate file name if it is specified. If the *file* name begins with !, it is taken as a command; ex invokes the command and pipes the given range of lines into the command as input.
	If you specify a *file*, it must not already exist, and the readonly option must not be on. These conditions can be overridden by using the flag !.
[1,$] wq [!] [>>] [*file*]	Is the same as write, except that it exits the editor immediately afterward (if the write is successful).
x[it]	Writes out the current file if it has been modified. ex then terminates.
[.,.] y[ank] [*buffer*] [*count*]	Copies the given line range to the specified *buffer* (a letter from a through z). If you do not specify a *buffer*, ex uses the unnamed buffer. You can use yank to copy text from one file, then edit a new file and put the copied text into the new file.
[.+1]z [*flag*] [*count*]	Displays the number of lines given by *count*. If you do not specify a *count*, ex uses the current value of the scroll variable. The lines are displayed with the given line located according to the *flag*. If *flag* is +, ex displays the given line and a screenful after that. If *flag* is ., ex displays a screenful with the given

line in the middle. If *flag* is -, ex
displays a screenful with the given line
at the end, and if *flag* is ^, ex displays
the screenful before that. Dot is left at
the last line displayed.

`[.,.] <[<...] [`*count*`]` `[`*flags*`]`	Shifts the given lines left by the value of the `shiftwidth` variable. If there are multiple < characters, each causes another shift of the same distance. Dot is left at the last line of the range. If you specify a *count*, ex shifts that many lines.
`[.,.] >[>...] [`*count*`]` `[`*flags*`]`	Shifts the given lines right by the value of the `shiftwidth` variable. If there are multiple < characters, each causes another shift of the same distance. Dot is left at the last line of the range. If you specify a *count*, ex shifts that many lines.
`[`*range*`] ! `*command*	If you do not give a *range*, ex submits the *command* to be executed by the command interpreter that the `shell` variable names. If you give a *range*, ex invokes the *command* with the contents of that line range as input. The output from the *command* then replaces that line range. Thus

`1,$!sort`

sorts the entire contents of the file.

ex makes several substitutions in
command before executing it. See the
Special Characters in ex *Commands*
section for details. If any such substitutions actually take place, ex displays the
new command line before it is executed.

If the file has been modified and the
variable `autowrite` is on, ex writes the
current file before calling the command.
If `autowrite` is off, ex gives a warning
message.

[$] =   Displays the line number of the given
                                          line, but does not change which line is
                                          the current one.

Ctrl-D   Displays the number of lines of text
                                          given by the scroll variable. Under
                                          DOS, Ctrl-D must be followed by Enter.
                                          Dot is left on the last line printed.

" *a line of text*   Any ex command beginning with " is
                                          taken as a comment.

[.,.] & [*options*] [*count*] [*flags*]

                                          Repeats the last substitute command.
                                          If *options*, *count*, or *flags* are speci-
                                          fied, they replace the corresponding
                                          items in the previous substitute
                                          command.

[.,.] ~ [*options*] [*count*] [*flags*]

                                          Repeats the last substitute command.
                                          However, it uses the last regular expres-
                                          sion as the regular expression in the
                                          substitute command. For example, if
                                          there has been a search since the last
                                          substitute, ex uses the search's
                                          regular expression rather than the
                                          substitute's. If *options*, *count*, or
                                          flags are specified, they replace the
                                          corresponding items in the previous
                                          substitute command.

Special Characters in *ex* Commands

When an ex command contains the % character, ex replaces the character with the
name of the current file. For example, if you are about to try out a macro and you
are worried that the macro may damage the file, you could say

```
!cp % /tmp
```

to copy the current file to a safe holding place. As another example, a macro could
use % to refer to the current file.

When an ex command contains the # character, ex replaces the character with the name of the alternate file. You can set the name of the alternate file with the read command as described previously. Thus, a command like

```
e #
```

tells ex to edit the alternate file. Using an alternate file can be particularly convenient when you have two files that you want to edit "simultaneously." The preceding command lets you flip back and forth between the two files.

When an ex ! command contains the ! character, ex replaces the character with the previous *command* line.

Option Variables

You can set options for vi and ex with the ex set command. For example

```
set autowrite
```

sets the autowrite option. You turn an option off by putting no in front of the name, as in

```
set noautowrite
```

In the descriptions that follow, variables that are off by default are preceded by no. The minimal abbreviation of each option is shown after the comma. Default values are shown after =.

noautoindent, ai   When autoindent is on and you are entering text, the editor bases the indentation of the current line on the previous line. In vi, you can change this default indentation by using the control keys Ctrl-D (to shift left) or Ctrl-T (to shift right). In ex, you can type a tab or spaces at the start of a line to increase the indent, or type Ctrl-D at the start of the line to remove a level. Under DOS, you will not see the new indent immediately. Ctrl-D places the current line at a zero indent level, restoring the indent level for the next line. 0 followed by Ctrl-D places the current line at a zero indent level, and the next line has this indent level as well.

	The variable `shiftwidth` defines the size of indent levels. Based on this value and the value of `tabstop`, the editor generates the number of tabs (Ctrl-I) and spaces needed to produce the required indent level.
`autoprint, ap`	When this option is on in `ex`, `ex` displays the current line after the following commands: `copy`, `delete`, `join`, `move`, `substitute`, `&`, `~`, `undo`, `<`, and `>`. Automatic line display does not take place inside `global` commands.
no`autowrite, aw`	When this option is on, the editor automatically writes out the current file if it has been changed since it was last written, and you execute any of the following commands: `next`, `rewind`, `tag`, Ctrl-^ (`vi`), and Ctrl-] (`vi`). Using `!` with any of these commands stops the automatic write. Note that the `edit` command is explicitly not part of this list.
no`beautify, bf`	When this option is on, the editor discards all control characters typed during `vi` Insert Mode, except Ctrl-L and Ctrl-I. You can still add control characters using the Ctrl-V escape mechanism. When `eightbits` is also on, the editor discards all eight-bit characters except accents, currency symbols, and punctuation.
`directory=/`**`tmp,`** `dir`	The editor uses three temporary files. They are created with unique names under the given directory. Any error on the temporary files is fatal.
no`edcompatible`	When this option is on, the editor attempts to make `substitute` commands behave in a way that is compatible with the `ed` editor (not discussed in this book).
no`ignorecase, ic`	When this option is on, the editor ignores the case of letters when matching strings and regular expressions.
no`list`	When this option is on, the editor displays tabs as `^I` rather than expanding them with

	blanks. It also indicates the ends of lines with $.
magic	When this option is off (nomagic), the metacharacters ^ and $ become the only ones with special meanings in regular expressions. All other metacharacters must be preceded by a backslash (\) to have their special meaning.
maxbuffers=**512**	This specifies the number of K units (1024 bytes) of memory that are used for the editor buffers. These are allocated in units of 16K. The default is 512, but if that is not available when the editor starts, maxbuffers is set to the number actually obtained. The editor needs at least 32K. Note that this is in addition to the code and data space required by vi, which can be as much as 128K. Changing maxbuffers has no effect.
nonumber, nu	When this option is on, the editor displays line numbers to the left of the text being edited.

paragraphs=**IPLPPPQPP LIpplpipbp**

	This list controls the movement between paragraphs in vi. Lines beginning with . followed by any pair of characters in the list are paragraph boundaries (such as .IP). Such lines are typically commands to text formatters like troff.
prompt	When this option is on, ex Command Mode prompts with a colon (:). (ex does not display prompts if it is not reading input from a terminal.)
noreadonly	When this option is on, vi does not let you write to the current file.
remap	If this option is on and ex expands a map macro, the editor then reexamines the expansion to see if it too contains map macros.
report=**5**	The editor displays a message whenever you issue a command that affects more

	than the number of lines you specify in this command.
restrict	When this option is on, all file names are restricted to the current directory. You may not call subcommands. This variable is automatically set if you invoke the editor with a command that starts with the letter r, as in rvi. Once the option is turned on, it cannot be turned off.
scroll=**window/z**	This sets the number of lines to scroll for the z (ex), Ctrl-D, and Ctrl-U commands.
sections=**SHNHH HU**	This list controls the movement between sections in vi. Lines beginning with . followed by any pair of characters in the list are section boundaries (such as .SH). Such lines are typically commands to text formatters like troff.
shell=	This is the name of the command interpreter to be used for ! commands and the shell command. The default value is taken from the SHELL environment variable. On DOS, if SHELL is not defined, ex takes the name of the command interpreter from the COMSPEC environment variable.
shiftwidth=**8, sw**	This sets the width of indent used by shift commands and autoindent.
noshowmatch, sm	If this option is on and you type a closing parenthesis) or a closing brace } in Insert Mode, the cursor moves to the matching open parenthesis or brace. It stays there for about one second and then moves back to where you were. This lets you note the relationship between opening and closing parentheses/braces.
tabstop=**8**	Sets tab stops for screen display in vi mode to multiples of this number.
taglength=**0**, tl	If this variable is non-zero, ex only compares tags for this number of characters.
tags=**tags**	The value of this variable should be a list of file names separated by spaces. These are used by the ex command tag and the vi

	command Ctrl-]. The files are typically created with the `ctags` program.
`term=`	This is set to the terminal type on entry to the editor. Under DOS, the variable only provides information; the editor ignores changes to it.
no`terse`	If this option is on, the editor displays messages in a very abbreviated form.
`warn`	When this option is on, commands with ! display a warning message if the current file has been modified. No message is printed if this option is off.
`window=`**24**	This variable gives the number of text lines available in `vi` mode. This is only provided for information; the value cannot be changed.
`wrapscan, ws`	If this option is off, forward searches stop at the end of the file and backward searches stop at the top. Otherwise, forward searches that reach the bottom of the file *wrap around* to the top of the file and keep going; similarly, backward searches that reach the top of the file *wrap around* to the bottom and keep going.
`wrapmargin=`**0**`, wm`	If this variable is non-zero in `vi` Insert Mode, when a line reaches this number of characters from the right of the screen, the current word moves down to the next line automatically. You don't have to press Enter.
no`writeany, wa`	If this option is off, the editor does not let a file marked [Not edited] overwrite an existing file.

Editor Initialization

Initialization code consists of one or more `ex` commands, to be executed by `ex` when it starts up. On DOS, initialization code can be obtained in several ways.

- If there is a file named `ex.rc` under the current directory, it is assumed to hold initialization code. This code is executed using an `ex source` command.

- Next, if there is an environment variable named EXINIT with a non-null value, its value is assumed to be initialization code and the code is executed.

- If EXINIT does not exist or has a null value, the editor attempts to find a file named ex.rc under your home directory. If you have an environment variable named HOME, the editor uses the value of this variable as the name of your home directory. If you have no HOME variable, the editor uses ROOTDIR as your home directory. The ex.rc file is executed using an ex source command. See Appendix E for more information on these environment variables.

The editor reads ex.rc as if it were a sequence of keystrokes typed at the beginning of an ex session. As a result, the contents of ex.rc must be the same as the characters you would type if you were in vi/ex. In particular, if the input contains an unusual character (such as a carriage return) that you would normally precede with Ctrl-V, there must be a Ctrl-V in the ex.rc file. If you are creating an ex.rc file with vi, you must type Ctrl-V twice to put a single Ctrl-V character into your initialization file, then Ctrl-V followed by the special character to put the special character into your initialization file. The initialization file must show both the Ctrl-V and the special character.

On UNIX systems, the editor goes through the same process but looks for files named .exrc instead of ex.rc.

Diagnostics

Possible exit status values are:

0   Successful completion.

1   Failure because of any of the following:

   Unknown option

   No such command from open/visual

   Missing lhs

   Missing file name

   System does not support job control

   Write forms are w and w>>

   Internal error: bad seek pointer

   Internal error: line out of range

   Internal error: line too long

Non-zero address required on this command

No lines in the buffer

Nothing to undo

Can't escape a new-line in global from visual

Global command too long

Argument list too long

File is read-only

No previous command to substitute for !

Command too long

No previous re (no previous regular expression)

Buffers are 1-9, a-z

Line too long

System does not support job control

Digits required after =

Nothing in buffer

Missing rhs

Too many macros

Recursive map expansion

Nothing to repeat

Last repeatable command overflowed the repeat buffer

Bad tag

No tags file

No such tag in tags file

Negative address—first buffer line is 1

Not an editor command

Unimplemented EX command

Wrong number of addresses for command

Mark requires following letter

Undefined mark referenced

Global within global not allowed

First address exceeds second

Can't use open/visual unless open option is set

No address allowed on this command

No more files to edit

No current file name

Extra characters at end of command

Not that many lines in buffer

Insufficient memory

Restricted environment

Command too long

Trailing address required

Destination cannot straddle source in m and t

No file name to substitute for %

No alternate file name to substitute for #

File name too long

Too many file names

Argument buffer overflow

Incomplete shell escape command

Regular expressions cannot be delimited by letters or digits

No previous scanning regular expression

No previous substitute to repeat

Can't escape new-lines into regular expressions

Missing [

Badly constructed regular expression

No remembered regular expression

Line overflow in substitute

Replacement pattern contains \d—cannot use in re

Replacement pattern too long

Regular expression too complicated

Can't escape new-line in visual

No such set option

String too long in option assignment

Limits

- Maximum number of lines: 65279 (64K - 256 - 1)

- Length of longest line: 1K (1024) bytes including \r\n

- Longest command line: 160 bytes

- Length of file names: 128 bytes

- Length of string options: 64 bytes

- Length of remembered regular expressions: 256 bytes

- Number of map, map! and abbreviate entries: 64 each

- Number of saved keystrokes for . in vi: 128

- Length of the *lhs* of map, map! or abbreviate: 10 bytes

- Max number of characters in a tag name: 30

- Number of characters in a : escape from vi: 128

- Number of characters in the global command: 256 including new-lines

- Requires 128K of memory plus maxbuffers K of auxiliary memory. maxbuffers can be set with the ex set command. On DOS, auxiliary memory is freed during Ctrl-Z, :stop, :!, :w !, .,.!, and :r ! commands. During start-up, maxbuffers is changed to reflect available memory; the editor needs at least 32K.

Portability

POSIX.2. X/Open Portability Guide. Most UNIX systems. MKS Toolkit. See portability notes throughout this document.

Files

/tmp/vinnnnn[abc]	Temporary files.
ex.rc	Start-up file.

See Also

```
sed
```

wc—Count of Lines, Words, and Bytes

Synopsis

```
wc [-lwc] [file ...]
```

Description

wc counts the number of lines, words, and bytes in text files. If you specify several files on the command line, wc produces counts for each file, plus totals for all files.

A word is considered to be a character or characters delimited by whitespace (spaces, tabs, and/or new-line characters).

wc counts bytes, not characters. This is a change from previous versions of wc, and one that is dictated by the POSIX.2 draft standard. There are several ways the number of bytes can differ from the number of characters.

1. On DOS, the end of the line is usually marked with a pair of bytes (carriage return and linefeed). In earlier versions of wc, this counted as a single character; now it counts as two bytes.

2. If you have a file containing multibyte characters, the byte count will be higher than the character count. (Mulibyte characters use more than one byte to represent a single character. They are needed in languages like Chinese, where there are so many characters you can't represent them all with a single byte.)

Options

The -c option only prints a byte count; -w only prints a word count and -l only prints a line count. The order of options can dictate the order in which counts are displayed. For example, -cwl displays the number of bytes, then the number of words, then the number of lines. If no options are specified, the default is -lwc: lines, then words, then bytes.

Diagnostics

Possible exit status values are:

0   Successful completion.

1   Failure because of an invalid command line option, or inability to open the input file.

Portability

POSIX.2. X/Open Portability Guide. All UNIX systems. MKS Toolkit.

See Also

```
vi
```

whence—Tell How Shell Interprets Command Name

Synopsis

```
whence [-v] name ...
```

Description

whence tells how the shell would interpret each name if you used it as a command name. It tells you whether a name is a shell keyword, alias, function, built-in command, or executable file. For executable files, whence gives the full path name.

Some UNIX systems have a similar command named which. The difference is that whence is built into the KornShell, while which is a separate command.

Options

-v gives a more verbose report.

Diagnostics

Possible exit status values are:

0   Successful completion.

1   Failure due to an invalid command line argument.

Portability

MKS Toolkit. On UNIX, whence is built into the KornShell, but is not in the Bourne Shell.

See Also

sh

Part IV

Appendixes

Bibliography and Suggestions for Further Reading

There are many UNIX books available for both the beginner and the advanced reader, and more books are published every day. The titles listed below are ones that I've found useful over the years—the list is certainly not exhaustive, but it should provide useful starting places for various topics.

Standards and Manuals

AT&T Inc. *UNIX System V Interface Definition.* 3rd ed. Englewood Cliffs: 1989.

Computer Systems Research Group, Computer Science Division, Department of Electrical Engineering and Computer Science, University of California. *UNIX User's Reference Manual (URM), 4.3 Berkeley Software Distribution.* Berkeley, California: 1986.

Institute of Electrical and Electronics Engineers. *IEEE Standard, Portable Operating System Interface for Computer Environments, IEEE Std 1003.1-1988* [POSIX.1]. New York: 1988.

Institute of Electrical and Electronics Engineers. *Information Technology—Portable Operating System Interfaces (POSIX)—Part 2: Shell and Utilities, P1003.2/D10.* New York: July 1990.

Institute of Electrical and Electronics Engineers.   *Information Technology—Portable Operating System Interfaces (POSIX)—Part 2: Shell and Utilities, User Portability Extension (UPE), P1003.2a/D5.*   New York: 1990.

X/Open Company Ltd.   *X/Open Portability Guide, XSI Commands and Utilities.*   Englewood Cliffs: Prentice Hall, 1988.

General UNIX References

Bourne, S.R.   *The UNIX System.*   Reading: Addison-Wesley, 1983.

Kernighan, Brian W. and Rob Pike.   *The UNIX Programming Environment.*   Englewood Cliffs: Prentice Hall, 1984.

Kochan, Stephen G. and Patrick H. Wood.   *Exploring the UNIX System.*   Carmel, IN: Hayden Books, 1989.

Smith, Ben.   *UNIX Step-by-Step.*   Carmel, IN: Hayden Books, 1990.

Topham, Douglas.   *The First Book of UNIX.*   Carmel, IN: Howard W. Sams & Company, 1990.

Waite, Mitchell, Donald Martin, and Stephen Prata.   *The Waite Group UNIX Primer Plus.*   Indianapolis: Howard W. Sams & Company, 1983.

MKS Documentation

Mortice Kern Systems Inc.   *MKS Toolkit Reference Manual.*   Waterloo, Ontario: 1991.

Mortice Kern Systems Inc.   *MKS Toolkit User's Guide.*   Waterloo, Ontario: 1991.

Mortice Kern Systems Inc.   *MKS RCS Tutorial and Reference Manual.*   Waterloo, Ontario: 1991.

Other References

Aho, Alfred V., Peter J. Weinberger, and Brian W. Kernighan. *The AWK Programming Language.* Reading: Addison-Wesley, 1987.

Bolsky, Morris I. and David G. Korn. *The KornShell Command and Programming Language.* Englewood Cliffs: Prentice Hall, 1989.

Hansen, August. *VI: The UNIX Screen Editor.* New York: Prentice Hall, 1986.

Holliker, William. *UNIX Shell Commands Quick Reference.* Carmel, IN: Que Corporation, 1990.

Kochan, Stephen C. and Patrick H. Wood. *UNIX Shell Programming.* Revised ed. Carmel, IN: Hayden Books, 1985.

Regular Expression Summary

This appendix provides a quick reference summary about regular expressions, which are first discussed in Chapter 5. The appendix provides a number of examples to clarify various points.

A regular expression lets you search for strings in text files. No regular expression can match the new-line character at the end of a line, so no regular expression can match strings that extend over more than one line.

Regular expressions may be made up of normal characters and/or special characters, sometimes called *metacharacters*. There are two types of regular expressions: *basic* and *extended*. These types differ only in the metacharacters they can contain.

vi and ed recognize basic regular expressions; all other UNIX commands recognize extended regular expressions. grep and sed recognize both basic and extended regular expressions, depending on the options used.

The basic regular expression metacharacters are:

```
.   ^   $   [  ]   \   \d   *   \+   \?   \{   \}   \(  \)   \<  \>
```

The extended regular expression metacharacters are:

```
.   ^   $   [  ]   \   \d   *   +   ?   {  }   |   (  )   \<  \>
```

The list below explains the meanings of these characters.

.   A dot character matches any single character of the input line.

^
: The ^ character does not match any character, but it represents the beginning of the input line. For example, ^A is a regular expression matching the letter A at the beginning of a line. The ^ character is only special at the beginning of a regular expression, or after the (or | character.

$
: This does not match any character, but it represents the end of the input line. For example, A$ is a regular expression matching the letter A at the end of a line. The $ character is only special at the end of a regular expression, or before a) or | character.

[abc]
: This expression matches any one of the characters found between the [and] characters. If there is a – sign in the expression as in [a–z], it stands for a range of characters; for example, [a–z] matches any lowercase character. If the first character after the [is a caret (^), the regular expression matches any character *except* the ones specified within the brackets. Other than this, regular expression metacharacters lose their special significance inside square brackets. To match a ^ character in this case, it must appear anywhere except as the first character inside the brackets. To match a], the] should appear as the first character inside the brackets. A – (dash) character loses its special significance if it is the first or last character of the class.

Within a character class expression (one made with square brackets), the following constructs may be used to represent sets of characters:

[:alpha:]
: Any alphabetic character

[:lower:]
: Any lowercase alphabetic character

[:upper:]
: Any uppercase alphabetic character

[:digit:]
: Any digit character

[:alnum:]
: Any alphanumeric character (alphabetic or digit)

[:space:]
: Any white space character (blank, horizontal tab, vertical tab)

[:graph:]
: Any printable character, except the blank character

[:print:]	Any printable character, including the blank character
[:punct:]	Any printable character that is not white space or alphanumeric
[:cntrl:]	Any non-printable character

\   This character is used to turn off the special meaning of metacharacters. For example, \. only matches a dot character. Note that \\ matches a literal \ character. Also note the special case of *d*.

d   For *d* representing any single decimal digit (from 1 to 9), this pattern is equivalent to the string matching the *d*th expression enclosed within the ( ) characters (or \\(\\) for some commands) found at an *earlier point* in the regular expression. Parenthesized expressions are numbered by counting (characters from the left.

Constructs of this form can be used in the replacement strings of substitution commands (such as the :s command in vi), to stand for constructs matched by parts of the regular expression. For example, in the following vi command

```
:s/\(.*\):\(.*\)/\2:\1/
```

the \1 stands for everything matched by the first \\(.*\\) and the \2 stands for everything matched by the second. The result of the command is to swap everything before the : with everything after.

re*   A regular expression *re* followed by * matches a string of zero or more strings that would match *re*. For example, A*B matches AB, AAB, AAAB and so on. It also matches just B (zero occurrences of A).

re+, *re*\+   With extended regular expressions, *re* followed by + matches a string of one or more strings that would match *re*. With basic regular expressions, the principle is the same, except that you must write \+ instead of just +.

re?, *re*\?   With extended regular expressions, *re* followed by ? matches a string of one or zero occurrences of strings that would match *re*. With basic regular expressions, the principle is the same except that you must write \? instead of just ?.

539

char{*n*} *char*\{*n*\}	In this expression (and the ones to follow), *char* is a regular expression that stands for a single character (a literal character or a .). Such a regular expression followed by a number in braces stands for that number of repetitions of a character. For example, X{3} stands for XXX. With extended regular expressions, you just use normal brace characters; with basic regular expressions you must put backslashes in front of the characters, as in X\{3\}. This principle applies to the constructs below as well.
char{*min*,} *char*\{*min*,\}	When a single-character regular expression is followed by a number in braces, and the number is followed by a comma, it stands for at least that number of repetitions of a character. For example, X{3,} is an extended regular expression that stands for at least three repetitions of X, while X\{3,\} is a basic regular expression meaning the same thing.
char{*min*,*max*} *char*\{*min*,*max*\}	When a single-character regular expression is followed by a pair of numbers in braces, it stands for at least *min* repetitions and no more than *max* repetitions of a character. For example, X{3,7} is an extended regular expression that stands for three to seven repetitions of X, while X\{3,7\} is a basic regular expression meaning the same thing.
re1¦*re2*	This expression matches either regular expression *re1* or *re2*.
(*re*) \(*re*\)	This lets you group parts of regular expressions. In extended regular expressions you just use the normal parentheses characters; in basic regular expressions you must put backslashes in front of the characters, as in \(and \).
\<	This matches the beginning of a word, where the beginning of a word is defined as the boundary between non-alphanumerics and alphanumerics (including the underscore character). This matches no characters, only the context.
\>	This construct is analogous to the \< notation except that it matches the end of a word.
	Several regular expressions can be concatenated to form a larger regular expression.

Examples

The following patterns are given as illustrations, along with plain language descriptions of what they match.

```
abc
```

matches any string containing the three letters abc, in that order.

```
a.c
```

matches any string beginning with the letter a, followed by any character, followed by the letter c (for example, a!c).

```
^.$
```

matches any line containing exactly one character.

```
a(b*|c*)d
```

matches any string beginning with a letter a, followed by either zero or more of the letter b or zero or more of the letter c, followed by the letter d. For example, this would match ad, abd, acd, abbd, accd, and so on.

```
.* [a-z]+ .*
```

matches any line containing a "word." In this case, a word consists of lowercase alphabetic characters, delimited by at least one space on each side. For example, this would match the line abc def g.

```
(morty).*\1
morty.*morty
```

The above expressions both match lines containing at least two occurrences of the string morty, e.g., morty drove morty's car.

```
[[:space:][:alnum:]]
```

matches any character that is either a white space character or alphanumeric.

For further examples of regular expressions, see the discussion of grep in Chapter 5.

Portability

The basic regular expressions are available on most UNIX systems. Extended regular expressions may not be. Systems compatible with POSIX.2 support the extended set.

Summary of File Name Generation with Glob Constructs

A command line argument containing glob constructs may be used anywhere that a path name or list of path names is valid. The shell expands each such argument into a list of all existing path names that have the form corresponding to the path name.

The following glob constructs are recognized by the KornShell:

?   Matches any single character in a file or directory name, except for a leading dot (.).

*   Matches zero or more characters, except for a leading dot (.), anywhere in a file or directory name.

[...]   Matches any single character given inside the brackets. Inside the brackets you can use ranges of characters. You specify a range by giving the first character in the range, a minus sign (–), and the last character in the range. For example, [a-z] stands for the lowercase letters. If you want to have a literal minus sign as one of the characters in the brackets, put it first or last.

[!...]   Matches any single character not given inside the brackets. You can use ranges inside the brackets. For example, [!a-z] matches any character that is not a lowercase letter.

If an argument contains glob constructs and you do not want the shell to expand the constructs, enclose the argument in single or double quotation marks. For example, in

```
find /lu -name "*.exe" -print
```

the shell won't expand the * because the * is inside quotation marks. However, find will indeed list all files ending in .exe, as requested.

Common Environment Variables

When the KornShell executes a program, it gives the program a set of variables, called the program's *environment*. Each variable has a name and a value. These variables are called *environment variables*.

Note that a shell variable is only an environment variable if the variable is passed to the programs that the shell executes. This means that a shell variable is only an environment variable if it's marked for export. This situation is different from DOS, where all variables are environment variables because all variables are shared by all executing programs.

The following variables are used by several commands in the MKS Tools and are frequently used on true UNIX and UNIX look-alike systems:

COLUMNS   If you set this variable to a numeric value, various commands use its value as the width of the output device (measured in columns). Usually, the output device is a display screen, but you can also use COLUMNS to set up wider lines for line printers or typewriter terminals.

ENV   The value of this variable should be the name of a file of KornShell commands, or else it should be the null string. When the KornShell is invoked in a way that is not a log-in shell (e.g., when you run a shell script), the KornShell executes the commands inside the file named by ENV before the shell does anything else. Thus your ENV file may contain definitions of aliases, shell functions, and so on that can be used by shell scripts.

HOME   This variable is set during the log-in process. Its value is the name of your home directory. Your home directory is specified in the /etc/passwd file (/lu/etc/passwd with MKS Tools), which also records such information as your log-in name and your password.

LINES   If you set this variable to a numeric value, various commands use its value as the number of lines available on the output device.

LOGNAME   This variable is set during the log-in process. Its value is your user name.

PATH   This variable is set to a default value by the log-in process. Normally, you would use your profile file to set your PATH. PATH lists the directories that the shell should search when it is looking for commands. On a true UNIX or UNIX look-alike, names in the PATH list are separated with colon (:) characters; with MKS Tools, names are separated with semicolon (;) characters. With MKS Tools, be sure to enclose the directory list in single or double quotation marks when you assign a value to PATH.

ROOTDIR   Because DOS has a multidevice file system, it's necessary to keep track of the standard root directory that holds information files (like /lu/etc). ROOTDIR contains a device name, and possibly a directory where all such files can be found. With the MKS Tools, ROOTDIR is always the name of the directory where you installed the MKS Tools package. By default, this is c:/lu. ROOTDIR is not needed on a true UNIX or UNIX look-alike system, because such systems have different ways of referring to devices.

SHELL   This variable should contain the full path name of the shell you are using. With the MKS Tools, the default is c:/lu/bin/sh.exe.

TERM   This variable serves little purpose with the MKS Tools, but on a true UNIX or UNIX look-alike system, its value is a string that tells the type of terminal you are using. Various programs that interact with the terminal (such as vi) make use of TERM. Typically, these programs look up information about your type of terminal in a file called a *termcap* file. Termcap stands for *terminal capability*, and the termcap file describes the special capabilities of various types of terminals, as well as any special keys or character sequences that such terminals use.

UNIX has the ability to interact with many different types of terminals from many different manufacturers. Historically, this has been one of UNIX's greatest strengths. However, UNIX terminal handling is a complicated subject, and one that is outside the scope of this book.

TMPDIR   By default, MKS Tools commands store temporary files under $ROOTDIR/tmp. To use a different directory, set TMPDIR to the name of the directory you want to use. Some UNIX systems use TMP instead of TMPDIR, while others use neither TMPDIR or TMP.

TZ   Commands that print times (and dates) use this variable to determine the time zone. On a true UNIX system, the TZ variable would be set in the global profile file so that all of the system's users will have the same time zone setting.

POSIX.2 Utility Summary

The list below gives capsule summaries of the utility commands required by Draft 10 of the proposed POSIX.2 standard. This list includes the commands that are built into the shell.

ar	Manages object libraries.
asa	Converts text with a FORTRAN-style carriage control into a normal POSIX text file.
awk	A report generator and prototyping language. awk has strong information retrieval and programming abilities.
basename	Obtains the basename component of a path name. The input is a path name. The output is that path name, without directory names, and (optionally) without an extension either. Useful in scripts, to strip suffixes like .c.
bc,dc	Simple desk calculator utilities.
break	Command to break out of a loop (for, while, UNTIL) in the shell programming language.
c89	A C compiler that conforms to the 1989 ANSI standard for C.
case	A conditional execution construct similar to the switch statement in C or the case statement in Pascal. Used in the shell's programming language.
cat	Displays the contents of one or more files.
cd	Changes the current directory and/or disk.
chgrp	Changes the group ownership of one or more files.

chmod	Changes file characteristics. For example, chmod can change the permissions on a file.
chown	Changes the owner of one or more files.
cksum	Displays checksums and block counts for one or more files.
cmp	Compares two files on a binary basis. Can be used to report offsets of each difference.
colon	This command is just :. It always returns a true exit status, and it is used as a do-nothing operation in the shell programming language.
comm	Finds common lines in two files. The files are assumed to be sorted.
command	Executes a simple command.
continue	Skips to the next iteration of an until, while, or for loop in the shell programming language.
cp	Makes a copy of one or more files.
cut	Displays portions of input lines.
date	Displays the date and time in a large variety of formats. Can also be used to set the current date and time.
dd	Copies and possibly converts data into other formats, and handles disks directly.
diff	Compares two text files, and displays the differences between them.
dirname	Similar to basename, but returns the directory names from a path name instead of the file name.
echo	Prints out its arguments.
ed	A text editor (line editor).
env	Displays all environment variables.
eval	Constructs a command by evaluating a string of expressions and concatenating the results.
exec	Executes a collection of commands, and opens, closes and/or copics a group of file descriptors.
exit	Terminates a shell script and returns an exit status.
export	Sets the export attribute for variables and functions (determining which functions and/or variables will be passed on to processes that are invoked later on).

expr	Evaluates an expression and prints the result.
false	A utility that always returns a non-zero status value. It is called `false` because a non-zero status value is interpreted as a "false" answer to a true-or-false question.
find	Prints out names of files that meet a certain set of criteria.
fold	Breaks up long lines into shorter lines. This is usually used when you want to display a file with lines that are too wide to fit on the terminal screen.
for	Repeats a collection of statements in the shell programming language, using a different value for a variable on each iteration.
getconf	Obtains information about the POSIX configuration (such as the settings given to various options when the system was set up).
getopts	Analyzes command line options to a shell script.
grep	Reads a file and displays lines that contain a given pattern of characters.
head	Prints the first few lines of a file.
id	Displays the name of the current user and any group affiliations.
if	Begins the usual `if-then-else` construct in the shell programming language.
join	"Glues together" two sorted, textual relational databases.
kill	Kills a running program or sends a signal to a process.
lex	Generates code that performs lexical analysis of input.
ln	Creates a link.
locale	Obtains locale-specific information (such as information on the native character set of the country where the UNIX system is running).
localedef	Specifies locale-specific information.
logger	Records a log message.
logname	Determines the log-in name of the user running the command.
lp	Sends data to a line printer.
ls	Sorts and lists the contents of a directory.

551

mailx	Utility for sending and reading electronic mail messages.
make	Command for automatically updating files that must be kept in synch with each other.
mkdir	Creates a new directory.
mkfifo	Creates a first-in, first-out special file (similar to a pipe, only it is given a name).
mv	Renames or moves files and/or directories.
nohup	Runs a job at a higher priority and makes sure that there is no hang-up (the job will not be delayed or put on hold).
od	Dumps a file in any of a number of selected formats (octal, hexadecimal, decimal, and so on).
paste	Concatenates the lines of one or more input files.
pathchk	Checks that a path name is valid and/or portable to other POSIX systems.
pax	Reads and writes special archive files for data interchange or for file backup and restoration.
period	Executes a file containing commands. The command is simply a . (dot). The name of this command was changed back to dot in Draft 11 of POSIX.2.
pr	Prepares and formats a text file for printing on a hard copy printer.
printf	Formats output according to a specified output description.
pwd	Displays the name of your current working directory.
read	Reads input from the terminal, possibly assigning the input values to shell variables.
readonly	Makes shell variables and functions read-only (which means that other processes can read their values but cannot change them).
return	Returns from a shell function or shell script, possibly specifying an exit status for the function or script.
rm	Deletes files.
rmdir	Deletes directories.
sed	A non-interactive text stream editor.
set	Sets shell options and assigns values to parameters.

sh	A shell (a command interpreter). This can be the Bourne Shell, the KornShell, or something else compatible with these shells. The sh command invokes a new copy of the shell.
shift	Used in manipulating arguments passed to a shell script or function.
sleep	Suspends execution for a specified amount of time. Primarily used in shell scripts.
sort	Sorts and/or merges data.
strip	Removes unneeded information from executable files (such as symbol tables and debugging information).
stty	Sets terminal options; in other words, this indicates how you want certain input sequences to be interpreted.
tail	Prints the last few lines of a file.
tee	Copies one input file to several output files (and also displays the input).
test	Determines if a given condition is true. This is used primarily in shell scripts.
touch	Changes the file change date for a file.
tr	Translates input characters into other characters. Can be used for such jobs as converting from uppercase to lowercase or encrypting data in a simple way.
trap	Sets up signal handlers for shell scripts.
true	Always returns a zero exit status (indicating "true" in true-or-false tests).
tty	Displays the terminal name.
umask	Sets default permissions for your files.
uname	Prints out configuration-specific information such as the host machine name, the operating system, the machine type, and so on.
uniq	Displays all the unique lines in a sorted file.
unset	Is the reverse of set—it discards values and attributes of shell variables and/or functions.
until	Is a traditional until loop in the shell programming language.
wait	Waits for a program to finish.

wc   Displays the number of lines, words, and characters in one or more files.

while   Is a traditional `while` loop in the shell programming language.

xargs   Constructs a command line and executes it.

yacc   Generates code for construing the meaning of input.

     The preceding list shows the commands that are part of the main body of the POSIX.2 standard. In addition, the POSIX.2 standard will eventually include a User Portability Extension, commonly called the UPE or POSIX.2a. The UPE includes various commands that are optional on a system that conforms with POSIX.2; for example, the UPE includes `vi`.

KornShell Editing Features

The KornShell has built-in facilities for interactive command editing and file name generation that not only aid in entering new commands but also let you modify and re-execute previous commands. This capability is distinct from that provided by the `fc` command, which passes previous command lines to a separate program for editing. The built-in facilities mimic the `vi` screen editor. You can enable the facilities with the command

```
set -o vi
```

and disable them with

```
set +o vi
```

Unlike full-screen editors, shell editing works through a one-line window, extending from the end of the prompt to the second to the last column. Multiline history entries are displayed with new-lines, represented as `^J`.

The number of columns on the output device is obtained from the `COLUMNS` variable if this variable is defined (see the man page for `sh`); otherwise, it is assumed to be 80. A command line that would extend into the extreme right column can be scrolled horizontally. If you try to move the cursor beyond the edge of the window, the line is scrolled to center the cursor in the window. The second to the last column will display a character indicating that you are only seeing part of the line: < indicates extra data off the left side of the screen; > indicates extra data off the right side of the screen; and * indicates extra data off both sides.

When the `vi` editing facilities have been enabled, the shell is initially in *Insert Mode* after each new prompt. Keyboard input is normally inserted at the current position in the current command line; the exceptions are the *action keys* listed below. (Note that in Insert Mode the cursor arrow keys are ignored.)

Backspace, Ctrl-H	Delete the character to the left of the cursor.
Ctrl-Z	Terminate the shell (which can cause a log out). On a UNIX system, you would use Ctrl-D instead.
Ctrl-W	Delete the word (a string delimited by whitespace) to the left of the cursor.
Ctrl-U, Ctrl-X	Delete the current line. Ctrl-U is MKS Tools only, not UNIX.
Ctrl-J, Ctrl-M, Enter	Execute the current line.
Esc	Switch from Insert Mode to Command Mode.
Ctrl-V	Take the next character literally; useful for entering any of the above characters as text.
\	Escape the following action key. If the next character is any of the above except Ctrl-J, Ctrl-M, or the Enter key, the \ is erased and the escaped character is entered literally; otherwise the \ is entered, and the next character is treated normally.

If you press the Esc key while you're in Insert Mode, the shell enters Command Mode, and keyboard input is interpreted as commands to reposition the cursor, scroll through the command history, delete or change text, or re-enter Insert Mode. In Command Mode, you will not see the commands you type in, but you will see their results.

Many commands may be preceded by a number called a *count*; this tells the shell to execute the command that number of times. Except where otherwise noted, the count defaults to 1.

The following sections describe the available commands. Commands are grouped together according to their purposes. In all command descriptions, *N* is a number serving as the count and may be omitted. Also, *c* stands for any character.

Cursor-Movement Commands

These commands reposition the cursor in the command line. The commands only work in Command Mode; to get out of Insert Mode and into Command Mode, press Esc.

*N***h**	Move back *N* characters.
*N***l**	Move forward *N* characters.
0 (zero)	Move to the first character on the line.

^	Move to the first non-blank character on the line.
$	Move to the last character on the line.
*N*w	Move to the beginning of the *N*th next word (where a word is a string of alphanumerics, or a string of non-blank non-alphanumerics).
*N*W	Move to the beginning of the *N*th next full-word (where a full-word is a string of non-blanks).
*N*b	Move to the *N*th previous beginning of the word.
*N*B	Move to the *N*th previous beginning of the full-word.
*N*e	Move to the *N*th next end of the word.
*N*E	Move to the *N*th next end of the full-word.
*N*f*c*	Move to the *N*th next character *c*.
*N*F*c*	Move to the *N*th previous character *c*.
*N*t*c*	Move to the character before the *N*th next character *c*.
*N*T*c*	Move to the character after the *N*th previous character *c*.
N;	Repeat the previous *f*, *F*, *t*, or *T* command.
N,	Repeat the previous *f*, *F*, *t*, or *T* command, but in the opposite direction.

Line Search

The following commands change to display a different command line.

*N*j,*N*+,*N*downarrow	Display the *N*th next command line from the command history. Using the Down Arrow key is MKS Tools-specific, because UNIX doesn't know if a particular terminal will have arrow keys.
*N*k,*N*-,*N*uparrow	Display the *N*th previous command line from the command history. Using the Up Arrow key is MKS Tools-specific.
*N*G	Display the command with history number *N*. If *N* is omitted, the shell displays the latest command (based on the vi G (go to) command).
N/*string*Enter	Display the *N*th command line, searching backwards, that matches *string*. If *string* is omitted, the shell uses the previous search string.

N?*string***Enter**	Display the *N*th command line, searching forward, that matches *string*. If *string* is omitted, the shell uses the previous search string.
*N*n	Repeat the last string search (/ or ?) command.
*N*N	Repeat the last string search, but in the opposite direction.

Text Change

The following commands alter the text in the current command line. Some of these commands operate on a text block, defined by a cursor-movement command immediately following the text change command. The descriptions designate the cursor movement by *M* (for movement). The text block extends from the current cursor position to the new position determined by the movement command.

i	Enter Insert Mode, inserting text before the character under the cursor.
I	Insert before first non-blank on line (equivalent to **^i**).
a	Move the cursor forward one character and enter Insert Mode, appending text after the character originally under the cursor.
A	Append to the end of the line (equivalent to **$a**).
*N***d***M*	Delete text block. If *N* is given, it is applied to the movement command *M*.
dd	Delete the entire command line.
D	Delete from the cursor to the end of the line (equivalent to **d$**).
*N***x**	Delete *N* characters to the right of the cursor (equivalent to *N***dl**).
*N***X**	Delete *N* characters to the left of the cursor (equivalent to *N***dh**).
*N***c***M*	Change text block; deletes block of text and enters Insert Mode. If *N* is given, it is applied to the movement command *M*.
cc	Change the entire command line.
S	Change the entire command line.
*N***s**	Change the next *N* characters, beginning at the cursor.
*N***p**	Paste *N* copies of the last block deleted by a text change command. Text will be placed immediately after the cursor position.

*N***P**	Like *N***p**, but text is placed immediately before the cursor position.
r*c*	Replace the single character under the cursor with the character *c*, and advance the cursor one position.
R	Enter *Replace Mode*, a special case of Insert Mode in which each character entered overwrites that under the cursor, and advances the cursor one position.
u	Undo the last text change to the current line. This is itself a text change command, so pressing **u** a second time "undoes the undo."
U	Undo all changes to the current line.
N~	Switch the case of the next *N* characters, advancing the cursor over them. (Uppercase letters turn to lowercase, and vice versa.)
N.	Repeat the last text change command. If *N* is given, it overrides the count originally given with the command.
*N*_	Append the *N*th argument from the previous command line and enter Insert Mode. If *N* is not specified, the shell appends the last argument from the previous command line.
*	Replace the current word with the list of file names that would match the word with a * appended. In the case of no match, the terminal will beep and the word will not be changed. Otherwise, the cursor is positioned at the end of the list and the shell enters Insert Mode.
\	Used to complete a path name. If there is only one existing path name that matches as much as you've typed, the shell completes the path name and adds a space after the complete path name. If there are several matching path names, the shell will expand what you've typed by adding all the characters that are common to all matching path names.
=	Lists all path names that match the current word.

Miscellaneous Commands

*N*y *M*   Yank text block. Does not alter the command
                   line or cursor position, but makes the text block
                   available to subsequent paste (**p** or **P**) com-
                   mands. If *N* is given, it is applied to the move-
                   ment command *M*.

yy   Yank the entire command line.

Y   Yank the rest of the line (equivalent to **y$**).

Insert a **#** at the beginning of the line and start a
                   new command line immediately. Essentially, this
                   turns the current line into a comment, so that
                   the line will be ignored.

*N***v**   Call the real **vi** editor to let you edit command *N*
                   from the history file. If you omit *N*, the shell lets
                   you edit the current line.

Ctrl-L   Redisplay the current line.

Ctrl-J, **Ctrl-M**, **Enter**   Execute the current line.

Warning

Selecting a previous history line for editing while at a secondary prompt (i.e.,
while entering a subsequent line of a new multiline command) may yield
unpredictable results.

Installing the MKS Tools Package

This appendix describes the process of installing the MKS Tools on your DOS system. You can use any release of DOS from Version 2.0 up.

Space Requirements

In order to install the MKS Tools, you need to have about 1 MB of space available on your hard disk. If you do not have this much free space, you will have to clear up some space for the software. To do this, back up some files you won't need for a while, then delete those files from your hard disk.

Choosing a Directory

Before you begin installing the software, you must decide where you want to store it. You must store it on a hard disk. If you only have one hard disk, this will be disk C; otherwise, choose a hard disk that has sufficient space to hold the software.

Next you must decide on a directory in which to store the software. By default, the installation procedure stores the software in a directory named \lu. You are strongly advised to accept this default, unless you already have a directory named \lu that is being used for something else.

If \lu is already being used for something else, decide on another name for the directory (such as \lux, short for *Learning UNIX*). During the installation procedure, you'll be asked to enter the name that you have chosen. The installation procedure automatically creates the directory if it doesn't already exist.

If You Don't Use *lu*...

Many examples in this book assume that the MKS Tools are installed under the \\lu directory. If you choose a different directory, remember your decision and adapt the examples accordingly. For example, if you choose to install the software under \\lux and an example asks you to type

```
ls /lu
```

you should type

```
ls /lux
```

instead.

Running the Installation Procedure

Insert the first MKS Tools diskette into drive A: or drive B:. If you use drive A:, enter the command

```
a:install
```

If you use drive B:, enter the command

```
b:install
```

The installation procedure displays a box asking Where do you want the Learning UNIX tools installed? At the bottom of the box, you'll see a line that already contains the name

```
c:/lu
```

which stands for the \\lu directory on the C disk. (This is your first taste of UNIX; UNIX uses the slash (/) in file names, where DOS uses the backslash.) If you want to accept the preceding directory, just press Enter. Otherwise, type in the disk drive and directory name that you have chosen and press Enter.

Next, the installation displays a box asking What user ID would you like to use? Your answer should be the name that you'd like to use when interacting with the computer (such as jim or juanita). The name can be up to eight characters long, and can contain letters or digits. You are advised to use lowercase letters, because UNIX traditionally uses lowercase whenever possible. When you've entered your chosen name, press Enter.

The installation procedure then begins copying files from the diskette to your hard disk. It does this using a command named `tar` (described in Chapter 5 of this book). Everything happens automatically, so you don't need to worry about how `tar` works right now; however, you'll see the word `tar` displayed on your screen while the copying takes place. (I thought you'd like to know what it means).

Depending on the type of diskettes your computer uses (5 1/4-inch or 3 1/2-inch), the installation procedure may ask you to change diskettes. If so, remove disk 1, insert disk 2 in the same drive, and press Enter.

When all the files have been copied from the diskette(s), the installation procedure displays the message

```
Installation Completed Successfully
Press ENTER to Continue.
```

Press Enter, and the installation procedure will terminate.

Stopping Partway Through

If you find you must stop partway through the installation procedure for some reason, you can stop the installation by pressing Ctrl-C or Ctrl-Break. The procedure will display `Interrupt?` This question asks if you really want to cut the installation short. If you do, enter y for *yes*; if you don't, enter n for *no*. Press Enter when you have entered your answer.

Starting the MKS Tools

To start the MKS Tools, enter the following commands:

```
cd \lu
lu
```

This starts the MKS Tools software. Always type the command as `lu`, even if you choose a different directory to hold the software.

The `lu` command reminds you what user name you chose during installation. You should use this name during the log-in procedure. For further information about logging in and using the MKS Tools, see Chapter 2.

New Students

If a new student wants to start the *Learning UNIX* lessons, simply run the installation procedure again as described previously. When the installation procedure asks for the directory where you want the UNIX tools installed, use the same directory used for the previous student. When the installation procedure asks for a user ID for the new student, enter an appropriate name; this name shouldn't be the same as any previous student's name.

Coexistence

If you install a new student according to the procedures described in the previous section, old students will find they can no longer log in. The reason is that the installation procedure gets rid of the old user's password information in the passwd file.

If old students want to be able to log in to the MKS Tools after new students have been installed, follow these steps.

1. Before you install a new student, log in to the MKS Tools and enter the command

   ```
   cp /lu/etc/passwd /lu/tmp
   ```

   This makes a copy of the old password file.

2. Install the new student, as described in the *Basic Installation* section in this chapter.

3. Log in to the new student's account and issue the commands

   ```
   cat /lu/etc/passwd /lu/tmp/passwd >/lu/tmp/pass2
   cp /lu/tmp/pass2 /lu/etc/passwd
   rm /lu/tmp/passwd /lu/tmp/pass2
   ```

   These commands concatenate the old and new password files and copy the concatenation to the proper directory.

MKS Tools Versus the MKS Toolkit

The MKS Tools are a subset of the MKS Toolkit, a collection of more than 160 programs that simulate the look and feel of UNIX on a DOS or OS/2 system. The MKS Tools are only intended to be an educational aid; they are not intended to give you the capabilities of the full MKS Toolkit. The most important differences between MKS Tools software and the corresponding MKS Toolkit commands are:

- The *Learning UNIX* version of vi can only write out a maximum of 100 lines of text. That limit is high enough that you should be able to experiment freely while you're using this book.

- Before you can execute any of the UNIX commands that come with this book, you must log in to the MKS Tools program (named lu under the \lu directory). The real MKS Toolkit does not impose this restriction—you can use MKS Toolkit commands at any time that you could use any other DOS command. For example, you can execute MKS Toolkit commands in response to the usual DOS C> prompt; you don't have to log in to use MKS Toolkit commands.

- The KornShell that comes with the MKS Tools will only execute other MKS Tools commands; for example, you can't execute spreadsheets or word processors while you are using the MKS Tools. With the real MKS Toolkit, the KornShell will execute any valid DOS program.

The following is a list of commands which are in MKS Toolkit but are not part of the MKS Toolkit that come with this book.

asa	awk	awkl	basename
c	calendar	cksum	clear
cmp	comm	compress	cpio
crypt	csplit	ctags	cut
dc	dd	deroff	dev
diff3	dirname	echo	ed
expand	expr	fg	file
fmt	fold	getconf	getopt
gres	help	id	jobs
join	kill	lc	line
logname	look	m4	mailx
man	mksinfo	nl	nm
od	pack	paste	patch
pathchk	pax	pcat	pg
printf	prof	ps	pwd

rev	size	sleep	spell
split	strings	strip	sum
switch	sync	tee	test
time	touch	tr	tsort
tty	uname	uncompress	unexpand
uniq	unpack	unstrip	uudecode
unencode	which	xargs	

Most of these commands are explained in Appendix E.

You Can Use Both!

It's possible to have both the MKS Tools and the MKS Toolkit installed on one DOS system. Because the MKS Tools work entirely within the /lu directory, they don't conflict with the MKS Toolkit, provided that the ROOTDIR for the full MKS Toolkit is *not* /lu.

Note, however, that the MKS Tools automatically change ROOTDIR to the directory where the MKS Tools are installed. Thus, when you quit using MKS Tools, ROOTDIR will be set for MKS Tools instead of MKS Toolkit. To use MKS Toolkit, you can either set ROOTDIR to the appropriate directory or just reboot the system.

Glossary

These following terms are used and defined in this book. Terms shown in *italics* are also defined in this glossary.

Abbreviation: In vi, a *string* that stands for another string. Whenever you type an abbreviation, vi automatically converts it to the associated string.

Access Time: A *file characteristic* that tells the last time that a person or program *opened* a file.

Alias: A name that you associate with a *string* in the *KornShell*. When the KornShell sees an alias name used in a location where a *command* could begin, the shell replaces the name with its associated string. In other words, an alias stands for the first part of a command.

Append: To add text to the existing contents of a file. You can do this with the *redirection* construct >>. There is also a vi command that appends new text to the text being edited.

Archive: A file whose contents preserve the contents of many other files and *directories*. In this book, the tar *command* creates and manipulates archives. Some UNIX and UNIX look-alike systems offer other commands (such as pax, cpio) that can also manipulate archives.

Argument: See *Command Line Argument*.

Arithmetic Expression: A sequence of arithmetic operations yielding a value.

Assignment: A *KornShell command* that gives a value to a *variable*.

Background Job: A program that is not a *foreground job*. See *Foreground Job* for details.

Backslash: The \ character. In the *KornShell*, the backslash is used as the default *escape character*.

Basename: The last part of a *path name*; the part that remains when you remove all the directory names. For example, in `dir1/dir2/file.c`, the basename is `file.c`. Also see *Dirname*.

Binary: A method of representing numbers and other kinds of information using only the digits 0 and 1.

Binary File: On UNIX, any file that is not a *text file*.

Block: A unit for measuring the amount of disk space used by a file. Typically, UNIX blocks are 512 *bytes*; however, this size can be different on different UNIX systems.

Body of a Function: The *commands* inside the definition of a *shell function*. For example, in

```
function cd1
{
    cd $1
    ls -x
}
```

the body of the function consists of the `cd` and `ls` commands.

Built-in Alias: An *alias* that is automatically defined for you when you start the *KornShell*. For example, *history* is a built-in alias; it is an alias that you do not have to define yourself.

Built-in Command: A *command* that the *shell* can execute directly; the shell does not have to search for a file that contains the program. For example, `set` and `alias` are commands built into the *KornShell*. `TYPE` and `DIR` are commands built into DOS's `COMMAND.COM` *command interpreter*.

Byte: The amount of computer memory used to hold a single character (such as a letter or digit). Different types of computers can have different byte sizes, but the most common size, especially in personal computers, is eight bits.

Case-Sensitive: A description of any software that treats upper- and lowercase letters differently. For example, the UNIX file system is case-sensitive. Thus, the names `FILE`, `file`, and `File` are all different file names and refer to different files. The opposite of case-sensitive software is case-insensitive or caseless software. For example, the DOS file system is case-insensitive; the names `FILE`, `file`, and `File` all refer to the same file.

Command: Any instruction to any piece of software. In this book, the most common type of command is an instruction to the *KornShell* to run a particular program. The standard programs on a system are sometimes called commands or utility commands.

Command Editing: The process of editing and reexecuting a *command* entered previously. Command editing features are offered by the *KornShell*.

Command File: A file containing instructions to a program. In particular, a `vi` command file is a file containing the kind of `vi` instructions that normally begin with a colon (`:`). In the instructions contained by such a command file, the colon is omitted.

Command History: A list of all *commands* recently executed by the *KornShell*. This list is recorded in the *history file*.

Command Interpreter: A program that reads the *commands* that you type in, and then executes them. Also known as a *shell*.

Command Line: An instruction to the *shell*, consisting of a *command* name followed by *command line arguments*.

Command Line Argument: A part of *command line*. Arguments provide information that tells a program what it should do. The most common command line arguments are *command line options* or *path names*. Command line arguments are separated from each other by *white space*.

Command Line Option: A *command line argument* that changes the default behavior of a program. On a UNIX system, simple command line options consist of a minus sign character followed by a single letter or digit, as in `-X`. More sophisticated command line options may consist of a minus sign followed by a keyword, followed by a value, as in `-ctime 1`.

Command Mode: In a `vi` editing session, the editor is in Command Mode anytime it waits for you to enter a *command*. See also *Insert Mode*.

Command Prompt String: The *string* that the *KornShell* displays when it wants you to enter a new *command*. See also *Secondary Prompt String*.

Command Substitution: A feature of the *KornShell*. When a *command line* contains a construct of the form `$(command)`, the shell executes the given `command` and collects its *standard output*. The shell then puts the output in place of the original `$(command)` construct and executes the resulting command line.

COMMAND.COM: The standard *command interpreter* on a DOS system.

Comment: An English-language description of what a *shell script* or *shell function* does. In the *KornShell*, a comment begins with a number sign character (#) and goes to the end of the line.

Component: See *Path Name Component*.

Contextual Cursor Movement: In `vi`, a way of moving the *cursor* through text. Contextual cursor movement depends on the nature of the text itself. For example, the `w` command moves the cursor to the beginning of the next word in the text. To do this, `vi` must examine the text to find where the next word starts.

Control Character: Generally a character that is not one of the printable characters (letters, digits, or punctuation characters). Various types of software put control characters into files to convey a special meaning. For example, word processors use control characters to indicate formatting information.

Control Structures: In the *KornShell*, a group of special instructions that perform special processing. Examples include `if` constructs, `for` loops, `while` loops, and so on.

Current Directory: Roughly speaking, the *directory* you are "working in." Usually when you want to refer to a file, you must give the name of the directory that contains the file, the name of the directory that contains that directory, and so on. To reduce typing, you can designate any directory as your current directory. You can then refer directly to files and *subdirectories* in your current directory without specifying all the containing directories. You can change your current directory with the `cd` command and display the name of your current directory with the `pwd` command. The notation `.` refers to the current directory. See also *Path name*.

Cursor: The marker on the display screen that shows where the next character you type will appear.

Default Options: With the *KornShell* and other software, the *options* that are in effect if you do not explicitly specify any options. For example, with `vi` the default tab stops are set every eight columns on the display screen.

Device: Any piece of equipment that can give information to or receive information from your computer, such as a hard disk drive, a floppy disk drive, a video display terminal, a mouse, or a printer.

Device Driver: Software that looks after interactions between your computer and a particular *device*. For example, there will be a device driver for each line printer attached to your computer; this software will look after all interactions with that printer.

Device Files: A UNIX file associated with a *device*. The file looks like a normal disk file; however, if you perform I/O on the file, it has the effect of performing I/O on the device. For example, the file `/dev/lp` may be associated with the line printer, and if you write data to `/dev/lp`, the data will appear on the printer.

Directory: A construct for organizing computer files. If you picture files as folders that hold information, a directory is like a drawer that can hold several folders. Directories can also contain subdirectories, which can contain subdirectories of their own. When you want the computer to find a particular file, the computer has to know the name of the file, the name of the directory that contains the file, the name of the directory that contains this directory, and so on.

Dirname: The first parts of a *path name*; the list of directory names. For example, in `dir1/dir2/file.c`, the dirname is `dir1/dir2`. See also *Basename*.

Encryption: The process of putting information into a specially coded form to keep the information secret. The reverse of encryption is decryption.

End-of-File: Something that indicates the end of the information that a file contains. This is often a special character. For example, the Ctrl-Z character is often used to mark end-of-file on DOS, and the Ctrl-D character is often used to mark end-of-file on UNIX. Another common approach is to record the number of *bytes* in the file, so that when a program has read that number of bytes, it knows it has reached the end of the file.

Environment: When using the *KornShell*, the collection of all features that can affect the execution of a *command*. This includes the current settings of all *shell options*, *shell functions*, *aliases*, *file descriptors*, and *variables*. Each executing program has its own environment.

Environment Variables: See *Variables*.

EOF: Short for *end-of-file*. Also commonly used as the name of a character or value signifying end-of-file.

Escape Character: A character used to "turn off" the special meanings of other characters. By default, UNIX software uses the *backslash* as its escape character. When you put the escape character in front of another character that has a special meaning (such as a *glob construct*), the escape character says that you want the second character to be taken literally instead of having its special meaning.

Executable: Able to be put into execution. An executable file is a file for which you have execute *permission* and which contains a program or *shell script* that the *KornShell* can execute.

Exit Code: The DOS terminology for a *status value*.

Expansion: To replace a special construct with its real meaning. For example, to expand an *alias*, the *KornShell* replaces the alias with the *string* associated with that alias. To expand a *variable*, the KornShell replaces the variable with its associated value.

Export: The act of one program passing information to another program. For example, when the *KornShell* exports a *variable* to another program, the KornShell passes the name and value of that variable to the program. If you want the KornShell to export a particular variable, you should mark that variable for export using the `export` command. As an alternative, you could use the command `set -a` to tell the shell to export all variables created in the future.

Field: A piece of data within a *record*. Usually, the fields of a record must be separated by special characters (such as blanks or commas).

File Characteristic: A piece of information about a file, such as the date and time that the file's contents were most recently changed.

File Descriptor: A number associated with an *open* file. Whenever a *process* wants to perform I/O on a particular file, the process identifies the file by specifying the file descriptor number. DOS sometimes uses the term *handle* for file descriptors. See also *Standard Input*, *Standard Output*, and *Standard Error*.

File Permissions: *File characteristics* that tell who can use a file and how those people can use it. There are three classes of permissions: owner permissions, which control use by the file's *owner*; group permissions, which control use by people in the file's *group*; and other permissions, which control use by everyone else. For each of these three classes there are three permission types: r permission lets you read a file, w permission lets you write to the file, and x permission lets you execute the file (as a program or *shell script*). These are often described in a *string* that gives owner, group, and other permissions in that order. For example, rwxr-xr-- stands for rwx permissions for the owner, rx for the group, and r for others.

File System: A collection of files and *directories* on a particular *device*. It is possible for a UNIX system to have several separate file systems. More loosely speaking, *file system* can refer to all the files and directories of a particular UNIX machine.

Filter: A general term for any program that reads in data from the standard input, "transforms" the data in some way, then writes out the result to the standard output. A simple example would be a program that reads in text, converts all letters to uppercase, and then writes out the result.

Folding: Displaying a long line of text by breaking it into several shorter lines on the display screen. For example, vi can fold a long line so you can read the line on the display screen; internally, however, vi keeps it as one long line instead of breaking it up into shorter lines.

Foreground Job: An executing program that can interact with the terminal. The opposite of a foreground job is a *background job*, a program that is running on its own and is shut off from interacting with the terminal. To start a program running in the background, put a & on the end of the command line that invokes the program. Background jobs are sometimes called *batch jobs*.

Glob Construct: A character or *string* that can be used in place of characters in a *path name*. Each glob construct stands for a particular pattern of characters; for example, ? stands for any single character, while * stands for a string of zero or more characters. When the *KornShell* sees a path name that contains a glob construct, the shell *expands* the construct into a list of all existing files with names that match the pattern given by the glob construct.

Group: A collection of users on a UNIX system. Groups are created by the UNIX system's administrators. Each group usually consists of a collection of people with something in common; for example, the administrators might set up a group for each project that a company is working on. A user can belong to any number of groups. One of these is designated the user's primary group, and the rest are considered secondary groups. Each group is identified by a name and a number.

Group Permissions: See *File Permissions*.

Handle: The DOS term for a *file descriptor*.

History File: A file used by the *KornShell* to record the commands most recently executed during this session. This file is always *open* while the shell is running. On UNIX systems, the history file is sh_history under your home directory; with MKS Tools, the name is sh_histo.

   Also, a file used by a revision control software package to record the history of changes made to another file.

Home Directory: A directory that usually serves as your personal directory when you use a UNIX system. When you first *log in*, your *current directory* will be your home directory. The name of your home directory is given by the HOME *variable*.

Initialization File: A file that contains instructions to be executed when a program starts up. For example, a vi initialization file contains instructions that should be executed when you start vi, before vi executes any instructions entered from the keyboard.

Insert Mode: In a vi editing session, the editor is in Insert Mode any time you are typing in text that is added to the text already shown on the screen. See also *Command Mode*.

Integer: A number that has no fractional part and no exponent. A whole number.

Interrupt: A signal that tells a program to stop what it's doing as soon as possible. UNIX systems often use the Ctrl-C or Del character to issue an interrupt. (Note: some programs can ignore interrupt signals.)

Kernel: The heart of an *operating system*. The kernel supplies services to all programs that execute under the operating system, and also keeps users and programs from interfering with each other. See also *Operating System*.

Kill: The action of manually terminating a *process*. On a UNIX system, this is commonly done with the kill command.

KornShell: A *command interpreter* developed on UNIX by David Korn. The KornShell is a descendant of the Bourne Shell, and accepts any input that the Bourne Shell accepts. The KornShell has many additional features that the Bourne Shell does not.

Line Editor: A type of *text editor* that takes input in a line-by-line mode. Editing commands appear on the screen as they are typed, and therefore interweave with any lines of text that are also on the screen. Contrast this with a *Screen Editor*.

Link: A name associated with a file. On a true UNIX system, a file can have more than one *path name*, and therefore more than one link. Because this is not true on a DOS system, this book does not examine links in any detail.

Linking a Program: Combining several *object files* and/or *object libraries* to produce an *executable* program.

Log In: The process of identifying yourself to the system and proving you are who you say you are. To begin using a UNIX system, you must log in; unlike DOS systems, you can't just turn on the machine and start working.

Log Out: The process of telling the *shell* that you are finished working. This ends your *session*. With the *KornShell*, you log out by entering the `exit` command. "Log off" is another term for log out.

Loop: A *control structure* that repeats a set of *commands* until a given condition is met.

Makefile: A file that describes interdependencies between other files. Used in connection with the `make` command, which updates files to keep them in synch with each other. The makefile also shows the commands needed to update the files.

Man Page: A description of a *command* in a UNIX reference manual. For example, the `ls` man page describes the `ls` command.

Merging: Combining several files into a single file. You can do this with the UNIX `sort` command.

Metacharacter: A character that can have a special meaning in a *regular expression*. For example, $ is a metacharacter that stands for the end of a line.

Modification Time: A *file characteristic* that tells the last time that a person or program changed the characteristics of a file, particularly the *file permissions*.

Mount: To associate a *file system* with a *device*. You must mount a device before you can use it. For example, if you want to write to a file on a diskette on a UNIX system, someone must issue a `mount` command that associates the diskette with a directory in the normal file system. Writing to a file under that directory has the effect of writing to the corresponding file on the diskette. Some devices can be mounted automatically when the UNIX system starts up; this varies from system to system.

Multitasking: Executing several programs simultaneously.

Multiuser System: An *operating system* that can be used by several people simultaneously, and that provides security measures that let people protect their programs and data from other users.

New-Line: A character or *string* that separates lines of text in a *text file*. On a keyboard, you generate a new-line by pressing Enter.

Null String: A *string* that contains no characters. Often written `""` or `''`.

Null Suffix: A file named *suffix* that contains no characters. For example, `file.` has a null suffix because it has a `.` and nothing afterward.

On UNIX, there's a difference between a file that has a null suffix and one that has no suffix at all. A file that has a null suffix has a `.` to show where the suffix begins, and no characters after the `.` (because the suffix is null). A file that has no suffix at all has no `.` in its name.

Object File: A file that contains all or part of a program, in a format that is close to the internal format used by the computing hardware. An object file is produced by compiling a *source file*.

Object Library: A file with contents that are constructed from several *object files*. Object files are put together into libraries, because some types of software work better with one large file than many small ones.

Opening a File: Asking the *kernel* to prepare a file for input or output. In order to open a file, a program must specify whether it wants to read the file, write to the file, or both. The kernel then checks to see if the program's user has appropriate *file permissions* on the file to perform such actions. If the file doesn't exist, the process of opening a file for writing creates the file. When the kernel opens a file, it assigns a *file descriptor* number to the file so that the program can identify the file in future actions.

Operating System: A collection of software that performs services for other programs and that enforces security measures to prevent programs and users from interfering with each other. An operating system can be divided into three parts:

- The *utilities*, commands for performing everyday operations, like copying or removing files

- The *shell*, which starts up the commands that the user wants to execute

- The *kernel*, which does the most basic work of the operating system, such as performing I/O. The kernel also supervises the programs and users who share the system.

Option: Something that controls or modifies the usual behavior of a program. See also *shell options* and *command line options*.

Owner of a File: Normally, the person who created the file.

Parameter: A symbol standing for an *argument*. In *shell scripts* and *shell functions*, the parameter $1 stands for the first argument, $2 stands for the second argument, and so on. These are called *positional parameters*, because the numbers refer to positions in the argument list. There are also special parameters that stand for lists of arguments and other information.

Parent Directory: A *directory* that contains another directory. For example, if dir1 contains dir2, then dir1 is the parent directory of dir2. The notation .. refers to the parent directory of your *current directory*.

Path Name: A description of how to locate a desired file. An absolute path name gives the full name of the file, beginning at the *root directory* and listing the sequence of directories that lead to the file. An absolute path name always starts with a slash (/) character, signifying the root. Here are some examples of absolute path names:

```
/etc              # name of a directory directly under the root
/dir1/dir2        # name of a subdirectory
/dir1/dir2/file.ksh  # name of a file
```

A relative path name describes how to find the file beginning at your *current directory*. You can identify a relative path name because it does not start with a slash. Here are some examples of relative path names:

```
sonnet            # name of a file under current directory
testdir/sonnet    # file under subdirectory of current directory
../sonnet         # file under parent of current directory
```

Path Name Component: Part of a *path name*, giving the name of a directory or file. For example, in /dir1/dir2/file.suf, the components are / (standing for the root), dir1, dir2, and file.suf. Components are separated by slash (/) characters. See also *Basename* and *Dirname*.

Pattern: Another name for a *regular expression*.

Pattern-Matching: The process of searching for *strings* of characters that conform to the pattern of characters specified by a *regular expression*.

Permissions: See *File Permissions*.

Pipe: A communication mechanism between two *processes* that connects an output *file descriptor* in one process to an input *file descriptor* in the other. Most commonly, the *standard output* of one process is connected to the *standard input* of the other.

Pipeline: A sequence of two or more *processes* connected by *pipes*. The *standard output* of each process becomes the *standard input* of the next process in the sequence. In the *KornShell*, a pipeline is written as

```
command ¦ command ¦ command ¦ ...
```

Placeholder: In the synopsis of a *command line* and in *command arguments*, a symbol that stands for a value. For example, in the command line synopsis

```
banner [-f fontfile] [-c char] [-w n] [text ...]
```

`fontfile`, `char`, `n`, and `text` are all placeholders. When you type in a real `banner` command, you replace these placeholders with real values. For example, you would replace the `text` placeholder with the actual text that you want `banner` to display.

Portable Character Set: The set of characters that are guaranteed to be valid for file names in any system conforming to the *POSIX* standards. The set includes the 26 upper- and lowercase letters used by the English language, the 10 digits, the underscore (_), the dash (-), and the dot (.).

Porting: Taking a program that works on one computing system and making whatever changes are necessary to get it to work on another.

Positional Parameter: See *Parameter*.

POSIX: The umbrella name for a family of standards developed by the Institute of Electrical and Electronics Engineers. These standards describe the features and behavior of UNIX-like *operating systems*.

Process: A program that is currently executing. A process includes the memory that the program occupies, the files it has open, the program's *environment*, and any other attributes specific to a running program.

Process ID: A number that serves to distinguish one *process* from another. The *kernel* assigns each process a unique process ID when that process begins executing. On a standard UNIX system, the `ps` command lets you determine the process ID of a particular process.

Profile File: An *initialization file* for the *KornShell*. A file containing KornShell *commands*, intended to be executed whenever the KornShell starts up. Typically, people use profile files to set *options*, define *aliases*, define *shell functions*, and in general, to do any work needed to set up their shell sessions. On a true UNIX system, profile files are named `.profile`; with the MKS Tools, profile files are named `profile.ksh`.

Rapid Prototyping: The process of creating a prototype version of a program as quickly as possible. The program may be considered a prototype because it has not been optimized for efficiency or because it only does a part of the work that a finished program should do. For example, suppose a program is going to interact with the user by displaying menus; you might make a prototype that only displays menus, without doing any other work. This prototype makes it easier to experiment with the appearance of the menus and to ask the users if they like what they see. Producing a prototype very early in the program design process often helps the programmers detect problems and correct them before they've invested a lot of work in an unsatisfactory approach.

Read-Only File: A file that you can read but not write to. Typically, you make a file read-only if you don't want to overwrite the current contents by accident.

Record: For the purposes of `sort`, a line in a *text file* that is broken into one or more *fields*.

Redirection: Typically, the process of sending the *standard output* of a program to a file instead of the display screen, or of reading the *standard input* of a program from a file instead of the keyboard. More precisely, redirection is the process of changing the association of files and *file descriptors* before running a program. In particular, `>file` redirects the standard output to `file`, while `<file` redirects the standard input from `file`.

Regular Expression: A *string* describing a pattern of characters. Special characters (called *metacharacters*) within the regular expression can specify additional criteria for the pattern of characters.

Return Value: Another name for a *status value*.

Reverse Video: Displaying dark characters on a light background.

Root: Short for *root directory*.

Root Directory: The main *directory* in a UNIX file system. All other directories and files are contained in the root directory or in subdirectories of the root directory.

Screen Editor: A *text editor* that shows the text you are editing, not the commands that you enter in order to edit it. Contrast this with *Line Editor*.

Script: A file containing instructions for a piece of software. For example, a *shell script* contains instructions for a *shell* (such as the *KornShell*); a `sed` script contains instructions for `sed`.

Search Path: A list of directories that a *command interpreter* should search in order to find commands that you want to run. On UNIX, your search path is given by the value of the `PATH` variable.

Search Rules: Another name for your *search path*.

Secondary Prompt String: The *string* that the *KornShell* displays when it wants you to enter another line of a multiline *command* (such as an `if` construct). Also see the *Command Prompt String* entry.

Session: A period of interaction with a piece of software. For example, a `vi` session lasts from the time you start `vi` to the time you quit. A *shell* session lasts from the time you start the shell (for example, at *log in*) to the time you quit using the shell (for example, at *log out*).

Shell: A program that reads your *commands* and executes them. Also called a *command interpreter*. See also *Operating System*.

Shell Function: A *shell command* made up of several other commands, comparable to a subprogram in a programming language. To define a function, you specify a set of commands to make up the function and a name for the function. You can then use the function name as if it were a command name. When a command line starts with the function name, the shell will execute all the commands that make up that function.

Shell Option: An *option* that controls the behavior of a *shell*. The *KornShell* has several options that let you change its usual behavior. For example, set -x tells the shell to display each command before the command is executed, showing all the *expansions* performed in the *command line*.

Shell Script: A *script* containing input for a *shell*.

Sorting Key: A description of a *field* or collection of fields in a record. The sort command uses sorting keys to specify how records are to be sorted. The sorting key tells which pieces of information are to be used in sorting and what sorting order is to be used. A sort command can have several sorting keys.

Source File: A text file containing instructions written in a programming language such as C or Pascal. A compiler program translates the contents of a source file into a form closer to the internal machine language used by the hardware, and writes this translated information into an *object file*.

Standard Error: The usual name for *file descriptor* 2 (two). By convention, programs write diagnostics and error messages to this descriptor. Usually, the descriptor refers to the display screen, but this can be changed by *redirection*. This descriptor is separate from the *standard output*, so that error diagnostics are still seen when the standard output is redirected.

Standard Input: The usual name for *file descriptor* 0 (zero). By convention, programs read input from this descriptor. Usually, the descriptor refers to the keyboard, but this can be changed by *redirection*.

Standard Output: The usual name for *file descriptor* 1 (one). By convention, programs write output to this descriptor. The descriptor usually refers to the display screen, but this can be changed by *redirection*.

Status Value: An *integer* that a program uses to indicate whether or not it was successful. When a program is invoked by the shell, the shell receives the program's status value when the program finishes execution. *Shell scripts* and *shell functions* can also produce status values when they finish execution, by using the return statement. Status values are also called *return values*, *exit status values*, or *exit codes*.

Stream: A "route" by which input travels to a program and/or output travels from a program. For example, if a program wants to write to a particular file, the program asks the kernel to *open* an output stream to that file. Each open stream in a program has its own *file descriptor*.

Stream Editor: A *text editor* that does not interact with the user. The user specifies a set of commands or a *command file* on the editor's command line, and the editor simply executes those commands on all specified files.

String: Any sequence of characters, as in abc. Strings are often enclosed in single or double quotation marks.

Subdirectory: A *directory* contained by another directory. The *root directory* is the only directory that is not a subdirectory.

Subshell: A *shell* that was started by another program (usually by another shell).

Suffix: The final part of a file's *basename*. Also called a *file name extension*. For example, in /dir/file.c, the suffix is .c. The DOS file system treats suffixes as special parts of file names. The UNIX file system does not offer any special treatment; on UNIX, users simply use suffixes as a convenient naming convention.

Superuser: A *userid* on UNIX systems, used for system administration tasks. The kernel allows the superuser to access any file, regardless of the permissions on that file, and to control all executing programs. The user number of the superuser is zero, and the user name is often root.

SVID: Short for **S**ystem **V** **I**nterface **D**efinition. A standard developed by AT&T to describe UNIX systems.

Temporary File: A file that a program creates while it is doing work, then deletes when the file is no longer necessary. For example, the sort command can create temporary files to hold partly sorted data; when sort finishes sorting the data, it gets rid of all the temporary files created during the sorting process. UNIX systems usually have a *directory* named /tmp where programs can store their temporary files. The MKS Tools use a directory named /lu/tmp for temporary files.

Termcap File: A file describing the capabilities of many different kinds of terminals. Commands like vi consult the termcap file to determine any special characters that might be used when interacting with your terminal.

Text Editor: A program that lets you create and modify *text files*. See also *Line Editor*, *Screen Editor*, and *Stream Editor*.

Text File: A file that contains readable text. Text files are broken into lines of text. Usually, these lines only contain "printable" characters: letters, digits, and punctuation characters. Contrast this with *binary files*, which often contain *control characters*.

UNIX: An operating system developed by AT&T Bell Labs.

Userid: A way of identifying a particular computer user. On UNIX, there are two types of userids: a user number (which is used internally to distinguish one user from another) and a user name (also known as a log-in name). Whenever you have to identify yourself to the computer (for example during *log in*), you enter your user name.

Utility: A standard command or program that accompanies an operating system. For example, every UNIX system has a `cp` command; `cp` is a standard utility program.

Variable: A name with an associated value. Variables are used to store information. When they are *exported* to other programs, they can pass the stored information on to those programs. The variables that the *shell* exports to another program are called the *environment variables* of that program.

Whitespace: A sequence of one or more spaces or horizontal tab characters. Whitespace is used to separate *arguments* on a *command line*.

Wild Card Construct: Another name for a *glob construct*.

Working Directory: Another name for your *current directory*.

X/Open: An international standard specifying requirements for UNIX-like *operating systems*.

Index

F

G

Q

R

T

593

W

X

Find The Latest Technology
And Most Up-To-Date Information
In Hayden Books

MKS Toolkit

ESSENTIAL TOOLS FOR DOS & OS/2

MKS Toolkit, the complete version of the MKS Tools tutorial software included in this book, provides more than 150 essential tools for DOS and OS/2. In fact, MKS Toolkit brings you a whole new world: the world of UNIX™ systems. MKS Toolkit is not just for programmers, but for anyone who wants greater productivity and fewer headaches.

MKS Toolkit offers an abundance of utility programs which can be linked together through pipes and I/O redirection to perform complex tasks. On-line manual pages explain how to use these tools. The installation program allows you to choose to install only the utilities you need—ideal for laptop users.

One of MKS Toolkit's major features is the MKS KornShell, a command interpreter and programming language all in one, allowing the user to write powerful scripts of commands either interactively or in an editor.

MKS KornShell - the smart command interface

MKS KornShell gives you total control of the commands you execute. For example, MKS KornShell keeps a record of the commands you type in and makes it easy to edit and re-execute previous commands. This can be a real time saver for repetitive jobs. But the shell also lets you create loops and functions like a programming language, making it even easier to handle jobs that repeat the same instructions several times.

MKS KornShell lets you have longer command lines (up to 8192 characters instead of the usual 128), more environment variables, aliases for commands, abbreviations for commonly used strings, and that's just a start. It's also compatible with the KornShell on UNIX systems, and offers all the features of the Bourne shell, plus C shell enhancements. You can also use a transient version of MKS KornShell to reduce the shell's memory requirements to about 20K.

MKS Vi

MKS Vi is the standard UNIX screen editor for DOS and OS/2. Unlike most DOS editors, MKS Vi has no limitations in file size, and provides a number of features especially important to programmers.

MKS AWK

MKS AWK is a powerful data manipulation and report generation language, compatible with the new awk (nawk) described in *The AWK Programming Language,* by Aho, Weinberger, and Kernighan (Addison-Wesley: September 1987).

Both MKS Vi and MKS AWK are also offered as separate packages.

System Requirements

MKS Toolkit runs under DOS 2.0 or above on the IBM PS/2, IBM PC family, and compatibles. Although it is not required, a hard disk is recommended for improved performance and convenience. The software is shipped on either 360K 5.25" or 720K 3.5" diskettes and is not copy protected. Please specify disk size when ordering. Full technical reference and tutorial documentation is also included.

Trademarks, Licences, and Copyrights

1. Trademarks

- MKS and MKS Toolkit are trademarks of Mortice Kern Systems Inc.
- UNIX is a registered trademark of AT&T.
- Xenix, MS-DOS, and MS-OS/2 are trademarks of Microsoft Corp.
- PC DOS is a trademark of IBM Inc.

2. Copyrights

3. Mortice Kern Systems Inc. Programming Licence Agreement

Special Offer!

Purchase your MKS Toolkit by filling out and returning this order form, and you will receive a 20% discount off the list price.

❑ **YES!** I would like to purchase the full MKS Toolkit so I can have the power of UNIX® on my DOS or OS/2 personal computer.

__DOS *$199.00* (List price $249 USD)

__OS/2 *$279.00* (List price $349 USD)

__DOS & OS/2 combination $*319.00* (List price $399 USD)

Prices subject to change after April 30, 1992.

○ 5 ¹/₄" media   ○ 3 ¹/₂" media

❑ **YES!** Please send me information on other MKS products.

❑ **YES!** Please send me site license and LAN pricing for the MKS Toolkit.

Method of Payment:

❑ Charge my: VISA _____ exp. ____/____

MC _____ exp. ____/____

AMEX_____ exp.____/____

Signature: _____

Phone: (___)_____ Fax: (___)_____
(required for credit card orders)

❑ Money Order   ❑ Check   ❑ C.O.D.
                                                (add $4.00)

Shipping or Mailing Address: Please type or print clearly.

Name_____

Company_____

Address_____

City_____

State_____ Zipcode_____ Country_____

For more information call MKS at (800) 265-2797 *(continental USA only)*
or (519) 884-2251

50% educational discount available to qualified educational buyers. Call MKS for details.
30 day money back guarantee

To order: Fill in the reverse side, fold, and mail

BUSINESS REPLY MAIL
FIRST CLASS MAIL PERMIT NO 11 LEWISTON N.Y.

POSTAGE WILL BE PAID BY ADDRESSEE

MORTICE KERN SYSTEMS INC
P.O. BOX 1266
LEWISTON N.Y.
14092 - 9957

LISTEN   SECOND EDITION

LISTEN

SECOND EDITION

JOSEPH KERMAN

UNIVERSITY OF CALIFORNIA AT BERKELEY

WITH VIVIAN KERMAN

WORTH PUBLISHERS, INC.

Listen

Second Edition

Printed in the United States of America

Library of Congress Catalog Card No. 75-28510

ISBN: 0-87901-053-3

Designed by Malcolm Grear Designers

Type set by Progressive Typographers

Music set by Music Typographers

Picture Editor: Anne Feldman

Printed and bound by R. R. Donnelley & Sons Co.

Cover: Detail of *La Parade* by Georges Seurat. Oil
on canvas, 1887–1888. Courtesy of the Metropolitan
Museum of Art, bequest of Stephen C. Clark, 1960.

Worth Publishers, Inc.

444 Park Avenue South

New York, New York 10016

Preface

This second edition of *LISTEN* incorporates a significant amount of reorganization and new coverage, while leaving undisturbed the salient features of the original. The main strengths of the book, as we have come to see them, are three. First, the emphasis is on music, rather than on music history, theory, or listening techniques in the abstract. As far as possible — though admittedly it is not *always* possible — theoretical and historical data are introduced not for their own sake, and not for the sake of "memorization," but in order to point up aesthetic qualities of actual pieces of music. Secondly, each of the main chapters begins with a general stylistic overview of the broad historical period in question; this serves as a conceptual focus for understanding the music that follows. And thirdly, short picture essays, set aside from the main text, convey some aspects of cultural history which can stir the students' interest and perhaps also stimulate their musical response.

It has been gratifying to find that when we have received positive (and sometimes enthusiastic) responses from users of the book, they have generally centered on these areas. These basic features are not ones that have been modified in the present revised edition.

The general format of the book has also been kept; the "look" of the volume remains much the same. But within this format, a good deal of revision has taken place. The most extensive changes have been made in the opening chapter, *A Vocabulary for Music.* This has been rethought and almost completely rewritten to make it just as crystal-clear, as simple, and as logical as possible. As before, only those technical concepts are introduced that are of direct importance to the aesthetic experience. And the little record allows this introductory chapter to make its points much more vividly than would be possible with words alone. Throughout Chapter 1, references to BAND 1, BAND 2, etc., guide readers point by point to music on the record, which is included in every copy of *LISTEN.*

Another revision — this one more in the nature of an addition — involves popular music. New sections have been added to the last three chapters: "Popular Music of the Nineteenth Century" in the chapter on *Romanticism,*

"American Popular Music: Jazz" in *The Early Twentieth Century*, and "Post-war Popular Music: Rock" in *The Electronic Age*. This arrangement was decided on because it seemed most logical, since *LISTEN* is organized along historical lines, to present this material, too, in historical context—not as an isolated phenomenon, hermetically sealed off from "classical" music, but as a part of the total cultural life of the time. We hope this coverage of popular music will meet a need that has been expressed by many users of the first edition. To meet another expressed need, an Appendix has been added containing biographies of the main composers.

In this second edition, the picture essays and the "line scores" have all been repositioned at the ends of the various subsections of the chapters, so that students will not be in danger of losing sight of the main text or get confused as to what to read when. The book should now be easier to deal with, easier to get around in. As to the "line scores," it is perhaps worth stressing that the book is quite complete without them; it has *not* been written on the assumption that students will actually be able to read music. But as many teachers have discovered, simplified scores of one kind or another are an added help to students who can follow along in a general way—and need not frighten the others.

The discussion of musical forms and genres has been systematized, expanded somewhat, and made more evident by the use of a regular series of headings such as "The Concerto Grosso," "Fugue," "The Trio Sonata," etc. These are added to the original composer and composition headings. Some instructors wish to stress discussions of genre and form and we believe that this, again, will make the book easier for them to use. To provide for a little more flexibility of use, too, a larger number of compositions is covered in this new edition. Some music that proved less successful for teaching purposes has been changed, and in certain chapters the material is presented in what we hope is a more effective sequence.

Finally, an improved eight-record album has been prepared for *LISTEN* and the various sides have been keyed in to the text by means of references next to the titles of the compositions. Ideally, of course, a record set for a book of this kind should include all the pieces covered, but a selection has to be made to keep the cost of the album within reason.

These, then, are the main changes that have been made in this revised edition. In conclusion, though, I should like to draw attention again to some elements that have not been changed, such as the three basic features mentioned at the beginning of this preface, and particularly to the first of these features. Introductory music courses should emphasize listening to music, not facts about it: everybody seems to be agreed on this point. The focus must be, always, on aesthetic experience. This has been my guiding principle as a teacher and writer on music for over twenty-five years, and it was the main idea I held in mind while writing, and rewriting, the present textbook.

JOSEPH KERMAN

Berkeley, California
February, 1976

Acknowledgments

This book would never have assumed its original, still less its revised, form without the collaboration of my wife, Vivian Kerman. Closely involved in planning the proportions, tone, and focus of the book, she has been able to keep a clear sense of perspective about it ever since. We are pleased to repeat the acknowledgments made in the first edition, to Walter Meagher and the many musicians and teachers who commented on early drafts of the various chapters—especially Clinton Elliott and Douglas Leedy; Professors Conan J. Castle, Jerald Graue, Donald Keats, and William B. Stacy; also Professors John D. Anderson, Ervin J. Dunham, John M. Glowacki, Paul D. Hilbrich, David M. Hollister, Paul Marshall, Jr., Thomas Regelski, Howard M. van Sickle, Milôs Velimirović, and Victor Yellin; and former Dean Robert M. Trotter. Harry N. Abrams, Inc., cordially granted permission to reprint some sentences by the second author of *A History of Art and Music*, by H. W. Janson and Joseph Kerman (Harry N. Abrams and Prentice-Hall, 1968). Professor and Mrs. Janson also provided us with some of our illustrations, as did also Messers. H. H. Arnason (the superb Houdon photographs), Sherwood Dudley, and Alfred Frankenstein. Sources of the pictures, music, and poetry are given on pages 413 to 415. For material on the record we are grateful to Folkways Records, Vox Productions, The New York Pro Musica, Société Française du Son, Jonathan Kramer, and CBS Records, Inc.

For their good advice about improvements for the second edition we are grateful to another group of musicians, teachers, and students, whose criticisms and suggestions—some of them extremely shrewd, thoughtful, and detailed—have been invaluable to the revision process. Our special thanks go to Carman Moore and to Professors Elaine Brody, John F. Bullough, Conrad Douglas, Herbert Golub, Henry J. Keating, Ted Kinnaman, Thomas N. Monroe, Sterling Murray, Jerry R. Perkins, Donald W. Pugh, Martha Rearick, Thomas Wright, and Martha Wurtz. We also wish to thank the many teachers who sent us the countless invaluable suggestions that resulted from their classroom experiences.

We are particularly grateful to Professor Sterling Murray for providing, in the excellent Instructor's Manual that accompanies this text, suggestions for teaching based on his own use of *LISTEN*.

Music on the Record

Contents

Picture Essays

CHAPTER 1   A Vocabulary for Music

A Vocabulary for Music

Music appeals to the ear and the mind, to the senses and the intelligence, to emotion and intellect. We cannot generalize very far about these components of music's appeal, if only because the musical experience seems to differ so much with different listeners. Some people are physically excited by listening to music; others are exhilarated by following its intricate patterns. Others will tell you that it gives them a sense of solace and serenity, and still others derive from it an almost mystical insight into the order of life, feeling, the cosmos. Everybody likes music of some kind, to some degree, and people's responses to it are various indeed.

But there is nearly always some combination of feeling and thinking in our response to music, some combination of emotional and intellectual elements. This is the case with popular music, just as much as with the more self-consciously "artistic" music of the concert hall. It is true that plenty of music lovers claim to enjoy music only for its emotional side and not for its intellectual side. Sometimes they proclaim this quite belligerently. But these people might ask themselves—for a start—whether the third or thirtieth time they listen to a song, a rock number, or a symphony, they feel the same "gut reaction" they felt the first time in just the same way. Is not memory now a consideration, and is not memory an intellectual process?

However this may be, listening again and again to particular pieces of music is clearly an activity of major importance. It is *the* basic activity that contributes to the love of music and to its understanding; such, at least, is the belief underlying the present book, which consists mostly of accounts of musical compositions—symphonies, concertos, songs, and operas—that are well worth listening to many times. The accounts are designed to clarify their contents and their aesthetic quality: what goes on in the music and how this affects us. Some material is also provided on the historical and cultural background of the various pieces, but the main emphasis falls on the music itself.

If a text is going to be of any real aid in the listening process, obviously it must be written in a language that fits the job at hand. We have to use a set of terms by which features in music can be referred to and described. A first task, then, is to develop a vocabulary for music—a special vocabulary that will allow the authors of this book to talk sensibly to the readers and that will form the basis for a meaningful dialogue between teachers and students.

No one is going to find this vocabulary entirely new. Its terms and concepts are, of course, the ones used by professional musicians; some readers will have met them before at their music lessons, at choir practice, or while playing with a group. However, there is a basic difference in the use we wish to make of these terms. The idea is not to probe "the elements of music" for their own sake, however important this may be to the specialist. Certainly the idea is not to learn how to make music, which is the musician's real province. What we need is a way of talking about music, not a way of making it: a vocabulary *for* music, not a vocabulary *of* music.

Our stake in musical notation also differs from the professional musician's. Again, the idea is not to write down music or read it accurately, but merely to follow it and gain a general sense of its patterns. Short music examples and simplified full-length "line scores" are not hard to learn to use, and once this is accomplished, the music becomes clearer. Following with the eye helps us to focus on the things we need to catch with the ear—helps us, that is, to listen.

Even when explained in this way, the prospect of learning a vocabulary for music often meets with some resistance on the ground that the terminology is unduly "technical." But if we want to talk with any degree of precision about any special field, we have to use its own special, technical language. In any case, "technicalities" aren't usually a problem when people have a lively interest in the subject matter. Understanding what is meant by *shortstop* and *double play* is all to the good even if you are not playing baseball but only watching it on television. Those are among baseball's technical terms.

One other point is worth mentioning in this connection. Technical usage often assigns to certain words meanings that differ somewhat from their everyday meanings. *Rhythmical* is one such word (and one of the first we shall want to consider); *sequence* is another. We are familiar with the problem from other fields, such as physics, which requires specialized definitions of such concepts as force, energy, and acceleration. In ordinary conversation the same terms can be used more loosely, of course. Even after taking a physics course, no one is likely to shrink from saying, "She is a forceful character" or "He doesn't seem to have much energy tonight." But for the purpose of understanding special fields, it is necessary to keep a clear idea of the limited meanings assigned to technical concepts: force and energy in physics, or rhythm, harmony, and melody in music.

No doubt the best way to grasp musical concepts and the terms that go with them is to actually perform music. Even on the simplest level, clapping hands or beating time helps explain rhythm and meter. Singing helps explain pitch and melody. Singing rounds helps explain counterpoint. However, this is a rather personal process, which cannot be aided much by a book, even if the book were furnished with step-by-step instructions like a cookbook. Instead, a record has been included with this book in order to make the discussion as concrete as possible. Remove the record and play it in connection with the reading; the dozen short excerpts on it have been chosen to illustrate the main points of this chapter as you read them.

With the record on the phonograph, then, let us proceed to develop our vocabulary for music. First we take up a series of concepts having to do with time: rhythm, meter, and tempo. Then we move on to the various properties of sound—dynamics, tone color, pitch—and from there to melody, musical texture, form, and finally, musical style.

Rhythm and Meter

Music exists in time, just as painting exists on a flat surface and sculpture and architecture exist in the three-dimensional world. Sounds mark off spans of time, as it were, just as lines and brushstrokes mark off areas on a painter's canvas. Arranging sounds in time, then, is the composer's basic task. He decides when every sound or note* of every kind is to occur, and thus sets up time relationships among all the points of his musical composition. Rhythm, in the most general sense, is the term referring to the whole time aspect of music.

RHYTHM

Composers can also stress certain sounds, or as it is more usually put, provide them with an accent. There are many ways of accenting a note: the simplest way is to have it played somewhat louder than its surroundings. (The painter, whose analogous task consists in tracing lines at the right places on his canvas, can accent the lines by heavy shading, for example.) In music, successive sounds follow one another sometimes directly and sometimes with short spaces of silence in between. But in any case, the time interval between notes is generally fixed with care, and so is the relative weight of the notes, that is, which of them are to be accented and which are not. No single feature of music, not even melody, determines the effect of music more crucially than the timing and weighting of notes: rhythm and accent.

ACCENT

The term *rhythm* can also be used in a less general sense—and usually is. We speak of "a rhythm" or "the rhythm of a particular passage" in order to refer to the specific time relationships within that passage. "A rhythm" is simply a particular arrangement of long and short notes. Thus we might say that a certain rhythm—for example, the beginning of *Good King Wenceslas*—consists of six notes of the same length followed by one of twice the length, four notes of the original length, then two of the double length, and so on.

But of course such things are usually expressed in musical notation, which has developed its own system of marks to indicate the relative lengths of notes. Some readers will already know this system, but those who are not

---

* The word *note,* common as it is, can prove to be slightly tricky in usage. It can mean either (1) a sound of a certain definite, single pitch and duration, (2) the written or printed sign for such a sound in musical notation, or even (3) one of the keys pressed with the finger on a piano or organ (as in "this note is stuck").

familiar with it should refer to page 8. The rhythm described above is notated most simply as:

With most music, the mind does not experience rhythms strictly in their own terms. Back of the rhythms, we instinctively hear a pulse of accented and unaccented <u>beats</u> in a simple, regular, recurring pattern. This pattern is called the <u>meter</u>. And while listening to a rhythm, we tend to organize it in our minds according to the regular beat-pattern of the meter:

BEATS

METER

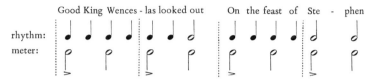

(The symbol > indicates a strong accent.) The process of beating time consists of marking out the strong (accented) and weak (unaccented) beats which make up the meter. It is a way of organizing time into simple units.

Basically there are two kinds of meter: duple (ONE two ONE two ONE two . . .) and triple (ONE two three ONE two three ONE two three . . .). In almost all the music we hear, one of these meters serves as the regular background against which the much more complicated course of the rhythm itself is measured or heard.

It is the interaction of rhythm and meter that supplies much of the real vitality of music. As the rhythm momentarily coincides with the meter, then goes its own way, and then perhaps even contradicts or obscures the meter, all kinds of variety and tension and excitement can result. A good example is the work of a first-rate jazz drummer (listen to band 1). Measure by measure, he whirls through a dazzling collection of different complex rhythms, all of them within the framework of the simple duple meter. The drummer controls accent, too, by hitting his drums hard or softly. The amazing thing is how the meter is invigorated by the complicated rhythmic play that goes on around it. How much more imaginative and lively our drummer is than the player of the big bass drum in a marching band, whose destiny is to beat out the ONE two ONE two ONE two of the meter and nothing more!

Marches and dances, which exist in order to stimulate body movements, always emphasize the meter in a strong, obvious way. Most popular music has a heavy beat, too, because meter gives rise to a very basic (and therefore "popular") emotional response. In other kinds of music, however, the metrical underpinning is not always emphasized, or even explicitly beaten out at all, in back of the rhythm. It does not need to be, for the listener almost always feels it under the surface. People will even imagine they hear a simple duple or triple meter in the steady dripping of a faucet or the click of a motor. The psychological reason for this probably lies in the fact that simple repetitive patterns of stress/unstress underlie so many of our basic life functions: the heartbeat, breathing, walking, as well as more obvious activities such as dancing and marching.

BAND 1

We observed a moment ago that the interaction of rhythm and meter is characteristic of most music. However, there are certain kinds of music that do without meter. Listening to them may help focus our understanding of both meter and rhythm.

BAND 2   Compare band 2, a drum solo from the Caribbean Islands, with the jazz drum solo on band 1. You may find them equally fascinating in rhythm, but you will scarcely be able to discern any simple recurring pattern of beats underlying the drumming on band 2. As a result, this highly exhilarating solo has a very different effect.

BAND 3   A second example of music without meter is the Gregorian chant on band 3, sung by a choir of Benedictine monks. Composed in early medieval times, music of this general style constituted the daily church music of Europe for many centuries. There is melody of a kind here—one that we are not accustomed to—but the rhythm strikes us as halting and indefinite, constantly fluctuating and devoid of bold accents. Once again, it is impossible to beat out a recurring metrical pattern behind this music. Perhaps, indeed, this was the point. As religious music of the Catholic Church, Gregorian chant had to be kept separate from the more physical manifestations of the world, such as dancing.

BAND 4   Yet another example of meterless music is the piece by a young American composer, Jonathan Kramer, on band 4. The various astonishing sounds appear to follow one another in an entirely random time sequence—which is not surprising, since in fact they were produced, and were intended to be produced, by chance. Obviously there is no metrical basis to be felt here.

All these are instances of nonmetrical music. But to think of them as unrhythmical is not correct. Like all other kinds of music, these pieces consist of sounds in time, and the time relation of sounds creates rhythm. "Unrhythmical music" is really a contradiction in terms, and to speak of "rhythmical music" is to be redundant. Granted that we often call music "rhythmical" when its rhythmic qualities impress us particularly. Some people, speaking even more approximately, call music "rhythmical" whenever the meter is strongly emphasized, as in dance music of all kinds, jazz, and rock.

There is no harm in such loose talk, but it does not get us very far in trying to develop a vocabulary for music. It does not allow for many shades of meaning. The jazz drummer and the Caribbean drummer are both "rhythmical." To distinguish between them, we need to say that whereas both employ highly intricate rhythms, and rhythms that are beautifully controlled, one works within a simple meter and the other does not. Speaking loosely, people might describe both the Gregorian chant and the Jonathan Kramer piece as "unrhythmical." To distinguish them, we need to say that Kramer uses utterly irregular rhythms, which capture something of the uncontrolled shock of unpredictability, whereas the chant rhythm is calm and purposeful, even though within limits it is free, elastic, and indefinite.

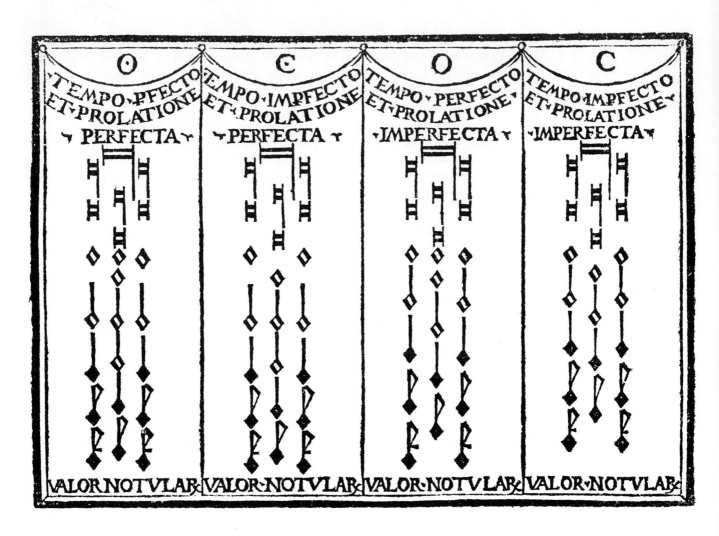

Musical Notation: Rhythm

This perplexing diagram was used to explain rhythmic notation in the fifteenth century, when notes had Latin names, diamond shapes, and much more complicated time relationships to one another. A simplified diagram is used to explain today's note values:

One whole note:

= 2 half notes:

= 4 quarter notes:

= 8 eighth notes:

= 16 sixteenth notes:

To make rhythms, composers use not just sounds but sounds alternating with short silences called *rests* (because the player rests—or at least, catches his breath). The following rests are equivalent in duration to the notes shown at the left:

Whole note rest
(below a line):

half note rest
(above a line):

quarter note rest:

eighth note rest:

sixteenth note rest:

These two diagrams of equivalent note and rest values show how diagonal "flags" (♪ ♪ ♪) can be run together as horizontal "beams" (♫ ♩ ♩), which are easier to read. The rhythm is the same. More flags or beams can be added to the note stems to halve the time values further, as required (♪♪♪, ♫♫♫). In a similar way, extra flags can be added to the short rests to halve their duration (𝄾, 𝄾).

Here is a simple music example showing how these rhythmic equivalents work. A *measure* (or *bar*) is the basic time unit chosen for a piece of music—in this case, a whole note. Measures are marked off by vertical *measure lines*. Each measure covers the same time span, one whole note, which is equivalent to two half notes (measure 1) or four quarter notes (measure 2) or eight eighth notes (measures 3 and 4):

Among the additional conventions employed in rhythmic notation, a dot after a note or rest lengthens it by 50 percent. Thus ♩. = ♩ + ♪ and 𝄽 = 𝄽 + 𝄾. To count out the following more complicated rhythmic equivalents, think of quarter-note beats. The whole note always contains four beats:

The *meter* of a piece is indicated by means of a *time signature*, a numeral or sign printed on the staffs at the very beginning and at points of change (if any) thereafter. The top digit in the numeral shows *how many beats* come in each measure. The bottom digit shows *what kind of note* represents the beat—half, quarter, eighth, etc.

Thus the most common time signature for duple time is ⁴⁄₄ ("four-four time": also written as 𝄴). Other familiar duple-time signatures are ²⁄₄ and ²⁄₂ (also written as 𝄵). Common signatures for triple time are ³⁄₄ and ³⁄₈. There are also *compound meters* involving 6s, 9s, and 12s. The familiar meter ⁶⁄₈ is essentially a duple meter, but with

each of the two main beats (ONE and *four*) subdivided into three (ONE two three *four* five six ONE two three *four* five six . . .).

Notice that the system of rhythmic notation deals only with the *relative* length of the notes and says nothing about their *absolute* duration. Hence the rhythmic notation alone does not tell us how fast or slowly a piece is to be played (see our discussion of tempo, page 10). What is more, the rhythm of *Good King Wenceslas* can be indicated quite correctly in several different ways, depending on which note is chosen for the basic beat:

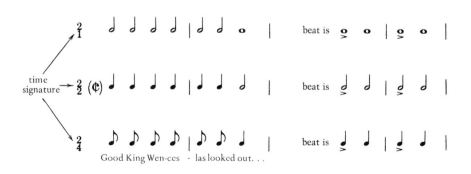

The symbol > indicates a strong accent, called a *sforzato* (Italian for "forced," also indicated by the abbreviation *sf*).

Tempo

Tempo is the term for the speed of music, fast or slow. In metrical music, it is the rate at which the basic, regular beats of the meter follow one another. Whereas rhythmic notation only takes account of the relative duration of notes, as we have seen, tempo takes account of their absolute duration in fractions of a second. This can be expressed quantitatively by indications such as ♩ = 126, meaning 126 quarter notes per minute. Such indications are called *metronome marks,* after the metronome, a mechanical or electrical device that ticks out beats at all practicable tempos.

When composers give directions for tempo, however, they generally prefer qualitative language, which leaves some latitude for different performers, different acoustical conditions in concert halls, and the like. Italian terms for tempo have become conventional, because in the period when these terms began to be used regularly, Italy dominated the musical scene in Europe:

COMMON TEMPO INDICATIONS	LESS COMMON TEMPO INDICATIONS
adagio . . . . . . slow	*lento, largo, grave* . . slow, very slow
andante . . . . . on the slow side, but not too slow	*larghetto* . . . . somewhat faster than largo
moderato . . . . moderate tempo	*andantino* . . . . . . somewhat faster than andante
allegretto . . . . on the fast side, but not too fast	*vivace, vivo* . . . . . lively
allegro . . . . . . fast	*prestissimo* . . . . . . very fast indeed
presto . . . . . . very fast	

Not all of these Italian words refer in their original meaning to speed itself, of course. Most of them are terms for a certain character or mood, which is associated in a very general way with a range of speed. In the last analysis, composers are less interested in speed for its own sake than in the character which a certain speed can give their music, and they feel safer in giving performers indications along these lines. *Vivace* is close to our "vivacious" and *allegro* actually means "cheerful." *Grave* is our word "grave" and *largo* means "wide" or "spacious." *Andante,* derived from the common Italian word for "to go," might be translated as "going along steadily."

Reading scores, you may come across some of these other terms used to indicate irregularities of tempo and tempo changes:

accelerando (*accel.*) . . . . gradually getting faster
ritardando (*rit.*), *rallentando* (*rall.*) . . . gradually getting slower
più lento, più allegro . . . . slower, faster
fermato (⌢) . . . a hold of indefinite length on a certain note
rubato . . . . . a short temporary change in tempo (see also page 225)

The most important terms to remember are the "common tempo indications" above. For when they appear at the top of a symphony movement, etc., they usually constitute its only heading or title. People refer to "the Andante" of Beethoven's Fifth Symphony, meaning a certain movement (the second).

Dynamics and Tone Color

Music is sound in time; we have discussed the time aspect of music in the last few pages, and now we come to sound itself. Sound may be said to have three distinct properties.* We shall take them up in order of increasing difficulty, starting with *dynamics* and *tone color* in the present section. *Pitch* and important matters that grow directly out of pitch—scale, melody, harmony—will be discussed at some length in the next few sections of this chapter.

DYNAMICS The general name for the volume of sound, the loudness or softness of a musical passage, is dynamics. Scientists measure it quantitatively in units called decibels; supersonic passenger planes were banned because their decibel count was over 110. Musicians use qualitative language (as is also true of their directions of tempo). Again, Italian terms have long been conventional:

forte (*f*) . . . . loud   *piano* (*p*) . . . . soft

mezzo forte (*mf*) . . . . medium loud   *mezzo piano* (*mp*) . medium soft

fortissimo (*ff*) . . . . . . very loud   *pianissimo* (*pp*) . . . very soft

One note played louder than the surrounding notes makes for an accent (page 9), and a long passage played at a louder dynamic than another will sound climactic by comparison. Terms for changing dynamics are:

crescendo (*cresc.*, $<$) . . . . gradually getting louder

diminuendo (*dim.*, $>$) . . . . gradually getting softer

TONE COLOR The notes that we hear in music, loud or soft, differ in general *quality* of sound, depending on the instruments or voices that produce them. Tone color and *timbre* are terms for this quality. Tone colors are almost impossible to describe, let alone notate; about the best one can do is use imprecise adjectives such as "bright," "warm," "harsh," "hollow," or "brassy." Yet tone color is one of the most immediate and easily recognized of musical elements. Many people know and can distinguish the sounds of various different instruments even though they cannot carry a tune or follow rhythms.

INSTRUMENTS The study of musical instruments is a very extensive and fascinating subject, touching on many other fields of knowledge. To study musical instruments, one also needs to study history, because instruments are known or documented from all historical periods; anthropology, because instruments are found among all the peoples of the world and there are remarkable parallels among them as well as differences; sociology, because instruments are used for love and war, religion, work, and recreation; and art, because men have always felt an urge to make the objects that produce their music into things of beauty. The student of instruments needs talented hands, too, in

---

* Science provides a relatively simple explanation for each one. Although the explanation is not of primary concern to musicians and listeners, it has an interest of its own, and a brief introduction to the science of sound is provided in the picture box on pages 38 and 39.

order to adjust and fix these very precisely made objects. An extraordinary number of different devices have been invented for the making of music, and the range of tone colors they can produce is almost endless.

Musical instruments can be classified in a number of ways. The standard categories for Western instruments are the following:

String instruments   including those which are played with a bow (violin, cello) and those which are plucked or hammered (guitar, harp, dulcimer)

*Woodwind instruments**   including hollow pipes, in which air vibrates to produce the sound (recorder, flute), and pipes containing reeds which do the vibrating (oboe, clarinet); here the air in the pipe acts as a resonator

Brass instruments   wind instruments with a special kind of cup- or funnel-shaped mouthpiece; when the player blows into this, his lips actually vibrate to produce the sound (trumpet, French horn)

Percussion instruments   in which something is struck to produce the sound (drum, cymbal, xylophone)

Keyboard instruments   piano, harpsichord, pipe organ, piano accordion

Today some of these instruments exist in forms in which the sound is amplified electronically (electric guitar). And the twentieth century has developed instruments in which the sound is generated, as well as amplified, by electronic means (electric organ, Moog synthesizer; see page 376).

In the chart on the page opposite, the main instruments of the symphony orchestra are listed and briefly characterized. The listings in large letters constitute the basic core of the orchestra, and the ones in small letters are more recent additions (see also the historical charts on pages 148, 224, and 331).

Then on pages 16 to 21 will be found a sampling of other instruments of the same general types used in Western music of past ages, in Western popular music, and in non-Western music—music from Africa, South America, and the Near and Far East. This will perhaps give some idea of the pervasive and sometimes quite unexpected distribution of instruments over the centuries and over the entire world.

In reading the orchestra chart on page 13, bear in mind that whenever instruments turn out to be successful and popular they tend to be made in several different sizes so that a broad range of pitches can be covered. Sometimes such "families" of instruments keep the same name (alto saxophone, tenor saxophone), sometimes not (oboe, bassoon). Families are shown on a horizontal line, starting with the highest in pitch at the left.

---

* So called because all these instruments used to be made of wood. Today flutes and piccolos are made of metal (there are even gold flutes).

Instruments of the Orchestra

STRING INSTRUMENTS

VIOLIN
The violin family, in four sizes, covers almost any pitch needed in symphonic music.

VIOLA
The "tenor" instrument, 2 or 3 inches longer than the violin.

VIOLONCELLO
Usually abbreviated to *cello*; the bass instrument, played between the knees.

DOUBLE BASS (also called STRING BASS and BASS VIOL) The deep bass instrument, up to six feet tall.

HARP The orchestra harp is a large instrument covering six and a half octaves.

WOODWIND INSTRUMENTS

PICCOLO
Short for *flauto piccolo,* Italian for "small flute."

FLUTE
Basically a cylinder with a side hole for blowing. The player holds it horizontally, blows down through the hole, and to control pitch covers or uncovers other holes in the cylinder (as on all woodwinds).

E♭ CLARINET
A small, high clarinet.

CLARINET
An elastic reed made of cane is fitted against a mouthpiece ("beak"). When held in the mouth and blown through, the reed vibrates against the beak.

BASS CLARINET
This rather long instrument is bent twice, like a saxophone.

OBOE
A double reed (two reeds clamped together with an air space in between) is held in the mouth and blown through. The reeds vibrate against one another.

ENGLISH HORN
Hopelessly named, this is *not* English and *not* a horn but just a "tenor" oboe.

BASSOON

CONTRABASSOON OR DOUBLE BASSOON
The bass members of the oboe family are so long that they have to be bent back on themselves several times.

BRASS INSTRUMENTS

TRUMPET   BASS TRUMPET
A long *cylindrical* tube (except for the very end, which flares out). The player blows into a small cup-shaped mouthpiece; his lips themselves actually vibrate, like a double reed.

The trumpeter controls pitch by *overblowing* (blowing in a way that produces overtones: see page 39) or by pressing valves which open or shut extra pipes linked to the main tube.

Mouthpieces of this kind, sometimes called "loose-lip" mouthpieces, are used with all the brass instruments.

TENOR TROMBONE   BASS TROMBONE
Low-range instruments essentially similar to the trumpet, but with pitch controlled by a sliding mechanism instead of by valves.

FRENCH HORN
A long *conical* tube wound into a handsome spiral shape. The funnel-shaped "loose-lip" mouthpiece and conical tube make for mellow tone. Pitch is controlled as on the trumpet.

TENOR TUBA   BASS TUBA
Low-range instruments similar to the French horn, but with conical tubes of somewhat different proportions.

PERCUSSION INSTRUMENTS

XYLOPHONE
Tuned wood blocks played with hammers.

TIMPANI (KETTLEDRUMS)
Large drums tuned to a definite pitch, used in sets of two or three. *Pedal timpani* are provided with a device to change pitch instantaneously.

TRIANGLE   CYMBALS, GONG, SNARE DRUM   BASS DRUM

Musical Instruments of the Orchestra

STRING INSTRUMENTS

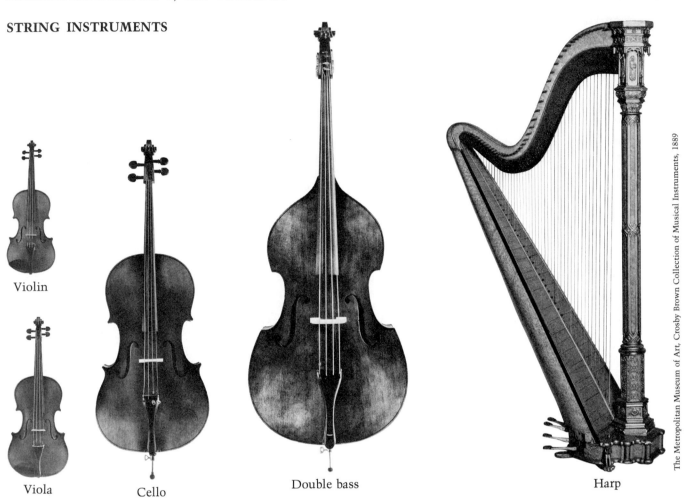

Violin

Viola

Cello

Double bass

Harp

The Metropolitan Museum of Art, Crosby Brown Collection of Musical Instruments, 1889

BRASS INSTRUMENTS

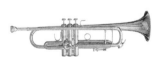

Trumpet

Trombone

French horn

Tuba

SCALE 15:1

WOODWIND INSTRUMENTS

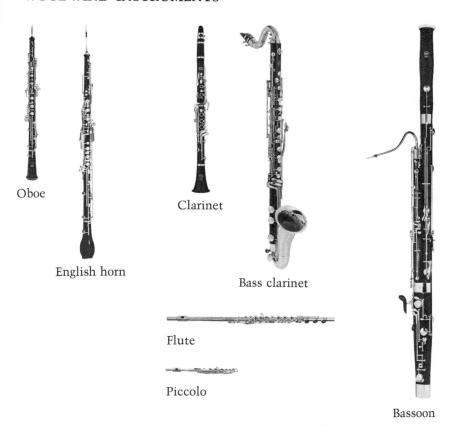

Oboe

English horn

Clarinet

Bass clarinet

Flute

Piccolo

Bassoon

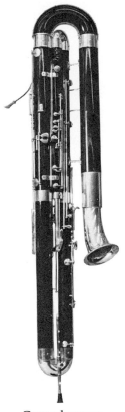

Contrabassoon
(Double bassoon)

PERCUSSION INSTRUMENTS

Timpani (kettledrums)

Cymbal

Triangle

SCALE 15:1

Musical Instruments in History and in the World

STRING INSTRUMENTS
VIOLIN TYPE

The main bowed string instruments of sixteenth-century Europe were the various members of the VIOL family. Roughly similar to the violins, they differed in details of construction, number of strings, tuning of the strings, etc. Also, viols had frets on their fingerboards, like guitars.

Viols gave way to violins because the latter are more brilliant in tone. But the largest member of the family, the VIOLA DA GAMBA ("knee viol"), survived into the eighteenth century. Bach wrote for it in the sixth Brandenburg Concerto, the *St. Matthew Passion*, and several fine sonatas. Three viols are pictured at the left of page 52.

A curious kind of mechanized violin is the HURDY-GURDY (see page 215).

HARP TYPE

The harp is a very ancient and widespread instrument. Types called the LYRE and the KITHARA were cultivated in Sumeria, Egypt, and Greece. Like all string instruments, harps require a soundbox or resonating air chamber to amplify the sound (unless electronic amplification is used, as in the skinny rock guitars). On harps, the soundbox is at the side or bottom.

Similar to harps, except that the strings stretch right across the soundbox, are ZITHERS, which are plucked, and DULCIMERS, which are played with hammers. The Japanese KOTO is a kind of zither. The HARPSICHORD (see page 138) is really a mechanized keyboard zither. And the PIANO is a keyboard dulcimer—open a grand piano and you can see the strings and hammers.

WOODWIND INSTRUMENTS
FLUTE TYPE

The OCARINA, a simple type of flute, has one of the most venerable ancestries of all instruments. Reindeer bones with holes, made into such flutes, were found in the prehistoric painted caves of Lascaux in South France.

The RECORDER resembles the flute but is held vertically and blown through a simple "chimney" or "whistle" mouthpiece. The tone is thin, easy to produce—but hard to keep in tune.

Ashmolean Museum, Oxford

Viola da gamba
(Italy, 1700)

Ancient
Egyptian harp

Medieval dance band: two shawms and sackbut (France, 1450)

OBOE TYPE

Many types of oboe flourished in Medieval and Renaissance Europe. Oboes were originally imported from the Near East, probably at the time of the Crusades. They must have been violent in tone, to judge from some of their names: BOMBARDE, POMMER, SCHRYARI, KRUMMHORN, RACKETT, SHAWM. For dancing in the late Middle Ages, the standard "group" consisted of two shawms and a SACKBUT or early trombone (called *haute musique,* "loud music").

Besides the harplike lyre and kithara, ancient Greece knew the AULOS, a double oboe, the instrument of Dionysus, god of wine. It must have required great wind pressure, for players wore straps to support their cheeks (see page 18).

CLARINET TYPE

Strange as it may seem, the MOUTH HARMONICA is basically similar to the clarinet, or to a whole set of clarinets—it contains one tiny metal reed for each note on the instrument. The ACCORDION is similar, but the player squeezes air from a bellows instead of blowing it and presses a keyboard and chord buttons. A keyboard is also used in the REED ORGAN or HARMONIUM, which provided the accompaniment for after-dinner hymns in many pious Victorian drawing rooms. Again, the sound is produced by a whole set of single reeds, blown by a bellows pumped by foot pedals.

SAXOPHONES are very close to clarinets in blowing and fingering technique. Most players can "double" on both instruments. First developed in the nineteenth century for military bands, the saxophone reached its peak a hundred years later in jazz. Some of the greatest jazzmen were or are sax players: Sidney Bechet, Coleman Hawkins, Johnny Hodges, Lester Young, Charlie Parker, Gerry Mulligan, and Ornette Coleman.

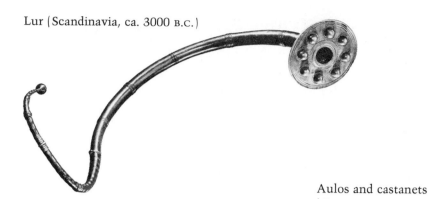

Lur (Scandinavia, ca. 3000 B.C.)

Aulos and castanets
(Greece, c. 350 B.C.)

BRASS INSTRUMENTS
TRUMPET TYPE

The CORNET and the FLUGELHORN are modern trumpetlike instruments with wider tubes and a more mellow sound. The BUGLE, made without any valves, or one at most, is therefore restricted to relatively few notes and can play only military fanfares. Silver trumpets were found in the pyramid tomb of the Egyptian King Tut-ankh-amon, ca. 1250 B.C. Amazing bronze-age trumpets called LURS have survived from Scandinavia, perhaps as early as 3000 B.C.

HORN TYPE

The SHOFAR, the traditional synagogue instrument that is still used to announce the Jewish New Year, belongs to the conical, French-horn category. It is a ram's horn blown through a brass-type mouthpiece.

EUPHONIUMS, SAXHORNS, SOUSAPHONES, HELICONS, and BARITONES are some of the many band instruments of the tuba type.

**PERCUSSION
INSTRUMENTS**
DRUM TYPE

By worldwide standards, the Western symphony orchestra is pitifully poor in percussion instruments, even though modern composers have added greatly to the traditional stock shown on page 13. Africa, which has produced the most intricate art of drumming known, is very rich in drums. Some are made of hollowed-out slit logs (SLIT-DRUMS), others of skins stretched over pottery or wood resonators of all shapes. Our BONGO DRUMS are of Cuban origin, played in sets with the fingers.

RATTLES, MARACAS (gourds), CASTANETS, WOOD BLOCKS, BELLS, and CYMBALS exist in a great variety and abundance in most cultures, as do BULL ROARERS—small drumlike objects swung around on a string. In our culture, they survive as carnival noisemakers.

CHIME TYPE

"Chimes" is a generic name for sets of tuned objects (bells, blocks, etc.) generally played with hammers, like a xylophone. Chimes have been developed most highly in Indonesia, where an elaborate court orchestra (GAMELAN) is made up chiefly of such instruments. They employ wood blocks (GAMBANG), bronze slabs (GENDER), bamboo pipes (ANGKLUNG), or metal disks or vases (BONANG).

Several chime instruments besides the xylophone are used in the West. The bright GLOCKENSPIEL, played with hammers, and the gentle CELESTA, played from a keyboard, both use steel plates. TUBULAR CHIMES are sometimes used in the symphony orchestra (as well as for doorbells). The VIBRAPHONE uses metal tubes which are kept in vibration by means of an electrical mechanism. As with the saxophones, the possibilities of this flexible instrument were first demonstrated in jazz, by such players as Lionel Hampton, Red Norvo, and the Modern Jazz Quartet.

Indonesia: gamelan orchestra with various chime and percussion instruments

Ghana: elephant-tusk trumpets

Ivory Coast: drummers

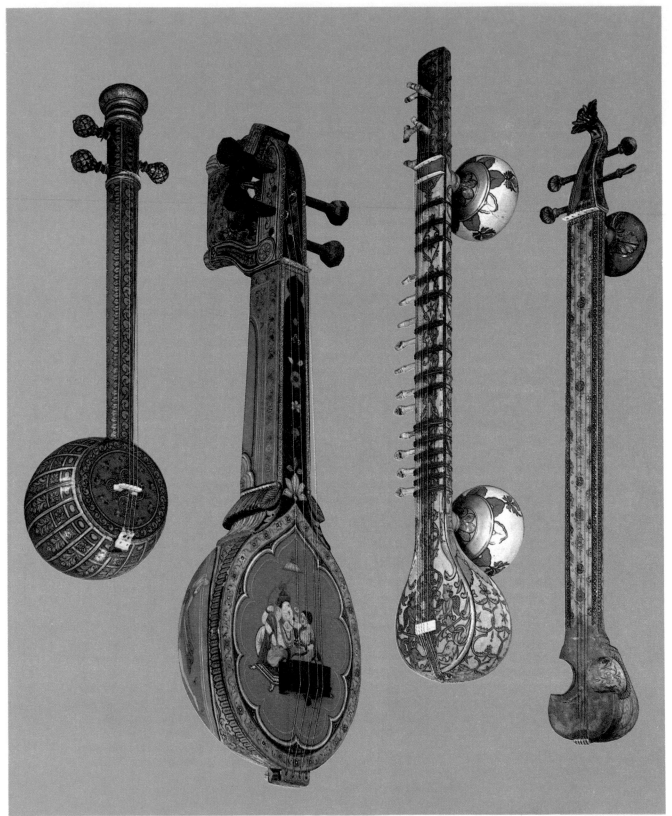

One very important type of string instrument has no regular role in the symphony orchestra: "strumming" instruments called LUTES, after the main early European variety. They include the GUITAR, MANDOLIN, BANJO, UKELELE, BALALAIKA, and the ELECTRIC GUITAR family. As with the violin family, pitch is controlled by stopping strings on a fingerboard which, however, usually has *frets* on it. Frets are little cross-bars across the fingerboard. They mark off the exact length of the strings required to get the right tuning.

In the Orient, lute-type instruments come in marvelous shapes and with extraordinary decorations. On the facing page, from left to right, is a SITARA, a LONG-NECKED LUTE, and two VINAS, all from India.

On this page, folksingers with lute-type instruments: Jean Ritchie with an APPALACHIAN DULCIMER and Ravi Shankar with an Indian SITAR. (But the Appalachian dulcimer is misnamed. Do you see why?)

Pitch: Scales

PITCH

Some sounds seem high, others low. This we hear instinctively—though we might be hard-pressed to say just how the adjectives "high" and "low" match up with our experience of the sounds in question. But the quality of "highness" or "lowness," which is called <u>pitch</u>, obviously figures centrally in the whole notion of music. If sound lacked this quality, music would be truly impoverished, a matter of rhythm, dynamics, and tone color alone.

Pitch, dynamics, and tone color are the three properties of sound. For sounds which are to be used in music, it is important that the pitch be focussed, rather than blurred or indefinite as it is in low or high noises. There are some musical instruments with indefinite pitch, of course—think of the bass drum and cymbals—but we don't expect to see them leading the band.

The experience of pitch is formed very early from the outside world. Birds sing and pet mice squeak in the upper pitch range, while thunder and motorcycles without mufflers make low-pitched noises. Men generally speak and sing lower than women do—and no doubt our first, most intimate acquaintance with pitch differences comes from the voices we hear during infancy. Shown below are the average vocal ranges of the common types of men's and women's singing voices as used in a chorus. (For those who are not familiar with musical notation for pitch, it is explained on page 26.)

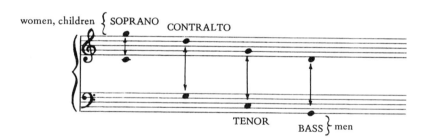

Trained singers, especially those trained for opera, often have astonishing vocal ranges, far beyond these averages.

In addition to this quality of "highness" and "lowness," there is another important aspect of pitch that everyone recognizes instinctively. (Or nearly everyone: tone deafness, like color blindess, afflicts only a small proportion of mankind.) If someone plays a series of higher and higher pitches—say an upward run on a piano—there comes a point at which the pitch seems in some sense to "duplicate" an earlier pitch. The new pitch does not sound identical with the old one, but somehow the two sounds are very similar in their different ranges or levels. They blend extremely well. They may almost seem to melt into one another.

OCTAVES

This auditory "duplication" is known as the phenomenon of <u>octaves</u>, a term whose origin will be explained in a moment. The scientific explanation for the phenomenon (see page 39) matters less to us than does the fact that people perceive it so generally and so easily. For instance, when men and women sing together, they sing in octaves, duplicating each other's song an octave or two apart. If you asked them, they would all say they are singing "the same tune," at different octave levels.

BAND 5 The effect of octaves can be heard on Band 5, an excerpt from a religious play with music—actually, a sort of opera—composed around A.D. 1200. The lively little tune is sung first by one monk (tenor) in a middle register, next by the choirboys (sopranos) in a high register, and next by the choir of monks (basses) in a low register. Then tenors and basses, then tenors, basses, and boy sopranos all sing the tune together. The tune sounds in three octaves simultaneously, blending perfectly.

As a result of the phenomenon of octaves, the full continuous range of pitches which exists in nature (and which is covered, for example, by a siren starting very low and going up higher and higher until we can no longer hear it) falls into a series of "duplicating" segments. About ten of these octave segments are audible to us. A large pipe organ covers all ten. A piano covers about seven. Two and a half are shown on the diagram on page 27.

It is interesting to consider the difference between these similar segments of pitch materials and the range of colors available to the painter. (Like pitches, colors also result from vibrations—light waves of different frequencies.) One difference is that the painter's palette extends all the way from red through orange, yellow, green, blue, and indigo to violet without any kind of duplication effect. Another difference is that the painter mixes his pigments at will and uses all the subtle shades between one primary color and the next. The musician, on the other hand, generally employs only a small limited number of fixed pitches in each segment.

The reason each segment is given the name *octave,* meaning "eight-span," is that at one time the music of Western Europe employed only seven different pitches, and then repeated the first one at a higher duplicating pitch, DIATONIC SCALE thus making a total of eight. The set of seven pitches is called the <u>diatonic scale</u>.

Scale is a term for the total pitch material that is considered to be available for making music. Although students are taught to "play scales" as though they were simple melodies, a scale does not necessarily have to imply a melody or any *order* of notes. It can be thought of simply as the store of notes available—seven per octave, in the diatonic scale. The set of white notes on the piano constitutes this scale, carried up and down through the octaves.

At a later point in history, five further pitch subdivisions were settled on between some of the others. The total now stood at twelve. These constitute the <u>chromatic scale</u>, the series of all the successive white and black notes on the piano keyboard or all the fretted notes on the guitar:

Until very recently, Western music used these twelve pitches, duplicated through all the octaves, and in principle no other pitches. Features of many instruments are designed to produce these particular pitches exactly: frets on guitars, carefully measured-out holes in flutes, and the tuned sets of strings in harps and pianos. Other instruments, such as the violin and the slide trombone, have a more continuous range of pitches available to them (as does a police siren or the human voice). In mastering these instruments, one of the first tasks is learning to pick out exactly the right pitches. We call this playing in tune. Singing in tune is a matter of constant concern for vocalists, too.*

INTERVAL

The space or distance between any two pitches is called an <u>interval</u>. Intervals take their names from the number of diatonic-scale notes between the two pitches, counting from the first pitch to the second inclusive:

SECOND THIRD FOURTH FIFTH SIXTH SEVENTH OCTAVE

As every chorus singer knows, when he has to sing one specific pitch after another, it is the interval between them that determines how easy or hard they are to sing and also how "easy" or tense the song will sound. Octaves, for instance, strike us as easy in both senses. Seconds distinctly do not.

This is true also when one sings or plays two notes simultaneously. "Singing in thirds," the practice of singing along with somebody else at the interval of a third higher or lower, used to be called "close harmony," a term suggesting the comfortable sound this creates. But try singing in seconds! We shall return to this question a little later, when we discuss harmony.

---

* It is true that many instrumentalists and all singers regularly perform certain notes *slightly* off tune for an important and legitimate artistic effect. "Blue notes" are an example. The fact remains that these "off" pitches are only small, temporary deviations from the main notes of the scale—the same twelve which, on instruments such as the piano, are absolutely fixed.

The Two Main Coordinates of Music

This is a good stopping-place for a moment of review, to see how far we have got in developing a working vocabulary for music. Since music on the most basic level is an art that deals with time, we started with aspects of time: rhythm, meter, and tempo. Then we moved on to the properties of sound: dynamics, tone color, and finally pitch. We are now ready to put time and sound together, as it were, and to consider melody and tunes, harmony and counterpoint.

For this purpose, it often helps to think of pitch and time as the two main "coordinates" of music. Just as a graph with stock prices and time as coordinates can help an economist to visualize the stock market with its slumps and rallies, so a graph with pitch and time as coordinates can help us to visualize music. In fact, musical notation comes quite close to this concept:

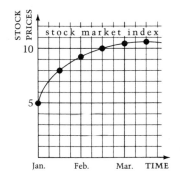

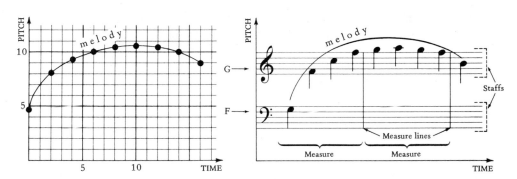

Low and high notes are positioned on a sort of grid, made up of rows of horizontal lines crossed with vertical ones. The horizontals mark off pitch, from high to low; they are grouped into *staffs* of five lines each (see page 26).

The vertical lines of the graph, the measure lines, mark off time (time in fractions of a second, rather than months and days, as on the stock market chart). Measures are the basic time units in music, as explained on page 9.

To see how the concept of musical coordinates can be put to use, consider a melody—that is, a series of notes of various pitches following one another in time. They can be plotted on the Pitch/Time graph with dots, with the pitch of each note (its "highness" or "lowness") indicated by its placement up or down, and with its position in time indicated by its placement from left to right. In an actual score, the big dots of the note-heads are "plotted" on the Staff/Measure-line grid in much the same way.

Musical Notation: Pitch

Musical notation for pitch begins by assigning letter names to the original seven pitches of the diatonic scale: A B C D E F G. Then the letters are used over and over again for pitches in the duplicating octaves. The octaves can be distinguished by qualifications such as "high C," "low C," or "middle C" or else by means of prime marks (c', c'', c''', etc.)

These pitches are notated on *staffs* (also called *staves*). A staff is a set of five parallel lines; each line and each space between lines accommodates a letter-name pitch. Each staff is calibrated or keyed in by a sign called a *clef* (French for "key"). What the clef does is to peg one of the five lines to one specific pitch. Then the other lines

and spaces are read in reference to this fixed point.

Thus in the treble clef, or G clef (𝄞), the spiral converges on the second line up, indicating that this is the line for the pitch G above middle C. In the bass clef, or F clef (𝄢), the two dots enclose the fourth line up; the pitch F below middle C goes on this line.

Adjacent lines and spaces on the staff serve to accommodate pitches with adjacent letter names. So all the other pitches find their place on the staff in relation to the fixed calibration points marked by the clefs.

Here is the notation for the pitch A in six different octaves, requiring two different staffs:

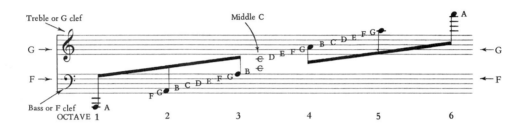

Also required are short *ledger lines,* to indicate pitches above and below the staffs. In the example above, notice how middle C is notated on one ledger line below the treble-clef staff, or else on one ledger line above the bass-clef staff.

Memory rules for identifying the staff positions are still current. Reading up on the treble clef staff, the spaces spell out the word "FACE" and the lines EGBDF can stand for "Every Good Boy Does Fine."

The subdivision pitches between the members of the

diatonic scale are not given letter names of their own. Nor do they get their own individual lines or spaces on the staff. The pitch between A and B is called "A sharp" (A♯, meaning higher than A) or "B flat" (B♭, meaning lower than B). The original pitches are called "natural," and it is sometimes necessary to specify this (A♮, B♮—A natural, B natural).

On the staff itself, the sharp, flat, and natural signs are placed directly ahead of the notes they qualify (see the music examples on pages 29 and 42).

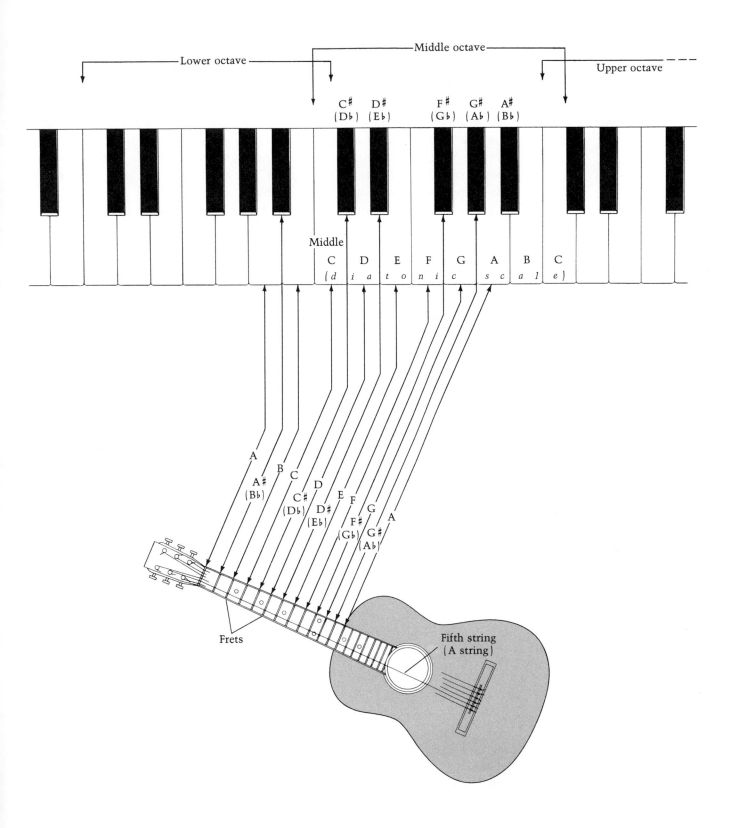

Melody and Tune

The pitches that make up music occur simultaneously or successively in time—usually both. As we have just seen, successive pitches can be plotted on the Pitch/Time graph as a line. A coherent succession of pitches is called a melody, and indeed musicians very commonly speak of "melodic line" or simply "line" in this connection. The importance of melody in the musical experience hardly needs to be stressed. This is an article of faith with musicians and music lovers of all descriptions.

Just as a line in a drawing can possess character and strike us as bold, firm, graceful, or delicate, so a melody can gain character from the succession of pitches in time from high to low, low to intermediate, and so on. A melody is a "line in time," with the direction and shape of the line given by the pattern of pitches. As the notes follow one another, each higher than the last, the melody seems to climb; a pair of low notes acts as a setback; a long series of repeated notes on the same pitch may seem to wait ominously—one develops an interest in how the melody is going to come out. In a satisfactory melody, the succession of notes is felt to hold together as some sort of meaningful unit.

BAND 3

For a very intricate and beautiful "line in time," listen again to the long Gregorian chant on band 3. At first hearing, we are likely to be impressed by the timeless, gentle, mystical quality which many people admire in all Gregorian melodies. The line floats vaguely, in an undisturbed and completely tranquil fashion. But some of the vagueness lifts as we listen to the melody several times and hear that it consists of three parallel sections—parallel, because they begin similarly and end similarly. They begin with the same two notes, sung on the syllable "A-" of the repeated word "*Agnus*" ("Lamb"). And they end with a passage of about a dozen notes which are almost, but not quite, identical.

Yet there are telling differences between the sections. Section 1 hovers around a few relatively low notes. Section 2 instantly climbs up higher, seeming more energetic and more expressive. But after this beginning it sinks down even lower in the middle, as though to balance or apologize. Section 3 mounts up to the highest note yet, a climax, and then descends in leisurely, graceful curves. The total melody comes to a very peaceful conclusion with that ending passage of a dozen notes which has been heard twice before—so similar, and yet so subtly different.

If you had trouble in catching these melodic features, even with repeated listenings, you may find it helpful to follow the score on page 33. In terms of the pattern of pitches and sheer number of notes, this certainly counts as a rich, complex melody. In rhythm, on the other hand, it is undeveloped and vague. Ordinarily, rhythm assumes major importance in determining the character of a melody, but Gregorian chants depend mainly on pitch.

Does such a thing exist as music without melody, that is, "unmelodic" music? In drum solos, perhaps; though even here, remember that certain drums do have clearly focused pitch—timpani and bongo drums, for instance—and if several such are used, there will be a rudimentary melody.

This is the case with the Caribbean drum solo on band 2. On the other hand, the Kramer composition on band 4 is genuinely unmelodic. The sounds were made by banging on a wrecked piano and then amplifying electronically. These noises have no definite pitch at all, in most cases.

BAND 6   The excerpt on band 6 comes from a symphony by Gustav Mahler, written in the early years of this century. Though we may not find the melody at all easy to sing or remember, or even to follow, a succession of pitches is certainly there, and the composer seems determined to convey some rather urgent effect with them. We might describe the result as a difficult melody, as a strained melody, or even (if we must) as an ugly melody. But as long as the music involves a succession of pitches and the mind can detect some kind of rationale in them, it has melody.

Some listeners, coming to music such as Mahler's for the first time, might be inclined to dismiss it as "unmelodic" or "unmelodious." Once again, this is loose talk which does not help in developing a vocabulary for music. When people call music "unmelodious," they probably mean that it does not strike

TUNE   them as having a <u>tune</u>—a simple, easily singable, "catchy" melody such as a folk song or a dance. In this book the word "tune" will be reserved for this use. A tune is a special kind of melody. "Melody" is a term that includes tunes, but also much else.

Several general characteristics of tunes can be enumerated. As you read the following, keep singing through to yourself *The Star-Spangled Banner* to provide your own illustrations of the various points.

PHRASE   ①   Tunes fall naturally into smaller sections, called <u>phrases</u>. To some extent, this is true of all melodies, but with tunes the division into phrases is especially clear and sharp. In tunes with words (that is, songs), the musical phrases generally coincide with the poetic lines. And since most lines in a song lyric end with a punctuation mark and a rhyming word, these features also serve to emphasize the musical phrase divisions:

> And the rockets' red *glare,*
> The bombs bursting in *air.* . .

Singing a song, one has to breathe—and one tends to breathe at the ends of phrases.

②   In many tunes, all the phrases are two, four, or eight measures long. (Measures are the basic time-units of music: see page 9.) Blues tunes, for example, typically consist of three four-measure phrases; hence the term "twelve-bar blues"—"bar" is another term for "measure." Almost all the phrases of *The Star-Spangled Banner* are two measures long. But one phrase

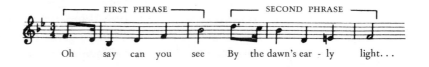

broadens out to four measures, with a fine effect: ("Oh say does that star-spangled banner yet wave. . . ").

Other phrase lengths, besides two, four, and eight measures, can certainly occur and can make for a very welcome contrast. But in general there will be a sense of "balance" between the phrases of a good tune, in terms of phrase lengths—and in other terms, too. Taken all together, the phrases of a tune add up to a well-proportioned whole.

③ Balance between phrases in a tune can be strengthened by means of melodic and/or rhythmic parallelism. Sometimes two phrases are identical ("Oh say can you see," "Whose broad stripes and bright stars"). Sometimes they have the identical rhythm but different pitches ("Oh say can you see," "By the dawn's early light"). Sometimes phrases have the same general *pattern* of pitches, but one phrase lies slightly higher or lower than the other ("And the rockets' red glare," "The bombs bursting in air"). Sequence is the technical name for this last arrangement, which occurs frequently in music and nearly always to good effect.

Of course, composers also take care to make certain other phrases contrast with their neighbors. They make one phrase short, another long, one phrase low, another high (perhaps even *too* high, at "O'er the land of the free"!). A tune containing some parallel phrases and some contrasting ones will seem to have logic, or coherence, and yet will avoid monotony. "Unity in variety" is a good slogan for artistic success of all kinds.

④ A tune has *form.* It has a clear, purposeful sense of beginning, a feeling of action in the middle, and a firm sense of winding down and concluding at the end. There will probably be a distinct high-point, either a single high note or a high passage, which the earlier part of the tune seems to be heading toward. Then the later part of the tune relaxes from this high-point ("And the home of the brave"), and reaches a very conclusive stopping-place at the very end. In a less conclusive way the music also stops at earlier points in the tune—or if it does not actually stop, at least it seems to settle. This happens after some of the interior phrases, such as "By the twilight's last gleaming" and "That our flag was still there."

The term for these stopping-places or settling-places is cadences. Cadences can be made with all possible shades of finality about them. The art of making cadences, indeed, is one of the most subtle and basic in all of musical composition.

Take any song you know and sing it through; all or nearly all of these features will hold true, just as in *The Star-Spangled Banner.* For example, Bob Dylan's *Blowin' in the Wind* is made up of four eight-measure phrases with strongly stressed parallelism among the first three of them. Indeed, phrase 1 ("How many roads . . . ") is repeated almost exactly by phrase 3 ("How many times . . ."). What is more, each of these phrases consists of two somewhat similar halves. Phrase 2 ("How many seas . . . ") begins like phrase 3—all this parallelism gives the song its haunting quality—but ends on a heavy, dragging cadence or stopping place. The contrast sounds almost

SEQUENCE

CADENCE

BAND 7

rich; the phrase sinks down instead of hovering in the air, inconclusively, as happens at the cadences of phrases 1 and 3. And phrase 4 makes a stronger contrast yet. It lies lower, and a striking sequence at the words "The answer, my friend, is blowin' in the wind" provides the tune with new energy and a new sense of direction: down. There is no melodic high point; the words do not allow it. In this tune it is the *lowest* pitch that stands out and lends special solidity, even bleakness, to the final cadence.

This kind of analysis can be applied to any tune, old or new. The mark of a good tune is a vital, intriguing set of melodic parallels, contrasts, and balances. Why do people like to sing one particular tune rather than another? Because of the words, perhaps. But also because there is a pleasure in going through again and again a good, shapely melodic pattern—a pleasure involving an appreciation of its comfortably balanced phrases, an anticipation of working up to its climax, and a feeling of accomplishment and relaxation at rounding it all off with a decisive final cadence.

At the same time, other music exists that does not consist of tunes, music which people probably do not sing much but which they seem to enjoy anyhow. Neither the longer, more ambitious rock numbers nor symphonies and concert music consist exclusively of tunes, though they generally have tunes or fragments of tunes embedded in them, along with much other material.

MOTIVE Such musical fragments are called <u>motives</u>. A motive can be as short as two or three notes—in any case, short enough so that its rhythmic and/or melodic character is easily recognized, and easily remembered when it comes back again. We listen differently to music built out of motives than to tunes. The experience is less direct and immediate, but also it is more diverse and broad-ranging and has potentialities for more powerful emotional expression.

In listening to music of this kind, we first recognize a motive and then lose it as something else is played. We wait for it to come back; when it does, it may be presented in such a way as to heighten its effect. There may be several such motives, coming back in order or out of order, in combination or in other new ways. Indeed, interest is likely to center not on the fragments themselves but on what happens to them. We listen not to the unfolding of phrases, one directly after another in a relatively short span of time, as in a tune, but rather to the way things are "worked out" over a much longer span.

THEME Another term used to refer to musical material is <u>theme</u>. This is just a general term for the basic subject matter of a piece of music. The themes of a political speech are the main points that the politician elaborates, enlarges, and develops. The composer of a symphony or a fugue treats his themes in somewhat the same way.

Themes vary in nature, depending on the type of music. For the themes of fast symphony movements, composers tend to use short motives of the type just described above. However, in a form such as the theme and variations (see page 182), it is traditional to use full tunes as the "themes," often taken from actual songs or dances. Band 1 contains the end of a variation on the "theme" *Tiger Rag.* For still other types of music, the basic elements of themes can be harmony or tone color (see page 257).

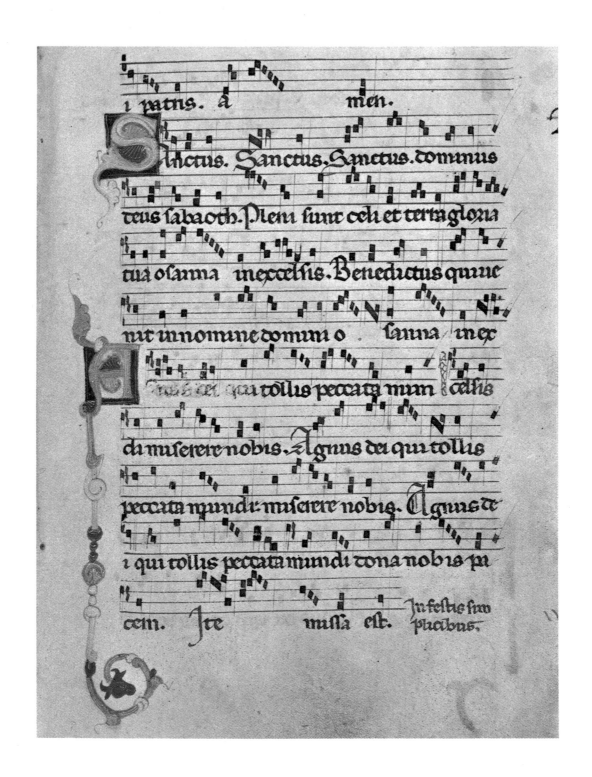

Gregorian Chant

The Gregorian chant melody of band 3, Agnus Dei, as it appears in an illuminated manuscript book of Catholic Mass music, dating from the fourteenth century. The melody begins on staff 6.

Some features of musical notation as it is known today can be seen here in an archaic form. Instead of our staff consisting of five lines, the music of the Middle Ages used four—drawn in red, which makes the notes themselves stand out beautifully. The notes are square or lozenge-shaped, not oval as in musical notation today. The three-dot mark at the beginning of each staff is the ancestor of our bass clef, marking the pitch F, which also consists of three elements (𝄢).

After the elaborately decorated, long-tailed initial letter A (staff 6), the next few letters (" . . . gnus Dei") have faded out over the centuries. The rest of the text is clear, however.

The main point for us is what this ancient musical notation lacks. It lacks all indications for rhythm and meter because this music has no meter and is vague and floating in rhythm. Though some notes have stems and others do not, this has nothing to do with their time values, all of which can vary considerably, within certain limits, according to the taste of the singers. And there are no measure lines. The small vertical strokes are only put in to mark the ends of phrases, not measures.

The preferred way of transcribing this notation, so that the music can be read today, is without meter indication, measure lines, or stems on the notes:

This page of the manuscript also includes some other Gregorian chants besides the Agnus Dei. They are all other sections of the Mass (compare page 57): the end of a *Gloria* (staff 1), a *Sanctus* (staffs 2 to 5 and the end of staff 6), and an *Ite Missa est* (end of staff 10).

Texture: Polyphony

So far, we have been discussing music as though at any moment only a single note is heard—as though in a span of time a single melody, rhythm, and tone color is experienced without accompaniment of any kind. This is, of course, rarely the case. It happens only in some special situations: when people sing by themselves, in archaic types of music such as Gregorian chant (band 3), or momentarily within larger pieces, for special effects of contrast.

Most music is more dense and complicated, deriving much of its effect from simultaneous sound factors, from what musicians call the "vertical" as well as the "horizontal" dimensions of music. Look back at the Pitch/Time graph which we discussed on page 25, and you will see that it is quite possible to plot more than one melody on it.

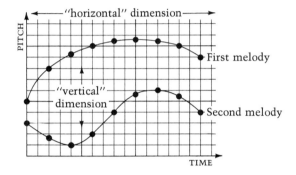

Melody exists in the "horizontal dimension" of music. The relation between simultaneous melodies or other sounds is perceived in the "vertical dimension."

TEXTURE

Texture is the term used to refer to the blend of the various sounds and melodic lines occurring simultaneously in a piece of music. The word is adopted from textiles, where it refers to the "weave" of the various threads—loose or tight, even or mixed. A cloth such as tweed, for instance, by design leaves the different threads clearly visible. In fine silk or percale, the weave is so tight and smooth that the individual constituent threads are hard to detect.

POLYPHONY
COUNTERPOINT
IMITATION

When two or more melodies are played or sung simultaneously, the texture is described as polyphonic, or *contrapuntal.** The latter term comes from counterpoint, which means the technique of working melodies together in a satisfactory way. *Imitative counterpoint*, or imitation, occurs when the various lines sounding together use the same or quite similar melodies (but at staggered time intervals, with one coming in shortly after another). Anyone who has ever sung a round has taken part in imitative polyphony: *Three Blind Mice, Row, Row, Row Your Boat*, and so on.

---

* We shall be using these terms interchangeably, though strictly speaking, polyphony refers to music in this texture and counterpoint to the technique of producing the texture.

BAND 8   Band 8 presents the beginning of an imitative polyphonic composition by a late seventeeth-century Italian composer, Arcangelo Corelli. First one violin, then another, then the cello enter at staggered intervals with the same lively melodic fragment. After the instruments are all playing, this fragment is not heard again just yet, but each instrument continues playing music that is similar in rhythm and melody. Presently the opening fragment returns in some of the instruments, one at a time, with the effect of stressing the imitative quality of the texture. For a score of this composition, see pages 114–115.

Non-imitative counterpoint occurs when the melodies are essentially different from one another. In popular music, the most impressive use of non-imitative counterpoint comes in traditional jazz, when the trumpet, clarinet, trombone, and other instruments are each improvising on their own simulta-

BAND 1   neously. An example appears in the Dixieland number on band 1, directly after the drum solo which was discussed above. Each instrument has its own interest and its own melodic integrity; each has its own kind of melody suited to the nature of the particular instrument; each seems to be trying to sound more brilliant and imaginative than the others. Listening to contrapuntal music of this kind, our attention shunts rapidly (and happily) back and forth from one instrument to another. At the same time, we may also appreciate the art by which they are all made to fit together.

BAND 6   Another example, from a symphony by Gustav Mahler, appears on band 6. Underneath the main high melody on the violins, another violin melody pursues its own course. Each melody sounds strained enough by itself, as we have already observed (page 29), but the overlapping, intertwining combination of the two makes for an even more intense total experience. At the end of the band, all the other instruments drop out, so that the non-imitative counterpoint between the two violin lines stands out with special clarity.

At the risk of pushing our graph analogy too far, we might draw the following lines to represent imitative and non-imitative polyphony, respectively. Below each graph is the same polyphony in standard musical notation:

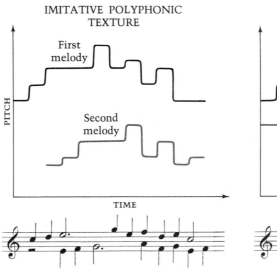

Texture: Homophony

HOMOPHONY

BAND 7

CHORD

HARMONIZATION

When there is only one melody of real interest and it is combined with other sounds that are markedly subsidiary, the texture is called <u>homophonic</u> or (more loosely) *harmonic*. The subsidiary sounds form "the accompaniment." A folk singer accompanying himself on a guitar or a dulcimer is spinning a simple homophonic texture (band 7).

Very likely the folk singer employs a number of standard groupings of simultaneous pitches which practice has shown will work well in combination. Any grouping of simultaneous pitches is called a <u>chord</u>. An imaginative guitar player will also discover non-standard chords and unexpected successions of chords in order to enrich his accompaniments.

We say that the folk song is <u>harmonized</u> when it is provided with subsidiary chords in this manner. Hymns offer another example of music in a simple homophonic texture, with each note of the melody underpinned by a single chord. The harmonizing can be done either by the organist or by the choir, with the various different voices contributing the notes that make up the chords. The soprano sings the hymn tune.

Represented below is a simple homophonic texture, in which the accompanying instruments or voices generally move simultaneously with the main melody. Each move creates a chord. Compare this graph with the ones on the previous page.

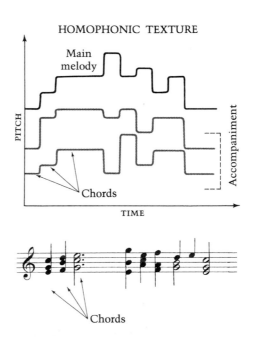

HOMOPHONIC TEXTURE

Different sets of chords can be used in the harmonization of any melody, and the overall effect of music depends to a great extent on the nature of these chords, or the <u>harmony</u> in general. This is especially true of music of the last 250 years, which is the most familiar to us. We easily recognize the

HARMONY

difference in harmony between Mozart and Mahler or between New Orleans jazz and rock. Play band 9, which contains three very short sections of music using different types of harmony. We might struggle to describe them as "stolid" in the first case, "sensuous" in the second, and "tense, restless" in the third, but in fact qualities of harmony are exceptionally difficult to characterize, except in highly technical language.

A pair of terms often used in discussions of musical texture is consonance and dissonance, meaning (roughly speaking) chords that sound at rest and those that sound tense, respectively. These qualities depend on the kind of intervals (see page 24) that make up the chords; octaves, for example, are consonant. When it is necessary to distinguish between different degrees of dissonant tension, the terms "high-level" and "low-level" dissonance can be used. Thus the first item on band 9 includes consonances and some low-level dissonances, whereas the third item includes mainly high-level dissonances as well as some low-level ones.

The real point about dissonant harmony is that we instinctively expect its feeling of tension to relax into the calm of consonant harmony, or at least to lower-level dissonance. (The technical verb used by musicians is *to resolve*.) Usually composers employ dissonance and consonance in conjunction, deriving artistic effect from the contrast or alternation between the two.

It is simplest to think of consonance and dissonance in reference to the chords of homophonic music. But the terms apply to polyphonic music, too. For as several "horizontal" melodic lines are arranged to go together in counterpoint, the "vertical" result at any individual moment is likely to be a standard chord. (At least, this is true for a good deal of polyphonic music.) Besides following the progress of the various lines, one cannot help hearing a succession of chords formed in this manner. And these chords will be consonant or dissonant, depending on the way the composer fits the individual melodic lines together.

Indeed, the alert reader will have sensed that in some situations the distinction between homophony (a single melody with accompaniment) and polyphony (several simultaneous melodies) will be hard to maintain. From the point of view of the choir singing a hymn, don't the altos, tenors, and basses all have melodic lines of their own, even though these may admittedly sound rather drab compared to the hymn tune in the soprano? Who is to say that the guitar accompaniment to a folk song doesn't have a modest melody, too?

In a way, then, homophony and polyphony are two ways of viewing or hearing the same set of simultaneous sounds. Homophony is the "vertical" view, polyphony the "horizontal" view. The distinction can sometimes come down to a matter of degree. However, while the chorus tenor and the guitarist may feel quite proud of the melodic lines they are producing, the listener may hardly notice them at all. Similarly, in a finely spun cloth, individual threads are there but no one discerns them individually (except the weaver). If only one melody stands out, the texture is called homophonic. As soon as another begins to attract attention too, the texture deserves to be called polyphonic.

The Science of Sound

Musical pitch was one of the first natural phenomena to be investigated scientifically in the Western world. Only astronomy goes back as far — and astronomy does not allow for direct experimentation, as the study of pitch does. Only later were light, mechanics, chemistry, and even medicine studied in a truly scientific way.

The pathbreaking investigations are credited to the Greek mathematician-philosopher Pythagoras, who lived before 500 B.C., before the time of Socrates, Plato, Archimedes, or Euclid. He is also famous for his theorem about right-angled triangles ($a^2 + b^2 = c^2$). Pythagoras discovered or codified numerical facts about the sounds produced by plucking strings. If we pluck a taut string, it gives out a certain pitch. Then if we pinch the string in the middle and pluck the half-length string, the new pitch is exactly an octave higher. Another way of saying this is that string lengths in the ratio 2:1 produce notes which sound at the octave. Strings in other simple numerical ratios — such as 2:3, 3:4, 4:5, 8:9 — produce all the other notes of the diatonic scale (page 23).

To the Greeks, this seemed fascinating and extremely significant. It showed that physical phenomena which can be detected by the senses (in this case, the sense of hearing) relate directly to mathematical abstractions which can be understood by reason. They did not know that falling bodies, light waves, electrons orbiting the nucleus of the atom, and so on, obey mathematical laws too. Nonetheless, Pythagoras went ahead and proposed the hypothesis that all nature is governed by number. This was quite an insight — though today we would put it a little differently, and say that natural phenomena can be described in terms of mathematics.

Pythagoras's experiments were repeated and discussed with great admiration and interest for more than two thousand years after his death. In the Middle Ages, they formed the basis of the university music curriculum. Shown here are woodcuts from a fifteenth-century music-theory book. Pythagoras is represented as a professor of the time demonstrating his musical theories using tuned bells, glasses of water, strings under different tension (with different weights attached), and pipes of different lengths. Perhaps, after all, there is something to the popular view that musical and mathematical talents go together.

What Pythagoras did not know — what was not grasped until the sixteenth century — was how sound is actually produced. Sound results from very small but very rapid vibrations that are set up in certain objects or bodies: in taut strings, plates, gongs, bells, and columns of air enclosed in tubes of one kind or another. One complete vibration is called a *cycle*.

The human ear can detect a considerable range of these vibrations, from around 16 cycles per second up to around 20,000. What sounds to us like an "average" musical sound—for instance, the A which is used to tune up at the beginning of a symphony concert—has a frequency of 440 cycles per second.

The three properties of sound are pitch, tone color, and dynamics:

1 *Pitch*, the "highness" or "lowness" of sound, depends on the speed or rate of the vibrations. The smaller the vibrating body, the faster the vibrations and the higher the sound (a piccolo encloses a smaller tube of vibrating air than does a trombone). If you blow across the top of a beer bottle as you fill it up with water, the sound becomes higher as the vibrating column of air above the water becomes shorter.

The phenomenon of octaves has to do with the remarkable fact that strings and other sound-producing bodies tend to vibrate not only along their full length but also simultaneously in halves, quarters, etc. Scientists call these fractional vibrations *partials*; musicians call them *overtones*. The sound of the overtones is very, very much softer than that of the fundamental note. But when a second string, half the length of the first, vibrates it also reinforces an overtone of the first (full-length) string. The ear receives this as a kind of "duplication."

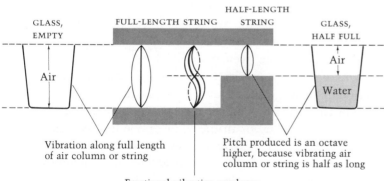

GLASS, EMPTY

FULL-LENGTH STRING

HALF-LENGTH STRING

GLASS, HALF FULL

Air

Air

Water

Vibration along full length of air column or string

Fractional vibration produces overtone an octave higher, in addition to main vibration

Pitch produced is an octave higher, because vibrating air column or string is half as long

2 *Tone color*—that indescribable quality of sound—depends on the amount and proportion of the overtones. In a flute the air column happens to vibrate largely along its total length and not much in halves or quarters, whereas violin strings vibrate simultaneously in many subsegments. This is what seems to account for the "white" tone color of the flute and the "rich" tone color of the violin.

3 *Dynamics* or loudness depends on the amplitude of the vibration, on how far or hard the string or air column vibrates. For example, in a guitar, loudness depends on how many sixteenths or thirty-seconds of an inch the string flares out when we pluck it. The harder we pluck, the louder the sound, of course. Players of wind instruments control dynamics by the wind pressure that they produce by blowing.

Form

Form is a general word with a long list of dictionary definitions. As applied to the arts, it is an important concept referring to the shape, arrangement, relationship, or organization of the various elements—of the words, phrases, meters, rhymes, and stanzas, to take poetry as an example. In painting, the elements of form are lines, colors, shapes, and so on.

In music, the elements are those that have already been discussed: rhythm, tone color, melody, and texture. In a musical piece of some length, the organization is carried out by means of repetitions of themes, whether they be tunes or motives (see page 31), by repetitions of rhythms, tone colors, and textures, and by long-drawn-out contrasts, balances, climaxes, cadences, and the like.

In this book we shall be speaking about musical form a good deal. This may come as a surprise to some readers. The fact is that over the years Western music has been very largely concerned with constructing long or relatively long pieces of music, such as Masses, fugues, symphonies, and operas. Everyone knows that music can easily make a nice effect for a minute or two. But how does it extend itself (and justify itself) onto a time span of ten minutes, half an hour, or two full hours?

This is the problem of musical form. Rarely have composers thought of music as a continuous stream, like Muzak or airline earphone music, which the listener can hook into absentmindedly at will, enjoying what he hears for as long as he happens to be paying attention. Rather, they have designed music as a specific sound experience in a definite time span, with a beginning, middle, and end and often with subtle routes between. Musical form is the relationship of these beginnings, middles, and ends.

It is a striking fact that non-Western music has never developed this concept of musical form very far. The special richness of Western music depends on form, and since this is our music, we can hardly help regarding richness of form as a positive value (though an oriental musician might think otherwise). The distinction between oriental and Western art music is perhaps clarified by thinking of the difference between a continuous decorative frieze around a wall and a wall painting, or mural. The frieze can be understood even when only a part of it is seen. But we can understand the mural only by seeing the whole thing. And as westerners, we would probably regard the mural as the more significant work of art.

However, analogies between musical form and other artistic phenomena can become deceptive if they are pushed too hard. Musical form is very much its own thing, as is equally true of form in any of the other arts. The special factor with music is the crucial importance of memory and also of anticipation, the reverse of memory. (The main talent involved in an "ear for music," in fact, is memory.) In grasping musical form, we are continuously putting together in our minds what we are hearing at the present moment, what we heard earlier in the piece, and what we feel we have been led to expect to hear later.

This is not as formidable as it may sound. Our discussion of tune, above, exemplifies musical form perfectly, and no one has any trouble exerting his memory and anticipation in order to appreciate musical form on this level, at least. In the various phrases of a tune, with their parallel features or contrasts, in the climax, the cadences, and so on, we have a microcosm of musical form in larger pieces.

For a symphony is, in a way, a tune "writ large" or blown up, and the mental process necessary to grasp its form is of the same kind. To be sure, a symphony requires more concentration for its comprehension than a tune. Composers are aware of the potential difficulty here, and they exaggerate their musical effects accordingly. In other words, the larger the piece, the more strongly the composer is likely to emphasize the features of repetition and contrast that determine the musical form.

We shall not go into the various types of musical form at this point in the book. Such discussions are best left until later, when we are actually listening to specific pieces of music. However, one aspect of musical form can be discussed in general terms here, the concept of <u>tonality</u>.

TONALITY

Any instrumentalist, and anyone who has ever tried to pick out a tune on the piano, knows that a tune that begins on C can also be maneuvered so that it begins on A, B, or any other note. The pitch relations can all be made to match, and the tune will sound "the same," only somewhat higher or lower. (In picking out a tune on the piano, you may have to experiment a little with the black notes.) Tunes or other passages that are located differently in this way are said to be in different *keys* or *tonalities*. Altogether, there are twelve different tonalities available, one for each of the twelve chromatic pitches in any octave.*

A tonality takes its name from one of the twelve pitches. There is always one pitch which sounds very *central* to the whole feeling of the passage, around which the music seems to gravitate, and on which it wants ultimately to settle and come to rest. If we are talking about a simple tune, this is the last note, the note that winds up the tune and makes the final cadence. (That is what cadence means—coming to rest on the most satisfying, central pitch of the tune. The art of making cadences and the art of harmonizing melodies both tie in directly with the problem of establishing a clear sense of tonality.) With melodies that are not clear tunes, and with other types of music, the concept of tonality may be more subtle. But in any case, the general feeling of centrality or focus provided by tonality is an important feature of most music.

Why bring up tonality at this particular point of our discussion rather than previously, during the treatment of pitch? The reason is that our main consideration is not so much the property itself but what composers do with it. Composers learned to *change* tonality in the course of a piece, that is, to move from one tonality to another—a procedure known as <u>modulation</u>. By doing this, they saw that they could obtain a striking means of contrast. And this could be used as an important factor in producing musical form.

MODULATION

* "Duplication" at the octave does not count as a change in tonality.

For example, if a phrase of a tune is repeated in a new tonality, this will cause a different (and more arresting) kind of formal balance in the tune as a whole than if it were repeated in its original tonality. In extended pieces, lengthy sections holding to a single tonality will sound more peaceful and stable than sections featuring constant modulation. Here is another basis for contrasts that composers can capitalize on for purposes of musical form.

BAND 7

On band 7, the first two stanzas of *Blowin' in the Wind* are sung in the same tonality. Then the guitar modulates suddenly, and stanza 3 is sung in an unexpected new tonality. Dylan did not actually write the song this way; this particular performing group added the modulation. Is it an improvement, in your opinion? Whatever you may think about this, you can't fail to feel the heightened effect that stanza 3 acquires by being presented in the new tonality. This is an example of how musical form can be based on changes of tonality, or modulation.

BAND 10

Band 10 is a section from the last movement of Beethoven's Fifth (*Emperor*) Piano Concerto. There are three piano passages interspersed with orchestral ones. The piano starts up the same tune each time, but each time in a different tonality. Indeed, the ends of the piano passages—the places where long scales work their way up from the left hand to the right and then down again—seem mainly concerned with hammering home the "central" feeling that is determined by each new tonality.

Between the three piano entries, however, modulations are carried out quite suddenly by the orchestra. Beethoven emphasizes the differences in tonality among the three piano passages by changing the piano's tune in other ways, too: in dynamics and in the melodic continuation after the first two measures. Striking changes of mood result. The tune sounds crisp the first time, soft and slightly tentative the second time, warmly glowing the third time.

In musical form, we said, the organization is carried out by, among other things, repetition of themes. Beethoven, a master of musical form, here achieves a kind of "shaded" repetition primarily by means of modulation.

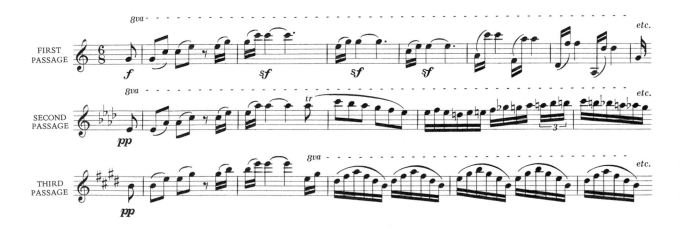

In the three piano passages, notice how the first measures in each have a similar look on the page (♪ ♫ etc.), even though they are notated at different pitch levels. Thereafter, the music is different each time.

It may be useful at this point to list the main standardized musical forms that we shall be discussing in this book, with page references:

passacaglia   page 93
fugue   page 95
ritornello form   page 100
dance form   page 118
sonata form   page 157
minuet and trio   page 173
rondo   page 175
theme and variations   page 182

People sometimes refer to symphonies, quintets, operas, oratorios, and so on as "musical forms." But this is another example of loose terminology that it is best to avoid in the interests of clarity. For all of these categories or types of music can be composed in different forms—that is, their internal order or organization can be of different kinds. We shall see that the last movement of a symphony by Haydn (No. 88) is in rondo form, whereas the last movement of a symphony by Brahms (No. 4) is in passacaglia form.

GENRE

The best term for these general categories of music is a borrowed French one, genre (zhahn'r). A genre is usually determined in part by the instrumental or vocal combination involved—a cantata is always sung, a symphony is for orchestra, a quintet is for five singers or instrumentalists. The main genres treated in this book are the following:

mass   page 64
madrigal   page 70
concerto grosso   page 100
trio sonata   page 112
suite   page 118
overture   page 127
opera   page 122
oratorio   page 122
cantata   page 132
symphony   page 171
string quartet   page 180
concerto   page 188
sonata   page 200
lied (song)   page 211
song cycle   page 212
Romantic "miniature"   page 230
étude   page 224
program symphony   page 240
symphonic poem   page 248

"Outer Form" and "Inner Form"

In most periods, artists have tended to employ certain
standardized patterns of form, what we shall call "outer
forms." These patterns have their fixed elements, but
they are always general enough to allow for many
possibilities of organization on the detailed level. Hence
the quality and feeling of works in a single outer form
can vary greatly—or to put it another way, works
adhering to a common outer form also have an
individual "inner form" of their own. Indeed, the
interplay of the two can be an important factor in the
aesthetic effect.

In literature, a familiar example of an outer form is the
sonnet, with its fourteen five-stress lines, its
standardized rhyme schemes, its tendency to pause
after eight lines and to reach a "point" or climax at
the very end. Within this framework, in their inner
form, sonnets can be as different as night and day:

Shall I compare thee to a summer's day?
Thou art more lovely and more temperate. |
Rough winds do shake the darling buds of May,
And summer's lease hath all too short a date. |
Sometime too hot the eye of heaven shines,
And often is his gold complexion dimm'd;
And every fair from fair sometime declines,
By chance, or nature's changing course, untrimm'd; |
But thy eternal summer shall not fade
Nor lose possession of that fair thou ow'st,
Nor shall Death brag thou wand'rest in his shade
When in eternal lines to time thou grow'st. |
So long as men can breathe or eyes can see,
So long lives this, and this gives life to thee.

— Shakespeare

A shilling life will give you all the facts: |
How Father beat him, | how he ran away, |
What were the struggles of his youth, | what acts
Made him the greatest figure of his day: |
Of how he fought, fished, hunted, worked all night, |
Though giddy, climbed new mountains; | named a sea: |
Some of the last researchers even write
Love made him weep his pints like you and me. |
With all his honours on, he sighed for one
Who, say astonished critics, lived at home; |
Did little jobs about the house with skill
And nothing else; | could whistle; | would sit still
Or potter round the garden; | answered some
Of his long marvelous letters but kept none.

— W. H. Auden*

It is not only the subject and the language that are so
different, it is the way the thought develops. Vertical
lines on the poems show how they divide up into
thought units. Shakespeare announces his "theme" in
the first two lines and then discusses it in beautifully
balanced two- or four-line units. In the modern sonnet
by W. H. Auden, the thought proceeds by fits and starts,
with brief, irregular units cutting across the lines.
Shakespeare moves steadily up and up to a climax in
his very elegant final line. Auden stops in the middle,
digresses, and jabs his way to a climax (or anticlimax?)
of three dull words.

These diagrams are architectural ground plans of
churches from various periods in history. Thin walls are
indicated by lines, and heavy masonry columns, etc., by
black areas. Christian churches traditionally follow the
same "outer form," in that they are built in the shape of
a cross and face in the direction of Jerusalem (east, for
us). But the ground plans show how widely the
architectural "inner forms" have ranged. One can
imagine how different these cruciform churches would
seem if one were actually in them.

* Copyright 1945 by W. H. Auden. Reprinted from *Collected Shorter Poems 1927–1957*, by W. H. Auden, by permission of Random House, Inc.

Salisbury Cathedral, 1220–1284

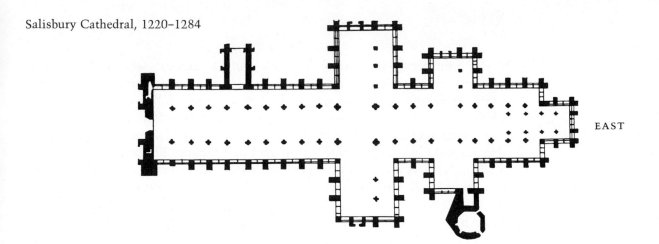

EAST

San Vitale, Ravenna, ca. 530–548

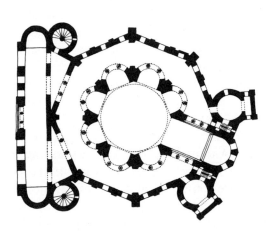

San Lorenzo, Florence, 1418–1446

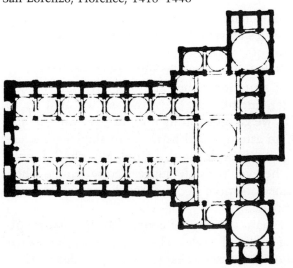

Christ Church, London, 1677

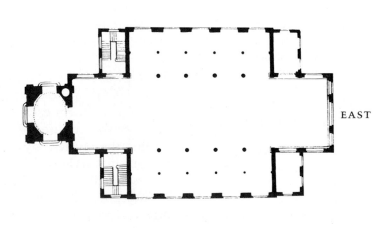

EAST

Style

Style, like form, is another of those broad, general, and rather vague words—general, but very necessary. The style of a tennis player is the particular way he or she reaches up for the serve, swings, follows through on the forehand, hits the ball deep or short, and so on. A life-style means the whole combination of things one does and doesn't do, the food one eats, the way one dresses and talks, one's habits of thought and feeling. The style of a work of art, similarly, is the combination of qualities that makes it distinctive.

In this book musical styles will be discussed in terms of the various qualities that have already been described in this chapter. One style may favor jagged rhythms, simple harmonies, tunes to the exclusion of all other types of melody, and may pay little attention to tone color. Another may exhibit a finicky preference for certain kinds of tone color. Another may concentrate on a special type of form. We shall not always be able to develop a clear, definitive list of such characteristics for each musical style, but we should at least be able to define intelligently some of the features that make styles different from one another and viable in their own terms.

It is possible to speak of the life-style of a generation as well as the life-style of a particular person. Similarly, in music a distinction can be made between the style of a historical period and the style of a particular composer. To a large extent Handel's manner of writing, for example, falls within the broader limits of his day. But there are some features that make his style unique. And perhaps this constitutes the measure of his musical genius. In forming our own tastes, we may arrive at a preference for baroque music above late romantic, and within baroque music we might prefer Handel to Bach or Vivaldi. We may also not care much for a certain style, such as modern jazz, yet still admire the individual style of a particular player or group.

In any historical period or place, the musical style must bear some relation to the life-style in general; this seems self-evident. A soul number by Stevie Wonder or Aretha Franklin summons up instantly the emerging urban black consciousness of the 1960s and 1970s. A country-music record would suggest something different, and so would a hard rock record. Indeed, is there anything that expresses today's life-styles so strongly—one might almost say, so passionately—as does popular music?

With older styles of music, although everybody recognizes in a general way that they relate to total cultural situations, the relations have rarely been demonstrated in a detailed and convincing way. Nevertheless, we shall try to suggest some of these relations as we go on to study the music of various historical periods. For each period, an attempt will be made to sketch some aspects of the culture, history, and life-style of the time. We shall briefly outline the musical style and wherever possible suggest correlations. Then the musical style will be examined in more detail through individual composers and individual pieces of music.

These individual pieces are our main concern, of course, not history or culture or any general concepts of musical style. This point may be worth stressing as we come to the end of the present chapter, a chapter designed to focus and sharpen the listening process; this book is called *Listen*, and it rests on the belief that the love of music depends first and foremost on careful listening to particular pieces. We are not primarily interested in how music can be seen to be a "good example" or "typical" of some musical style or period. But we *are* interested the other way around, in what history and style can do to illuminate music. If a glimpse into the cultural history or the life-style of a period can shed light on the musical style, fine; for certainly, understanding the musical style in general can contribute to an appreciation of individual pieces of music. It may seem paradoxical, then, but in this indirect way, history too can help us to *listen*.

Musical Notation: Scores

The music example from Beethoven's *Emperor* Concerto on page 42 provides an occasion for explaining or clarifying features of musical notation. This should enable the reader to follow the music examples and line scores included in this book. Here is the example again, with various features keyed for discussion purposes:

Some features have already been covered:

1. the relative length of notes — ♩. ; ♩ ; ♪ and ♫ ; ♪ and ♫
2. signs for sharps (♯), flats (♭), and naturals (♮)
3. the tempo indication, allegro (fast)
4. the clef, which calibrates the pitches in respect to the lines and spaces on the staff. The treble clef (𝄞) indicates that the second line up on the staff is set at G above middle C. All the other lines and spaces work in relation to this.
5. the meter indication (*time signature*); 𝄶 sets up a compound meter (page 9), with six beats in all (ONE two three *four* five six, ONE two three *four* five six. . .)
6. dynamic marks: *f* for loud, *pp* for very soft, *sf* for a strong accent (*sforzato:* equivalent to >).

New features in the example are the following:

7. the indication "8va —" directs the passage to be played an octave higher. Without it, the printer would have to resort to endless small lines above the staff (*ledger lines*), which are messy to read.
8. curved lines can have two meanings: (8A) Above notes of different pitch, they are *slurs,* indicating that the notes are to be played smoothly (*legato*) rather than in a crisp, detached fashion (*staccato*). (8B) Above notes of the same pitch, they are *ties,* indicating that the notes are "tied" together; the second one does not sound separately and the total length of the sound equals the combined length of the two. Ties allow for irregular note lengths which are not covered in basic rhythmic notation and allow notes to be held across the measure line.
9. the sharps and flats placed on certain lines and spaces at the beginnings of staffs are called *key signatures.* They mean that in the following music, whenever a note occurs on the line or space in question, the flat or sharp of the pitch is to be played rather than the regular, or "natural," pitch.

Thus, in measure 4 of staff 2, when Beethoven wants the pianist to play a regular D, not D♭, he has to write a natural sign (♮) before the note in order to cancel the effect of the key signature. A moment later he writes ♭ before G to obtain G♭—and then to cancel *that,* he writes ♮ for the next note.

10. "3" within a bracket (*triplet*) means that the three sixteenth notes above it are shortened so that they occupy the time normally taken by two.
11. "*tr*" for "*trill*" directs the pianist to alternate the A♭ with B♭'s, played as fast as possible. (At this tempo, he can perhaps fit in four or six notes total.)

Shown below is a *score,* the beginning of the full score of the famous "Hallelujah" chorus from Handel's *Messiah.* This score is keyed to the same numbered points listed on the opposite page. In scores, each instrument and voice that has its own independent music gets one staff (the piano or harpsichord gets two—one for each hand). Simultaneously sounding notes and measure lines are lined up vertically. A song requires only three staffs, one for the voice and two for the piano, but band and orchestra scores may have as many as forty or fifty (see page 374).

In the "Hallelujah" chorus score, notice that the voices and oboes are completely silent for the first three measures, as indicated by whole-note rests (see page 8). The trumpets and timpani (kettledrums) don't come in at all on the first page.

To follow music with a full score takes considerable experience and agility—the eye has to keep scanning up and down and across like a television camera. For the sake of simplicity, the longer music examples in this book have been reduced to "line scores," in which the main musical events are shown measure by measure on a single staff. It is not hard to follow music on two staffs, such as piano scores (page 176, etc.), or on three (pages 114 and 115).

CHAPTER 2   1500–1600   The Sixteenth Century

1500–1600   The Sixteenth Century

We take it as a matter of course that music and the other arts are available to all. Time, patience, a little money, incentive—incentive is the main thing: if we care enough, we can all come to enjoy painting, architecture, poetry, or music. But this was not always the case. Before the invention of printing in the fifteenth century, books were few and jealously guarded; access to written literature was counted a rare privilege. Architecture—exterior architecture—was always visible to those on the spot, but easel paintings were not, prior to the institution of public museums and the invention of photography in the nineteenth century. Only in our own century has a major new art form, the movies, grown up on a mass basis. In the past, the arts belonged to a small elite.

Music, too, or at least the most elaborate and highly developed music, used to be heard and cherished by only a small fraction of the population. Two major forces led to its democratization: a sociological development in the eighteenth century and a technological advance in the twentieth.

The technological advance we know very well: it is the invention of sound recording. Today millions of people of all classes who rarely attend actual musical performances hear music every day thanks to cassettes, records, and broadcasts. Popular music is geared to the tastes of this mass audience—and to the packaging and promotional routines of today's music industry.

The sociological development was the institution of concerts. Occasions on which music is presented to the general public, at a price, did not always exist; they came into being in the eighteenth century. These concerts served the rising bourgeois or commercial classes of Europe—hardly a "mass audience," but nevertheless one that was much wider than before. These people paid their money and expected a concert to be something of an occasion. They demanded (and got) music of a certain substance and dignity: symphonies, concertos, and the like, which they could think of as impressive "masterpieces."

What were music making and listening like in the days before concerts and records? We should give this at least a moment's thought before turning our attention to old music. For old music was designed by and for people whose view of music was very different from our own. If we come to it with modern expectations, this can lead to misunderstandings and disappointments.

Music in Church and Court: The Middle Ages

For us today, the paramount influence of the Christian Church on the history of Western music is not easy to conceive. For hundreds of years from the beginning of the Middle Ages, the Church was the only source of intellectual and artistic life. It remained a major force all through the Renaissance, and it was still important at the time of Bach, in the eighteenth century. The great monasteries, cathedrals, and court chapels were the main centers of music. All composers were churchmen, and all musicians got their training as church choirboys. (Exception must always be made for popular musicians, minstrels, and jongleurs who as a class already had a reputation as vagabonds. Alas, we know next to nothing about their music because the only people who wrote music down were monks and other clerics.)

From the point of view of the Church, music's role was to make the all-important church services more impressive and solemn. Musicians did for the church services what the architects of the great Gothic cathedrals did for the places of worship, and what the illuminators of manuscripts did for the books preserving Holy Writ. They produced work fully comparable in beauty, but they produced it for God, not for man — and certainly not for the great masses of men. Peasants and other ordinary people could hear local folk music, an occasional song from a vagabond minstrel, and not much else. They were denied "art music" along with the jobs, money, and leisure linked to any class other than that which they had been born into.

GREGORIAN CHANT   The earliest music of the Church was Gregorian chant.* This is melody sung in a free rhythm, without any accompaniment, as we have already seen (pages 7 and 28). Each of the various church services — and in the monasteries, monks observed at least nine every day — had numerous sections, and each section had its own Gregorian chant. In principle, too, the sections changed daily, depending on whether it was an ordinary weekday or Sunday or a special day such as Christmas or Easter. So there had to be thousands of different chants, all carefully worked out to enhance the particular service element in question. Composing this music was less a matter of free invention than of small additions and adjustment to a sacrosanct, traditional prototype. And listening to it was — not so much listening as worshipping, while allowing music to expand the devotional experience.

It is therefore not surprising that this music should strike us differently than later music. It was conceived in an entirely different sociological context. It was designed not for an audience but for the performers — the worshippers — themselves. Hearing Gregorian chant or later church music of the Middle Ages, one feels less like a "listener" in the modern sense than like a privileged eavesdropper, someone who has been allowed to attend a select occasion which is partly musical, but mainly spiritual. The experience is an intimate and tranquil one, cool and, to some listeners, especially satisfying.

---

* So called because the basic repertory was assembled and codified under Pope Gregory the Great around A.D. 600. But many of the chants had been composed much earlier, and many more were composed later and added to the strictly "Gregorian" repertory.

A momentous development in Western music came to a head around the year 1000. This was the development of polyphony, that is, two or more melodies sung simultaneously (see pages 34 and 35). As far as we can tell, polyphony did not arise simply because people liked the rich sound of two melodic lines in combination and the resulting harmony. Rather it arose as another way of enhancing the church services, this time at second remove. Polyphony was a way of enhancing the Gregorian chant, which itself enhanced the services. One monk would still sing the traditional chant as required at the proper point in the service, but now another monk would sing another, non-Gregorian melody simultaneously with it. The result was called ORGANUM organum (plural: *organa*):

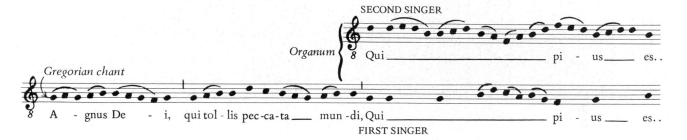

This example uses the stemless notes of Gregorian chant notation (see pages 32 and 33), without any indication of rhythm, for in the earliest organum the rhythm was free, just as in Gregorian chant itself. At a later point, definite rhythms were introduced into organum—no doubt because this made it much easier to keep the two simultaneous melodies in step. Organum flourished in the twelfth and thirteenth centuries, at the newly built Cathedral of Notre Dame in Paris. We even know the names of some composers, Masters Leonin and Perotin. Perotin astonished the musical world by writing organa for as many as four polyphonic voices.

At this period we also hear for the first time of important court music. The princely courts of Europe were another major institution, besides the Church, which fostered music. Over the long span of the Middle Ages, as the kings and barons gained political power at the expense of the Church, they also assumed leadership in artistic support. From the twelfth and thirteenth centuries, the Age of Chivalry, a large group of court songs has been preserved, TROUBADOURS the songs of the troubadours of South France, the trouvères of North France, TROUVÈRES and the Minnesingers of Germany and Austria. ("Minne" means ideal or MINNESINGERS chivalrous love.) They wrote crusaders' songs, dialogues, laments for a dead prince, and especially songs in praise of their ladies.

These pieces bear the names of knights and princes—and even some kings. Perhaps some of them wrote the words only, leaving the music to be composed by their musician-servants, the jongleurs. However, the music is simple enough so that it is not beyond a moderately musical knight: just a pleasant and not very long tune, in most cases, without any indication of accompaniment. (Though once again, perhaps the jongleurs played along with their masters, providing simple polyphony.) Some of the songs have a haunting charm that still touches us today: the "Palestine Song" by Walther von der Vogelweide, *Robin m'aime* by Adam de la Hale, and *Ja nuns hons pris* by Richard I of England, the crusader-trouvère-king known as the Lion-Hearted.

The fourteenth century has been compared by some historians to the twentieth, for it was a time of the break-up of tradition, uncertainty, corruption, and misery. A plague called the Black Death carried away an estimated twenty-five million people. The Papacy was actually thrown out of Rome and for a while two rival Popes claimed the allegiance of European Christendom. As the Papacy grew weaker the courts grew stronger, and with them, court

VITRY

music. The main composers, Philipe de Vitry (1291–1361) and Guillaume de

MACHAUT

Machaut (ca. 1300–1377) were both churchmen—Philipe ended up his life as a bishop—but they were political churchmen who served the French court.

Philipe de Vitry wrote some interesting songs in Latin commenting on

CHANSON

political events of his time, and Machaut wrote many chansons, elegant love songs in French for voice with or without instrumental lines in polyphony.

MASS

Machaut also composed one polyphonic Mass, the first famous example of a genre which later became very important (see page 57). His "Mass of Notre Dame" builds its polyphony over the traditional Gregorian chant, following (in a much more complex way) the practice of Leonin and Perotin before him.

DUFAY

The greatest composer of the mid-fifteenth century was Guillaume Dufay (ca. 1400–1474). Like Machaut, he wrote many beautiful court songs for voice and instruments, among them *Se la face est pale* and *Adieu m'amours.* But Dufay wrote much more church music, including ten Masses. Some of these, again, are based on Gregorian chants; the force of medieval tradition was still strong. But other Masses use material from court songs (such as his own *Se la face est pale*) and even popular songs (*L'homme armé*—"The Man at Arms," named after a house in Cambrai, Dufay's home in North France). Such use of worldly, nonreligious elements in sacred music would have been unthinkable in earlier times. It shows the influence of the powerful new secular movement called the Renaissance (see pages 62 and 63). Significantly, Dufay travelled to the cradle of the Renaissance, the city of Florence in North Italy, and served for several years as a singer in the Papal Chapel at Rome.

Notice that we have said nothing about purely instrumental music. From its origins in the Church, Western music inherited a basic commitment to vocal music. The function of church music was to present religious words; indeed, musical instruments were actually forbidden by the early Church on account of their association with dancing and other secular pursuits. In the later Middle Ages, both church and court music were sung with instrumental participation, but purely instrumental music was little cultivated.

If anything, the vocal orientation of music was strengthened by attitudes stemming from the Renaissance in the fifteenth and sixteenth centuries. But the Renaissance also began to provide a rationale for purely instrumental music, which took its first real strides in the sixteenth century. At the same time, vocal music reached heights that have never since been matched. Before studying the main features of sixteenth-century musical style, we should look at some of these underlying Renaissance attitudes.

The Mass

A solemn moment from the Mass, the most important of Roman Catholic services. In this daily rite, the participants reaffirm their direct connection with Christ by reenacting the Last Supper and partaking of the symbolic bread and wine (Holy Communion). Elements of this service remain in many Protestant religions.

A lengthy, intricate ceremony, invested with solemn action and visual display, the Mass contains many parts which are to be sung or chanted. For music, too, contributes powerfully to an atmosphere of solemn worship. Over many centuries, this music was Gregorian chant. But later, the Church encouraged composers to reset texts from the Mass to "contemporary" music — always on the condition that the musical style would strike the listener as decently religious. Composers have not always pleased prelates in this respect.

The favorite parts of the Mass to set to music were those that occur in every Mass rather than those that vary during the church year. Then the music could be used at any time, not only at Christmas, Lent, Easter, Ascension, or whenever the particular text was used. Five parts were settled on, which do not even follow one another in the service and whose texts differ considerably in length and religious function.

The *Kyrie* is a brief prayer near the beginning of the Mass (with words in Greek, not Latin — a relic of the very earliest days of Christianity). The *Gloria* is a long hymn to the Trinity. The *Credo* is a recitation of the Christian's long list of beliefs. A shorter hymn, the *Sanctus*, occurs at the climactic stage, when the celebrating priest raises the bread and wine for all to see (the Elevation of the Host). The *Agnus Dei* is another short prayer near the end of the Mass. We have already discussed a Gregorian Agnus Dei (page 28; band 3).

It is this group of five texts — Kyrie, Gloria, Credo, Sanctus, Agnus Dei — that has been set to music by countless composers, from Guillaume de Machaut in the fourteenth century to Igor Stravinsky in the twentieth. Mozart, Haydn, and Beethoven each wrote a number of Masses. Sixteenth-century composers wrote most of all; Palestrina went over the hundred mark.

A particularly solemn and special Mass is celebrated when someone dies. The Requiem Mass, as it is called, omits the Gloria and the Credo and adds a number of other prayers and hymns. The requiem hymn *Dies irae* ("Day of wrath") achieved the status of a veritable musical symbol of death and its terrors; its ancient Gregorian tune was worked into quite a few symphonic pieces by nineteenth-century composers (see page 245). Fine Requiem Masses were composed by Mozart, Hector Berlioz, Giuseppe Verdi, and Gabriel Fauré.

Music and the Renaissance

"The Discovery of the World and of Man" We can take our departure from this famous phrase, coined to sum up the spirit of the Renaissance (see pages 62 and 63). Man, rather than God, became the measure in the arts as well as in philosophy, science, politics, and even religion. What this meant, to put it in the most general terms, was that artists tried to make their work more directly relevant to man's needs and desires. And they began to reinterpret the world around them—the architect's world of space and stone, the painter's world of images, the musician's world of sound—in new ways to meet these new ambitions.

Music had always exhibited the power to delight man's senses and stir his feelings. These were attributes that Renaissance musicians now wanted to exploit. Turning their attention to the sensuous side of music, they began to develop purely instrumental styles: keyboard music (for organ or harpsichord) and music for groups of string or wind instruments. They began testing novel tone colors and planning carefully for them in compositions.

There was also a growing interest in harmony. Medieval music had been polyphonic in texture, a fact which does not in itself preclude harmony (indeed, as we noted on page 37, most polyphonic music creates some sort of chords, and hence harmony, as a by-product of its simultaneously sounding melodic lines). But earlier music had tended to concentrate on the "horizontal" aspects of polyphony at the expense of the "vertical." People now learned to listen for "vertical" chords and to relish them for their sensuous quality. Clearly homophonic textures also came into use in this period. It is no accident that the concept of the chord was first introduced in the sixteenth century.

Listening to this music, then, we are aware that it has a firm harmonic basis. Nonetheless, there is something strange about the *kind* of harmony involved. It is not the chords themselves so much as the way they are used, the way they follow one another. For sixteenth-century harmony lacks a clear sense of tonality, the principle of centrality around the focal point of a single note that we discussed on page 41. Chords seem to succeed one another in a relatively aimless and indefinite manner—though what may strike us at first as aimless can later seem fluid, subtle, and evocative.

MODAL HARMONY The term <u>modal</u> is used for harmony of this sort. Compared with the harmonic style of more familiar music, the modal harmony of the sixteenth century sounds unpredictable and lacking in tension. It followed carefully considered principles of its own, principles that made for a delicate, sensuous quality unlike that of any other music.

Music as an Expressive Force Renaissance composers also turned their attention to music's emotional side, its power to stir human feelings. Bringing up this subject means broaching a famous problem which has given rise to lengthy philosophical controversies (and to many lengthy student bull sessions). Everyone agrees that music has something to do with emotion;

many people are also convinced that music can be said to "express" emotion. But how does it do this? And just what are the feelings involved?

Men of the Renaissance thought they had answers to both these questions. The feelings involved are those described or implied by the words, phrases, and sentences of vocal music. And the way music "expresses" those feelings is by supporting the words, by making what the words say more vivid and convincing. It was through the interplay of music and words that the Renaissance composers sought to infuse their work with new human relevance.

Hence the continuing high prestige of vocal music in the sixteenth century. The most important composers concentrated on vocal music—mainly music for small groups of singers and for choirs. They worked constantly to refine the relationship between words and music. And in common with the architects, painters, and poets of their time, they were able to take some encouragement for their own interests from classical antiquity. Although next to no ancient Greek music survived, there were many impressive accounts of it that stressed its extraordinary ability to stir the emotions. Only music with words did this, according to the Greek writers, and the Renaissance tended to treat anything the ancient Greeks and Romans did or said as gospel.

Music and Words   Concern for the relationship between words and music took two forms. First, composers tried to make sure that the words could be understood. They employed what is called accurate <u>declamation</u>; that is, they had words sung to rhythms and melodies that approximated normal speech patterns. This may seem elementary and obvious, but listen again to the Gregorian chant on band 3: how little the early Middle Ages cared about the audibility or comprehensibility of the words! This is true also for music of the later Middle Ages. The Renaissance was the first era in which words were set to music naturally and clearly, vividly, and beautifully.

Second, composers tried to match their music to the *meaning* of the words. Passages with gloomy texts were given relatively long-drawn-out notes, a low range, and dissonant harmonies. On a more detailed level, single words such as "run" and "fly" were set to rapid notes, and phrases such as "He ascended into heaven" were set to brilliant high ones. Often one can see this on the page, even without the sound—as in this Elizabethan madrigal of 1597:

Fly,   Love, a - loft   to heav'n to seek out   for - tune...

The term <u>word painting</u> is used for this practice. Word painting could become mechanical and silly, as when in Italian music of the time the word *occhi* ("eyes") was set as two whole notes (o o). But when skillfully used, it could intensify the emotion inherent in words in a striking way, as Renaissance doctrine demanded. Developed in the sixteenth century, word painting has remained an important resource in all later music.

DECLAMATION

WORD PAINTING

The Style of Sixteenth-Century Music

Two different kinds of music were employed in vocal compositions of the sixteenth century. One kind was music of a homophonic texture—essentially a melody accompanied by chords (see page 36). In most cases these chords would be sung by other singers, either soloists or chorus members; hymn singing in parts stems directly from the Renaissance. Homophony certainly brings out the words clearly, and we have mentioned the growing interest in chords for their sensuous quality as such.

The other kind of music, imitative polyphony, was the most important texture of the time. It occupied the main energies of sixteenth-century composers, who raised it to a very high level of refinement. Imitative polyphony also reflects the ideals of simplicity, moderation, and balance which characterize the visual arts of the High Renaissance (see pages 68 and 69). For by its very nature, imitative texture depends on a perfect balance among multiple voice parts. First one voice begins with a musical theme designed for the words in question; soon another enters singing the same theme at a higher or lower pitch level, then a third, then a fourth, and so on, while the earlier voices continue with new melodies artfully contrived to fit in with the newcomers without swamping them. Before the section ends, perhaps each voice will sing the main theme again. Each voice has its own shapely melody drawn from a single source. None is a mere accompaniment or "filler," and none stands out for long over any of the others. The whole texture is alive and even, a web of similar melodies all beautifully coordinated.

The ideal of calm and balance permeates the sixteenth-century musical style in other ways. Tempo and dynamics are constant factors, or at least, the composers rarely gave any specifications for them; we must assume that in most cases a "golden mean" was invoked. Such basic musical elements as rhythm and melody are very restrained in character. The rhythm is fluid, devoid of sharp accents, and quietly shifting all the time—so much so that the meter is often obscured. It is a significant fact that sixteenth-century music was still, like Gregorian chant, written without measure lines (or bar lines). For measure lines mark the meter. This music had a definite meter—unlike Gregorian chant—but composers did not think of stressing it.

The melody is fluid, too; it never goes very high or very low, and the ups and downs are carefully balanced. It often reminds us of the smooth, oscillating flow of Gregorian chant. Calm, controlled, considerate of their fellows, shunning all obvious gestures: these rhythms and melodies almost recall the Renaissance ideal of good breeding. Rarely does the music of the sixteenth century settle into the easy swing of a dance rhythm, or into the clear patterns of an actual tune.

As a matter of fact, detailed analysis reveals that these rhythms were put together from a surprisingly limited stock of different note values, and the melodies from an equally limited stock of intervals. The real point, however, lies not in the analytical data but in the special feeling that such limitation creates. This music can sometimes strike us as vague, but as we listen more closely—and always listen to the words as well as the music—we may catch something of its flexibility, sensitivity, and quiet expressive force. Does it perhaps remind us of a wonderfully musical and subtle speaking voice? The sixteenth century would have been pleased to think so.

The last few paragraphs have brought out some of the characteristics of the central style of the sixteenth century. Here is a brief summary of these characteristics, following the order of the terms as taken up in the opening chapter, "A Vocabulary for Music."

In *rhythm*, sixteenth-century music is fluid and dignified, with few surprises. The *meter* is not emphasized strongly at all, but though it is often obscured, a duple pattern usually prevails. The *tempo* is, or should be, moderate (beware of performances and recordings in which the tempo is deathly slow). *Tone color* was not an artistic resource that was much exploited at the time. In any piece, it remained basically the same: a group of solo singers or a choir, perhaps with some instruments doubling the choral parts. The ideal of calm moderation extends also to the *dynamics*.

The *melody* moves in a calm and elusive way. Sixteenth-century composers knew tunes perfectly well, in folk music and dance music, but they did not often employ them in their most elaborate music (any more than twentieth-century composers do). Two kinds of *texture* existed side by side: homophony and especially imitative polyphony, which strikes as pure a balance as possible among the various voices of the choir. The *harmony* that we hear in both of these textures seems clear enough chord by chord, but the chords do not follow one another in such a way as to give a clear sense of central *tonality*. Hence the floating, indecisive quality of sixteenth-century harmony, the quality of "modal" harmony.

As for the *form*, this simply follows the words. The composer took the text he was setting, divided it into small verbal segments, and set each one with new imitative or homophonic music. The words also provide the key to the expressive range of sixteenth-century music. Careful declamation and word painting, the Renaissance musician believed, tied his music to the words and thus allowed the words to make their emotional effect more vividly.

These style characteristics appear most consistently in the Roman Catholic church music of the time. Despite the strong secular stirrings of the Renaissance, sacred music was still very important, and it is with church music that we associate the most famous composers of sixteenth-century Europe: from the Netherlander Josquin Desprez at the turn of the century to later figures such as the Englishman William Byrd, the Spaniard Tomas Luis da Victoria, the Netherlander Orlande de Lassus (or Orlando di Lasso), and the Italian Giovanni Pierluigi da Palestrina. Working in Rome, for some years at the Papel Chapel, Palestrina refined the Renaissance church style to an unparalleled degree, so much that it is sometimes called "the Palestrina style."

In the secular and the instrumental compositions of the time, a number of style characteristics are handled somewhat differently. Indeed, they are handled in a way that begins to forecast the music of later centuries, as we shall see.

The Renaissance

Renaissance is the name given to a complex historical movement that worked deep changes in Europe during the fifteenth and sixteenth centuries. In the words of the historian Jules Michelet, the Renaissance involved "the discovery of the world and of man." Medieval society was stable, conservative, authoritarian, oriented toward God. The Renaissance laid the groundwork for the world we know today, a dynamic society oriented toward man.

Only when the habit of accepting authority was weakened could "the discovery of the world" proceed very far. Columbus and Copernicus questioned for themselves; they did not accept ancient doctrine handed down by philosophers convinced that the world was stable and man's knowledge of it fixed once and for all by God. Pythagoras and his authoritative experiments on sound were mentioned on page 38. In the sixteenth century people finally began to examine these experiments critically, revise them, and supplement them. The discovery of vibrations as the source of sound was made by the Venetian mathematician G. B. Benedetti around 1560.

The painting, sculpture, and architecture of the Renaissance have probably been more admired than those of any other period. This is the age of Donatello, Botticelli, Leonardo da Vinci, Raphael, Michelangelo, Titian, and many other famous artists. A strong interest in perspective showed the painters' concern for the world around them (even if they still often painted the afterworld, too). Artists developed new and more sensuous techniques, such as oil painting on canvas, and revived forgotten ones, such as sculpture in bronze. Sensuous subjects reappeared for the first time in centuries. Renaissance sculptors and painters unhesitatingly depicted nudes—seldom seen in the Middle Ages except in a moralistic context, such as that of Adam and Eve expelled in shame from Eden.

Here the Renaissance followed a new authority: not the Church, but classical antiquity. The ancient Greeks and Romans provided a powerful stimulus through their humanistic philosophy and political structures, their wonderfully rich languages and literatures, their sculpture, coins, murals, and architecture. Art and artifacts were dug up and studied with great industry by scholars of the time. But not only this: strenuous efforts were made to imitate classical styles, to bring them into contemporary life. People even scrutinized Greek writing about music theory to see what inspiration it might provide for sixteenth-century composers.

Our illustration shows a relief sculpture of the early Renaissance by Luca della Robbia. It comes from the *cantoria*, a large marble gallery or choir loft built for the singers of Florence Cathedral. Luca decorated this with sculptured panels showing musical scenes. We may imagine these choirboys singing the imitative polyphony that was soon to become the chief musical style of the Renaissance. Full of life, self-contained and self-confident, they are taking the same sensuous pleasure in their singing that Luca evidently experienced in sculpting their handsome bodies.

Less contained are the figures on one of the other panels, who supposedly are enacting these phrases of the psalmist: "Praise Him with the timbrel and dance . . . praise Him upon the loud cymbals." But they certainly look more like ancient Romans than ancient Hebrews. Place Luca's group next to a group from a Roman marble sarcophagus, as on the facing page, and his classical inspiration is very clear.

The Sixteenth-Century Mass

Josquin Desprez (ca. 1450–1521)
"PANGE LINGUA" MASS (ca. 1510)   *Side 1*

The five sections of the Mass, as explained on page 57, have been set to music by composers from the time of Guillaume de Machaut in the late Middle Ages to our own day. Naturally, there is not much connection in musical style between a fourteenth-century Mass and a twentieth-century one—even less connection, perhaps, than exists between portraits or love poems of these particular centuries.

In the sixteenth century, the Mass was one of the two main genres of Catholic Church music (the other was the motet: see page 67). At this period the Mass was a composition for voices alone, sung by a small choir. One of two textures was employed for the successive fragments of the Mass text: imitative polyphony on the one hand, homophony on the other. Generally some of the same themes would be used in the various movements. These themes might be derived from Gregorian chant, from a motet, or from a song; less frequently, they were composed freely for the occasion.

Josquin Desprez was born and trained in a part of Europe that was famous in those days for its musicians, the Netherlands (more precisely, North France and Belgium). Guillaume Dufay came from the same province. In his early years, Josquin wrote music rather like that of Dufay, and he actually composed two Masses based on the popular song *L'homme armé* following the older master's example. But in later years, he developed the perfectly balanced High Renaissance style which has been described on the previous pages. Josquin's music was much admired during and after his lifetime, and sixteenth-century composers took his late Masses as models for their own work.

One of these late Masses, the "Pange lingua" Mass, is perhaps Josquin's greatest masterpiece. It is a four-part composition, that is, a composition for four different voice parts. (The actual voices would have sounded different in Josquin's day from the standard modern choir of soprano, alto, tenor, and bass; for one thing, the soprano and alto would have been sung by boys.) Ideally, this Mass should be sung on Corpus Christi Day, a Church feast dedicated to the true body of Christ in the Eucharist, which comes every year on the seventh Thursday after Easter. For as the name of the Mass indicates, the music takes many of its themes from the traditional Gregorian chant "Pange lingua" which is sung on this feast.

The first section of the "Pange lingua" Mass (and of every other Mass) is the Kyrie. This sets the words of a simple prayer in three subsections:

Kyrie eleison.	God have mercy.
Christe eleison.	Christ have mercy.
Kyrie eleison.	God have mercy.

A brief passage of imitative polyphony covering a small text segment and based on a single motive (or sometimes on two used simultaneously) is called a <u>point of imitation</u>. For the first Kyrie subsection, Josquin employed a point of imitation involving seven entries of this theme*:

(Can you hear all seven of them? The order of the voice entries is *tenor, bass*—wait—*soprano, alto*—wait—*bass, tenor, soprano*.) The theme seems to catch wonderfully the mood of self-abasement and reverence appropriate to prayer. Josquin did not invent the theme—it was derived from the Corpus Christi chant, as can be seen from the above example—but he gets credit for choosing it and for shaping it so beautifully, especially at the end.

The Christe subsection has two points of imitation, for the words *Christe* and *eleison* respectively; the motives of these points are rhythmically similar. The second Kyrie subsection has two short points of imitation, used one after another for the same words (*Kyrie eleison*).

In the four remaining sections of the Mass—the Gloria, Credo, Sanctus, and Agnus Dei—innumerable new points of imitation are heard, but now they are interspersed with occasional small text segments set in a homophonic style. The second half of the Gloria begins with a passage in which the contrast between polyphony and homophony is used for a fine expressive effect:

Qui tollis peccata mundi,	You who take away the sins of
MISERERE NOBIS.	the world, have mercy upon us.
Qui tollis peccata mundi,	You who take away the sins of
SUSCIPE DEPRECATIONEM NOSTRAM.	the world, relieve our transgressions.

Capital letters show where Josquin set the text in a homophonic texture, small letters where he employed imitative polyphony. The effect is as though one or two persons are timidly evoking Him who takes away the sins of the world, and then the whole congregation—or the whole of Christendom—is urgently responding with the prayer for mercy and relief. This music gives a strong, almost a dramatic sense of communal worship.

The characteristic "modal" sound of the harmony, apparent throughout, strikes us most at the conclusions of the main sections, perhaps—at the largest cadences (see page 30). Somehow this music never comes to rest. The characteristic metrical flexibility of sixteenth-century music can be illustrated by another example from the Gloria. Although the "Pange lingua"

---

* The music examples in this chapter have measures indicated by dots instead of lines (see page 9), in deference to the fact that sixteenth-century composers did not indicate measures in any way. Meter was rarely emphasized.

Mass is mainly in triple meter, here the rhythm seems to contradict this:

The imitations in the tenor and bass voices fall into a regularly repeating rhythmic pattern, a pattern of five half-note beats ($\frac{5}{2}$). Only at the end of the example, as the imitations move up into the alto and soprano voices, does the music follow triple meter ($\frac{3}{2}$). Flexibility of meter goes along with modal harmony to give this music its floating, slightly indefinite quality.

Not all of Josquin's compositions share the sober, reverential tone of the "Pange lingua" Mass. His motet setting the lament of King David on the death of his son Absalom is a more anguished work. On the other hand, the well-known motet *Ave Maria* conveys an unforgettable mood of bright, childlike innocence. Josquin also wrote polyphonic French songs, or chansons, as Dufay had done before. Some are melancholy but others are swift-moving, deft, and humorous: *Petite Camusette, Fault d'argent,* and *Basies moi.*

This expressive range, together with his technical skill and imagination, gives Josquin a preeminent place among the older composers. He is also the first composer to exhibit some distinctively modern traits. He wrote a motet on the Psalm "Remember the word to thy servant, upon which thou hast caused me to hope" as a reminder to the French king that his salary was due. There exists an interesting letter to Duke Hercules I of Ferrara, who needed to hire a musician for his court chapel, saying that Josquin was the best available, but recommending against him because he had a reputation for independence and would not necessarily produce music on order. The Duke engaged Josquin anyway; Renaissance noblemen competed with one another to maintain the most elegant musical, artistic, and literary establishments. And Josquin made sure that his employer will always be remembered by musicians (or by musicologists, in any case). He wrote a Mass based on a theme derived from the Duke's name in the following curious manner (*doh re mi* used to be sung as *ut re mi*):

H E R C U L E S	D U X	F E R R A R I E	
re ut re	*ut*	*re fa mi re*	
D C D	C	D F E D	→ D C D C D F E D

The Sixteenth-Century Motet

MOTET   The term motet can be a confusing one, for it has been used over many centuries to denote vocal compositions of many different kinds. (The word "sonata," as we shall see, presents the same problem.) In the sixteenth century, the motet was a relatively short piece in Latin for voices alone, composed to a text taken from one of the Catholic service books, the Latin Bible, or some such source. The motet differs from the Mass primarily in scope, not in style. For again the various successive text segments were set in one of two textures: imitative polyphony on the one hand, homophony on the other.

All the famous sixteenth-century composers (see page 61) wrote dozens of motets. Lassus wrote more than a thousand, which were published with some awe after his death under the title *Magnum Opus Musicum* (*A Great Work of Music*). We have already mentioned Josquin Desprez's setting of King David's lament, *Absalon, fili mi,* and his *Ave Maria.* Another beautiful Josquin motet is *Tribulatio et angustia,* a setting of a few well-chosen Psalm verses telling of the dark night of the soul. The four voices sing in imitative polyphony throughout. Word-painting is handled in a typically restrained way; the music surges up slightly but very effectively at the words *"et nomen Domini invocavi"* ("and I called on the name of the Lord") to make a climax in the last line.

Later in the sixteenth century, more homophony and more word-painting appeared in motets, as well as in Masses. Palestrina (ca. 1525–1594) begins *Tu es Petrus* with a homophonic section in the three upper voices, echoed by the three lower ones. Then the texture grows more polyphonic and at the words *"claves coelorum"* (the keys to heaven), one voice after another soars up to its highest range in imitative counterpoint. This motet was sung at Papal coronations in Rome, where Palestrina attained the informal status of "official" composer to the Catholic Church. Its text is the punning pronouncement by Jesus from which the Popes, as successors of St. Peter, derived their authority: "You are Peter [meaning *rock* in Greek] and on this rock I shall build my Church."

Perhaps the most emotional of sixteenth-century composers was Tomàs Luis da Victoria (1548–1611), a Spaniard who worked for years in Rome. His Passion motets, such as the almost entirely homophonic *O vos omnes,* seem to reflect a personal involvement with Christ's suffering such as was recommended in the *Spiritual Exercises* of St. Ignatius Loyola, founder of the Jesuit Order, a contemporary and countryman of Victoria.

Many church choirs today sing some motets by the Elizabethan composer William Byrd (1543–1623). Byrd's *Ave verum corpus* begins homophonically, with some magical chords, and ends with a touching prayer in a half-homophonic style, in which the soprano voice is answered by the three others in the choir singing as a group. *Non vos relinquam orphanos* begins with a point of imitation combining two motives, one for the opening words and the other for the word "alleluia." It ends with a new rich cascade of alleluias; such polyphonic alleluia endings were something of a specialty with this composer.

Raphael

Balance, order, moderation, dignity, and gravity were especially prized in the Renaissance. The classical ideal of the "golden mean" was held up as a model for human behavior—though it cannot be said that this ideal was always attained at the murderous courts of the Sforza, Medici, and Borgia princes. Today's (or yesterday's) ideas about etiquette go back to the Renaissance. Gentlemen were advised to do everything in moderation, to walk, dance, and ride gracefully without abrupt movements, and never to seem overeager, boastful, or aggressive. (They were also advised to play the lute—but not to give the impression of playing too well, like professionals.)

The Shakespeare sonnet on page 44 shows how Renaissance poetry achieved effects of moderation and gravity through its balanced proportions.

The same spirit infused the visual arts in what is called the High Renaissance, the great age of Leonardo da Vinci, Michelangelo, and Raphael, around the beginning of the sixteenth century. Leonardo's *Mona Lisa* and *The Last Supper* are familiar to all. The simple, weighty pose of Mona Lisa, without any other figures, objects, or even ornaments to distract attention from her, reflects the ideal of the age. So do the smooth, echoing curves of her face, breast, hands, and clothing and the timeless dignity of her mysterious look. *The Last Supper* is an almost evenly balanced picture, with its inevitable yet undramatic focus on Christ sitting quietly at dead center. Around Him all the Apostles are gesturing actively, yet the whole effect is curiously grave and beautiful.

Consider also our two *Madonna and Child* pictures by Raphael. (Raphael painted many variants of this scene, all of them great favorites.) The Virgin in the first picture looks as unruffled as Mona Lisa—her face just as symmetrical, her clothing just as sober and smooth. From her central position she seems to control the picture; since the children play on the left side, she turns slightly as though inviting us to consider the other side, too. Her extended bare foot seems to serve as a horizontal counterpoise to the boys' bare flesh. For vertical balance, the landscape rises, high and rather dense, on the boys' side.

The second picture is even more impressive in terms of balance. Raphael has contrived to bring two more figures into a design he had developed for only three.

The same equilateral triangle enclosing the group, the same central figure that turns, the same foot, the same landscape—and the same calm, dignified repose emanating from all the figures and faces, adult and infant alike.

At the risk of becoming over-fanciful, a musician might compare the first Madonna to a piece of perfectly balanced polyphony for three voices, which Raphael then rescored for five voices in the second Madonna. For in sixteenth-century music, too, this general ideal of balance and simple dignity came strongly to the fore.

Raphael Sanzio (1483–1520) was a younger contemporary of Josquin Desprez, whose "Pange lingua" Mass is discussed on pages 64 to 66. Both men were favorites of the famous art-loving Pope Leo V in Renaissance Rome.

Madrigal, Fa-la, and Lute Song

Thomas Morley (1557–ca. 1603)

HARD BY A CRYSTAL FOUNTAIN (1601)   *Side 1*

IT WAS A LOVER AND HIS LASS (1600)   *Side 1*

England did not feel the full impact of the Renaissance, which had evolved in Italy during the fifteenth century, until the reign of Queen Elizabeth (1558–1603). Shakespeare has given his name to this Golden Age, which also produced the scientist-philosopher Sir Francis Bacon, the architect Inigo Jones, and the "Renaissance man" Sir Philip Sidney—poet, literary arbiter, courtier, lover, and gallant soldier. Raleigh brought back tobacco from Virginia (named after the Virgin Queen), and Drake dropped anchor near San Francisco as he plundered his way around the world. Music, too, flourished more vigorously in England at this time than at any other, before or after. Among the leading composers were William Byrd and his pupil Thomas Morley, who devoted his main efforts to the English madrigal.

MADRIGAL

The madrigal, the chief secular vocal form of the late sixteenth century, resembles a motet in that it is a relatively short piece set to a relatively short text. The text, however, is not a selection of religious prose in Latin but a poem in the vernacular (the local language). Nine times out of ten it is a love poem, ranging in sentiment from heartsick to playful, from melancholy to erotic. Some Elizabethan love sonnets, by Sidney and others, appear as madrigal texts.

The musical style of the madrigal, too, basically resembles that of the motet and the Mass. Different sections in homophony or imitative polyphony come one after another, employing clear declamation and some word painting. But with a decisive change of emphasis: there is more homophony, less (and less complex) polyphony, and a great deal more word painting.

Hard by a crystal fountain is not an amorous madrigal but a patriotic one, written for a brilliant choir of six voices. Morley edited a publication called *The Triumphs of Oriana*, to which all the madrigalists of the day were invited to contribute a madrigal ending with the same refrain:

> Then sang the shepherds and nymphs of Diana:
>> "Long live Fair Oriana!"

Oriana was a mythological name for Queen Elizabeth, and the nymphs and shepherds of Diana (the goddess of chastity) were her subjects. The text of Morley's madrigal is given on page 73.

In sectionalizing this text for musical setting, Morley nearly always followed the line divisions. Capital letters show where he set the text in a homophonic style, small letters where he used polyphony. But we are bound to note that the distinction between homophony and polyphony does not always stand out sharply, especially in the more slow-moving sections, where a half-homophonic, half-polyphonic texture emerges. The polyphony is neater and simpler than in Josquin or Palestrina, and the harmonic style less modal:

In its clearer treatment of rhythm, meter, melody, and tonality, the madrigal evolved its own more modern version of the sixteenth-century style.

It also developed a more intimate relation between words and music. In Morley's madrigals, the declamation of the words brings out their ordinary speech quality in a lively, natural way. In addition, a great many of the individual words are neatly "painted" and thus pointed up: "crystal," "fountain," "sleeping," "filled," "heaven," "barren," "mountain." The dense polyphony for the last two lines—denser than anywhere else in the madrigal: see the example above—gives a vivid impression of the shepherds and nymphs trying to outdo one another in calling out their congratulations: "Long live Fair Oriana!"

Some other fine madrigals by Morley (their texts appear on page 73) are:

I go before, my darling, for two voices only. The lovers' mutual pursuit is charmingly illustrated by long contrapuntal passages.

April is in my mistress' face, for four voices. In this simple, epigrammatic madrigal, the word painting is delicate: a rich harmony and a rather sensuous rhythmic slow-down for the September in the lady's breast, followed by a severe-sounding contrapuntal motive for the "cold December" in her heart. The mood is thoughtful, even a little melancholy.

Phyllis, I fain would die now, a realistic dialogue madrigal for seven voices, divided into two choirs, one high and one low, to speak for the two lovers. At first, as he makes advances and she rejects them, the two choirs sing in alternation (the word "die" had a double meaning in Elizabethan poetry and drama). But finally the choirs come together in vigorous polyphony—an amusing representation of a lovers' tussle, punctuated by cries of "no no no no" from both "Phillis Quier" and "Amintas Quier."

FA-LA OR BALLETT

Morley also wrote the popular dance songs *Now is the month of Maying*, *Sing we and chant it,* and *My bonny lass she smileth,* which are still great favorites of choirs and madrigal groups. These pieces belong to a genre called the fa-la, after their long refrains sung to the syllables "fa la la." Though fa-la's are usually classified with madrigals, they are really dance songs: clear, simple tunes sung through several times to different poetic stanzas. An alternative name, *ballett,* shows that these tunes were also intended for dancing, like popular tunes of all ages.

LUTE SONG

However, the most tuneful pieces written by the Elizabethans were lute songs (or lute "ayres," as they called them). These are simply solo songs with a number of stanzas and an accompaniment for the lute, the guitar-like instrument which was widely popular all over Renaissance Europe. Sometimes the accompaniment also includes a bass string instrument. A delightful lute song by Morley is set to words found in Shakespeare's *As You Like It,* where it is sung by two young boys: *It was a lover and his lass.* On pages 74 and 75 this piece has been arranged for piano and also for guitar, so that today's guitarists—acoustic guitarists only, please!—can also play it. The voice line can be sung or else played on a melody instrument such as a recorder, a favorite in Renaissance times. The piece reminds us, if we needed reminding, of the steady current of popular music running below the more "artistic" and complicated music of the Renaissance and of all other periods. The earthy tone certainly contrasts with the spirituality of the Mass and the elegance of the madrigal.

Which is not to say that Morley's songs lack artifice and skill in the composition. In Chapter 1 we mentioned that any good tune displays various kinds of melodic parallelism, balance, contrast, and organization in terms of a miniature musical form. Notice how Morley has balanced all the main text lines by ending each one of them with three descending notes (and/his/lass; fields/did/pass; Lovers/love the/Spring), and how he has expanded the "ding-a-ding" refrains by the device of sequence (see page 30).

A very charming place comes in measures 24 and 25, which shift for a moment into $\frac{3}{4}$ time—an example of the rhythmic flexibility which we first observed in the "Pange lingua" Mass of Josquin Desprez. Perhaps, too, some word painting was intended by all those teeming sequences; do they not convey a sense of the gay burgeoning and blossoming of springtime? Even the most earthy of Renaissance compositions, then, could borrow some "artistic" techniques from the Mass and madrigal to considerable profit.

Texts of Madrigals by Thomas Morley

Hard by a crystal fountain
Oriana the fair lay down a-sleeping.
THE BIRDS THEY FINELY CHIRPED, THE WINDS WERE STILLED;
Sweetly with these accenting the air was filled.
THIS IS THAT FAIR, WHOSE HEAD A CROWN DESERVETH
Which heaven for her reserveth.
LEAVE, SHEPHERDS, YOUR LAMBS KEEPING
Upon the barren mountain,
AND NYMPHS ATTEND ON HER AND LEAVE YOUR BOWERS
FOR SHE THE SHEPHERDS' LIFE MAINTAINS AND YOURS.
THEN SANG THE SHEPHERDS AND NYMPHS OF DIANA:
"Long live Fair Oriana!"

I go before, my darling;
Follow thou to the bower in the close alley.
There we will together
Sweetly kiss each other
And like two wantons dally.

April is in my mistress' face
And July [*pronounced* Ju'*ly*] in her eyes hath place;
Within her bosom is September—
But in her heart a cold December.

AMINTAS:	Phyllis, I fain would die now.
PHYLLIS:	To die O what should move thee?
AMINTAS:	For that you do not love me.
PHYLLIS:	I love thee! plain to make it,
	Ask what thou wilt, and take it.
AMINTAS:	O sweet, then this I crave thee:
	Since you to love will have me,
	Give me in my tormenting
	One kiss for my contenting!
PHYLLIS:	This unawares doth daunt me;
	Else what thou wilt I grant thee.
AMINTAS:	Ah, Phyllis, well I see then
	My death will thy joy be then.
PHYLLIS:	O no, no, I request thee
	To tarry but some fitter time and leisure.
AMINTAS:	Alas, death will arrest me,
	You know, before I shall possess this treasure.
BOTH:	No, no, dear, do not languish;
	Temper this sadness,
	For time and love with gladness

Once ere long will provide for this our anguish.

Thomas Morley, *It Was a Lover and His Lass*

It was a lov-er and his lass, With a hey, with a ho, and a hey no - nie

no, and a hey_____ no - nie no - nie no, That o'er the green corn-

fields did pass in Spring - time, in Spring - time, in Spring - time, the on - ly pret - ty

ring time, When birds do sing, hey ding - a - ding - a - ding, hey ding - a - ding - a - ding, hey

1.

It was a lover and his lass,
With a hey, with a ho, and a hey nonie no,
That o'er the green cornfields did pass
In Springtime, the only pretty ring time,
When birds do sing, hey ding-a-ding-a-ding.
Sweet lovers love the Spring.

2.

Between the acres of the rye,
With a hey, with a ho, and a hey nonie no,
These pretty country fools would lie
In Springtime, the only pretty ring time,
When birds do sing, hey ding-a-ding-a-ding.
Sweet lovers love the Spring.

3.

This carol they began that hour,
With a hey, with a ho, and a hey nonie no,
How that a life was but a flower
In Springtime, the only pretty ring time,
When birds do sing, hey ding-a-ding-a-ding.
Sweet lovers love the Spring.

4.

Then pretty lovers take the time,
With a hey, with a ho, and a hey nonie no,
For love is crowned with the prime
In Springtime, the only pretty ring time,
When birds do sing, hey ding-a-ding-a-ding.
Sweet lovers love the Spring.

Venice

Venice, the island city of canals, lies on a tidal lagoon of the Adriatic Sea near the northeast corner of Italy. This location was ideal for trading with the Near East and with Northern Europe and for resisting attacks from the mainland. Wealthy, liberal, and cosmopolitan, Venice developed a more representative form of government than any of its rivals. In the sixteenth century it became a showplace, one of the most brilliant and powerful of the Italian Renaissance city-states.

The glorious topography of Venice, highlighted by the Italian sun and the blue Adriatic, seems to have enlivened the spirit of its inhabitants. They built their city in flamboyant, varied architectural styles employing building materials of many colors, collected from their trading routes. The great Venetian painters—the Bellinis, Titian, Tintoretto, Veronese—specialized in warm, rich colors. Parades and pageantry, on land and on water, were a special feature of life in the "Serene Republic." They still are today, as our picture of the Grand Canal shows.

Perhaps, then, it is more than a play on words to describe Venetian music of the sixteenth century as "colorful." In vocal music, Venetian composers added more and more voices to the polyphonic texture, reaching as many as twelve or sixteen. They divided these big choirs into two, three, or more sections singing "stereophonically." With musical forces like this, one has to have a conductor; this institution seems to have been invented by the Venetians.

Instrumental music, too, was particularly developed in sixteenth-century Venice. Giovanni Gabrieli, organist of St. Mark's Cathedral, the greatest church in Venice, was the first composer who systematically indicated exactly what instruments were to play some of his canzonas, ricercars, and sonatas. St. Mark's itself is a huge circular church with two choir lofts on opposite sides—an ideal location for multichoir music of the kind written by Gabrieli.

Instrumental Music of the Renaissance

As we observed earlier, instrumental music of the sixteenth century had a double handicap to overcome, for it had no place in the long tradition of church music or in the newly influential theories of the ancient Greek writers. Sometimes instrumentalists simply played along with the singers in vocal music, and sometimes they played vocal music by themselves. For instance, Benvenuto Cellini boasts about how beautifully he and some friends once played a motet on wind instruments for the Medici Pope Clement VII. (Cellini was a leading sculptor and goldsmith, who also left a famous racy and vainglorious autobiography.) Around 1525, when this took place, hardly any music existed that was designed first and foremost for instruments.

But as composers and their audiences grew more interested in the sensuous qualities of tone color, they felt a need for music written especially to bring out the best qualities of the particular instruments. At last they took what seems to us a very elementary step, and specified precisely what instruments were to play in their compositions. Previously they had allowed the pieces to be performed by string instruments, woodwinds, or brass at choice—a permissive attitude which can still be traced in the music of the late baroque period.

There are two broad categories of instrumental music in the Renaissance. The first consisted of dances: the slow and formal *basse dance*, the sober *pavane* in duple meter, the livelier *galliard* in triple meter, the rowdy *volta*, and numerous others. These Renaissance dances prepared the way for the better-known dance music of the baroque era which followed. The greatest composer of dances in the sixteenth century was the English motet composer William Byrd, though his music did not circulate very much outside his own country.

The other broad category of Renaissance instrumental music consisted of pieces patterned in a general way on the vocal music of the time. Chansons and motets—remember Benvenuto Cellini—were the principal models. There were many different subspecies, with different titles; we shall take up just a few.

Giovanni Gabrieli (ca. 1555–1612)

CANZONAS (1597)

SONATA PIAN' E FORTE (1597)   *Side 1*

Venice, famous for its love of brilliance in all walks of life, provided fertile soil for the development of instrumental music. The leading Venetian composer was Giovanni Gabrieli, first organist of St. Mark's Cathedral. This was a position parallel in eminence to that of Palestrina in Rome. Besides much two- and three-choir vocal music, Gabrieli wrote magnificent compositions for choirs and instruments, organ music, and pieces called *canzonas* and *ricercars* for groups of instruments alone.

Gabrieli's canzonas do not all have the instruments specified, but they sound quite exciting when played by modern brass instruments. In any of these pieces, the basic form of the Mass and the madrigal—a string of homophonic or imitative polyphonic sections—is easy to recognize. But as in the madrigal, only more so, the rhythm, meter, melody, and harmony all seem simpler and clearer than those of the more austere church style of Josquin and Palestrina. The homophonic sections sometimes sound like simple dances in triple meter. Often two groups of instruments echo one another in brilliant fashion.

Furthermore, canzonas usually include some large-scale repetitions of the musical sections, in patterns such as A A B C C, A B B C B D, and A B C D A. Composers sensed that without words to hold the listener's attention and give him some reason to follow from one section to the next, the music required some other kind of interest. The repetitions give a jog to the memory—an interesting jog, let us hope—and provide the compositions with a certain cohesiveness and order.

Like the madrigal, then, instrumental music could be said to speak the basic sixteenth-century musical language with its own modern accent. The tendency toward repetitions was a step away from the church style. A further step, a step toward the exploitation of dynamics, was taken in one of Gabrieli's best-known works, the *Sonata Pian' e Forte. Sonata* means "sounded" or "piece that is sounded" (we shall see a good deal more of this term later), and *pian' e forte* means "soft and loud."

Here is a composition with the instruments carefully specified and divided into two groups: a low group consisting of three trombones and a violin and a higher group consisting of three trombones and a *cornetto* (not a cornet, but an archaic instrument resembling a curved recorder played with a type of trumpet mouthpiece; modern performances often substitute an oboe). The two groups alternate and echo, playing now loudly, now softly, and coming together for occasional massive climaxes. With the whole texture enlivened by darting rhythms and rich harmonies, the iridescent play of instrumental tone colors makes a sumptuous effect.

The *Sonata Pian' e Forte* does not include any large-scale repetitions of sections, such as occur in the canzonas. Apparently Gabrieli judged that the novel tone colors and dynamic contrasts would be enough to maintain interest. The echo idea, it is interesting to realize, was adapted to instrumental music from vocal music, from the two-choir style used in dialogues such as Morley's *Phyllis, I fain would die now.* Gabrieli's work ushered in a long period of experimentation with various ideas—the echo idea was only one—for the style and form of purely instrumental music. These efforts led eventually to such forms and genres as the fugue and the concerto grosso of the baroque period and, ultimately, to the symphony and the sonata of later times.

Music of the sixteenth century was never intended for concerts, and therefore we can hardly be surprised (though we may be very sorry) that it plays so small a role in the concert repertory today. A work such as Josquin's "Pange lingua" Mass does not belong in a concert hall but in an ancient chapel, where it can be experienced as part of a religious ritual. Morley's madrigals should be sung with good friends around a table. Gabrieli's canzonas should be heard in St. Mark's Cathedral, echoing from choir loft to choir loft across the vast nave, or else in the famous plaza outside, with the instruments glistening in the sunlight and the brilliant sounds whipped by sea breezes off the Adriatic.

All this can put today's listeners at a disadvantage. For the institution of public concerts — one of the major determinants of modern musical life, as we have pointed out — has subtly influenced all our expectations about composing, performing, and listening to music. Paradoxically, though, there is some comfort to be had from the other major development in our musical life, sound recording. We take records so much for granted, and they play such a central role in college music courses, that a moment's consideration of their good and bad features is definitely in order.

Like other kinds of technology, recording technology has its disadvantages, and these should always be borne in mind. The perfect reproduction of a single performance on records can seem like the one right performance of the piece in question; these "frozen" interpretations tend to make people forget the fresh excitement that always attends a good live performance. Furthermore, records are great levelers, making their own identical milieu for music of diverse kinds. Television gives us golf matches, movies, interviews, and news shots of plane crashes and famines, but there is no denying that the individuality and full savor of actual events are dulled by the inevitable 24-inch frame. Something similar takes place with all the different kinds of music available on records.

But when all is said and done, records are great liberators, freeing us to hear a fantastic abundance and variety of music. Perhaps they are even on the way to freeing us from the concert mentality. We listen to what we want when we want it, with as many replayings as we wish and under conditions we choose for ourselves. Records have opened up to us the music of remote and previously enigmatic cultures — for example, the music of India — and also a far wider range of our own Western music than was ever heard in the traditional concert hall. Music of the Renaissance has been one of the main beneficiaries. Those who acquire a taste for sixteenth-century music soon come to appreciate its scope, variety, sophistication, and sensitivity. These are as impressive in the music of that era as in the music of later times.

CHAPTER 3   1700–1750   The Late Baroque Period

1700–1750   The Late Baroque Period

Music in the period from approximately 1600 to 1750 is usually referred to as "baroque," a term adopted about fifty years ago from the field of art history. More recently, some musicians and musicologists have objected to the use of this term, not without reason, as well as to the use of the terms "classical" and "romantic" for later periods. Still, nobody seems to be able to do without some kind of chronological terminology for styles, and the reasons for the objections probably do not need to disturb readers of this book. We shall use the term "baroque" simply as a general name for a musical style, and we shall speak of "baroque music" without trying to probe into the inner meaning or implications of the word itself.

In actual fact, most of the baroque music heard today dates from 1700 to 1750, a subperiod sometimes classified as the "late baroque." Bach and Handel were the greatest composers of this period, and among the very good composers were Alessandro Scarlatti and Antonio Vivaldi in Italy, François Couperin and Jean Philippe Rameau in France, Domenico Scarlatti in Spain, and Georg Philipp Telemann in Germany. The discussion of the present chapter will center on the late baroque period.

Both early and late baroque music are heard a good deal nowadays, more than at any time since the seventeenth and eighteenth centuries. The story of the revival of this music would make an interesting chapter in the history of musical taste. The composers we have just mentioned were not remembered and continuously played after their death; after around 1750 baroque music went out of fashion with a vengeance. Even the music of so great a composer as Bach went underground, as it were, surviving in copies written out by some of his students, which were passed on from one generation to the next. Bach was "rediscovered" in the nineteenth century, and most of baroque music waited until the twentieth, until after the First World War and particularly after the Second. Why this was so is not altogether easy to say. But whether we find it strange or not, many music lovers today seem to feel closer to this music, written over 250 years ago, than to some more recent styles.

Monteverdi

The late Renaissance and the early baroque periods were both dominated at the start by composers of unusual genius. Around 1500 it was Josquin Desprez, and around 1600 it was Claudio Monteverdi. Born in 1567, Monteverdi followed Gabrieli in the great musical establishment at St. Mark's Cathedral, Venice, and died there in 1643.

Monteverdi has been called "the last great madrigalist and the first great opera composer," a neat phrase that sums up his role in bridging the Renaissance and the early baroque. In his ten books of madrigals and related pieces, published between 1584 (when he was seventeen) and 1638, musicologists can trace the breakdown of the madrigal of Morley's generation (see page 70), until it was a madrigal in name only. Both in technique and in feeling, it has been transformed into a truly baroque genre. And the first masterpiece of opera was Monteverdi's *Orpheus*, written in 1607, only a few years after opera was invented.

Perhaps the most essential baroque feature about Monteverdi's later music is its intense, even exaggerated emotionality. This almost startles audiences of today at occasional performances of his operas *Orpheus* and *The Coronation of Poppaea* (Poppaea was the ambitious, scheming mistress of the Roman Emperor Nero). Monteverdi also pioneered many techniques used by the late baroque composers, such as trio texture (page 112), arias (page 125), and recitative (page 123). His recitative style is more moving than that of any other baroque composer, with the possible exception of Bach.

Monteverdi was especially fond of the ground bass form, similar to the passacaglia form used by Bach (page 93). Some well-known Monteverdi pieces employing ground basses are the extraordinarily emotional *Lament of the Nymph* and the lyrical *Zefiro torna* ("Spring breezes return": a so-called "madrigal" for two tenors and instrumental bass—an example of vocal trio texture).

Not many portraits of the early composers have survived, nor many of their letters (let alone autographs, that is, actual scores written in their own hands: compare page 104). For Monteverdi, we are lucky to have three portraits and many letters, which reveal the anxieties and stresses he experienced as he wrote music that listeners often misunderstood and critics sometimes attacked. This surprisingly modern frame of mind seems to have taken its toll on the composer's appearance as he grew older, to judge from the three portraits.

The Style of Late Baroque Music

After listening to a late baroque piece carefully all the way through, we may be surprised to realize how soon all the basic material is set forth and then, after that, how regular and repetitious the music is. It seems as though the composers had set about with some enthusiasm to wring their material dry, spin it out methodically to the maximum extent, and in general exhaust its possibilities. Once these composers got hold of a musical idea, they never let go. A prime fact about baroque music is its thorough, systematic, even rigorous quality.

This does not mean that baroque music is unemotional. Quite the reverse: the same thoroughness and system applied to the expression of feeling led to new emotional intensities, as we shall see in a moment. (Would you say that rock music is unemotional because the technique of rock, too, is pretty persistent?) But before coming to the matter of expression, we should consider some technical features—rhythm, form, melody, texture, and tone color.

Rhythm is the basic element of music, and the thorough, singleminded quality of baroque music shows up most obviously in its regularity of rhythm. These rhythms are not complicated; they are designed for wear. A single rhythm or closely similar rhythms may continue to be heard throughout a whole piece or a major section of a piece. The meter nearly always stands out, emphasized by certain instruments playing in a clear decisive way (all very different from sixteenth-century music). Baroque music is brimming with energy, and the energy is channeled into a highly regular, determined sort of motion—"sewing-machine rhythm," as it has been called by none-too-friendly critics.

Careful listening may also reveal another aspect of regularity in the methodical turnover of chords: what musicians call a regular *harmonic rhythm.* That is, a baroque piece tends to change chords every beat, every measure, or at some other set interval (this must not be taken absolutely literally, but it is a fair statement of the tendency).

Dynamics Another very steady feature of baroque music is dynamics, or level of loudness. As with Renaissance music, scores rarely were marked with loud and soft indications (f and p), and once a dynamic was chosen or set, it continued at about the same level for the whole section—sometimes even for the whole composition. Or in certain kinds of music, such as the concerto grosso, with its orchestra and group of solo instruments (page 100), two different dynamic levels were set up in alternation, one after the other.

TERRACED DYNAMICS

This arrangement is often referred to as terraced dynamics. Its origin goes back to the two-choir style of the late sixteenth century, which we discussed in connection with Giovanni Gabrieli's *Sonata Pian' e Forte.*

Do not imagine that baroque music was performed at an absolutely dead level of dynamics. Instrumentalists of the time would make small changes in dynamics to bring out rhythmic accents, and singers allowed themselves to sing high notes louder than low ones. But natural variations of this kind were played down; gradual buildups from soft to loud, and the like, were not used.

Musical Form   Exhaustive, too, was the baroque concept of musical form. In some favorite musical forms of the time, a single musical idea, or theme, continues throughout the piece with scarcely a moment's letup. Two clear examples are the passacaglia and the fugue. And just as the baroque composer tended to minimize sharp contrasts in rhythm or dynamics, so also he preferred not to incorporate many sharply contrasting themes in his pieces and play them off against one another. Now, to be sure, contrast is a relative matter; all music has some contrast, or it would amount to a single unvarying note. But music of this period employs less contrast than music of later ones. In extending his music through time, singlemindedness was the baroque composer's basic attitude.

Where he did work to achieve contrast was *between* musical pieces, not *within* them. We shall observe very extreme contrasts in technique and feeling between the successive movements of the concerto grosso, for example, or between the two pieces that make up the Agnus Dei of Bach's Mass in B minor. The impression is always that of a massive confrontation and a standoff. Only later did the Viennese composers bring serious contrast into a single movement, as though to show that there are several sides to every question and that the answer has to reconcile them all. The treatment of contrast is a central aspect of the Viennese style, as will be seen in the next chapter.

Melody   In melody, baroque music tends toward complexity. Composers liked to push melodies to the very limits of ornateness and density. We may grasp and enjoy these long, intricate melodies, with a wealth of "decorations" added to the main direction of the line, but if we try to sing them, we find ourselves getting lost—they rarely fall into anything as simple as a tune. Even their appearance on the page seems to tell the story:

The sign ⌒ in the first bar directs the performer to add yet another extra detail of melodic decoration. Compare also the score written by Bach shown on page 104, and the first item on band 9 of the record.

BAND 9

Not all melodies of the time are as ornate as this, and there are some general exceptions to the rule, such as the simpler dance tunes in Handel's *Fireworks Music* (page 118). On the other hand, plenty of baroque dances, including some by Handel, are unusually intricate, so that they could scarcely have been used for actual dancing but must have been enjoyed simply as pieces of music for listening. They still are.

An easily recognized feature of baroque melodies is their frequent use of sequence (page 30). They repeatedly seem to be catching hold of a motive or some other figure and working it methodically through several pitch levels. Sequences, almost entirely absent from the central style of Renaissance church music, provided baroque music with one of its most effective means of forward movement.

Texture: The Continuo The standard texture of baroque music was polyphonic (or contrapuntal). This was also the case with music of the sixteenth century, but composers now had the means to carry the principle further. Large-scale baroque pieces spin a web of contrapuntal lines which seem to have been designed to fill every nook and cranny of musical space-time. Bassoons, bass viols, and organ pedals may play the lowest line, while the other string instruments stake out their places in the middle, with oboes and flutes above them—doubtless also overlapping—and the trumpets piercing their way up into the very highest and most brilliant reaches of the sound universe. The density achieved in this way is the more impressive because all the sounds are alive, as it were—alive because they are moving, because they are all parts of moving contrapuntal lines.

Again, some exceptions ought to be noted: homophonic orchestra ritornellos (page 100), such as occur in the concerto grosso and other forms; the massive homophony in Handel choruses; and Bach's wonderfully expressive hymn harmonizations, or *four-part chorales* ("four-part" because there are four notes in each chord and "chorale" from the German word for hymn). Yet it is no accident that these textures appear *within pieces that elsewhere feature polyphony*. The concerto ritornello alternates with the polyphonic texture of the solo-instrument passages. Handel's choruses include both homophonic and polyphonic sections. And the Bach chorales come at the end of long church cantatas, where they have the effect of calming or settling the intense, complex polyphony of all the preceding music (just as, on a smaller scale, even a strictly polyphonic piece has to settle ultimately into homophony—that is, into a single chord at the final cadence).

How does baroque polyphony differ from that of the sixteenth century, as found in such works as Josquin's "Pange lingua" Mass and the Gabrieli canzonas? The answer has much to do with the harmony underlying the counterpoint itself, and here the baroque characteristically systematized Renaissance practice. Renaissance "modal" harmony sounds strangely indecisive, as though it had come about as a result of the combination of contrapuntal lines, half accidentally. But baroque composers conceived a harmonic scaffold first, then fitted the contrapuntal lines into it. The point is that they had evolved the important concept of tonality (page 41), whereby every chord has its place in relation to the others in creating the feeling of order and centrality. Consequently, a clear harmonic framework of a tonal nature had to come as the starting point. It is this clear harmonic framework that we hear, essentially, as the feature that distinguishes between baroque and sixteenth-century polyphony.

The central importance of harmony appears in the universal practice of CONTINUO *figured bass*, or *basso continuo* (usually abbreviated to just continuo). The great majority of baroque compositions include a part for a chord instrument — organ, harpsichord, even guitar — which plays simple chords while the other instruments are playing melodies. The *general* form of the chords is indicated by a numerical shorthand below the bass notes, but the *specific* form is left to the player, who has to engage in a certain amount of improvisation in order to "realize" the continuo. The term "figured bass" stems from this numerical shorthand, which can be seen on the score on pages 114 and 115; the term "continuo" indicates that the chords run continuously throughout the piece. These continuo chords are the solid framework against which the contrapuntal lines of baroque music trace their intricate, airy patterns.

Why didn't the composers tear down the scaffold once it had served its purpose and leave the music entirely to the contrapuntal lines? First, because of their passion to fill up musical space. The continuo instrument could cover every note in every chord over several octaves, even if the contrapuntal lines occasionally missed one. Second, because the continuo instrument provided a welcome reinforcement of the regular metrical pattern. The lively, brittle tone of the harpsichord continuo punctuating almost evey beat is a hallmark of baroque music. We have heard the quieter sound of an organ continuo on band 8.

BAND 8

Tone Color Yet tone color in itself is no more a central feature of this style than it is of Renaissance style. True, there are characteristic "baroque sounds," which may delight us and which we do not meet elsewhere: the recorder, the bright baroque organ, the ever-present harpsichord, and the "festive" orchestra featuring high trumpets and drums. Nevertheless, a significantly large amount of music was written in such a way that it could be shifted from one instrumental or vocal group to another. Handel arranged parts of his oratorio *Messiah* as a concerto grosso; Bach arranged some of his Brandenburg Concertos as church cantatas. Apparently the original tone color as such was not critical. If it had been, the composers would not have sanctioned changing it, let alone taken the first steps themselves.

For this reason, baroque music has proved to be highly flexible, adapting to various kinds of arrangements in later years. In the 1930s, Bach was arranged for the large modern symphony orchestra by the American conductor Leopold Stokowski and for jazz band by more than one enterprising arranger. In the 1960s, Bach moved over to the Swingle Singers and the Moog Electronic Synthesizer.

Purists among baroque-music fans complain that these arrangements trick up the music in tone colors the composers never dreamed of and would probably despise if they had. We can go along to the extent of agreeing that the arrangements certainly do not constitute any improvement. Yet the fact that they are possible at all, without killing the music entirely, shows that tone color was secondary in the baroque composer's scheme of things.

The Emotional World of the Baroque Composers at the time were much concerned with music's expressive powers. They had no doubt that music could mirror a wide range of human feelings, and they attacked the problem of bringing this about with their usual relentless drive. The result can be very powerful and yet in a curious way also impersonal. For it is hard to feel that these men were trying to mirror their own emotions in music; rather, they seem to have tried to isolate emotions in the abstract and then depict them as singlemindedly as possible. The exhaustiveness of their musical technique made for a similar exhaustiveness of emotional effect. As the rhythms and themes are repeated over and over again, the music hammers away at a single feeling, intensifying it and magnifying it to a remarkable extent. Sadness in baroque music is presented as the deepest gloom, gentleness as sentimentality, cheerfulness as pomp and splendor, joy as wild jubilation.

These are exaggerated sentiments; the people who experience them would seem to be larger than life. This may prove puzzling until we understand an important fact about the baroque age: its fascination with the theater. Both the spoken theater and the opera took great strides in the seventeenth century, and their impact on people's minds can be compared to that of the movies and television in the twentieth. The baroque theater concentrated on grandiose gesture and high passion, on ideal emotions expressed by ideal human beings. Kings and queens were shown performing noble actions or vile, experiencing intense feelings, reciting thunderous tirades, and taking part in lavish stage displays. How these personages looked and acted can be seen in the picture on page 121, which also finds them in a typically extravagant setting.

Theatricality is a key to the emotional world of baroque art, whether in music, the visual arts, or poetry. In baroque paintings people tend to be posed in stagelike attitudes. Architectural interiors, and even the formal gardens of the time, look like stage sets. Or take a characteristically high-pitched passage from a poem of 1717 by Alexander Pope, in which Heloise is dreaming of her lover Abelard:

> Oh curst, dear horrors of all-conscious night!
> How glowing guilt exalts the keen delight!
> Provoking demons all restraints remove,
> And stir within me every source of love!
> I hear thee, view thee, gaze o'er all thy charms,
> And round thy phantom glue my clasping arms . . .
> I shriek, start up, the same sad prospect find,
> And wake to all the griefs I left behind.

The exaggerated words for the intense emotions, the grandiloquent phrases, and even the gestures that are suggested—clasping, gazing, starting up—all seem to have come straight from the theater.

There is nothing "false" about theatrical emotion, as we know from the strong effect it has on us in the theater or at the movies. It has the virtues of great intensity, clarity, and focus; it has to, or it would not reach its audience. The actor analyzes the emotion he is required to depict, shapes it and probably exaggerates it, and then methodically projects it by means of his acting technique and craft. It is not his personal emotion, though for the moment he makes it his own. We may come to feel that baroque composers proceeded in much the same manner, not only when they composed operas—actual stage works set to music—but also oratorios, church cantatas, and even instrumental music.

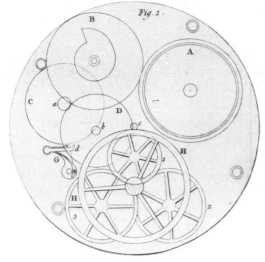

Fig. 1.

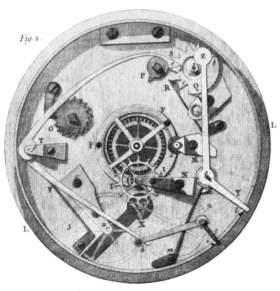

Fig. 2.

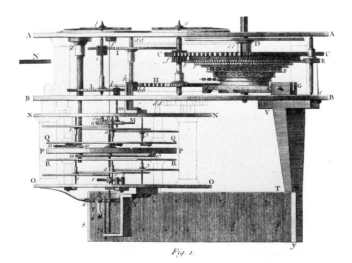

Fig. 1.

The Scientific Temper

That man's reason, coupled with accurate observation, could gain control over natural phenomena was an exciting idea that became more and more pervasive during the baroque period. Emerging from the spirit of inquiry that had developed in the sixteenth century, the idea took support from a veritable flood of scientific discoveries in the seventeenth. Galileo, Kepler, and Newton laid the foundations of modern astronomy, mechanics, and physics. Harvey discovered the circulation of the blood, Boyle produced a vacuum, Leeuwenhoek observed protozoans. And Newton and Leibniz, in independently inventing calculus, found the mathematical tool to make sense out of all this new observation and discovery.

One symptom of the new confidence in human knowledge was the undertaking of great comprehensive encyclopedias—the famous one prepared by the French Encyclopedists and the more modest *Encyclopaedia Britannica*. The first true dictionary of music dates from this period, too. Another symptom was the extensive development of scientific instruments of all kinds. Since music is the art of sounds in time, perhaps the best symbols for baroque music are time-measuring instruments: clocks, watches, and chronometers, which baroque craftsmen brought to a fantastic level of accuracy.

Among the philosophers, Locke and Hume transferred the habit of scientific observation into a cold, hard look at man's nature and thought processes. Others, such as Leibniz, actually tried to investigate God by the quasi-mathematical methods that had worked so well in other areas. They came up with the notion of God as the "Great Watchmaker," a sort of supertechnocrat regulating man and the world by the application of scientific laws.

Musicians, too, responded to the new intellectual climate, though less directly and no doubt less consciously. Late baroque composers favored intricate melodies, dense polyphonic textures, regular, methodical rhythms, and formal plans which allowed them to pursue a single musical idea rigorously in repetitions of all kinds (see pages 85 to 86). We can detect in all this an ambition to stake out the field of music, as it were, and fill it in systematically—an ambition based on the conviction that all the elements of music could be investigated, encompassed, and controlled at man's will. A similar conviction underlay the bold efforts of scientists, philosophers, technicians, and craftsmen of the time.

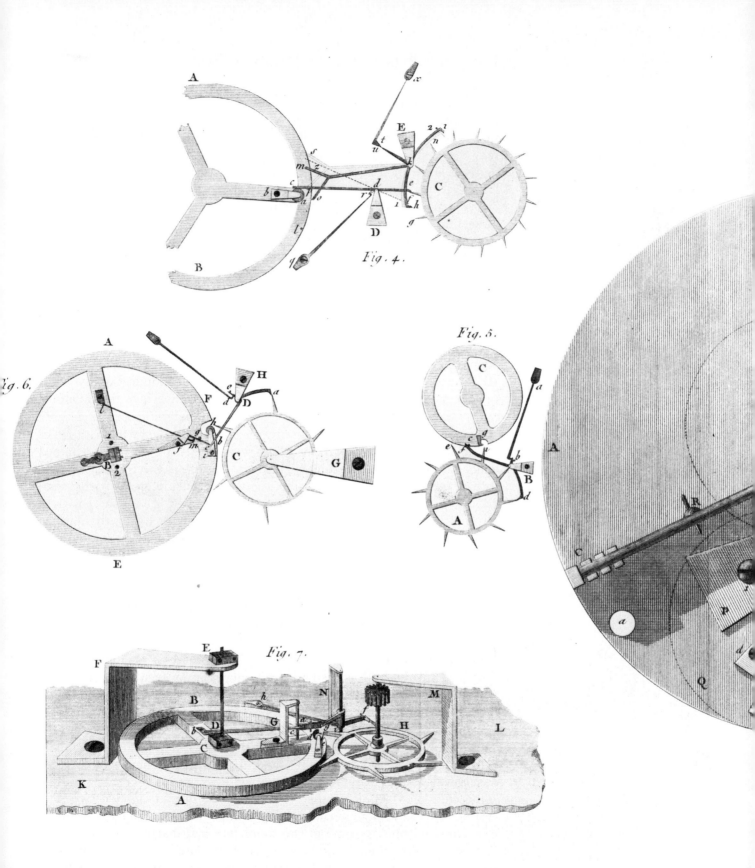

Fig. 4.

Fig. 5.

Fig. 6.

Fig. 7.

Johann Sebastian Bach (1685–1750)

The baroque period was a great age for the theater; it was also a great age for the crafts. Furniture making, metalworking, wood carving, and musical-instrument making were all highly developed (page 98). Composing music was regarded as another such craft. It may be hard for us to grasp this, perhaps, since the romantic idea of the composer is so firmly ingrained: the lonely genius working over each masterpiece as a long labor of love expressing his own individual personality. But the baroque composer thought of himself as a servant with a master to satisfy, a craftsman with a job, turning out music on demand (and on schedule) to fill a particular requirement. This is why many pieces of baroque music seem relatively anonymous, as it were. They strike us less as unique masterpieces than as excellent examples of their type — their style — of which there are many other equally excellent examples.

Crafts are the products of long family traditions, and the Bachs were the most famous, and the largest, of musical families. Over the generations they supplied a relatively small area of central Germany with dozens of musicians; all the surviving male members of Johann Sebastian's huge family became musicians, too, some of them major composers in their own right. One feels that from the start Bach was conditioned (if not always happy) to accept his "place." He served first as church organist in several sleepy towns, then as a musician at the petty courts of Weimar and Cöthen. He never attained a major court position, settling instead as cantor of the Thomasschule at Leipzig, which was a large and important town but no great artistic center.

Outside of Leipzig, Bach's music was little known. As for the position of cantor, that was the highest one within the hierarchy of the Lutheran Church, but it was hedged in by bureaucratic restrictions which would have exasperated even a less independent spirit than Bach's. He had to compose music and manage the choirs for the big churches in town, every Sunday of the year as well as Christmas, Easter, Ascension, and so on; he was supposed to teach music and Latin in the choir school (the Thomasschule); and he was forbidden to play the organ in the church services, since that was the prerogative of other officials.

Bach gained an awesome control over all the craft aspects of music. He also exhibited an unusually systematic and encyclopedic turn of mind. It is not that he had studied the scientific discoveries which so interested his time (page 90), but he seems to have absorbed the scientist's confidence in reason and calculation as guides for all man's activities, including music. Thus, within many of his compositions, there is a decided element of calculation in the layout of the musical form, as we shall see. Bach also developed a mania for collecting his music together in orderly sets following some clear plan. Among these are *The Well-tempered Clavier*, two sets of twenty-four preludes and fugues in all possible tonalities. This was almost the first effort to employ some of the more rare and distant tonalities; it was Bach's way of proving that this could be done. The last thing he wrote, *The Art of Fugue*, is another "demonstration" work, containing seventeen different canons and fugues composed from the same brief theme.

Saying all this about Bach could give rise to the idea that his music must be remote, intellectual, and unemotional. This is far from the case. One or two pieces in *The Art of Fugue* may be on the dull side, but the others are profound, brilliant, powerful, highly expressive. They are among the most miraculous pieces written in the whole baroque period. Bach's unmatched control over musical materials and processes—his unmatched sense of craft—allowed him to probe deeper into emotional states than any of his contemporaries. Whether in bold jubilation or in quiet meditation, he constantly amazes us by the variety of feeling he is able to convey in music.

BACH   PASSACAGLIA AND FUGUE FOR ORGAN (c. 1715)   *Side 1*

In the Passacaglia and Fugue for Organ, Bach built a very interesting large-scale piece of music from a single short theme. It is hard to think of many more rigorous, singleminded pieces in the whole musical repertory. Yet there is nothing dull about it; this brilliant essay in organ virtuosity is a tribute to the high level of organ technology, organ playing, and composition for the instrument in eighteenth-century Germany (see page 98). And what is especially clear in this piece is the way in which musical form contributes to a musical effect—in this case, an effect of massive, exhaustive cumulation.

PASSACAGLIA   A passacaglia is a special type of theme and variations (page 182) employing a short theme in the bass register. First, the theme is heard quietly, without accompaniment. It is played on the organ pedals:

There follow no fewer than twenty variations, in which this short theme appears in different guises or with different accompaniments above it. Often it appears exactly as shown in the example, the variations consisting simply of fresh contrapuntal lines above or below it. At other times the theme is somewhat obscured, though never so far that the listener loses it entirely. Through it all, Bach pours forth an inexhaustible supply of fascinating musical ideas, which seem to spring up under the organist's fingers in the spirit of an inspired improvisation.

We develop a sort of "double listening" for a piece like this, listening at one and the same time to the theme (which hardly ever changes) and to the material presented with it (which changes constantly, variation by variation). This is not hard to do, no harder than it is to take in a distant view while also admiring someone in the foreground. Our interest and pleasure in the piece depend on our double awareness of the fixed element—the regular, stately recurrence of the eight-measure theme—and the ever-new additions to it.

Bach has imposed a master plan upon the twenty variations. At first the variations hold to the original form of the theme, by and large, while building up methodically from the quiet beginning to a level of considerable vigor. Then suddenly changing this procedure, Bach starts to manipulate the theme in miscellaneous freer fashions. Finally a third group of variations returns to the original form of the theme, in the organ pedals — very loud, emphatic, and triumphant in spirit. Bach plans his passacaglia in a three-part form, then, with the general pattern *buildup–digression–climactic return.* In detail, the buildup proceeds as follows:

Variations 1 and 2: Quiet, mainly homophonic

Variation 3: Contrapuntal, with flowing rhythms

Variations 4 and 5: Contrapuntal, with faster rhythms — the same in each case (♫♩♫♩♪), but variation 5 more intense

Variations 6, 7, and 8: A still faster rhythm (♪♫♩♩) and scales: first upward, then downward, and then upward and downward together, for an obvious climactic effect

At this point, Bach departs from this orderly scheme and directs his attention to alterations of one kind or another within the theme itself:

Variation 9: The "digression" begins as the upper imitative figure (marked with a bracket) infects the theme in the bass rhythmically, as it were:

Original form of the theme:

The pedals play what may be described as a decorated version of the theme.

Variation 10: Played in a detached fashion with chords, the theme in the bass sounds like mere accompaniment to the scales above it. This is a surprise in view of the contrapuntal texture of the music up to this point.

Variations 11, 12, and 13: The theme moves away from the bass and into the higher regions, with an effect of brightness and liberation.

Variations 14 and 15: The theme disappears entirely, though we sense its background presence from the pattern of harmonies associated with it. As though to emphasize his rather precarious action in dropping the theme, Bach makes these two variations the quietest since the beginning of the piece.

Then the last group of variations follows, the climactic return. With the theme back in the organ pedals, each of the new accompaniments above it seems more impressive than the last. One interesting device, used at the very end, consists of a pair of interlocking figures played repeatedly at exactly the same pitches, even though the theme, of course, is moving through different notes:

A general term for such repeated elements in music is <u>ostinato</u> (Italian for "obstinate"). Here the ostinato is actually in duple meter, although the theme continues in triple meter (the measure lines go with the theme). This superimposition of two different meters gives the climax of the passacaglia its special breathless, swirling quality.

After twenty variations, Bach has exhausted the possibilities of this way of treating his theme. But he has not exhausted the theme itself. In the second part of the Passacaglia and Fugue he treats it in a new way, as a *fugue;* this is sufficiently different from the passacaglia form, he believes, to lend fresh interest to what is by now a very old story. Let us take advantage of this clean break in the middle of the Passacaglia and Fugue for a brief discussion of fugue in general.

Fugue

<u>Fugue</u> is one of the most important musical forms perfected by the baroque, and it counts as one of the most impressive cultural products of the entire age. Bach is the recognized master of the form; his great fugue collections *The Well-tempered Clavier* and *The Art of Fugue* have already been mentioned. In his earlier years Bach featured fugues in all his more flamboyant virtuoso organ pieces, such as our Passacaglia, the Fantasy and Fugue in G minor, and the well-known Toccata and Fugue in D minor. Certainly neither he nor his audiences ever regarded fugues as dry or "intellectual."

Put simply, fugue is systematized imitative polyphony. The Renaissance invented imitative polyphony; the baroque, characteristically, systematized it. A typical Renaissance work, such as Josquin's "Pange lingua" Mass, consists of successive "points of imitation" (page 65); in each point, a small melodic figure associated with one verbal phrase of the Mass text is imitated once or twice through all the voices before the composer moves on to the next verbal phrase and its new figure.

If we can now conceive of a single point of imitation extended to last for an entire coherent piece, the result is a fugue. Or to define it another way: a fugue is a polyphonic composition for a fixed number of voices or instruments, built on a single theme, called the <u>fugue subject</u>, which enters systematically in all the voices.

At frequent intervals throughout a fugue, then, the subject will appear in one voice or another: at the top of the texture, at the bottom (the bass), or else tucked away in the middle surrounded by other polyphonic lines. The subject appears in different tonalities, too. Although the modulations (page 41) in a fugue are not too obvious—not as obvious as those illustrated by bands 7 and 10 of the record—without modulations a fugue would get badly bogged down.

The entries of the fugue subject are spaced off by passages called <u>episodes</u>, made up of melodic fragments, motives, sequences, sections of polyphony, etc., often derived from the subject. Episodes present nothing strikingly new; the idea is not to make any truly arresting contrast. In its attitude toward the aesthetic axiom "unity in variety," the fugue leans to the side of unity. And it is characteristically baroque in this.

Many fugues have one feature that provides some relief from this one-sided devotion to a single idea. This is the presence of a <u>countersubject</u> or countersubjects, distinctive contrapuntal lines which accompany the subject regularly. Countersubjects may be introduced for the first time either at the first statement of the fugue subject or, usually, at subsequent statements; they tend to stand out from the subject because of their particular melodic or rhythmic profiles. Episodes in fugues freely make use of material from the countersubjects as well as from the subject itself. The fugue in Bach's Passacaglia and Fugue has two countersubjects:

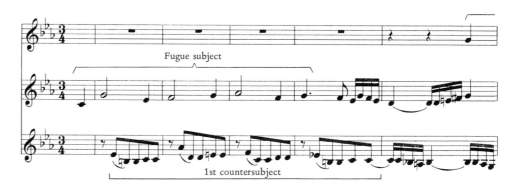

Notice how systematically the rhythms are arranged—the subject moving in half and quarter notes, countersubject 1 in eighths, countersubject 2 in continuous sixteenths.*

Why does Bach judge that treating his passacaglia theme as a fugue will give it renewed life, after he has already wrung it dry through the twenty variations? First, the theme is reduced from eight measures to four, which makes things sound brisker and more urgent; furthermore, the episodes are all of different lengths, so that the regular, stately eight-measure pattern is ruptured. Second, the fugue subject modulates: it modulates for the first time at its second appearance, as is indeed obligatory with fugues. After hearing the theme twenty-two times in the same tonality, to hear it somewhere else is a true breath of fresh air. Third, new interest is added by the countersubjects.

And in relation to these, Bach develops a plan that could almost be called mathematical. Three contrapuntal lines—high, middle, and low—can be changed around the octaves in six permutations:

HIGH:	subject	subject	cs 1	cs 1	cs 2	cs 2
MIDDLE:	cs 1	cs 2	subject	cs 2	subject	cs 1
LOW:	cs 2	cs 1	cs 2	subject	cs 1	subject

(where cs stands for "countersubject"). Bach uses five out of the six possibilities, so that the same three-part combination is heard in five slightly different ways. Sometimes the second countersubject rattles away in the pedals; at other times it fades into the middle of the texture. Sometimes the main subject sounds out like a tune at the top of the texture; at other times it serves as a rocklike support in the bass. In its different way, this fugue is as rigorous a musical structure as the passacaglia, and again the structure is in the service of the musical effect.

Through the repetitions of the theme in the passacaglia and the subject in the fugue, the music has built up great cumulative momentum, like some gigantic flywheel. Bach's final task is to apply the brake, which he does with the help of a particularly flamboyant stop on a very unexpected chord. Then the piece grinds to a halt with a long majestic cadence. The organist must pull out all the stops at this point. There is something highly theatrical about this conclusion, which may make us think of the sweeping gestures of the larger-than-life saints and angels on a baroque painted ceiling (page 131).

For other baroque fugues, which differ enormously from this one in emotional effect, see the discussion of Corelli's Trio Sonata in F minor, with a score (pages 114–115), the "Amen" chorus from Handel's *Messiah* (page 128), and the *"Dona nobis pacem"* of Bach's Mass in B minor (page 141). As we have already stated, fugue was one of the great art forms perfected in the baroque period. But it did not die out afterward. It was still found to be a richly expressive medium by Viennese, romantic, and early twentieth-century composers.

---

* The very sharp-eared listener may detect that the melody of countersubject 1 is actually derived from the passacaglia theme (measures 4 to 5). Countersubject 2 owes its dull melodic shape to its intended use on the organ pedals. Playing fast passages with two feet is not easy unless the notes are pretty close together.

The Organ

The baroque period witnessed the perfection of many musical instruments — the violin of Stradivarius, the harpsichord, the guitar — but none went through a more impressive development than the organ. Especially in Germany, the craft of organ building and design reached a level that has never been matched, though in recent years some builders have come a long way toward recapturing the sound of the "baroque organ." Organ technology supported whole schools of organ composing, culminating in the great fugues and chorale preludes of Johann Sebastian Bach.

The organ is one of the most venerable, as well as the most powerful, of Western instruments. The basic principle — a tuned set of pipes, fed by air from a bellows and controlled from a keyboard — goes back to the early Middle Ages. Musicians of that period soon saw the advantage of having several sets of pipes of different acoustical properties, with alternate air-feeding channels. This allowed the use of different tone colors and dynamic levels.

But early organs rarely went beyond a dozen such sets of pipes, or *stops,* as they are called. It remained for the baroque to systematize and extend this principle enormously. Important organs of Bach's time had up to eighty stops, methodically deployed to cover all pitch ranges, to include a great variety of tone colors, and to provide a wealth of possibilities for the blending of sounds.

Stops with a soft, fluty quality, nasal-sounding "reeds," and so-called "strings"; very high stops and very low ones; "solo" stops and stops designed to fill combination sounds — organs grew so complex that the pipes had to be divided into several sections. Each section, in an enclosed case of its own, could be played separately or coupled with others. Among names for these sections were the *great organ, choir, positive,* and *pedal.* The last of these, containing the lowest and some of the noisiest pipes, was of course the one played on a special bulky keyboard by the feet, the pedal board.

The subtle blending of the tone colors of the various stops was a great art among baroque organ builders. Their practical knowledge of acoustical science appears from their development of an ancient type of stop called a *mixture,* which actually gives each note *several* pipes tuned to several different partials (page 39). Played alone, mixtures sound blurred or even out of tune, but in combination they add just the topping required to give the tone color special brilliance.

It is as though the organ builders set about to cover the whole of "musical space" as they could conceive it in the mind or discern it by the ear. And they sought to dominate another kind of space — the kind they could see — by means of the physical design of their instruments. The organ of Wilhering Abbey, Austria, built in 1733, shows how organ design fitted in with baroque church architecture. If the organ pipes did not catch the light pouring in from the great recessed window, we might mistake them for just one more decorative element in this busy, exciting space. For the pipes look like serrated columns reaching up to the ceiling and holding it up, one level above the sculptured columns at the sides. The intricate wood carving of the chambers enclosing the pipes runs into the sculptured figures, which seem to be on the point of soaring across to meet their opposite numbers on the ceiling painting and the bas reliefs.

The main pipes in the photograph constitute the so-called "great organ" and the pedal; the smaller set in the middle makes up the positive. The console, where the organist sits, is hidden behind the positive.

The Concerto Grosso

The concerto grosso is the most important orchestral genre of the baroque period. Basic to this genre is confrontation between a group of soloists and the total orchestra. Indeed, the word "concerto" comes from the Latin *concertare*, which means "to strive together"—a rather vivid derivation which accurately indicates a joint contest between soloists and orchestra.

The concerto grosso involves more contrast than do most other baroque genres, then. But the contrast is still not as marked as it is in later types of music. For a distinctive fact about the concerto grosso is that several soloists play as a group. This means that individually they cannot lose themselves in brilliant virtuoso fireworks (as happens in later solo concertos); extreme contrasts between soloists and orchestra are ruled out. Furthermore, the soloists were usually not special "artists" hired at a high fee when they were on tour, but simply the best regular members of the orchestra. When the solo parts had rests in the score, these "first-desk men" (as we would call them) played right along with the orchestra parts. The whole system was not conducive to the star psychology.

In Bach's Fifth Brandenburg Concerto, as we shall learn in a moment, an interesting development takes place before our very ears. One of the solo instruments, the harpsichord, breaks free for a time and, while the other instruments watch silently, launches into a long, brilliant, almost improvisational passage of personal display. This gives us a clear glimpse into the future: the virtuoso solo concerto for a single instrument, already present in the baroque period, will become the norm (page 188).

In Bach's time, the concerto and the concerto grosso most often consisted of three movements, though the number was flexible—much more so than in later forms such as the symphony. A <u>movement</u> is a constituent member of a larger piece. Ordinarily, the boundaries of a movement are clear enough; it ends with a strong cadence and a full stop. (Yet there are exceptions: within some larger pieces, one movement runs into another after an expectant pause, a special transitional passage, or some such device.) The several movements in a single work often employ different meters and tonalities and they always employ different tempos, fast and slow. They nearly always employ different themes.

MOVEMENT

Generally, the first movement of a concerto grosso is an extroverted piece in fast tempo. The second movement is slow and quiet. The third movement is fast again—if anything, faster than the first.

RITORNELLO FORM

The first movement typically employs <u>ritornello form</u>, another favorite baroque means of musical architecture. This form depends on the alternation of two musical ideas or groups of ideas, one of which belongs to the orchestra and the other to the solo group. <u>Ritornello</u> is the name for the orchestra material, which tends to be shorter and more homophonic. *Ritorno* is the Italian word for "return"; the function of the ritornello is to come back again and again within the movement as a key element of the form.

RITORNELLO

BACH   BRANDENBURG CONCERTO NO. 5, FOR FLUTE, VIOLIN,
HARPSICHORD, AND ORCHESTRA (1721)

Bach wrote his set of six Brandenburg Concertos in 1721 for the Margrave of
Brandenburg, a minor nobleman with a paper title: Brandenburg had recently
been merged into Prussia, the fastest-rising state in Europe. Probably the
composer expected some preferment, but he received none. Let us hope that
he at least got a good fee, for these works are now regarded as the finest examples of the concerto grosso written in the late baroque period. Bach, with
his encyclopedic turn of mind, decided to write each concerto for a different
combination of instruments, some of them never used before or after. Brandenburg Concerto No. 5 employs a solo group consisting of flute, violin, and
harpsichord, with a small orchestra of string instruments plus harpsichord.

First Movement   A concerto grosso usually begins with the ritornello. The
present ritornello is loud, vigorous, straightforward in quality, and basically
homophonic in texture. (Every once in a while, though, the bass takes on an
independent melodic character and begins to sound like a real polyphonic
line.) The melody itself is agreeable and easily recognized but, like so many
baroque melodies, becomes more complicated as it proceeds:

We can probably learn to sing the first phrase, a, after a couple of tries, but
after that things get difficult. There is no clear stop between phrases b and c,
as the melody begins to wind around itself in an intricate, decorative manner.
Yet undoubtedly it is just these features that give the melody its strength and
its flair.

Once the ritornello ends, with a very solid cadence, the three solo instruments enter with rapid imitative counterpoint. They tend to dominate
the rest of the movement, introducing new themes and exchanging fragments
in all kinds of artful ways. Occasionally the orchestra breaks in again with
parts of its ritornello (phrase a, phrase b, or phrases a + b), in various different tonalities. For the rest, the orchestra sometimes plays accompaniment
to the soloists as they spin out their contrapuntal web. Gradually the harpsichord outpaces the flute and the violin, until at last it seizes the stage and
plays its lengthy virtuoso passage. (As we have already said, the virtuoso
harpsichord passage in this concerto grosso is an unusual feature.) Finally the

orchestra returns with a full-length statement of the ritornello, verbatim—the first time all of it has been heard since the piece began.

If we were to count the ritornello fragments between the full statements at the beginning and end of this long movement, we should arrive at about seven. A diagram of the movement could be prepared as follows (R stands for the whole ritornello, [R] for a fragment of it):

R *solo* [R] *solo* [R] *solo* [R] *solo* [R] *long* [R] *solo* [R] *solo* [R]   *long*   R
abc   a   b   b   b *solo* a   ab   b *harpsichord* abc
                                                             solo

However, the point is not the number of ritornello fragments or the details of the diagram but the general sense we have of the ritornello acting as a sturdy, reliable support for the rapid and sometimes fantastic flight of the solo instruments. The instruments may sometimes forget themselves, as the harpsichord in particular seems to do, but the ritornello is always there, ready to bring them back down to earth and to remind the listener of the original point of departure. This is the real feeling behind ritornello form. The ritornello may be compared to the solid metal setting for the more brilliant jewels in a crown or, better, to the piers of a bridge holding up the soaring spans. These slightly fanciful similes are correct to the extent that the ritornello, setting, and piers serve as supporters for the solo passages, jewels, and spans, which in each case occupy the centers of interest and importance.

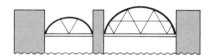

Second Movement After the forceful first movement of a concerto grosso, a movement that is relatively quiet is needed as a relief. Working in a world of terraced dynamics (page 85), the baroque composer had a very simple way of achieving this: leave half the instruments out. Thus in the Fifth Brandenburg Concerto, the slow movement employs only the three solo instruments—flute, violin, and harpsichord—plus a cello to reinforce the harpsichord left hand playing the continuo bass (page 87).

Chamber music is the general term for music to be played by small groups—in practice, groups of from two to nine musicians. Unlike orchestral music, it sounds best in a small concert hall or a large room of a house (or a baroque palace). The Brandenburg slow movement, and many another concerto grosso slow movement, would be entirely at home in a baroque chamber-music piece, such as a trio sonata (page 112). Chamber music can be more complex as well as more intimate than orchestral music, and Bach makes a rather subtle movement of considerable length out of two main motives:

These motives are also heard in inversion, meaning that all their melodic intervals are reversed; wherever the original motive goes up, the inversion goes down, and vice versa. Conceived in the abstract, inversion may seem like a merely mathematical device, but here it sounds perfectly elegant and natural:

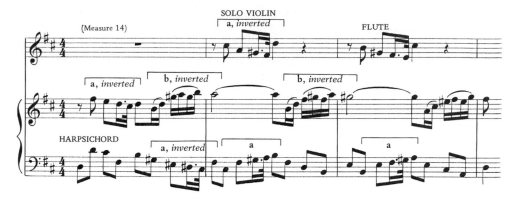

Third Movement The full orchestra returns in the last movement, which is probably the finest of the three. The fast dancing compound meter (page 9), with its triple component (ONE two three *four* five six), provides a welcome change after the duple meter of the two earlier movements.

The ways Bach finds of playing off the soloists against the orchestra are more varied and interesting in this third movement than in the first; on the other hand, the orchestra and soloists do not have contrasting material. The whole piece grows out of a single darting theme, introduced at the very beginning by the soloists:

Sometimes this seems to be treated as a fugue, but at other times it is developed more freely than the fugue form usually allows. One imaginative detail is a rather song-like melody which emerges from the theme after a time:

Tempo and meter remain the same, but the rhythm feels markedly slower, as indicated by the dotted half notes which come in every other measure. When the rhythms marked r and s were first heard within the main theme itself, they were indistinguishable from the body of that theme, but now they sound strikingly different: they seem to be no more than little decorations to the dotted half notes which are slowing down the rhythm.

The structure of this movement is as complex and ingenious as the mood is high-spirited and airy. You may notice that a large section of music—nearly eighty measures—at the beginning of the movement returns verbatim at the end, like a huge ritornello.

Bach's Musical Handwriting

A score copied by Johann Sebastian Bach. To judge from
this score, Bach would not have minded our speaking of
"winding lines" in reference to baroque melodies; his
handwriting seems unconsciously to have mirrored the
quality of his melodic style. And his impressive powers
in weaving together five different contrapuntal melodies
are mirrored by the really ingenious way in which he
manages to write them all down on two staffs. This is an
organ prelude and fugue; nowadays we make things
easier and always put organ music on three staffs, one for
each hand plus one for the pedal (see pages 95 and 96).

In decorative terms, this intricately crowded,
fluid-looking score shares some of the characteristics
of the visual art of the time. We spoke of the
baroque composers' urge to fill up "musical space." Here
we see Bach actually filling the tiny space that was left
at the end of the third line, even though this meant
breaking the measure in two—a rare occurrence in music
writing.

Antonio Vivaldi (1678–1740)

CONCERTO GROSSO IN A MINOR FOR TWO VIOLINS AND ORCHESTRA, OP. 3 NO. 8* (1715)

Side 2

The Venetian composer Antonio Vivaldi, one of the most important international musical figures of his day, is a composer who has come to the fore in the baroque-music revival of the last twenty years. He wrote quantities of church music and operas, but he was especially industrious as a composer of concertos, of which over 450 (!) are known. The Concerto Grosso in A minor for Two Violins and Orchestra appeared in 1715 as one of a group with the charming title *L'Estro Armonico* ("Harmonic Fancy").

This work shares a number of the general features that have been pointed out in Bach's Brandenburg Concerto—the emphatic orchestra ritornello in the first movement:

the busywork of the solo sections, making much use of sequences:

as well as the quiet slow movement for a reduced orchestra and the lively last movement. At the same time, we shall probably also sense that the whole piece has been conceived from a simpler point of view. The texture is thinner, and the melody is less subtle, especially in the solo passages. Technique relates to expression; Vivaldi's expressive range is relatively limited and also externalized, lacking the depths that seem to be lurking even in Bach's simpler compositions.

---

* *Opus* (abbreviated Op.) is Latin for "work." Opus numbers are assigned by composers or publishers when musical pieces are printed, as a means of distinguishing them—a pressing necessity when a composer writes as many concertos, for instance, as Vivaldi did. Twelve Vivaldi concertos were published together as Op. 3; our particular concerto was the eighth of the set.

Sometimes pieces are distinguished not by opus numbers but by numbers assigned in a musicologist's catalog of the composer's music. Most familiar are the K numbers used for Mozart's music, after the catalog by a certain Ludwig von Köchel (pages 180, 186).

First Movement   The first movement of the Vivaldi concerto appears on pages 108 and 109, in a simplified, full-length score of a type we shall call a "line score." If we follow the piece through with this score, it should help us hear the rigorous structure underlying a typical late-baroque concerto grosso movement. Follow the music line by line without stopping at the ends of lines (which have sometimes been made to come out at different lengths in order to isolate and thus distinguish the ritornellos, solos, etc.) A line score shows only the most important melodic lines in the music.

The fairly long opening ritornello actually falls into four separate subsections, here labeled "main theme," "sequence," "cadence-phrase 1," and "cadence-phrase 2." After the solo violins enter, the orchestra interrupts with one or another of these subsections or several in a row until all are well represented by the time the movement comes to a close. It is as though the composer had laid out the ritornello on a drawing board, snipped it into sections, and then methodically shifted these into place. The solo sections, too, have many similarities among them, as is indicated on the line score.

However, several of the ritornellos and solo sections do come in different tonalities, which gives the piece interest and drive. And in spite of the almost mathematical structure, there are some unpredictable elements (see the markings on the line score):

1. The new figure introduced by the solo violins at the end of solo 2, which the orchestra can hardly wait to pick up in ritornello 3 (page 108, lines 10 and 11)

2. The forceful repetition of the special new cadence at this same ritornello, a repetition in a different tonality (page 108, last line)

3. The energetic new upbeat figures that launch ritornellos 4 and 6 (page 109, lines 2 and 7)

Perhaps we especially appreciate these more spontaneous elements; perhaps we appreciate them all the more because they appear within an otherwise formal structure.

At the beginning of solo 3, a motive (page 31) derived from the opening ritornello grows more and more important. In the ritornello, it appeared directly after the main theme, in the form of a short imitative ostinato (page 95). In solo 1 it was referred to briefly and rather freely, but now it dominates the solos, developed into sequences of various kinds.

A diagram for this movement on the pattern of the one given for Bach's Brandenburg Concerto No. 5 (page 102) runs as follows:

R	*solo*	[R]	*solo*	[R]	*solo*	[R]	*solo*	[R]	*solo*	[R]	*solo*	[R]	*solo*	[R]
abcd		d		b, etc.		a		c		a		bd		d

Second Movement The second movement of the Vivaldi concerto begins with a passacaglia theme:

First presented alone by the orchestra, like a ritornello, this theme later serves to conclude the movement. Between these appearances, the solo violins weave contrapuntal lines that are gentle and wistful. Meanwhile, the orchestra plays the passacaglia theme quietly or makes new phrases out of the theme's two motives. The treatment is much freer than that of Bach's Passacaglia and Fugue for Organ.

Third Movement The last movement is a strong, brilliant piece of the same general nature as the first. The ritornello is shorter, and comes back less often than the first-movement ritornello does. Furthermore, the orchestra here is not restricted to its opening ritornello material, but introduces some definite new ideas—they are rather fantastic in quality—during the later course of the movement. And rather surprisingly, a warm, songlike solo theme appears among the customary rapid-moving figures for the two violins. This theme seems to move more slowly than the rest of the movement, and its expressive quality, too, recalls the slow movement rather than the first or third.

Was Bach also struck by this theme, and could he have had this very piece in mind when he wrote the songlike passage we discussed in the last movement of the Fifth Brandenburg Concerto (page 103)? Baroque music was often rearranged for different instruments, with a resulting change in the original tone colors, as has been pointed out before. This concerto of Vivaldi's was one of several that Bach arranged for organ or harpsichord—evidence of his admiration for Vivaldi and his interest in keeping abreast of modern developments in Italian music.

In fact, Bach's organ arrangement is just as likely to be heard nowadays as Vivaldi's original. The organist should play the orchestral passages on the pipes of the "great organ," which is the heaviest of the various sections into which organs are divided (see page 98), and play the solo passages on the "positive," a smaller and more delicate section. In this way the terraced dynamics of Vivaldi's piece will be maintained exactly, and the form will be just as clear. Neither composers nor audiences at the time would have been much bothered by the change in tone color between the two versions. Listen to them both and see if you agree.

An Early Eighteenth-Century Park

View of a baroque park. The seventeenth-century idea
that reason and calculation could control natural
phenomena shows up very clearly in the planning of
parks and gardens. In a baroque formal garden and its
surrounding park, everything was rigorously laid out
according to geometrical plans. Lawns and flowerbeds
were planted in neat shapes, and walks laid out straight
beside them. Bushes were clipped down, even carved
into shapes, and shrubs were planted at regular
distances. Waters were run into channels and fountains.
It was also very characteristic to have the whole garden
prominently furnished with classical statues, which
seem to stand guard lest the poor plants try to be bushes
and trees and flowers rather than elements in the master
plan created by man's reason.

Formal gardens were not new to the baroque period, but one new feature was the emphasis on long vistas reaching far into space, guided by long lines of shrubbery, lawn, or water. Past the lawn in our photograph, which already extends for a great distance, there is an endless straight canal bounded on either side by high trees. The baroque landscape architect shared his fascination with space with the contemporary stage designer and ceiling architect (see pages 120 and 131).

This view is of a German park, designed in 1722, at the castle of Nymphenburg near Munich. (It was the setting of a well-known movie of the 1960s, *Last Year at Marienbad.*) The park has been considerably simplified since the eighteenth century — as appears from the old print below — but the general formal layout remains the same.

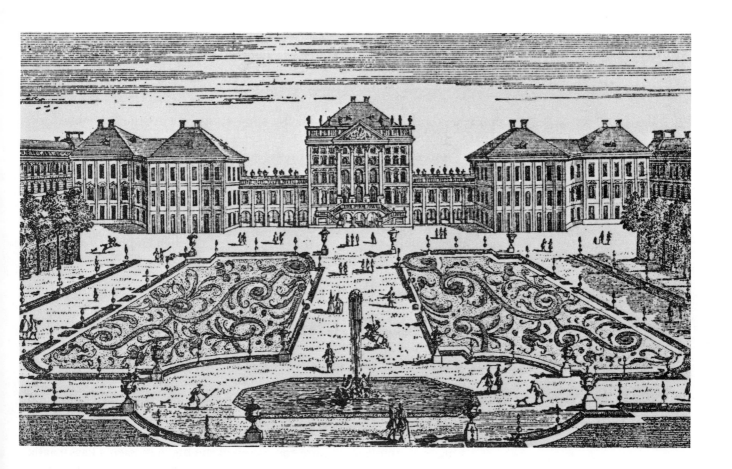

The Trio Sonata

Arcangelo Corelli (1653–1713)
TRIO SONATA IN F MINOR, OP. 3 NO. 9 (1689)

TRIO SONATA

If the main orchestral genre of the baroque was the concerto grosso, the main chamber-music genre was the trio sonata. This is not an easy term to define. Originally the word *sonata* simply meant "sounded," "something sounded," or "a piece that is sounded," as distinct from *cantata*, "a piece that is sung" (page 132). The trouble is that musicians have used these terms over many centuries for compositions of vastly different styles and forms. When Giovanni Gabrieli wrote his *Sonata Pian' e Forte*, the term was new and could cover almost anything—including the one-movement orchestra piece in echo style that we examined above, on page 79. In the baroque period, the sonata was a chamber-music piece for from one to half a dozen instruments, consisting of several short movements—the number was not fixed—in a variety of different forms. Later the term sonata was used in a more limited sense, as we shall see.

The adjective "trio" is also, alas, open to misunderstanding. *Trio* means "three"; the trio sonata is written for three *main* instruments, usually two violins and a cello (or two flutes and a cello, or two oboes and a bassoon). But in addition a continuo player (page 87) fills in harmonies at the harpsichord or organ; he performs a subsidiary, supporting role to the others. A trio sonata, then, is a baroque sonata for three main players plus a subsidiary player—four in all.

Arcangelo Corelli was the first of the great line of Italian baroque violinist-composers, a line that also included Antonio Vivaldi. Corelli lived earlier than the other composers represented in this chapter; his music influenced all of them and in many ways set the style and the standard for late baroque music.

Corelli's Trio Sonata in F minor, Op. 3 No. 9, consists of four short movements: slow, fast, slow, and fast again. (This is a common arrangement, but there is really no standard formal plan for the movements of a trio sonata or even a fixed number of them.) Corelli's second movement, a brisk fugue, appears on band 8 of our record; its score is shown on pages 114 and 115.

BAND 8

Each of the three main instruments has its own staff of music, while the continuo chord instrument (organ) reads from the same staff as the cello. With his left hand the organist plays exactly what the cello is playing, and with his right hand he fills in chords according to the numerical shorthand below the staff (figured bass: see page 87).

This fugue is simpler and more concise than the fugue in Bach's Passacaglia and Fugue for Organ (and hence easier to follow from a score). The piece begins with each of the main instruments—violin 1, violin 2, cello—playing the fugue subject in order. Then, after an episode, there are two further entries of the subject, slightly altered in rhythm: see the very beginning of line

2 in the line score. The second of these new entries, played by the first violin, follows the first entry at a shorter time interval than before, a common device in fugues, called <u>stretto</u>. Stretto automatically makes for an effect of tension and excitement.

Another episode modulates to a new key, and at its conclusion a new stretto develops in all three voices: see the beginning of line 3. (The term "voice" is always used for the polyphonic lines in a fugue, even when they are not sung but played by instruments.) The three-voice stretto represents a climax of intensity, after which the music seems spent. It soon winds down to a closing cadence in the original tonality. Notice that the countersubject in this fugue is heard only once at its full length, appearing afterwards only in fragments.

An important factor in the effect of all trio sonatas is the sense of contest between the two high instruments, that is, the two violins. Although in some passages they complement one another—in the third movement of this Corelli sonata, for example—these occasions seem to be temporary truces. Ordinarily the two violins play against one another, taking each other's measure, clashing, crossing, and vying for top position. Obviously fugue fits in very well with this sense of contest, for every time one violin plays the fugue subject, it stands out over the other—only to give up its place a moment later. Stretto simply heightens this effect, which is present in the episodes also.

To make an interesting contest, the contestants should be fairly evenly matched. In ten out of the twenty-eight measures in Corelli's fugue—ten out of the twenty-six measures during which both violins play—the second violin tops the first.

Corelli, Trio Sonata, Op. 3 No. 9: Second Movement

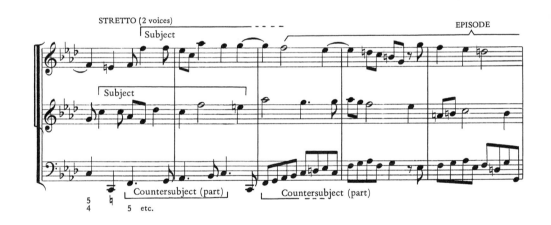

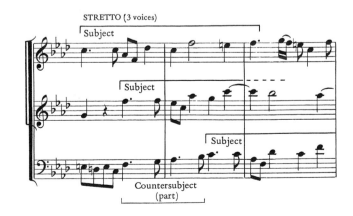

An Early Concert

A concert in London's Vauxhall Gardens, the famous "pleasure garden" of the middle and upper classes. Laid out as a formal garden, Vauxhall received its smart bandstand in 1732. Here Handel's *Fireworks Music* was rehearsed before an admiring crowd of 12,000 people. Music was a regular attraction, together with good food, pleasant walks, and blazing lights at night—all for a shilling's admission. Music was one of the pleasures that the middle class came to enjoy and was ready to support. The concert shown here actually took place later, in 1785.

On the introduction of concerts, and their impact on music making and music listening, see page 53. Indoor concert series were also established in the eighteenth century, such as the *Concert spirituel* in Paris, the *Tonkünstler Societät* concerts in Vienna, and the "Academy of Antient Music" in London. The first concert hall opened in 1748 in a University town, Oxford.

The orchestra, well furnished with Handelian "festive" trumpets, has not been depicted too gently by the painter, Thomas Rowlandson. But none of Rowlandson's subjects has been spared. In the alcove at the left, leading literary lights of the day, including Dr. Samuel Johnson and James Boswell, are seen attacking a large meal. The amorous youth at the right is the Prince of Wales, later King George IV, here shown at the start of a career which was to be marked by unusual debauchery. Indeed, what is most interesting about this picture is the leveling of royalty, nobility, middle class, and even artisans such as the musicians. "Democracy" as we think of it was still some time off, in England or elsewhere, but the rigid class boundaries of old were beginning to break down, at least in certain situations, such as that of the "pleasure garden."

George Frideric Handel (1685–1759)

Handel was a very different type of personality from Bach. He counts as an exception among composers of the time in not stemming from a family of musicians. Indeed, a little story used to be told about how he had to brave his father's displeasure and practice secretly at night by candlelight. Perhaps because he lacked musical roots, he traveled widely from his native Germany and gravitated to the glamorous and lucrative world of the theater—a world far removed in spirit from Bach's organ lofts. After apprenticeship in the opera houses of Germany and Italy, Handel came to England, where he seems to have sensed perfectly the aspirations of the rising middle class. In London, which was rapidly becoming the world capital, he made a career for himself as an opera composer, impresario, and musical entrepreneur.

His career had its ups and downs, but for a musician, Handel enjoyed quite unusual fame and fortune. At his death in 1759, an admiring nation had him buried in Westminster Abbey under a grandiose baroque monument.

Like Bach, Handel was a formidable organ virtuoso and a phenomenal worker. His famous oratorio *Messiah*, which lasts for more than two hours, is said to have been written in twenty-four days. Few musicians today would even be able to copy it out in that time. And like all composers of his day, only more so, Handel was constantly rewriting and rearranging his old music for new occasions. This is another reflection of the craft spirit in baroque music; when Handel or Bach were required to provide music for some one-time ceremony at court, they tried to rewrite it later with new words as an opera or a church cantata, which could then be performed again. They would no more put it on a shelf to gather dust than a silversmith would abandon a candelabrum that was for some reason no longer salable.

As for Handel, he also extended this economical practice to other men's music: an appreciable number of his pieces were "borrowed" from other composers, sometimes with an ingenious new addition by Handel and sometimes plain. The interesting point is that baroque musical style is so uniform that he could do this without exciting comment. We can scarcely imagine anyone getting away with this in the individualistic art world of today.

Though Handel was primarily an opera and oratorio composer, he by no means neglected the instrumental forms of his day, such as the concerto grosso. He produced a fine set of twelve for two violins and orchestra, the same solo combination as used by Vivaldi in the piece discussed above. His best-known instrumental works preserve the memory of great outdoor festivities in London. The *Water Music* was composed for an aquatic fête on the River Thames in 1717, and the *Royal Fireworks Music* was composed to celebrate the end of the War of the Austrian Succession (sometimes known as King George's War) in 1749. These works and these occasions remind us of the role Handel took for himself as musical spokesman for eighteenth-century England, expressing its satisfactions, its values, and its aspirations. The popular tone which he achieved on such occasions, and for which he had to bend his normal style only slightly, still has a very strong appeal today.

The Suite

FIREWORKS MUSIC (1749)

Outdoor music needs to be simple in form as well as popular in tone. Handel cast both the *Water Music* and the *Fireworks Music* in the form of the suite. This was a term used in the baroque period for a miscellaneous collection of dances, usually with a preliminary movement of some size to introduce them.

There were many different kinds of baroque dances. Each had some kind of distinctive rhythm and pace which made it as easy to recognize as a waltz or a polka might be today. Some of the most popular baroque dances were the following:

Allemande   a dance in a moderately slow duple meter, with much subdivision of the beats

Courante   a dance in a moderately slow triple meter, a companion to the allemande. A characteristic of the courante was that the normal triple meter ONE two three or ONE two *three* four *five* six was often re-interpreted as a compound duple meter (see page 9): ONE two three *four* five six.

Sarabande   another slow, sober dance in triple meter, with a slight accent on beat two—ONE *two* three

Gigue (*jig*)   a fast lively dance, typically in $^6_8$ meter

Minuet   a dance in solid triple meter, simpler than the others mentioned above

Baroque dances consisted of two sections roughly equal in length, each repeated, i.e., played twice in immediate succession. The dances themselves sometimes came in pairs, and when they did it was usual to play one, then the other, then the first one over again—an A B A form. Dance form will be discussed further on pages 173 and 174.

A composer with a systematic turn of mind, such as Bach, would develop a standard plan for a suite. Bach's suites for keyboard (there are six each, entitled French suites, English suites, and partitas) are all built around the same four dances: the allemande, the courante, the sarabande, and the gigue. Handel and other composers preferred to vary their choice of dances. For the *Water Music* and the *Fireworks Music*, we may as well say that Handel used the suite form as a kind of grab bag, into which he threw an informal array of lively ideas. It is not a matter of life and death to hear all the dances in order; for modern performances, conductors sometimes pick and choose among them.

The *Fireworks Music* was written for a big band: a total of sixty trumpets, French horns, oboes, bassoons, and drums. Later Handel arranged it to include string instruments; today it is usually heard in this version.

The long sectional preliminary movement defies formal classification, like much of Handel's music. In the first section, the grand pompous tone and the dotted rhythms recall the *Grave* part of the French overture (page 127), and in the second section, the alternation of "solo" sections for trumpets and horns recalls the concerto grosso. However, the main point about music of this kind is its verve and forcefulness. Few composers have been as successful at creating this effect as Handel. The rhythms in the second section keep changing (over the steady triple meter) until they reach this splendidly energetic rhythmic and melodic climax:

Following this opening number comes a series of different dances. The first is a sprightly item in duple meter, of the type called the *bourrée*. Next comes a slow-swinging *siciliana*, in compound meter ($\frac{12}{8}$), featuring the French horns; this is entitled *"La Paix,"* which is French for "Peace." (Why should a German composer working in England put a French name on a piece of music written to celebrate the end of a war against France? Probably because at this time it was a French habit to provide dances in suites with special titles of one kind or another, and the French were admired as specialists in dance music.)

The next piece is called *"La Réjouissance,"* meaning "Rejoicing"—military rather than peaceful rejoicing, to judge from the brisk martial tone. This would have made a perfect quick march for the redcoats, whose baroque military pomp fared so poorly thirty years later in the American colonies.

A majestic *minuet* in triple meter, the simplest of all the dances, concludes the suite. It alternates with another, quieter minuet, producing an A B A form; in both minuets, it is easy to hear the repetitions of the two internal sections (see page 118; the sections are all eight measures long). Outdoor band music needs plenty of repeats, and Handel left directions for repeating several movements of the *Fireworks Music* with varying instrumentations.

The rehearsal of the *Fireworks Music* at Vauxhall Gardens, the famous pleasure garden of the London middle and upper classes (see page 116), was attended with great approval by twelve thousand persons. At the celebration itself, which was led off by a hundred brass cannons, everything went wrong: the great set piece caught fire, the crowd stampeded, two spectators died, and the man in charge of the fireworks had a mad fit. Music should stay indoors.

Opera of the Baroque

We have spoken of the grand theatrical quality that characterizes much of the art of the baroque age (page 89). The theater flourished at that time, and so did opera, which had been invented around the beginning of the seventeenth century in Italy and soon spread all over Europe. Then as now, stage display was an extremely important factor in opera. Music, poetry, costume, stage architecture and painting, action, ballet — this dazzling blend of artistic elements gratified the baroque passion for comprehensiveness. Of all art forms, opera is perhaps the one which best sums up the spirit of the period.

This fascinating picture was painted to celebrate the opening of the Royal Theater in Turin, Italy, in 1740. The leading scene designer of the time, Giuseppe Galli Bibiena, produced a characteristic set (one of many for the single opera): a grandiose representation of a baroque palace interior, loaded down with elaborate ornament. Notice how extremely symmetrical and mathematical it is. Notice also the special emphasis on vast spaces, both at the back of the set and also, thanks to some ingenious illusion, at the top. The set suits to a tee the royal characters of the opera, whose larger-than-life emotions can be read clearly enough from their stage attitudes. One hand on his hip and the other extended in a grand gesture, the Prince is performing an act of impossibly noble forgiveness while the Princess, in remorse, turns and shudders in her handkerchief.

Also characteristic is the deliberate blurring of distinctions between architecture and painting and between the stage set and the theater itself. The columns, proscenium arch, painted ceiling, and painted drapery of the theater all blend together with the set — part of which is solid, while the rest is painted on backdrops. Even the boxes are pressed into decorative service, like the organ pipes in the baroque church on page 99.

Besides its accurate representation of the opera orchestra, the picture offers much else of sociological interest. The best box seats were actually over the stage, so that we could say that the audience and the actors blend together, too. But clearly many of the audience were less interested in the opera than in conversation or looking around at society. Boys are selling oranges and sherbet, and there is even what looks like a security guard.

Baroque Opera and Oratorio

HANDEL   *SAMSON*, ACT II, SCENE iv (1743)   *Side 3*

OPERA

If Handel was first and foremost an opera composer, the reason was that for an ambitious musician of his time, opera was at the center of the action. Opera—drama set to music—was the favorite genre of music lovers in the eighteenth century, fascinated as they were by things theatrical. Its influence was pervasive, so that the Bach church cantatas, to mention one significant non-operatic form, can scarcely be understood without some knowledge of opera.

Furthermore, the emotional world of the arts of the time, music as well as painting and sculpture, seems to have revolved around the stage. It was pointed out above that the grand gesture and high passion of the baroque theater encouraged composers to think of feelings in extreme, intense forms. The majestic theatricality of a baroque opera scene finds its emotional analog in concerto grosso movements, virtuoso organ pieces, and other instrumental music of the period.

ORATORIO

Handel's most famous compositions, his oratorios, are highly operatic in form and spirit. The leading expert on these pieces, Winton Dean, always refers to them as "dramatic oratorios." The dramatic oratorio is a long religious piece in English, cast in semi-dramatic form, with characters, dialogue, plot, action, and even division into separate acts—all this, even though Handel was not thinking of actual stage performances. Oratorios were intended to be performed in the concert hall, not in the theater and not in church. But their audience was the opera audience, and it is not surprising that many oratorios take very well to stage production, as experience in recent years has shown.

LIBRETTO

Typically, Handel would start from an Old Testament story. Then the rudimentary skeleton of a story line in the Bible would be fleshed out by the *librettist*, the writer of the libretto (Italian for "little book"), containing the words of the oratorio or opera. The librettist would supply subplots and even add new characters in order to make the whole thing more like a play. He would also fit in extensive passages for Handel to set as choruses.

For the chorus assumed a central role in the dramatic oratorio, modeled ultimately on the role of the chorus in classical Greek drama. While the characters act out their story, the chorus speaks for the people of Israel or else for the heathen tribes with whom the Israelites were always warring. The chorus comments on the action, shows how the fate of the individuals reflects on the fate of nations as a whole, and draws the final moral.

Handel's *Samson* was written in 1743. We can listen to Act II, scene iv as a fine example of baroque oratorio and also (stretching things a little) as a fine example of baroque opera. The basis of the story is found in a small number of verses in The Book of Judges 16:21–31. This the librettist expanded greatly, leaning heavily on the famous play *Samson Agonistes*, written seventy-five years before by John Milton. For any purely literary quality in this libretto, we can thank Milton rather than Handel's librettist, who helped himself plentifully to lines and whole passages from the original play whenever he could. (And Handel "borrowed" music, as we shall point out in a moment.)

After having been betrayed by Delilah, Samson was captured by the Philistines, blinded, chained, and put to work in prison. At the beginning of Act II, scene iv, a mighty Philistine warrior, Harapha, comes to taunt him. The blind Samson immediately challenges him to fight, and after much blustering Harapha retires in disarray. The scene ends with an intense prayer by the Israelites for deliverance from the Philistines. Samson and Harapha obviously stand for their respective nations and gods, and Samson's final triumph will be seen as a vindication of Israel and Jehovah. This idea is thoroughly biblical, but the incident itself was made up by Milton and is not found in the Scriptures.

The table below shows how the action of the scene is divided into musical numbers of three kinds: recitative, aria, and chorus. A *duet* is simply a joint aria for two singers.

	Recitative	An Israelite (Micah) tells Samson of the arrival of the Philistine champion, Harapha. He has come to taunt Samson; Samson at once challenges him to fight, but Harapha says he scorns to fight a blind man.
1.	Harapha (bass voice): ARIA, "Honor and arms"	Harapha enlarges on this sentiment in a blustering tone.
	Recitative	Harapha continues blustering, but now it is Samson's turn to goad him.
2.	Samson (tenor) and Harapha: DUET, "Go, baffled coward, go!"	The two warriors confront one another, in the same musical piece. Though Harapha insults Jehovah, Samson gets the better of the name-calling match.
	Recitative	Stung by Harapha's blasphemies, Micah asks why, if Dagon the god of the Philistines is a true god, they do not ask him to destroy Samson's strength, which obviously still worries Harapha.
3.	Israelites: CHORUS, "Hear, Jacob's God"	The Israelites pray to Jehovah to help them in their affliction.

RECITATIVE In the table, we have purposely not given the recitatives numbers, as a small way of indicating that these items are in a sense submusical. Recitative, from the Italian word meaning "recite," is a technique for reciting words to minimal music, that is, just enough music to maintain musical continuity without lapsing into plain speech. (The term is also applied to a whole number written in this technique, as in the table above.) The voice brings the words out clearly and vividly, following the free rhythm of language carefully and mirroring the natural ups and downs that occur as we raise our voices at a question, lower them to speak "asides," or cry out in excitement. The technique is used primarily for lengthy dialogues, the giving of directions and information, and all the other necessary but prosy lines that go into a dramatic piece.

The instrumental part in a recitative is minimal, too—usually just a series of chords played by continuo instruments (page 87). A low instrument such as a cello plays bass notes, while the organ or harpsichord fills in occasional chords above it. Hence the term secco recitative ("dry" recitative):

SECCO RECITATIVE

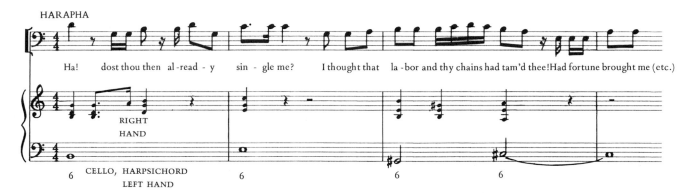

If, as occasionally happens, other instruments are brought in to sustain the chords, the result is called accompanied recitative. But "accompanied" is almost too strong a word; the chords merely provide the singer with basic support and make sure he keeps on the right pitch. Just as the vocal part in recitative does not make distinctive melodies, so the instrumental part does not get organized with any of the devices of musical form. In this, recitative differs sharply from the aria (see below).

ACCOMPANIED RECITATIVE

Only a few composers try to get much of an artistic effect out of recitative. Most are happy enough if listeners will simply accept it as a necessary device to keep the oratorio or opera going. If recitative still strikes you as an unnatural and exaggerated way of handling words, you have a point—though it is one that English and American composers have worked hard to counteract. The truth is that recitative does not take very easily to the English language. It was invented in Italy, and Italian is spoken in a much more excited and even musical fashion than our language is, especially in moments of high dramatic tension.

In our opening recitative from *Samson* (a secco recitative) the statements of Samson, a tenor, are stiff but short and biting: "The way to know were not to see but taste"; "Boast not of what thou wouldst have done—but do." Harapha, though, is a bigmouth bass who enjoys rolling his tongue around grandiloquent blank-verse lines:

Ha! dost thou then already single [i.e., pick on] me?
I thought that labor and thy chains had tam'd thee!
Had fortune brought me to that field of death
Where thou wrought'st wonders with an ass's jaw,
I'd left thy carcass where the ass lay dead!

The reference is to Samson's famous exploit of slaying a thousand men with the jawbone of an ass. Finally Harapha comes to the point, with the words "To combat with a blind man I disdain," and launches at once into his aria enlarging on these sentiments. (In Milton, incidentally, he takes another look at Samson and adds "And thou hast need much washing to be touch'd.")

ARIA

No. 1: Aria, "Honor and arms" (Harapha) An <u>aria</u> is a piece for solo singer and orchestra which, unlike recitative, has real musical profile and coherence. In a baroque aria, the words rarely add any new ideas; indeed, the dramatic situation after it is over remains the same as at the beginning—the same, except in terms of emotional credibility. The aria enlarges *musically* on the sentiments expressed *verbally* at the end of the recitative; the aria is a soliloquy, meditation, tirade, or address during which the character can "get out his feelings." For this, the composer needs the various techniques of musical form on all levels: clear melodies, recognizable rhythms, motives, repetitions, ritornellos, whatever. Unlike recitative, arias tend to repeat their words many times, to music that is often related though not identical. It is as though the character is mulling over his emotions.

In Harapha's aria "Honor and arms," clear melodic ideas emerge at once and are repeated many times along with their associated words (all very different from the preceding recitative). A long orchestral ritornello (page 100) appears at the beginning of the aria, at the end, and at many points in between; it has the forthright character of a concerto grosso ritornello, and it performs a similar function in terms of the musical form. "Honor and arms"

DA CAPO ARIA

belongs to a highly stylized aria form known as the <u>da capo aria</u>, in which the large opening section returns after the second section: a three-part A B A form. Although this tiresome arrangement is well suited to the tiresome Harapha, the second A section is sometimes cut in performances and recordings.

As for the musical material itself, baroque composers often worked ingeniously to match up musical details with the text so as to achieve effects of illustration. In this they followed (and systematized) the practice of word painting in Renaissance music (page 59). Thus the fanfare-like music at the words "Honor and arms" evokes military trumpet calls associated with military arms. When Harapha sneers that it would be a poor victory to "glory" over Samson, he sings *coloratura,* that is, many rapid notes to the single syllable "glo–." This would seem to equate empty glory with ornateness and display. In the second (B) part of the aria, Harapha's scorn is well depicted by the melodic line:

Vanquish a slave *that is half slain!*
So mean a triumph I disdain!

All this makes the piece more vivid, and the formal repetitions perhaps make it bombastic. In any case, we have a much keener impression of Harapha after he has exposed his feelings in the aria than beforehand, when he was only talking about them in recitative.

No. 2: Duet, "Go, baffled coward, go!" (*Samson and Harapha*) In the next brief secco recitative, Samson repeats his challenge, then dismisses Harapha contemptuously in the angry duet "Go, baffled coward, go!" A duet is an aria for two singers in which they develop their own sentiments. Samson simply enlarges upon the sentiments of his recitative. Harapha is reduced to taunting Samson back by reminding him that he has been deserted by Jehovah.

The vigorous counterpoint in the ritornello sets the stage well for this concise scene of confrontation. Samson's sharp exclamations ("Go!" and "Fly!") are quite lifelike, as are also the furious coloratura which he lapses into when he speaks of his "wrath" and the mocking pathetic tone in which he sings "go, baffled coward, baffled coward, baffled coward . . ." in a descending sequence. Samson certainly gets the best of the encounter. Harapha cannot even think up his own music—he merely adjusts his words to music originally invented by Samson—and he appears to have retreated in confusion at the end, while Samson is still shouting at him. The very last word, however, is reserved for the orchestra, which once again winds up the piece in the manner of a miniature ritornello form.

No. 3: Chorus of Israelites, "Hear, Jacob's God" This mighty six-voice chorus shows fine expressive use of musical texture. After a brief secco recitative by one of the Israelites, Micah, we can practically see the Israelites surging together to utter the homophonic exclamations "Hear, Jacob's God! Jehovah, hear!" and then stumbling in one at a time to sing the imploring contrapuntal motive "save us, save us." There is a remarkable solemnity coupled with urgency in this slow prayer—which Handel "borrowed" note for note from an earlier oratorio composer, Giacomo Carissimi!

Original or not, this chorus presents an excellent picture of a psychological low point for the Israelites. If we listen to the whole oratorio, we will observe them gradually taking heart, chorus by chorus, as the drama slowly swings in their favor. And over the long haul, Samson, too, progresses—from gloom and despair at the beginning of the oratorio, to firmness, pride, anger (as we have seen), and finally to ecstatic faith in Jehovah. Each stage of his psychological progress is represented by a full-scale aria; the baroque composer could enter intensely into the feelings of the moment and expand them into several minutes of single-minded repetition. At last Samson attains the physical and psychological strength to pull down the Philistines' stadium and kill thousands of the enemy, along with himself.

With this splendidly grandiose action—performed offstage, unfortunately, though a baroque theater designer would have given his eyeteeth to stage it—the drama sails majestically to a close. There remain only lengthy laments for the dead Samson and a song and chorus in praise of Jehovah. Handel was in his element in music of this kind. No composer has ever surpassed him in musical effects of majesty and splendor.

HANDEL   *MESSIAH* (1742)

Composed in 1742, *Messiah* (not *The Messiah*) is the most famous and beloved of Handel's oratorios. It is exceptional among them in several respects. The subject comes from the New Testament rather than the Old; the words are taken directly from the Bible rather than from a newly written libretto; and there are no characters or plot line. Perhaps it is just as well that we do not have to listen to the story of Jesus expressed in the eighteenth-century verse of Handel's librettists.

Nevertheless, *Messiah* employs the same operatic form as that which we saw in *Samson:* a series of recitatives, arias, and choruses. The difference is that the solo singers of recitatives and arias do not represent particular Bible characters but instead voices from the Christian community, just like the chorus. They tell the story of Christ's birth, suffering, and resurrection with more emphasis on ideas than on actual Bible incidents.

Oratorios and operas of all periods begin with an orchestral number called
OVERTURE   the <u>overture</u>. (A practical reason behind this convention is simply to get the audience seated.) In baroque times, the most common type was the so-called
FRENCH OVERTURE   <u>French overture</u>, which had been developed at the court of Louis XIV in the seventeenth century. This consisted of two parts: a slow and decidedly pompous section most typically entitled *"Grave"* (the French pronunciation, *grahv,* or sometimes the Italian, *grah-veh*) and a vigorous, fast, fuguelike section. Sometimes the *Grave* section returns at the end (A B A). Not only did Handel provide such an overture prior to Act I of *Messiah,* he also wrote a sort of choral *Grave* section to launch Act II of the oratorio, the splendid chorus "Behold the Lamb of God":

The dotted rhythm* continues throughout, but once again, as in the chorus "Hear, Jacob's God" in *Samson,* Handel's imitative texture alternates effectively with strong homophonic sections, especially for cadences.

---

* A dotted rhythm is one featuring many alternations of short and long notes, notated with dots, such as ♪ ♪♫ ♪♫ ♩ .

Almost every one of the fifty-odd numbers in *Messiah* is a gem, and we can only pick and choose among them for brief comment. The celebrated "Hallelujah" chorus, which serves to conclude Act II in unparalleled triumph, is largely homophonic in texture, employing the "festive" baroque orchestra featuring trumpets and drums with special brilliance (see the score on page 49). It may remind us of the *Fireworks Music,* and indeed, all baroque composers tended to praise the works of God in much the same spirit as they celebrated the exploits of great princes. The "Amen" chorus—actually the third part of a longer chorus, "Worthy is the Lamb"—is, on the contrary, polyphonic. A fugue with a clear countersubject (page 96), it concludes the oratorio with solemnity and magnificence:

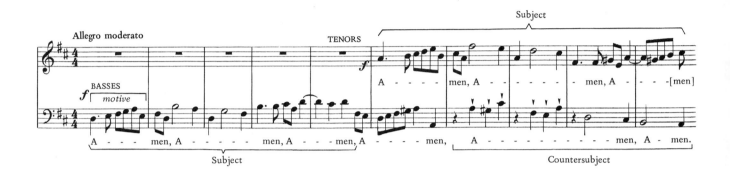

The grand subject is intoned first by the bass voices, then by tenors, altos, and sopranos, followed by the two violin sections of the orchestra. The basses have the subject twice more, then (eight measures later) the altos—but then Handel abandons the subject as a whole, concentrating instead on contrapuntal treatments of a short motive from the very beginning of the subject. He also uses the motive upside down (inversion, page 102):

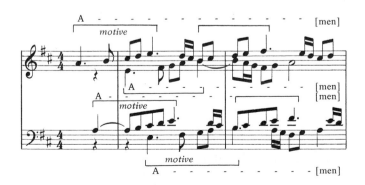

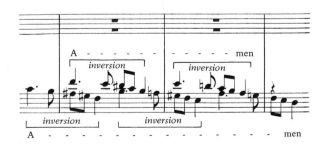

The arias in *Messiah* range in mood from the rousing vigor of "The trumpet shall sound" (bass) to the pastoral gentleness of "He shall feed his flock" (alto and soprano) and from the pathos of "He was despised" (alto) to the serenity of "I know that my Redeemer liveth" (soprano). The last is an especially fine testimony to Handel's skill as a melodist — the hauntingly tuneful first phrase, for example:

I know that my Re - deem - er liv -eth

Although the words change considerably as this aria proceeds, Handel avoids any really striking new musical ideas, preferring to have the orchestra return from time to time with this fragment of tune and also with a second figure:

In arias, as in other kinds of music, baroque composers tended to emphasize a single sentiment rather than to deal in contrasts.

And yet we may have some difficulty with this aria, at least if we try to accept it as a deeply personal religious statement. The soprano expresses serenity and confidence in her Redeemer, even perhaps complacency, but she seems to be strangely unmoved by the religious concepts behind such words as "He shall stand at the latter day upon the earth" and "though worms destroy this body." Like many arias, this one is likely to strike us mainly as an expression of the singer's pleasure at her own musical abilities, to which we respond gratefully with pleasure of our own.

An equally beautiful number, the opening tenor solo in *Messiah*, perhaps provides a clue to the feeling of the oratorio as a whole. Its key words, "*Comfort* ye, my people" and "Speak ye *comfortably* to Jerusalem," Handel was careful to emphasize over all the other words around them. Listening to the tenor's congratulations, it must have been easy for a contemporary audience to identify Jerusalem with London (or British Dublin, where *Messiah* was premiered). Music and conventional piety were both among the comforts of the rising English middle class.

The establishment religion was the Church of England, or Anglicanism. Like other religions in certain stages in their development, eighteenth-century Anglicanism had come to a point where smugness and status overshadowed spiritual values. Many Englishmen were beginning to turn to the new Methodist movement to alleviate their discomfort with this state of affairs.

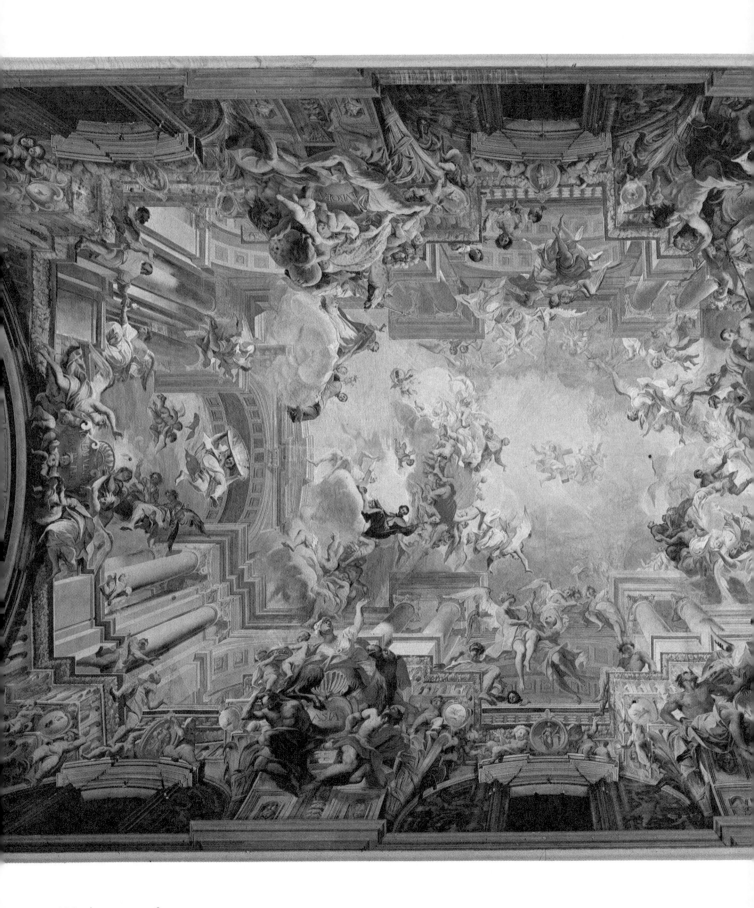

Baroque Ceiling Painting

Ceiling paintings are perhaps the most astonishing products of the baroque artistic imagination. Sometimes covering the entire ceiling of a church or a hall in a palace, they give the impression that the roof has suddenly been thrown open to reveal a miraculous vision of the dome of heaven. Angels, cherubs, saints, and mortals spin around in the clouds, lose themselves in the sun's rays, or spill back into the church itself. Great winds are all but visible in the swirling drapery. Vast spaces and ecstatic, violent motion—or rather, vast spaces in violent motion: this was the essential illusion cultivated by the ceiling painters. Shown on these two pages is the apotheosis, or ascent to heaven, of St. Ignatius Loyola, founder of the Jesuit Order, on the ceiling of the church dedicated to him in Rome.

The twin illusions of space and motion are created by the most sophisticated application of the laws of mathematical perspective. In our illustration, for example, all the "architecture" is painted on the flat ceiling (compare the theater set on page 121). There are some points of contact between ceiling painting and dense baroque polyphony, such as is found in the Sanctus of Bach's Mass in B minor (page 140). This, too, gives a sense of powerful, complex movement filling all the reaches of "musical space" from the lowest notes on the organ pedals to the highest of flute and trumpet tones. And only Bach's very impressive control over the craft of counterpoint enabled him to gear all this musical movement into the total breathtaking effect.

St. Ignatius himself would have been happier with the music of his own century, the sixteenth century, music by Palestrina or Giovanni Gabrieli or William Byrd. But if this baroque depiction of his apotheosis calls for music—and who can doubt that it does?—it is music such as that of Bach's Sanctus.

Baroque Cantata and Mass

BACH

CANTATA NO. 140, *WACHET AUF, RUFT UNS DIE STIMME* (1731)

Side 3

We are likely to find a deeper spiritual quality in the religious music of Bach, in spite of the difficulties caused by the words being in German. This is partly because Bach was a more genuinely introspective composer than Handel and partly because he was writing directly for the Church. Always remember that Handel wrote his oratorios (even *Messiah*) to be performed in a concert hall for an audience that was accustomed to opera. Bach wrote his religious music for particular church services and, what is more, tailored it closely to the specific content of those services.

In the Lutheran Church of Bach's day, there were prescribed Bible readings and prescribed hymns for every Sunday of the year, as well as for the feasts of Christmas, Easter, Ascension, and so on. The readings set the tone of the service and provided the basis for the sermon. For every Sunday and feast day, Bach had to reflect the religious content of the service in his <u>cantata</u>, which is a general name for a composition in several movements for voices and instruments—usually soloists, chorus, and orchestra.* As cantor of the Thomasschule in Leipzig, Bach was required to provide church cantatas for the full year—a stupendous task, which must have kept him composing constantly for some time after he was appointed. Over two hundred Bach cantatas have survived.

CANTATA

The way in which a cantata could reflect its service was through the words of the libretto, of course. The words would refer to the readings of the day and enlarge upon them. Thus Bach's Cantata No. 140, *Wachet auf, ruft uns die Stimme*, composed for a certain Sunday in autumn, refers to the prescribed reading for that Sunday:

There were ten girls, who took their lamps and went out to meet the bridegroom. Five of them were foolish, and five prudent; when the foolish ones took their lamps, they took no oil with them. . . . As the bridegroom was late in coming they all dozed off to sleep. But at midnight a cry was heard: "Here is the bridegroom! Come out to meet him." With that the girls all got up and trimmed their lamps. The foolish said to the prudent, "Our lamps are going out; give us some of your oil." "No," they said; "there will never be enough for all of us. You had better go to the shop and buy some for yourselves." While they were away the bridegroom arrived; those who were ready went in with him to the wedding. . . . Keep awake, then; for you do not know on what day your Lord is to come. (Matthew 25:1–13)

---

* In addition to church cantatas, Bach also wrote secular cantatas for court or civic celebrations. The basic meaning of the word *cantata* is "sung" or "piece that is sung"—compare the word *sonata*, page 112.

Whether Bach and his librettist cared for this rather stern parable we have no way of knowing. It was there, and they had to use it. But maybe it is significant that the librettist says nothing about the discomfiture of the foolish girls and dwells only on the joys accorded to the wise.

CHORALE An even more intimate way in which a cantata could reflect its service was through one of the chorales (from the German word for "hymn") which were specified for the occasion. To the congregation, the words of the chorale would probably be even more familiar and vivid than the Bible words themselves. Those were churchgoing days, and everybody learned their hymns by heart in early childhood, the words right along with the tunes. What is more, the congregation would be singing the same chorale at the same service. Thus if a composer used that chorale tune in his cantata, he gained a sense of immediacy and a kind of participation by the congregation. This could only make the service into a more meaningful religious experience.

And so Bach incorporated into Cantata No. 140 all three verses of the chorale of the day, *Wachet auf, ruft uns die Stimme.* In fact, the cantata libretto is built around (or within) the three hymn verses in a symmetrical way, as the following table shows:

1. Christians: CHORALE (verse 1),   As though by a watchman at midnight,
   "Wachet auf, ruft uns die Stimme"   the prudent girls are exhorted to awake and prepare for the coming of the Bridegroom.

   Recitative (secco)   The daughters of Zion are told that the Bridegroom is coming at once.

2. The Soul and Jesus: DUET,   "Savior, I await Thee; when wilt Thou
   "Wann kommst du, mein Heil?"   come?" "I come; I open the door to heaven."

3. Christians: CHORALE (verse 2),   Zion rejoices at the coming of Jesus,
   "Zion hört die Wächter singen"   the Son of God.

   Recitative (accompanied)   Jesus promises to support and cherish the Soul.

4. The Soul and Jesus: DUET,   "My Friend is mine; nothing will
   "Mein Freund ist mein"   separate us." "I am thine; you will come with Me to joy."

5. Christians: CHORALE (verse 3),   Glory to God.

   "Gloria sei dir gesungen"

Compare this with the table for the scene from Handel's oratorio *Samson,* page 123. Handel's librettist added new characters, not in the basic Bible story, and arias for these characters to sing. Bach's librettist added recitatives and duets to the basic material of the chorale.

In this cantata, only verse 3 of the chorale is presented in a straightforward way, that is, in a way that might fall within the range of actual congregational singing. This verse 3 (No. 5 in the cantata) is a simple but masterly four-part harmonization of the chorale, with all voices and instruments joining together to provide solid chords. In the other two verses, Bach changed the chorale in tempo, meter, rhythm, and accents—though not in pure melody—as indicated below:

The entire chorale tune is printed above only at verse 3. It is a grand tune, by the way, and much of the popularity of this cantata comes from our pleasure in hearing the tune with Bach's various additions and decorations. (We might stop for a moment to sing the chorale and to analyze it along the lines suggested on page 29. Notice the symmetrical phrase-repetitions, the fine high climaxes, and the excitement provided by the successive shortening of the phrase lengths up to the very end, when an "echo" of the sturdy third phrase makes a very satisfying cadence.)

In verses 1 and 2 of the chorale (Nos. 1 and 3 in the cantata), Bach does not present the whole tune consecutively but in a "gapped" form. The lines are separated by rests (as indicated in the example above) and embedded within a much longer and more complex musical structure. Such a movement has the aspect of a meditation on the chorale verse, or an interpretation of it from a musical point of view. On a larger scale, indeed, we could think of the entire cantata as a meditation on the entire three-verse chorale.

No. 1: Chorale, "Wachet auf, ruft uns die Stimme" (*"Awake, the voice cries to us"*) This is the most complex movement in the cantata and an impressive testimony to Bach's structural powers. The chorale itself is sung by the sopranos so slowly that it seems like a solemn framework, as though it were sounding impassively on great bells. There is more activity in the material sung by the lower voices of the chorus (the altos, tenors, and basses) and much more in the orchestra, which consists of strings, three oboes, and organ playing the continuo.

The orchestra begins with a long ritornello full of different motives, alternating between violins and oboes, while the bass keeps up a steady marchlike pace. Perhaps Bach meant this ritornello to suggest the approach of the wedding procession:

After the chorale begins in the sopranos, fragments of the ritornello continue to weave their way in and out of the chorus parts. And when the chorus stops for short periods between the lines of the chorale, the march can still be heard following its vigorous course.

There is an impressive place where the lower voices seem to forget themselves in joy at the word "alleluia," and the soprano has to wait with the chorale while they spin out jubilant imitations:

These imitations take up the most vigorous of all the motives in the original ritornello (marked x on the first musical example on page 135). After the chorale is over, the lower voices stop, too. The orchestra concludes with a repetition of the whole ritornello. Thus the chorale is actually enclosed and solidified by a ritornello form.

*No. 2: Duet, "*Wann kommst du, mein Heil?*" ("*When wilt Thou come, my Savior?*")* A rather emotional secco recitative for tenor announces that the Bridegroom is at hand and that the girls should make ready. This really repeats the message of the previous chorale verse, No. 1, but brings it onto a more personal plane.

The duet that follows is like a tiny opera scene. The bass voice, representing the Savior, or Bridegroom, answers worried questions from the soprano, representing the Christian Soul, or one of the girls who is not quite ready yet. Bach is at his most baroque in the melodies of this duet. As we listen to the skittering solo violin of the ritornello (see the example on page 86) and the two intertwining vocal lines, we may well see winding lines before our eyes, lines swirling like the arms and legs and drapery of the baroque ceiling on pages 130 and 131. But a characteristically steady rhythm in the bass and continuo seems to hold rein on all the ornament and all the anxiety.

This duet is in a free type of da capo form (page 125), free in that the second A section, with the original words and music, is not exactly the same as the first (A B A'). The other duet, No. 4, is in strict da capo form (A B A).

*No. 3: Chorale, "*Zion hört die Wächter singen*" ("*Zion hears the watchmen calling*")* Another "gapped" chorale with ritornello, this piece uses the same general form as that of the opening movement, although it is simpler in style and texture. The ritornello consists of only one melodic line plus continuo; the chorale itself is sung by the chorus tenors only. The rest of the choir is silent. The well-known ritornello melody is both firm and gentle, and it sounds so self-sufficient that we are pleasantly surprised when it fits in with the chorale tune—a particularly clear example of how non-imitative counterpoint can make an interesting effect.

We have mentioned a number of times the tendency of baroque composers to rearrange their music for different instruments. Bach arranged this cantata movement also for organ. In this version, the ritornello is played on one set of pipes, the chorale tune on another, the continuo bass on another (the pedals).

CHORALE PRELUDE

This was an economical way of making pieces of the type known as the chorale prelude, a composition for organ based upon a chorale tune. Such works were a staple with the Lutheran organists of the baroque period. The congregations knew the tunes and the words so well that a wealth of religious associations would be set up simply by the organ music, even without any singing.

Bach composed dozens of chorale preludes afresh, using almost all the familiar hymns of his day. Together with his organ fugues, these pieces make up a body of organ music that by common consent far surpasses that of any other composer, of any time. Listen to Bach's organ chorale prelude *Wachet auf* after listening to the cantata movement, and see which of the two tone colors you prefer.

No. 4: Duet, "Mein Freund ist mein" (*"My friend is mine"*) In an accompanied recitative (page 124), the bass voice reassures the Soul in an even more personal and warm tone than was used in the tenor recitative preceding the earlier duet, No. 2. And in the duet No. 4 itself, all anxiety has passed, as the voices blend happily together beneath the smiling tunes and curlicues of the solo oboe. More than one commentator has observed that as far as the music is concerned, this duet could be representing the billing and cooing of a newly married peasant pair as well as a colloquy between Soul and Savior. Perhaps that is why the piece sounds convincing.

No. 5: Chorale, "Gloria sei dir gesungen" (*"Glory be sung to Thee"*) The third and last verse of the chorale is sung in a simply-harmonized, homophonic version, making a very solid conclusion. This forthright statement has the effect of resolving all the doubts, tensions, and complexities noted earlier in the cantata.

Indeed, if we think back—or "listen back" in memory—we realize that Bach has arranged a deliberate succession of moods in this cantata. Here, just as in Handel's *Samson*, the baroque composer has isolated a series of emotional moments and then exaggerated each emotion in a musical number. Bach moves from considerable tension (No. 1) to anxiety and apprehension (No. 2) to calm solidity (No. 3) to simple joy (No. 4) to exultation (No. 5). In religious terms, the Christian Soul prepares in several psychological stages for the coming of God and, after some qualms, accepts Him. It is not incorrect to speak of a dramatic progression in the cantata as a whole and to say that this has been achieved by a semi-operatic form.

Bach, as we have mentioned, wrote a great many church cantatas, of which over two hundred have survived. Almost all of them incorporate chorales, though some do no more than bring a single simply-harmonized verse at the very end of the cantata. Others employ chorales more extensively, including the well-known Cantata No. 4, *Christ lag in Todesbanden* (Christ lay in death's bonds). There are no recitatives in this cantata. The six numbers use the words and music of the six verses of a sturdy old Easter hymn written by Martin Luther himself.

Bach's famous Passions are settings of the story of Christ's last days and his crucifixion, designed for Good Friday services. The story itself was taken word for word from one of the Gospels: hence the titles *Passion According to St. Matthew* and *Passion According to St. John*. The librettist then interspersed this biblical material with many recitatives, arias, choruses, and chorales. Basically, then, passions are like oratorios, except that they include chorale numbers, as in church cantatas. In the *Matthew* Passion, the sad and gentle "passion chorale," so called, *O Haupt voll Blut und Wunden* (O sacred head sore wounded), returns many times with different simple harmonizations: a wonderfully expressive devotional effect.

The Harpsichord

The harpsichord: for the baroque period, the universal keyboard instrument, and for us today, the source of the most characteristic "baroque sound": the crisp bright sonority of metal strings rapidly plucked by mechanized quills.

The great rise in popularity of baroque music over the last twenty years has caused a resurgence of interest in this ancient "historical" instrument. Nowadays Bach's keyboard suites and fugues are generally performed on the harpsichord, as he intended, rather than on the modern piano, which was not developed until after his death and which distorts the quality of his music. And baroque orchestral music is generally heard today with the clear rhythmic sound of the harpsichord aerating it—a welcome change from the customary thick, dreary performances of half a century ago.

All this has been made possible by a new wave of harpsichord building. A new handmade instrument can be bought for less than the price of a grand piano. There are also firms that make kits from which you can construct your own harpsichord! One is illustrated above. While we can hardly describe home harpsichord building as a major leisure industry, over ten thousand instruments have been made from these kits. This surely represents a very respectable number of Americans who are engaged in an activity of devoted historical restoration.

In their own way, the harpsichord kit builders are going back to the craft spirit of old in trying to fashion their instruments from raw (or relatively raw) materials. Baroque harpsichords themselves were beautifully crafted, in terms of both the sound produced and the cabinetwork. Sometimes they were also elaborately decorated with paintings, designs, or wood inlay. A seventeenth-century instrument decorated in this way is shown on the facing page.

A harpsichord looks something like a small piano, and its basic "works," a set of tuned strings activated from a keyboard, are essentially those of the piano. The difference comes in the way the sound is generated. On the piano, sound is produced by striking the strings with soft, felt-covered hammers. These are controlled by a rather complicated mechanism (the *action*). The complication is required to permit slight changes of finger pressure to achieve all possible dynamic shadings, from very soft to very loud, and then to have the sound stopped, or damped, when the fingers are lifted off.

On the harpsichord, sound is produced by plucking the strings with small hard quills, one per string, activated from the keyboard. Hence the sharp, brittle sound. Harpsichord action and damping are simple and direct (which is fortunate for the kit builders).

As follows from the brief discussion above, the harpsichord does not allow for changes in dynamics. (It was to meet this situation that the hammer instrument was developed in the eighteenth century—and at once entitled the *pianoforte* or *fortepiano*, "loud/soft.") The best that harpsichord builders could do was add another set of slightly different strings with slightly different quills, controlled from a second keyboard. Thus one could obtain terraced dynamics, as on the organ, though the range was not so great.

Italian harpsichord: The Metropolitan Museum of Art, Gift of Susan Dwight Bliss

Although Bach was a Lutheran, the most immense composition he ever wrote was a Roman Catholic Mass. He began it in the hope of impressing a Catholic prince and gaining an important court position; the maneuver failed. Even Masses at this time were written in a semi-operatic form—without recitatives, to be sure, but with a succession of arias, duets, and choruses. Each one expresses the emotional quality of the successive fragments of the Mass text in the usual baroque fashion.

It can sometimes be quite revealing to consider the differences among settings of the same text, such as the immemorial Mass text, by composers of different eras. In the late Renaissance, the Mass was regarded as a coherent experience; Josquin's "Pange lingua" Mass is level, cool, and unified in style, in spite of all its effective small-scale contrasts. The same is true of the Masses of Palestrina or Byrd. But the more dynamic and theatrical atmosphere of the baroque turned the Mass into a vivid series of emotional tableaus. Bach seems to be constantly shifting back and forth from agonized repentance in certain numbers to ecstatic jubilation in others. Where Josquin stands back from the Mass text and sets it to music with a sense of decorum and balance, Bach plunges in, stressing all the contrasts, paradoxes, and elements of wonder inherent in it.

As with Handel's *Messiah*, from Bach's Mass in B minor we can only pick and choose at random among the many superb pieces on which to comment. The Sanctus is superlative, a six-voice chorus (two soprano parts, two altos, tenor, bass) with a "festive" orchestra, consisting of strings, flutes, oboes, trumpets, and drums. As the voices and instruments pursue their contrapuntal lines—some of them ornate, others emphatic, but all intricately bound together—the musical space almost seems to sway with the change of the framework harmonies determined by the continuo. We can visualize numberless angels singing praises to God ("Holy, holy, holy, Lord God of Hosts!") as they swirl around in the clouds and drapery of a great baroque ceiling—under which, indeed, this music would have been performed (see pages 130–131). As the Mass text moves on to the phrases "Heaven and earth are full of Thy glory" and "Hosanna!", Bach provides new musical ideas of similar brilliance from a seemingly inexhaustible supply.

Turning to the final part of the Mass, the Agnus Dei, we see that Bach has read the text thoughtfully and decided to emphasize the contrasts within it. The first section encompasses the words *Agnus Dei qui tollis peccata mundi, miserere nobis* (Lamb of God . . . have mercy upon us). This Bach sets as a personal utterance, a grief-stricken aria for alto voice with a ritornello in the strings which seems to stumble and halt. Here it is easy to picture—indeed, it is hard not to picture—some deeply suffering sinner, prostrate in prayer, out of a baroque dramatic oratorio. Mary Magdalene, perhaps. Bach sets the second section, *Dona nobis pacem* (Give us peace), more impersonally, as a fugal chorus which expresses confidence in the glory of God and the inner peace that he will provide. The two sentiments in the two sections are never reconciled, only placed in dramatic contrast with one another.

The fugue that concludes the Agnus Dei is one of the densest ever composed by Bach or anyone else. It has a tight subject imitating itself at very close time intervals:

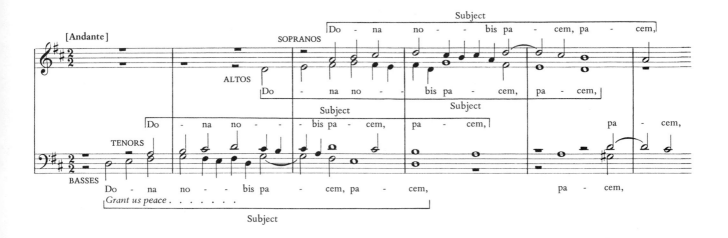

In other words, the fugue subject is presented immediately in stretto (page 113). Usually composers reserved stretto for points of climax later in their fugues; remember the fugue in Corelli's Trio Sonata in F minor (pages 114 and 115). Bach could afford to throw it away at the beginning.

A fugue with words brings out those words very strongly, of course. The words are repeated over and over again with the fugue subject. In this chorus, the impression is that all the nations of the world are trooping in, one by one, with the demand for peace—and also all the trumpets of the world: halfway through the fugue, the piled-up subject entries in the voices soar up to the roof of heaven as the trumpets add brilliant new entries of their own. This fugue has a second subject, or motive, which moves in relatively fast notes, but it has hardly any episodes. All emphasis is on the clamor for peace, endlessly repeated by the subject.

For those who like figures, Bach's fugue brings in the subject twenty-eight times in its total of forty-six measures! This certainly counts as a rigorous structure, which would doubtless have delighted any of the eighteenth-century systematic thinkers and scientists who knew about music. Yet the effect is not one of dry calculation but one of overwhelming glory. We may think back at this point to the fugal "Amen" chorus which concludes Handel's oratorio *Messiah*. Whether we prefer Handel's more casual, bold, and loose-jointed fugue style or Bach's marvelously tight constructions is largely a matter of taste. Each in his own way, the two great composers end their large works in the grandiose, exhaustive fashion that is typical of the baroque period. Each fugue makes a personal statement within the baroque conditions of system and structure on the one hand and grand theatrical gesture on the other.

CHAPTER 4   1775–1825   The Viennese Style

1775–1825   The Viennese Style

In the second half of the eighteenth century, a new musical style was developed by several great composers active in Vienna, the capital of Austria. Geographically, Austria stands at the crossroads of four other musical nations: Germany, Czechoslovakia, Hungary, and Italy. In political terms, too, Vienna at the time was central. As the capital of the powerful Hapsburg Empire, covering parts of Hungary, Czechoslovakia, Yugoslavia, and Italy, she was plunged into every European conflict of the time and was exposed to all the new cultural currents and shades of opinion. During the years in question, Vienna lived through the absolutist monarchy of Empress Maria Theresa, enjoyed the liberal, "enlightened" rule of Joseph II, and was overrun by the revolutionary French armies of Napoleon. After 1815 Vienna submitted to Europe's first modern police state, the counterrevolutionary regime of Prince Metternich.

Through all this, a remarkable group of composers worked in an environment that buzzed with music. Often they worked in close personal contact with one another. Gluck, Haydn, Mozart, Beethoven, Schubert—musicians can point with pride to this galaxy of great composers and compare the accomplishments of Viennese music with those of other such rich cultural flowerings at other times and other places: art in Renaissance Florence and Venice, for example, or literature in Elizabethan England.

The new musical style developed by the Viennese composers is traditionally referred to as "classical." Recently, however, musicians and musicologists have been objecting to this term even more strongly than to the term "baroque," and in this book we shall take the plunge and eliminate it entirely. For unlike the term "baroque," the term "classical" can lead to real misconceptions. The notion that the music takes its inspiration from ancient Greece is only the first of these. It is true that in the visual arts and literature of the time there was much interest in Greek and Roman models and that this interest extended to such areas as furniture and dress design. But even in the visual arts "neoclassicism" was only one trend among others and was part of a larger tendency, as is suggested by our illustration on page 178. In music, the influence of classical antiquity counts for so little that it can safely be ignored.

A second, worse misconception is that a "classical" style has to be entirely serene and unemotional. But we shall see that it was exactly the Viennese composers—first Haydn and Mozart, then Beethoven and Schubert—who pioneered a new degree of personal involvement and expression in their music. Music in this period reaches a new subtlety, a new depth in its depiction of emotion. And certainly events of the time did nothing to promote serenity; rarely has civilization been so shaken as by the revolutions of this age. Perhaps the American Revolution of 1776 was far enough away to be ignored somewhat, and perhaps the ominous effects of the Industrial Revolution were not yet apparent. But the French Revolution of 1789 traumatized the whole of Europe. As the proudest of all monarchies fell to an uneasy coalition of the middle and lower classes, the whole basis for the class structure and governance of Europe was thrown in doubt. Anarchy, atheism, socialism, the guillotining of kings, a general reign of terror—these were the specters of the time. There followed a quarter of a century of Napoleonic wars, during which Europe wondered whether this revolution might overrun the world. Deep passions and ugly forces had arisen which shook man's faith in reason. The arts in this period could not and did not remain calm, stable, and above the fray.

In discussing the general features of the Viennese musical style, we shall find ourselves contrasting it directly with the baroque style. Every rising generation reacts against the older generation to some extent, and this tendency is particularly clear with the music that grew up in this time of revolutions. We shall also need to bear in mind the difference, or at least the change in emphasis, between the early Viennese style of Haydn and Mozart in the 1770s and 1780s and the late Viennese style of Beethoven's music after 1800, shared from around 1815 on by Schubert. As will be pointed out, this late Viennese style includes some clear forecasts of romanticism.

The Character of the Viennese Style

Rhythm Thoroughness, singlemindedness, and massive power are qualities that come to mind in considering baroque music. With Viennese music, the key qualities are flexibility, variety, and contrast. These qualities can be discerned in all the elements of musical technique—in rhythm, dynamics, tone color, texture, melody, and form. And a new sensitivity of feeling grew up in this music as a result of its new technique.

We have said before, and it bears repeating, that of all the elements of music, rhythm and motion are the ones that contribute most centrally to its effect. Viennese music is highly flexible in rhythm. While the meter and tempo remain constant throughout a single movement or large section, the rhythms of the various themes or of the subsections tend to contrast sharply. While the number of beats per measure and the speed of these basic beats remains constant, the first theme may move in half notes and quarters, followed abruptly by the second theme moving in eighth notes and sixteenths, and so on. (See, for example, the first music example from Mozart's

Clarinet Quintet on page 181.) Within themes, too, rhythmic surprises are frequent. The music slows down and speeds up, stops suddenly, presses forward by fits and starts, or glides by as though on ball bearings.

All this gives a sense that the music is moving in a less predictable, more exciting way than baroque music does. We shall hear evidence of this in all compositions by the Viennese composers: in Beethoven's Fifth Symphony, with its driving first theme and its gentle second one, in Mozart's highly dramatic opera ensembles from *Don Giovanni*, and even in quiet songs such as Schubert's *Der Lindenbaum*.

Dynamics Instead of using the steady dynamics or the terraced dynamics (page 85) of the earlier period, composers now worked extensively with gradations of volume. The words for growing louder (*crescendo*) and growing softer (*diminuendo*) first came into general use at this time. Orchestras of the mid-eighteenth century were the first to practice long crescendos — which, we are told, caused audiences to rise up from their seats in excitement. Doubtless these passages were subtly managed in terms of rhythm, too.

The clearest sign of the new flexibility in dynamics was the rise in popularity of the piano. The foremost distinction between the piano and the omnipresent harpsichord of the baroque era was in dynamics. The harpsichord could manage only one sound level, or at best a few slightly different terraced dynamics. The new *pianoforte* or *fortepiano* ("loud/soft") could produce a continuous range of dynamics from soft to loud (pages 138 and 139). It attracted composers because they wished their keyboard instruments to have the same flexibility in dynamics that they were teaching to their orchestras.

Even the organ, whose different sets of pipes had led most directly of all to terraced dynamics when they were connected in or out, was now fitted with a device to allow for crescendos and diminuendos. This was a type of Venetian blind controlled by the player which either muffled the sound or allowed it to come forth full blast. The so-called *swell mechanism* is a fixture in all nineteenth- and early twentieth-century organs.

Tone Color: The Orchestra The Viennese composers also devoted increasing attention to tone color. And of this, the clearest sign is the development of the symphony orchestra. For the first time, orchestral music was distinguished clearly from chamber music. Instrumental resources could no longer be changed around so easily for any particular piece, and an orchestral piece could no longer look like a chamber-music piece (remember the slow movement of Bach's Fifth Brandenburg Concerto). The orchestra was made more forceful and various in tone color, while chamber-music groups were made more intimate and flexible. The orchestra as standardized in this period forms the basis of the orchestra of later times.

The foundation of the Viennese orchestra was a group of *string instruments:** about twelve violins, divided into two separate groups ("first vio-

---

* Today's symphony orchestras include about three times as many string instruments in each category, without a proportional increase in the winds. To play Mozart and Haydn properly, modern orchestras have to cut down on their forces sharply.

THE VIENNESE ORCHESTRA
(As in Mozart's Overture to *Don Giovanni*)

Strings: violins 1, violins 2, violas, cellos, double basses

Woodwinds: 2 flutes
2 oboes
2 clarinets
2 bassoons

Brass: 2 French horns
2 trumpets

Percussion: 2 timpani

lins" and "second violins"), about four violas, and about three cellos, with a few double basses playing the same music an octave lower. With the strings as a framework, *woodwind instruments* were added on the outside, generally in the highest range. More or less in the spirit of decorative frosting, pairs of flutes, oboes, clarinets, and bassoons served to provide variety in certain melodic passages as well as strengthen the string sounds in loud passages. And *brass instruments* were added on the inside, as it were, in the middle range. Pairs of horns and trumpets served as solid support for the main harmonies, generally limiting their activity to occasions such as cadences (page 30) when the harmonies needed to be made particularly clear.

Learning to identify the various instruments of the orchestra by name is not important in itself, but it does help us to distinguish the various sounds—and this certainly *is* important if we are to appreciate the increasingly sensitive use that composers made of tone color in their total musical effects. Names and brief descriptions of the main orchestra instruments were given on page 13. The best way to sharpen one's awareness of different tone colors is simply to listen to a lot of music with information as to what is playing—information that will be provided systematically in this book.

Texture   The predominant texture of Viennese music is homophonic. Again and again in Viennese compositions, a single melody with a simple chordal accompaniment is heard, something that comes up much less frequently in baroque music. The new texture arose partly as a reaction against baroque polyphony. Polyphony struck the new age as heavy, pedantic, and unnecessarily complex.

But the new texture was not merely a negative reaction. It was also a positive move in the direction of flexibility, for music with many contrapuntal lines that have to fit in with one another simply cannot be fast on its feet. And as a result of this simplification of texture, harmony could receive more subtle treatment than before. The reasons are of the same order: when composers did not have to find places for all notes of their chords in individual contrapuntal lines, they could more easily refine chords for their own sake.

Along with the preference for homophonic textures went an interest in rendering them more precise. There is a great difference, obviously, between homophony made up of chords held steadily on one set of organ pipes, and the same chords played in rapid, light repetition by string instruments. In their desire to calculate carefully the precise tone color given to accompaniment chords, the Viennese composers jettisoned the continuo (page 87), which had spread its thick chord patterns over nearly all baroque music. They no longer took the easy way out, relying on the continuo player to fill in the harmony at his own convenience. Composers now wanted it filled in exactly to their own specifications.

Yet it is important to realize that Viennese composers used counterpoint, too. They used a more delicate type of counterpoint than that of the baroque, but they were not ready to give up the richness and variety of effect achieved by polyphonic textures. In fact, they gained a sharper awareness of the expressive possibilities of polyphony. For polyphony was now generally used to give the impression of tension, of one line rubbing against another. The development section in Viennese sonata form, a section whose principal quality is tension, almost invariably involves some contrapuntal textures; and sonata form was the most important musical form of the time.

Melody: Tunes   In the melodic writing of this period, a significant feature is the emphasis on tunes. The Viennese composers stood much closer to popular and folk music than did their predecessors of the baroque. In the music of Joseph Haydn—the real founder of the new style—there is an unquenchable popular lilt which people have often traced to his native folk music. Haydn, Mozart, and Beethoven wrote many dances for the ballrooms of Vienna. Beethoven arranged dozens of folk songs for various instrumental and instrumental-vocal combinations, including Scottish, English, and Irish numbers such as *Auld Lang Syne, The Last Rose of Summer,* and *Paddy O'Rafferty.*

It is therefore not surprising that many of the short themes in Viennese symphonies strike us as tuneful. These themes consist of phrases which, in another context, might have gone on to make excellent songs. And often entire tunes were worked into larger compositions. For example, the theme-and-variations form (page 182) grew popular, both for separate pieces and for movements in larger pieces. As the "theme" in this form, the Viennese composers took a regular tune (not a bass, as was the case in Bach's Passacaglia for Organ, discussed on pages 93 to 95). Sometimes they even took actual popular songs or folk songs. Beethoven wrote variations on *God Save the King* and *Rule Britannia;* Mozart wrote variations on *Baa Baa Black Sheep,* which he knew as the French song *Ah, vous dirai-je, maman;* and all composers of the time wrote variations on current hits from the opera.

When they made up tunes of their own for variations, these usually turned out to be of the same type. The German national anthem (*Deutschland Über Alles*—the tune of the hymn *Glorious Things of Thee Are Spoken,* or sometimes *Praise the Lord, ye Heavens Adore Him*) was composed by Haydn and used by him for a theme-and-variation movement in a string quartet, the so-called Emperor Quartet, Op. 76 No. 3.

Another form that grew more important was the rondo (page 175). This form, too, takes its point of departure from a full-fledged tune, which comes back many times during the movement in a more or less unchanged form.

Finally, there is a special convention established by Viennese composers for symphonies, sonatas, and chamber-music pieces: the inclusion of a dance movement in nearly every one. Music lovers tend to take this convention for granted, but we ought to notice that it represents a real change from the baroque. Baroque composers had also written dances, as we have seen, but they had segregated them into dance suites, in which whole sets of complex and simple dances stand side by side. Other important baroque forms, such as the concerto grosso and the trio sonata, do not necessarily include any dances.

The one dance type that figures in the earlier Viennese symphonies and sonatas was the *minuet*. This dance began as one of the simplest baroque types (Handel used one to end the *Fireworks Music:* see page 119). Some Viennese minuets are simple and genuinely tuneful; others are less so, and Beethoven transformed the minuet into an explosive kind of movement which he christened *scherzo* ("joke"). But even with these reservations, the omnipresent minuets and scherzos of the Viennese period presented a clear mandate for tunefulness and simple melodic structure.

Musical Form Composers whose ideal was flexibility and variety found themselves facing a special problem: How was all the variety to be held together as a coherent whole? This was a matter of musical form, which is the aspect of music that concerns its total extension in time. Viennese composers worked with contrasts of themes, rhythms, tone color, dynamics, tonality, and all the rest; by the use of certain principles and certain formal schemes, they managed to make all these contrasts live together harmoniously in the same universe. These two principles—contrast and coherence—can be seen as yet another large-scale application of the aesthetic maxim of "unity in variety."

The main formal scheme developed in this period is the so-called *sonata-allegro form*, or *sonata form*. We shall examine it in detail later. At this point, we need only observe that although sonata form and other Viennese forms might at first strike some people as rigid and constraining, at least on the conceptual level, in actual fact these forms accommodated or made possible a quite amazing variety of music. There are sonata-form movements that sound elegant and fluid and others that sound forceful and driven by fate; there are playful rondos and melancholy ones. There are even tragic-sounding minuets.

Sonata form, in particular, seems not to have inhibited the Viennese composers at all but rather to have served them as a stimulus to endless possibilities. As with the sonnet in literature and the cross-shaped plan in church architecture, mentioned on page 45, the "outer form" of sonata form was flexible enough to encompass a great range of different "inner forms."

Working to achieve coherence, after having employed so much contrast, the Viennese composers felt a need to include long passages of repetition in their music. This, too, has struck some people as rigid and as unnecessarily formal. But just as in the architecture of a Greek temple or a Cape Cod cottage, a generous amount of repetition is required here to produce a satisfying effect. Without these large-scale stable repetition areas, the music would really lack stability and a sense of coherence.

Of course, this is hard to prove since the composers didn't write any music which does, in fact, lack coherence. A test can be suggested, however. If you listen carefully to about half of a Viennese symphony or sonata movement and then take the stylus off the phonograph, the effect will be distinctly frustrating. Some connection will be missing; you want to know how the music "comes out"; the composer's real point has not yet been driven home. But although it may be unconventional to say so, you can listen to half of a baroque piece and still get a fair enough idea of the composer's meaning without staying to the end.

On first hearing a variety of Viennese music, it is not uncommon to be impressed as much by the differences between the earlier and later styles as by the similarities. The music of Haydn and Mozart may seem light and neat, possibly charming, and possibly (though mistakenly!) somewhat superficial. Beethoven is likely to seem forceful and dramatic. But on listening further, we discover works by Mozart, too, that are passionate, intense, forceful, and dramatic—some of his greatest works, in fact: the Symphony in G minor and the opera *Don Giovanni* are famous examples. And some of the greatest compositions of Beethoven emanate deep serenity and gentleness. One that will be discussed later is the Piano Sonata in E major, Op. 109.

Variety, once again, is a central fact about the expressive quality of the music by the Viennese composers. Moreover, after getting to know one of their pieces well—really well—we may also become more than a little disenchanted with any easy label that critics attach to it. Music that seems "passionate" at one moment can easily become "serene" at the next. The music changes—that was the point of our discussion of Viennese musical form—and it changes in a way that may indeed seem to mirror emotional experience. For if we attempt to analyze such experience within ourselves, we must realize that it is constantly changing, complex, and fluid. With baroque music, perhaps, static words such as "mournful" and "jubilant" will do, more or less; the baroque composer distills emotion and projects it with relative simplicity—with something of the same single-minded intensity as is employed by a great actor, as we have suggested (page 89). In presenting shifting feelings, equivocations, conflicts, and resolutions, the Viennese composer is the more sensitive psychologist.

Looking at the vivid portrait busts by the sculptor Houdon on pages 152, 153, 168, and 169, anyone might despair of guessing his "secret" and yet feel sure that in addition to his technical skill, he possessed unusual powers of discernment into human personality and feeling. With his contemporaries, the great Viennese composers, the secret certainly begins with their exciting new flexibility of musical technique. But over and above technique, each in his own way drew upon remarkable stores of human insight. For many listeners, their music rings truer in emotional terms than almost any other music that has been written before or since.

The Enlightenment

The Enlightenment is the name given to an important current of thought in eighteenth-century Europe and America. It developed out of the faith in man's reason that had led to the great scientific discoveries of the baroque period. Now, however, the emphasis veered away from the purely intellectual and scientific toward the social sphere. Less intent on controlling natural forces than on turning them to universal benefit, men tried to use their reason to solve questions of public morality, education, sociology, and especially political science. The American Constitution and the Federalist Papers constitute the Enlightenment's most tangible and impressive product. This period also saw the beginning of several social science subjects: economics (Adam Smith) and demography (Malthus). Meanwhile scientific research moved in the direction of technology, which put science to a social use. By 1800, the Industrial Revolution was well under way.

Social injustice came under strong fire in the eighteenth century. So did entrenched religion — and not only from intellectuals. Many people turned to Methodism, the new popular religion concentrating on salvation, evangelism, and the Christian life; this met their needs more closely than did the rituals and doctrinal subtleties that dogged Catholic and traditional Protestant worship, each in their own ways. Meanwhile philosophers expressed skepticism about miracles, hellfire, the sacraments, and so on, such as had never been voiced before. There were currents of agnosticism and even outright atheism.

"Mock on, Mock on, Voltaire, Rousseau:
Mock on, Mock on: 'tis all in vain!
You throw the sand against the wind,
And the wind blows it back again. . . ."

wrote William Blake, incensed by Enlightenment attacks and satires on religion. The names of these two French thinkers are always mentioned in connection with the Enlightenment: Voltaire (pictured to the left) the older and more far-ranging, Rousseau (right) the younger and more equivocal. An amazingly diverse and influential man of letters, Voltaire produced a stream of philosophical, scientific, and legal essays, satires, stories (*Candide*), plays, poems, tracts, and slanted history, all in the service of a tireless crusade for tolerance and humanity. Judicial torture, for example, owed its repeal in France to Voltaire.

The activities of Rousseau were more focused: whatever his subject, this passionate man always came around to blasting the social institutions of his day as forces stifling the individual. He was Europe's first self-announced "alienated" intellectual; perhaps none has ever impressed his contemporaries more. Rousseau was something of a composer, too, and a widely read music critic. Predictably, he favored simple music, close to the heart of the "natural man" and far from what he considered the repressive formalism of late baroque music. If Rousseau had been born in our time, he would be turning up as an aging, argumentative fan at pop-music events.

After the middle of the eighteenth century, concert music too moved closer to the "natural man." One thinks of the dances in Viennese symphonies, songs such as Schubert's folklike *Der Lindenbaum,* and the simple, moving, hymnlike type of melody that comes up in the slow movement of Haydn's Symphony No. 88 and the last movement of Beethoven's Piano Sonata in E, Op. 109 (see pages 150, 173, 202, and 212). Beethoven's Ninth (*Choral*) Symphony includes a famous hymn to universal brotherhood. One could also say that the more precise psychological depiction of Mozart's operas reflects the new respect for man's individual nature.

This is not to say that Mozart, Haydn, and Beethoven were directly influenced by Rousseau. If they had read his criticism, they would have sniffed, and if they had heard his music, they would have laughed. Yet Rousseau, Voltaire, and other thinkers of the time radically changed the intellectual climate, and this was something composers and their audiences reacted to, whether they knew it or not.

Wolfgang Amadeus Mozart (1756–1791)

As is well known, Mozart displayed extraordinary musical talent at an early age and was taken around Europe as a child prodigy. He played, improvised, and composed special music for Vienna, Munich, Amsterdam, Venice, and Rome. He charmed Queen Marie Antoinette, and he delighted the English so much that his London concert tour was extended for longer than a year. Without knowing it, young Mozart was placed in the position of being the harbinger of a whole new concept of the musician, the concept of "artist" rather than "artisan." Yet he came from a solid, lower-middle-class musical family, and his father's intention was always to have Wolfgang follow in his footsteps as court musician to the Archbishop of Salzburg, in central Austria.

In London, Mozart was the subject of a learned essay on infant psychology by an eccentric scholar of the time named Daines Barrington. Alas, while people were much intrigued by unusual talent in the child, they were not yet ready to respond to genius in the adult. Mozart's adult life was one long disappointment. He himself contributed to this by giving up his court position and going to Vienna, the center of the musical universe, where he tried to make a career for himself as an independent musician. By this action, he seemed to be saying that it was impossible for the artist to continue in a servant role and that genius must work untrammeled. Even Handel had not cut himself off entirely from the traditional bonds, and Handel, a bachelor, was much better able to take care of himself than was Mozart, who was impractical, sensitive, "difficult" in personal relationships, and blessed with a wife who was less effective in money management than in childbearing. Despite some moments of success, Mozart lived in poverty and illness, dying after only ten years in Vienna at the age of thirty-five.

Of all the great composers, Mozart is the hardest to characterize and the hardest to get to know. Perhaps there has to be one great composer who wears a Mona Lisa smile. But behind the smile—underneath the light and formal surface of much of his music—there is a fantastic intelligence at work, and the more one listens, the more one marvels at the shades of subtle feeling that Mozart is able to convey. This is not to speak of the considerable body of his music that is not light at all—the dark, intense compositions which demolish the old-time view of Mozart as the composer of charming nothings. Furthermore, no composer ever produced music more effortlessly and spontaneously, whether in respect to the themes themselves or to the way they fit together as coherent pieces. Perfection came to him easily.

Mozart wrote many letters which happen to be preserved. In them he appears sharp and sensitive, good-humored and self-aware, shrewd and sympathetic about people and events—enormously likable, in fact, even today, though he stands so far away from us in time. It is no accident that he was a special master of opera. Mozart could depict psychological character in music with a skill that has never been exceeded by composers of later times. We may come to feel that his activities as an opera composer spilled over into his instrumental compositions, giving them, too, a vivid sense of personality in spite of exteriors that may appear formal and restrained.

The opera *Don Giovanni* contains some of Mozart's most serious and even tragic music, as we might guess at once from the impressively solemn slow music that begins the overture. In the discussion of the baroque oratorio, page 127, it was mentioned that operas and oratorios in all periods begin with an orchestral number, the overture; *Don Giovanni* is no exception. The solemn slow section of this overture leads in to a longer section in fast tempo.

This introduces us immediately to the vivacity, alertness, and high contrast which mark the Viennese style. The delicate, keen-sounding opening theme ends with a little wind-instrument fanfare which contrasts abruptly:

One can almost hear one set of characters mocking another. As the music rushes ahead, there are sharp changes in dynamics and decided stops in the rhythm, stops which announce the arrival of new themes. After one of these stops, another theme, bristling with internal contrast, appears:

The gruff beginning and the twittering continuation give the effect of speedy repartee. Thus there is actually sharp contrast *within* these themes, short as they are, as well as contrast *between* one theme and the next. "Tuneful" is not a word we would apply to this overture, perhaps, except for one small idea:

This might have turned into a pleasant tune, like a folk song, if Mozart had not been more interested in a total effect of helter-skelter activity.

All the themes are presented in a homophonic texture, accompanied by the simplest of chordal backgrounds. But as the music proceeds, the gruff part in the second example also figures in extended contrapuntal passages. As for tone color, the orchestral sound glitters constantly, whether in loud passages or in soft. Better yet, tone color is used in an integral way to bring out the character of the musical material. The fanfare in the first example would sound pale if it were not played by the wind instruments, in contrast to the strings earlier in the theme. The contrapuntal treatments of the second example would lack bite if the imitations were not staggered between strings and winds.

Map labels:

North Sea

ENGLAND · London

PRUSSIA · Berlin

POLAND · Warsaw

UNITED NETHERLANDS

SAXONY

Brussels · Bonn

AUSTRIAN NETHERLANDS

Prague

BOHEMIA (Czechoslovakia)

VIENNA

Paris

Strasburg

BAVARIA

Salzburg · Eisenstadt

Budapest

HUNGARY

Basel

SWITZERLAND

AUSTRIAN EMPIRE

FRANCE

Milan · Venice

Belgrade

SERBIA

ITALY

Mediterranean Sea

Adriatic Sea

Rome

1786

Vienna

The Austrian Empire in 1786, showing the importance and centrality of Vienna. Also shown are sites associated with the great Viennese composers:

Salzburg, the beautiful city where Mozart was born, which is today a favorite tourist attraction largely on account of that fact. Although Salzburg is really a part of Austria, it used to be an independent state ruled by an Archbishop, and so was not included within the Austrian Empire.

Eisenstadt, the location of the country palace of the Esterházy family outside Vienna, where Haydn worked for so many years of his life. For a painting of an opera performance in the Esterházy palace theater, see pages 184–185.

Bonn, Beethoven's birthplace, today the capital of West Germany.

Sonata Form

The fast part of the Overture to Mozart's *Don Giovanni* is also an example of sonata form. This will require discussion at some length, for sonata form is the most important form developed by the Viennese composers. Characteristically, it is the form which more than any other exploited and systematized the new interest in contrast. In particular, sonata form employs contrast of thematic material and contrast of tonality (see the discussion on pages 41 and 42).

There is no problem in understanding what is meant by contrast of thematic material. When a Viennese composer starts a piece with a theme consisting of nothing more than a few memorable rhythms and then directly afterward goes into a long suave tune, he achieves an effect of contrast simply by the juxtaposition. Contrast of tonality, however, is a more difficult concept. It was pointed out on page 41 that melodies can be played in different tonalities, which sound different in some sense. (You can verify this by trying to pick out a tune at the piano—*America*, for instance—starting first with the note C and then with the note F♯.) But contrast means more than mere difference: it implies a feeling of opposition, even confrontation. How does a composer obtain such a feeling between two tonalities and use it for aesthetic purposes?

EXPOSITION

A piece in sonata form begins with a large section of music called the exposition. In the first tonality (which is that of the piece as a whole; in Mozart's Symphony in G minor, the first tonality is G minor), a main theme is presented. This theme may be a tune or a group of small phrases that sound as though they want to grow into a tune. Or the theme may consist of nothing more than a few small motives of a memorable rhythmic character. (The term *motive* was defined on page 31).

Soon after the main theme is well established, there is a change in tonality, or modulation, as it is called, which gives a sense of dynamic forward movement. The part of the exposition that accomplishes this is called the bridge or *transition*. The composer tries to make the modulation not too smooth, at least in rhythm, so that there will be some tension in the way the new themes, now to be introduced, "set" in the new tonality. To contribute to this tension, the new themes usually contrast with the first theme in melody and rhythm, as well as in tonality.

BRIDGE

The group of new themes in the new tonality is called the *second group*. The most striking of them is usually called the *second theme*, and the last one, which is always so constructed that it makes a very solid ending, may be called the *cadence theme*, or *closing theme*. The end of the exposition is marked by a loud series of repeated cadences. Unfriendly critics in the nineteenth century spoke of "presenting arms" at this juncture of sonata-form movements.

DEVELOPMENT

The following section, the development, works with, or "develops," earlier themes and motives. These are broken up, recombined, extended, and in general shown in unexpected and often exciting new contexts. Much use is made

THE VIENNESE STYLE | 157

of counterpoint. In tonality, the development section moves around restlessly; there is constant modulation, constant change of tonality. We have the impression of a purposeful search for the proper position for the music.

After a time—usually after the tension has built up considerably—the last modulation in the development section returns to the first tonality. The passage that accomplishes this is sometimes called the *retransition*. With a real sense of relief or resolution, we next hear the themes of the exposition come back in their original order (or something close to their original order). Hence the name for this third section, the <u>recapitulation</u>.

RECAPITULATION

But there is an important difference: everything now remains in the same tonality (the first tonality). Stability of tonality is very welcome after the instability of the development section—and what is more, the old material now has a slightly new look. Thus the strong feeling of balance between the exposition and the recapitulation (A B A′) is a weighted balance, because the second A section (A′) has achieved a new solidity.

If even more solidity seems to be needed, another section is added at the end, as though to deliver concluding remarks on the subject matter of the movement. This <u>coda</u> (meaning "tailpiece"; a general term, not restricted to sonata form) is generally subsidiary and quite brief in Mozart's work, but Beethoven and Schubert expanded it greatly.

CODA

Diagrams of various sorts have been devised in order to try to clarify sonata form. Here is one, in which the changes of tonality are indicated by different vertical levels of a continuous line:

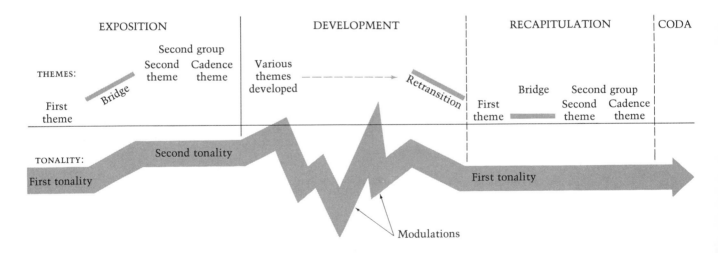

It is surely no accident that the terminology of sonata form—exposition, development, recapitulation—resembles the terminology of the drama. Sir Donald Tovey, one of the most perceptive writers about music, observed that Viennese music has a "dramatic" quality, as compared with the "architectural" quality of baroque music. In a complex Viennese sonata, the themes seem almost like people to whom things are happening. They seem to change, grow, have adventures, and react in relation to other themes.

Listening again to the Overture to *Don Giovanni,* we can hear how the fast section of this falls into sonata form and how this form holds the dizzy contrasts of the piece together as a convincing and interesting totality. It may help to follow the line score on pages 160 and 161.

Exposition   The main theme appears twice, but the second time, instead of being mocked by the wind-instrument fanfares, it shoots off purposefully in a new direction. After a firm stop, the *bridge* commences with an especially busy rhythm, forecasting its role in making the modulation. Note also the abrupt changes in dynamics.

Another firm stop, and the *second group* makes its sharp contrast to everything that has gone before, in terms of both melody and tonality. After a brief dialogue between flute and oboe comes the loud *cadence theme* (a part of the second group). It sounds conclusive, and a high-spirited, amusing passage of "presenting arms" makes it sound doubly so.

Development   This begins directly with the second theme. Already at the second playing of the gruff part of this theme (line 5, measure 5), an interesting melodic change occurs—a "development." Soon a contrapuntal treatment of this gruff part begins to modulate repeatedly. Underneath the polyphony in the winds, we may be able to hear the other part of the second theme twittering away in the strings simultaneously. (By the way, this part of the second theme sounds suspiciously like a part of the main theme; see line 1, measures 6 and 7.) The modulations land in a tentative-sounding tonality.

Here the main theme is played, complete with fanfares (line 6). Then another modulation prepares for a series of modulating sequences (page 30) on the second theme. These add an unexpected new serious note—a real "development" in mood, we might say (line 7). After all this activity, a *retransition* high in the strings leads us with a sense of relief to the original tonality and the main theme, back in its original form.

Recapitulation   As is often the case with Mozart, the recapitulation in this overture follows the exposition closely. Mozart makes the minimum changes necessary to achieve the all-important sense of stability by keeping all themes and sections in the original tonality. Can you hear where these changes come, without looking at the line score?

Only one is really obvious, and this change is of a kind that would never occur in a symphony. It is conceivable only in an opera overture. After the "presenting-arms" passage at the end of the recapitulation, suddenly the second theme appears and modulates once again, rather slyly, leading to a mysterious halt which breathes expectancy. The point is that the curtain goes up at this very moment, to reveal a mysteriously darkened stage. The mood of the first scene is going to be very different from the brightness of the overture. Mozart carries off a dramatic stroke even before the curtain goes up, by running the overture directly into the action rather than coming to a formal stop.*

* One is irresistibly drawn into the opera at this point! However, for class purposes some may prefer to postpone the subject of opera and now examine some other movements in sonata form and in other Viennese forms: page 170 following.

Mozart, Overture to Don Giovanni: Fast Section

* Same music as the previous measure

Opera Buffa

DON GIOVANNI: INTRODUCTION TO ACT I *Side 3*

In the late eighteenth century, comic opera grew to equal in importance the serious opera that had monopolized the grandiose theaters of the baroque. The new flexibility of style was well suited to the casual, swift, and lifelike effects that are the essence of comedy. Mozart wrote some German comic operas; he also composed Italian comic operas for Vienna, just as Handel, another German, had once written Italian operas for London.

OPERA BUFFA

Serious Italian opera was called *opera seria;* comic Italian opera was called opera buffa. The techniques employed in Mozart's *Don Giovanni* are the techniques of *opera buffa,* techniques that could have been made possible only by the new style.

But *Don Giovanni* itself is neither a comic opera nor a tragic one. It is a thought-provoking mixture of both—what might be called today a "dark comedy." It seems to represent Mozart's opinion that events have both an element of farce and an element of tragedy, and that life's experiences cannot be safely pigeonholed. We have already seen evidence of this ambivalence in the Overture, with its two sharply contrasted sections, and we shall see more evidence in other numbers of the opera.

The story gave Mozart his cue. Don Giovanni is the Italian name for Don Juan, the semilegendary Spanish lover. The rambling tale of his endless escapades and conquests always stirs up appreciative chuckles, often with a bawdy undertone; certainly the subject belongs in *opera buffa.* But in his relentless, utterly selfish pursuit of women, Don Juan ignores the rules of society, morality, and God. He commits crimes and sins, and not only against the women he seduces. In one instance, he kills the father of one of these women, and this action—the killing of the Commandant—is taken as the symbol of his generally evil life. As the legend goes, Don Juan, when hiding in a graveyard, is reproached by the marble statue which has been erected over the Commandant's grave. He arrogantly invites the statue to dinner; the statue comes and drags him off to hell. On the literal level we may find this hard to take, but below the surface there is a serious allegory, indeed a profound one, which is stressed by Mozart's music.

ENSEMBLE

The opening musical number, or introduction, is an ensemble. This is the general term for musical numbers in *opera buffa* sung by two or more people. Like a duet in a baroque opera or oratorio (we heard one for Samson and Harapha in Handel's oratorio *Samson),* an ensemble depicts different sentiments of the various characters simultaneously. But it also depicts these sentiments changing, for in the course of an ensemble, the action proceeds and the situation changes. Almost always this involves musical changes—in tonality, in themes, and even in tempo. One of the most potent forms developed by the Viennese composers, the *opera buffa* ensemble extended the range of musical drama immeasurably.

The darkened stage reveals a single character. From his grumbles, we can tell that he is a servant, the traditional comic servant in the drama of all ages. Always work, never a word of thanks, no sleep, bad food—a marvelous musical figure depicts his complaints:

The nagging quality achieved by the sudden fortes and sforzatos and the jerky rhythm would be impossible without the flexibility of the Viennese style. (The actor could invent some action in synchronization with these sforzatos; for instance, he could slash away spitefully at an innocent tree.)

This music is over in a moment, and a fragment of real tune shows what is really eating our man. *"Voglio far il gentiluomo!"* he sings: "I want to play the gentleman"—the gentleman who, he goes on to tell us, is in the house with the lady while he, Leporello, has to stand guard outside. In a stroke we have Leporello's character, the clue to all his actions in the opera: he wants to be Don Giovanni. Every man, in one corner of his feelings, wants to be a Don Juan. As for Leporello, when he later comes to sing his big aria, *"Madamina"* (page 165), he cannot even talk about himself but instead spins a fantasy about his master's amorous adventures.

But for all his intensely human features, Leporello is also a bit of a clown, as we can tell from the *"no, no, no's"* injected into his complaining. Hearing a noise, he goes into hiding. There is a vigorous modulation and change of theme as Don Giovanni runs onto the stage, trying to shake himself free from the grasp of Donna Anna, the latest of his women. Just how far Don Giovanni

has gotten with Donna Anna is a famous unanswered question, but in any case she is determined to unmask him in order to identify him and put in motion the customary Spanish revenge. There is a new dark urgency to the music as they argue in angry, short musical phrases, sometimes singing separately, sometimes together. Meanwhile, Leporello chatters away simultaneously in a faster rhythm, as shows up clearly in the second example on page 164. He is half enjoying the scene, though he knows it may spell trouble. This juxtaposition of different sentiments—the two principals on the one hand, Leporello on the other—shows how vividly *opera buffa* ensembles can point up dramatic situations.

Another modulation and another deepening change of mood: Donna Anna's father, the Commandant, has been awakened by her shouts. He enters with sword drawn. When Don Giovanni refuses to fight an old man, the Commandant calls him a coward, an insult that cannot be borne. As the two Spanish grandees square off, Leporello's background remarks (words and music) take on a significant new tone: he is now genuinely frightened. The music tells us that the duel is somber and formal, fought according to the rules of swordsmanship. A loud dissonant chord is held for a moment in the orchestra, and we know that the Commandant has been mortally wounded.

The last section of the introduction, a trio (Donna Anna has run off), allows the three men to stop and think and express their individual reactions. Tempo and mood change completely. The Commandant groans his last; Leporello mumbles in horror; Don Giovanni muses with a strange mixture of grimness and sympathy on the incredible course of events. Since all of these three male roles are assigned to the bass voice, or to the slightly higher bass-baritone, the tone color is especially dark and strange. Though this trio lasts only a short time, it stays in the memory as one of the most haunting parts of the opera. One feels that Mozart has made his characters equal to the emotional demands of a sudden, meaningless death.

The overture, we remember, had not really stopped but had merged into the beginning of the introduction. Now the introduction itself trails off without a true cadence into a passage of secco recitative, as Don Giovanni and Leporello try to collect themselves in the darkness. Secco recitative is (by definition: see page 124) a dry business, but here it makes a wonderful contrast with all the tragic intensity as the two men get back to the glum realities—enlivened by some bad jokes from Leporello, which are not appreciated by Don Giovanni. This abruptly restores the mood of comedy in which Leporello's grumbling had begun the opera. As the opera continues, there are constant abrupt changes of this kind.

MOZART *DON GIOVANNI:* ARIA, *"MADAMINA"* (LEPORELLO'S CATALOG ARIA)

It is a little later in Act I that Leporello gets to sing his main aria, which recounts Don Giovanni's amorous exploits: *"Madamina, il catalogo è questo"* ("Lady, this is the catalog"). He sings it as a kind of mocking excuse or explanation for Donna Elvira, another one of Don Giovanni's women who has been deserted by him. The fast, casual singing style, with its raucous wind-instrument interruptions, is ideal for Leporello to rattle off the catalog of his master's conquests: 640 in Italy, 91 in Turkey, and so on. The patter singing in Gilbert and Sullivan is derived from this very style. At the place where Leporello chalks up the record (*"Ma, ma, ma in Ispagna son già mille e tre"* —"But . . . but . . . but in Spain, already a thousand and three!"), the music slows down suddenly for a second, a perfect representation of the tall-story teller stopping for effect — rolling his eyes, no doubt, and shooting up his eyebrows. The Viennese composers' new flexibility of style could be used for very comical purposes.

The second half of the aria, a slow minuet during which Leporello catalogs the women according to physique rather than nationality, includes amusing details of illustration. There are pompous long notes when he speaks of *"la grande,"* the tall girl whom Don Giovanni flatters as *"maestosa"* ("majestic"), and repeated chucking noises for *"la piccina"* ("the petite girl"). Best of all is the dry cackle of the bassoon when Leporello remarks that although Don Giovanni will seduce old women, his "predominant passion" is for young beginners. At the end there is an aura of broad innuendo in the music at his words to Elvira: *"You* know how it goes!" (*"Voi sapete quel che fa!"*). Can we not imagine, only too well, an impolite stage gesture accompanying the very last notes in the orchestra here? We can be sure that Mozart did.

MOZART   *DON GIOVANNI:* FINALE TO ACT II   *Side 4*

Let us not attempt to recount the whole complicated plot of *Don Giovanni.* The hero pursues several more women, but ultimately things close in on him. In numerous ensembles and arias, some serious, some comic, the personalities of the characters are all made marvelously clear through the music. At last comes the scene in which the Commandant's statue arrives to dine with Don Giovanni and Leporello, in the finale of Act II, the last act.

FINALE   The word <u>finale</u> is used in music with two similar meanings. It can refer to the last movement of a work with several movements, such as a concerto grosso or a symphony. Or it can refer to the ensemble that concludes an act in an *opera buffa* (or any opera of later times). *Opera buffa* finales are the longest and most complex of ensembles, usually involving everyone in the cast and encompassing an entire lengthy scene of dramatic action.

Only after the Act II finale has been going on for some time, in a spirit of slapstick comedy, does the statue finally arrive, on a loud dissonant chord held in the orchestra. This chord is especially chilling if we remember it as the same one we heard when the Commandant was killed, in the Act I introduction. We certainly remember the music he now sings as the same solemn music we first heard at the beginning of the Overture:

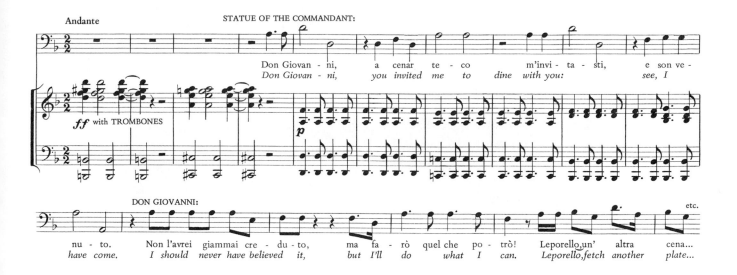

Like a recapitulation in sonata form, the return of this earlier music helps make the opera into a coherent whole, with a consistent message.

In the gripping scene that follows, each character sings quite different music. The statue delivers slow rhythms that are truly marble-encased. Don Giovanni speaks in vigorous, manly accents. Meanwhile, Leporello, from underneath the dinner table, chatters in terror and even makes compulsive jokes; when the statue invites Don Giovanni to dinner with him, Leporello babbles, *"Oibò! oibò! tempo non ha, scusate!"*—"Too bad! too bad! he hasn't the time, please excuse him!" As the statue demands repeatedly that Don Giovanni repent (*"Pentiti! pentiti!"*), the orchestra plays again the somber music accompanying the duel in the Act I introduction. Don Giovanni proudly refuses. The music gets faster and more furious. A chorus is heard from the underworld, flames burst out, and Don Giovanni sinks screaming into hell. His final cry is parodied by a shriek from Leporello—terrified, but quite safe—and after this grisly scene ends, there is another sudden switch to the world of comedy as the various characters return to sing (among other things) a cheerful moral: "That's the way all sinners end up."

The trouble is, we are still shaken by the statue. The musical pressure he applies is terribly impressive, and Don Giovanni's bravery in resisting this reveals itself in every musical phrase he utters. Sinner or not, he has a consistency and integrity that we cannot help admiring. Don Giovanni is an "existential man," who refuses to live by the "absurd" standards of society and follows his own course—here, frank self-gratification—to the end, even if it dooms him. The "absurdity" has been made very clear by the comedy. Don Giovanni simply could not repent his ways and never look at another woman.

Is this something that we in the twentieth century are reading into this old *opera buffa?* We would never do so if Mozart's music were not so sensitive and so convincing. The music is so "intelligent" that we cannot help thinking closely and sympathetically about all the people in Mozart's operas—not only Don Giovanni but also Leporello and all the others.

Jean-Antoine Houdon

One of the most impressive artists of the late eighteenth century was the French sculptor Jean-Antoine Houdon (1740–1828). His work deserves to be better known, especially in the United States, where he voyaged in 1785 in the company of Benjamin Franklin. He did portrait busts of Washington, Jefferson, Franklin, John Paul Jones, Robert Fulton, and that other, more famous French visitor to our shores, Lafayette.

It is said that a sitting for Houdon was often a battle, with the sitter trying for days to hide his true personality and Houdon inevitably catching it in the end. His psychological penetration was remarkable, enabling him to portray exactly the personalities of the most diverse types. The emergence of this quality in Houdon can be linked with similar qualities in Jane Austen's novels (*Pride and Prejudice* was written in 1796) and in Mozart's supreme operas (*Don Giovanni* is discussed on pages 163 to 167). Many musicians feel they can sense the same sort of psychological subtlety and accuracy in Mozart's instrumental music, too. For thanks to its new flexibility of style, the music of the Viennese masters is constantly changing in a way that seems to be modelled on emotional experience.

Houdon's portrait of Voltaire (page 152), one of his most famous, shows us not only a man of extraordinary sharpness and humor—that we would know from reading the great philosopher's works—but also one of deep humanity, warmth, and charm. We are instantly drawn to this old gentleman. Rousseau (page 153; in bronze rather than marble) is another proposition: complex, intense, resolute, and dangerously ironic. And Franklin: look hard at page 168, and you will soon get the uncomfortable feeling that the marble is looking back at you, coolly sizing you up and figuring out how you can best be used to advantage.

Houdon is also famous for his busts of women and exceedingly pretty little girls. A certain Madame de Sérilly, above, has been caught with an indescribable look—devious, even furtive, and yet possibly also coquettish. Will some cunning scheme succeed in getting her out of a compromising situation, or will she have to rely once again on her beauty? This complicated and intriguing court lady could almost be a countess in some *opera buffa* by Mozart.

Joseph Haydn (1732–1809)

Haydn was a member of yet another musical family. His brother Michael also became an important composer, who, as it happens, worked beside Mozart's father at the court of the Archbishop of Salzburg. Joseph for most of his life served a noble family of Hungarian music lovers, the Esterházys, whose estate was situated forty miles outside of Vienna. An unusual painting of an opera performance at this estate is reproduced on pages 184 and 185; Haydn is conducting from the harpsichord.

The Esterházy family also had palaces in the city, and Haydn was the most famous composer around Vienna when Mozart arrived there in 1781 and became his friend. A year after Mozart's death, in 1792, young Beethoven came to Vienna to study with the sixty-year-old master, then at the very crest of his fame. Thus Haydn formed a personal link among the main members of the Viennese school.

It is an ironic fact that if Haydn had died at the age of thirty-five, like Mozart, he would hardly be remembered today. All his great music, and there are huge quantities of it, was written after he had passed that age: some sixty symphonies (out of a grand total of over a hundred) and a like number of string quartets, as well as piano sonatas, piano trios, Masses, and two celebrated oratorios. These last are *The Creation* and *The Seasons*, written to words translated from the English nature-poet James Thomson. *The Seasons* consists of descriptions of the four seasons (a strange subject for an oratorio!), and *The Creation*, too, though its real subject is God's creation of the world according to Genesis, spends much loving care in portraying His created natural objects. These works reflect the new respect for nature that grew up in this period, a respect that is very evident in contemporary landscape architecture such as that illustrated on page 178.

Perhaps the earthy tone which is often apparent in Haydn's music is another reflection of this intellectual current. Or perhaps it resulted from Haydn's own humble background. The latter does not, however, explain the sophistication, subtlety, and even musical "wit" that Haydn achieved in symphony after symphony and string quartet after string quartet. It was really Haydn who pioneered the Viennese style, and he handled it with a mastery that was not exceeded by any of the other composers.

It is gratifying to read that after his retirement from the service of the Esterházys, Haydn was invited on two occasions to visit London, then the world capital. He was wined and dined by society, even royalty, and presented with an honorary degree by Oxford University. He was applauded for his magnificent set of twelve *London* symphonies, and even drawn into a discreet autumnal flirtation with a widow (memorialized in the dedication of some of his best piano trios). Probably no other great composer has ever been so handsomely lionized abroad—though plenty of instances can be cited with performers, from the sopranos of the eighteenth and nineteenth centuries to the rock stars of the twentieth.

The Symphony

The symphony—a large, impressive concert piece for orchestra—is the most famous genre developed by the Viennese composers, and probably also the most important. It is not for nothing that we commonly speak of the *symphony* orchestra or *symphony* concerts. The standard symphony consists of four good-sized movements. First comes a fast movement, which may be preceded by a relatively short passage of slow music, called the *slow introduction.* Then there is a slow movement, than a minuet movement, and then another fast movement. Occasionally the order of the middle two movements is reversed.

In nearly all of their first movements, Viennese composers employed sonata form. Let us trace this through in the first movement of Haydn's Symphony No. 88, again in some detail. This will supplement our discussion of sonata form in Mozart's *Don Giovanni* Overture, for the treatment of form by the two composers, and hence the effect of their pieces, is very different.

The Symphony No. 88 is scored for a rather small orchestra, without clarinets (compare page 148)—and, oddly enough, the trumpets and drums do not play at all during the first movement. The slow introduction to this movement is short, too, and rather routine—at least by comparison with that of the Overture to *Don Giovanni.* Later, Haydn took a cue from Mozart and made his symphony introductions longer and more involved than this.

Exposition   The fast part of the movement begins with a lively little tune with a folk-like swing about it:

It soon dawns on us that in this movement Haydn is not going to wait till the development section to start developing his main theme. Part of this theme, a motive marked mainly by its rhythm, r, is heard repeatedly. In one of its manifestations, it serves as a bridge, changing tonality:

This reaches a strong cadence (though there is no complete stop), and the dynamics drop to a hush for the second group. Even the second theme has rhythmic connections with the original main theme:

Still another version of motive r is present in the cadence theme, which is initially played by the wind instruments alone:

After a firm but brief concluding passage, the exposition finally comes to an expectant halt.

In symphonies and sonatas (but not in overtures), composers often allow the performers of sonata-form movements the option of repeating the exposition — and even the development plus recapitulation, too. Since this particular symphony movement is quite brief, conductors often do repeat the whole exposition at this point. Such repeats do not include the slow introductions.

Development   The development begins by quietly working over fragments of the main theme. There are many modulations, going through tonalities that sound very tentative. The rhythms, too, sound tentative until a sudden forte starts up a new phase of development. This is resolutely contrapuntal, a riot of confusion in which the bridge, second theme, and cadence theme are all heard in and around the reigning rhythm r. But each has a new quality. The second theme is no longer quiet, the bridge no longer points in any clear direction, and the cadence theme no longer makes a firm cadence.

Another expectant stop, and we realize with a real sense of relief that the recapitulation is about to restore order.

Recapitulation   The first theme returns, safely in the original tonality but with a delightful new feature: a cool counterpoint is added high above it by a flute. Then the bridge is completely rewritten, the second group is abbreviated, and a short coda reminds us yet again (as if we need reminding!) of the first theme. The very last bars bring up an amusing new echo version of motive r:

Although this symphony movement employs sonata form as clearly as the Overture to *Don Giovanni* does, the two pieces hardly sound similar at all. Haydn treads the fine line between providing just enough contrast among his various themes to keep the interest up and making the themes similar enough in rhythm to create confusion and fun. We may lose track of the themes in this speedy movement, but in that case the joke is on us. We should be ready to laugh with Haydn (or at any rate, smile inwardly with him) as he runs the modest, even rustic theme through all those improbable developments. His ingenuity in finding new ways of making the familiar rhythm of motive r sparkle—down to a new idea in the very last bars—seems unlimited. It is qualities of this kind that make people speak of wit in Viennese music, and especially in music by Haydn.

Haydn's control of sonata form ensures that the piece does not sound rambling or arbitrary. He may loosen the reigns pretty far in the recapitulation, but while we are enjoying the relaxed sense of freedom in the presentation, we can tell that the exposition material is all arriving in the original tonality. Imaginative treatment of form only adds to the sense of exhilaration and high spirits.

Second Movement   The second movement of Symphony No. 88 is a glorious example of the Viennese composers' affection for tunes. A better way to put it might be *intoxication* with tunes, for in this case the movement contains scarcely any music besides the main melody—a remarkable circumstance, especially since the melody is really quite short:

Notice how many dynamic marks Haydn has put in to gain an expressive effect. Does this tune, lovely as it is, overstay its welcome? It appears no fewer than seven times. Haydn means to lend it fresh interest by presenting it in different tonalities and by adding little counterpoints above it, but he cannot bear to have them disturb the tune too much. This warm, direct, and somewhat hymn-like tune shows another side of Haydn, one that is just as typical as the "wit" in the earlier movement.

MINUET AND TRIO

Third Movement   The third movement of a typical Viennese symphony is a minuet and trio, as we said above. A few brief points about dances were made in the course of the discussion of Handel's *Fireworks Music*, page 118. These need to be extended at this point.

Baroque dances usually consist of two parts, roughly equal in length. Each part is repeated, that is, played twice in succession before the music goes on, and the dances tend to come in pairs, alternating in an A B A pattern. The second dance in such a pair is called the *trio* (a curious name until we learn that at one time it was often scored for three instruments; the reduction in scoring made for an effective contrast with the other dance). Thus a minuet and trio simply amount to a minuet plus another minuet—probably contrasting in mood—after which the original minuet is played a second time. However, on this second occasion the internal sections of the original minuet are each played only once, rather than twice, as in the first playing.

A baroque minuet movement can be charted as follows:

Minuet	Trio	Minuet
A	B	A
‖:a:‖:b:‖	‖:c:‖:d:‖	a b

The a's, b's, c's, and d's stand for the internal parts of the minuets. The signs ‖: and :‖ tell the player to make an exact repeat of the music between them.

The Viennese composers generally extended the internal form of their minuets and trios so that the music of the first part (a or c) comes back again, either exactly or with some alterations, at the end of the second part. In other words, their minuets developed internal a b a structures, and the two parts of the dance were no longer roughly equal in length. Most Viennese minuet movements fall into one of the following schemes:

	Minuet	Trio	Minuet
	A	B	A
	‖:a:‖:b a:‖	‖:c:‖:d c:‖	a b a
OR			
	‖:a:‖:b a':‖	‖:c:‖:d c':‖	a b a'

Prime marks indicate that the second a and c embody significant extensions or alterations of the first ones.*

The two Haydn sonata minuets on pages 176 and 177 ought to be well within the range of most beginning pianists. The first minuet is in the ‖:a:‖:b:‖:c:‖:d:‖ a b form that occurs more commonly in baroque music; the second is in ‖:a:‖:b a':‖ ‖:c:‖:d c':‖ a b' a form. Characteristically, Haydn employs phrases of different lengths: 10, 10, 12, and 12 measures in the first minuet; 8, 8, 6, 8, 4, and 6 measures in the second. This would probably confuse anyone who tried to dance to them, but it makes them more interesting as pieces of music for playing or listening.

Do you notice anything peculiar about the first minuet and trio?

Back to the minuet of Symphony No. 88—which like very many Haydn minuets, has a rollicking country-dance feeling about it. The trio contrasts by its quiet dynamics, but here, too, a rustic element is introduced by the low drone notes held by the violas and bassoons. They seem to evoke peasant instruments such as bagpipes or a hurdy-gurdy (see page 215). This "popular" tone did not prevent Haydn from putting in many ingenious details: for instance, the disguised return of c' in the trio.

---

* Strictly speaking, and in spite of the diagram, the two A's are different, for the second A lacks the internal repetitions of the first. But this difference is not considered "significant" enough to earn a prime mark. A change of melody, harmony, or number of measures would be.

Fourth Movement Haydn's last movement is a <u>rondo</u>. The rondo is a relatively simple form in which one main tune alternates with other tunes or with other sections of music in a pattern such as A B A C A D A or A B A C A B A, etc. The main tune here (A) is a cheerful, busy item:

There is an element of tease in this tune because it sounds suspiciously like the main theme of the first movement; certainly it relies on a single motive (the first ten notes) almost as consistently—and twice as comically. Notice the sudden jolts in dynamics. The tune falls into an ‖: a :‖: b a′ :‖ scheme, with a "witty" touch at the end of section b, in the first half of measure 24. The last two notes (two D's) run right into a′, the return of a, which begins with an upbeat consisting of the same two D's.

The high points in a rondo come with the returns of the main tune, A. So Haydn makes these returns as interesting and amusing as possible by playing around with two upbeat D's ahead of time in a deceptive fashion:

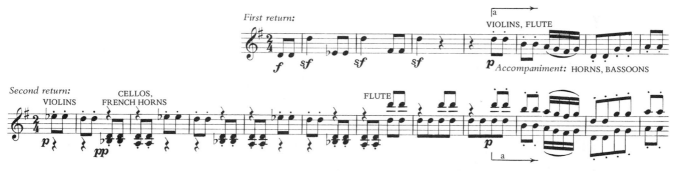

Do you hear how this last return to A enlarges on the run-in to a′ within the theme itself? As has been indicated above in the example, Haydn makes some effective changes of tone color in the returns of A, in spite of his relatively small orchestra. The dynamics are also neatly controlled.

This particular rondo can be charted as A B A′ C A Coda. (In A′, the little a′ within the tune is much changed.) Just as in the first movement of the symphony, fragments of A are constantly poking their heads into the other sections. The result is again a high-spirited and rather brainy piece with a high degree of unity. The combination of qualities such as these with strong rhythms and good-humored, folk-like melodies is Haydn's special hallmark.

Haydn, Minuet from Piano Sonata No. 41 in A (H.26)

Minuet da Capo
*(i.e., play the Minuet
again without internal repeats)*

Haydn, Minuet from Piano Sonata No. 35 in A♭ (H.43)

Minuet da Capo

A Late Eighteenth-Century Park

Between this park and the baroque park shown on page 110, the change in concept is striking indeed. Nature is no longer sternly controlled but is allowed to run free and delight us with its rich and rather mysterious random arrangements. Yet it is important to understand that this landscape is every bit as artificial, and just as precisely calculated, as the other. It has all been laid out and planted to create the impression of "wild" vegetation in an especially engaging manifestation. The paths were planned to seem to wander aimlessly, wild flowers were transplanted, and the lake was dug with carefully irregular outlines. Whereas the early eighteenth-century park seems cool and serene, the late eighteenth-century one seems soft, gentle, inviting.

Both parks employ "classical" features: rows of statues and urns in one case, a little imitation Greek temple in the other. But whereas in the baroque park the classical element serves to emphasize the park's regularity and man-made quality, the temple here seems to peep out accidentally from under the great trees. It seems to be a natural—at any rate, a most pleasing—outcome of the landscape rather than something imposed upon it. If we refer to the visual arts of this period as "classical" or "neoclassical," then, we should realize that classical elements were not used for their own sake but for their associations.

The view is from the beautiful garden at Stourhead, England, which was designed between 1750 and 1780. Today it looks much the same as in those times, as is shown by the old engraving; it formed a perfect site for Stanley Kubrick's period movie *Barry Lyndon*.

Viennese Chamber Music

The Viennese composers wrote chamber music (page 102) for all kinds of instrumental combinations. Beethoven wrote a popular septet for clarinet, bassoon, French horn, violin, viola, cello, and double bass. Haydn wrote numerous trios for an archaic instrument called the baryton—not a baritone horn, not a baritone singer, but a peculiar sort of bass viol with additional strings to pluck. The main chamber-music combinations of the time were the piano trio (piano, violin, cello) and, most important of all, the string quartet (violin, violin, viola, cello).

PIANO TRIO
STRING QUARTET

String quartets have a reputation for being esoteric, and many listeners have the feeling that they must be dull. This is not the case; Haydn and Mozart wrote as many beautiful quartets as symphonies, and Beethoven's sixteen examples include some of his very greatest music. But it is true, of course, that in tone color and dynamics, the string quartet medium is more restrained than (say) the symphony orchestra. You have to listen carefully enough to get past the level of tone color to the real muscle of the music—to rhythm, melody, and texture. As an introduction to Viennese chamber music, we shall take Mozart's Clarinet Quintet, a work which adds the more colorful clarinet to the four standard string-quartet instruments.

MOZART   QUINTET FOR CLARINET AND STRINGS, K.581 (1789)

Side 6

Mozart's Clarinet Quintet (he wrote only one) was composed not long before his death. It shares a mood common to much of his late music, a mood rather different from the busy, brilliant confidence of the fast section of the Overture to *Don Giovanni*. Some of the same brightness is present, but there is also a quality of serenity and a tinge of lassitude and regret.

This Clarinet Quintet is a fine example of the new interest in tone color among the Viennese composers—especially fine, perhaps, because it is so unflashy and restrained. How well Mozart understood the clarinet and how fully he exploited its possibilities! He let it perform brilliant runs and hold mellow long notes (which sound much more effective than long notes on a violin); he had it play sensuous tunes and carry hard, driving rhythms; and he used the vibrant low register with special imagination, as though scooping up cups of water from a dark well. If today the clarinet is recognized as the richest and most flexible of all woodwind instruments, that is because Mozart showed composers after him how to capitalize on all its resources of tone color. Certainly the Clarinet Quintet cannot be conceived of as transposed for some other solo instrument, as might be the case with a baroque concerto grosso.

First Movement   The first movement of the Clarinet Quintet counts as a quiet one by the standards of other music of the time, such as Haydn's Symphony No. 88 or Mozart's Overture to *Don Giovanni*. It is nevertheless considerably more varied and dynamic than a baroque piece would be. The four string instruments, without the clarinet, play the peaceful main theme:

But the vivid interruption by the clarinet marks this instrument at once as a force of energy within the group. The clarinet introduces the next figure, too. This begins by sounding like a fluid continuation of the main theme, but soon shows signs of pressing forward into new territory, and we recognize it as the bridge. After an abrupt stop, the second group makes a definite contrast through its tone of muted agitation:

Agitation increases when the clarinet takes up the theme in an expressive new version. Then another theme, the final-sounding cadence theme, starts to wind up the exposition—

—though at the very end it is the main theme that returns in the violin to make the big cadence.

To begin the development section, the clarinet emerges slowly from the depths to play the main theme once again. But this statement sounds really fresh, and therefore counts as "development," for at least two reasons. First, we hear at last the theme with the rich, "liquid" tone quality of the clarinet. Second, we hear it suddenly in a new tonality, which provides a gorgeous new glow.

The interruption following the theme now has to be played by the violin, and the rest of the development consists of vigorous treatment of this interruption (which is surprising material for development, consisting as it does of neutral-sounding passage-work). There is much unrest; the interruption figure passes from one instrument to another, from one tonality to another. Finally things calm down into a little retransition passage, which is clearly preparing for the return of something familiar to stabilize all the previous action.

As usual with Mozart, the recapitulation by and large parallels the exposition, though of course all the music remains in the same tonality. Consequently the section sounds settled and essentially at rest, even though in the second group the clarinet grows more and more emotional. The clarinet also takes the lead in a very lovely extension of the cadence theme. It introduces some transitory new figures, before a brief restatement of the first theme concludes the recapitulation, just as it had concluded the exposition. The cadence theme has been extended, but there is no coda.

Second Movement The second movement of Mozart's Clarinet Quintet centers around a long slow melody for the leading instrument. The two violins are directed to put on mutes to muffle the tone.* If we respond to this melody, and its glorification of the sound of the clarinet, the movement will stand out as a tranquil oasis in the middle of the other, more active movements. None of the other Viennese composers, not even Schubert, wrote such beautiful slow movements. On the other hand, if we do not warm to the melody—and taste for melody is sometimes a very personal thing—the movement will probably not offer much of interest. The clarinet plays the long melody twice, at full length, in just the same way, with only a rather wispy passage of scales and dialogues with the first violin to separate the two statements.

Third Movement The minuet movement of the Clarinet Quintet happens to be furnished with two trios, a rather rare occurrence which results in an A B A C A arrangement. It can be thought of as a simple type of rondo (page 175). The internal dance parts are repeated only in the first A, in B, and in C.

The minuets of chamber-music pieces, especially those by Mozart, naturally tend to be more elegant than the more robust minuets of symphonies. Here the first trio, B, scored for the string instruments alone, recaptures the disturbed tone of the second group of the first movement. The second trio, C, is an accompanied clarinet solo, emanating a peculiarly Mozartian grace, though obviously he meant it to sound countrified. Perhaps he even meant it as a tribute or a compliment to his friend Haydn, who made a specialty of rustic-sounding minuets (page 174).

THEME AND VARIATIONS

Fourth Movement Another relatively simple form was used by Mozart for the last movement of the Clarinet Quintet, the <u>theme and variations</u>. This starts with a lively and somewhat innocent-sounding tune:

There follow five variations, sections in which the composer runs through the theme again, measure by measure, from beginning to end, varying certain aspects of it while keeping other aspects constant:

---

* Violin mutes are small clamp-like devices which fit on the part of the instrument that holds the strings up from the body, the so-called *bridge* (not to be confused with the bridge section in sonata form). See the diagram on page 364. Mutes for French horns, trumpets, trombones, and tubas are large conical wedges that fit into the open ends of these instruments.

It is hard to make a general rule about the theme-and-variations form since the elements that composers vary and keep fixed differ from period to period. We are acquainted with Bach's Passacaglia for Organ (a special kind of theme and variations). But what is true of a baroque passacaglia may not be true of a Mozart quintet movement — or of a twentieth-century jazz piece (see page 356).

Variations in the Viennese style maintain the dimensions of the theme in measures, the phrase structure of the theme, including the position of the cadences, and the main outlines of its harmony. The melody itself tends to change from variation to variation, though sometimes Mozart keeps the original melody, too (see the beginnings of variations 1 and 4 — though at the ends of these variations, the melody gets lost again). In variation 4, it is the rapid passage-work played by the clarinet simultaneously with the tune on the violin that counts as the "variation."

The point of the variations is to obtain many contrasting moods out of the same theme, which is transformed but always still discernible. Variation 2 seems rather nervous, and variation 4 brilliant. Variation 3 captures once again that note of agitation which briefly clouds all the earlier movements of the quintet, and variation 5 may remind us of the tranquil slow movement. For here Mozart changes the tempo for the first time, to an adagio (slow). After this meditative, nostalgic slow variation, part of the theme returns in its original melodic form, but a little faster. The movement concludes with some new continuations and repeated cadences in the Viennese manner.

Opera Buffa

A performance of an *opera buffa* at the Esterházy castle near Vienna, probably a work by Joseph Haydn, and probably in 1775. Haydn worked for the Esterházy family for most of his life. The composer himself is shown playing the harpsichord.

Light and flexible, comic opera (*opera buffa*) typified the operatic world of the late eighteenth century, just as heroic opera (*opera seria*) characterized the baroque. If we place this picture next to the illustration of the baroque opera on page 121, everything in the comparison seems to stress the difference. Instead of the grandiose, architectural set designed for great princes and princesses, we have here an intimate and unassuming country scene, well stocked with painted animals. The people are grouped on the stage lightheartedly, in contrast with the self-serious poses of the baroque actors. The young Italian ladies are clearing up some comic complications with the visiting Turks.

The colors show a new lightness of spirit, too. Instead of the deep, rich tints of the baroque picture, this one employs light blues, greens, and yellows, with the charming brick-colored coats of the orchestra men making a bright contrast, which we might be tempted to compare with a musical contrast in the Viennese style. Even the architecture of the theater seems to be on the light side. The big columns are flattened out and marbled so that they do not attract much attention to themselves.

"Storm and Stress"

Vivacity and serenity, perhaps, are the typical moods explored by the early Viennese composers. Within this broad general description, they found an inexhaustible fund of variety, as is shown by the various movements of Mozart's Clarinet Quintet and Haydn's Symphony No. 88—to look no further. But it is important to understand that these same composers also probed into the darker emotional regions. They did not do this so very often, but when they did it was always almost with a very powerful effect. Their first efforts in this vein come from the 1770s and seem to reflect a general current in the arts of this time known as "Storm and Stress," or *Sturm und Drang* in German.

This was a short-lived but intense movement which we can now see as a preview of Romanticism. The German theater was jolted by a number of furious revolutionary plays (one of them entitled *Sturm und Drang*), and German literature by the most famous of all novels of unrequited love and suicide, *The Sorrows of Young Werther* by Johann Wolfgang von Goethe. Some painters, too, reached for more somber subject matter. Storm scenes became popular, and the strange Swiss-English artist Henry Fuseli began setting down such macabre visions as *The Nightmare* (see page 239).

The Viennese composers approached the "Storm and Stress" mood in some of their most memorable compositions, as we already know from Mozart's *Don Giovanni*. Haydn wrote a number of symphonies in the 1770s that are much more moody and intense than his No. 88. The same can be said of one of Mozart's most famous and greatest pieces, the Symphony No. 40 in G minor.

MOZART   SYMPHONY IN G MINOR, K. 550 (1788)   *Side 5*

In the following short discussion of Mozart's symphony, we shall single out only a few of its admirable features for special notice. Once again, the main theme of the first movement is presented homophonically—so much so that the accompaniment starts up one measure ahead of the theme itself:

The subdued nervous tension of this theme, a blend of refinement and great agitation, stamps the first movement unforgettably. The theme contains motives which will go through extensive alterations in the course of the development section. The second theme is divided between the strings and woodwinds:

This is repeated at once with the role of the instruments reversed, the strings taking the notes originally played by the winds, and vice versa. The instrumental alternations contribute something absolutely essential to the character of the theme and serve to show Mozart's fine ear for tone color.

In this movement, the contrast in tonality between the first theme and the second is particularly clear. So is the feeling of their both being held to the same tonality in the recapitulation. Mozart gives the recapitulated second theme a wonderful new quality of pathos, and he provides the cadence theme with unexpected emotional depths.

The second movement, also in sonata form, is a calm and very beautiful interlude. The minuet and trio fall into the usual A B A form (without any second trio, as in the Clarinet Quintet). The minuet itself, however, has been transformed in spirit from the usual easygoing dance; it is as though the mood of the first movement has been made more gloomy and intense. Part of this effect comes from its contrapuntal texture, especially in the second part of the minuet proper. As we have said, counterpoint usually means tension to a Viennese composer, whereas a baroque composer uses it as a normal and neutral stylistic element.

A serious symphony requires a serious, dramatic last movement. Mozart would not have ended this symphony, as he ended the Clarinet Quintet, with a form such as theme and variations, which tends to emphasize repetition and decoration rather than contrast and forward movement. Once again he turned to sonata form, beginning with this tense, brusque, explosive theme:

A particularly angry transformation of this theme opens the development section:

This modulates furiously and sets up a mood of conflict which the recapitulation brings under control only with difficulty.

This movement—indeed, this symphony as a whole—forecasts a significant change of emphasis in the Viennese style that is usually associated with Beethoven. Musical contrast is seen in psychological terms as serious tension, conflict, or strife. As the "Storm and Stress" movement warned, the seemingly stable society of Mozart and Haydn's youth was perched on a powder keg. When this exploded, music soon reflected the shocks.

The Concerto

SOLO CONCERTO

On page 100 we discussed the baroque concerto grosso at the time of Vivaldi and Bach in terms of the basic concerto idea. This basic idea—the contest or contrast between a group of soloists and the orchestra—was refined as the eighteenth century progressed. The contrast was made sharper and sharper; the norm became the <u>solo concerto</u>, with a single soloist, who was that much freer than the solo group and could be treated as a formidable virtuoso. At the same time, the orchestra was growing. The Viennese orchestra was much more flexible and powerful than the baroque concerto orchestra. So the balance between two such forces presented a real problem—but it was the sort of problem that brought out the best in the great composers of the time.

Listening to one of their concertos, then, we find ourselves listening to a constantly shifting give and take between two opposing forces. It is a fascinating contest, in which neither side can ever emerge definitely as the winner. To put it in general terms, the art of the Viennese concerto was to pit the soloist's greater mobility, brilliance, and expressive abilities against the orchestra's increased power and variety of tone color.

MOZART PIANO CONCERTO NO. 24 IN C MINOR, K. 491 (1786)

Mozart's C minor Piano Concerto is another of his intense, "dark" compositions reflecting some of the same forces that erupted in the "Storm and Stress" period. The opening orchestral theme, for example, is remarkably forceful and even tragic in quality. Notice how perfectly this theme has been designed for the orchestra; it would not sound well on the piano and the piano never plays it. Then the first theme which the piano does play, when it finally comes in, has a flexible "solo" quality which would not suit the orchestra. By the use of such characteristic themes, and by many other means, Mozart gives sharp individuality to the two forces in his concertos and works out complex patterns of interplay between them.

The first of the three movements of a Viennese concerto employs sonata form—or rather, a somewhat complicated adaptation of sonata form made to accommodate the special contrasts alluded to above. Another special feature of concerto first movements is the <u>cadenza</u>. This comes just before the end. In this concerto, after the last playing of the tragic theme, the orchestra falls silent; in a spell of solo virtuosity, the pianist shows his mettle by making new versions of the themes, indulging in brilliant feats of virtuosity, and so on. (But today cadenzas are usually written out, not improvised.)

CADENZA

Second Movement A beautiful slow rondo in the form: A B A C A Coda. The high points in a rondo are the returns of the main theme, A; the piano always takes charge at these moments, playing its thoughtful, rather wistful opening tune. The contrasting sections B and C are played by the orchestra woodwinds, answered by the piano. Mozart's sensitivity to tone color is again in evidence: compare the tense, melancholy quality of section B, featuring the oboes, with the smooth, luminous quality of section C, featuring clarinets.

Third Movement This concerto finale is not a rondo, as would be more usual, but a set of variations on a bleak-sounding march tune, played by the orchestra:

Variation 1: Not surprisingly, the piano shines in all the variations, but Mozart keeps a sense of balance by beginning the variations alternately in the piano and in the orchestra. The whole of variation 1 belongs to the piano. It sounds at once more personal—more fluent, more anxious—than the orchestra.

Variation 2 (double): A double variation is one in which each half of the theme is varied differently in the repetition. So if the theme is diagrammed ||:a:||:b:||, variation 1 will be ||:a':||:b':|| and variation 2 will be a'' a''' b'' b''', etc. The woodwinds in the orchestra, featuring the oboes, lead off with a'', answered by rapid runs in the piano as a'''.

Variation 3 (double): With a sudden change of mood, the piano starts a furious version of the march tune, which is freely repeated by the orchestra.

Variation 4 (double): A much quieter, consoling variation is initiated by the woodwinds again, but this time featuring the clarinets (remember section C of the slow movement). The orchestra quietly shows that in tone color, at least, it is clearly master.

Variation 5 (double): As though to show *his* abilities, the piano plays continuously all through this double variation, beginning with an expressive contrapuntal version of the tune and continuing in the raging style of variation 3.

Variation 6 (double): Light-hearted, airy counterpoint in the flute, oboes, and bassoons is answered in a free repetition by the piano.

Variation 7: Repetitions are omitted from this variation, as the orchestra (with the piano in close dialogue) returns to its original version of the march tune. Then, after a short cadenza, there follows a short but very moving coda. It starts like another variation, for piano alone, in $\frac{6}{8}$ time, and then proceeds more freely. The piano keeps reiterating a despairing little figure, but the more tough-minded orchestra brings the movement — and the whole concerto, with its almost bewildering array of dark emotions — to an abrupt, forceful cadence.

Ludwig van Beethoven (1770–1827)

Probably no figure in any of the arts meets with such a strong universal response as Beethoven. People may respect Michelangelo and Shakespeare, they may admire Leonardo da Vinci and pity Van Gogh, but Beethoven instantly summons up a powerful, positive image: that of the tough, ugly, angry genius forcing out one deeply expressive masterpiece after another in the teeth of adversity. His music has enjoyed broad-based, uninterrupted popularity from its own day to the present; today its place is equally secure with unsophisticated listeners and with the most learned of musicians. The bicentennial of his birth in 1970 produced, among other things, a commercial edition on records of his complete output, a package running to seventy-five LPs. His themes have been turned into pop songs. His beetling brows have been emblazoned on T-shirts. He has been immortalized by a comic strip.

While the popular Beethoven image has been much romanticized over the years, it has a solid basis in fact. His life was not very interesting in terms of outer events, but there was one shattering inner event: at the age of thirty he began to lose his hearing. The effect of this calamity could be compared with that of a craftsman having both hands amputated. Even if one could compose with the "inner ear," no musician had ever existed purely as a composer; one had to play, conduct, run a musical establishment. But thanks to his genius and to his uncompromising personality, Beethoven made himself into a pure composer, and he forced the aristocracy of Vienna to support him at it, more or less on his own terms. Whereas Mozart had starved in Vienna, Beethoven made a living and even amassed some stocks and shares.

His capital, we might say, was a new concept of artistic genius which society was now ready to support. Beethoven did not create this concept, but he exemplified it powerfully for his own age, and he still exemplifies it today. No longer a mere craftsman, the artist suffers and creates; endowed not just with greater talent but with a greater soul, he suffers and creates for mankind. Music was no longer held down to bodily appurtenances like the ear or the fingers. It existed in the highest reaches of the artist's spirit.

Beethoven is sometimes linked with the French Revolution. The outer connections are slight, even though from a distance he did dedicate one of his greatest works, the *Eroica* ("Heroic") Symphony, to Napoleon, only to scratch out the dedication in a rage when he learned that the liberator had turned tyrant (see page 197). The inner connections are more significant, perhaps. To Beethoven's generation, the French Revolution represented an ideal of perfectibility, not so much of society (as Beethoven himself acknowledged in his scrapped dedication) as of human aspiration. That is what the triumph over deafness meant to Beethoven, and also to those of his contemporaries who were swept away by his music and watched his accomplishment with awe.

And that is what generations since have cherished in Beethoven's music. As we listen to the *Eroica* Symphony, we surely suspect that it had less to do with Napoleon than with the composer's own self-image. The sense of heroic striving and inner conquest is what emerges so magnificently in Beethoven's most famous compositions.

His output has been categorized as belonging to three periods. The first of these reminds us of his close connections with the earlier Viennese composers, for in his first hundred works or so, Beethoven followed in the footsteps of Mozart and Haydn. There is certainly a highly individual flavor in the first-period works—as witness, for example, the well-known *Pathétique* Sonata and indeed many other of his early piano sonatas. But Beethoven was not one of those composers who step forward with something dazzlingly new at a very tender age. After a slow development, he arrived at the second period, the characteristically "heroic" period of the *Eroica* Symphony, the Fifth and Seventh Symphonies, the Overture to *Egmont*, the *Appassionata* Sonata, and most of his other best-known works. Then at the end of his life a new style evolved, which is now regarded as Beethoven's greatest. We shall return to the third-period compositions later.

BEETHOVEN   SYMPHONY NO. 5 IN C MINOR (1807–1808)   *Side 7*

The tag "Fate knocking at the door," which is always associated with Beethoven's Fifth Symphony, sounds as if it were a romantic invention, but apparently it originated with the composer himself. Over the course of the four movements, the listener seems to experience not just the conquest of fate but a complete demolition of it. The first movement—the actual "fate" movement—is one of Beethoven's greatest sonata-form pieces, and the scherzo is an amazingly imaginative creation. As an introduction to Beethoven's strengths, as well as his excesses, we can hardly do better than this most famous of all symphonies.

First Movement Coming to the first movement of Beethoven's Fifth Symphony after the music of Haydn and Mozart, one is likely to be struck most forcibly by the differences. Beethoven was always a conspicuously "unpretty" composer even in his first-period pieces, which stay closest to the older masters. In second-period pieces such as the Fifth Symphony, the tremendous energy and sheer power seem like a far cry from the elegance and wit of the earlier Viennese style.

But we discover something interesting if we try to pinpoint the actual stylistic features that make us think so. One such feature is the thorough saturation of the music by a single motive (♪♩♩♩), which occurs constantly and seems to grow in endless versions. Others are the breathless sense of development, the many emphatic cadences preceded by extended preparatory material, the short sections of music in sharp contrast, and the long passages of balanced repetition. All these features we know from Haydn and Mozart. Haydn's Symphony No. 88 even carries a single motive through the entire first movement with something of the same consistency and sense of growth.

What is the real difference, then? Not the basic style itself, but the way it is being used—or, rather, the expressive purpose it is being used for. The Viennese style was flexible enough so that a composer with a certain frame of mind could take it in deadly earnest. Beethoven insisted on treating musical contrast not as a source of humor, as Haydn did, but as a source of conflict, a confrontation. In the development process, he saw not merely a stimulating exploration, as Mozart often did, but a struggle—sometimes a struggle to the death. A recapitulation is more than the occasion of relief and stability; to Beethoven it is a moment of exultation, rescue, triumph, consummation. As we study Beethoven pieces, we shall find ourselves employing the same terms as we did for earlier Viennese music; but the adjectives will be very different.

Exposition (*"Confrontation"*)   The example below shows how the famous motive (♪♩♩♩) first forms the rhythmic substance of the main theme, then begins the bridge, and even mutters away underneath the quiet, song-like second theme, which in other ways contrasts so obviously with everything else:

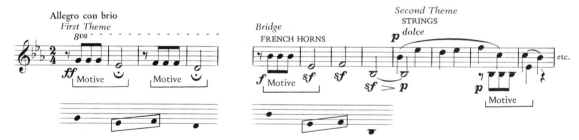

The bold horn call, which serves as the bridge, behaves like an unusual example of the type in many ways, but it does one essential thing very clearly: it really cements the new tonality and with power and authority clears the terrain for the second theme.

The example also shows how the first theme and the bridge both consist of a similar aggregate of four pitches (never mind the rhythm, for the moment). The bridge can be regarded as a kind of broadening out of the first theme, hinging on the two middle pitches. Does this seem like an artificial way of thinking of these two themes? Any doubts on this score will be dispelled by Beethoven's own actions in the development section and coda.

Remember that it was the Viennese convention to allow an optional repetition of the exposition in sonata form (page 172). Generally, conductors do indeed repeat the present exposition, after a stormy passage (featuring the main motive once again) has led from the second theme to a strong cadence.

Development ("Struggle") As is often the case, the beginning notes of this development section make an immediate modulation, the first of many restless changes in tonality that electrify the section. The present modulation sounds like the crack of doom, thanks in part to Beethoven's orchestration, simple as it is (the effect is created mainly by two French horns). For a time the first theme is developed, leading to an earsplitting climax, then the bridge. In the following passage, Beethoven extracts the two middle pitches of the bridge, which we mentioned above, and echoes them between high wind instruments and lower strings:

Then at the end of the example, he actually breaks them in two and starts echoing just a single note! This kind of development process is called *fragmentation.* It may seem a bit crazy to point to a single half note in the middle of a score and say that it was "derived" from the middle of some particular theme. Yet because of the way in which Beethoven has led up to this point, each of these single half notes is heard as a logical and enormously tense outcome of the fragmentation of the bridge theme.

Beethoven is famous for the tension he builds up in sonata-form movements prior to the recapitulation. In the Fifth Symphony, the hush at this point becomes almost unbearable. Finally the whole orchestra seems to grab the listener by the lapels and shake him back and forth, shouting the motive again and again until finally the first theme settles out, safe and sound in the original tonality. Now, this is much the same technique as that used by Haydn in preparing the humorous returns of his rondo theme in Symphony No. 88 and elsewhere. The opening motive of a theme is played over and over again until it serves as the kickoff of the theme itself. But in place of Haydn's wit, Beethoven gives a sense of tremendous achievement.

Recapitulation ("Consummation") Very close to the exposition, except for an expressive slow solo for the oboe—an extremely original and affecting moment. Everything holds to the original tonality.

Coda Long, action-packed codas are a feature of Beethoven's movements in sonata form. The stormy passage at the end of the recapitulation does not come to a cadence, as it did in the exposition, but instead plunges headlong into a violent climax reminiscent of one in the development section. Then this powerful concluding idea appears:

Compare the bottom line of this with the example on page 192. Here the *pitches* of the main theme are played in the *rhythm* of the bridge, and then those two middle notes—the common ground between the themes—are emphasized by a long downward sequence. This does not strike us as an abstract demonstration of ingenious theme-building. It adds something important to the loudness and rhythmic drive of this passage: a sense of tightness and wonder, wonder that the basic themes of the movement can be expanded into ever-new emotional gestures. The triumph over fate is the triumph over musical raw materials.

Second Movement After so tense and urgent a beginning, Beethoven deliberately made the second movement of the Fifth Symphony relatively gentle in tone and relaxed in form. Like the second movement of Haydn's Symphony No. 88, this piece centers on a single short tune, which appears seven times in relatively simple variations:

The tune reaches a climax at the end, a climax with something of the character of a fanfare.

We have stressed the Viennese composers' affection for tunes. Beethoven's melody may not be as beautiful as Haydn's, but perhaps the movement makes up for this by its interesting form. A second theme, not altogether unrelated to the first, appears and sounds even more like a fanfare:

This songlike movement has its moments of mystery and more than one hint of not-so-distant military music. It ends firmly with the first fanfare.

SCHERZO

Third Movement The very interesting third movement is a free <u>scherzo</u>. Beethoven developed this type of movement out of the Viennese minuet and used it as a substitute. The meter is triple, as in the minuet, but the tempo is faster. As for the mood, when Beethoven refers to a "joke" (*scherzo*, in Italian), we may think instead of an impatient and sometimes explosive rush.

Beethoven's earliest scherzos took over the form of the minuet and trio:

Scherzo	*Trio*	*Scherzo*
A	B	A
‖: a :‖: b a' :‖	‖: c :‖: d c' :‖	a b a'

Later he often expanded the form to A B A B A Coda, and ignored some or all of the internal ‖:a:‖:b a':‖ and ‖:c:‖:d c':‖ plans. The present scherzo runs as follows:

Scherzo		Trio				Scherzo	
A		B				A' ⟶	
	‖:c:‖ d	c'	d	c''			
						New orchestration	

There are striking differences of tone color in this piece. In the scherzo part (A), contrast between two themes—a quiet, somewhat ominous one and a raging, loud one—is heightened by the instrumentation. Cellos and double basses answered by woodwinds play the first theme, whereas French horns play the other. The trio (B) begins with the double basses alone—an unusual, gruff sound which does perhaps constitute a "joke." Then in section c'' and in the whole of A', the orchestration changes radically. Pizzicato strings (plucked with the finger instead of being played with the bow) and a brittle-sounding oboe replace the smooth and raging sounds heard before. Everything is transformed into a quite unexpected mood, a mood approximating mystery, numbness, even terror.

PIZZICATO

Fourth Movement   The point of this change in tone color appears in the sequel, the most unusual idea in this symphony: Beethoven runs the ghostly scherzo right into the blaring last movement. Thus the latter has the very literal effect of triumph over some sort of adversity. The transitional passage between the movements features another famous tone color in its ominous drumbeats on the timpani (the rhythm is that of the second scherzo theme). Then after a huge crescendo, the last movement introduces trombones and a piccolo for the first time, over and above the normal forces of the Viennese symphony orchestra (page 148).

Again in sonata form, this last movement adopts the accents of a military march to create a steady mood of rejoicing. Perhaps in mood it is a bit exaggerated, though in making such a judgment we should give due weight to its role in balancing the grim struggle of the earlier movements. The coda of this movement is one of the most emphatic in all music.

But whether we find the movement as a whole exhilarating or merely exhausting, we should be able to appreciate another highly original stroke of musical form at the retransition, the passage leading from the development section to the recapitulation. The second theme of the scherzo reappears for just a moment, a complete surprise (and even a change in tempo and meter, from $\frac{2}{2}$ back to $\frac{3}{4}$). This theme now sounds neither raging nor ghostly; it seems instead like a dim memory. It has come to tell that the battle has been won. Fate and terror alike have yielded to Beethoven's forceful, optimistic vision.

The Age of Revolutions

Revolutions are never the work of the oppressed masses alone. Financial interests come into play, intellectuals argue the case, and artists plead the cause. And none of these people can foresee the end of the course of events once it is put in motion. The American Revolution led to a stable, rational political order that was the admiration of the liberal world for years after the Enlightenment. The French Revolution backfired in political terms, though it left an unforgettable legacy to romanticism and the European consciousness.

Our first picture is of the Boston Massacre of 1770—which some historians say was a case of justified self-defense on the part of British soldiers provoked by an ugly mob. However this may be, this propaganda picture was widely promulgated, and by none other than Paul

Revere. Some think the amateur artist was Revere, too. An inflammatory poem was added:

Unhappy Boston! see thy sons deplore
Thy hallow'd walks besmear'd with guiltless gore,
While faithless PRESTON and his savage Bands
With murd'rous Rancour stretch their bloody Hands;
Like fierce Barbarians grinning o'er their Prey
Approve the Carnage and enjoy the Day. . . .

Thus stoked, the memory of the Boston Massacre smoldered for five years until the American Revolution broke out.

The second picture illustrates a bitter irony of the kind revolutions breed. Napoleon was first hailed by liberals

as the savior of the French Revolution, but they discerned an ominous new turn when he had himself crowned Emperor in 1804. Beethoven, who was about to call his latest symphony "Bonaparte" in admiration, hastily scratched out the dedication and substituted the neutral title *Sinfonia Eroica* ("Heroic Symphony"). And Napoleon's imperialistic policies led France into calamitous campaigns in Spain and Russia. With a ferocity that had scarcely been matched in all of Europe's endless wars of the previous century, the Spanish people rose up against oppression by a country that had only recently overthrown its own oppressors. France lost 300,000 troops in Spain alone, a number about equal to the total population of Paris in those days.

The French atrocities in Spain found a great painter to record them, Francisco Goya. Besides the famous painting shown below, *The Third of May, 1808,* Goya did a series of etchings called *The Disasters of War,* some of which are too ghastly to be reproduced in an ordinary book.

It was no news in 1808 that war was disastrous. What was new was the passion with which some artists were now identifying with popular causes and using their art to plead those causes. There was a very new sense of the artist's importance and authority. Goya and even Beethoven are cases in point, and only sixteen years later, Byron died in Greece, where he had gone to fight and write for that nation's independence. Whatever historians might tell us, can we believe that the executions of May 3 were "justified"?

BEETHOVEN   OVERTURE TO *EGMONT* (1809)

Another composition in Beethoven's heroic mold is the Overture to *Egmont*, written to precede a play by Johann Wolfgang von Goethe, the most famous literary man of the time. Beethoven also wrote a good deal of other incidental music for *Egmont*, including songs, background music, and a concluding "Symphony of Victory." The play tells of the unjust oppression of the Dutch by the Spaniards in the sixteenth century and of the martyrdom of their hero, Prince Egmont. Beethoven was much attracted to subjects of this kind. Some elements of the *Egmont* story appeared in the one opera he composed, *Fidelio.*

Like the Overture to *Don Giovanni*, the Overture to *Egmont* consists of a slow introduction and a fast sonata-form movement. The sonata-form part is conceived much more simply than the first movement of the Fifth Symphony. Unlike the symphony, the overture does not revolve around a single striking motive. The development section is shorter and less exciting, and the recapitulation does not make such a shattering effect.

On the other hand, there are interesting relations between the themes of the slow introduction and those of the main movement, relations which bear witness once again to Beethoven's control of musical form. The determined theme that opens the slow introduction (Beethoven's mark means "Sustained but not too much so"):

turns up in a faster, angrier version as the second theme of the sonata-form movement that follows later:

Back in the slow introduction itself, a brief motive moves haltingly through various instruments until it finally seems to gather speed; then it runs right into the main theme of the fast part of the movement. Notice the first three notes of this theme in the cellos—they have the same melodic contour as the motive:

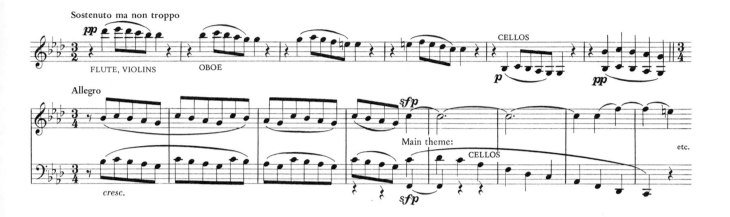

This passage may remind us of the transition between the scherzo and the last movement of the Fifth Symphony. The single low note (it is for double bass) on the offbeat, just at the point where the main theme evolves out of the motive, is a characteristic Beethoven rhythmic touch which gives the passionate main theme extra urgency and unrest. *Sfp* means a sforzato (*sf*) followed by a sudden hush (*p*, *piano*).

This sonata-form movement features another sensational coda. First, the second theme is played by all the instruments as loud as possible. Then a brief silence—designed to recall the brooding slow introduction—leads to a very enthusiastic section of new, marchlike music in a new meter (duple meter). Beethoven called this the "Symphony of Victory," for Goethe demanded that such a thing occur when Egmont goes to his execution at the end of the play. Beethoven's overture, then, illustrates an important heroic feature of the story which is to follow.

This coda even outdoes the last movement of the Fifth Symphony for insistent wild rejoicing. Beethoven makes fine use of his French horns (four of them) and trumpets and also throws in a piccolo. Now we realize why he pulled his punches at the beginning of the recapitulation. He wanted to obtain the maximum effect at the start of the "Symphony of Victory" in the coda.

The Sonata

The term <u>sonata</u> is a confusing one, with multiple meanings, as we have remarked before (page 112). We know its adjectival use in the term "sonata form," the name for the scheme employed in the first movements of Viennese compositions—among them overtures, symphonies, quartets, and also (as it happens) sonatas. As a noun, "sonata" refers to a piece in several movements for a small number of instruments or a single one. The most important type of sonata in the baroque period was the trio sonata (page 112), as exemplified by Corelli's Trio Sonata in F minor.

In reference to music of the Viennese period, the noun "sonata" is restricted to compositions for one or two instruments only. Sonatas were composed for violin and piano, cello and piano, and so on. Mozart wrote one for bassoon and cello. But most sonatas were designed as solo pieces for the favorite new instrument of the time, the piano.

Some piano sonatas adopted the general movement plan of the symphony: an opening fast movement (in sonata form, perhaps with a slow introduction), a slow movement, a minuet or scherzo, and another fast movement. However, there was also a tradition of forms in three or even in two movements, and it was this more intimate tradition that Beethoven followed in composing his Piano Sonata in E, Op. 109.

BEETHOVEN   PIANO SONATA IN E, OP. 109 (1820)   *Side 6*

At the end of Beethoven's life, in his so-called third period, his style moved in a direction of greater serenity, subtlety, and introspection. The music loses some (though not all) of its earlier tone of heroism; it loses all of its earlier heroics. The control of contrast and musical flow becomes even more potent than before, and there is a remarkable sense of concentration. A new freedom of form leads to a range of expression that can only be called miraculous, encompassing all the strength of Beethoven's earlier music together with a new gentleness and spirituality.

As we might expect, the music of Beethoven's third period does not often employ the "heroic" orchestral forms, such as the symphony, the concerto, and the overture. He now preferred the string quartet and the piano sonata. As a young man, Beethoven had made his name in Vienna as a virtuoso pianist, and although now he was stone-deaf and never played in public, he continued to be drawn to "his" instrument, the instrument which allowed him a maximum sense of intimacy and flexibility. Amazingly, his "inner ear" still enabled him to develop fascinating new piano tone colors.

First Movement The brief first movement of the Piano Sonata in E is the freest in form and the most subtle in mood. Two expressive themes contrast in every possible way, even in tempo and meter:

The first of these themes barely murmurs its way into our consciousness, whereas the second breathes considerable passion and draws on some brilliant piano effects. Both themes sound inconclusive, even fragmentary, and they follow one another so suddenly that the flow of the music does not sound like that of a sonata-form movement or a rondo. This is true even though these two themes return later in a sort of climactic recapitulation. Instead of undergoing "fragmentation" (page 193) or any of the usual development procedures, the first theme grows into long, smooth, melodic lines:

At the end, after the "recapitulation," new ideas seem to emerge spontaneously, as though from a quiet well of melody. There is an air of flickering meditation about this movement, a strange combination of tenderness and fantasy.

Second Movement The very fast (prestissimo) second movement is an ingenious hybrid. It conveys the brusque mood of the traditional scherzo that Beethoven regularly placed in the center of his large pieces. But being a piece in sonata form, it runs through the drama of confrontation, struggle, and consummation that he regularly placed at the beginning—for example, in the first movement of the Fifth Symphony and in the Overture to *Egmont*. The difference in position makes all the difference in the effect. It is one thing to place a dramatic sonata-form movement at the beginning of a long piece, where it necessarily sets the tone for everything that follows. It is quite another thing to place it as an interlude between two quiet movements.

The line score on pages 204 and 205 shows how concisely and yet how strictly and lucidly Beethoven now employed sonata form. Everything seems to be expressed with a minimum of fuss and a maximum of directness; there is not an ounce of fat. The development section focuses hard on an unexpected detail of thematic material, the bass line underneath the main theme (marked with a square bracket in the line score). It is treated in counterpoint, inverted, and "fragmented."

Then at the recapitulation, this bass line is twisted around and placed high *above* the theme when the theme is repeated. This touch, immensely strong and sinewy, shows Beethoven's ability in these years to derive the greatest effect out of the smallest details. Notice, too, the expressive extension of the bridge in the recapitulation and the solid hammer strokes that constitute the coda.

In third-period works such as this, Beethoven seems almost able to match the impressive, forceful accomplishments of his second-period symphonic movements in half the time.

Third Movement   The last movement, the longest and obviously the weightiest of the three, concludes the sonata on a note of quiet spirituality. This movement is a theme and variations. In form it is comparable to the last movement of Mozart's Clarinet Quintet or of his C minor Piano Concerto (pages 182 and 189), though the mood and tempo are very different.

Beethoven uses as his theme a serene, hymn-like tune, both halves of which are repeated (eight measures each). Some of the fine points of this tune are the wonderful "deep" harmony at X, the sequence (page 30) at the beginning of the second half of the tune (Y), and the rich cadence in a new tonality at Z.

The variations depart much farther from the theme than those of Mozart's Clarinet Quintet or the C minor Concerto or, indeed, those of any earlier piece by Beethoven. We have the feeling that extraordinary depths are being plumbed within the theme, that its inner nature and possibilities are being exposed in an unparalleled manner. At first the variations may sound remote, but as we listen closely and allow for changes in tempo, we hear that they follow strictly the eight-measure structure of the tune with its cadences. Listen especially for the points mentioned above—X, Y, and Z; they all turn up one way or another in the variations, often with a very unusual effect.

Variation 1: Beethoven has transformed his hymn almost into a romantic reverie. The treatment of the sequence Y is very striking.

Variation 2 (double): A so-called "double variation," in which each half of the theme is varied differently in the repetition. (See page 189. If the theme is diagramed ‖: a :‖: b :‖ variation 1 will be ‖: a' :‖: b' :‖ and variation 2 will be a'' a''' b'' b'''.) This variation seems to dissect the theme, display all the nerves and tendons, and then put everything back together again.

Variation 3 (double): This cheerful variation, with its country dance rhythms, may remind us of Haydn. Strictly speaking, this counts as a double variation, too, though the differences are less apparent than with variation 2.

Variation 4: A languorous, highly decorative variation. In the second part, at the sequence Y, a cloud of fury blows up and then passes as suddenly as it had begun.

Variation 5 (double): A fast, firm-sounding contrapuntal variation, based on a motive derived from the first notes of the theme. Extensive imitations of this motive (plus a new scalewise countersubject) are fitted into the eight-measure pattern, cadences, sequences, etc. After the usual thirty-two measures $(8 + 8 + 8 + 8)$ have gone by at a steady forte, the last eight are repeated quietly as preparation for variation 6.

Variation 6 (double): In this remarkable double variation, the accompaniment speeds up under a broken version of the theme until violent trills and passage-work create an astonishing welter of piano sound. There is a feeling that we are on the verge of some enormously powerful and solemn revelation; then this feeling gradually subsides.

To conclude, the theme returns exactly as it was at the beginning but without the repeats. The effect is of a profound quietude. Far from seeming redundant or anticlimactic, the theme seems newly and unexpectedly rich as it harks back over all the vast resources that have been explored within the boundaries of its single melodic unit. The simple—even innocent—device of bringing the theme back at this point shows Beethoven's masterful control over musical form. He achieves an almost mystical effect: the still voice after the hurricane.

DEVELOPMENT ⟶

bass figure

Damper (left)
pedal on

etc.

8va

etc.

cresc.

8va
tr

* In piano music, curved brackets enclose staffs that are played by the right hand and left hand simultaneously. The left hand is not always shown in this line score, though of course it continues all the way through the piece.

Beethoven's Musical Handwriting

Beethoven was the first composer whom people viewed as a solitary genius struggling to produce masterpieces in the face of affliction. One fact that contributed to this image was his practice of working out his pieces very carefully and laboriously, sketching the themes, transitions, and so on, on music paper again and again until they finally came out right. Few earlier composers had the time or the temperament for such perfectionism. Beethoven never threw out his old sketches; he clung to them as though feeling unconsciously that their record of the creative process was a part of his real life.

A typical Beethoven sketch — our example is for the Ninth Symphony — is an all-but-indecipherable scrawl in which the impatience and struggle of genius seem to be set down in graphic form. It is a loaded comparison to place this picture against the sample of Bach's handwriting shown on page 104, perhaps. For this is a rough sketch and that is a finished copy. Still, after making allowances, we can see in these two pictures the changeover from the old concept of the composer as "artisan" to the new view of him as "artist." Developed by the romantics, this concept is still with us today, though many contemporary composers are fighting against it.

Franz Schubert (1797–1828)

STRING QUARTET IN A MINOR (1824)

Side 8

Schubert was the only true native among the famous Viennese composers. Born in Vienna in 1797, he lived very unspectacularly and died of typhoid fever when he was only thirty-one, shortly after the death of Beethoven. It is said that Schubert was so shy he never even introduced himself to the formidable older master, whose music impressed him, and disturbed him, greatly.

Schubert did not achieve fame during his lifetime, but that was hardly to be expected of a composer who was so young and so self-effacing. He took pleasure in the admiration his music received from his close circle of friends, the so-called "Schubertianer" (see page 210). And he lived to see nearly a hundred of his works published—piano pieces and sonatas, songs and choruses, some chamber music, and the most delightful waltzes imaginable. This number would exceed the wildest dreams of a thirty-one-year-old composer of our time, and it testifies to the rich musical culture which supported the Viennese composers. Even today, by the way, Austria devotes *one-fifth* of its total state income to music and the other arts.

Schubert is popularly known as an outstanding song composer. So he was; but in addition, the symphonies, sonatas, and chamber-music works of his last years rank beside the masterpieces of Haydn, Mozart, and Beethoven. The general style and formal assumptions of the Viennese composers remain at the basis of these instrumental compositions of Schubert's, together with some new features of his own. The most striking of these, one that will hardly cause surprise coming from a song composer, is the increasing use of long song-like tunes in his instrumental pieces. The first movement of Schubert's Quartet in A minor is a case in point.

First Movement Even before hearing the long tune, we are struck by a restless, haunting accompaniment figure which serves as a sort of introduction:

When first mentioning the string quartet, on page 180, we made the obvious point that in tone color and dynamics, the quartet medium is more restrained than, say, the symphony orchestra. But it is also more intimate and subtle. The unique color of this introduction-figure, combining the winding second violin with the throbbing viola and cello underneath, could only have been produced by a string quartet. The figure will be heard many times during the first movement, always with a moving effect.

Here at the beginning it leads into a long, melancholy tune, during which Schubert seems to forget that he is starting up a sonata-form movement which is supposed to be dramatic, forward-looking, contrast-oriented, etc. True, in the recapitulation he pulls himself together and abbreviates the tune somewhat.

Notice the last measure of the example, which starts the bridge passage. The *ff* motive employed here has been forged out of the beginning of the tune itself—motive a, with a forceful alteration in rhythm and with an impatient trill added to the second note. This expert detail shows that Schubert knew very well the distinction between a typical sonata theme and a long tune. His innovation was unashamedly to incorporate long tunes into his sonata-form movements anyway.

The development section dwells on the main theme, or tune. It is treated in imitation, modulating. Then the motive marked b is fragmented out for especially vehement polyphony, and a particularly beautiful retransition follows. The coda, too, uses the main theme, which obviously occupied the center of Schubert's affections.

Second Movement The form of this slow movement, and also that of the last movement, follows a sort of modified sonata form:

Sonata Form

EXPOSITION		DEVELOPMENT	RECAPITULATION		C O D A
1st theme	2nd group		1st theme	2nd group	

Modified Sonata Form

EXPOSITION		RECAP	BRIEF DEVELOPMENT	ITULATION	C O D A
1st theme	2nd group	1st theme		2nd group	

This plan is fairly "strict" and not new with Schubert; his use of it serves to stress his traditional orientation. It must be admitted, though, that in listening to these two movements, we feel encouraged to lose ourselves in the many charming melodies rather than concentrate on form and coherence. Here is the first theme of the second movement:

Schubert thought well enough of this tune to come back to it several times. He used it in an orchestral piece written to accompany a play called *Rosamunde*, and as the basis for a theme and variations for piano, the Impromptu in B♭, Op. 142 No. 3. It is quite interesting to compare the treatment of the tune in the quartet with these others, especially the piano variations.

Third Movement With its marvelous mood of hushed mystery, this movement certainly makes an original transformation of the usual straightforward, spirited minuet. Soon after the beginning (does it not recall the beginning of the first movement?), we hear a kind of dream waltz starting up and fading out again. This "minuet" actually uses a musical idea from one of Schubert's songs, *Die Götter Griechenlands* ("The Gods of Greece"), to words by the famous poet Friedrich von Schiller:

> Beautiful land of Greece! where art thou?
> Come back again, o age of Nature's flowering. . . .

So here (at last!) is a touch of "classical" antiquity in Viennese music. Yet the classical reference has much the same quality as the little temple in the park shown on page 178. Schiller is lost in feelings of nostalgia for times past, and with Schubert this nostalgia becomes almost romantic. Note especially the deep, throbbing modulation at a', the return of a within the traditional ‖:a:‖:b a':‖ form.

Fourth Movement Again Schubert employed the modified sonata form shown in the diagram on page 208. Contrast in tonality is especially clear between the first and second group in the exposition, between the delicate, sprightly opening theme and the wary, mock-ominous theme in the second group. The "misplaced" development section, although short, works its way up to quite an aggressive climax.

But once again it is the tunes themselves that occupy the center of attention. They have an unmistakable popular-music lilt about them; this delightful movement is much lighter in tone than the three earlier ones. We are reminded of the fact that before Johann Strauss, Schubert was the greatest of the Viennese waltz composers. However, since this movement is in duple time Schubert could not evoke the waltz, a triple-time dance. His first and second themes recall two other popular dances of the time, the écossaise and the galop.

Schubert Among His Friends

Although there is some reason to consider Schubert as one of the early romantic composers, there is not much in his biography to make one think of a typical romantic career in the style of Byron, Chopin, or Edgar Allen Poe. For a time he worked as a low-level schoolteacher, like his father. Though he entertained ambitions as a theater composer, he lacked utterly the force and the wile necessary to succeed in that field. He gained himself a few private pupils among young ladies of the aristocracy and upper middle classes, but old anecdotes suggest that he felt more comfortable in the company of the maids downstairs. He was happiest of all in the small devoted circle of his friends, who called themselves the "Schubertiania" and provided him with friendship, admiration, and money for the better part of his brief composing life.

At a musicale among the Schubertianer, Schubert is at the piano, surrounded by a group of warm admirers. Most of them seem to be charming young people, except for the distinguished older gentleman next to the composer — Michael Vogl, a retired opera singer, who was almost the only influential friend Schubert had. Vogl sang his songs in public and introduced them to publishers. His voice was a high baritone, and Schubert wrote directly for him. As a result, songs such as *Die Winterreise* sound best when sung by this kind of voice, though they are also often performed by sopranos, tenors, and basses.

The Schubertianer prided themselves on their universal artistic tastes, ranging from music to poetry and painting. The man who drew this pleasant picture, Moritz von Schwind, drifted into the Schubert circle at the age of seventeen. He later became a leading German painter, but he never forgot the musical enthusiasms of his youth. (Schwind himself is the second mustache to the right of Schubert.) In the 1860s, he painted a rather dreadful series of scenes from famous operas on the foyer walls of the Vienna Opera House, where they can still be seen today.

The Lied

SCHUBERT   *ERLKÖNIG* (1815)   *Side 8*

DIE WINTERREISE (1826)   *Side 8*

Over six hundred songs were written by Schubert in his short lifetime, half of them before he was twenty. Sometimes people refer to them by the German word for song, which is *Lied* (plural: *Lieder*—pronounced "lead," "leader"). Schubert's *Lieder* range very widely in form and scope and sentiment. Some are lovely tunes sung through identically for several stanzas of poetry; this is called strophic form. Other songs provide new music for the later stanzas, in order to reflect the changing words of the poem. The usual term for this technique, *durchkomponiert* in German, translates into English as "through-composed."*

STROPHIC AND THROUGH-COMPOSED SONGS

Familiar examples of Schubert strophic songs are *Heidenröslein* and *An Silvia* ("Hedge Rose" and "To Silvia"), and of through-composed songs, *Gretchen am Spinnrade* and *Erlkönig* ("Gretchen at the Spinning Wheel" and "Elfking"). The latter is set to a terse ballad by the famous poet Johann Wolfgang von Goethe; a ballad is a poem or song that tells a story. Though in fact Schubert did not write many "story" songs, *Erlkönig* is probably his most famous composition.

Goethe's poem is given on page 217. It tells of a father riding frantically through the night with a delirious child who thinks he hears the voice of the demon Elfking. The Elfking first invites the child to join him, then cajoles him, then threatens and assaults him. The father tries to quiet the child, but he is dead when they reach town.

Schubert writes different music for the three different voices—music that gets higher and higher as the tension increases. Each "voice" characterizes the speaker perfectly, and differentiates him from the others. What, then, holds the song together as an artistic unity? The piano accompaniment has agitated repeated notes, suggesting the horse's hooves on this grim ride, and these keep going throughout until just before the journey's end. During the Elfking's first and second stanzas, when the child hears him half asleep, the horse's hooves are muted. But they pound away furiously in the king's third stanza; when the Elfking threatens him with force, the child is wide awake in terror. A wonderfully imaginative touch—and Schubert was only eighteen when he thought it up.

---

* A neater, seventeenth-century English term was "through-set." "Strophic song" refers to something very simple and familiar, of course, and the term needs to be used only when it is necessary to draw a distinction between strophic and through-composed setting. Almost all folk songs are strophic songs; so are *Blowin' in the Wind* and *It was a lover and his lass* (pages 30 and 74–75).

His masterpiece of song composition, written near the end of his life, is a set of twenty songs collectively called *Die Winterreise* ("The Winter Journey"). This is a song cycle, a group of songs with some kind of loose connection—at the very least, there will be a common idea running through all the poems. In the present case, we are to picture a young man disappointed in love who takes a journey through the countryside in wintertime. The various sights he sees remind him of his bitter experience and despair. Each sight forms the subject of one of the songs in the cycle, and in many songs, the piano accompaniment illustrates some element in the nature scene. A carrion crow wheels in the winter sky, hounds rattle their chains at night, a last leaf is blown helter-skelter from a tree, and a begger-musician plays his instrument with fingers numb from cold.

Der Leiermann ("The Hurdy-Gurdy Man") is the final song in the song cycle. (Texts from *Die Winterreise* are given on pages 215 and 216.) The poet sees an old beggar-musician playing in the snow, with no one to listen or put a penny in his plate; this old man, he thinks, reflects his own condition. What is famous about this song is the economy of means by which Schubert achieves his musical picture of hopelessness. Except for the question at the end,

> Strange old man—shall I go with you?
> Will you play your music to songs of mine?

the song is strictly strophic, two stanzas with the same tune—and what a numb tune it is, with its regular rhythm and monotonous phrase structure. The piano accompaniment is frozen, too, with the same left-hand chord droning away in every measure in order to invoke the sound of the archaic peasant instrument (page 215). Yet in mood this accompaniment strikingly recalls the figure that opens Schubert's Quartet in A minor: compare the example on page 207. Schubert has indeed contrived to make the hurdy-gurdy play "songs of mine," songs of his own.

Der Lindenbaum ("The Linden Tree") achieves quite another mood. Seeing a fine tree, the poet recalls how peacefully he used to rest under it as a boy, and this stirs memories of a folklike melody. Indeed, in Germany this nostalgic melody has since attained the status of a folk song. A feature that distinguishes the song as such from a folk song is the piano introduction, which seems to suggest rustling leaves and also, perhaps, distant hunting horns in a dark forest. Is it too much to say that the poet, and Schubert with him, shared some of the same warm feeling toward nature that is exhibited by the landscape architect whose work appears on page 178?

This piano introduction, transformed in mood, makes an impressive contrast in the middle of the song, as the poet passes the linden tree in a driving storm in wintertime. But for once the benign summer image dominates. The song ends very much as it began, with the original tune. Notice the ironic undertone, however; the poet is now thinking of another kind of "rest."

A more complex song is *Der Wegweiser* ("The Signpost"). Here the poet meditates sadly on the directions his life has taken; there will be no return from the path he has to follow now. As is Schubert's habit, the song begins with a piano introduction and a tune. But in the remaining stanzas of the poem, there are only suggestions of strophic form; the bleak tune never returns exactly. Schubert grows more and more obsessed with the chief motive:

Moderato
pp

Was vermeid ich denn die We - ge, wo die andern Wandrer gehn,
Why do I avoid the roads   *used by other travellers,*
suche mir versteck-te Stege durch verschneite Felsen - höhn?
and seek hidden paths   *among the snow-bound rocks?*

This is ultimately "developed" into a long series of repeated notes, the quiet tolling of a knell underlining the suggestion of death at the end of the poem. Although the feeling of this song is romantic, even sentimental, the treatment of motives shows Schubert's technical adherence to the Viennese style.

If we were to listen to the whole of *Die Winterreise,* we might observe this motive coming back quietly in song after song. It provides a certain musical unity to the whole song cycle, in addition to the poetic unity.

At the beginning of this chapter, we took note of some differences between the earlier Viennese style, as practiced by Haydn and Mozart, and the later style, as practiced by Beethoven and Schubert. In discussing these later composers, we have mentioned a number of features that look forward to romanticism: Beethoven's image as suffering genius, his heroism and taste for revolutionary drama, his freedom of form in the third period; Schubert's special affection for song and lengthy melody and his nostalgic nature worship and sentimentality. An argument can be made for classifying these composers as early romantics.

But as a matter of fact, one can argue that the origins of romanticism in music go back even earlier. As the "Storm and Stress" movement blew up in literature and the visual arts in the 1770s, a new emotionalism in music erupted which still echoes loudly in Mozart's G minor Symphony and C minor Piano Concerto (written in the 1780s). Rather than joining these arguments, we have preferred to stress the continuity between the Viennese composers, as determined first and foremost by their flexibility of musical technique and by the breadth and subtlety of emotional expression that this made possible. The new expressivity was pioneered by Haydn and Mozart, then extended by Beethoven and Schubert. To this common factor may be added the geographical and personal contacts among these men and the excellent use they all made of such forms as symphony, quartet, sonata form, minuet, and scherzo.

The truth of the matter is that the style boundary between the Viennese (or "classical") and the romantic periods in music is less sharp than that between the baroque and the Viennese. In Germany, musicologists now acknowledge this and speak of a single "classical-romantic" period. The break between the earlier and later Viennese styles is also less sharp than that between Beethoven and Schubert, on the one hand, and Chopin, Schumann, and Berlioz, on the other. Let us now turn our attention to these early romantic composers.

The Hurdy-Gurdy

This curious and very ancient instrument consists of a set of strings in a sound box. These are not made to sound by means of bowing or plucking; instead, a wooden wheel turned by the player rubs continuously against the strings. Rosin is a help, but the hurdy-gurdy can never have made a very refined sound. It was used almost exclusively for popular music in the streets or on the village green, but Haydn wrote some concertos for the instrument on the commission of a player who was none other than the King of Naples.

Like another famous popular musical instrument, the bagpipe, the hurdy-gurdy used many long drone notes. Composers often imitated this sound in their "art music," and it is possible to detect signs of a changing attitude toward the common people, under the influence of Enlightenment ideas, in the way they treated it. Baroque composers were interested only in creating a simple and piquant result. (For a familiar example, listen to the so-called "Pastoral Symphony" in Handel's oratorio *Messiah*.) Haydn, in such works as the trio of the minuet in Symphony No. 88 (page 174), is inclined to poke fun at the peasant musician, who does not seem to be quite sure when to shift his drone notes. He seems to lose count in the melody line, too. It is affectionate fun, though, and if we listen closely, perhaps the peasant gets the last laugh, for these pieces are as artfully put together as any of Haydn's music, given their small scale.

As for Schubert, in his famous song *Der Leiermann* ("The Hurdy-Gurdy Man," page 212), the simple countryman has now become a figure of pathos, from whom (significantly) the poet can learn appropriate feelings:

Strange old man—shall I go with you?
Will you play your music to songs of mine?

This rather harrowing hurdy-gurdy man was painted by the seventeenth-century French artist Georges de La Tour.

Texts of Schubert Songs

Der Leiermann

Drüben hinterm Dorfe steht ein Leiermann,
Und mit starren Fingern dreht er, was er kann.
Barfuss auf dem Eise wankt er hin und her,
Und sein kleiner Teller bleibt ihm immer leer.

Keiner mag ihn hören, keiner sieht ihn an,
Und die Hunde knurren um den alten Mann.
Und er lässt es gehen, alles wie es will,
Dreht, und seine Leier steht ihm nimmer still.

Wunderlicher Alter, soll ich mit dir gehn?
Willst zu meinen Liedern deine Leier drehn?

The Hurdy-Gurdy Man

Over there, beyond the village, a hurdy-gurdy man stands,
Grinding away with numbed fingers as best he can.
He staggers barefoot on the ice
And his little plate remains ever empty.

No one wants to hear him, no one looks at him,
And the dogs snarl about the old man.
But he lets the world go by,
He turns the handle, and his hurdy-gurdy is never still.

Strange old man—shall I go with you?
Will you grind your music to my songs?

Der Wegweiser

Was vermeid ich denn die Wege,
Wo die andern Wandrer gehn,
Suche mir versteckte Stege
Durch verschneite Felsenhöhn?

Habe ja doch nichts begangen,
Dass ich Menschen sollte scheun,
Welch ein törichtes Verlangen
Treibt mich in die Wüstenein?

Weiser stehen auf den Wegen
Weisen auf die Städte zu,
Und ich wandre sonder Massen,
Ohne Ruh, and suche Ruh.

Einen Weiser seh ich stehen
Unverrückt vor meinem Blick;
Eine Strasse muss ich gehen,
Die noch keiner ging zuruck.

The Signpost

Why do I avoid the roads
Used by other travellers,
And seek hidden paths
Among the snowbound rocks?

I have committed no crime—
Why should I shun mankind?
What is this foolish desire
That drives me into the wilderness?

Signposts stand on the roads,
Pointing toward the towns;
And I wander ever onward,
Restless, yet seeking rest.

I see a signpost that stands
Immovably before me;
I must travel a road
By which no one has ever returned.

Der Lindenbaum

Am Brunnen vor dem Tore
Da steht ein Lindenbaum;
Ich träumt in seinem Schatten
So manchen süssen Traum.

Ich schnitt in seine Rinde
So manches liebe Wort;
Es zog in Freud und Leide
Zu ihm mich immer fort.

Ich musst auch heute wandern
Vorbei in tiefer Nacht,
Da hab ich noch im Dunkel
Die Augen zugemacht.

Und seine Zweige rauschten,
Als riefen sie mir zu:
"Komm her zu mir, Geselle,
Hier findst du deine Ruh!"

Die kalten Winde bliesen
Mir grad in's Angesicht,
Der Hut flog mir vom Kopfe,
Ich wendete mich nicht.

Nun bin ich manche Stunde
Entfernt von jenem Ort,
Und immer hör ich's rauschen:
"Du fändest Ruhe dort!"

The Linden Tree

By the well before the gate
There stands a Linden tree;
In its shade I dreamt
Many a sweet dream.

In its bark I carved
Many a word of love;
In joy as in sorrow
I felt ever drawn to it.

Today I had to wander
Past it at dead of night,
And even in the darkness
I closed my eyes.

And its branches rustled
As if they were calling to me
"Friend, come here to me—
Here you will find rest."

The cold winds blew
Straight into my face,
My hat flew from my head—
But I did not turn round.

Now I am many hours' journey
Away from that place;
But I always hear the rustling:
"There you would find rest!"

Erlkönig

Wer reitet so spät durch Nacht und Wind?
Es ist der Vater mit seinem Kind;
Er hat den Knaben wohl in dem Arm,
Er fasst ihn sicher, er hält ihn warm.

'Mein Sohn, was birgst du so band dein Gesicht?'
'Siehst, Vater, du den Erlkönig nicht?
Den Erlenkönig mit Kron und Schweif?'
'Mein Sohn, es ist ein Nebelstreif.'

'Du liebes Kind, komm, geh mit mir!
Gar schöne Spiele spiel ich mit dir;
Manch bunte Blumen sind an dem Strand,
Meine Mutter hat manch gülden Gewand.'

'Mein Vater, mein Vater, und hörest du nicht,
Was Erlenkönig mir leise verspricht?'
'Sei ruhig, bleibe ruhig, mein Kind:
In dürren Blättern säuselt der Wind.'

'Willst, feiner Knabe, du mit mir gehn?
Meine Töchter sollen dich warten schön;
Meine Töchter führen den nächtlichen Reihn
Und wiegen und tanzen und singen dich ein.'

'Mein Vater, mein Vater, und siehst du nicht dort
Erlkönigs Töchter am dustern Ort?'
'Mein Sohn, mein Sohn, ich seh es genau:
Es scheinen die alten Weiden so grau.'

'Ich liebe dich, mich reizt deine schöne Gestalt;
Und bist du nicht willig, so brauch ich Gewalt.'
'Mein Vater, mein Vater, jetzt fasst er mich an!
Erlkönig hat mir ein Leid's getan!'

Dem Vater grauset's, er reitet geschwind,
Er hält in den Armen das ächzende Kind,
Erreicht den Hof mit Müh und Not;
In seinen Armen das Kind war tot.

The Elfking

Who rides so late through the night and the wind?
It is the father with his child.
He holds the boy in his arm,
Grasps him securely, keeps him warm.

'My son, why do you hide your face so anxiously?'
'Father, do you not see the Elfking?
The Elfking with his crown and tail?'
'My son, it is only a streak of mist.'

'Darling child, come away with me!
I will play fine games with you.
Many gay flowers grow by the shore;
My mother has many golden robes.'

'Father, father, do you not hear
What the Elfking softly promises me?'
'Be calm, dear child, be calm—
The wind is rustling in the dry leaves.'

'You beautiful boy, will you come with me?
My daughters will wait upon you.
My daughters lead the nightly round,
They will rock you, dance to you, sing you to sleep!'

'Father, father, do you not see
The Elfking's daughters there, in that dark place?'
'My son, my son, I see it clearly:
It is the gray gleam of the old willow-trees.'

'I love you, your beauty allures me,
And if you do not come willingly, I shall use force.'
'Father, father, now he is seizing me!
The Elfking has hurt me!'

Fear grips the father, he rides swiftly,
Holding the moaning child in his arms;
With effort and toil he reaches the house—
The child in his arms was dead.

CHAPTER 5   1825–1900   Romanticism

1825–1900 Romanticism

Of all the terms used to describe style in the arts, "romantic" is no doubt the most familiar and the most evocative. Originally applied to literature of the early nineteenth century, the term conveyed attitudes that became so widespread that the word had to spill over into many other areas of life. The use of "romantic" to mean "amorous" dates from the nineteenth century and derives from the artistic movement—though love was only one of several important themes of romanticism.

In music, the term "romantic" is applied to music from near the beginning of the century to its end, a longer span than in any other art. Over this period, music shows rather more continuity of style than do literature and painting. At the basis of this musical continuity, perhaps, is a philosophical idea, a new concept of music and its role, which took a firm hold on the European consciousness.

Literary romanticism dwelt on a number of important themes, among them the glorification of romantic love, nostalgia for the past, and a new enthusiasm for nature (see pages 228, 247). For poets and artists of the time, these were ways of getting to the real heart of romanticism: the insistence on spontaneous personal emotion. Men and women were determined to experience life to the full and to express what they experienced just as fully. Especially in Germany, romantics began to see that of all the arts, music could express inner experience most deeply and freely. Deeply, because music is closest of all to the subjective, instinctive springs of emotion, what we now call the unconscious. Freely, because the musician's imagination is not tied down to matter-of-fact words and statements (like the poet's) or to the representation of things (like the painter's.) Music seemed the perfect outlet for an age that insisted above all on the value of individual emotional expression.

This concept of music was widely held by musicians as well as other artists and thinkers. It found definitive formulation in the works of Arthur Schopenhauer, a much-read German philosopher who influenced the composer Richard Wagner at a critical period of his career. Wagner's opera *Tristan und Isolde*, one of the most characteristic products of romantic music, practically spells out Schopenhauer's philosophy (page 256). Music gained enormous prestige and status. "All art aspires to the condition of music," wrote a famous nineteenth-century critic, Walter Pater. Indeed, music was taken much more seriously in the nineteenth century than ever before—or after. Which may help to explain why nineteenth-century music continues to dominate the concert repertory and why Schopenhauer's views are shared in a general way by many people today who have never heard his name.

Emphasis on the importance of personal feeling naturally entailed new prestige for the artist himself. Composers and performers no longer regarded themselves—and no longer allowed themselves to be regarded—as craftsmen serving society, but rather as free spirits expressing their own souls with a genius not granted to the common run of mankind. "My nobility is *here*," Beethoven is supposed to have said, pointing to his heart, and people believed him. The pianist-composer Franz Liszt started his career playing in drawing rooms where a silk cord separated him from the aristocratic listeners, but he lived to be sought out by these same people on terms of equality. Liszt's well-publicized liaisons with a countess and a princess may be taken as signs of the changing times. (An admiring throng around Liszt, including the countess, is pictured on page 276).

All of this will cause us something of a problem as we examine the features of romantic musical style. Since the main artistic value at the time was the expression of personal emotion, every artist labored to evolve a personal style. And since individuality was at a premium, we shall find talking about musical style in general terms considerably harder than spotting novelties and innovations. To be sure, all nineteenth-century composers shared some common interests, which will be discussed in the following pages. But one such common interest was to sound different from everybody else.

Another way of putting the problem is in terms of the distinction between "period styles" and "individual styles," a distinction that was made when the concept of musical style was first introduced (page 46). The romantic period is the point in musical history when the balance shifted decisively in the direction of individual styles. If someone were suddenly to play us a piece of earlier music—by switching on a car radio, for instance—we might identify it at once as baroque and then puzzle over whether it was by Vivaldi, Bach, or Handel. With a romantic piece, our first reaction would probably be: "That sounds like Chopin [or Berlioz, Wagner, or Strauss]." Whether or not we would also add dutifully that the piece sounded romantic, the center of our interest would be on its individualistic qualities. And certainly that is where the composer would have wanted it to be.

The Style of Romantic Music

Romantic Melody and Harmony   It is not easy to characterize romantic melody and harmony. To a large extent, they go together. The melodic lines tend to have richness and intensity, and the harmony contributes to this by winding up great tensions and then providing great relief at points of relaxation. Each in his own way, composers developed the knack of making their melodies passionate, dreamy, supercharged, intimate, or whatever shade of emotional coloring they sought to convey.

Sometimes these melodies grew so demonstrative and effusive that the effect may strike some listeners unpleasantly. This is a risk run by romantic artists in general, though it is overcome by the best of them. However, most listeners warm instinctively to romantic melody and to its typical harmonic underpinnings. It is familiar to us from its echoes in the more emotional popular music of the present and in what used to be called the "sweet" music of the jazz and swing eras.

Besides using harmony to support emotional melody, composers began to relish it for its own sake. Fascinating untried chords and juxtapositions of chords were explored, for it was found that harmony could contribute potently to those mysterious, ethereal, rapturous, or sultry moods that were so greatly enjoyed at the time. This was a true novelty, compared with the practice of earlier composers. Harmony began to encroach on the territory of tone color itself. There are even some themes in Romantic music which gain their memorable character from harmony, rather than from melody or rhythm, as in earlier music (see the example on page 257 and the "magic sleep" theme in the line score on page 262).

The Expansion of Tone Color   Tone color had been treated with considerable subtlety by the Viennese composers, but the romantics seized on this aspect of music with particular enthusiasm and gave it special development. They invented new musical instruments, greatly improved old ones, coaxed astonishing new sounds out of all instruments, and combined sounds in unheard-of ways. For the first time in Western music, the sheer sensuous quality of sound assumed major artistic importance, on a level with rhythm, melody, and form. Bach and Beethoven wrote carefully for the various instruments, of course, but in one sense they seem to have applied their instrumental "colors" as a last touch, over and above the "drawing," that is, the real foundation of notes and structure. This is generally not so with the romantic composers, fascinated as they were by the emotional possibilities of pure sonority. For Chopin or Berlioz, piano sound or orchestral sound is primary. Their music can no longer be thought of in abstract terms apart from its particular tone color.

The orchestra was expanded enormously. Compare the early romantic orchestra shown on page 224 with the typical Viennese orchestra on page 148. Indeed, the age was fascinated by the orchestra, both as an independent entity, in symphonies and the like, and also as a newly rich accompaniment to opera. On the whole, chamber music languished. If people today automatically think of the symphony orchestra whenever they think of "classical music," that is a holdover from the nineteenth century.

As though to symbolize all this, some of the main composers of the time wrote major textbooks on orchestration, the technique of writing most effectively for each orchestral instrument and combining them to produce the best

AN EARLY ROMANTIC ORCHESTRA
(As in Berlioz's *Fantastic Symphony*)

Strings:	violins 1, sometimes divided into 3 sections
	violins 2, sometimes in 3 sections
	violas, sometimes in 2 sections
	cellos, sometimes in 2 sections
	double basses, sometimes in 4 sections
	2 harps
Woodwinds:	2 flutes, one sometimes playing piccolo
	2 oboes, one sometimes playing English horn
	2 clarinets, one sometimes playing high clarinet (E♭ clarinet)
	4 bassoons
Brass:	4 French horns
	2 cornets
	2 trumpets
	3 trombones
	2 bass tubas
Percussion:	4 timpani (two players)
	bass drum, cymbals, side drum
	chimes (tubular bells)

blends. The texts by Hector Berlioz (1844, with important expansions by the late romantic composer Richard Strauss, 1905) and Nikolai Rimsky-Korsakov (1913) are still studied with profit, after all these years.

ÉTUDE

With a similar concern for tone color in mind, pianist-composers of the romantic period wrote studies for piano, or <u>études</u>, as they are called in French—a field which till then had been left mainly to humble pedagogues. Needless to say, the études of Frédéric Chopin and Franz Liszt are a far cry from the mournful finger exercises of Czerny and Hanon, which afflict so many beginning pianists. They train the fingers ingeniously for certain special technical problems, but at the same time they are marvelous pieces of music, among the finest written by their composers. One will be briefly discussed later, page 232.

Dynamics and Rhythm Dynamics were often controlled very closely by the romantic composers. As they sought greater contrasts for more and more expressive effects, they tried to mark dynamics on their melodies with a precision sometimes amounting to fussiness. Where the eighteenth century had been content with the signs *ff*, *f*, *mf*, *p*, and *pp* (page 11), the nineteenth needed to go up to *ffff* and down to *ppppp*.

In rhythm, the flexibility that had been discovered by the Viennese composers was capitalized on and extended. Not only did composers now want certain passages to be slowed down or speeded up, but they expected performers to treat the meter freely all along, or at least in certain "expressive" passages. A style of playing was encouraged in which the meter is constantly "stretched" slightly and then compressed again—or, when the meter is handled strictly, the melody stretches so as to be slightly out of phase with it. Listen, for example, to the way the third beat of the triple meter tends to be played in a good performance of a Viennese waltz, such as *The Blue Danube*. This is called <u>rubato</u>, "robbed" time.

RUBATO

An artistic rubato can be sensuous and teasing, though the meter is always clear; indeed, rubato can make the meter seem more interesting and elegant. Excessive rubato is vulgar or spineless or both. It is up to the performer to tread the fine line, for composers have never tried to notate rubato precisely.

The Problem of Form in Romantic Music   Spontaneity was an important goal of the romantic movement. (Though we may reflect that spontaneity was becoming harder all the time to achieve in such areas as harmony and orchestration, in which the composer now had to acquire more refined skills and learn more "rules" than earlier composers had needed.) And if there was any area in which the romantic composer wanted to be (or to seem) free and spontaneous, it was the area of musical form. The music should bubble out moment by moment, irrepressible and untrammeled, like churning emotion itself. Yet the music had to avoid real formlessness, lest the listener lose track of the musical thought and simply stop listening.

On page 44 the distinction was drawn between "outer forms," such as the sonnet or sonata form, and the "inner form" of individual works of art. It was natural for romantic composers to stress inner form and pay less attention to outer forms. When they did use outer forms such as sonata form, theme and variations, rondo, and so on, they sometimes worked within the form so freely that it becomes a fine point whether the scheme is really there at all—a fine point, and usually a useless argument. For, more and more, composers found themselves creating a new inner form for every new composition. This was hard to do, much harder than the task of the Viennese and baroque composers with their outer forms, and it is not surprising that not a few romantic pieces strike us as rambling and disorganized.

Thus we shall not be able to produce a list of "forms" for the romantic period to match those of, say, the baroque—ritornello form, passacaglia, fugue, da capo aria, and the rest. What we can do is make a two-sided point about the scope or size of romantic compositions. Also we can identify two general formal principles of the era: the *principle of the literary program* and the *principle of thematic unity*.

"Miniature" and "Grandiose" Compositions   The point about scope or size is this: romantic compositions show an interesting tendency to be either considerably shorter or else considerably longer than most earlier music. Some composers cultivated "<u>miniatures</u>," pieces lasting just a few minutes—in particular, short songs and piano pieces. This music conveys a brief but particularly intense whiff of emotion. The composer is able to commune with the listener in the most intimate possible way.

ROMANTIC "MINIATURES"

Short pieces were written in earlier times, of course, as movements within larger compositions—Viennese minuets in symphonies, baroque dances in suites—where their effect was balanced by other movements. But in the romantic era, short pieces often come singly and stand out more clearly as individuals in their own right.

Other composers (or sometimes the same ones) moved in the opposite direction, toward what we shall call "grandiose" pieces. They planned larger and larger symphonies, cantatas, and operas. The number of movements, the performing forces, and the total time span were all increased. Starting with the generously augmented romantic symphony orchestra, composers would then pull in all kinds of added performers: solo singers, a chorus or several choruses, and in one famous instance, even four extra brass bands (the Requiem Mass by Hector Berlioz). With words added, the total effect was laced with poetry, philosophical or religious ideas, a loose story line, and/or dramatic action. The listener was to be impressed (even stupefied) by a combination of great thoughts, opulent sounds, grandiose emotions, and sheer length.

The "Principle of the Literary Program" This principle emerged from the determination of the romantic composers to make music expressive. As we mentioned above, they believed that music comes close to the basic sources of human emotion and therefore can express spontaneous feeling deeply and freely, even without further explanation. At the same time, the nineteenth century abounded in music associated with ideas, stories, evocative titles, and the like. One way or another, these were expressed in words, words which would in some sense "explain" the emotional content of the music.

Perhaps there is indeed a contradiction here. But we must remember that the romantics were less interested in building consistent aesthetic theories than in pursuing all possible ways of maximizing emotional effect. In this spirit, they enthusiastically explored combinations of music with whatever literary elements they thought could enrich it.

The grandiose choral-orchestral compositions which we have just mentioned are a case in point, with their philosophical or narrative texts "expressed" in music. Opera flourished mightily, too (see page 254). As for the romantic "miniatures," songs already had poetic texts, and the nineteenth century saw a wonderful outpouring of lyric poetry in all languages to supply the composers. Piano pieces, lacking the advantage of literary associations, were often furnished with atmospheric titles: either general ones such as *Songs without Words, Ballades, Woodland Sketches*, or else somewhat more specific ones—*Dream of Love, The Poet Speaks, Rustle of Spring.*

Finally, composers began to write large-scale instrumental pieces bearing not only titles but literary "programs," actual stories or at least descriptions of emotional impressions arranged in some order. Step by step, the music follows the program and illustrates or reflects it. The principle of program music looms large in nineteenth-century music.

Much ink has been spilled about this matter by aestheticians and amateur philosophers. How closely, if at all, does the music really illustrate the program? Does the program "explain" the music? If you are played the music without being told the program, could you tell it from the music? Does (or should) the music make complete sense on its own terms, even if perhaps we can see that the program does add another dimension to it?

But the point is that the romantics did not *want* to be without the program. They did not particularly *want* the music to "make sense on its own terms." They wanted the combination of dimensions provided by both. There are some people who tend instinctively to summon up "pictures" in their minds when listening to music. Perhaps this habit should be frowned upon as far as baroque, Viennese, or modern music is concerned, but it fits in perfectly with the spirit of romanticism.

The "Principle of Thematic Unity" This is the other broad principle that can be identified in romantic music. To put it simply, composers tended more and more to keep some of the same themes running through all the many movements in their large works. In the "grandiose" compositions mentioned above, this served to provide a measure of unity to pieces which otherwise might have seemed straggling and formless.

That puts it simply; but in practice things worked out in a rather more complicated way. We shall experience several different levels of thematic unity in nineteenth-century music. In some compositions, themes from one movement come back literally and obviously in subsequent movements. In others, free variations of a theme are used successively either in different parts of one movement, or in all the movements of a piece. This procedure differs from the theme-and-variations form of the baroque and Viennese periods (page 182), in which the "theme" is usually an entire tune, the variations go all the way through the tune, and the variations follow one another directly, in an orderly series. It is best to use a special term, <u>thematic transformation</u>, for the variation-like procedure applied to relatively short themes, at relatively wide intervals of time, in nineteenth-century music.

In still other romantic pieces, we hear themes with even looser relationships among them. They bear a mysterious family resemblance, one which may be very hard to pin down. Clearly different, they nonetheless show vague similarities, though these similarities are too slight to count as variations by the standards of Viennese music (or even as transformations by the standards of romantic music).

This last phenomenon raises some fascinating questions: how is the line drawn between "variations," "transformations," and "vague similarities"? How about similarities which are so slight that some people (such as the composers) can hear them but other people cannot, at least not on the conscious level? Indeed—most fascinating of all—may there not be vague similarities that create the impression of unity subliminally, on a subconscious level, as though by some musical "hidden persuader"?

This notion would have delighted the romantics, with their view of music as the inner language of unconscious emotional experience. Vague similarity rather than precise recall, suggestion rather than outright statement, atmosphere rather than discourse, feeling rather than form: all these go to the heart of romanticism. We shall not be able to appreciate romantic music fully if we approach it in a literal frame of mind. In much of this music, the "inner form" is tied to the principle of thematic unity, and this is something that requires ears that are not only sharp, but also imaginative, exploratory, and more than a little fanciful.

THEMATIC
TRANSFORMATION

Romantic Nostalgia for the Past

Two important preoccupations of early romanticism were fascination with nature and fascination with the past, especially the Middle Ages. Taste in fiction moved away from "contemporary" subjects (*Tom Jones, Robinson Crusoe*) to tales of historical adventure and romance (*Ivanhoe, The Hunchback of Notre Dame, The Cask of Amontillado*). Many early romantic poems were set in olden times: Sir Walter Scott's *Young Lochinvar*, John Keats's *La Belle Dame sans Merci*, Samuel Taylor Coleridge's *Kubla Khan* and *Christabel*, and Alfred Lord Tennyson's *The Lady of Shalott*.

Our picture illustrates a later and longer poem by Tennyson, *Idylls of the King*, which was begun in 1857 and became one of the great best sellers of Victorian England. The king is Arthur, the legendary king of sixth-century England, and the poem recounts the tales of the Knights of the Round Table and the Holy Grail in such a way that they seem vaguely relevant to the standards and ideals of the nineteenth century. Longfellow's *Hiawatha* is another example of this kind of work, a grandiose blend of romanticism, nostalgia, and middle-class patriotism. The best example of all is Richard Wagner's four-night opera *The Nibelung's Ring*, based on the most famous of German medieval myths (see page 258). Incidentally, the Arthurian legends were also a rich source for Wagner, yielding him the subjects of his operas *Lohengrin, Parsifal* (whom Tennyson called "Sir Percivale"), and *Tristan und Isolde*.

Many other opera composers chose romantic subjects from the past, among them the stories of Joan of Arc, Ivanhoe, Francesca da Rimini, Mary Queen of Scots, and of course Faust—a great favorite. Composers also sometimes experimented with real or simulated old music to give their compositions an antique flavor. We shall see Berlioz importing a Gregorian chant into his *Fantastic Symphony* (page 245). There was something of a cult at this time for the music of the famous sixteenth-century composer Giovanni Pierluigi da Palestrina (see page 61). Palestrina lived in the Renaissance, long after the Middle Ages, but he was about the earliest composer whose music was known to the nineteenth century.

Romantic interest in the past was less historical than nostalgic. Poets and their readers loved the past for the pleasantly high feelings it could stir up. Thus our artist (Gustave Doré, the most famous of nineteenth-century book illustrators) thought nothing of drawing King Arthur's costume and castle in a style that is fully six hundred years too late. The later period was, visually speaking, more "romantic"; compare the castle with the nineteenth-century fantasy castle of King Ludwig II (page 252). Other romantic features of this particular picture are the grisly skeletons and the sentimental response to them conveyed by the droop of Arthur's head (and also his horse's!).

Romantic "Miniatures"

Romantic "miniatures," for piano solo or voice and piano, are short pieces which convey a particularly intense, intimate whiff of emotion (page 225). They are easy to listen to, because they are short and tend to concentrate on a single very striking musical idea. To be sure, this idea is usually so special, and of such limited applicability, that it could not keep up interest for too long. Obviously "miniatures" have less meat on them than bigger works. But no doubt there will be people who relish these highly-flavored snacks and do not care so much for heavy four-or-five-course romantic symphonies and the like.

The later Viennese composers already reflected the fashion for "miniatures." Beethoven wrote some piano pieces called *Bagatelles* (meaning "trifles"; one of them is no more than twelve measures long), and Schubert made a specialty of songs, as we have seen. The chief romantic composers of "miniatures" include two who are not treated in detail in this book, Felix Mendelssohn (1809–1847) and Franz Liszt (1811–1886), as well as Brahms, Schumann, and Chopin.

Frédéric Chopin (1810–1849)

MAZURKA IN A MINOR, OP. 17 NO. 4 (1830) *Side 8*

ÉTUDE IN C MINOR, OP. 10 NO. 12 (REVOLUTIONARY ÉTUDE) (1832) *Side 8*

BALLADE IN G MINOR, OP. 23 (1840) *Side 9*

Chopin is remembered first, perhaps, for his wonderful feeling for tone color. Himself a superb pianist, he revolutionized the technique of playing the piano, so that it became an ideal medium for romanticism instead of the rather matter-of-fact instrument of earlier times. He created entire new sound areas of pianistic melancholy, languor, and delicacy; and on the other side, he developed a range of power and brilliance that far outshone the barnstorming virtuoso pianists of his day. Besides his sensitivity to tone color, Chopin had an equally fine ear for melody and harmony and a great instinct for rhythm. Faint or bright, there is always a sparkle to his music, a rhythmic sparkle in addition to the exquisite piano sound.

With a fastidiousness that marked all his actions, Chopin limited the range of the music he wrote more sharply than any other important composer. Besides two early piano concertos and three sonatas, he wrote almost exclusively "miniatures" for piano solo. Their titles form a romantic gallery. The famous *nocturnes* are dreamy night pieces or serenades; the *impromptus* are supposed to sound like improvisations; the *études* have been mentioned above (page 224). There are also *ballades*, which do not have specific ballad poems as programs but only mean to suggest the aura of some thrilling tale of yore. And there are *preludes*—preludes to nothing, which end expectantly and leave the listener dreaming of what might ensue.

More conventionally, Chopin wrote some scherzos (page 194) and numerous dances for piano: waltzes, mazurkas, and polonaises. The latter two are Polish dance types; Chopin was a patriotic Pole even though his father was originally French and he himself lived in Paris. He wrote mazurkas and polonaises partly out of nostalgia for the land of his birth, partly to satisfy the Parisians' fascination with exotic foreign music, but most of all, because these dances gave him the opportunity to experiment with novel melodic and harmonic effects inspired by Slavic folk sources.

The Mazurka in A minor, Op. 17 No. 4, is said to have been sketched by Chopin when he was only fourteen. It opens with an atmospheric, floating introduction of four measures:

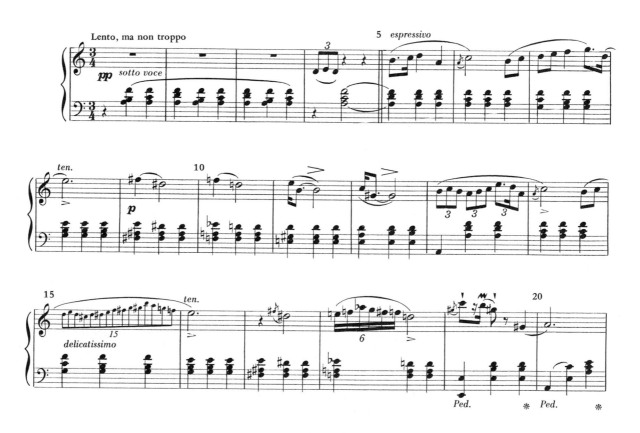

Unlike the usual purposeful introduction of a Viennese piece, this romantic introduction seems to grow up imperceptibly out of a great void, as though we have to bend an ear to catch its mysterious, delicate rustle. The identical four measures return at the end of the piece, leaving us suspended—for the piece does not come to a true cadence (page 30) at all. As this music fades away, we should assume a pensive attitude, half musing upon the melancholy mazurka itself and half yearning for these delicate sounds to start up again in the silence. A truly romantic stance, this, if we achieve it.

The mood of melancholy is most unusual for a mazurka, for in real life this is a bright and rather hard dance. Chopin views it through his own special filter; only the characteristic dance rhythm (♪ ♩ ♩ ♩), slowed down greatly in tempo, refers hauntingly to the folk origins of the mazurka dance type. The delicious sliding harmonies in measures 9 and 10 are typically romantic and typically Chopinesque.

So is the right-hand writing in measures 13, 18, and especially 15. Here a vague sensuous shimmer of sound, further blurred by the sustaining (right-foot) pedal, deliberately hides the rhythm, melody, and harmony in a wash of piano color, at least for a moment. We can draw an analogy between the obscuring of musical elements by tone color in Chopin's music and the obscuring of lines by actual color in romantic paintings such as those of Turner (page 246).

In any good performance of Chopin, the pianist will apply some rubato (page 225), slightly contracting and expanding the meter at many points. This adds even further to the emotional sheen.

In another mood, Chopin's well-known Étude in C minor makes its introduction (not shown) out of a torrent of fast piano runs. These continue in the left hand below a melody which catches the romantic spirit at its most hectic and its most magnificent:

Chopin marked this melody *appassionato,* "impassioned." Just when it seems to have calmed down to an ominous hush, the fury bursts out again for a sudden loud conclusion. Whether or not this piece reflects the composer's patriotic indignation at the Russian capture of Warsaw in 1831, as has been said, the nickname *Revolutionary Étude* seems fair enough.

Both of these pieces are short and simple in form. Our mazurka is a stripped-down dance form (a a b a | c c' c c'' | a coda); compare the minuet form on page 174. The *Revolutionary Étude* really consists of one long tune repeated with a new ending (A A').

A longer and more ambitious work is the Ballade No. 1 in G minor. Though there is no real story to this "ballad," perhaps the solemn, almost "speaking" introduction does seem to say "once upon a time" before the main business begins. This takes the form of a tune with a brooding quality:

Notice that while the melody contains many eighth notes (indicated by the upward stems in the music), Chopin has directed that some of these melody notes be sustained (as indicated by the downward stems). This is another good, if quiet, example of Chopin's skill in manipulating piano tone color.

There are two further themes, embedded in a great variety of brilliant piano writing:

Although all three of these melodies are quiet when first heard, they return with different dynamics and in different moods. The first tune grows menacing from the point marked with the asterisk on, and the second tune rages in triumph. A form diagram for the piece must include a reference to the dynamics:

INTRODUCTION	MAIN SECTION	CODA
Largo	Moderato	Presto con
	A---→ B C A B B C A	fuoco
	p pp pp $pp < ff$ ff ff ff $pp < f$	*il più forte*
		possibile

The Ballade in G minor contains within itself something of the wide range of Chopin's sentiment. This extends from gentle to violent—most violent of all at the final cadence:

The markings for the coda (page 158) of this ballade mean "very fast, with fire" and "as loudly as possible." But even in the most violent passages, Chopin never seems to lose his control or his sense of refinement.

Chopin was greatly admired for a hundred years after his death, during the great age of piano music. Doubtless this age is now passing (see page 391). There are fewer great piano virtuosos and popular-music pianists; children are less docile about practicing their scales; young composers tend to employ one of the new electronic composing machines rather than "work at the piano." It will be a pity if the popularity of Chopin's music suffers on this account. He was the most exquisite of the early romantic composers—the most poetic, some would say, of all the great composers.

Chopin and George Sand

The composer Frédéric Chopin and Mme. Aurore Dudevant (George Sand), painted by their friend Eugène Delacroix, the greatest of the French romantic artists. Delacroix's portrait of Chopin radiates a sense of agony and self-absorbed passion, qualities which we may rather doubt would have struck a Houdon so forcibly (page 169). Here one romantic artist portrays another, consumed by the common fire of their genius.

When the romantics spoke of emotional freedom, what they generally meant first was free love, and it is no coincidence that many artists of this time had intense and often irregular love affairs, which they made no effort to hide. Chopin, Berlioz, Liszt, Verdi, and Wagner can be mentioned among the musicians. As for George

Sand, she was a distinguished novelist, feminist, and champion of sexual freedom who also lived for a time with the poet Alfred de Musset. There had been literary ladies before in France (the "bluestockings") and elsewhere, but the romantic period was the first in which they began to preach and practice women's liberation. Besides adopting a male name, Sand sometimes wore men's clothes and was famous for her cigars.

From her photographs we know she was not beautiful, but evidently Delacroix considered her extremely feminine. He has depicted her sensuousness and rich magnetism marvelously — the "romantic" woman behind the plain face. (The cigar is there, too, but notice how Delacroix has de-emphasized it.)

Robert Schumann (1810–1856)

CARNAVAL (1834)

Another distinguished pianist-composer of the early romantic period was Robert Schumann. Like Chopin, he was happiest with "miniatures," short piano compositions and songs. But unlike Chopin, Schumann always wanted to write music on a larger scale: symphonies, chamber music, cantatas, fugues, even an opera. He also tended to group his songs together in song cycles (page 212) and to write piano pieces in big sets held together by some sort of program.

His style of writing for piano is just as individual as Chopin's but denser and less brilliant. One of Schumann's favorite directions to place on his music was the German word *innig*, meaning "inward," "introspective," "intimate"; he substituted a certain warmth and privacy for Chopin's more polished, refined style. This results as much from his harmony and melody as from his piano writing. But of course we cannot hope to find words to catch the musical character of these two composers, any more than we could really describe two of our close friends to someone who does not know them. Each composer emerges from his music as a fully rounded individual, and we can get to them only by immersing ourselves in their compositions.

Carnaval is a series of twenty relatively short piano pieces, linked both by means of similar themes and by a vague program. At a masked ball, the first piece, "Pierrot," arrives, followed by "Harlequin," "Coquette," Schumann himself in two separate manifestations, his friends "Estrella" and "Chiarina," and Chopin—the latter represented by a condensed little nocturne in which one romantic composer imitates another perfectly, and with perfect authority and affection. "Paganini" also arrives—Niccolo Paganini, the fabulous violinist of that time who was said to be in league with the devil. Schumann does his best to translate Paganini's fiddle fireworks into pianistic terms.

For the last number (No. 20), they all join in a rollicking "March of the David League against the Philistines." This was a make-believe society of Schumann's, consisting of young spirits banded together against the Goliath of middle-class society and its conservative musical tastes. To show how unconservative he was, Schumann put his David March into triple meter. It includes a pompous old "Grandfather Dance" to stand for the Philistines, and a bit of Beethoven's "Emperor" Piano Concerto to cheer the David League along in their good fight.

Notice how many of the numbers in *Carnaval* feature the same three notes—A♭, C, B—near the beginning of their melodies. This counts as a rather direct application of the "principle of thematic unity" that was mentioned above (page 227). Can you hear the thematic similarity between some—any—all of these pieces, and does hearing it add anything to your enjoyment of *Carnaval*? What is more fascinating yet, those three notes are derived from the name of the German town *Asch*—for the German names for A♭, C, and B happen to be *As*, *C*, and *H*. Asch was the home of Schumann's current girl friend, Ernestine von Fricken—"Estrella." (He later married "Chiarina"—Clara Wieck.) To this day musicologists are puzzling about Schumann's use of private "codes" of this kind.

PIANO CONCERTO IN A MINOR (1841–1845)

Of Schumann's larger pieces, his single Piano Concerto is one of the best. The first movement is in sonata form, but handled very freely. An explosive little introduction (piano) is followed by the gentle main theme of the whole concerto (woodwind instruments, line 1):

But as soon as this theme is repeated by the piano, we know in a flash that the tone color of the piano suits it best. The rest of the movement contains some very interesting versions of the main theme, in which tempo, mood, and other aspects are changed. These are not true variations, since they do not last all the way through the theme, but for one or two measures they act like variations. This is an instance of thematic transformation, one of the characteristic levels of thematic unity employed by romantic composers (page 227).

The version on line 2 of the example appears in the second group of the exposition (and also, of course, in the recapitulation). It is played by the orchestra with animated (*animato*) figures in the piano. The slower version of line 3 begins the development section, after a vigorous orchestral passage has modulated into a new dreamlike tonality. Here a dialogue—a sort of joint meditation—is set up between the piano and the orchestra clarinet. Then ultimately the marchlike version of line 4 arrives. It serves as a bright coda for the movement, directly after an introspective, richly expressive cadenza. But this cadenza was written out by Schumann. He did not trust the pianist to improvise his own.

Second Movement Schumann calls it *Intermezzo*, meaning "interlude"—almost as though to apologize for its intimate, shadowy, almost casual quality. This movement is in a simple A B A' form. The A section sounds like a tender whispered conversation between piano and orchestra. A nostalgic melody in the cello and some other instruments forms the B section.

At the end of A', we are surprised to hear the orchestra playing a tentative bit of the main theme of the first movement, while the piano makes puzzled comments (line 5 of the example). These hints soon lead into a brisk theme—a decisive beginning for the last movement (line 6).

The asterisks on the example indicate how Schumann has tried to provide thematic unity between the themes of his different movements. The theme of the last movement is actually "derived" from the main theme of the opening movement, for the new theme centers on the most important notes in the first measures of the old one. Whether we can *hear* this, as well as *see* it, is another question; certainly this is an example of the "vague similarities" that were discussed above (page 227). By means of the tentative little passage at the end of the second movement, Schumann has done his best to lead us by the hand (or by the ear) so that we do hear the themes in this way.

Third Movement The last movement of this concerto is in sonata form, like the first. The second theme is intriguing because it seems to move twice as slowly as the rest of the movement; notice how ingeniously Schumann makes the two different tempos run into one another. This second theme is another of his triple-time marches. The development section starts with a stiff contrapuntal passage, which we may feel to be out of place in a romantic work. The coda, after a firm final statement of the main theme, goes into a splendid spin with a new theme for the piano.

At one point within the second group, after the double-slow second theme, the piano passage-work sounds a little like Chopin. Evidently Schumann had picked up some pointers when doing his *Carnaval* portraits.

It is interesting that Schumann originally planned the first movement of his Piano Concerto in A minor as a complete piece. He added the other movements later. This first movement could hardly be described as a "miniature," but it is still true that prior to the romantic period, composers would not have thought of writing a single concerto-like movement by itself. Nor would they (or could they) have written concertos on such an intimate scale—with such an intimate tone of voice—as that of Schumann's first two movements.

Romanticism and the Macabre

In their pursuit of all emotional sensation, the romantics did not neglect the netherworld of fantasy, dream, and nightmare. Like other romantic preoccupations this can be traced back to the late eighteenth century. A weird picture by the Swiss-English painter-poet John Henry Fuseli, *The Nightmare* (1781), catches the combination of horror, irrationality, and sexuality that enters into romantic effusions in this vein. We see something of the same combination in *The Sick Rose,* a powerful short poem by another painter-poet and a friend of Fuseli's, William Blake:

O Rose, thou art sick!　　　Has found out thy bed
The invisible worm,　　　　Of crimson joy;
That flies in the night,　　　And his dark crimson love
In the howling storm,　　　Does thy life destroy.

Besides ordinary historical novels, this period also saw the rise of the Gothic novel, which spun elaborate tales of ghosts and tortures of old. Sanguinary old ballads were dug up and greatly relished. Fantastic stories became popular, among them *Frankenstein* — forerunners of our own science fiction.

Composers did their best to provide weird chords and terrifying orchestral sounds as their contribution to this aspect of romanticism. Giuseppe Verdi, in his opera *Macbeth,* composed such music for the witches and the visions they summon up for Macbeth's benefit. Richard Wagner, in his opera *The Flying Dutchman,* depicted the legendary ghost ship and its spectral crew. And in the *Fantastic Symphony,* Hector Berlioz's "Dream of the Witches' Sabbath" bears comparison with Fuseli's *Nightmare.*

The Program Symphony

Hector Berlioz (1803–1869)
SYMPHONIE FANTASTIQUE (*FANTASTIC SYMPHONY*) (1830)
Side 9

One of the most attractive and flamboyant figures of the early romantic period, Hector Berlioz moved firmly in the direction of "grandiose" compositions. He was an enthusiastic breaker of tradition, a shocker of the bourgeoisie, and a superb orchestrator, unmatched in some ways until the time of Gustav Mahler and Claude Debussy (see pages 286, 309). Berlioz could manage orchestral effects of breathtaking delicacy, but in his own time he was famous for effects that were so forceful—he once planned to use thirty-two timpani in a piece—that people have solemnly debated whether his decibel tolerance may have been greater than that of normal people. One of the endless series of cartoons he inspired is shown on page 264.

Berlioz hit upon a plan, which is simplicity itself, for combining the two romantic principles discussed above: the principle of the literary program and the principle of thematic unity. Write a large symphony with a literary program concerning some person; then in each movement, have this person represented by a single tune which can be treated to variation or transformation. The result is called a program symphony.

PROGRAM SYMPHONY

Produced in 1830, when Berlioz was only twenty-six years old, the *Fantastic Symphony* is certainly one of the most sensational pieces in the whole history of music. The written-out program consists of a general statement and then guidelines for the various movements:

A young musician of morbid sensibility and ardent imagination is in love, and has poisoned himself with opium in a fit of desperation. Not having taken a fatal dose, he falls into a long sleep in which he has the strangest dreams, wherein his feelings, sentiments, and memories are transformed by his sick brain into musical ideas and figures. The beloved woman herself has become a melody which he finds and hears everywhere as an *idée fixe* [a "fixed idea," an obsession; the *idée fixe* melody is usually heard in variation or transformation].

IDÉE FIXE

So the *Fantastic Symphony* counts as the first example of turned-on music—or at least, so it seemed. Everybody knew, or soon came to know, that Berlioz was suffering from unrequited love for the Irish actress Harriet Smithson, who had taken Paris by storm with her Shakespearean roles. Was the program a piece of veiled autobiography, or was it merely a skillful advertising device?

In any case, audiences at the time may well have found the symphony psychedelic in its use of tone color, which was produced by an unprecedentedly large orchestra (page 224) used in the most original ways. Also very original was the notion of having a single theme turn up in all the movements of symphony (there are five, lasting fifty minutes) as a reminder of the musician's beloved. This *idée fixe* must be quoted in full; Berlioz's long melodies are distinctive and much admired:*

Like Schubert in the Quartet in A minor (page 207), Berlioz places this long tune in a sonata-form movement and breaks parts of it off to use as motives for the development section. Whether the effect is as "organic" as with Schubert is a question, especially considering the greater length of the Berlioz piece.

In any case, the tune shows many typical features of romantic melody, such as the excited rising or surging movement in bars 1–2 and especially in bars 5–8. The whole of line 2 seems like a passionate struggle to inch higher and higher up the scale, gaining one note and then losing three. Bar 19, just before the cadence, provides a positive shudder of emotion.

Notice, too, the profusion of dynamic marks in this tune, added by Berlioz to ensure just the right expressive quality. There are also many other marks; with the romantic composers, one has to become something of a linguist to follow all their directions. Compare this brief glossary for the *idée fixe* with the lists of more ordinary terms on pages 10 and 11:

canto espressivo	an expressive song
*poco **sf***	accented, but not too strongly
dolce	sweetly
cresc. poco a poco	gradually getting louder
animato	animated
ritenuto	held back (in tempo)
a tempo	at the original tempo
*poco **f**, poco rit.*	somewhat loud; somewhat slowed down

---

* In this example, note values have been halved and the odd measure lines omitted to facilitate reading. The *idée fixe* in its original notation appears on the first line of page 242.

To illustrate the shifting nature of the hallucination, Berlioz transformed the *idée fixe*—in rhythm, especially—for its appearances at other stages of the dream:

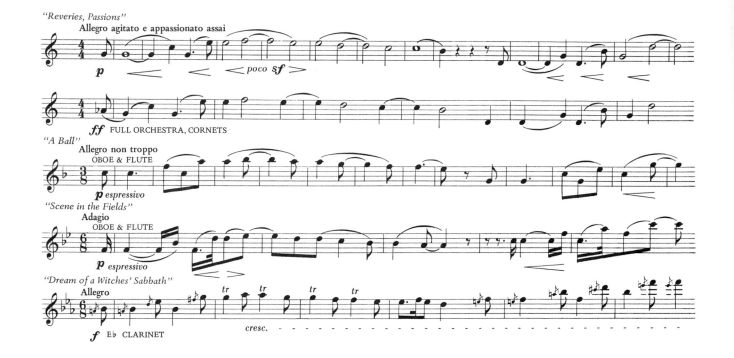

First Movement: "Reveries, Passions"

First he remembers the uneasiness of mind, the aimless passions, the baseless depression and elations which he felt before seeing her whom he loves. Then the volcanic love which she instantly inspired in him, his delirious agonies, his jealous furies, his fits of tenderness, his religious consolations.

His first memories are depicted not by the *idée fixe* but by another long tune—a halting, passionate melody which is perhaps even more striking. (It was taken from a love song written by Berlioz when he was eighteen.) The symphony does not even begin directly with this tune but opens with a short quiet run-in; this typically romantic touch suggests that the music grows up imperceptibly out of silence. This early part of the movement hardly sounds like the introduction to something else, as did the slow openings of Mozart's

Overture to *Don Giovanni*, Haydn's Symphony No. 88, or Beethoven's Overture to *Egmont*. It sounds more like a short movement in its own right.

After the appearance of the *idée fixe*, the movement picks up speed and follows sonata form—but very loosely. The *idée fixe* serves as the main theme. Some of the finest strokes run counter to the principles of the Viennese composers: for instance, the many striking slowdowns and the arresting up-and-down chromatic scale (page 24) that crops up in the development section without any noticeable connection with anything else. Near the end, the *idée fixe* returns noisily at a faster tempo (see the second line on page 242). And at the very end, the "religious consolations" mentioned in the program are clearly apparent in the music, still animated by fragments of the *idée fixe*.

Second Movement: "A Ball"

At a ball, in the midst of a noisy, brilliant fête, he finds his beloved again.

A symphony needs the simplicity and easy swing of a dance movement, and this episode in the opium dream conveniently provided one. It is a waltz rather than a minuet or scherzo; the *idée fixe*, in a lilting triple meter, appears in the position of a trio (see line 3 on page 242). However, the internal dance structure of a b a, etc., which is usual in earlier dance movements but which might restrain the "spontaneity," does not occur. Two prominent harp parts are featured in the score of this movement; Berlioz wanted each to be played by "at least two instruments."

Third Movement: "Scene in the Fields"

A summer evening in the country; he hears two herders piping in dialogue. This pastoral duo, the location, the light rustling of trees stirred by the wind . . . gives him a feeling of unaccustomed calm. . . . But she appears again, his heart breaks. . . .

The "pastoral duo" at the beginning of this long country scene is played by an English horn (evidently the boy herder) and an oboe (the girl), backstage. At the end of the movement, the English horn returns to the accompaniment of distant thunder sounds, played with Berlioz's favorite sponge-tipped sticks on four differently tuned timpani. Alas, the girl oboe is no longer to be heard.

In between these pipings, the movement is built on another long tune, first played by violins and flute, then later by violas, cellos, and four bassoons. When the *idée fixe* finally arrives (line 4 on page 242) it is interrupted by angry sounds, which swell up to a surprisingly forceful climax.

Fourth Movement: "March to the Scaffold"

He dreams that he has killed his loved one, that he is condemned to death and led to execution. A march . . . accompanies the procession . . . Finally the *idée fixe* appears for a moment . . . to be cut off by the fall of the axe.

This is perhaps the most impressive movement in the symphony, despite the grisly or ludicrous effect (depending on how you look at it) of the final guillotine chop and snare-drum roll. Besides the blaring march tune in the wind instruments—Berlioz wrote some highly impressive pieces for band—there is another theme, treated in counterpoint:

On two occasions, this appears at a higher octave in an extraordinary divided orchestration, a memorable instance of Berlioz's novel imagination in tone color:

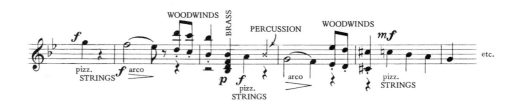

Pizz. (for *pizzicato*) means that the violin strings are plucked with the finger. *Col arco* means "with the bow."

Fifth Movement: "Dream of a Witches' Sabbath"

He sees himself at a Witches' Sabbath. . . . Unearthly sounds, groans, shrieks of laughter. . . . The melody of his beloved is heard, but it has lost its character of nobleness and timidity. . . . It is *she* who comes to the Sabbath! . . . She joins the diabolical orgy. The funeral knell, burlesque of the *Dies Irae.* . . .

Berlioz really lets himself go in this movement, adding the element of parody to the sensational orchestral effects already pioneered in the earlier movements. As he himself points out, the "noble and timid" *idée fixe* theme sounds cheap and raucous when played by the squeaky high clarinet, the E♭ clarinet, and when changed to a fast jig rhythm (line 5 in the example on page 242). A similar burlesque rhythm is applied to one of the most solemn and famous of all Gregorian chants, the Dies Irae, which is introduced with church-bell sounds:

Below two of Berlioz's versions, this example shows the beginning of the original chant in modernized Gregorian notation (the absence of stems on the notes reminds us that chant rhythm is supposed to be free; see page 33).

The Dies Irae was and still is sung only at Masses for the Dead, or Requiem Masses (page 57). In Catholic France, an audience would have recognized it instantly. The effect of its burlesque treatment must have been shocking—and graphically illustrative of a Black Mass at the obscene witches' revels summoned up by Berlioz's drugged imagination. The early romantics enjoyed trafficking in the macabre and the diabolical (page 239).

After taking revenge on Harriet Smithson by parodying her into an old hag, Berlioz does not, in fact, have her cavort much with the other revelers. The movement ends with a contrapuntal combination of the Dies Irae and another dynamic theme illustrating the witches' dance.

Compared with works like Beethoven's Fifth Symphony and Schumann's Piano Concerto, the *Fantastic Symphony* may seem rather undisciplined in form. One cannot always sense the "logic" linking one musical event to the next. Later program symphonies by Berlioz do better in this respect; we should not forget that the *Fantastic Symphony* was his first major effort, an amazing production for a composer aged only twenty-six. Later he wrote symphonies entitled *Harold in Italy,* based on the once-famous epic poem by Lord Byron, and *Romeo and Juliet,* after Shakespeare. Shakespeare's plays greatly attracted the romantics because of their loose formal structure and their strong emotions. They attracted Berlioz also because of Miss Smithson, the Shakespearean actress, who by this time had become his wife.

But in any case, formal "logic" was not the chief concern of Berlioz or many another romantic composer. What we appreciate in his music is its flamboyance and imaginativeness, both in the extraordinary orchestral sounds and in the unpredictable sequence of the novel musical ideas. Compared with the Fantastic Symphony, the Schumann Piano Concerto can seem rather tame. The last few decades have witnessed a distinct Berlioz revival; our own music, too, places less emphasis on logic than on flair.

Romanticism and Nature

An important facet of romanticism was a fascination with nature. William Wordsworth established a new tone of reverence and admiration for nature in English poetry, and he was followed in this by Keats, Shelley, Tennyson, and all the other great romantic poets. We may also recall the sentimental nature images of the poet of Schubert's *Die Winterreise* (page 212).

The English also excelled in painting landscapes and seascapes. William Turner's *The Slave Ship* (1839), originally entitled *Slavers Throwing Overboard the Dead and the Dying—Typhoon Coming On*, shows a frail ship buffeted by the elemental forces of nature, including fantastic fishes (or are they, too, victims of the typhoon?). Turner's astonishingly bold use of color and free treatment of forms convey an unforgettable sense of the majesty, mystery, and menace of nature.

It may seem unfair to suggest comparing this highly imaginative painting with "real" nature as laid out in the parks illustrated on pages 110 and 178. But the point is that the romantics were less interested in "reality" than in imagination, less concerned with nature for its own sake than with the feelings that nature stirred within them. They were ready to heighten nature, even distort it, if this would increase the emotional effect. In Turner's picture, though the plight of the slaves is dire, viewers can enjoy the thrill of the mighty swirls of yellow water and the blood-red fog while remaining safely outside the picture frame. Like historical novels, such pictures allowed the mind to roam over wild feelings that were safely distant from Victorian reality.

Composers shared in this romantic enthusiasm for nature by writing program music (page 226). Felix Mendelssohn's *Hebrides* Overture (*Fingal's Cave*) has passages that sound a little like the orderly beating of waves, and even a romanticized foghorn; Mendelssohn himself was a talented watercolorist. The "Scene in the Fields" from Berlioz's *Fantastic Symphony* includes the sounds of shepherds piping and a thunderstorm (page 243). Other musical landscapes of a somewhat later period are Bedřich Smetana's *Vltava* (a river, also known as the Moldau), Richard Strauss's *Alpine Symphony*, Claude Debussy's *Clouds* (page 309), and so on.

The Symphonic Poem

Peter Ilyich Tchaikovsky (1840–1893)
ROMEO AND JULIET (1867–1880) *Side 10*

SYMPHONIC POEM

After Berlioz, the program symphony did not flourish widely. Composers who wanted to follow him in writing orchestral program music seem to have found the system too inflexible. They tended to write program music in one long movement, employing a great variety of forms: sonata form, rondo, theme and variations (all treated very freely), and most often, unique "inner forms" designed for the particular occasion, to match the particular program. The best general name for these pieces is symphonic poem, though the term *tone poem* and others are also used.

A key figure in this development was Franz Liszt (1811–1886). A colorful and historically important composer, Liszt started his career as a piano virtuoso, the greatest of his day, producing brilliant or delicate piano "miniatures," in which all of Chopin's innovations were extended and exaggerated. He then turned to conducting and writing orchestral music. In his two program symphonies and his many symphonic poems, Liszt made a speciality of thematic transformation (see page 227), extending Berlioz's concept of the *idée fixe* and its variations. Though his symphonic poems were famous at the time, today only one of them is likely to be encountered at symphony concerts, and that rarely: *Les Préludes*, which has a cloudy program taken from the French romantic poet Alphonse de Lamartine.

A symphonic poem that is more often heard today is *Romeo and Juliet* by the Russian composer Peter Ilyich Tchaikovsky. A generation or two ago, Tchaikovsky was everybody's favorite romantic composer; perhaps he still is today. His long list of popular works includes symphonies, which we shall discuss briefly later, and brilliant concertos for piano and for violin. He wrote many operas and ballets, including *Swan Lake*—the most famous of all ballets—and the Christmas favorite *The Nutcracker*. Besides *Romeo and Juliet*, his program-music pieces include two others based on Shakespeare, *The Tempest* and *Hamlet*; Shakespeare was greatly admired in the romantic era, as we remember from the case of Berlioz. And there is *1812*, a patriotic number commemorating the Russian victory over Napoleon in that year, the subject also of Tolstoy's great novel *War and Peace*. Tchaikovsky introduces both the French national anthem (the *Marseillaise*) and a Russian hymn into this piece and has them battle with one another. It is program music with a vengeance.

However, *Romeo and Juliet* treats Shakespeare's play more tactfully and only in rather general terms. Indeed, Tchaikovsky did not call it a symphonic poem but rather an "overture-fantasy." Still, once we know the title we easily identify the three main themes with elements in the drama. The high, surging melody must stand for the love of Romeo and Juliet. The very agitated theme suggests the deadly vendetta between their two families or, more generally, the fate that stands between these "star-cross'd lovers," as Shakespeare calls them. The religious-sounding theme stands for the kindly Friar Laurence, who devises a plot to help the lovers which goes fatally wrong.

Romeo and Juliet begins with a slow introduction, as low clarinets and bassoons play the Friar Laurence theme. Notice the solemn slow wind chords interspersed by strumming on the harp, an instrument which Berlioz had introduced into the orchestra (see page 243) and which Tchaikovsky liked particularly. Someone, we feel, is getting ready to narrate a serious, tragic tale. The slow introduction works up to a climax over a dramatic timpani roll.

The tempo changes to allegro and we hear the vendetta (or fate) theme. It is made up of a number of short rhythmic motives, which Tchaikovsky puts to use at once for development; this section too works up to a climax, when part of the theme is punctuated with sensational cymbal claps. The highly romantic love theme is played first of all by the English horn doubled by the violas—a mellow sound. It is followed by a curious but affecting passage constructed out of a little sighing figure:

This gradually turns into a contrapuntal accompaniment for the love theme, played by the French horn. The sigh is beginning to turn into a sob:

Tchaikovsky repeats these themes and develops them in various ways. He does not try to follow through the story step by step, any more than Berlioz does in the *Fantastic Symphony*. In the sections where the Friar Laurence theme and the vendetta theme are developed vigorously together, we may get the impression of a battle between the forces of good and evil; and at the end, we cannot miss a reference to the tragic outcome of the play. The tempo slows down again, and part of the love theme appears in a mutilated version over funeral drum taps in the timpani. The sighing theme, too, is now heard in a very mournful transformation.

However, the mood is not entirely gloomy; the storyteller (he may be Friar Laurence, perhaps) seems to derive solace and inspiration from his tale. The harp strumming is resumed, and the love theme returns for the last time in a new cadential version, surging enthusiastically upward in a way that is very typical of Tchaikovsky. An impressive final cadence is made up of some of the rhythms of the vendetta theme, over another dramatic timpani roll.

Richard Strauss (1864–1949)

DON JUAN (1887–1888)

The symphonic poems of Richard Strauss (which he preferred to call "tone poems") are more involved than those of Tchaikovsky. *Don Juan* goes back to the subject of Mozart's opera *Don Giovanni:* the legendary Spanish lover who pursues women insatiably and is finally doomed for his sins. Strauss took his inspiration not from the old legend itself but from a long, extravagant version of it by the nineteenth-century German poet Nikolaus Lenau. The program consists of excerpts from the poem:

Fain would I run the circle, immeasurably wide, of beautiful women's endless charms, in a full tempest of enjoyment, to die of a kiss at the mouth of the last one. O friends! would that I could fly through every region where beauty blossoms, fall on my knees before each one, and conquer. . . .

I shun satiety and the exhaustion of pleasure; I keep myself fresh in the service of Beauty. . . . The breath of a woman that today is the odor of spring may perhaps oppress me tomorrow like the air of a dungeon. . . . Indeed, passion is always and only the *new* passion. . . . Away, then, to triumphs ever new, while youth's fiery pulses race!

Beautiful was the fire that urged me on. It has spent its rage, and now silence remains . . . the fuel is all consumed, the hearth is cold and dark.

No doubt the lengthy opening theme refers to the hero:

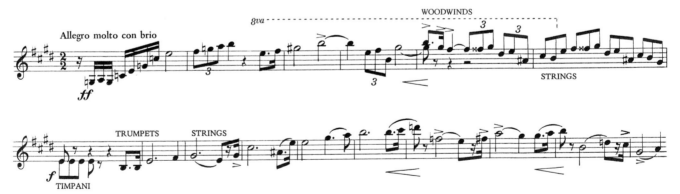

Do you detect some similarity to the *idée fixe* of Berlioz's *Fantastic Symphony?* The vehemence, ardor, and spontaneous flow of this music carry all before it, or so Strauss means to suggest. His own vaulting style of romantic melody is also employed to very good advantage in the warm love scene that follows, at a slower tempo. It starts out like young love at first sight, but toward the end, we clearly hear Don Juan's impatience to get on to the next "tempest of enjoyment," as Lenau puts it. (We should not blame anyone for tiring of this particular lady, with her saccharine solo violin.)

Don Juan's original theme returns, and soon he launches into a new adventure—with a more mature woman, it would certainly appear, someone more sensual and relaxed. But this second love scene also ends in disillusion. Note the wonderfully rich sound of the oboe in this scene; such orchestral opulence was one of the proudest accomplishments of the romantic composers.

Then a bold new theme blares out in the French horns, a revival of noble wanderlust in Don Juan:

For a moment, we can picture him chafing to leave while the lady wheedles him to remain. He gets away, and in a long developmental section, this bold new theme is added to Don Juan's original musical material.

Suddenly there is a sharp break in the music. This place is usually explained as illustrating the death of Don Juan, which comes about in Lenau's poem through a duel; sensing that his youth has "spent its rage," our hero allows himself to be run through. Mournful memories of both women are heard in the orchestra, on various woodwind instruments and on the inevitable solo violin. However, before dying, Don Juan apparently remembers his whole career, in a passage that has the feeling of a sonata-form recapitulation. This passage includes both his original theme and the bold new one of the example above. Then the music sinks down, and the piece ends on an extended note of pathos.

The unique "inner form" of *Don Juan* may be diagramed as follows:

				Developmental					D
				Passage	D		Remembrance		E
DON	Love Scene	DON	Love Scene	NEW	DON	U	DON	NEW	A
JUAN	No. 1	JUAN	No. 2	THEME	JUAN	E	JUAN	THEME	T
THEME	(*slower*)	THEME	(*slower*)		THEME	L	THEME		H

To compare Strauss's *Don Juan* with Mozart's *Don Giovanni* (pages 163 to 167) is to observe how romanticism transformed the half-scurrilous, half-moralistic old legend. If Strauss's hero strikes us as more immediately dashing and ardent, that may be because he tends to dramatize himself—both in the poem and in the music, furnished as it is with generous helpings of brass and percussion, vigorous rhythms, and bold, overreaching melodic leaps. His women are sentimental, and he plays along.

Mozart's Don Giovanni, completely un-introspective, follows his nature unhesitatingly and faces the consequences when they happen to catch up with him. Strauss's Don Juan is always harping on the theme of his heroism, comparing his conquests, and worrying about the coming termination of his amorous career. He has no sense of humor at all about his adventures, as Mozart's Don Giovanni does. When Don Giovanni dies, he doesn't think of any of his women but only (as always) of himself. And he dies with a shriek of agony at the torments of hellfire, not with a sob or a sniff, as in Strauss.

Wagnerian Castles

Nineteenth-century German architecture: two sides of the coin. Shown below is Wagner's Festival Theater at Bayreuth. At the left, the castle of Neuschwanstein, built after 1867 by the extravagantly romantic young King Ludwig II of Bavaria. Bavaria was the largest state in Germany, though Prussia was the most powerful. Ludwig was later declared insane, on equivocal evidence, and deposed.

Neuschwanstein, perched on a lonely mountain, overlooking a dramatic gorge and waterfall, is a romantic fantasy in stone. Everything about it tells of the nineteenth century's yearning for the past, for the Middle Ages of fairy tale and myth: the picturesque turrets, the great keep, the Minstrel's Hall, the ancient-style furniture, the leaded-glass windows. Such yearning also made Ludwig, from his boyhood on, into a deep admirer of Wagner and Wagner's operas celebrating medieval German myths. On his accession to the throne at the age of eighteen, he brought the composer to his court and for a time gave him unlimited support. For Wagner, whose fortunes were then at a low ebb, this was indeed the action of a fairy godfather, and it was the decisive turning point in his career.

What did Wagner do with the support? Besides maintaining himself on a scale of personal luxury that was the talk of the time, he built a special theater in the little Bavarian town of Bayreuth exclusively for the performances of his operas. There are very few frills on this building; it is a solid lump of nineteenth-century architecture, as functional as a factory. Today, while poor King Ludwig's castle is maintained by the state as a curiosity which tourists can visit for a small fee, the Bayreuth Theater is still putting on Wagner festivals and selling out every summer, at stiff prices, exactly as Wagner had planned a hundred years ago. The rest of the year the theater is dark. It is hard to think of any other artist who ever carried off such an impressive act of entrepreneurism.

Romantic Opera

Romantic composers and their audiences alike were fascinated by the possibilities of combining music with literature and ideas in general. The atmosphere that produced the program symphony and the symphonic poem was also very conducive to the development of opera. It also meant that many (though not all) composers and librettists began thinking hard about the meaning and "message" of their operas, and viewing the genre as a sort of serious drama in music rather than simply as entertainment. Not surprisingly, opera flourished all over Europe in the nineteenth century even more brilliantly than before.

Many romantic novels supplied the subjects for romantic operas: for example, Sir Walter Scott's *Ivanhoe*, *Kenilworth*, *The Lady of the Lake*, *The Pirate*, and *The Bride of Lammermoor*. Just as people today like seeing the movie or television version of a popular book, so people in those days enjoyed the "opera version." Remarkably few romantic operas have truly original stories, in fact. Mostly they go back to novels, or stage plays, or (in the case of Richard Wagner) to old medieval legends.

And many operas touched in one way or another on sensitive political issues—so sensitive, that the police-state censors were kept working overtime. French opera, in particular, developed into a very elaborate and pompous entertainment called "grand opera," featuring huge crowd scenes and historical stories about revolutions, uprisings, religious wars, and so on. It seems clear that for the Parisian middle classes, "grand opera" served as a sort of safety valve in the highly unstable political situation of the time.

Political motives were also central for the two greatest masters of romantic opera, working within rather different operatic traditions: Giuseppe Verdi in Italy (page 265) and Richard Wagner in Germany.

Richard Wagner (1813–1883)

Richard Wagner probably had the most fascinating career of all the great composers. We can hardly do justice to all its facets, but one aspect of it deserves to be brought out. This is Wagner's remarkable ability to play both sides of the nineteenth-century scene—not only the romantic, artistic side but also the materialistic. For in spite of hardships over a great many years, Wagner finally emerged as a success symbol which might have been the envy of any nineteenth-century businessman.

He was an incredible sponger, living in a style of ostentatious luxury on borrowed money which he never paid back. His love life featured some sensational and widely discussed conquests. He treated people as ruthlessly as any robber baron. In his middle years he gained the support of royalty and started to dabble in power politics, a subject which, along with every other, he had written about in endless books and articles.

But perhaps his most impressive accomplishment of all was to build: not in sound, but in bricks and mortar. He designed a special theater in Bayreuth, Germany (page 253), for the sole purpose of producing festival perform-ances of his own operas. These events fairly hypnotized artists and intellec-tuals of the time. Bayreuth soon became a flourishing commercial venture, and a hundred years later, under the direction of Wagner's descendants, it is still doing very nicely with yearly Wagner festivals.

All this was possible, of course, only because Wagner impressed the world so deeply as a romantic composer and, even more, as *the* ultimate romantic artist. He brought all the arts together into what he called the "Combined-Art-Work" (*Gesamtkunstwerk*) to which he devoted virtually all his atten-tion as a composer. This was his own special type of opera—except that

MUSIC DRAMA Wagner always insisted on calling it by the high-sounding name of "music drama."

In Wagner's "music drama" the music shares honors with the drama, the philosophy, and the poetry—all provided by Wagner himself—and also with the stage design and acting. (No other opera composer has ever specified de-tails of sets and acting so carefully; our line score on pages 261 to 263 reproduces only a fraction of Wagner's stage directions.) His operas are pro-foundly emotional, as suited the romantic temperament. They deal with weighty philosophical issues, or so at least Wagner and his admirers believed, and they do so under the symbolic cover of old medieval German legends. This was another romantic feature, one which anticipated Freud, with his emphasis on myths (for example, the myth of Oedipus) as embodiments of the deepest unconscious truths.

Wagner was a great conductor and a superb orchestrator. He raised the orchestra to a new importance in opera, with the help of his famous system
LEITMOTIVS of leitmotivs, or leading motives. These are simply motives associated with some person, thing, or idea in the drama. By playing leitmotivs, the orchestra can "tell the story" and thus do what the program symphonists were doing, only better. Sometimes the leitmotivs grow very tiresome: whenever the hero draws his sword, for example, the orchestra dutifully comes up with the "sword motive." On the other hand, they could be used very subtly to show what was going on in the hero's mind even when he was saying something else. Wagner also became extremely skillful at transforming leitmotivs so that they expressed unexpected shades of developing meaning.

The theory, in any case, was that leitmotivs, being music, could state ideas in *emotional* terms, over and above the intellectual terms provided by mere words. This was a logical end result of romantic doctrine. Furthermore, the complex web of leitmotivs provided the long "music dramas" with thematic unity of a particularly rich sort. On both counts, psychological and technical, leitmotivs were ideally calculated to impress the nineteenth century.

Two persons helped to inspire Wagner's great secular hymn to love, *Tristan und Isolde.* One was the philosopher Arthur Schopenhauer, whose books Wagner had just discovered. The other was the wife of one of his patrons, Mathilde Wesendonck, with whom he was having a love affair.

Schopenhauer had made a particularly powerful formulation of the general romantic view of music's great importance in the scheme of things. According to his philosophy, life consists of "the Will," or inner feelings and drives, and "Appearances," or ideals, morals, reason, and everything else. He believed that the Will has complete power over Appearances, and that the only real outer manifestation of the Will is through music.

For Schopenhauer, the dominance of the Will was the source of life's misery. Wagner, less pessimistic, decided to write a "music drama" that would glorify the all-powerful Will through music—which, as Schopenhauer would have had to admit, was most appropriate. The aspect of Will would be sexual love, and the story would be taken (as usual) from an old legend.

Tristan und Isolde, then, is not just a love story or even just a great love story. It is that, but also more. It is a serious (and successful) effort to show passion as the ruling force, almost a religious principle, that transcends every other aspect of worldly Appearance. Thus when Tristan and Isolde fall in love, the Will first overpowers her fierce pride, which had previously branded Tristan as her blood enemy. It also dissolves Tristan's heretofore perfect chivalry, the *machismo* of the medieval knight, which had demanded that he escort Isolde safely to her marriage to King Mark, his uncle and liege lord. Love overcomes the marriage itself; they meet adulterously. Love negates the mortal sword wound received by Tristan after the affair is discovered. Apparently he simply cannot or will not die until Isolde comes to him. Then, after he dies in a kind of ecstasy in her arms, she herself sinks down in like rapture and expires also.

At this point (if not earlier) the plot passes the bounds of reality, of course—which was exactly Wagner's point. Once Tristan and Isolde have drunk the love potion that was conveniently provided by the original legend, they seem to move in a realm where conventional attitudes, the rules of the world, and even life and death have lost their powers. In fact, this opera's transcendental quality brings it very close to mystical or psychedelic experience. What the prudish, materialistic middle-class audiences of the time made of something that subverted their values so completely is hard to say. We can suspect that they accepted it as a kind of fantasy, one that they could enjoy while denying themselves (and others) emotion in their actual lives.

In any case, the Prelude to *Tristan und Isolde* is one of the most impressive and justly celebrated of nineteenth-century compositions. ("Prelude"—*Vorspiel*—is Wagner's special name for "overture"; remember that he insisted on calling his operas "music dramas" to distinguish them from other people's mere operas.) It opens with a slow motive treated in a free threefold sequence (page 30). The ending harmonies of the motive, in particular (measures 2–3, 6–7, 10–11), create a remarkably sultry, sensual, anxious feeling:

This is an example of a romantic theme which derives its essential character from harmony rather than from melody or rhythm. It becomes the chief leitmotiv of the long opera to come, associated with a rich compound of meaning, including passion, yearning, and release in death.

The motive is heard many, many times in the Prelude. After the huge climax in the middle of the piece, releasing tension that has built up to an almost unbearable pitch, the motive returns in an imaginative free variation of its original threefold sequence. Otherwise, the Prelude consists of a marvelous dark churning of emotion, produced partly by incessant sequences and partly by Wagner's very characteristic trick of avoiding cadences. The music constantly shifts in tonality (modulates); every time it seems ready to stop, it surges ahead, as though feeling cannot be satisfied. Love can be satisfied only by death, by the great cadence accompanying Isolde's death at the very end of the opera.

The passage leading up to this cadence is known as the "*Liebestod*" ("Love Death"). An orchestral arrangement of this passage, leaving out Isolde's singing line, is often tacked onto the Prelude to make a sort of informal symphonic poem (though it is not spoken of as such, for some reason). The sense of ecstasy and growing release is very powerful. The sequences continue; the motives now sound freer and less contorted than those of the Prelude. The orchestration, dense and very rich throughout, also grows lighter, though it is able to support an even more ecstatic climax than that of the Prelude. At the very last cadence of the "*Liebestod*," the main motive of the Prelude (measures 2–3, top line) returns once again, now radically transformed to suggest that love's yearning has reached its transcendent goal.

Except for this cadence, the music of the "Liebestod" is basically identical to a section that Tristan and Isolde sang at the height of their passionate love scene in Act II of the opera. To the nineteenth century, at least, this music seemed dangerously sexual in its connotations. It may not grab us that way, but remember that there were no "adult" movies or frank novels in those days. The most suggestive elements in the arts, before *Tristan*, were the ankles and knees (*never* the thighs!) of female ballet dancers.

However this may be, there can be no doubt that *Tristan und Isolde* is made of stronger stuff, emotionally speaking, than other romantic pieces. Even our relatively brief orchestral excerpt shows this, and if we subject ourselves to the entire five hours of the uncut opera, the effect can be truly overpowering. By its successful expression of intense emotion, *Tristan und Isolde* approaches not only the ideal of Schopenhauer but also that of the romantic nineteenth century as a whole.

Wagner's *Der Ring des Nibelungen* ("The Nibelung's Ring"), an opera lasting for four separate evenings of three to five hours each, surely counts as the very limit of a romantic tendency which we mentioned on page 226, the tendency toward the grandiose. Wagner required this length of time, perhaps, because of the extent of the material he wanted to cover. *The Ring* encompasses large portions of the most famous of all the old Germanic legends, involving gods and goddesses, giants and dwarfs, magical events and very human actions, all in a great variety of obscure and bloody incidents straggling over many decades.

Yet in back of all this tedious mythology, Wagner had a modern tale to tell. The basic theme is the corruption of the world through people's greed for money (gold) and the power it buys. In the guise of mythical gods, gnomes, and warriors, one group after another in modern society is shown destroying itself in the pursuit of gold. George Bernard Shaw accurately described *The Ring* as a devastating attack by a romantic artist on the capitalist middle-class values of his day. Wagner was a revolutionary activist in his youth and had been thrown out of Germany as a result (page 271). This enormous work is one outcome of his early political passions.

The first opera of the four is *Das Rheingold* ("The Rhine Gold"). First we see the gold in its original, "natural," and thus innocent state in the possession of some mermaids in the River Rhine. (Wagner designed a stage machine to make them swim.) But it is stolen from them by a race of dwarfs and then by the gods themselves, who mortgage it to a race of giants. The dwarfs are called Nibelungs, and they forge the gold into a ring: hence the name of the total opera. For Wagner, who was a notorious antisemite, the ugly dwarfs also served as a hint that the first race to be corrupted by gold was the Jews. But the "establishment" is shown moving in on them at once, as represented by the king of the Germanic gods of mythology, Wotan (from whom we get Wednesday, "Wotan's day"). The main message of the opera is the degeneration of Wotan's realm—that is, nineteenth-century Germany—as a result of his lust for gold.

When one of the dwarfs steals the gold in the first place, he is really chasing the mermaids themselves. To get the gold, he consciously renounces love, that is, turns his heart forever from gentleness, affection, and charity. This was an ingenious way of turning the old myth into a commentary on the bias of the middle classes toward hard work and discipline and away from emotion. At the next stage, when Wotan steals the ring from the dwarf, he doesn't give up anything, at least not right away. Everything is managed by guile and cruelty: *The Rhine Gold* shows gold corrupting all who touch it, including even the king of the gods.

The next opera is *Die Walküre* ("The Valkyrie"). In Germanic mythology, amazon goddesses called Valkyries served the heroes of old in Valhalla with a pleasant combination of warlike companionship and feminine (if statuesque) charm. The Valkyrie in question is Brünnhilde, Wotan's favorite daughter.

We can skip the involved details of the plot, important as they are for a full understanding of the opera, since we shall be concentrating on only a single scene.

Suffice it to say that Brünnhilde, disobeying orders, has intervened to save a mortal whom Wotan, with great reluctance, had agreed to kill in the course of his pursuit of the ring. Brünnhilde had understood Wotan's inner feelings and acted accordingly, but the law demands that Wotan punish her disobedience. Apparently, the mildest fate available for her is to be turned into a mere mortal woman and placed in a deep sleep on a mountain ringed with fire, where the first true hero who climbs through can claim her as his bride. Sleeping Beauty has many sisters in folk tales and the world of mythology.

The last scene of the opera is usually called "Wotan's Farewell," his last farewell to Brünnhilde. We are likely to forget about punishment and gold and get caught up in Wotan's anguish. He feels this deeply, for not only is Brünnhilde his favorite daughter, she is the only person with whom he has any real contact and mutual sympathy (his unsatisfactory married life has been displayed earlier in the evening). In other words, Wotan realizes that he, too, is going to have to renounce love—a fact that is made clear by a leitmotiv in the orchestra. Before the four-day opera ends, Wotan will also renounce his power and will see his entire world go up in flames.

The scene consists of three parts, each beginning with a statement by Wotan (sung by a bass-baritone) and ending with a lengthy orchestral passage. If we follow Wotan's words with care on the combination libretto-line score on pages 261 to 263, we shall observe that Wagner the poet has inserted many complicated thoughts that Wagner the composer is able to bring out by means of nuances in the vocal melody and details of accompaniment. Both intellectually and emotionally, Wotan is a figure of great interest and stature. But as is Wagner's way, the emphatic orchestral passages at the end of his statements are almost more impressive than what Wotan actually sings.

Part 1 Wotan refers to some of the more superficial reasons he will miss Brünnhilde and describes the ring of fire. The orchestral web while he is doing this is rich and complex. Thus at his mention of the fire, a striking leitmotiv dances and sparkles and modulates in the high strings and flutes. No one will have any trouble associating this leitmotiv with the *magic fire* that is going to surround the sleeping Valkyrie.

Brünnhilde can be wakened and won only by a mortal hero who is "freer than I, the god," that is, by someone who has not been tainted by the gold and who is therefore morally freer than Wotan. Just before he says this, the most striking motive that has yet been heard in the scene swells up in the trombones. Wagner hopes that the audience will instantly accept this strong, bold music as a musical prophecy of the *hero-to-come.**

---

* This music is traditionally called the "motive of Siegfried," for that is the name of the hero who, in fact, arrives next evening. But of course we do not know that yet; we have only a vague but portentous awareness that Brünnhilde will not be left sleeping forever.

The orchestral conclusion to Part 1 continues with an emphatic passage depicting a great surge of love between Wotan and his daughter. After a heavy cadence in the brass, the instruments circle down with a short, repeated motive, which clearly has a lulling quality. This *slumber* leitmotiv has been heard before, and it comes again and again in the scene, blended into the other music with the greatest ingenuity and expressivity.

Part 2   Wotan speaks more personally of his love for Brünnhilde before putting her to sleep with a kiss. His long, slow "Farewell Song," the most tuneful part of the scene, gives us perhaps the most moving impression of his deep feelings. When at last he "kisses her godhead away," a sober motive is played by the English horn, a leitmotiv previously associated with *renunciation of love*. Is this Wagner's way of commenting for the benefit of the audience, or is it his way of showing Wotan's own awareness, in back of his actual words? Probably the latter, given the highly self-aware picture of Wotan that has been built up during the opera—indeed, even during the earlier part of this scene.

The orchestral conclusion to Part 2 begins with the famous leitmotiv of Brünnhilde's *magic sleep*. The harmonies are what are so magical—and tender. The still orchestration (first winds and harp, then strings) conveys an unforgettable effect. Thereafter, a long, slow, musing passage of rich music incorporates memories of Wotan's "Farewell Song." Toward the end, a strikingly brief motive is heard twice in the lower brass instruments. It is not surprising to learn that this ominous leitmotiv has to do with the idea of *fate*.

Part 3   The last part of the scene begins with a blatant motive in the trombones; Wotan is a primitive warrior-king as well as a good father. This motive stands for the *law* which Wotan is bound to uphold—by force, it would appear. He summons the god of fire, Loge. The final tableau of the opera sounds as splendid as (we hope) it looks; the *magic fire* and *slumber* motives blend together into Wagner's most opulent orchestral sound. Thrice Wotan strikes flame from the rock with his great spear. Then he departs, after uttering a curse to protect Brünnhilde from all cowardly suitors; but with his usual sixth sense, he finds himself singing his curse to the music of the *hero-to-come*. This impressive forecast prepares the way musically for the next opera, *Siegfried*.

The orchestral conclusion to Part 3 includes a new recollection of Wotan's "Farewell Song" and, as the ultimate determinant, the motive of *fate* (also heard at the end of Part 2). Everything is wrapped up in gorgeous sound and flickering red lights. Wagner would have enjoyed today's light shows.

But for all his interest in decor and stage machinery, in poetry and philosophy, Wagner was first and foremost a musician. The principal element in his formidable "Combined-Art-Work" was music. As we have seen, it is the music—the system of leitmotivs—that makes the essential point at every juncture of Wotan's Farewell. When Wotan realizes that he must renounce love, when Brünnhilde falls into her magic sleep, when the god of fire enters, even when Wotan prophesies the coming of Siegfried, the moment is invested with musical significance by means of an appropriate leitmotiv.

Wagner, Die Walküre: Wotan's Farewell. Line Score*

PART 1 WOTAN, OVERCOME AND DEEPLY MOVED, TURNS EAGERLY TO BRÜNNHILDE, RAISES HER FROM HER KNEES, AND GAZES WITH EMOTION INTO HER EYES. HE SINGS:

> Farewell, thou valiant, glorious child!
> *Leb' wohl, du kühnes, herrliches Kind!*
>
> Thou holiest pride of my heart, farewell, farewell, farewell!
> *Du meines Herzens heiligster Stolz! Leb' wohl, leb' wohl, leb' wohl!*
>
> If now I must leave thee and nevermore greet thee,
> *Muss ich dich meiden, und darf nicht minnig mein Gruss dich mehr grüssen,*
>
> if never again mayst ride beside me, nor bear me a cup of mead at banquet,
> *sollst du nun nicht mehr neben mir reiten, noch Meth beim Mahl mir reichen,*
>
> if I must abandon the child I love, thou laughing delight of my eyes—
> *muss ich verlieren dich, die ich liebe, du lachende Lust meines Auges—*
>
> such a bridal fire for thee shall be kindled as ne'er yet burned for a bride!
> *ein bräutliches Feuer soll dir nun brennen, wie nie einer Braut es gebrannt!*
>
> Threatening flames shall flare round the fell;
> *Flammende Gluth umglühe den Fels;*

> Let withering terrors daunt the craven! Let cowards fly from Brünnhilde's rock!
> *mit zehrenden Schrecken scheuch' es den Zagen; der Feige fliehe Brünnhilde's Fels!*
>
> For one alone shall win the bride, one freer than I, the god!
> *Denn Einer nur freie die Braut, der freier als ich, der Gott!*

BRÜNNHILDE SINKS IN ECSTASY ON WOTAN'S BREAST; HE HOLDS HER IN A LONG EMBRACE AS THE ORCHESTRA PLAYS:

SHE THROWS HER HEAD BACK AGAIN AND, STILL EMBRACING WOTAN, GAZES WITH DEEP ENTHUSIASM INTO HIS EYES.

* In this line score, the language of the translation has not been modernized but retains Wagner's involuted and, as he thought, medieval-sounding quality.

PART 2 WOTAN RESUMES:

Thy brightly glittering eyes that smiling oft I caressed, when valor won them a kiss as reward,
Der Augen leuchtendes Paar, das oft ich lächelnd gekos't, wenn Kampfeslust ein Kuss dir lohnte,

when childish lispings of heroes' praise from thy sweet lips flowed forth;
wenn kindisch lallend der Helden Lob von holden Lippen dir floss;

those gleaming, radiant eyes that oft in storms on me shone when hopeless yearning
dieser Augen strahlendes Paar, das oft im Sturm mir geglänzt, wenn Hoffnungssehnen das

my heart had wasted, when world's delight all my wishes wakened through wild sadness —
Herz mir sengte, nach Weltenwonne mein Wunsch verlangte, aus wild webendem Bangen:

For the last time, lured by their light, my lips will give them love's farewell!
zum letzten Mal letz' es mich heut' mit des Lebewohles letztem Kuss!

On a more blessed Mortal those eyes will open; but for me, Immortal, they close forever:
Dem glücklicher'n Manne glänze sein Stern: dem unseligen Ew'gen muss es scheidend sich schliessen.

For thus I, the god, turn from thee; thus I kiss thy godhead away!
Denn so kehrt der Gott sich dir ab, so küsst er die Gottheit von dir!

HE CLASPS HER HEAD IN HIS HANDS.

HE KISSES HER LONG ON THE EYES. SHE SINKS BACK UNCONSCIOUS IN HIS ARMS. HE GENTLY BEARS HER TO A LOW MOSSY MOUND.

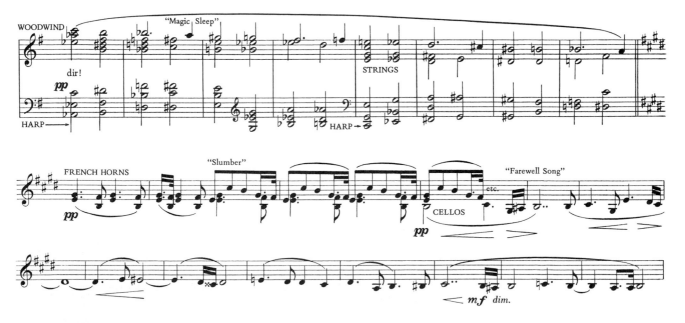

HE TURNS SLOWLY AWAY, THEN AGAIN TURNS ROUND WITH A SORROWFUL LOOK.

PART 3 WOTAN STRIDES WITH SOLEMN DECISION TO THE MIDDLE OF THE STAGE AND DIRECTS THE POINT OF HIS SPEAR TOWARD A LARGE ROCK. HE CALLS UPON LOGE, THE GOD OF FIRE:

Loge, hear! attend!
Loge, hör'! Lausche hieher!

When first I found you, a flickering flame, you fled from me in a devious blaze;
wie zuerst ich dich fand, als feurige Gluth, wie dann einst du mir schwandest, als schweifende Lohe;

I caught you then; I release you now! Appear, and wind thee in flames round the fell!
wie ich dich band, bann' ich dich heut'! Herauf, wabernde Lohe, umlod're mir feurig den Fels!

Loge! Loge! attend!
Loge! Loge! hieher!

A FLASH OF FLAME ISSUES FROM THE ROCK, WHICH SWELLS TO AN EVER-BRIGHTENING FIERY GLOW.

WOTAN STRETCHES OUT HIS SPEAR AS IF CASTING A SPELL.

He who my spearpoint's sharpness feareth, ne'er cross the flaming fire!
Wer meines Speeres Spitze furchtet, durchschreite das Feuer nie!

HE LOOKS SORROWFULLY BACK AT BRÜNNHILDE.

HE LOOKS BACK AGAIN.   HE DISAPPEARS THROUGH THE FIRE.

(End of opera)

"Noise"

As these Parisian cartoons of the mid-nineteenth century show, romantic music had to face a good deal of hostility from the conservatives of the day. They were offended by its overemotionalism, puzzled by its harmonies, and bored by its great lengths. But when people don't like new music and are not quite sure what it is that is bothering them, they usually complain about the *noise*.

The first cartoon is captioned "Field Marshal Berlioz." Cool, immaculate, his hair flying with correct romantic abandon, Berlioz leads an orchestra that includes a cannon, a rotating machine to strike the drum, and a tuba player with a sadistic glint in his eye. All this is having its effect on the critics, who cower among the coffins.

— Tu mènes ton oncle à l'Opéra, mais le pauvre homme est sourd !
— Justement, il a voulu profiter de l'occasion pour voir le *Tannhauser*.

The second cartoon refers to the first opera by Richard Wagner to be produced in Paris, *Tannhäuser*. "You're taking your uncle to the opera? But the poor old gentleman is deaf." "Precisely, my dear chap: and he wants to take advantage of it to see *Tannhäuser*."

As a matter of fact, *Tannhäuser* did indeed offer something for Uncle to see: a voluptuous ballet at the Court of Venus, which Wagner, against his better judgment, had inserted into the opera to make it more palatable to Parisian taste. But the work was hooted off the stage, a famous fiasco which owed as much to anti-German intrigues as to the undoubted novelty and "noise" of Wagner's musical style.

Giuseppe Verdi (1813–1901)

Giuseppe Verdi, the greatest of Italian opera composers, lived through almost the entire romantic era. His first sweeping success, *Nebuchadnezzar* (mentioned on page 271), dates from around 1840, the time of Chopin's Ballade in G minor and Schumann's Piano Concerto. His magnificent Shakespeare operas *Otello* and *Falstaff* date from around 1890, the time of Strauss's *Don Juan* and the Brahms Fourth Symphony. Throughout this long career, one that naturally encompassed many changes of style, Verdi worked steadily at the depiction of powerful emotion, like all his contemporaries. He worked at this with remarkable fidelity, and a case can be made that Verdi brought out the best of musical romanticism through all its changing phases.

People are inevitably drawn to compare and contrast Verdi and Wagner, the two masters of nineteenth-century opera. The heart of the contrast lies in Verdi's unswerving emphasis on the singing human voice. He never allowed the voice to be overshadowed for long by the orchestra, as Wagner with his leitmotivs often did, and he entertained no such grandiose ideas as that of Wagner's "Combined-Art-Work" (page 255). Opera was a singing art to Verdi, and generations of Italians before, during, and after his lifetime have enthusiastically agreed with him.

Verdi still employed recitative and arias, though not exclusively. Of course, these forms had changed greatly since the times of Handel or Mozart. Many of Verdi's arias might be described as strophic songs (page 211) with orchestra, in his own highly emotional, exuberant melodic style. Some of his most familiar music consists of timeless tunes such as *"La donna è mobile"* from the opera *Rigoletto,* the "Anvil Chorus" from *Il Trovatore, "Celeste Aïda"* from *Aïda,* and the duet from the Tomb Scene of the same opera, which we shall deal with presently.

But although people have always loved Verdi's tunes, in his own day the dramatic side of his operas was admired especially. First and foremost he was interested in people, people placed in dramatic situations where violent, exciting actions bring out equally violent emotions. Verdi sought out librettos full of breathtaking situations, and to match these in music, he was able to turn his melodies to remarkable dramatic use. Wagner, on the other hand, was principally interested in philosophical ideas and relied more on harmony and orchestration than on singing per se; the famous *"Liebestod"* of *Tristan und Isolde* (page 257) still makes satisfactory music with the voice part left out (!). Wagner was a fine psychologist in music, as we have seen, but at best his gods and Valkyries and mythical princesses are "larger than life." They lack the immediacy of Verdi's vibrant and very human characters.

There are interesting similarities and contrasts, too, between Verdi and Wagner in their records of political activism. Each of them in his own way cared intensely about the world around him (page 271). One could scarcely name two figures further removed from the popular image of the unworldly artist working in an ivory tower.

The plot of *Aïda* is thoroughly romantic (in the sense of amorous). The young Egyptian general Radames and the beautiful Ethiopian slave girl Aïda are in love, but Radames has aroused the passion of the Princess Amneris—a *femme fatale* in every sense of the word. Prodded on by the Egyptian priesthood, Amneris's father, the King of Egypt, is waging a holy war against Ethiopia. Aïda, prodded on by *her* father, persuades Radames to reveal the secrets of his battle plan. But Amneris has eavesdropped on their tryst out of jealousy, and she turns him over to the all-powerful priests for justice.

At the beginning of Act IV, the last act, Amneris proceeds with her plan. She offers to intercede and save Radames if he will return her love. To her astonishment, he refuses, saying he regrets his actions and would prefer to die rather than live without Aïda. Amneris, whose nature is wildly passionate under the best of circumstances, rises to a perfect fever of rage, distress, and self-blame in this scene (scene i), but there is nothing she can do; Radames is led off by his guards. Now read on (and listen).

Act IV continues with the so-called Judgment Scene (scene ii). Wearing ominous white hoods, like members of the Ku Klux Klan, the priests march through the palace on their way to the crypt below, where Radames's trial will take place. Their tread is depicted by the sinister-sounding motive shown at the beginning of the following example:

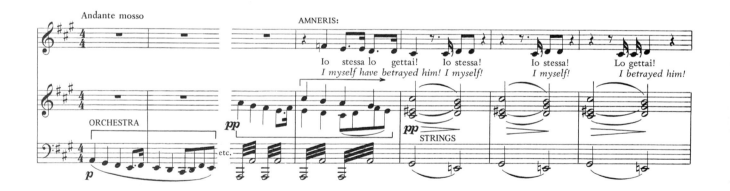

Though Verdi rarely used leitmotivs—they were very much Wagner's trademark (page 255)—this motive does, in fact, occur many times in the course of *Aïda* to signify the idea of the implacable priesthood. However, the motive is treated more simply and more melodically than it would have been in Wagner's hands.

Remember that when this brief march sets in motion the inexorable series of events leading to Radames's death, Princess Amneris has scarcely had time to collect herself and recover from her shock. She is almost too distracted to sing connected tunes, a rare condition indeed for ladies in nineteenth-century opera. Instead she utters broken phrases:

Oime! morir mi sento! Oh! chi lo salva?	Alas! death overcomes me! Oh, who will save him?
E in poter di costoro	And I betrayed him into *those* hands,
io stessa lo gettai! Ora, a te impreco,	I, I myself! Curses on you,
atroce gelosia, che la sua morte	foul jealousy, which now prescribes his death
e il lutto eterno del mio cor segnasti!	and everlasting regret in my heart!
Ecco i fatali,	Here are the inevitable,
gl'inessorati ministri di morte:	inexorable ministers of death:
Oh! ch'io non vegga quelle bianche larve!	Ah! let me not see those white hoods!

As the march recedes into the depths, Amneris, in a passage with strangely beautiful harmonies (see the end of the example above), bleakly repeats over and over again that she is to blame. Verdi is usually praised for his melodies, but like most romantic composers he could also employ harmony in an individual and effective way. This passage is an example. Amneris may have spoken these words before, but only now does their true impact sink in upon her.

With Amneris, we hear but do not see the trial in the crypt below. As the court is an ecclesiastical one, the proceedings begin with a prayer, sung in a solemn, chantlike chorus, without orchestra. Amneris responds with a prayer of her own:

This is the first of several magnificent phrases in which Amneris expresses her emotions, or to put it more accurately, hurls them across the footlights at us. Especially effective is the way in which Verdi aims unerringly for the high notes in the singer's range (Amneris is a mezzo-soprano, a voice type between soprano and contralto). These phrases never coalesce into regular tunes, though they could do so easily. For this highly dramatic scene, Verdi contents himself with single melodic phrases, which depict the unbearable grief of the unfortunate princess in a particularly intense, concise way.

The priests end their prayer on a note of naked force, as the motive of their march blasts out on the trombones. Now the hearing begins. The High Priest (Ramphis) puts the case for the prosecution:

Radames! Radames! Radames!	[The name echoes thunderously round the vault, on brass instruments.]	You revealed your country's secrets to the foreigner:
Radamès! Radamès! Radamès!		*Tu rivelasti della patria i segreti allo straniero:*

Defend yourself!	[The priests repeat]	Defend yourself!	[But Radames does not; we hear only a muffled drum roll.]	He is silent. Traitor!
discolpati.		*Discolpati.*		*Egli tace. Traditor!*

Amneris, hearing this from above, breaks into another tremendous sob of passion:

Ah   pie - tà!   eglieè inno - cente, Nu - mi,   pie - tà,   Nu - mi,   pie - tà!
Ah have pity!   *he is innocent,*   *gods have pity,*   *gods have pity!*

The High Priest intones two further accusations:

Radames! Radames! Radames!   ⎡ Echo: wind   ⎤   You deserted the encampment on the day preceding the battle. . .
Radamès! Radamès! Radamès!   ⎣ instruments ⎦   *Tu disertasti dal campo*   *il dì che precedea la pugna. . .*

and

Radames! Radames! Radames!   ⎡ Echo: wind   ⎤   You broke faith, your country perjured, your King, your honor. .
Radamès! Radamès! Radamès!   ⎣ instruments ⎦   *Tua fè violasti, alla patria spergiuro, al Re, all'onor. . .*

At each new accusation, Radames remains silent, as before, and is greeted by the same shout of "Traitor!"

And at each new shout, Amneris delivers herself of another outburst. The music is essentially identical all three times, except that the second and third times are each one note higher. This seemingly minor alteration makes for a splendid intensification, for in voices a single note makes a remarkable difference in terms of excitement. Verdi arranges things so that, for her third outburst, Amneris is singing in the highest, most thrilling part of her vocal range.

After the third condemnation, the priests pronounce judgment without further ceremony. They do so in a coarse, marchlike tune, punctuated by harsh rhythmic explosions in the orchestra:

Ra - da - mès,   è deciso il tuo fa - to;   degliin fa - mi la morte tuạ - vrai;   sot - to
Radames, your fate is decided.   *A traitor's death will be yours:*   *beneath*

l'a - ra del Nume sdegna - to,   sotto l'a - ra del Nu - me sde - gna - to a te vivo fia schiuso l'a - vel.
the altar of the god whom you scorned   *you shall be buried alive.*

If they had sentenced Radames using the music of their original chant, there would at least have been the semblance of ecclesiastical dignity, but this particular tune reflects the savage relish with which they shout their fatal words. They are no longer priests but vengeful men.

Another cry from Amneris, and the priests emerge from the vault, marching to the same motive with which they had descended a few minutes before (in the example on page 266). Amneris confronts them on the way up, with yet another of her passionate phrases:

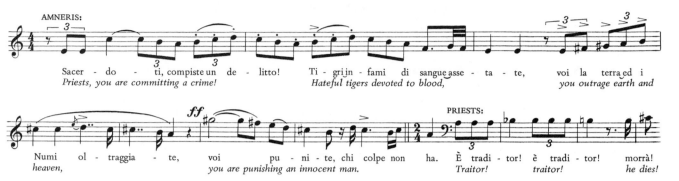

This melody is clearly related to the priests' sentencing song. Contemptuously, they merely address three words to her: "Traitor! he dies!" ("*È traditor! morrà!*"). Amneris tries again and again with a new lament, but they pass swiftly off, leaving her alone on the stage. All but inarticulate with despair and humiliation, she hurls a wild curse at them:

Empia razza! anatema su voi!   Evil hierarchy! a curse on you!
la vendetta del ciel scenderà!   May the vengeance of heaven descend on you!
anatema su voi!   Curse you!

All through this powerful dramatic scene the tension has been built up masterfully. A brutal onslaught of orchestral sound discharges it, and the curtain falls.

AÏDA, ACT IV: TOMB SCENE

Like the Judgment Scene, the Tomb Scene (scene iii) that follows includes action on two separate horizontal levels. This time we see both. Below, the large tomb in which Radames has been left to suffocate after the tomb has been bricked up. Above, the temple of Phtha, with the altar under which the priests have promised to bury him.

The mournful, hushed sounds that introduce the Tomb Scene represent a marked contrast to the intensity of the Judgment Scene. Yet we may notice that they are made up of a motive taken from the orchestral music accompanying Amneris's final curse in that scene. Radames hardly has time to express the hope that Aïda may live happily before he hears a sound in his tomb. Aïda has secretly hidden in it, in order to die with him.

After some accompanied recitative (page 124), each sings a short aria-like section, consisting of several melodic phrases. Radames, a tenor, speaks very tenderly of the pathos of Aïda's coming death. Aïda, a soprano, already a little delirious from the thin air, speaks of the future joys of heaven.

Then Verdi mounts his impressive final tableau. The priests, now accompanied by priestesses, file into the temple above, singing a hymn with a near-Eastern flavor. It celebrates the great god Phtha ("*Immenso Ftha*"). Below,

Radames and Aïda begin their final duet, a farewell to the sorrows of earth and a welcome to eternity. It is a famous instance of Verdi's simple and yet highly effusive melodic style:

Notice how the melodic line is rooted around just a few notes: high and low G♭ and D♭. This feature gives the melody a unique ethereal quality, as befits a couple who are going to die from lack of oxygen a few minutes later. Another feature that does the same is the high accompanying haze of the strings which swell up ecstatically later.* We sense that these young people are already far out of this world, perfectly attuned to one another—they sing the same tune in octaves—in a love that transcends death itself. Was this Verdi's answer to Wagner's *Tristan und Isolde*? It is interesting to try to sense the difference in effect as these two composers portray a "love death" from very different standpoints.

Before the final curtain, a figure in mourning enters the temple above to pray. A broken woman, drained of all the emotion revealed in her desperate scene with the priests, Amneris can only whisper in a monotone: "Peace, peace, I implore!" ("*Pace t'imploro!*"). The different sentiments of the various characters are made more vivid by simultaneous contrast: we saw this principle already at work in the *opera buffa* ensemble (page 163) of Mozart's day. Amneris's grief is set directly against the ecstatic, otherworldly togetherness of Radames and Aïda.

Simultaneously, too, the priests continue their implacable chanting; in fact, they sing the last words in the scene ("*Immenso Ftha*"). One of the things Verdi wanted to show in this opera, below the level of the personal story, was the repressive effect of organized state religion. Like all Italian liberals, Verdi regarded the Papacy as a force for reaction; he was a "free-thinker"—the characteristically romantic euphemism for "atheist"—and bitterly anticlerical. There is no question that in his very unsympathetic picture of these ancient Egyptian priests, in both the Tomb Scene and the Judgment Scene, Verdi was making a not-so-subtle political point for his own time.

---

* Still another way in which Verdi achieves the ethereal quality of this passage is by insisting that the very highest note sung (B♭; see the asterisk in the example) be very quiet, rather than loud, as it would ordinarily be sung—and as, in fact, it *is* sung in almost all performances, unfortunately. The romantic composers are particularly vulnerable to irresponsible performers. This whole duet also is often performed with excessive rubato (page 225).

Viva Verdi!

An Italian political drawing of 1859. The agitators scrawling *"Viva Verdi!"* ("Long live Verdi!") on the wall were the inventors of our modern-day acronyms: Verdi's name spelled out <u>V</u>ittorio <u>E</u>mmanuele, <u>Re</u> <u>D</u>' <u>I</u>talia — Victor Emmanuel, King of Italy, the symbolic leader of the Italian struggle for national unification.

It is interesting to compare Verdi and Wagner in the matter of their politics. Wagner as a young radical (over thirty, at that) incited revolutionary riots and had to go into exile for many years. This was in the Revolution of 1848, which broke out all over Europe but was soon put down; Wagner was associated with the famous anarchist Bakunin. But as he came close to the seats of power in later life, he grew much more reactionary. Wagner has been branded as an intellectual precursor of Nazism — a charge with a clear basis in fact, though it requires a considerable amount of qualification. Verdi, who never played the role of an active revolutionary, remained a staunch liberal to the end of his long life.

While Wagner's "music dramas" were élite productions, Verdi's operas were widely popular, the popular art of the Italian people in an age without television and movies. Again and again these operas show noble oppressed peoples suffering under tyrants, though of course in a disguised form to get around the censors. One Verdi melody, almost forgotten today, the song of the Israelite slaves in his biblical opera *Nebuchadnezzar*, became a semiofficial hymn in the Italian struggle for liberation — a parallel to the *Marseilleise* in revolutionary France or *We Shall Overcome* in America during the 1960s. A famous line in Verdi's opera *Attila* (Attila the Hun) shook the rafters every time it was sung in revolutionary Italy: "Give me Italy, and you can have the world!" (*"Avrai tu l' universo, resti l'Italia a me!"*). Verdi's practical nationalism can make the musical nationalism of such composers as Moussorgsky seem rather trifling by comparison.

When Garibaldi and Cavour between them ousted the Austrians and a united Italy was established in 1861, Verdi was made an honorary deputy in the first Italian parliament. Probably no other composer has ever received so fine a tribute from his nation.

Nationalism

NATIONALISM

Giuseppe Verdi was not the only nineteenth-century composer to place his art in the service of political nationalism, nor was Italy the only country engaged in a struggle for independence. The Czechs revolted against the Austrian Empire, the Poles rose up against Russia, and Norway broke free of Sweden. All over Europe, people were becoming more conscious of their history and destiny, their national character, and their artistic heritage.

This gave rise to a musical movement, also called nationalism, which involved the incorporation of national folk music into concert pieces and operas. Generally, nationalist composers wrote program music or music with words, in which the programs and texts stress national themes of one kind or another. Nationalism also involved a desire to make local music independent of Europe's traditional culture leaders: France, Italy, and the German countries. Now, composers working in these countries had the advantage of working within long-established, fully accepted traditions; they did not have to do anything specially "national" to gain attention and respect. Thus, although Verdi was definitely a *political* nationalist, we do not speak of him as a *musical* nationalist.

Nationalism flourished in outlying countries, then—among them Spain, Britain, Norway, Denmark, Czechoslovakia, Poland, and Russia. The origins of the movement go back to the polonaises and mazurkas of Chopin (see page 231), and it continued as an important force in the early twentieth century. American nationalist composers first appear in this latter period (see pages 348–351).

Sometimes musical nationalism had no more profound *raison d'être* than the pleasure audiences get from hearing folk music at symphony concerts, whether their own folk music or someone else's. Frenchmen wrote Spanish music, Russians wrote Italian music, and Czechs wrote American music (Georges Bizet's *Carmen*, Peter Ilyich Tchaikovsky's *Capriccio Italienne*, Antonin Dvořák's *New World* Symphony). These pieces serve the same function as travelogues, perhaps. Yet even this "nonpolitical" music had the effect of emphasizing the exotic and unique qualities of nations. Romantic individuality had become a national as well as a personal ideal.

Modest Moussorgsky (1839–1881)
PICTURES AT AN EXHIBITION (1874)

Of the nineteenth-century nationalist composers, the Russians were probably the most successful, and of the Russians, Modest Moussorgsky was probably the most original. *Pictures at an Exhibition* is an interesting sample of nationalist program music. It illustrates a memorial exhibition of pictures by a minor artist and architect called Victor Hartmann, a friend of the composer's who had recently died. Despite his German name, Hartmann came from a Russian family and cared deeply about getting Russian "motives" into his work, just as Moussorgsky did. Not all of Hartmann's pictures are unmistakably Russian (nor are all of Moussorgsky's musical pictures), but the most impressive ones are, such as his vision of the Great Gate of Kiev (page 275).

Pictures at an Exhibition was written for piano solo, as a series of piano "miniatures" joined in a set, such as Schumann's *Carnaval* (see page 236). In 1922 the set was orchestrated by the composer Maurice Ravel, and this is the form in which it has since become popular. Though Ravel's orchestration is more modern, light, and smooth than Moussorgsky's would have been, the general spirit is probably fair enough to the original conception.

"Promenade" As a way of giving some overall musical unity to the set of different pictures, Moussorgsky hit on a plan that is as simple and effective as it is ingenious. The first number, "Promenade," does not refer to a picture yet but depicts the composer walking around the museum. Then the same music recurs several times in very free variations, to show the promenader's changes of mood. The promenade theme recalls a Russian folk song:

—since, of course, Moussorgsky thought of himself as typically Russian.

Ravel orchestrated the theme first for brass instruments, later for woodwinds and strings. Quintuple meter ($\frac{5}{4}$) is a distinct rarity, and having this meter alternate with $\frac{6}{4}$ is rarer yet. The metrical anomaly gives the impression of blunt, unsophisticated folk music—and perhaps also of walking back and forth without a clear destination, as one does in a museum.

1. "Gnomus" Moussorgsky's titles are sometimes fanciful and obscure; "gnomus" refers to a drawing of a nutcracker carved like a gnome. The nut is cracked between his heavy jaws, the two handles form his long legs, and he has no body at all. A little child could be frightened by such an object, perhaps. Moussorgsky writes music that sounds suitably macabre, with a lurching rhythm to illustrate the gnome's clumsy walk on his handle-legs.

"Promenade" Quieter now, the promenade music suggests that the spectator is musing as he moves toward the next picture.

2. "Il vecchio castello" "Ye Olde Castle" (in Italian) must have been one of Hartmann's more conventionally romantic pictures. A troubadour sings a mournful tune outside a medieval castle. Ravel in 1922 used an alto saxophone for this tune, something Moussorgsky almost certainly would not have done back in 1874, when saxophones were still relatively new inventions and strangers to the symphony orchestra. Nonetheless, the tone color of the saxophone is highly evocative, and so are the bleak bassoons that Ravel puts underneath it.

Moussourgsky had created his own effect of bleakness by having a single note, G♯, sound constantly in the bass during every single measure—a simple type of ostinato (page 95). Is the troubadour's song Italian, Russian, or neither?

"Promenade"; 3. "Tuileries: Children Quarreling after Play" First the boys are heard, then the girls, apparently; the rhythm is supposed to suggest their petulant squabbles. The Tuileries is a park in Paris. A few years before Moussorgsky wrote the *Pictures,* the neighboring palace of the same name was burned to the ground by revolutionaries.

4. "Bydlo" A ponderous Polish cattle cart, depicted with strong peasant accents in the music, is heard approaching, clattering by, and receding into the distance again. The tuba solo sounds excellently clumsy here.

"Promenade"; 5. "The Ballet of the Chicks in Their Shells" For this absurd subject—costume designs in the form of big eggs, intended for a ballet—Moussorgsky wrote appropriately comical and not particularly Russian-sounding music. He marked this piece *Scherzino* ("little Scherzo") *and Trio.* Notice the illustration of chicks clucking, on clarinets, flutes, and piccolo.

6. "Two Polish Jews, One Rich, One Poor" Once a composer gets the nationalist idea, he is as glad to employ Polish or Jewish folk accents in his music as Russian. Here Moussorgsky draws a vivid contrast between two residents of the Polish ghetto, a pompous, rich Jew and a skinny, whining beggar. Ravel uses rapidly repeated notes on the muted trumpet, another unusual orchestral sound. The total effect is that of a none-too-gentle parody.

First we hear one character, then the other, then both of them together; the technique recalls that of the *opera buffa* ensemble (page 163). And indeed, Moussorgsky's illustrative and parodistic techniques were employed to best advantage in the field of opera. His operas have nationalistic subjects: *Khovanshtchina, The Fair at Sorotchinsk,* and greatest of all, *Boris Godunov,* based on a play about an early Russian czar by Alexander Pushkin, the famous Russian romantic poet.

"Promenade" The original piano piece includes another promenade here, but for some reason Ravel cut it out. He has Nos. 5, 6, 7, and 8 played consecutively, without pause.

7. "The Marketplace, Limoges" Another picture from Hartmann's wide travels. Limoges is in the south of France, but the music will do for busy marketplaces anywhere.

8. "Catacombs: Sepulchrum Romanum" Moussorgsky lapses into Latin to make these Paris catacombs, containing ancient Roman tombs, sound more mysterious. He made a speciality of the macabre, as we know from *"Gnomus."* The harsh, weird harmonies he concocted for these slow chords create a very strange effect, and Ravel's orchestration adds to it: all brass and woodwinds, with no strings except double basses.

"Promenade: Con mortuis in lingua mortua" Apparently the previous picture makes the promenader meditate upon the recent death of Hartmann as he

walks slowly away. A halo of strings (a piano tremolo in the original) covers the promenade theme; this is Moussorgsky speaking "the language of the dead" (*lingua mortua*).

9. "The Hut on Fowl's Legs (Baba-Yaga)" In Russian folklore, the witch Baba-Yaga lives in a hut supported by chicken feet. She grinds up human bones to eat in a mortar and pestle, which also serves her as a broom for flying. In Moussorgsky's music, she is certainly a raunchy old lady with a strong Russian accent. This piece, which lasts longer than the preceding ones, falls into an obvious A B A' form, leading directly to No. 10.

10. "The Great Gate of Kiev" The longest number, and the climactic one, this illustrates a fabulous architectural design by Hartmann shown below. It was never executed. Moussorgsky summons up in the imagination a solemn procession with clashing cymbals, clanging bells, and chanting priests. Two Russian melodies appear, a forceful one and a quieter, hymnlike one, in addition to the promenade theme. The ending is very grandiose, for grandiosity forms an integral part of the Russian national self-image — and of many others, unfortunately.

The Great Gate of Kiev, by Victor Hartmann

Liszt Among His Friends

A popular picture of the nineteenth century, purporting
to show the great pianist-composer Franz Liszt playing
to a group of celebrities of his time. From left to right,
the novelists Alexandre Dumas, Victor Hugo, and
George Sand (page 235), the violin virtuoso Niccolò
Paganini, the opera composer Gioacchino Rossini, and
Liszt's mistress Countess Maria d'Agoult. The fact that
the painter was quite ready to put the Countess in this
picture shows how much it was taken for granted by this
time that an aristrocrat and a commoner could live
together—if the commoner was a famous artist. Liszt is
presumably playing some deeply intimate "miniature" for
piano (see page 225).

The expressions on the listeners' faces show that the
painter, at least, believed that romantic music penetrates
into the very souls of those who participate in it. To
compare this picture of music making with earlier ones
is to see how romanticism changed attitudes toward
music in the later nineteenth century. Music is no longer
a casual entertainment (page 116) or a pleasant,
warm, social pastime (page 210); it is the occasion for
communion—almost a seance.

Perhaps the most amusing detail in this picture is the
somber bust of Beethoven on the piano, a bust that
looms much larger than the heads of any of the people.
Liszt gazes hungrily upon it for inspiration.

The Late Romantic Symphony

As we have seen, the program symphony of Berlioz and Liszt was one of the exciting new genres of the early romantic period. Ordinary, non-programmatic symphonies continued to flourish at this time, along with works in associated genres, such as concertos and sonatas. Schumann, for instance, wrote four symphonies and one concerto each for violin, cello, and piano.

If anything, later in the nineteenth century the production of non-programmatic symphonies was stepped up. Partly this was a matter of prestige, for ever since Beethoven, composers felt that somehow they were being judged on their ability to produce impressive symphonies. Some composers produced just nine symphonies, like Beethoven. Many of the great favorites on today's (or yesterday's) concert programs were written by symphony composers of the late romantic period:

Antonin Dvořák (1841–1904), a very prolific Czech composer whose warm, sunny melodies have caused people to compare him to Schubert. The best known of his nine symphonies is No. 5, "From the New World." Some of the themes are said to reflect Negro spirituals—which Dvořák could have heard in 1892–1895 when he was directing the National Conservatory in New York, a predecessor of Juilliard.

Peter Ilyich Tchaikovsky (1840–1893), whose symphonic poem *Romeo and Juliet* we have already studied. Like Moussorgsky and most Russian composers of the time, he was influenced by nationalism and put folk songs in his early Symphony No. 2 ("Little Russian"), No. 3 ("Polish"), and No. 4. The Symphony No. 5 in E minor contains a very famous French horn tune in the slow movement. The dance movement is a waltz, as in Berlioz's *Symphonie Fantastique*. The "Pathétique" Symphony No. 6 in B minor features some interesting innovations: a movement in $\frac{5}{4}$ time (compare Moussorgsky, page 273), and a slow movement placed at the very end of the piece, rather than in the middle. Characteristically, it is marked *Adagio lamentoso*.

Anton Bruckner (1824–1896), a distinguished Austrian cathedral organist—not the usual niche for a composer of symphonies, and one that may help explain the somewhat ponderous quality of his nine examples. As a symphony composer, too, Bruckner was unusual in being deeply influenced by Wagner. His music has slowly grown in popularity since his death, first in Austria and now everywhere else.

Symphonies in the romantic tradition continued to be written at a great rate in the early twentieth century, too. Among the main composers are Jean Sibelius (1865–1957: 7 symphonies), Ralph Vaughan Williams (1872–1958: 9 symphonies), Roy Harris (born 1898: 7 symphonies), and Dmitri Shostakovich (1906–1975: 15 symphonies). Many of these works continue to show some nationalistic features—Finnish, English, American, and Russian, respectively.

And for their time, all of these men were and are conservative to some degree. This was already true of Johannes Brahms, the greatest of all the late nineteenth-century composers of symphonies and associated genres.

Johannes Brahms (1833–1897)

SYMPHONY NO. 4 IN E MINOR (1885)   *Side 12*

Brahms is a strange case. Born in the dour industrial port city of Hamburg, he gravitated toward Vienna, once the city of Mozart and Beethoven but by that time the city of Johann Strauss, the Waltz King. Here Brahms became, musically speaking, more Catholic than the Pope, soberly upholding the ancient Viennese style even while Vienna was drifting off in other directions. In his youth, Brahms even went so far as to sign a foolish manifesto condemning the "modernist" music of Liszt, Wagner, and others. He never wrote program music or operas but concentrated instead on straight symphonies, concertos, and many chamber-music works.

In these, Brahms steadily cultivated sonata form, variations, and all the other Viennese musical forms. Almost alone among the important composers of his time, he made no special effort to pioneer striking new harmonies or tone colors, in spite of his unquestioned mastery in these areas. He wrote many "miniatures," songs and piano pieces, but he never ventured even as far as Beethoven had into the "grandiose" possibilities of romanticism.

It might sound as though Brahms can be written off as a dull conservative, then—like some other composers of his and later generations. The fact is, though, that he had a good deal to add to the Viennese style: a grand sweep of romantic melody and harmony and an enormously impressive musical technique. Technique in music does not count for everything, but it can take a composer a long way, and Brahms cultivated the elements of musical craft with great sophistication and power. And it must be understood that even in his string quartets in sonata form, his music does not sound like imitation Haydn or Beethoven. What is similar—what is "traditional"—is the musical *flow:* the general rhythmic feeling and the way the themes are built, run into one another, contrast, and develop. The sentiment is very different, and here Brahms found as individual a voice as that of any of his contemporaries.

Brahms's Fourth Symphony was his last (he had waited till the age of forty before feeling ready to undertake his first in the form immortalized by Beethoven). He wrote no fewer than three movements of the Fourth Symphony in sonata form. Then for the fourth movement, he chose a passacaglia—a form that had scarcely been used since the time of Bach. It could almost pass as another manifesto, proclaiming Brahms's traditional orientation to a new generation of modernists.

First Movement   Traditionally, the first movement of a symphony is the richest and most involved of the four. Brahms's Fourth is no exception. To begin a sonata-form movement with a long gentle melody was a romantic practice that we have seen in Schubert and Berlioz (pages 207 and 241):

(The little swells, up and down, on the half notes in measures 9 to 12 show the romantic composer's concern for expressive dynamics in his tunes.) Then the long theme actually starts to repeat itself, in a variation featuring woodwind scales. However, the pace of the exposition picks up skillfully, and a procession of contrasted themes follow—mostly stronger themes, including some stiff trumpet fanfares.

The development section opens with the main theme, which now starts to modulate at the point where motive x is marked on the example. Then, after many episodes, the retransition (end of the development) is based on the same motive x. This echoes back and forth among the various instruments as though they were groping their way through a fog toward the original tune and the original tonality. (The conductor must not neglect to bring out the little dynamic swells.) When the theme looms up at last, it is slowed down into deep, mysterious long notes; the original rhythm is resumed only at measures 4 and 5. This effective moment shows something of what Brahms had to contribute to the Viennese style: he could create a sense of profound mystery at the recapitulation, a point that Mozart had generally treated as a release and Beethoven as a triumph. After measures 4 and 5 of the theme in the recapitulation, notice how strictly the music follows that of the exposition.

Second Movement   The second movement of the Fourth Symphony provided Brahms with an especially good opportunity to deploy his own variety of romantic melody. Though he cared mainly about the two mellow tunes, he found it most effective to hold them together in a modified sonata form, a plan that we have seen used by Schubert (page 208):

Sonata Form

EXPOSITION	DEVELOP-MENT	RECAPITULATION		C O D A
1st theme 2nd group		1st theme	2nd group	

Modified Sonata Form

EXPOSITION	RECAP	BRIEF DEVELOPMENT	ITULATION	C O D A
1st theme 2nd group	1st theme		2nd group	

The movement begins with a series of solemn introductory French-horn calls, entirely unharmonized. They run into the first theme:

Andante moderato
CLARINET

pp
VIOLINS PIZZICATO

Though the orchestration may not sound strikingly brilliant or unusual here, it deserves a moment's pause. The clarinet (upward stems) plays the tune in one rhythm, while the strings play it pizzicato (page 244) in a slightly different rhythm (downward stems). Which is the true rhythm of the tune? We cannot tell, but what we do hear is that the string rhythm reiterates the rhythm of the introductory horn calls. Thus by drawing a connection between two musical ideas, the orchestration makes a quiet point about musical form.

Clarinets and French horns, favorite components of Brahms's characteristic burnished tone colors, continue to dominate the tune as a whole. Its phrases are neatly balanced in the best Viennese fashion:

a	b	(a′)	c	a	b′	
4 measures	4	2	7	4	4	
Clarinet ----→	French horn		Clarinet, etc.	French horn	Clarinet ----→	

After this ends, the music swells into a forceful bridge passage. The lush second theme turns out to be a slower, smoother version of this very bridge:

Perhaps this ingenious detail of musical form makes the tune sound even more sensuous and relaxed, by comparison with its excited ancestor the bridge.

In the recapitulation, which soon comes around, the clarinet no longer plays in the first theme (we shall appreciate the reason for this in a moment). Halfway through phase c of the theme, a brief, angry development section begins, as is shown in the diagram on page 279. This development works over the motive of the horn calls and of the strings in the first theme.

Ultimately the bridge returns; so does the second theme, in a creamy new orchestration. What is more, it now appears loudly a second time, in variation. This, in turn, ends with a suave fragment of melody that was in danger of being forgotten: the cadential phrase (b′) of the first theme, further varied, and played by the long-lost clarinet, which celebrates by performing an extra little cadential flourish.

The movement concludes at last with a coda, built out of the original horn calls. But now they are harmonized in a solemn, rich way; they have matured immeasurably as a result of all the development of the horn-call rhythm. The overall sense of growth in this movement—the special contribution of sonata form—is as impressive as the sheer beauty of the melodies themselves.

Third Movement   In the third movement of this symphony, the relatively lively rhythm and a number of musical surprises make it safe to infer that Brahms was thinking of a Beethoven scherzo. But once again he wrote the piece in sonata form, with a slowdown recapitulation providing an even more unusual effect than that of the first movement.

Fourth Movement The last movement, a passacaglia, holds to this archaic form as tenaciously as does Bach's Passacaglia for Organ, which we discussed on pages 93 to 95. The grim eight-measure theme is followed by no fewer than thirty strict variations, prior to the free (but not entirely free) coda. Unlike Bach, Brahms does not keep his theme in the bass most of the time. Like Bach, however, he divides his chain of variations into three groups, numbered A 1 to 11, B 1 to 4, and C 1 to 15 on our line score (pages 282 and 283).

As usual with baroque or Viennese variations, these variations, too, reflect most clearly the phrase structure of the theme—here, a single eight-measure phrase—and also its harmonies. The melody itself appears in many guises. Sometimes its presence is more obvious (for example, in variations A 1, A 3, C 3, C 6, and C 9), at other times less so, particularly in group B. This was certainly by design, for Brahms obviously meant B to contrast with A and C, even slowing down the tempo for this reason. But rather than marking a new tempo, he wrote each measure exactly twice as long as before. For those interested, asterisks have been placed over the telltale melody notes in some of the group B variations.

The group B variations place an unexpected island of tenderness and pathos in the flood of gloomy, vehement sentiment of groups A and C, a flood which abates only occasionally. Perhaps the piece as a whole conveys a sense of heroic striving against the limitations imposed by the relentless theme.

These thirty variations bear impressive testimony to Brahms's technique and to the great fertility of his imagination. (Yet we may also feel they lack something of the breathtaking unpredictability of the variations in Beethoven's Piano Sonata in E, Op. 109; see page 202). The variations do not come in a random order, of course, as indeed the three-part structure (A B C) already begins to show. Group C acts as a "recapitulation," for C 1 sounds like the original theme, up to the cataclysmic new counterpoint in measures 4 to 8. Variations C 9 to 11 act as another "recapitulation"; they amount to a heightened version of A 1 to 3. Moreover, many pairs or larger groupings of variations go together with a sense of growth: A 4, 5, and 6; A 8 and 9; B 3 and 4; C 4 and 5; C 9 and 10; and C 12 and 13. And although we described the coda above as "free," the passacaglia theme can still be heard storming its way through to the very end of the movement.

The Fourth Symphony reveals Brahms in a very typical mood, a compound of earnestness, energy, and strong rich emotion. In the first movement, the earnestness has an aura of nobility about it, and in the last movement, the nobility hints at an element of tragedy. There is a sense of iron control, too, which puts something of a crimp on Brahms's romanticism; this strenuous music can also strike us as velvety and world-weary by comparison with the enthusiastic accents of Chopin, Berlioz, or Wagner. Unlike the other romantic composers, Brahms is rarely unpredictable. His music radiates the security and solidity that are provided only by a mature mastery of musical form.

The Industrial Society

The age of romanticism was also the age of materialism. While artists concentrated on private emotion, others devoted themselves to the industrial and commercial development that made the nineteenth century a prototype of the society we know today. The Industrial Revolution, based on the scientific discoveries of the seventeenth century and the technological advances of the eighteenth, was at its height. This was the age of the robber barons, the age of the twelve-hour factory shift, industrial disease, urban blight, and the unregulated child labor so vividly described by Dickens.

How did all this fit in with romantic ideals — and, indeed, not just ideals, but accomplishments? It is hard to avoid the conclusion that the arts, especially in the later nineteenth century, served many people as a kind of fantasy world, a never-never land of feeling. The Victorians could enjoy this world while denying themselves and others such emotions in their real lives. We also notice that in the later part of the century the relationship between artist and society became significantly more ambivalent. People still respected the artist, true, but they were increasingly shocked by his actions and increasingly reluctant to accord him decent support.

Artists reacted in different ways. Some were content to become "bohemians" — forerunners of the nonconformists, expatriates, dropouts, and hippies of later times. Others were more aggressive. Wagner first pilloried nineteenth-century capitalism in his earlier *Ring* operas (see page 258) and then turned it to his own advantage, by enlisting industrialists and bankers as supporters of his schemes. Still other composers could make no real accommodation in matter or in spirit. The resignation we sense in the music of Brahms and the half-nostalgic, half-desperate anxiety in Mahler both suggest that the uneasy quality of life in this era infected many of its finest artists.

As the nineteenth century drew to a close, philosophical and religious writings and the mood of music, art, and poetry increasingly reflected the tensions of society. These tensions, due in large part to unbridled industrialization and to new forces that rose to counter it, finally give rise to the combination of political factors that exploded in the catastrophe of World War I.

Gustav Mahler (1860–1911)

SYMPHONY NO. 4 (1901)   *Side 12*

A late romantic symphonist whose tendencies were more modern than those of Brahms was Gustav Mahler. One of the leading conductors of his time—among the positions he held was director of the New York Philharmonic Orchestra—Mahler composed almost exclusively for orchestra. He wrote nine symphonies (plus one "unfinished symphony," the tenth) and several orchestral song cycles, including *The Song of the Earth,* which is an impressive essay in oriental mysticism. Songs crept into his symphonies, too, together with many other features that the conservative Brahms symphonies excluded. Most of Mahler's symphonies and *The Song of the Earth* are unusually long and may be viewed as yet another plateau in the grandiose tradition of romantic music.

First Movement   Mahler begins with a few measures of what one commentator has called "farmyard noises" (besides the clucking sounds produced by flutes, clarinets, and sleigh bells, there is another reason for this appellation, as we shall see later). These measures serve as an unusual introduction to a sonata-form movement. The main theme, a long, graceful, sunny melody:

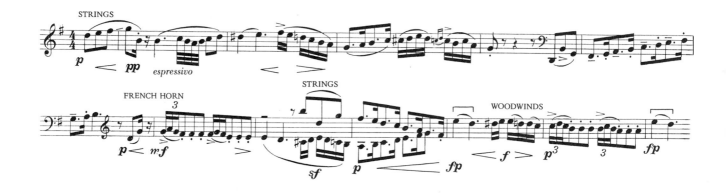

is repeated at once, whereupon it starts to accumulate interesting new contrapuntal lines. It will do this more and more as the movement proceeds.

Indeed, an important general feature of Mahler's style is a renewed emphasis on counterpoint. This fits in closely with his highly original style of orchestration. He repeatedly picks individual instruments out of the orchestra to play momentary solos, which are heard in counterpoint with other lines played by other "soloistic" instruments. The changing combinations can create a fascinating kaleidoscopic effect, for the various bright strands are made not to blend but rather to stand out in sharp contrast to one another.

To facilitate this, Mahler often lightened his orchestration so far that it hardly sounds like the typical late romantic orchestra of Wagner or Strauss. At times it even sounds like Haydn. Or more exactly, it sounds like a full-scale romantic orchestra that has somehow been persuaded to behave like a huge chamber-music group.

The highly sentimental second theme—a Mahler trademark—is appreciably slower than the first. Earlier we mentioned that the romantic composers tended to treat tempo more flexibly than their predecessors; with Mahler, the tempo changes many times within each movement. A rather rustic-sounding cadence theme appears in yet another tempo, after which the "farmyard noises" and the main theme return in their original tonalities.

Is this not the beginning of the standard exposition repeat, as sanctioned in most sonata-form movements (page 172)? No, for the main theme acquires a second set of new contrapuntal lines and leads off in a new direction. Instead of the bridge and the warm second theme, we hear a new cadence theme, one that emanates a deeply peaceful atmosphere. The movement could almost end right here.

Mahler does not hesitate to handle sonata form very freely, then. But from here on, he follows the orthodox plan. In an unusually long development section, motives from the exposition are worked over exhaustively. There are many quite obvious modulations, many strong changes in mood, and also this new theme:

Finally, out of the welter of sound the main theme turns up again—but at first it is distorted in tonality, orchestration, and even in rhythm (the longer notes of measures 1 and 2 in the example on page 286 are extended almost beyond recognition). Only with measure 3 does the theme regain its original aplomb. Thus Mahler catches something of the humor of a typical Haydn recapitulation; and the feeling of returning to a long-lost original tonality (measure 3) is even clearer than is usual in Haydn.

The various exposition themes now return in their expected order. But the bridge is now sporting a new contrapuntal line: the theme shown above, which appeared first in the development section. Once again, the "farmyard noises" start off the last section, a long coda concentrating on the main theme and that peaceful second cadence theme. If anyone was wondering about measures 1 and 2 of the main theme, they are accounted for in this coda.

Our discussion has deliberately stressed the many formal features in this movement that recall Viennese practice. Yet we may get the strange impression that whereas a composer such as Brahms *uses* Viennese features, Mahler is *quoting* them in a self-conscious, even nostalgic spirit. We shall return to this point in a moment.

Second Movement   In this symphony, the dance movement comes second, rather than third, as is more often the case. It is a haunting waltz vision, with two slightly slower trios (A B A′ B′ A″). An oddly tuned gypsy violin sparkles its way through the A sections, sounding restless and faintly grotesque. In the two trios, moreover, is there not a suggestion of sentimental German beer-hall tunes that have somehow been spiritualized onto a higher plane? It is hard to pin down, but there is something disturbing about the "tone" of this movement.

Third Movement   The slow movement that follows is clearly the center of gravity of this symphony. In intensity and seriousness, to say nothing of sheer length, it overshadows the other movements in a way that rarely or never happens in earlier symphonies.

Two contrasting thematic ideas are used, A and B. Tranquil and spiritual in mood, A is a long, rambling melody played mainly by the string instruments. (After sixteen measures, it starts to sprout new contrapuntal lines, like the main theme of the first movement.) Notice the slow rhythmic bass below, which is heard with various modifications all through A and still beats away during the long-drawn-out cadence before the entrance of B. This bass continues to sound throughout the movement, serving as a device to unify all the sections except B′ and the coda:

A	B	A′	B′	A″	INTERRUPTION	CODA
		Free variation; faster than A		In several different tempos and meters		In the mood of A, but with thematic touches of B

Section B is slower than A and much more disturbed and emotional. In particular, a great deal of anguish is extracted from the violin motive marked with the square bracket:

As appears in the example, this motive surges up and up, becoming an insistent, excruciating cry of passion tinged with despair. The very last form of the motive illustrated, covering an octave, is also heard again and again in the wind instruments.

The tendency of romantic composers to unify their compositions thematically has been mentioned more than once (pages 236 and 255). We ought to recognize this particular motive (with a thrill, Mahler hopes) as a climactic element of the main theme of the first movement: see the example on page 286. Consider also the moment when A'', the second free variation of A, has subsided to a huge quietistic plateau of sound, which surely seems like the end of the movement. Suddenly, without the least warning, there is a loud interruption, a vision of almost unsupportable ecstasy, and the theme that blares out in the brass is the new theme from the development section of the first movement (shown on page 287).

Anyone who picks up these hints and listens closely for this kind of thing will soon discern an elaborate underground network connecting very many of the themes and motives. Mahler has labored to make the entire symphony into a single thematic unit.

Fourth Movement The last movement is a quiet song for soprano, set to a curious, naive folk poem about the joys of heaven. In a note to the singer, Mahler insists that there must be no suspicion of parody, yet anyone might wonder about a composer of such world-weary sophistication treating poetry with such a strong peasant or childlike quality. Here is verse 1:

Wir geniessen die himmlischen Freuden	The pleasures of heaven make us joyous
D'rum tun wir das Irdische meiden,	And earthly ones we shun that annoy us.
Kein weltlich' Getrümmel hört man nicht im Himmel!	In heaven no rustle is heard of earth's bustle,
Lebt Alles in sanftester Ruh'!	Deep peace reigns all around.
Wir führen ein englisches Leben!	An angel's life we're living, yes,
Sind dennoch ganz lustig daneben!	But we're quite cheerful nonetheless:
Wir tanzen und springen, wir hupfen, wir singen!	We dance in a ring, we skip and we sing,
Sankt Peter im Himmel sieht zu!	Saint Peter in heaven looks down!

The last line is set off solemnly from the others, in a kind of imitation Gregorian chant:

Peasants of old rarely ate meat, except what they managed to poach, so their idea of heaven was startlingly carnivorous. Various saints who are associated with animals have them slaughtered and eaten in verse 2: St. John and his lamb, St. Luke and his ox. (The butcher is none other than Herod, though how he got into heaven is not explained.) And sure enough, the "farmyard noises" of the first movement come in cheerfully at this point, introducing this verse and also the remaining ones. The last line of verse 2 is "The angels bake the bread" ("*Die Englein, die bakken das Brot*"), set as in the example above.

Verse 3 talks about vegetables, fruit, fish—and more meat. The last line is

"St. Martha must be the cook!" ("*Sankt Martha die Kochin muss sein!*"), set as in the example, again.

Verse 4 tells of the exquisite music in heaven. Our innocent poet pictures St. Cecilia, the patron saint of music, in a dazzling costume of the kind illustrated on pages 184 and 185:

Cäcilia mit ihren Verwandten	Cecilia and all her relations
Sind treffliche Hofmusikanten!	Are excellent court musicians!

The last words, "It wakes all things to joy" ("*Dass Alles für Freuden erwacht*"), are set to a melody similar to that used before, but now blended into the general flow. The whole verse is deeply serene and quiet; the ending fades away into nothing. The last sound of this symphony is the lowest note on the double basses alone, marked **ppp** and *morendo* ("dying away").

This movement may amuse and delight us, but we must admit that it makes a most unusual ending for a great symphony. Indeed, as we think back, each of Mahler's movements seems decidedly ambivalent in mood. Despite some moments of intensity in the development section, the first movement is curiously neat and cut and dried; its main gestures do not sound romantic at all but hark back to a more innocent, "objective" ideal. This movement is almost a parody—to be sure, an affectionate, sentimental parody—of a Viennese symphony.

The mood of nostalgia is particularly strong in the last movement, with its naive poem and its sophisticated-naive music to go with it. In the second movement, there is a disturbing air of distortion and pain, and in the great slow movement, there is an exaggeration of emotion that slips past the bounds of "normalcy." For a piece to start as gently as this one does and then reach those half-hysterical, bittersweet throes of passion—all cannot be well in the composer's world. These are the first signs in music of a turn-of-the-century disillusion, a disillusion with the false confidence of the Victorian world that would soon turn to ashes.

Perhaps they are subtle signs; perhaps only listeners with some experience of romantic music will sense them at first. But compare Mahler with Brahms or Richard Strauss, composers who enter fully into the spirit of romanticism, expressing their individual emotions—whether gloomy, as with Brahms, or enthusiastic, as with Strauss—to their heart's content and satisfaction. Mahler cannot accept romanticism, but neither can he shake it off. He is caught in ambivalence. The undertone of anguish in his music—or *Angst*, to use a German word combining the meanings of anguish, anxiety, dread, malaise—has probably contributed to its significant revival in the last twenty or thirty years and helps to explain its growing popularity.

Minstrel Shows

Popular music of all ages is associated with the popular theater—and most kinds of popular theater are inconceivable without music. In the 1840s a new kind of semi-theatrical entertainment grew up in the northern cities of America, the minstrel show. Its basis was a stylized comic vision or parody of black life and character. This was served up as a sort of variety show consisting of songs, dances, instrumental numbers, jokes, and comic skits, performed by white men (never women) in blackface, using gawky gestures and the broadest of broad dialect accents.

Minstrel songs ranged from the raucous to the sentimental: southern Negroes were supposed to joke about possums and blue tail flies, and northern Negroes were supposed to yearn nostalgically for the old plantation. But some diluted strains of genuine black folk music were carried over into these songs. The rhythmic features of ragtime and early jazz were foreshadowed by the main type of minstrel dance, the banjo jig. The banjo, the minstrel's favorite instrument, came from the plantations and ultimately from West Africa.

Our playbill shows what two bits would get you by way of entertainment in New York in 1859. Among other things advertised is a medley of "popular Ethiopian airs," a "Local Banjo Song," and the premiere of that most famous of all minstrel numbers, *Dixie*. Notice also the "Burlesque Italian Opera" with such characters as Mlle. Pickle Hominy, Count no-Count MacCaffery, and Signor Houlihan Stuffhisowni. Popular art often parodies more elevated genres, genres (like Italian opera) which it has grown up in reaction to.

As for the parodying of supposed Negro traits which is at the very heart of the minstrel show, that has been described (by whites) as "good-humored." Maybe so. But black Americans today are not likely to take a kind view of the minstrel tradition, even though it shows that the nation was already finding black musical sources more interesting and valuable than any others. It is a shaming fact about the American popular theater that many of its genres have been built squarely on exploitation. The minstrel show was one such genre; burlesque was another.

Popular Music of the Nineteenth Century

POPULAR MUSIC

So far in this chapter (and in all the others, too) we have been discussing music of the concert hall, the opera house, the church, and the cultivated drawing room. During the nineteenth century, an extensive body of music grew up which both its composers and its listeners placed in a quite distinct category. Since then, popular music or *light music* has been an increasingly important feature of the cultural scene.

FOLK MUSIC

It is important to understand the difference between popular music and folk music. Before the present century, folk music flourished essentially in a peasant environment. It was simple, anonymous music which was not written down but passed on from father to son over many generations: traditional dance tunes for fiddle or some other instrument, and ballad tunes without fixed accompaniment. Ballads are songs that tell a story, rather than just expressing a sentiment such as love (as in most twentieth-century popular songs) or depression (as in the blues). Consequently ballads contain many stanzas, sung over and over again to the same tune (strophic form: see page 211). While rural communities remained basically unchanged, folk ballads such as *The Three Ravens* and *Barbry Allen* were sung in much the same way from the sixteenth and seventeenth centuries in England to the early twentieth century in Appalachia.

BALLAD

The nationalist composers understood this perfectly well. When they worked folk music into their operas and symphonic poems (see page 272), they did so in order to evoke something simple and old-world.

Popular music, on the other hand, was up-to-date music written for people in towns, not in the country—and for fairly well-off people in towns, not for the workers who served nineteenth-century capitalism. In the days before trade unions, the men, women, and children who worked a twelve-hour shift in the mines and factories had little energy and less money for elaborate musical pleasures. Groups or classes that had the leisure for listening to music, but did not want to take it too solemnly—then as now, this was the audience for popular music. The difference is that today these groups and classes have multiplied enormously.

Dances and songs, composed according to the fashion of the day, are the staple of popular music of all times. Such dances and songs are often written in the first place for theatrical or semi-theatrical entertainments. Here are just a few examples of nineteenth-century popular music:

Dances Social dancing was much more widespread a hundred years ago than it is today. Among the many different dances—each with different steps, of course—were the écossaise, polka, quadrille, galop, schottische, and, the most popular of all, the waltz.

And the most famous of nineteenth-century dances were the waltzes of the Strauss family. A peculiarly Viennese phenomenon, they were nonetheless received enthusiastically all over the world and still remain great favorites.

In works such as *The Blue Danube* or *Tales from the Vienna Woods* by Johann Strauss the Younger, several short waltzes in a row (usually five) are contrasted in melody and orchestral tone color. But the characteristic waltz lilt—triple meter with a slight accent on the third beat: ONE two *three*—keeps going steadily throughout. For use at light concerts and band performances in the park, the waltzes are provided with a slow introduction and a coda using motives from the waltzes themselves—an obvious bow to more traditional composers, and also a sign of some defensiveness, perhaps, or even inverted snobbery.

But traditional composers could never quite match the spontaneity and sparkle of the best Strauss waltzes. There is a story about Brahms being asked to autograph a lady's fan at a ball in Vienna. He wrote down the first few measures of the waltz that happened to be playing, which was *The Blue Danube*, and added under them the words "not, alas, by Johannes Brahms."

Songs   Every nation had its popular songs. The most talented and the most beloved of American song writers was Stephen Foster, who died in the last year of the Civil War, 1864. Though the great majority of Foster's songs are sentimental numbers such as *I Dream of Jeanie with the Light Brown Hair* and *Beautiful Dreamer*, he is remembered mostly today for minstrel songs such as *Oh Susanna, Old Black Joe, De Camptown Races*, and *The Old Folks at Home. The Old Folks at Home* (*Swanee River*) was popular indeed: it sold forty thousand copies in the first year of publication alone.

Popular Theater   Johann Strauss, "The Waltz King," also composed *light operas* or <u>operettas</u>. Operettas always have humorous or half-humorous plots which come to a happy ending, and they employ spoken dialogue in between the musical numbers, rather than recitative. Strauss's best operetta, *Die Fledermaus* (*The Bat*), is still performed at opera houses all over the world. Not surprisingly, some of its most successful numbers are written in waltz time.

The most vital type of American popular theater, the minstrel show, we have discussed on page 291. At the end of the century operettas became popular here; the greatest early hit was *Babes in Toyland* by Victor Herbert (1903). From here it was only one step to the twentieth-century musical comedy or "musical."

In England, a unique series of operettas was composed by Sir Arthur Sullivan in conjunction with the comic poet W. S. Gilbert. Gilbert in his librettos poked fun at various features of Victorian society, ranging from the Houses of Parliament (*Iolanthe*) to fashionable young ladies' enthusiasm for refined poets like Swinburne and Oscar Wilde (*Patience*). And Sullivan in his music poked fun at the musical theater of his time. He did this by imitating the serious style of standard Italian opera and even of Wagnerian "music drama" at moments in his operettas which were not serious in the least. Apart from "in"-references of this kind, Sullivan's music is uncomplicated and tuneful, a perfect foil for the very clever and amusing (and frequently outrageous) rhymes of his collaborator.

Popular music existed in earlier times, but it became a special force during the nineteenth century. One reason for this was that composers in the main romantic tradition were now making increasing demands on the listener, demands both intellectual and emotional. It was really Beethoven who started it, with his heroic aspirations and effusions in symphonies such as the *Eroica* and the Fifth. Schumann edited a magazine attacking the simple music of his time and demanding a more elevated tone from composers. When Wagner called his music "the Music of the Future," he was serving notice on listeners of the present that they would have to strain in order to understand his complicated message. Nineteenth-century symphonists wrote longer and longer symphonies which hypnotized the listener and drained him emotionally.

Not everybody chose to play in this particular ballgame. Many people with money to spend on music preferred to support composers who were ready to cater to simpler tastes, and who were able to bring a good deal of skill and talent to the task. A sharp distinction between "serious" and "light" music did not exist in the days of Handel or Mozart. It was really a by-product of romanticism, of the attitudes and ambitions (and pretensions) of the romantic composers.

As the twentieth century dawned, "serious" music grew more and more esoteric, as we know. It grew less and less capable of filling the needs of the mass market for music. And at just the same time, this market began to expand very significantly. The lower classes were becoming more affluent; indeed, class and financial barriers at last started to crumble in many countries, especially in America. One by one, powerful new technologies were developed for the dissemination of music to the mass market—phonograph records from 1900 on, radio from the 1920s, sound movies from the 1930s, and ultimately television. It is no wonder that in the twentieth century, popular music has grown so phenomenally in importance, variety, and artistic vitality. We shall see something of this in the next two chapters.

CHAPTER 6 1900–1950 The Early Twentieth Century

1900–1950   The Early Twentieth Century

No convenient name has yet been given to the musical style of the early twentieth century. For years people simply spoke of "modern music" or "contemporary music," until finally it became too embarrassing to be calling music written at the time of Wilbur and Orville Wright "modern," fifty years after the event. Airplanes continued to change after 1903, and so did musical style. There came a point at which one could no longer ignore successive innovations following the 1900–1925 period.

After World War II, in particular, music and the arts experienced radical new developments—as radical as jet and rocket propulsion in the field of aeronautics. These developments will occupy us in the next, and final, chapter. Postwar music, which counts as "contemporary" at least for the period during which this book is written (and probably also for the period when it will be read), represents a sharper break with tradition than has been seen in a very long while. From the standpoint of the 1970s, the music of the early twentieth century can be seen as a final extension of romanticism. It is an extreme, even wild offshoot of romanticism, perhaps, but an offshoot nonetheless.

As one indication of this, major composers around 1900 such as Gustav Mahler (page 286) and Claude Debussy remained firmly bound to the past in one way or another, even while showing tendencies that mark the new style. Even the most "advanced" figures in early twentieth-century music preserved some ties with romanticism, though in their most mature music these ties were stretched pretty far. And this, as will become apparent, is not something that can be said of the important figures who led music in new paths after 1950.

World War I

Those who are inclined to think of violence as unique to our times should read the history of the late nineteenth and early twentieth centuries: the mass slaughter in Paris following the commune of 1871, bloody labor strife throughout the industrial world, anarchist assassinations (President McKinley was one victim), and the vicious suppression of suffragette demonstrations. In an increasingly unstable society, in which the rich got richer and the poor grew more resentful, many artists responded with despair and apprehension. Their mood found expression in technical methods involving excesses and distortions of all kinds.

Then after nearly fifty years of peace, or armed truce, Europe drifted into a catastrophic war that everyone had seen coming and everyone was powerless to prevent. Estimated casualties over the four years: 40 million military and civilian dead from war, famine, and epidemic and 20 million wounded. It was really more than Victorian optimism about industrial progress could survive.

While World War I scarcely lacked for man-to-man ferocity, it introduced its own new kind of horror: technological weapons which left the individual soldier, sailor, and civilian more helpless than ever before. Previously, even machine guns had been of limited efficiency; in our Civil War, the sensational new weapon was the rifle, accurate and effective over five times the range of previous shoulder weapons. Now there were tanks on the land, submarines in the sea, and in the air, strafing from airplanes (in 1914, barely off the drawing boards) and bombing from zeppelins. Over the trenches drifted clouds of poison gas that left thousands of the "fortunate" survivors with permanently crippled lungs.

There is a well-known psalm, Psalm 137, that includes the verses: "There those who carried us away captive demanded of us a song. How can we sing the Lord's song in a strange land?" In dissonant times composers write dissonant music.

Early Twentieth-Century Style

Discussing romanticism on pages 221 to 222, we took account of the emphasis on individuality associated with this movement. "Individual" styles loom large, and the "period" style is not easy to pin down in terms of particular harmonic, melodic, textural, and rhythmic features. Composers responded to a common set of romantic attitudes, but each responded very much in his own way.

This is even more true of music in the early twentieth century. Composers in this period showed an increasing tendency to go in different directions and to find themselves in different camps, "schools," or "isms." This tendency appears in the other arts as well, and some of the musicologists' names for these "isms" are borrowed from literature or painting. Impressionism, expressionism, serialism, and neoclassicism will all be discussed in the pages to come. And "antiromanticism," though it is not a label in standard use, accurately describes a primary impetus of many early twentieth-century composers.

These labels should be used with discretion. We should not imagine that they will answer all our questions about modern art—they can raise new questions of their own. Composers often complain that once they have been pigeonholed into some "school," people will not listen to their music with open minds and accept it on its own terms, but think instead about how "typical" it is of the school. Still, these school names represent an honest (if not always adequate) attempt to puzzle out a complex musical situation. Twentieth-century music just presents more problems than earlier music, as is well known to the ordinary listener. If it's any comfort, he may as well also know that some of these problems exist for a considerable number of professional musicians as well.

The label composers enjoy least of all, perhaps, is "conservatism." Yet conservatism has become a striking feature of modern composition (as well as of listening habits). We have discussed a conservative figure of the late romantic era, Johannes Brahms (page 278); for every one composer like Brahms in the nineteenth century, a dozen composers in the twentieth have turned decidedly toward the past. Usually they have been oriented toward the late romantic period, though in some cases they have gone back to even earlier music. Neoclassicism is a general term for the latter tendency (see page 335).

There is no rule saying that a composer has to follow the latest "advanced" developments in order to write great music or even good music. One test is the survival of his music in the concert hall; another is its continuing use in the musician's studio. Brahms appears to have passed these tests with honor, and so have some conservatives of the early twentieth century.

Besides the polarities of style indicated by the schools mentioned above, the early twentieth century also saw impressive developments in popular music. Here America took the lead over Europe—as indeed she was beginning to do very emphatically in other areas too. Jazz started out as a relatively spontaneous and simple style, but it became much more sophisticated and "artistic" from the mid-1920s on. Indeed, the dichotomy between popular and "serious" music was blurred (though never quite breached) by repeated efforts to combine the two. These efforts came from both sides: from traditional composers such as Igor Stravinsky, Darius Milhaud, and Aaron Copland and from jazzmen such as George Gershwin, Bix Beiderbecke, and Duke Ellington.

Music in the early twentieth century, then, was enormously rich and diverse—or fragmented and confusing, depending on the way you look at it. Popular music of various kinds, "advanced" music, conservative music, different schools: all these competed for the listener's attention.

An Early Twentieth-Century Style? We might indeed wonder whether there is anything that holds all this diversity together. Can we really speak of a coherent "early twentieth-century style" in music?

A cohesive style did not exist as it had in the baroque and Viennese periods, or even in the romantic period. Like it or not, this negative fact is part of the whole point: life in general has become incredibly more diverse and fragmented in our century, with results that we all perceive. Nevertheless, some generalizations can be offered, for certainly some common factors exist. Turn on the radio, and there is usually no question about whether or not we are listening to a twentieth-century piece, whatever "ism" it may adhere to.

Involved is what might be described as a massive stretching and straining at musical elements. They have not yet snapped, but it is astonishing how far they seem to give. Melody, for example, becomes so "sprung" that the tuneful quality sometimes is lost entirely. Changes in another important area, harmony, will be discussed on pages 302 to 305. Rhythm, tone color, musical form, even the physical capabilities of instruments—in all these areas, composers seemed bent on exploration, liberation, and the exploitation of extremes.

It is possible to go further and speak of a deliberate policy of distortion applied to all or nearly all the traditional elements of music. A number of works can be cited as examples, all written within a few years of one another (around the time of World War I) by composers of widely differing orientations and backgrounds:

La Valse ("The Waltz"), a symphonic poem of sorts by the French composer Maurice Ravel. Ravel's hatred for Germany, shared by most Frenchmen of the time, expressed itself as hatred of German and Austrian music. Although he never wrote out a program for *La Valse*, the piece suggests a grand society ball that starts out quietly, grows more and more frantic, and finally explodes into violence. Surely this was a metaphor for Europe in the decades prior to World War I. As the momentum increases, a popular waltz by Johann Strauss, *Tales from the Vienna Woods*, is torn apart, exaggerated, orchestrated in brutal ways, and made to seem a perfect symbol of everything ugly in German culture (from a patriotic Frenchman's point of view, that is). The final cadence comes on a screaming discord.

Pierrot lunaire ("Moonstruck Pierrot"), an extremely famous song cycle for soprano and five instruments by the most "advanced" composer of this time, Arnold Schoenberg. The songs are written to slightly crazy poems by a minor Belgian poet of the time named Albert Giraud. Schoenberg knew them in German translation. An example:

Mit einem phantastischen Lichtstrahl	With a fantastical beam
Erleuchtet der Mond die krystallnen Flakons	The moon lights up the crystal flagons
Auf dem schwarzen, hochheiligen Waschtisch	On the black, high-holy washstand
Des schweigenden Dandys von Bergamo.	Of the tongue-tied Bergamo dandy.
In tönender, bronzener Schalle	In the bronze and resonant basin
Lacht hell die Fontäne, metallischen Klangs.	The fountains laugh like the sound of metal.
Mit einem phantastischen Lichtstrahl	*With a fantastical beam*
Erleuchtet der Mond die krystallnen Flakons.	*The moon lights up the crystal flagons.*
Pierrot mit wächsernem Antlitz	Pierrot, his countenance waxen,
Steht sinnend und denkt: wie er heute sich schminkt!	Considers and broods: how'll I make up today?
Fort schiebt er das Rot und des Orients Grün	He thrusts aside rouge and Orient green
Und bemahlt sein Gesicht in erhabenem Stil	And paints up his face in a dignified style—
Mit einem phantastischen Mondstrahl.	*With a fantastical moonbeam.*

To match this, Schoenberg supplied suitably spooky music, which lacks not only the tune that one might expect to find in a song, but also lacks connected melody of any kind. The instruments play sudden short spurts and surges, all seemingly dissociated. They seem to be straining mightily at their natural limits. As for the voice, it does not exactly sing or exactly speak but engages in a strange in-between style invented by Schoenberg. This "talksing"—in German, <u>Sprechstimme</u>—creates an effect of near-hysteria.

SPRECHSTIMME

General William Booth Enters into Heaven, a song by the American composer Charles Ives. In these years, Ives wrote a number of works that include distorted American folk and religious music, sometimes used for parodistic effects. In the present song, the gospel hymn *Cleansing Fountain* is treated to a series of "unnatural" harmonies which make a none-too-gentle comment on the religious consolations offered by General Booth's Salvation Army. In this, Ives seems to have agreed with the bitter tone of his poet, Vachel Lindsay.

Beyond Distortion   Early in the century many people were outraged by painters, poets, and musicians who engaged in distortion of this emphatic kind. Over fifty years later, the same reactions are still sometimes met with. Why doesn't the painter just paint a face instead of double noses and inside-out ears? Why doesn't the composer just write tunes instead of strange combinations of seemingly arbitrary sounds?

Behind these questions lies an unspoken confusion between art and escapism. This, we have suggested (page 285), was especially common in the late romantic era, and it is easy to understand the indignation of early twentieth-century listeners at the distortions they were confronted with. People do not like to have their established values twisted and then torn to shreds before their very eyes—or ears. But composers of the early twentieth century were followers of the romantics in at least this respect: they regarded music not as an escape from life's realities but as an essential comment upon them. And life in this century has not been so pretty—a circumstance for which artists and composers, after all, are not the ones responsible.

Artists tend to discern and express such things before other people do, however. Consequently they tend to get blamed, like the unfortunate messengers in Greek drama who are sacrificed for bringing bad news that they had no hand in creating.

If life is all that unpleasant, then, who needs art to reflect it with its own brand of unpleasantness? A reasonable question, to which two reasonable answers can be given. The first involves the psychological fact that art seems to fulfill deep and essential needs in the human consciousness. Man needs to create art and he needs to consume it, almost as much as he needs to work and play and make love. (Crusaders against distortion in art always want artists to produce painting, poems, music of a different kind; very, very rarely do they advocate a total art moratorium.) The other answer involves an aesthetic fact, or at any rate, an observation about art that has held up throughout history. Art has a miraculous way of renewing itself. After every great artistic revolution, unexpected new styles emerge which embody unexpected new kinds of beauty. What is interesting about twentieth-century music is what happened next, the evolution of a new musical language "beyond distortion."

Clearly, composers felt that the technical and emotional principles of romanticism were used up. They could no longer subscribe to them, any more than people could any longer buy optimistic Victorian theories of endless social progress under the industrial society. The case of Gustav Mahler is instructive in this regard; in his music, as was suggested on page 290, a deep ambivalence toward romanticism shows itself in many ways. Composers first tended to express their impatience with romanticism in parody and distortion for distortion's sake. But soon afterwards—or, actually, at the same time—they began to make something else out of the fascinating bent lines and sprung rhythms that their experiments in distortion had turned up. Composers searched for a new language to replace the language of the past. The various schools or "isms" are best regarded as individual gropings in this direction.

Harmony: Consonance and Dissonance   Exploration of the extremes, distortion, the evolution of a new language beyond distortion: in the early twentieth century these three stages can be observed in almost all the elements of music. They are most obvious with melody, perhaps. The eighteenth-century Viennese composers had brought tunes to the fore in their music, and the romantics had used tunes as the most emphatic means of conveying emotion. Advanced composers now wrote tunes that were, at best, distorted; we heard one on band 6 of the record (by Mahler, 1909). Then they abandoned tunes altogether. This happened in *Pierrot lunaire* (1912); and even in popular music, it finally happened in the modern jazz of the 1950s.

The same three stages are also apparent with early twentieth-century harmony. Harmony grew more and more dissonant, tense, and complex. At first, growing dissonance was the outcome of the exploration of new sounds. Then it was employed to distort the established order. Then it became the foundation of an entirely new language.

The concepts of dissonance and consonance were discussed on page 37. These concepts rest on the psychological fact that certain chords (consonant chords) sound stable and at rest, whereas others (dissonant chords) sound tense and need to "resolve" to consonant ones. Some dissonant chords are more tense than others, so that it is necessary to distinguish between "high-level" and "low-level" dissonances. When there is enough high-level dissonance around, low-level dissonance can sound relatively stable, that is, relatively consonant.

If we haven't spoken much about these two qualities up to now, that is because for the listener they have been relatively unobtrusive. Dissonance might almost be described as the harmonic fuel necessary to keep music running. One thing that gives baroque music its characteristic springy quality is the alternation between low-level dissonance and consonance. One thing that gives romantic music its characteristic surging quality is the alternation (a different kind of alternation) between higher-level dissonance and consonance.

However, things began to change in the early twentieth century, as harmonic exploration took two related steps. Composers first investigated higher and higher levels of dissonance. A traditional dissonant chord has four or five different notes. But here is an example of a dissonant chord combining *seven* of the twelve possible notes from the chromatic scale (X):

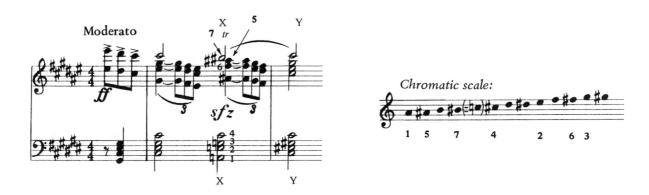

This dissonance was used for an effect of distortion, distortion for the sake of ugliness. It comes at the revolting climax of Richard Strauss's opera *Salome* (1907), as Salome kisses the mouth of John the Baptist's chopped-off head on the plate. But in the best orthodox manner, the dissonance resolves to a consonance (chord Y).

Composers took the second step when they started to tinker with the consonant harmonies. They still wanted the contrast between stable and tense sounds and then the effect of resolution. But since the level of dissonance was now so high, they considered that the stable sounds could be made more complex and tense also. High-level dissonance resolved to low-level dissonance, rather than to consonance. And paradoxically, once a clear norm of consonance was lost, so was any clear sense of distortion.

Here is a (highly schematic) graph to help explain these developments:

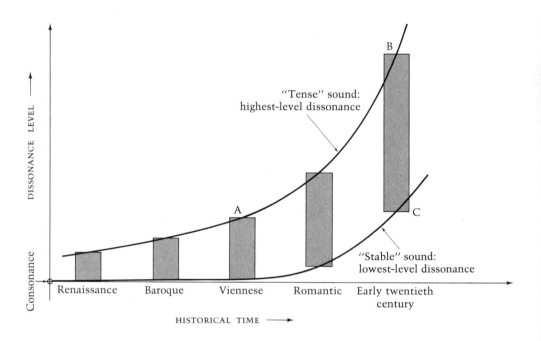

The range between stable sound and tense sound in early twentieth-century music (represented by the block *CB*) was at least as great as that in earlier periods. However, the level of the stable chords (represented by point *C*) might run as high as the highest-level dissonance used by composers in the Viennese period (point *A*). So no wonder this new music grated on the sensibilities of listeners who were still attuned to the music of Haydn and Beethoven.

Tonality and Atonality Closely related to developments in harmony were developments in tonality. Tonality is the feeling of centrality, or focus around a single note, that we get from simple tunes and from much (though not all) of music in general. As modern harmony grew more dissonant, tonality often grew more indistinct. Listen, for example, to the third excerpt in band 9 of the record. Finally some music reached a point at which no clear center can be detected at all, a condition known as <u>atonality</u>.

Just as the term "dissonance" is ambiguous, or at any rate allows for different degrees (high-level and low-level), so tonality and atonality are not open-and-shut concepts. Some music sounds very firmly rooted in one place; other music gives only a tantalizing impression of focus around a general area. Many pieces that listeners early in this century called atonal—often as a term of abuse—can be heard on close listening to have a subtle sense of tonality after all. Really thoroughgoing atonality waited for electronic and chance music of the late 1950s.

Also, we should not forget that tonality had already been weakened by earlier composers, at least in certain sections of their music. The Viennese composers weakened tonality every time they started up those continuous modulations in the development sections of their beloved sonata form (page 157). The result was to strengthen the feeling of solidity at the return of the original tonality, at the recapitulation. Could not the shifting tonality of a development section be used throughout the piece, without the effect of "resolution" achieved by the recapitulation?

CHROMATICISM

Richard Wagner had done exactly this. For example, the Prelude to *Tristan und Isolde* (page 256) continuously shifts in tonality; this is just the feature that gives the piece its striking mood of sultry, never-to-be-satisfied yearning. The technique by which Wagner achieved this is called chromaticism, the very liberal use of all twelve notes of the chromatic scale (page 24). Tonality depends on one note standing out from the rest in the ordinary (diatonic) scale: for example, C in the C-major scale C D E F G A B. When all twelve chromatic notes appear so frequently, the centrality of any single note is automatically weakened.

Wagner's chromaticism was a significant forecast of the coming trend toward atonality. To be sure, *Tristan und Isolde* achieves resolution at the end—after several hours—in the closing notes (the cadence) of the famous "*Liebestod*" (page 257). In advanced pieces, twentieth-century composers now weakened even a final, cadential feeling of tonal centrality.

Tune, harmony, tonality: all are closely related. The emancipation—or, as some would say, the cutting adrift—of melody, harmony, and tonality all went together. This joint emancipation counts as the central characteristic of early twentieth-century style.

It created difficulties for listeners and also for composers. The imminent danger of unregulated chaos spurred many of the latter into ingenious and imaginative new systems of aural logic; one of these, serialism, will be discussed later. But it also resulted in an enormous expansion of horizons for composers of all persuasions—not only members of the avant garde but also relatively conservative composers, and popular musicians, too. It was only this emancipation that made possible the new ranges of expressivity explored so brilliantly by Stravinsky, Webern, and Schoenberg in the first category; Bartok, Copland, and many others in the second; and George Gershwin, Duke Ellington, and Kurt Weill in the third. The excitement these composers felt at the intoxicating wealth of new resources that had opened up for them almost seems to vibrate in their music. Some of the vibrations can still be caught by listeners today.

Impressionism and Cubism

To exemplify the sheer sensuousness of impressionist painting and music, there is probably nothing better than an impressionist nude. This Renoir could almost be an illustration for one of Debussy's seductive water sirens (page 311). Impressionist painters did not try to depict shapes and objects so much as the *impression* shapes and objects give when they are bathed in actual light. To this end they evolved a painting technique involving iridescent patches of color. Notice how the technique softens the lines around the girl's body and renders the flesh as soft as the water and the clump of rushes in the background. The rushes and the water are painted in a particularly exaggerated impressionist way, with blue, green, red, and yellow patches of color.

An amusing contrast is Marcel Duchamp's *Nude*

Descending a Staircase, one of the most famous (or notorious) of early twentieth-century paintings because of the scandal it caused at the New York Armory Exhibition of 1913. Half a century later, we are probably not so appalled at the thorough destruction of the female form in this picture. Obviously, the painter was interested not in accurate representation but in abstract "composition," that is, in the arrangement of planes and shapes on the surface. It is pointless to criticize pictures of this kind for distortion; they have reached a stage "beyond distortion." Duchamp was investigating a new language in painting, cubism, which was also beginning to interest such artists as Juan Gris, Georges Braque, and Pablo Picasso.

Impressionism

Claude Debussy (1862–1918)

THREE NOCTURNES—*CLOUDS, FESTIVALS, SIRENS*
(1893–1899)   *Side 13*

Claude Debussy occupies the border area between the romantic and early twentieth-century styles. From the vantage point of the 1970s, his romantic allegiances are evident enough: in his investigation of marvelous new tone colors for orchestra and also for piano, in his rich harmonies, and in the unquestionably emotional quality of his music. Around 1900, the novelties of his style stood out more clearly. For instance, the tone colors, magical as they are, avoid the heavy sonorities that were usual at the time and concentrate instead on blurrings of delicate shades of sound. His harmonies, rich as they are, are also strangely vague, seeming to float easily and naturally without ever finding a true focus or cadence place. And while the total effect is certainly sensuous, it is also remarkably intimate and refined. Debussy shrank from the emphatic, broad emotion deployed by the other late romantic composers.

It might be said, in fact, that Debussy's passion was the avoidance of the obvious, whether in emotional effect or in the technical features that help create that effect, such as tone color and harmony. This characteristic also extends to melody. Debussy's themes and motives (he hardly ever uses actual tunes) are nearly always fragmentary and tentative. There will be just a whiff of melody, a tantalizing suggestion of a tune, and then it will fade away into the shifting tone colors and sinuous harmonic flow. A little later, many composers abandoned tune, in the conventional sense, entirely. In light of this development, Debussy counts as a transitional figure of great significance.

There does seem to be something characteristically French about Debussy's music, with its almost exaggerated emphasis on subtlety and refined understatement. Debussy was proud to think so; he hated the German composers and their blatant overemotionality (as he might have put it; Debussy was a sharptongued music critic as well as a composer). His music may even make us think of elegant French cuisine, by comparison with the hearty sauerbraten being served up across the Rhine by Richard Strauss and Gustav Mahler. A more conventional (and less fanciful) comparison links Debussy with

IMPRESSIONISM impressionism, the painting style evolved by French artists a few years earlier. Besides a similarity in feeling, there are also analogies in technique (see page 308). Debussy's musical style is often described as impressionistic.

Debussy's Three Nocturnes for Orchestra might be categorized as small symphonic poems (page 248), though they have no stories. They are illustrative pieces, and in this area it is probably safe to say that Debussy has never been matched, before or after his own time. The first nocturne, *Clouds*, is a pure nature picture. The second, *Festivals*, evokes mysterious nighttime fairs or parades. The title of the third nocturne, *Sirens*, refers to the legendary seamaidens who tempt lonely sailors and pull them into the deep.

Clouds The beginning of *Clouds* is shown below in a simplified score:

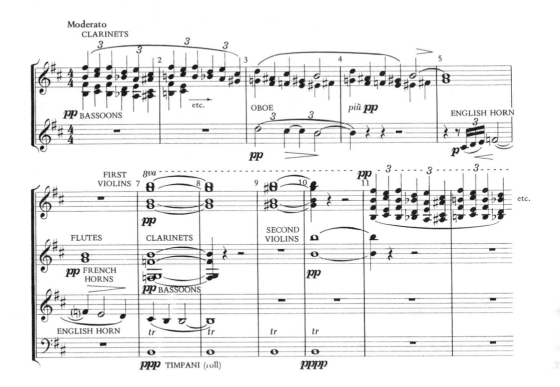

We may well find the theme of measure 1 a wonderfully atmospheric representation of great cumulus clouds, moving slowly, almost imperceptibly yet steadily, without any possibility of check or control. But at the same time we would also have to admit that as a theme, the chords of measure 1 circle around in a most inconclusive fashion. They make no strong declarations, and they lead nowhere definite. This is also true of the figure starting in measure 5 for the English horn. Yet even this muted gesture, with its vague rhythm and its fading conclusion, seems sufficient to exhaust the composition and bring it to a near halt in measures 7 to 10. How different these themes are from the bold ranging theme beginning Richard Strauss's *Don Juan* or from the brief but taut and expectant theme beginning Wagner's *Tristan und Isolde!* It is exactly this wispiness that gives Debussy's music its novelty and its particular expressive effect.

In terms of orchestration, too, Debussy's "sound" differs sharply from that of Gustav Mahler, another great innovator in orchestration of the same period (page 286). Mahler treated the orchestra more and more contrapuntally. Each instrument tends to stand out against the others like a little romantic hero striving for his own say in the world. Debussy has some contrapuntal effects, but not many — you can't have counterpoint without melodic lines, and he was much less interested in melody than in color and harmony. Thus in contrast to Mahler's orchestra, Debussy's is a single, delicately pulsing entity to which the individual instruments contribute momentary gleams of color. An analogy can be drawn with the paint blobs of an impressionist picture, which fade into the overall lush effect.

Listen to the first few measures of *Clouds,* and note especially the composite tone color at measure 7. As the English-horn figure starts to fade, it is covered by a unique and magical sound blended together out of a low drum roll, a middle chord on the clarinets and bassoons, and an exquisitely high chord on the first violins. (They are actually divided into six groups in order to play this chord, though only four show in the example.) The sound grows even more strained as G♯ replaces G (measure 9). Then both G and G♯ seem to dissolve, leaving a single octave B hanging in the second violins, as the drum roll fades to **pppp.** When the first theme is resumed by the high violins (measure 11), it sounds somehow thinner and also more sensual, like a glint of moonlight at the corner of the clouds.

As for Debussy's celebrated harmony, a good example appears just two measures after the above example concludes:

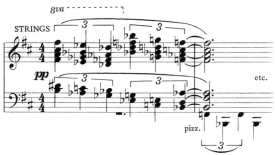

BAND 9   This passage appears in the middle of band 9 of the record. Those who can pick it out on the piano will see that the remarkably gentle, murmuring effect is caused by a long succession of chords of the same form (called major ninth chords), which slip by without causing a clear sense of tonality. This usage was individual with Debussy and has been much imitated since, as in this once-famous song of the 1930s, Duke Ellington's *Sophisticated Lady:*

Clouds might be said to fall into an A B A' form. B is a new theme played by flutes and harp, and there is a suggestion of A returning at the end. But only the faintest suggestion. Debussy shrinks from clear formal outlines, and one feels that the musical form here is much more fluid than that of A B A structures observed in other music. Mainly what we hear at the end, as the suggestion of A, is the English-horn figure and the timpani roll—suggesting distant thunder clouds, perhaps. Did Debussy have the "Scene in the Fields" from Berlioz's *Fantastic Symphony* in mind when he wrote this conclusion? It might prove interesting to compare the two passages (see page 243).

Festivals This is a more active piece, and in some ways a more conventional one. It has a clearer structure (A B C A′) and a good healthy climax in the C section, which seems to represent a spectral parade heard from afar and then coming nearer and nearer until it is blaring in our ears. But unlike the oxcart in Moussorgsky's "Bydlo," page 274, it does not go off down the road again. The far-off parade is orchestrated unforgettably. Three muted trumpets play the march tune, while two harps join the timpani and pizzicato strings—all marked **ppp**—in beating out the meter.

The march tune itself is fascinating. Its rhythms are straightforward enough, but the harmonies cause a striking distortion of what would be "normal" march music. We spoke above of distortion employed by early twentieth-century composers for effects of harshness or parody; here distortion is being used for quite another effect—fantastic and (we would have to say) highly romantic. These marchers in the night are wearing mysterious costumes and carrying strange flares, it seems, or else we are viewing them through some kind of tinted, scented fog. Probably everyone would agree that the distorted march music here is more beautiful, not less, than a "normal" Sousa march.

Near the end of *Festivals*, after the rushing, glittering first theme (A) has returned, the music slows down. A melancholy figure—brief, as usual—hovers in the oboe and other wind instruments, while the cellos and double basses rumble away quietly in the background. The mood recalls the ending of *Clouds*, though the musical material is not the same.

Sirens The third nocturne returns to the wispy technique of *Clouds*, employed now for a much more sensual effect. These shadowy, melting, endlessly caressing sirens are Debussy's answer to the overheated blandishments pictured in so much late romantic music. Remember the ladies in Richard Strauss's *Don Juan*, for example (page 250). (For a daytime siren by the impressionist painter Renoir, see page 306.)

The orchestra employed to create the remarkable tone colors in the Nocturnes actually counts as modest in extent, at least according to the standards of Strauss and Mahler. But in *Sirens* Debussy made one striking addition: female voices. The singers are provided with no words, only vowels—and not even these, on occasions when they are directed to hum. Singing without VOCALISE   words, called <u>vocalise</u> (rhymes with "ease"), was an innovation that composers did not pick up again until the 1950s, though in a rather different spirit, as will be seen in the next chapter. Again there is a suggestion of A B A′ form, with two themes for the sirens in Debussy's typical aimless, winding style:

We may come to feel that in among the watery shadows and half-lights of Debussy's music, a strange family resemblance links these two themes to the clarinet and English-horn themes, respectively, of *Clouds*.

Impressionism and Post-Impressionism

Another impressionist picture: *Field of Poppies* by
Claude Monet, one of the founders of impressionist
painting. Contrast this with a similar scene — a landscape
with figures — by Vincent Van Gogh, the great
"post-impressionist" painter, whose brooding, strong,
disturbed, and increasingly unnaturalistic vision was an
important precursor of early twentieth-century
expressionism. The human beings in Monet fit in with
nature as easily as do the poppies; in Van Gogh they are
overwhelmed by nature. Van Gogh painted many
versions of this scene, some of them darker and more
boldly distorted than this one. Sometimes two, three, or
a dozen moons blaze in the inky sky.

We can perhaps take Van Gogh's *The Evening Walk* as
an illustration of Act III, scene ii of Alban Berg's opera
Wozzeck—the moonlit murder scene (page 316). The
illustrative music of that scene oddly recalls the
impressionistic music of Debussy, and in examining
these two landscapes, too, we can detect similarities of
technique. Both Monet and Van Gogh used disconnected
daubs of color with which to make their very different
effects; both Debussy and Berg used disconnected
fragments of melody and tone color.

Expressionism

Debussy's reaction against the overemotionalism of late romantic music was shared by many other French composers and also by foreigners in Paris such as Igor Stravinsky. Most of these composers turned their backs also on the delicate sensuousness of Debussy's style and evolved styles of their own that were hard or brittle, tough or dry, and in any case decidedly unromantic. In France, the most outspoken antiromantic composers of this time moved in the direction of simplicity and even triviality.

In Germany and Austria, however, composers pressed forward with music that was increasingly emotional and increasingly complex. More and more they found themselves exploiting extreme emotional states, ranging to hysteria, nightmare, even perversion and insanity. Perhaps this was their response to the state of the world that they were coming to see as more and more desperate, or perhaps this seemed the only way to go, once all the more usual emotional states had been exhausted. This movement, which had important precedents and parallels in literature and painting, is called expressionism.

The first decade of the twentieth century saw the first works of Sigmund Freud, with their revolutionary new analysis of the significance of dreams, the power of unconscious emotional drives, and the central role of sexuality. Freud's psychology was to become one of the main currents of modern thought, but at first it made its effect mainly in Germany and Austria. Directly or indirectly, German expressionist literature, art, and music came under the influence of Freud's ideas.

Alban Berg (1885–1935)
WOZZECK, ACT III (1917–1919)   *Side 13*

A famous work combining expressionist poetry and music was mentioned above: Arnold Schoenberg's song cycle *Pierrot lunaire*. The best-known product of expressionist music is the opera *Wozzeck*, by Schoenberg's student Alban Berg. (The pronunciation is *Votseck*, with the first syllable rhyming with "lots.") *Wozzeck* is perhaps the most arresting opera of its time, a work that sums up, if not all aspects of the early twentieth-century consciousness, at least one essential aspect of it. In this respect, *Wozzeck* occupies a position parallel to Wagner's *Tristan und Isolde* in the nineteenth century.

And between these two works the contrast could hardly be more complete. Set in the courtly Middle Ages of romantic fantasy, *Tristan und Isolde* shows how personal emotion unites the lovers in ecstasy and allows them to transcend the demands of society and, indeed, of life itself. Wagner's view of human aspirations and relationships was optimistic, indeed triumphant. *Wozzeck* is set in a slum. It shows the individual crushed by society into madness and catastrophe. Even human communication is an impossibility, to say nothing of love.

Berg's deeply pessimistic attitude recalls that of another characteristic artist of the early twentieth century, Franz Kafka. Kafka's novels and stories show modern man trapped by a great impersonal system he can neither influence nor understand. In *The Trial*, for instance, Joseph K. (he is even denied a real name) stands trial for a crime which is never revealed to him. He wanders through the novel as though in a nightmare, trying to discover the reason for his oppression. But neither his judge nor his lawyer nor his priest will enlighten him. Finally he is taken to the outskirts of town and stabbed in the heart, no wiser than before.

Joseph K. has turned out to be a recurring, all-but-mythical figure in the twentieth century. One version of him appears as the brainwashed "hero," Smith, in *1984*, George Orwell's ominous prediction of life in the future under Big Brother. A current comic (or tragicomic) version of him is the man who gets a wrong credit-card charge and is unable to communicate with the computers, which ignore his checks, cut off his credit, repossess his furniture, and cancel his auto insurance. Franz Wozzeck is an inarticulate and impoverished soldier, the lowest member of the military machine. He is troubled by visions and tormented for no apparent reason by his sadistic captain and by the regimental doctor, who uses him for scientific experiments. His mistress sleeps with his NCO, who beats up Wozzeck when he makes some objection. Finally Wozzeck murders his mistress, goes mad, and wanders into a lake. Passersby hear him drowning but make no effort to save him.

The third and last act of this opera, containing the final catastrophe, is divided into five short scenes linked together without pause by orchestral interludes.

Act III, scene i: Marie's Room Wozzeck's unfaithful mistress Marie is shown in a short scene of morning-after repentance. First she reads a few verses from the Bible, punctuated by cries of anguish, then she fondles her child and tells it a little story:

"Neither was guile found in his mouth." *Lord God, Lord God, do not look at me!*
"And the Pharisees brought unto him a woman taken in adultery. Jesus said unto her: Neither do I condemn thee, go, and sin no more." *Lord God!* . . .

Once there was a poor child and he had no father or mother — they were all dead — and there was no one in the world, and he was hungry and cried all day and all night. . . .

"And stood at his feet weeping, and began to wash his feet with tears, and kissed his feet, and anointed them with ointment." *Savior, if only I could anoint your feet! Savior, you had mercy on her — have mercy on me also!*

Berg treats Marie's utterances in this scene in different vocal styles. When she is reading or narrating, she simply speaks, against a relatively gentle orchestral background, or else engages in "talk-sing" (*Sprechstimme*), derived from Schoenberg's *Pierrot lunaire* (page 301). On the other hand, her wailing cries of anguish are genuinely sung, mostly on high, intense notes which can hardly be said to coalesce into recognizable tunes. This makes Marie seem psychologically very different from earlier operatic figures whom we have heard, such as Wotan or Aïda. She is closest to Princess Amneris, but if Amneris is distraught to the point of tantrum, Marie is truly hysterical. The orchestral background for her outcries is also characteristically intense and dissonant and does not fit in noticeably with her singing line. This establishes the general level of atonality (page 304) that will be held through most of the act.

A blackout follows, and a short orchestral interlude runs from this scene into the next. The music surges up violently, with the trombones prominent. The audience has an opportunity to reflect in complete darkness upon Marie's misery and her desperate situation.

Scene ii: A Woodland Path by a Pond   Wozzeck takes Marie on a walk and speaks to her disconnectedly about their life together, her beauty, the darkness, and the blood-red moon they see rising. Her terror increases. In a sudden rage, he knifes her to death. Again, the words in this scene are sung in a dissociated style which sounds like neither recitative nor aria. Wozzeck's statements seem decidedly schizophrenic, ranging from tender at one second to coarse and violent at the next. The stabbing itself is very ugly, accompanied by a driving drumbeat.

What can we make of the orchestral music behind the singing? In its weirdly beautiful way, it is illustrating the nighttime scene: the black water of the pond, the shadows, the crickets and frogs and other woodland sounds. Berg has even learned something from the illustrative music of Debussy, but the effect of his scene is as different as—night from day, nightmare from daydream. If a score by Debussy recalls an impressionist landscape by Monet, this one by Berg recalls an ominous, brooding landscape by Van Gogh (page 313).

This scene also underlines the ambiguity of the term "atonality," an ambiguity that was stressed in the discussion above. Since neither the singing nor the orchestral music fits into conventional tonality, the effect may seem chaotic at first. Yet a single tonal center (the note B) is omnipresent in this scene, which in its own way counts as more "tonal," in that it is chained to one central note, than almost any other piece of music. A really attentive listener should be able to detect the same note sounding in every single bar, in high or low octaves, played by one instrument or another. The note B grows overpowering when the drum begins its beat; Marie's final shriek covers a two-octave B; and then in the blackout after the stabbing, the single note B is played by the whole orchestra in two gut-bursting crescendos. Don't turn down the phonograph if this famous passage hurts your ears—it is supposed to. (It is also hard on the stagehands, who are allowed just about twenty-one seconds to make the scene change.)

Scene iii: An Inn   If Wozzeck seemed close to insanity during the murder, he now enters into pure nightmare. In a sordid dive, he seeks consolation from Marg'ret, a friend (or perhaps one should say a colleague) of Marie's. Berg's idea of a honky-tonk piano opens the scene:

Here harmonic and rhythmic distortion of what might be a "normal" jazz piano is used for grotesque effect—an expressionist use of distortion, as contrasted to Debussy's impressionist use of it in the march in *Festivals* (page 311). Marg'ret gets up on the piano and sings a song, also distorted:

Suddenly she notices blood on his hands. It smells like human blood. In a horrible climax to the scene, all the people in the inn come out of the shadows and close in on Wozzeck to lynch him. But he escapes in the blackout, as the orchestral interlude surges frantically and furiously.

Berg contrived a very original musical form for this scene, a form that contributes directly to the dramatic effect he sought. The entire scene is built on a single short rhythm, repeated over and over again with only slight modifications—*but presented in many different tempos.* This twitching rhythm has been marked above the two previous musical examples, first at a fast tempo, then at a slow one. Perhaps its most obvious presentation comes when Marg'ret first notices the blood:

Even if the listener catches only a quarter or a tenth of the times this rhythm comes, the hypnotic effect of this rhythmic ostinato (page 95) contributes powerfully to the sense of nightmare and fixation.

Scene iv: By the Pond Wozzeck returns to the scene of the murder, and again the orchestra engages in nature illustration, making strange, macabre sounds, so different from those of Debussy. Wozzeck's mind has quite cracked. He shrieks out for the knife ("*Das Messer!*"), discovers the corpse ("*Mörder!*"), and sees once again the bloodred moon ("*Der Mond ist blütig. . . .*"). Finally he walks into the pond—which seems to him to be filled with blood—in order to wash himself and dispose of the murder weapon.

At this point, his two principal tormentors of Acts I and II, the Captain and the Doctor, happen to walk by. They hear the vivid orchestral gurgles and understand that someone is drowning, but like people watching a mugging on a crowded New York street, they make no move to help. The Captain speaks the last words of the scene: "Come on, Doctor! Let's get out of here!" He uses plain speech again, not song, but it is speech that rises shrilly in terror: "*Kommen sie, Doktor! kommen sie schnell!*" Even the tormentors of this life, we realize, are driven by tormenting demons of their own.

So far, the orchestral interludes between the scenes have all been very brief. As a result the drama presses to its catastrophe with great urgency. Now, however, Berg writes a slow, lengthy interlude in which great waves of pity for Wozzeck well out from the orchestra into the darkened auditorium. Obviously Berg identified with Wozzeck, and he agonizes with him in a series of great orchestral climaxes. The almost unbearable emotionality of this interlude recalls the slow movement of Mahler's Fourth Symphony (page 288), though the style is more atonal. By Berg's standards, however, the beginning and the end of this interlude are relatively tonal. If the score sounds crowded, that is because it finds place for all the many leitmotivs (page 255) which have been running through the opera, in Wagnerian fashion, to symbolize persons and feelings.

As the interlude sobs to a close, there is a sudden whoosh of harp, celesta, and winds, synchronized with the stage lights flashing on again for the next scene. The sound was borrowed from Debussy's *Festivals.* Here it may remind us of movie technique, when the camera cuts suddenly to a new image. In fact, the whole dramatic setup of *Wozzeck,* with its brief, intensely focused scenes running into one another, is a remarkable forecast of movie technique—forecast, because when Berg started to write his opera in 1917, the cinema was hardly taken seriously yet. Those who have seen the famous early German expressionist movies *The Cabinet of Dr. Caligari* and *M* may find in them a spiritual affinity with Berg's expressionist musical score.

Scene v: Epilogue. The Street Outside Marie's House. Next Morning The next scene is bright and clear, a sunlit morning, featuring high instruments from a reduced-size orchestra. They are playing some of the most ravishing sounds in the whole opera—but Berg is preparing to twist the knife in the wound. A group of children sing a ring-around-a-rosy game, whose melody is once again distorted:

CHILDREN:

Ringel, Ringel Rosenkranz, Rin - gel reih'n! Ringel, Ringel, Rosenkranz, Rin...
Ring around a rosy, a pocket full of posy...

The child of Marie and Wozzeck is also there, playing on a hobbyhorse; we hear his little switch and his giddap exclamations ("Hop, hop! Hop, hop!"). With a cruelty that is not uncommon in small children, the others come up and taunt him: "Hey you, your mother's dead!" He does not seem to understand. "Come on and see!" Hesitantly, he follows them off, as the curtain falls to quiet sinister-sweet orchestral sounds.

The message is unmistakable. Just as the Captain shares the horror of Wozzeck's world, so also does the child. He is in for a nasty shock as he goes out to the pond (though perhaps he has been prepared for it by the kind of stories his mother had been telling him). His world, too, the daytime world of everyday children's games, is peopled by tormentors he cannot understand.

So ends an opera which many people consider to be one of the most gripping theater pieces of the century. Berg's skill at the musical depiction of insanity is really uncanny, but this very virtuosity may suggest some interesting questions. Was Wozzeck actually hounded and driven mad in an objective sense? For that matter, was Joseph K. actually accused, tried, and subjected to the fearful runaround described in *The Trial*? Or is each of these works perhaps a brilliant analysis of the paranoid personality, on a symbolic level? The age of Freud, an age fascinated by neurosis and psychosis, has found in Franz Kafka and Alban Berg artists who reflect its concerns.

Anton von Webern (1883–1945)
FIVE ORCHESTRA PIECES, OP. 10 (1913)

Another expressionist composer who developed a highly individual "new language" was Anton von Webern. He grew up in the world of late romanticism, surrounded by the grandiose musical structures of Strauss and Mahler—and his teacher Arnold Schoenberg could rack them up with the best. Webern turned his music about-face, toward concentration, brevity, atomization, and quiet: quiet even unto silence. His compositions are almost all extremely brief. The Five Orchestra Pieces last 12, 14, 11, 6, and 32 measures, respectively! Webern's entire musical output has been recorded on four LP records.

His music is famous for its "atomized" melodic lines, lines shared among the different instruments, with one instrument often playing just one or two notes before another takes over. This breaks up the music into kaleidoscopic flashes—successive flashes and also simultaneous ones. With the beginning notes of the Five Orchestra Pieces, to take a famous example, it is tempting to write out the music with little spaces between instruments:

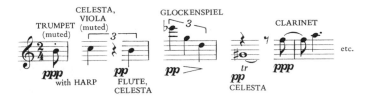

And as this example suggests, with its muted trumpet, murmuring celesta, and near-silent clarinet, Webern explored the most exquisite and excruciating limits of musical delicacy. For the rich brocade of romanticism and the subtle silk of impressionism, Webern substituted a unique texture of glittering lace.

His music is thoroughly atonal; it is also athematic, lacking tunes, motives, and obvious repetitions. (If the reader has been growing weary of all the A B A diagrams in this book, he can now start listening to music without repetitions, music that never comes around again to a second A.) In place of tonality and motive, Webern achieves a remarkable quality by giving heightened significance to the individual notes, which he somehow turns into separate little sources of tremendous energy. The orchestration plays a big part in this effect by isolating the notes and pointing them up so sharply.

The fourth of the Five Orchestra Pieces is shown below—the whole of it, in a full-length line score:

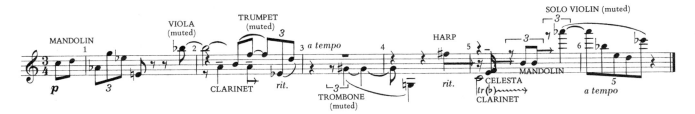

Webern's incessant *p*, *pp*, and *ppp* marks have been omitted from this score (elsewhere he also writes "scarcely audible," "fading," and "as light as possible"). While a strange, "sprung" melody is traced by the main instruments, other instruments enter with notes that are quietly repeated several times in various rhythms and then fade away entirely. These are indicated in the line score by arrows—the clarinet in measure 2, the harp in measure 4, the clarinet, celesta, and mandolin in measure 5. Meanwhile the main melody itself migrates from the mandolin to a single note in the viola, to the trumpet, down to the trombone, and then up very high in the violin.

Though the piece is written in ¾ time, the meter is scarcely apprehended. The rhythm complex is expressive, and involuted. Each note seems to have been edged into place with a hushed sense of special urgency. And it has been well observed that in Webern's music, the rests (the silences) are as expressive and "pregnant" as the notes themselves. Listen hard to the rests in measures 1 and 4—and measure 6.

Everybody knows that to get the maximum dissonance from two notes on the piano, the two notes should be adjacent—B and C, for example, or C and C♯. An examination of the score above shows Webern constantly working with adjacent notes of this sort, either simultaneously or successively, in one octave or another:

Measure 1	mandolin A♭ to G, and then E♭ to E♮
2	viola B♭ + clarinet A
	trumpet E♭ to D
2–3	clarinet A to trombone G♯
4	trombone G♯ to G♮
	trombone G to harp F♯
5	celesta E + F
	clarinet C + mandolin B
6	violin D to E♭

To hear all this would take sharp ears, certainly. But even if they are not heard specifically, these constant dissonances help create the quiet, tense, edgy atmosphere that always seems to underlie Webern's music.

In later years, Webern followed Schoenberg in adopting serialism, but his serial music sounds less like Schoenberg than like early, pre-serial music by Webern. Brevity and concentration remained his ideals.

There is some truth to the witticism that Webern was a composer who always quit when he was ahead. When his pieces end, we want more—or at least, we wonder why they ended quite as early as they did. Almost without realizing it, we find ourselves concentrating more intently on these tiny pieces than on longer ones by other composers. Not only is Webern working harder, infusing each note with unique energies, but the listener, in partnership, is listening more anxiously too.

What we hear is a curious blend of subdued yearning and pixieish imagination. Though at first the music may seem all charm, the strongly emotional nature behind it soon makes itself felt (most strongly, perhaps, in the third of the Five Orchestra Pieces). But the expressionist vision has been remarkably distilled; it is as though passion is being viewed through the wrong end of a telescope. As in a Japanese haiku, Webern's music carries an intense whiff of suggestion; then thoughts and questions resonate in the ensuing void:

閑さや岩にしみ入る蟬の聲

Shizukasa ya iwa ni shimiiru semi no koe

The silence;
The voice of the cicadas
Penetrates the rocks.

—Basho

Music and Painting: A Conjunction

For all the differences between the arts of music and painting, there are times when strikingly similar techniques can be observed in both. In post-impressionist and expressionist paintings (pages 313 and 328), successive liberties were taken with visual reality. Then early in the twentieth century, some painters took the great step and abandoned the representation of visual reality altogether. These painters went "beyond distortion" in seeking to make an artistic language in abstract visual terms. Their kind of abstraction is not the art language of today, to be sure, any more than Schoenberg and Stravinsky determine today's language in music. But the abstract art of the early twentieth century produced an impressive body of work which made today's art possible. Much the same thing can be said about early twentieth-century music.

Duchamp (page 307), Picasso, and the other cubists in Paris took one route to abstraction. The Germans took another. Both Paul Klee and Wassily Kandinsky were associated with the composer Arnold Schoenberg, who was also an artist at one time during his career, in a group called "The Blue Rider" (after the title of a little magazine). They took their steps toward abstraction at the same time that Webern and Schoenberg were moving toward music without tonality and without themes, before World War I. In spirit, Klee reminds us of Webern, perhaps, and Kandinsky of Schoenberg or Berg.

Both Kandinsky and Klee were very closely involved with music. In these years Kandinsky provided many of his paintings with musical titles such as *Improvisation* and *Fugue*; ours is entitled *Great Fugue* — the name of a celebrated string-quartet piece by Beethoven. Klee actually hesitated between a career in music or in art. His half-whimsical, half-frantic *Drawing with Fermata* indicates that he was well acquainted with the musicians' slang term for a fermata, "bird's eye." (Fermata is a hold of indefinite length on a note, chord, or rest.)

Arnold Schoenberg (1874–1951)
PIANO CONCERTO (1942)

Of all the advanced composers of this century, Arnold Schoenberg was the most keenly aware of the problem caused by ever-broadening dissonance and atonality. The problem, to put it simply, was the clear and present danger of chaos. In the 1920s Schoenberg made an impressive effort to impose a kind of order or control over the newly emancipated elements of music. This resulted in the *twelve-tone method,* later known as <u>serialism</u>.

SERIALISM

As a basis for such control, Schoenberg felt he had to find a way of guaranteeing that the level of atonality and dissonance in his music would remain more or less constant. With this in mind, he went a step or two beyond Wagner's chromaticism (page 305), the nineteenth-century technique that looked forward to atonality. Wagner used all twelve notes of the chromatic scale very freely; Schoenberg determined to use them all systematically.

Schoenberg chose a special arrangement, or ordering, of the twelve chromatic notes and then kept this fixed for the composition in question. Another composition would have a different arrangement. This ordering is called the *twelve-tone row* or <u>series</u>; hence the term "serialism." Then, in principle, Schoenberg composed by writing the notes only in the order of the series—and before starting over again, he always went through the entire series of twelve without any backtracking. This guaranteed that no single note would become too prominent and thus receive any shade of tonal centrality.

SERIES

Since for this purpose it makes no difference which way round the series goes, Schoenberg also composed with the series in certain different manipulations that still kept its essential character. Called *retrograde* (backward), *inversion* (upside down), and *retrograde inversion* (upside down and backward), they are illustrated below together with a basic series:*

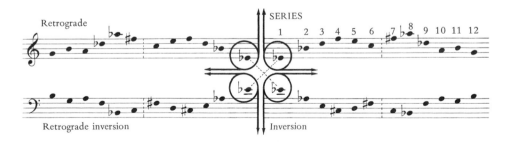

The series controls pitches, in a sense, but it does not say anything about rhythm, nor does it specify which octaves the various notes come in. Thus on

---

* Schoenberg did not invent, though he did systematize, inversion and retrograde. We encountered inversion in Bach's Brandenburg Concerto No. 5, page 102, and retrograde in the minuet from Haydn's Sonata No. 41, page 176.

page 326, the identical basic series, retrograde, inversion, and retrograde inversion can be written out with some notes an octave higher or lower.

Another important possibility is to *transpose* the series (and its retrograde, inversion, and retrograde inversion), that is, move it bodily up or down from one pitch level to another. The basic series shown above, beginning E B D . . . , may be transposed down to D A C . . . or to A E G . . . (see page 326), etc. With all these extensions, it will be seen that the twelve-tone method leaves the composer plenty of flexibility.

It is hard to learn about serialism for the first time without finding the whole thing pretty strange. (But equally strange things were happening in other arts during the exact same period; think about our illustrations of paintings by Duchamp, Klee, and Kandinsky.) Serialism may strike some people as a bold, ingenious and highly imaginative attempt to open up new artistic horizons. It may strike others as arbitrary and crabbed, a force stifling music's true spontaneity.

The healthiest reaction, perhaps, is plain curiosity about how the music actually comes out. For getting worked up one way or another about musical technique *in the abstract* is a deeply futile exercise. Listen at this point to the beginning of Schoenberg's Piano Concerto. Does it sound imaginative or does it sound crabbed?

The series shown on page 324 is one used in this concerto. The piece opens with a quiet tune, played by the pianist's right hand. This tune comes out of the series in a relatively simple way, as appears from the music on the next pages. Of the four phrases of the tune, phrase 1 follows the *series* itself, phrase 2 the *retrograde inversion* transposed, phrase 3 the *retrograde*, and phrase 4 the *inversion* transposed. There are a few "free" notes, marked with asterisks, and some note repetitions. You will see that the rhythm has nothing to do with the series. The series notes are sometimes rhythmically very prominent, and at other times they go by almost without being noticed.

This is a clear example of twelve-tone writing, but such a simple one that it cannot be described as typical. In fact, it is exceptional for actual tunes to be made out of a twelve-tone series or for a series to be treated as a tune. A series serves as a source of motives and harmonies, as the raw material for the musical elements rather than the actual musical substance itself. It is not even a scale but an orientation of notes in the chromatic scale. The way in which the left-hand accompaniment (shown on page 327 only for phrase 1) is derived from the series shows a level of complexity that is more usual. Measures 7 and 8, for example, cover the entire series:

except for note 12, G, which appears in the right hand.

How does serialism impose a "new order" on the increasingly free and chaotic elements of music? To continue our technical discussion (with apol-

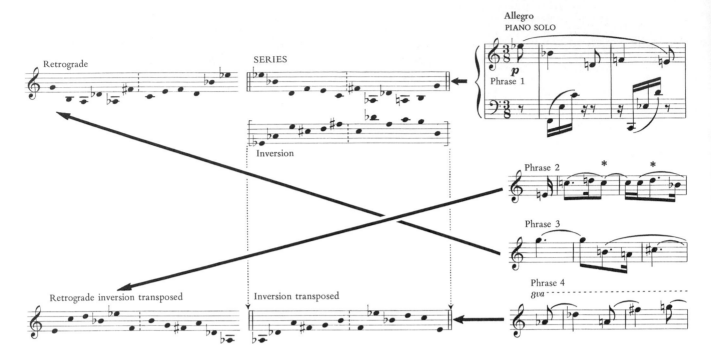

ogies—but it can't be helped if we are to understand the concept behind serialism, let alone hear it), it should now be pointed out that the important thing about the series is not the twelve notes themselves but rather the *intervals* between them. (See the definition and brief discussion of intervals on page 24.) When a twelve-tone series is used in inversion, retrograde, retrograde inversion, or transposition, the notes change from their original series locations. *But the intervals between adjacent pairs of notes all remain the same.* The intervals in our series can be tabulated as follows:

INTERVALS IN THE SERIES OF SCHOENBERG'S PIANO CONCERTO

Name of Interval*	Number of Chromatic Notes in the Interval	Occurs between the Series Notes that are Numbered:	Number of Times the Interval Comes in the Series
Semitone	1	4 and 5	1
Whole tone	2	7 and 8; 10 and 11	2
Minor third	3	3 and 4	1
Major third	4	2 and 3; 5 and 6; 9 and 10; 11 and 12	4
Fourth	5	1 and 2; 8 and 9	2
Tritone	6	6 and 7	1

* All larger intervals reduce to one of the six listed here if the notes are shifted in the octaves until they are as close together as possible.

Every serial composition has its own series and hence its own special sound—its own "twelve-tonality," one might say—determined by the intervals and *their* ordering. In the Schoenberg concerto, the interval of the

major third is prominent while the semitone and the tritone have been minimized. Throughout the work, then, certain melodic and harmonic patterns recur and stamp the music with a unique character.

Indeed, serialism can be regarded as the end result of an important tendency of nineteenth-century music, namely, the tendency to seek strong means of unity within individual compositions. We have observed the "principle of thematic unity" in the music of Schumann, Berlioz, Wagner, and Mahler, and we have spoken of the various levels on which it operates: recurring themes, thematic transformation, and subtle or even subliminal similarities (page 227). On its own rather different level, serialism carried out the ideal of unity that the romantic composers were working toward.

We also mentioned that this causes a problem for listeners, because the similarities or relationships can become so subtle that only the composers and their friends may be able to hear them. This problem comes up again with serial music—urgently. The relationships of serial music are not at all easy to hear; they demand, in fact, a radically new kind of musical perception. Was it this very feature that made serialism so fascinating to so many composers?

In the 1920s and 1930s, three of the leading figures associated with expressionism in music adopted the technique in a thoroughgoing way. These composers—Schoenberg, Berg, and Webern—have been called the "Second Viennese School," the first being, of course, the "school" of Haydn, Mozart, and Beethoven over a hundred years earlier. Then in the 1950s, a great number of composers of all generations, from Stravinsky down to the very youngest, adopted serialism and indeed extended it in ways that Schoenberg would scarcely have recognized. In the 1960s, the influence of serialism diminished.

Even composers of the early twentieth century who stood apart from the Second Viennese School sometimes adopted certain features of serialism. We shall see an example in the Violin Concerto No. 2 by Béla Bartók.

Expressionist Heads: Schoenberg

Further examples of expressionism in art, this time in the treatment of a head. The artist was the composer Arnold Schoenberg, who in the years around World War I had an active interest in painting, too. Expressionist distortion is especially evident in the first picture, entitled *The Critic*. Seldom do composers show any love for critics, though it should be noted that quite a few composers have been practicing critics themselves: Carl Maria von Weber, Berlioz, Schumann, Hugo Wolf, Debussy, and in this country Virgil Thomson.

The other picture is a self portrait; compare it with the photograph of Schoenberg, taken a few years later. And this photograph itself suggests two interesting observations. First, there are many ways of taking a photograph; the somber background, the harsh lights, and the rather weirdly different treatment of Schoenberg's two ears are "artistic" contributions by the photographer. Compared with the snapshots in your family album, this counts as an expressionist shot. The photographer, Man Ray, an American expatriate in Paris, was also one of the first to use photography as an abstract medium, as early as the 1920s.

The other observation concerns the long-range effects of the invention of photography in the early nineteenth century. This was a major encroachment by technology on art. Painters could talk all they wanted about the "inner truth" of painted portraits as compared with photographs, but gradually people who had been used to buying and commissioning pictures, in the aristocracy and the middle class, began to find their desire for accurate representation satisfied better—and much more cheaply—by photography. (The first famous composers who were photographed were Berlioz and Chopin.) Therefore, artists turned elsewhere, to the various levels of distortion represented by post-impressionism, expressionism, and beyond.

An analogy can be found in music. In the nineteenth century, as we have seen, the middle-class audience began to find their hankering for catchy tunes and dancelike rhythms nicely satisfied by the skillfully written types of popular music that evolved at the time. There were the waltzes of Johann Strauss, the operettas of Gilbert and Sullivan, and the pleasant band numbers that used to be played every Sunday in the park. As a result, serious composers looked beyond music based on simple tunes and rhythms, to the "new languages" of Debussy, Stravinsky, and Schoenberg.

Igor Stravinsky (1882–1971)

LE SACRE DU PRINTEMPS (THE RITE OF SPRING) (1913)

Side 14

One of the greatest of twentieth-century composers, Igor Stravinsky in his long career touched on many of the characteristic attitudes of his era and became a prisoner of none of them. His early work followed the romantic nationalism of Moussorgsky and other Russian composers. Young Stravinsky gravitated to Paris with a lively organization called the *Ballets Russes*. This Russian ballet company astonished the blasé Parisian public for many years with its exotic spectacles combining the newest and most sensational in dance, music, folklore, scenery, and costume design. Famous and soon-to-be-famous artists worked for the *Ballets Russes:* Matisse, Chagall, Braque, Rouault, Picasso.

The first three scores Stravinsky did for the *Ballets Russes* remain to this day his best-known pieces. Written from 1909 to 1913, they reveal an interesting progression toward more and more abstraction within the nationalist mold. The first of them, *The Firebird,* spins a romanticized fairy tale about Prince Ivan Tsarevitch, the ogre Kastcheï, and the magical Firebird. Its rich, half-oriental setting is matched by beautifully colored folk music and orchestral sound worthy of Debussy himself. But the next ballet moves from the steppes to the urban marketplace. *Petrouchka,* the story of a carnival barker and his puppet, encouraged Stravinsky to put a hard, satirical, mechanical edge on his folk material. Finally, *The Rite of Spring* boldly and brutally evokes the fertility cults of prehistoric Asian tribes. Here Russian folk music, drastically simplified, is treated as the source of primitive rhythmic and sexual energy rather than picture-postcard charm.

At its first performance, *The Rite of Spring* caused a near riot, the audience was so shocked at the dissonant sound in the orchestra pit and the suggestive choreography on the stage. Stravinsky employed an absolutely colossal orchestra, as though to show the world how well he could control the chief engine of musical romanticism. Compare this orchestra with the Viennese and romantic orchestras tabulated on pages 148 and 224. Almost a symbol of prewar opulence in musical terms, the orchestra of *The Rite of Spring* was twice as large as anything Stravinsky cared to use again.

The Rite of Spring has no real story; Stravinsky even said that he preferred to think of the music as a concert piece. However, the score bears many inscriptions indicating that the ballet is to portray a number of fertility rites of various kinds, culminating in the ceremonial choice of a virgin for sacrifice. Apparently she is danced to death (in the concluding "Sacrificial Dance"). It is dubious anthropology but effective theater.

The first part or act of the ballet is entitled "Adoration of the Earth." The interior sections run into one another directly, but there is usually little difficulty in determining when the new ones begin.

AN EARLY TWENTIETH-CENTURY ORCHESTRA
(As in Stravinsky's *The Rite of Spring*)

Strings:	violins 1, violins 2, violas, cellos, double basses, divided in many different ways
Woodwinds:	1 piccolo 3 flutes, one sometimes playing second piccolo 1 alto flute
	4 oboes, one sometimes playing second English horn 1 English horn
	1 high clarinet (E♭ clarinet) 3 clarinets, one sometimes playing second bass clarinet 1 bass clarinet
	4 bassoons, one sometimes playing second double bassoon 1 double bassoon
Brass:	8 French horns, two sometimes playing tenor tubas
	1 high trumpet (D trumpet) 4 trumpets 1 bass trumpet
	3 trombones 2 bass tubas
Percussion:	various timpani, bass drum cymbals, gong, tambourine, triangle

Introduction The famous opening theme is played by a bassoon at the very top—indeed, a little past the top—of its normal register. Early twentieth-century composers tended to stretch and strain at all elements of music, including the ordinary capabilities of their instruments. The bleating bassoon is joined by odd hootings on other woodwind instruments, forming a highly dissonant contrapuntal web. The whole effect is indeed introductory, for what is played by the bassoon, followed by oboe, high clarinet (E♭ clarinet), and trumpet, sounds rather like a static series of preliminary fanfares.

"Omens of Spring. Dance of the Adolescents" Probably this is where the original audience broke loose. The beginning of this dance is marked by heavy, harsh repetitions of a single dissonant chord in the strings, thirty-two times in all. However, sforzatos (>) (page 9) reinforced by short fat chords played by eight (!) French horns provide accents on the most unexpected beats:

The result is a contradiction of ordinary regular meter. Instead of eight standard measures in $\frac{2}{4}$ or $\frac{4}{8}$ meter containing four eighth-note beats each—

8×4—which the notation would suggest, Stravinsky makes us hear 9 (or $4 + 5) + 2 + 6 + 3 + 4 + 5 + 3$. The exhilarating effect is heightened when lively new fragments are played against the repeating chords. Among these are the first of several fragments of made-up folk song:

Stravinsky repeats these fragments over and over again at the same pitch but with slightly different rhythms and at slightly different lengths. This is Stravinsky's own variety of ostinato (page 95); the technique is illustrated in the third excerpt of the above example (the square brackets cover the repetitions). Like Debussy, Stravinsky tends to concentrate on small melodic fragments, but whereas Debussy usually abandons his fragments as soon as he decently can, Stravinsky keeps twisting and turning his, like a dog worrying a bone.

There are nearly 170 measures in this dance, and in all but two of them, some instrument plays the four even eighth notes (♪♪♪♪) prominently. This kind of metrical insistence was unknown in conventional music. To understand the impact of *The Rite of Spring* in 1913, remember that at the time, few Europeans were used to the steady beat of jazz (let alone rock).

"The Play of Abduction"   A whirlwind of brilliant rhythms, with much frantic work for the drums. This section ends with another good example of Stravinsky's rhythmic irregularity:

It is possible to hear this passage in a number of ways; something like the following jagged and highly complex metrical pattern emerges:

$$3 + 10 + 3 + 9 + 11 + 2 + 6 + 6 + 6 + 6 + 2 + 6 + 4 + 6 + 8 + 2 + 6$$

"Round Dances of Spring"   After a moment of respite, in an introduction featuring trills on the woodwind instruments, a slow, dragging dance is built out of the third folk-song fragment of the "Dance of the Adolescents" (in the sec-

ond example above). The very strong downbeat makes the meter as hypnotic as that of any hard rock number—except for an occasional added or skipped beat every once in a while, which always has a powerfully invigorating effect. This dance reaches a relentless climax with glissando (sliding) trombones, gong, and big drum. A sudden fast episode, and then the introduction returns to conclude the section. The introduction tune is played by a fascinating combination of high clarinet (E♭ clarinet) and alto flute two octaves apart.

"Games of the Rival Tribes"   Another fast dance with two more folk-like fragments treated in ostinato:

"Procession of the Sage"   One soon comes to realize that ostinato is an essential feature of Stravinsky's style, the feature that contributes more than any other to its "primitive" quality. Here four tubas play a lumbering ostinato, during which we can imagine a huge masked shaman borne aloft by half of the dancers, while the others leap and gesture around them.

"Adoration of the Earth. Dance of the Earth"   "Adoration of the Earth" is performed briefly by the Sage, then everyone joins in the short and breathless "Dance of the Earth." The rhythmic irregularity is more exciting than ever, though in fact this entire dance is built over an ostinato repeated about thirty times:

First played by the double basses, this ostinato becomes more audible when the basses are joined by bass clarinets and bassoons.

Notice that all the sections of *The Rite of Spring* end by simply stopping, without preparing for cadences in any special way. This is particularly apparent in the fast vehement sections, in which Stravinsky seems to lower his head and charge; the music usually gets louder and louder until it is turned off as though by a switch. This effect is striking in "The Dance of the Earth." We may indeed regard this as a "primitive" treatment of musical form.

What is conspicuously absent from *The Rite of Spring* is emotionality. Tough, precise, and barbaric, this music is as far removed from Debussy's impressionism or Berg's expressionism as it is from the old-line romantic sentiment of Strauss or Mahler. In later pieces, Stravinsky abandoned the barbarism—and lost most of his audience. But the dry, precise quality remained, and so did the characteristic irregular rhythms. Throughout his life they provided Stravinsky with a powerful strategy of movement, a sense of springing, racing, fencing, propelling, all rolled into one—a quality of movement unlike that of any other composer. Rhythm is at the heart of Stravinsky's viable "new language" for music.

Stravinsky and Duchamp

A nostalgic photograph of two of the pioneers of early twentieth-century art, taken near the end of their lives: Igor Stravinsky (left), composer of *The Rite of Spring*, 1913, and Marcel Duchamp, painter of the early cubist shocker *Nude Descending a Staircase*, 1912 (page 307). Duchamp, a tireless avant gardist, even concocted a piece of music around this time that looked past Stravinsky (and past Ives: see pages 348 and 349) to developments of our own era. His *Erratum musical* is a set of random notes drawn out of a hat, to be sung without any clues as to their time duration.

From the nineteenth century on, the various arts have grown together through (among other things) increasing contacts among composers, painters, and literary men. Stravinsky was associated with a long list of artistic figures of the twentieth century: Sergei Diaghilev, George Balanchine, Pablo Picasso, Jean Cocteau, André Gide, W. H. Auden, Evelyn Waugh, and Aldous Huxley.

The cast is international. Though Stravinsky was a Russian, he spent most of his life abroad, one of the first of a depressingly long list of twentieth-century artists who were driven from their homes by political regimes that they would not accept or that would not accept them. When the Russian Revolution broke out in 1917, Stravinsky stayed in Paris with his friends of the *Ballets Russes*, became a French citizen, and did not visit Russia again until he was past eighty.

In 1939, when France was invaded, Stravinsky moved again and came to Los Angeles. America provided a haven for a remarkable number of European composers (as well as performers and musicologists): Stravinsky, Schoenberg, Bartók, Darius Milhaud, Paul Hindemith, Bohuslav Martinů, Ernst Křenek, Kurt Weill, and others. This hospitality—doubtless disinterested—stimulated our own musical life in a deeply significant way.

Neoclassicism

STRAVINSKY   *ORPHEUS* (1948)

NEOCLASSICISM

We have pointed out that in his three famous ballets for the *Ballets Russes*, Stravinsky treated his nationalist folk material in an increasingly abstract way. Soon after *The Rite of Spring* he dropped folk material entirely. The process of abstraction once completed, he went on to evolve his own new musical language, mainly out of his very individual treatment of rhythm and meter. When Stravinsky adopted neoclassicism, he became by word and deed the leading anti-romantic composer in Paris, even though he never formed a "school." Neoclassicism was an important movement involving a return to the musical ideas of the centuries before romanticism—mainly to the eighteenth century, but sometimes to earlier ones too.

What the neoclassicists wanted to recapture from music of the preromantic past was its cool, clean, business-like quality by contrast with the over-inflated music (as they considered it) of the nineteenth century. Since certain formal principles are directly associated with this quality, the neoclassicists made a point of adopting old forms such as fugue and ritornello form as used in the concerto grosso. They also imitated the instrumental ensembles of the past, and in extreme cases they even borrowed actual old music. Neoclassicism was a widespread movement—more widespread than impressionism and expressionism and much more widespread than serialism. Paris was its center, but it was also popular in America, especially in academic circles.

Stravinsky's turn to neoclassicism can be traced in several more of his ballets. In *Pulcinella* ("Punch," 1920) and *Le Baiser de la Fée* ("The Fairy's Kiss," 1928), large sections consist of rewritings of earlier pieces. Stravinsky's sources were the late baroque composer Giovanni Battista Pergolesi in the first case and the late romantic composer Peter Ilyich Tchaikovsky in the second. By carefully calculated changes, sometimes very tiny changes, he contrived to make this old music enter into his own world of rhythmic irregularity and dissonance. As an anti-romantic composer, Stravinsky must have approached Tchaikovsky's sentimental song *None but the Lonely Heart* in an especially gingerly spirit. The result, in one of the dances in *The Fairy's Kiss*, is just about as emotional as a team of psychologists reporting on a physiological study of emotion.

Later ballets, such as *Orpheus* and *Agon*, do not rewrite specific pieces by earlier composers but invoke the style of earlier music in an increasingly subtle way. With *Orpheus*, the subject is classical, too—truly classical, not "neo": the legend of the greatest of all ancient Greek singers. When his wife dies, Orpheus charms his way by means of his music into Hades; he succeeds in winning her back on the condition that he not look at her until they have journeyed back to earth. But overcome by love and by her pleadings, he looks and loses her forever. Thereafter he renounces all contacts with women—not an uncommon option among the ancient Greeks—and is torn to pieces by female bacchantes whom he has repulsed. Apollo conducts the soul of Orpheus up to heaven.*

When the curtain rises, Orpheus is seen and heard playing a dirge for his wife Eurydice on his kithara (page 16); Stravinsky uses a harp. This music returns movingly near the end of the ballet—an element of musical form that would have earned an approving nod from Mozart or Beethoven. The song by which Orpheus charms Pluto into releasing Eurydice, played by a pair of oboes, recalls a baroque aria:

Then the beautiful section during which the two undertake their fateful journey back to earth is arranged as a "classical" A B A′ form, in which both A and A′ are scored for string instruments alone. Although this seems like astonishing asceticism for a composer who had once squandered the fantastic orchestral riches of *The Rite of Spring,* it fits in with the growing abstraction of Stravinsky's language in every other way. Characteristic irregular rhythmic passages still occur—notably the scene of the bacchantes—but while the actual rhythm is no less exhilarating, the total effect is less heavy and frantic.

Another bow to the past comes in the final scene, in which Apollo leads Orpheus up to heaven. Harp music alternates with a sort of slow fugue for two French horns, accompanied by a strange, thin, ascending melody. Stravinsky claimed that the tone color he devised for this melody, by putting together a muted trumpet and a violin playing close to the bridge,[†] evokes the sound of a medieval fiddle.

In addition to all this, we are likely to be struck by a restrained but pure and poignant lyricism at many points in *Orpheus.* The song-like quality was not new to Stravinsky—remember the folk-song fragments in *The Rite of Spring* illustrated on pages 332 and 333—but it had become refined and abstracted from obvious folk accents. "Art music" of the early twentieth century certainly never made any wholesale renunciation of melody. It is just that Stravinsky's kind of melody is cool, muted, understated, and utterly divested of romantic exaggeration. For his time, it was a more appropriate type of lyricism than the effusions of an earlier era. It may still be, for ours.

---

* In spite of all its equivocal aspects, this story with its testimony to the power of music has exerted a powerful attraction for composers. Very famous Orpheus operas were written by the early baroque composer Claudio Monteverdi (see page 84) and the Viennese composer Christoph Willibald von Gluck, to say nothing of a saucy parody by the nineteenth-century operetta composer Jacques Offenbach. Among movies about modern-day Orpheuses are *Black Orpheus* and an *Orpheus* by Stravinsky's friend Jean Cocteau.

[†] The bridge and other components of the violin are illustrated in the diagram on page 364.

Ballets by Stravinsky

Scenes from ballets by Stravinsky. In his early years, Stravinsky worked closely with the *Ballets Russes* under the impresario Sergei Diaghilev. Diaghilev was a fabulous personality with an uncanny knack of bringing together just the right artists, composers, and dancers to produce magical results. After World War II, Stravinsky was identified even more closely with the New York City Ballet under the great choreographer George Balanchine. A Russian refugee, first to France and then to America, like Stravinsky, Balanchine made the New York City Ballet into just about the finest in the world.

Pictured above and on the following page is the colorful folkloristic ballet *The Firebird*, 1909, Stravinsky's first great success and still one of his best-loved compositions. The backdrop was designed by the painter Marc Chagall.

Scenes from the neoclassic ballet *Orpheus,* 1948, appear above: Orpheus being comforted by his friends after the death of Eurydice, and the bacchantes' dance.

The pictures on page 339 are of the last piece Stravinsky composed specifically for ballet, *Agon* (Greek for "contest"). Written for Balanchine between 1953 and 1957, *Agon* still has a neoclassical aspect, for it is set up rather like an old dance suite (page 118), including a sarabande, a galliard, and three varieties of an esoteric Renaissance dance, the bransle, which Stravinsky must have hunted up in history books.

But *Agon* was also the first work that Stravinsky composed with a twelve-tone series. (Count the number of dancers; Stravinsky specified this number with care.) After World War II Stravinsky changed style once again,

adapting atonality and serialism. In dance terms, too, the process of abstraction is now complete, as one can gather from the pictures on page 339. Lacking any story, *Agon* is meant to be danced in rehearsal clothes—leotards and tights—and without scenery or properties. The dance is about pure movement, just as the music is about pure note relationships in time.

Stravinsky did not write only ballets, of course: he wrote three symphonies, a Mass, operas and oratorios, songs, piano pieces, chamber music, and so on. Still, among the great composers he will be remembered as the one who contributed most to ballet and received most from it. It cannot be accidental that a musician who was so keenly interested in rhythm should have been associated all his life with the world of dance.

Twentieth-Century Nationalism

Stravinsky started out his career in the Russian nationalist tradition of Moussorgsky and others, but soon moved off to a whole series of different new styles. Some other composers of the twentieth century started out with nationalism and stayed with it. The evocation of folk music remained a central element of their style—perhaps *the* central element—as was no longer the case with Stravinsky after the early 1920s.

These composers are generally counted among the twentieth-century conservatives (see page 299). Nationalism was a movement born of the nineteenth century, and there was undeniably something reactionary about continuing in this path fifty or more years later. However, all the new nationalists laced their music with twentiety-century style characteristics, such as high-level dissonance and complex, irregular rhythms, and a few of them were innovators in their own right. They developed their own musical languages combining the old and the new in various interesting ways.

Béla Bartók (1881–1945)

VIOLIN CONCERTO NO. 2 (1938)   *Side 14*

The Hungarian nationalist composer and folklorist Béla Bartók is a case in point. In the years around World War I, Bartók moved in the vanguard of musical experimentation along with Schoenberg and Stravinsky. He evolved a distinctive rhythmic style, as vigorous as Stravinsky's but more earthy, more closely involved with the literal rhythms of folk dance. (A famous "rhythm" piece by Bartók is the *Allegro barbaro* for piano. Its name tells the story.) He also pioneered new methods for harmonic and formal organization. Over and above this, Bartók never hesitated to try features that other composers had pioneered. He was always an eclectic, and opinions differ as to whether this enriches his music or makes it seem a bit disjointed. In his Violin Concerto, certain details will remind us of both Stravinsky and Schoenberg.

Yet in many ways Bartók always kept up his lines of communication with the nineteenth century. If he did not produce any symphonies, he did favor other old forms: he wrote six magnificent string quartets and a like number of concertos—for a modern composer, a considerable number and one that indicates a conservative orientation. Bartók also continued the tradition of romantic emotionality in his music (particularly in his latest music, interestingly enough). He shunned neither romantic melody nor the characteristic harmonies that go with it.

Back of all his music is the impressive harvest of Bartók's extensive field-work as an ethnomusicologist (see page 347). Even at its most complex and radical, the fabric of his music glitters with threads spun out of the rhythms of Hungarian folk dance and the accents of Hungarian folksong. In the last analysis, this was more important than questions of radicalism or conservatism to Bartók, and probably will be to his listeners too.

First Movement   The Bartók Violin Concerto harks back in a nationalist spirit to Hungarian folk music, and it also harks back to the traditions of romantic concert music. It was written to take its place in the repertory of great virtuoso concertos which grew up in the late nineteenth century. The image that Bartók evokes is that of the gypsy violinist, with all his flair and exhibitionism, his whimsy, and his throbbing emotionality. This personage first regales us in the rhapsodic main theme, after some introductory chords played by the orchestra:

The long, sweeping melody grows more and more passionate, even though the harmony grows more dissonant at the same time. Hungarian folk accents are provided by the rhythms marked by the square brackets on the above example, rhythms which divide the half-note beat into patterns consisting of a short note or notes followed by a longer one.*

   The second theme, in contrast, is a thoughtful dialogue between the solo violin and the orchestra, in which they try out different versions of a twelve-tone series:

We have discussed Schoenberg's invention of serialism as a means of organizing atonality (pages 324–327). The wide influence of the technique was also mentioned. Here is an example, from a composer who actually had, at least in this concerto, little stomach for atonality—so little, that he kept a single note, A, going continuously all through the nineteen measures of the theme. Bartók found a use of his own for Schoenberg's technique, then. Here serialism does not provide atonality but instead gives the impression of very free rambling over a very firm anchor of tonality.

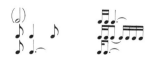

* The name "Scotch snap" has sometimes been applied to these rhythms, or at least to the simpler ones, for they come up frequently in Scottish folk music: "Should a *body* meet a *body* Comin' through the rye," and so on. But as Bartók could have demonstrated very well, they are characteristic of other folk traditions also, including the Hungarian.

The theme with the strongest folk quality is the brief cadence theme:

This gets positively boisterous, as the imitative counterpoint grows more and more dissonant.

The first movement of the Bartók Concerto is in sonata form (pages 157 to 159). The development section may surprise us a little by working with the orchestra's passive introductory chords rather than with some of the more vigorous thematic material, and by introducing a prominent inversion of the main theme (compare with the example on page 342):

Inversion, it will be recalled, is one of the characteristic processes of serialism (although this theme is not the serial one). After a retransition derived from the folklike cadence theme, the recapitulation includes a forceful new passage in the brass, derived ingeniously from the main theme. In this recapitulation, the second theme and the bridge are much compressed.

At this stage, we ought to have gained enough experience of sonata form to appreciate the effects Bartók obtains by manipulating it as he does. We can sense, too, how conservative the movement is in its form—which is to say, in the way it moves on a basic level. Conservative, even though the harmony is often dissonant, even though one theme is constructed serially, and even though the last thirty seconds include a passage of truly Stravinskian rhythm. The kind of gestures the themes make, the nature of thematic development and thematic derivation, the flow in and out of the climaxes, and the rather facile way in which the sections connect to one another—all this Bartók does along quite traditional lines.

Notice the highly expansive, sentimental place near the end of the piece, after the cadenza (page 188). It could have come right out of Richard Strauss or Gustav Mahler. To the anti-romantics of the 1920s, this passage would have been about as welcome as a gypsy violinist in one of their jazz cabarets.

Second Movement   The second movement is also traditional in aspect, a straightforward theme and variations (page 182) built on a relatively simple tune. With its warm and yet slightly melancholy or elegiac mood, this tune has a definite folk quality, even though it winds around in too complex a way for an actual folksong:

A diagram of this tune might be a b c | b' b'' d d. The melody falls into two somewhat similar halves, with the second half initiated by a free sequence (b' b'') built on the second short phrase (b) from the first half. The second d is played by the orchestra, more loudly and with new harmonies, but the melody is the same as that of the first d.*

Six variations follow. Unlike the strictest variations of earlier periods, they do not hold to the length of the phrases nor to their harmonies. However, the general *contour* is followed—the first phrase always goes down, the second goes up, the third arches higher still before coming down again, and so on—so that the relation between the variations and the original tune is not hard to hear. Folk singers, too, often follow the general contour of a song rather than exact details of melody and rhythm. Contour was a basic criterion in Bartók's own classification system for the Hungarian folksong.

The example on page 345 shows just the beginning of the six variations, lined up with the beginning of the theme (phrase a only). The orchestral repetition of phrase d is not incorporated into the variations, except the first.

After the heavy cadence ending the tune, *variation 1* begins in a rather uncertain spirit and gains impetus slowly. During phrases a, b, and c, the solo violin is accompanied only by occasional notes on the timpani. In *variation 2*, the violin ruminates in long, rich, rhapsodical lines. Meanwhile the orchestra builds up an interesting sonority, one that is a favorite with Bartók: piled-up dissonances in the high woodwind instruments, while scales tinkle and plunk in the harp and the celesta.

Variation 3 is urgent and rhetorical. *Variation 4* is mysterious: the violin plays smoky trills over a quiet, stripped-down version of the theme in the lower strings of the orchestra. (You may have to listen closely to hear them on some records.) There is a big slowdown in the middle of this variation; then the violin joins the orchestra in imitative counterpoint for phrases b', b'', and d.

---

* However, this does not begin to cover all the fascinating aspects of the tune, which deserves as much careful study as anyone is prepared to give it, even apart from the variations. It is a fine example of expressive melody in twentieth-century idiom. Notice how all the phrases except the last (d) begin by repeating the cadence notes of the previous phrase. This gives the body of the tune its meditative quality; the phrases seem to go back and brood over the previous statement. And it makes the climactic phrase d stand out with special force and expansiveness. Bartók intensifies this by having the orchestra repeat phrase d loudly, accompanied by new and frankly romantic harmonies.

In *variation 5*, the one fast variation (*Allegro scherzando*), the violin whirls along with a triangle, a side drum, and a piccolo in sharply irregular rhythms. *Variation 6* is a sort of distorted march, with strange light twitchings in the violin, pizzicato strings in the orchestra, and drum rolls played on the rims of the instruments.

Finally, the tune returns almost unchanged in melody, to conclude the movement and restore the original image after all these new interpretations. This formal device goes back to Mozart and Beethoven (see pages 183 and 203). Bartók goes further than these earlier composers by having his tune played an octave higher reharmonized, and reorchestrated in such a way as to create a strikingly new effect. And the orchestra finally makes its repeat of phrase d once again, after this had been cut out of the variations. But instead of loud romantic harmonies, the instruments now play pinprick dissonances. The celesta reminds us of variation 2, and the very last notes of all, on the timpani, summon up in a flash the feeling of variation 1. The tune has lived through all the variations, but it has forgotten nothing. Clear-eyed, ethereal, and penetrating, it is now somehow beyond melancholy, even beyond sweetness.

Third Movement   As we have seen, the romantic composers liked to link up movements in their symphonies and other large works by means of thematic transformation (page 227). This nineteenth-century idea still interested Bartók; he made the entire third movement of his Violin Concerto a transformation of the first. Theme by theme, passage by passage, and section by section, the third movement goes right through the first movement, turning out all the material in a new version.

Everything is now in triple meter rather than duple, as before; generally there is a lighter, more boisterous, and sometimes also a parodistic feeling. How often we come upon parody effects in twentieth-century music! If you really know the first movement of Bartók's Violin Concerto, listening to the last is rather like seeing someone in a fun-fair distorting mirror—or, better, like seeing a movie that is run at a faster speed and shown through a distorting lens.

Here is the main solo theme (illustrated along with its free inversion, which turns up in due time):

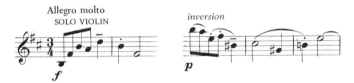

And the serial second theme, perched over the note A, once again:

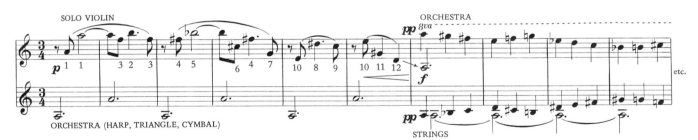

The orchestra seems to have forgotten the series, and it hurriedly invents a slightly different one, which it presents simultaneously in inversion. There are also transformations of the cadence theme (very brief!), the march theme in the development, the inversion of the main theme, the retransition based on the cadence theme, the forceful new brass passage in the recapitulation—and even an expansive, sentimental passage near the end, in which the gypsy violinist now starts to play saccharine waltzes.

But there is a kind of good-hearted mockery in his effusions. All in all, this movement provides a dazzling array of ideas, high-spirited and never too serious, miscellaneous, and often somewhat whimsical. Perhaps what holds this wealth of ideas together is the solo violin, who presides over all the proceedings with such genial and brilliant authority.

© G. D. Hackett, New York

Bartók in the Field

The composer Béla Bartók worked the rhythms of folk dance and the accents of folk song into all, or almost all, his music. In this he was an heir to the tradition of romantic nationalism; indeed, Bartók may be judged the most successful of all the nationalist composers. In his music the folk element always sounds deeply integral, never merely tacked on like an appliqué.

This is surely not unrelated to the fact that Bartók was also a professional folklorist. He published numerous pathbreaking studies on the music of his native Hungary and also that of other countries. Nearly a quarter of his total music publications consist of sets of folk-song arrangements and the like. Some nineteenth-century nationalists limited their contacts with "the folk" to what they could see out the windows of their well-heated Moscow apartments. Bartók actually got out into the field.

Composers of the baroque period worked and lived like skilled craftsmen. Romantic composers, who tended to regard themselves as geniuses, often thought they had something to tell the world as writers on philosophical and critical matters. It is perhaps fitting that the twentieth century should provide an important composer who was also an important research scholar—an ethnomusicologist. That a major composer should have been deeply influenced by work in the social sciences is another sign of the times; anthropology was one of the exciting new intellectual disciplines of the early twentieth century. Around the time Bartók was investigating folk music in the Balkans, the British folklorist Cecil Sharp was conducting his famous field studies of Anglo-American folksong in Appalachia.

Our illustration shows Bartók busy at his research, having a back-country girl sing a song into a primitive recording device. This photograph was taken in 1908, when recordings were very new. It may make us smile, for as far as these solemn peasants were concerned, the camera, too, must have been a new and doubtless awe-inspiring instrument. They are well scrubbed and decked out in their national costumes (the bashful girls on the right did not get to wear shoes because they were unmarried).

Charles Ives (1874–1954)

CENTRAL PARK IN THE DARK (1906)

THE UNANSWERED QUESTION (1906)   *Side 15*

Why America produced no considerable composers in the nineteenth century, when we produced such painters as Mary Cassatt and Winslow Homer and such writers as Herman Melville and Emily Dickinson, is an interesting question. It was only in the 1920s and '30s that a sizeable group of native composers emerged who could stand beside the composers of Europe. The output of our first major composer dates from around 1900 to 1920. He was Charles Ives, the son of a Civil War military bandmaster and music teacher of Danbury, Connecticut.

A great many of Ives's pieces have "American" subjects: *Lincoln, the Great Commoner*, the *Concord* Sonata for piano ("Concord, Mass., 1840–60"), *Some Southpaw Pitching*, and the *Holidays* Symphony in four movements called *Washington's Birthday, Decoration Day, The Fourth of July*, and *Thanksgiving*. Very often he employed fragments of American music: folk songs, popular songs by Stephen Foster, gospel hymns, ragtime—sometimes in great profusion. In the words of a historian of American music, Ives's music "emphatically declared that in its vernacular tradition American music had an artistically usable past."

Ives was our first important nationalist composer, then. But he was also a great deal more than that: a true American "original," a man with amazingly radical ideas about music, and an insatiable experimenter with musical materials. Working in isolation, Ives anticipated many of the most famous musical innovations of the early part of the twentieth century, and many innovations of the later part, too.

During his youth, the American musical climate was not at all friendly to modern trends. The main composers—men like Edward MacDowell (1861–1898) and Ives's own teacher at Yale, Horatio Parker (1863–1919)—wrote in a very dull traditional style. Partly for this reason, and partly out of inner conviction, when Ives got his B.A. he did not enter the musical profession but went into insurance. He did music on weekends and in the evening, while pursuing a lucrative business career during the day. He never mixed with musicians, and for years made little or no effort to get his innovative works performed or published.

All the while he was developing his unique mystical notions about music, notions which have been linked to nineteenth-century New England transcendentalism. To Ives, the actual sound of music seems to have counted less than the idea of music-making as a basic human activity. As a result, he believed that all kinds of music are equally valid, whether popular or sophisticated, whether simple or wildly dissonant, whether played on or off tune. What mattered was people's communal joy in music-making. Believing also that every musical experiment has equal validity, Ives launched into visionary projects such as no other composer of the time would have considered. He hated neatness and gentility; music for Ives had to have a grand Whitmanesque sweep.

This is true even of some of his shorter works. *Central Park in the Dark in "The Good Old Summer Time"* purports to be a "slice of life" offering sounds of a hot New York evening: placid but highly dissonant night noises, interrupted by snatches of ragtime echoing from nearby saloons. "A Contemplation of Nothing Serious," Ives called this piece. But he called *The Unanswered Question* "A Contemplation of a Serious Matter" and provided it with an astonishing metaphysical program:

The strings play **ppp** throughout, with no change in tempo. They represent "The Silences of the Druids" who know, see, and hear nothing. The trumpet intones "The Unanswered Question of Existence" and states it in the same tone of voice each time. But the hunt for the "Invisible Answer" undertaken by the flutes and other human beings [*i.e.,* clarinets and oboes *ad lib*] gradually becomes more active and louder. The "Fighting Answerers" . . . seem to realize a futility, and begin to mock "The Question"—the strife is over. . . . After they disappear, "The Question" is asked for the last time, and the "Silences" are heard beyond in "Undisturbed Solitude."

What is so novel here is the concept of three distinct levels of music which do not fit together in the least, in the terms of traditional polyphony. Ives even insisted that the strings, trumpet, and flutes, etc., sit well apart at different places on the stage. They each play streams of music in utterly different styles, without any fixed rhythmic or contrapuntal relationship.

Other Ives pieces employ equally unheard-of ideas. In *Psalm 90* for chorus, organ, and bells, low C sounds continuously in the organ pedals for the whole length of the piece—nearly eleven minutes. Playing the *Concord* Sonata, the pianist has to use his elbow as well as his fingers, also a special wooden block which holds down sixteen notes at once. The Second Symphony ends with a chord incorporating all twelve notes of the chromatic scale in several octaves (poor Richard Strauss! compare page 303). Ives wrote *Three Pieces* for two pianos tuned a quarter tone (half a semitone) apart, and several works in which certain elements can be played, or not played, or played in different ways, depending on the performer's choice.

These were indeed ideas born before their time. Small wonder that Ives's music never attained popularity during his lifetime, and had to wait until the musical atmosphere had cleared for it after World War II. Indeed, it may make more sense to regard Ives as an isolated prophet of our newest music, rather than as another denizen of the musical world of Stravinsky, Schoenberg, Bartók, and Copland. The man exists, as it were, between chapters.

Were Ives's remarkably forward-looking ideas realized successfully in his actual compositions? That is not always certain. As though anxious to protect his amateur status, Ives insulated himself off from the musical life of his time, avoiding not only the response of music critics and audiences but even the informal give-and-take comments of other musicians. He could experiment away, without really following his experiments through to their logical conclusions. But that was part and parcel of his deeply quirky, deeply original musical personality. It was left for composers of the post-1950 period to assume (or to avoid in their turn) responsibility for the Pandora's box of musical notions that Ives had set loose half-secretly some fifty years before.

Aaron Copland (1900–   )

EL SALÓN MÉXICO (1936)

APPALACHIAN SPRING (1945)

Side 15

An aspiring young American composer around 1920 found more options open to him than the young Charles Ives did in 1898. The musical climate was much more favorable to new ideas, partly because America had been growing more aware of all things European, including European new music. This trend was accelerated by the First World War. Composers of the 1920s associated themselves with European modernism as Ives never had done. Aaron Copland and Roy Harris went abroad to study, in the Paris of Stravinsky and the other anti-romantic composers. Roger Sessions learned from a "modernist" Swiss composer who had settled in this country, Ernest Bloch.

Copland made his debut in the mid-1920s with a number of concert pieces employing jazz elements. His most successful work in this vein is *El Salón México*, which deals in South American popular music, including a few actual songs (El Salón México was the name of a Mexico City dance hall). In this exhilarating piece, Copland skillfully recreates the feeling of highly metrical popular music by means of rhythms that are not metrically simple at all. In the jazzy opening, for instance, the rhythms are much more irregular than any that would have been used by popular musicians, at least in 1936:

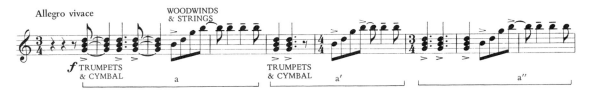

This is a Stravinskian ostinato of the type discussed on page 332. The three sections marked by square brackets sound roughly parallel, but the rhythms differ (the figures are obtained by counting eighth notes between accents):

a:	3 + 3 + 3	3 + 2 + 2 + 3 (or 2 + 1)
a′:	2 + 4	3 + 2 + 3
a″:	3 + 3 + 2	3 + 2 + 2 + 3

Why did Copland go to this trouble? Because the steady metrical beat of South American popular music is dull and soporific, that's why. If you have any doubts about this, you might ask yourself which is more genuinely exciting, the highly irregular climax of *El Salón México* or the incessant, climaxless beat of a bossa nova band. It is no accident that the better rock groups of the 1960s began introducing rhythmic irregularities into their beats.

Stravinskian rhythms appear everywhere in *El Salón México*. Nonetheless, Copland's music is milder and more conservative than Stravinsky's. The harmony is less dissonant, the tone less austere, and the style less inventive and "far out." Perhaps the heart of the comparison is this: Stravinsky used folk music as a stepping-stone to a new musical language, whereas Copland always expresses the nationalist composer's love of song and dance for their own sake. In his compositions, song and dance rarely fail to make themselves clearly felt.

In his role as an American nationalist composer, Copland journeyed all across the continent, and he also journeyed through time. The ballets *Rodeo* and *Billy the Kid* are Western in setting and include cowboy songs. *The Tender Land,* an opera about farm life in the corn belt, includes a big square-dance scene and some country ballads. (Copland's *The Tender Land* is to American opera what Richard Rogers's *Oklahoma!* is to musical comedy.) Copland wrote music for a movie version of *Our Town,* the well-known play by Thornton Wilder about a turn-of-the-century New England village. He wrote *A Lincoln Portrait,* for speaker and orchestra, and a fine song cycle to texts by Emily Dickinson, the nineteenth-century poet from Amherst, Massachusetts. Some of the songs include echoes of old hymns. *Appalachian Spring,* a ballet about Pennsylvania in the early 1800s, incorporates a melody sung by the Shakers, an extremist religious sect founded in the mid-eighteenth century.

This ballet was choreographed and danced by Martha Graham, the great lady of American modern dance. She conceived of "a pioneer celebration in spring around a newly built farmhouse in the Pennsylvania hills in the early part of the last century." From his ballet music, Copland arranged a concert piece (or suite) consisting of some seven sections, running directly into one another:

Section 1 is a very still, clear, static passage of a kind that Copland has made very much his own. It seems to catch the spirit of a vast silent landscape at dawn, perhaps, or just before dawn. In *section 2* "the bride-to-be and the young farmer-husband enact the emotions, joyful and apprehensive, their new domestic partnership invited." After a lively dance has begun, a new, slower melody—something like a hymn—looms up in counterpoint, first in the wind instruments and then in the strings:

A slower version of this new figure, in a new rhythm and with hymnlike harmonies, forms the main substance of *section 3.*

The next two sections pick up the tempo: *section 4* evokes a whirling square dance and *section 5* is a danced sermon by a revivalist and his followers. Both sections include quiet statements of the hymn. Then in *section 6* an agreeable Shaker tune, *A gift to be simple,* is played by a clarinet and followed by five variations. The variations are little more, really, than repetitions of the tune with new harmonies, in different tonalities, and in slightly different tempos.

Finally, after some music described as "like a prayer," the hymn and the landscape music return once again (*section 7*). The ballet concludes very quietly. Perhaps the housewarming celebrations have gone on all night and we are now experiencing another clear gray dawn, a reminder of the many lonely dawns the pioneer couple will face together in the years to come.

Bird

In the 1940s a group of black musicians founded a major new jazz style called "Bebop" or "Bop." The greatest of them was Charlie "Bird" Parker, who was born in 1920 in Kansas City, one of the country's best jazz towns. In this 1953 picture, he is shown playing the alto saxophone along with some other famous innovators: Thelonius Monk (piano) and Charlie Mingus (string bass).

The term "bebop" arose from the explosive rhythmic effects of the new style. Instead of dividing measures into the usual four quarter-note beats, Parker would divide them into eight faster eighth-notes. ("That horn ain't supposed to sound that fast," an older saxophonist complained on first hearing Bird.) Then he would accentuate off-beats, and employ startling complex rhythmic patterns. Using novel notions of melody and harmony, he fashioned a gently flowing improvisation style remarkable for its lyricism, freshness, and emotional expansiveness. His saxophone tone could be

hard at times, but he could also make it sound as luscious as the "sweetest" of swing arrangements.

The artist who lives in misery, as though driven by the demon of his own creativity, and finds fulfilment only in his art—this is a favorite romantic stereotype. It fits Beethoven, Tchaikovsky, and Mahler, to some extent, but it never fitted any musician as grimly as it did Parker. He was on drugs from the age of fifteen, and in later years could not control his immoderate drinking and eating. He would miss dates, make terrible scenes, and—too often—play poorly. Already a legend in his own lifetime, Parker died at the age of thirty-four after surviving a suicide attempt and a stay at a California mental institution.

His nickname "Bird," incidentally, which had nothing to do with music—he was very fond of chicken and called them "yardbirds"—suggested whimsical titles for some of his greatest recorded numbers: *Bird's Nest*, *Yardbird Suite*, and *Ornithology*.

American Popular Music: Jazz

Popular music in America has always been deeply involved with black folk music. Not only have black Americans evolved very vital musical genres of their own, but ideas from black music have also been taken over and modified by white musicians for the white mass audience. This happened in one way or another with minstrel music in the nineteenth century (see page 291), with ragtime and jazz in the early twentieth, and with rhythm and blues in the 1950s. The whole process can be regarded as enrichment or as a type of exploitation, depending on your point of view. It is also true that on another, perhaps deeper level, the process shows up an instinctive community of feeling among blacks and whites, a common national fund of musical response.

In any case, and for whatever reasons, American popular music found an instant formula for international success. The characteristic accents of American music have spread throughout the world more insidiously than Coca-Cola; by now the popular music of Venezuela, Sweden, Turkey, and Japan all bear the tell-tale marks of American style. The ultimate accolade came in the 1960s, perhaps, when the famous "Liverpool sound" of the Beatles, deeply influenced by American rock and roll, came back from Britain to deeply influence the course of popular music here.

The tell-tale marks are rhythmic ones. Our popular music of the early 1900s did not sound very different from anyone else's as far as melody and harmony are concerned. But it was performed in a rhythmic style that was truly revolutionary, one that made for a clear break with traditional concert music. The breach, incidentally, has never been healed in a lasting way, despite the efforts of Aaron Copland (see page 350) and many other composers on both sides of the fence.

This may be a time to review the concepts of rhythm, meter, and accent introduced on pages 5 to 7. The new rhythmic style involved a special kind of SYNCOPATION syncopation, syncopation being a term for the displacement of some of the main accents of music away from the normal metrical beats of the measure (such as ONE two ONE two) to some other position in it. Simple syncopation, sometimes called metrical syncopation, displaces the accents in a melody from the first beat (ONE two ONE two) to the second (one TWO one TWO). This comes up now and then in almost all music—as witness our musical example on page 250, measure 3, and many others. Black American music used a lot of syncopation of this simple kind, but that was just a beginning. It also developed syncopation of a more subtle kind, called beat syncopation. Here many of the accents are displaced *just a fraction of a beat* away from the normal metrical beat, or from some other clearly defined position in the measure.

The process is not easy to describe and quite impossible to indicate accurately in musical notation. But the effect is immediately familiar to us. The melody picks up a lively yet easy drive, the basic regular meter seems to get a new springy quality, feet are set tapping and fingers begin snapping irresistibly. When this happens, the music is said to *"swing."* And according to most people's rather loose definition, music that swings in this way means some kind of jazz.

JAZZ

More strictly speaking, jazz is a very interesting and imaginative performance style that grew up among black musicians around 1910 and has gone through a series of astonishing developments, decade by decade, up to the present day. The rhythmic style of jazz was derived from ragtime, a type of piano music associated especially with Scott Joplin around 1900 (the term is also used for some band music of the period). To modern ears, the reserved and even slightly stiff quality of Joplin piano rags such as *Maple Leaf* and *The Entertainer* gives them a special kind of cool charm.

RAGTIME

Jazz added one vital element. True jazz involves not only "swinging" rhythm (as in ragtime) but also the idea of *improvisation.* A jazz soloist never plays a song the way he hears it or sees it written down on paper. Indeed, he never plays it in the same way twice. He always improvises *around* a song, "swinging" the rhythm in new ways, adding brilliant high notes and fancy runs, embellishing the main notes of the melody, and adding little interludes (called *breaks*) of his own invention—all on the spur of the moment. He performs, in fact, spontaneous *variations* on his basic material. With its own modern American accent, jazz employs a much-used musical form that we have seen in various periods of the past (see pages 93, 183, 203, 281, 345).

Jazz players sometimes—especially in recent times—vary a song so freely that the melody is disguised beyond recognition. However, the basic harmonies of the song are played in the background by instruments such as piano, organ, vibraphone, or guitar, which together with string bass and drums make up the so-called *rhythm section* of a jazz band. (A poor name for it: these instruments play the basic *meter* of the song, not the rhythm, and also play the basic harmonies.) What is more, jazzmen sometimes improvise simultaneously. The result is a particularly exhilarating and particularly clear type of polyphony (see page 34 and band 1 of the record). Jazz polyphony of this kind is often compared with baroque polyphony such as that of the Bach Brandenburg Concertos; the rhythm section plays much the same role as the baroque continuo (page 87).

BAND 1

Jazz is a special performance style, then; it is not a special kind of music. It is a performance style primarily for instruments, only secondarily for voices—even though its basic material comes from vocal music. Jazzmen took their basic material from both white and black musical sources, from *popular songs* and the *blues.*

Popular Songs The early twentieth century in America was a golden age of popular song, composed mainly but not exclusively by white musicians. The names of the song writers of those days may not in all cases be remembered, but their songs are: *St. Louis Blues* (W. C. Handy), *Alexander's Ragtime Band* (Irving Berlin), *Because* (Jerome Kern), *Sophisticated Lady* (Duke Ellington: see page 310), *I Got Rhythm* (George Gershwin), *Begin the Beguine*

(Cole Porter). The traditional form of the popular song consists first of a 32-measure "chorus" in an A A B A pattern, with each section eight measures long. The chorus is preceded by a less important (and less memorable) "verse" of eight or sixteen measures. This form was used for almost all popular songs until the advent of rock music; it is the most common form at the basis of jazz.

Most of these songs were stereotyped love songs. They also served for dancing—for the omnipresent foxtrot, the Charleston, and Latin American varieties like the tango, the rumba, and the beguine. And as in the nineteenth century (see page 293), popular songs went hand in hand with the popular theater. Many famous songs originated as numbers for Broadway musical comedies (or "musicals") or for Hollywood movies. The name of the first "talking picture" in 1926 was, significantly enough, *The Jazz Singer*. The livelier songs and show tunes were written to "swing," and even the slower, more sentimental numbers could be performed in jazz style (according to the strict definition as well as according to the loose one).

BLUES | *The Blues* The blues is a special category of black folksong expressing loneliness, desertion, trouble, and depression. Some of the most moving and powerful of jazz records are improvisations on blues. The most common form consists of three four-measure phrases ("twelve-bar blues"), repeated many times as the blues singer develops his or her thought by improvising more and more new (or half-new) verses. Simple in form and strong in emotional content, the blues continued to influence popular music strongly in the 1950s and '60s, as we shall see.

The blues also has a distinctive scale and melodic style, evolved by black folksingers for their laments. Jazzmen took over many aspects of blues melody into their improvisatory style. "Blue notes," notes which deviate slightly from the normal pitch, became as characteristic of jazz as the "swinging" accents which deviate slightly from the normal metrical beat.

Even the instrumental technique of jazz developed a strikingly vocal quality, reminiscent of the blues. The mellow saxophone was particularly susceptible to this kind of development; but inventive players also stretched the capabilities of the clarinet, trumpet, trombone, guitar, string bass, and (unlikely as it may seem) even the piano in this direction. Amazing things were done with special mutes for brass instruments (see page 182). Along with "swinging" rhythm and improvisation, the flexible, vocal quality of instrumental sound counts as a third main characteristic of jazz.

Listen to one of the early records by Louis Armstrong, one of the greatest and most imaginative of jazz trumpeters. In the 1920s Armstong cut over a hundred ten-inch, 78-rpm discs as the leader of small bands of from four to seven musicians with names like *The Red Hot Peppers, Louis Armstrong's Hot Five*, and *The Dukes of Dixieland*. It is a good idea to acquaint yourself with the basic popular song or blues tune, if you do not already know it, in order to appreciate the wonderful variations that Armstrong contrives around it. For unlike theme and variations movements by Mozart or Brahms, jazz variations do not ordinarily begin with a statement of the theme in its unvaried form. The records include several "choruses," that is, several runs through the song by different soloists improvising separately or by the whole group improvising together. Often Armstrong himself sings one chorus, in his own inimitable vocal style—humorous, inventive, and decidedly reminiscent of his own trumpet playing.

The climactic group choruses at the ends of most of the records preserve jazz polyphony at its best. The forceful voice of the trumpet presenting its improvised variation, sounding like an elegant, joyful shout; the clarinet zooming up and down again in faster notes; the trombone underpinning the other instruments with march-like support notes and characteristic sliding progressions—all this fits together miraculously over the basic chords and meter hammered out by the so-called rhythm section: piano, drums, banjo or guitar, and string bass or tuba.

Though it is impossible to indicate jazz accurately in musical notation, as we have said, a rough sketch of an Armstrong solo can give some idea of the way jazz variations depart from the basic song. Here is the beginning of a 1927 recorded version of *Willie the Weeper* (*Side 16*):

At first Armstrong stays fairly close to the basic tune, but the second time through he varies it more freely. Freer still are the trombone and clarinet "choruses" which follow after the verse, and so is Armstrong's great final chorus in polyphony with the rest of the band.

Although the idea of improvisation is basic to jazz, not everything that people call jazz is actually improvised. Especially when bands got bigger, the musicians' parts were carefully written out (or "arranged") in a style that imitated improvisation. It is well to distinguish between actual improvised jazz, such as that of Louis Armstrong's early records, and arranged "big band" jazz or swing, as it came to be called in the 1930s (a noun this time, not a verb as in "the music swings"). There was an undeniable loss in spontaneity, but there was also a gain in sophistication, smoothness, and surety. And in many cases big-band arrangements allowed for a few moments of improvisation by the band leader or some other star.

It was through the big bands that jazz became widely popular with the American mass audience — that is, with the mass white audience. Some black musicians carried the ideal of jazz improvisation along more and more interesting and complicated paths, but they were not much heard. When most people thought of jazz, they thought of the glamorous swing bands which played at nightclubs and hotel ballrooms and college proms and over the radio. Benny Goodman, Glenn Miller, Count Basie, Duke Ellington, Guy Lombardo, Lawrence Welk, Woody Herman — these were household names all over America in the 1930s and '40s.

Ragtime, New Orleans, Chicago, and Kansas City jazz, swing, boogie, bebop, modern jazz — a bewildering variety of jazz types emerged from the beginnings around 1900 to the present day. It would take us beyond the scope of this book to go into them in detail, though jazz enthusiasts distinguish minutely between them all and relish the individual style of every player whose work is preserved on records. Indeed, it is a striking fact that jazz, which started out as a popular entertainment deplored by musical snobs and others, now forms the subject matter for refined connoisseurship. Jazz today has lost some of its popular quality, undoubtedly. But if in some sense it has approached the condition of "classical" music, that will not be regarded as such a bad thing by all listeners.

Perhaps the different types and styles of jazz, which are so carefully studied by the jazz buffs, can be compared with the different "isms" of twentieth-century music which we spoke about at the beginning of this chapter — impressionism, expressionism, serialism, neoclassicism, and the rest. Variety and multifariousness is a characteristic of all the music of this century, whether it is destined for the dance hall or for the concert hall. Another common feature seems to be the feeling of liberation experienced by all composers, their excitement at the wealth of new resources that had opened up for them. One can sense this in the jazz improvisations of Armstrong and Parker, just as in the composed music of Schoenberg, Ives, and Stravinsky.

CHAPTER 7   1950–   The Electronic Age

1950–   The Electronic Age

We have seen that the early twentieth century witnessed a rapid evolution in all musical elements used by the romantics. There was a heady, urgent quality about musical developments in the years before World War I. It was almost as though composers felt that time was running out. Discussing the prewar musical scene, on pages 299 to 305, we noted a characteristic quality of stretching and straining, a quality that seemed to affect all the individual elements of music. In the mid-twentieth century, after World War II, they snapped—and they snapped resoundingly.

Revolution, not expansion or evolution, animated the advanced musical circles of the 1950s. Not everybody participated in this revolution, of course; there were conservative (and even counter-revolutionary) composers in the 1950s, and there still are today. Nonetheless, after about a quarter of a century no one can miss the deeply radical thrust of post-1950 music. We sense this in our bones as we listen to new music today, and we sense it in our heads as we try to think about it. For there are increasingly frequent occasions when none of the traditional terms and categories seems to apply anymore.

For example, in a really advanced composition of the 1950s, 1960s, or 1970s, there may be no melody, because (often) there is no pitch. (Listen to band 4 of the record.) In music without any melody, the combination of melodic lines that makes up polyphony obviously cannot be experienced. And without melody and pitch, the whole question of dissonant and consonant harmony—which was endlessly discussed fifty years ago, which occupied the best minds among musicians, and which drove conservative listeners up the wall—has simply been bypassed. Sometimes meter goes, too. It is not just made highly irregular, as in Stravinsky; it is eliminated altogether. When this happens, people begin experiencing rhythm in a new way. Rhythm is still present—whenever notes exist in time, rhythm exists too—but somehow it does not seem to count. This is a truly extraordinary outcome for music, which is (or was) preeminently the art of sound relationships in time.

BAND 4

Most extraordinary of all, perhaps, are new concepts in the general area of musical form. The idea of a meaningful progression from one part of a tune or piece to another part; the feeling of beginnings, middles, and ends; themes, repetitions, climaxes, developments, recapitulations, cadences—all these are thrown open to question. Some composers conceive of a kind of music in which there is no particular reason for any one sound to follow or precede another. They compose by fitting notes together in some random way or by having performers play things in a chance order.

In short, the "Vocabulary for Music" developed at the beginning of this book, which helps to a degree in following older music, seems now to be in the process of becoming obsolete. We find we cannot use it and get results, any more than we can use English to communicate with one of those artificial intelligences which more and more are coming to control our existence. We need Fortran, Snobol, or whatever today's computer language is. Some kind of new vocabulary, too, is sorely needed to talk about today's music.

What lay behind the abandonment of so many of the traditional elements of music in the 1950s and beyond? Composers seem to have felt it necessary to clear the air of all the music they knew. They needed to reconsider the primitive basis of their art—what we once referred to as the main coordinates of music: pitch and time (page 25). To some extent, this attitude arose in reaction to the complex, intellectual music of the earlier twentieth century. Yet the curious thing is that at the same time highly intellectual tendencies came strongly to the foreground. Never before have such complex mathematical theories been advanced to explain or justify music, and never before have people been asked to puzzle over such abstruse musical analyses. Paradoxically, primitivism and intellectualism went inseparably together.

Both were needed, to judge from results. The extraordinary new sound worlds of today's music could never have been explored without radical thought processes, and they could not even have been approached if composers had not started anew from music's primitive beginnings. Yet admittedly, back of the primitivism of postwar music there has also been a current of nihilism and even violence. Pieces have been written which grow louder and louder until people have hurried out of the concert hall with their ears aching. This is a familiar syndrome in popular music, too, with its menacingly powerful amplifiers. In the 1960s people worried about the association between music and other kinds of violent behavior, such as the mass hysteria occasioned (and to some extent encouraged) by stars such as Elvis Presley and the Beatles. At a mass outdoor rock festival at Altamont, California, in 1969, Hell's Angels were hired as bodyguards for the Rolling Stones; a man who drew a knife was shot to death as movie cameras rolled, recording the event for posterity in the Stones' film *Gimme Shelter.*

Recently signs of violence appear to be diminishing in and around music. It may not be much comfort, but it is still true, to point out that revolutions characteristically pass through a violent first phase before viable new syntheses are established. In both "classical" and popular music, we can now begin to make out the outlines of late twentieth-century style—but only the outlines. It will still take a little time before the dust settles and we can view our astonishing new music in full depth and perspective.

World War II

Estimated casualties in World War II: 20 million dead, 34 million wounded. (Compare page 298.) The Hiroshima A-bomb, which killed approximately 100,000 people, had an explosive force equal to 20,000 tons of TNT. Thermonuclear warheads of the 1970s go up to the equivalent of 5 million tons of TNT. For a musical response to Hiroshima, see page 372.

The nuclear bomb is the towering symbol for our time of the dominance of technology. Sociologists and psychologists have not yet been able to determine the effects of this and other technological advances on our life-style in the mid-twentieth century. What has it done to the consciousness of two generations to grow up under the threat of world destruction—destruction, moreover, that might be set off by some Dr. Strangelove or even by a malfunctioning computer, like the computer HAL in Stanley Kubrick's disturbing movie, *2001*? It is a little like the threat of hellfire in the past, except that the people of Hiroshima and Nagasaki have actually experienced our hellfire.

Television, computers, supersonic airplanes, DDT, Xerox copies, the pill: every phase of our lives has been changed by technology. Compared with some of these things, electronic sound production and reproduction may seem like rather small matters. The fact remains, however, that music has probably responded to the technological revolution of the mid-twentieth century more profoundly than any of the other arts, including literature, painting, architecture, and even the movies. See pages 365 and 366.

Late Twentieth-Century Style

One of the first demands of advanced composers after World War II was for new sound materials. Among other things, they tried to attack standard musical sources for unexpected new effects. Singers had to learn not only how to perform *Sprechstimme* (page 301) and various kinds of *vocalise* (page 311) but also how to lace their performances with hisses, grunts, clicks, and other "nonmusical" noises. Pianists were told to stand up, lean over the piano, and pluck at the strings or bang them with rubber mallets.

Then some modern-jazz players discovered a way of blowing wind instruments such as the clarinet so as to produce chords, two or even three notes sounding simultaneously. This might astonish your high school band director, and neither he nor you would be enchanted by the tone color which comes with such chords. But a new sound, and a very weird one, it certainly was.

People also looked hard at the violin and other string instruments. Ordinarily, violin strings are bowed within the main part of their length, away from the *bridge*, the attachment which holds the strings up from the violin itself, and the *tailpiece*, the attachment which fastens down the ends of the strings. But one can also obtain noises by playing right on the bridge, right on the tailpiece, or at some point between them, where the strings are stretched tight and not tuned. One can also tap on the wood.

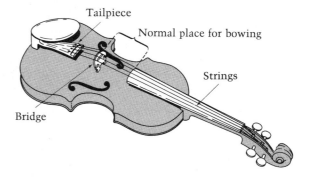
Tailpiece
Normal place for bowing
Strings
Bridge

Such procedures begin to sound more like curiosities than really fruitful sources of new sound. If knocking or scraping sounds are wanted, why not invent special percussion devices rather than maul $13,000 Steinways and $80,000 Stradivarius violins? A practical reason: because once performers have been hired, the presence of clarinets and violins and pianos can be counted upon, which would not be true of newly invented percussion devices. A symbolic reason: because these procedures convey an attitude both contemptuous and innovative toward the very basis of traditional music-making. And a musical reason: because composers usually want swift alternation between these new sounds and the traditional ones produced by the same instruments.

However, when it comes to producing new sounds, the poor old musical instruments of yore are no match for the magnetic tape recorder, the electronic sound generator, and the various related machines that go with them.

We can take the plunge and speak of our age in music as the "Electronic Age," so strong a mark has electronic technology left on the composing, performing, and listening procedures of the post-1950s.

Electronic Music The electronic sound generator can *generate* sounds from scratch; the microphone and recording machine can *reproduce* them. The key technological advance was the development of magnetic tape, which makes it very easy for the results of sound generation or reproduction to be stored, handled, and copied. Also doctored; tapes can be subjected to all kinds of manipulation, both physical (cutting and splicing, speed change, tape loops) and electronic (echo chambers, filters, mixing, etc.).

Of course, electronic generators are just as likely to come up with "non-musical" sounds—noises, without clear pitches—as "musical" ones, with clear pitches. Something of the almost endless range of possibilities can be suggested here:

MUSIQUE CONCRÈTE

Reproduced Non-musical Sounds (Noises) Traffic noises, amplified breathing, waterfalls—the sounds of life can be tape-recorded, stored, manipulated, and plugged into musical compositions at will. This is called musique concrète ("concrete music")—an odd term, for it is hard to understand why a waterfall is more "concrete" than a woodwind instrument.

Reproduced Musical Sounds A famous piece involving taped musical sounds is *Song of the Children* by the German composer Karlheinz Stockhausen, one of the most influential figures in postwar music. Stockhausen made a tape of a musical performance, of a hymn sung by a boy. He then used the tape in the composition again and again, after manipulating it in various ways. Sometimes the tape was cut up into half-second fragments separated by silences; sometimes it was superimposed upon itself (rerecorded, or dubbed), so that the effect is of a whole group of boys singing.

WHITE NOISE

Electronically Generated Non-musical Sounds (Noises) An endless variety of noises can be produced by generators. A familiar example is white noise, the hissing sound formed when every frequency of the audible spectrum is presented at the same intensity. (The color white is formed when every frequency of the visible spectrum is represented at the same intensity; "white" noise suggests the absence of tone "color.") Generators are also very good at producing sliding sounds, like sirens; you merely twist a dial.

Electronically Generated Musical Sounds Machines can also produce musical sounds, a resource that was already put to use in an instrument of the 1920s called the theramin, and in the Hammond organ of the 1930s. And machines can do this with deadly accuracy. Generators can be adjusted to provide any precise pitch, down to quarter tones and tenth tones in between our regular chromatic-scale notes, if such refinements are wanted. Rhythms, too, can be controlled with a mathematical precision beyond the abilities of mere human beings. Furthermore, as electronic apparatus became more and more sophisticated and computers came into play, all combinations of overtones (page 39) were made instantly available. They are mixed in with the main pitch and influence the tone color. The electronic composer does not have to rely on performers to be able to play the exact pitch, rhythm, or tone color that he has in his "mind's ear" or can calculate.

The one thing machines cannot do is duplicate human performance, with its subtle vagaries and tricks, its little inaccuracies of pitch and rhythm—its "personality," as we say. But of course, to duplicate human performance would be a futile exercise indeed. (As the man said to the washing-machine salesman, "What can your machine do that my wife can't do cheaper?") The whole point of working with electronic machines is that they suggest new sounds, new ways of connecting sound, whole new modes of sound experience that do not resemble standard music. Similarly, computers do not "think" like human beings, whatever some people say. They may think like someone's notion of an "ideal" human being, just as an electronic synthesizer may make music like an "ideal" instrumentalist or singer—but that is quite another matter.

Does all this make electronic music "inhuman," then? No, for there is a human being behind it, and we can trace the play of mind and emotion in an electronic piece just as well, or almost as well, as in an older composition designed for performers. Perhaps one way in which the two kinds of music differ can be expressed as follows. Between the composer of older music and the audience stands the performer. The performer can have the effect of enriching, renewing, or popularizing (or bungling!) the human gesture made by the composer. Between the composer of electronic music and the audience stands a machine. The machine is either a neutral factor, or it may make the composer's gesture seem more distant.

Certainly electronic music is "cooler" and more impersonal than older music. Electric guitars are more impersonal then saxophones. Given the growing impersonality of every aspect of life in the twentieth century, this hardly comes as a surprise.

On the Boundaries of Time   Time and rhythm mark the area in which modern music has made the most radical moves of all. Electronic devices can control rhythms of unprecedented complexity. But this is only one part of the story.

Earlier in the twentieth century, strange things had been done with time and rhythm by Anton von Webern, composer of extremely brief pieces full of highly compressed, intense musical gestures (pages 319 to 321). These we might describe as short time segments of high "intensity." The post-1950s have seen, among other things, music of exactly the opposite character. In a composition by the American composer Terry Riley, *In C*, the instruments repeat little melodic figures which spell out only three extended harmonies, one at a time, each lasting for about fifteen to thirty minutes (according to an estimate by the composer). This we would call a very long time segment of very low density indeed. With both Webern and Riley, we measure time—because we have no other way—in the same units: minutes and seconds. But one minute of Webern feels completely different from one minute of Riley. Like the difference in feeling between one minute at the end of a tied football game and one minute in the middle of an all-night run in a truck crossing South Dakota.

Webern was, in fact, one of the chief influences on advanced music of the 1950s. Composers were fascinated by his intense, seemingly disconnected notes, with their flickering colors and their highly complex rhythmic relationship. Rhythmic relationships were made more and more complicated. Musicians knew how to divide up a measure or a beat into 3, 4, or even 5 equal spans, but when composers also wanted divisions into 7, 11, and 13 and wanted these divisions to sound at the same time as some of the others, performers were in deep trouble. Machines were the only safe means for getting the desired results.

Composers also investigated the idea of treating rhythm according to serial principles. Twelve-tone series had been used by Webern directly after the concept was introduced by Arnold Schoenberg in the 1920s (page 324). These early serialists established a fixed order of the twelve different *pitches* of the chromatic scale and held to this order with various modifications (inversion, retrograde, etc.) throughout a piece. The new serialists of the 1950s set up a fixed pattern of twelve different *note lengths* and held to this pattern with various modifications (running backward, speeding up, etc.) throughout a piece. This was a peak of the new intellectualism in music.

RHYTHMIC SERIES   In the example below, showing such a <u>rhythmic series</u>—twelve notes of twelve different lengths—the numbers indicate the number of thirty-second notes in the notes above them:

This excerpt comes from a two-piano piece called, perhaps appropriately, *Structures;* it was written by Pierre Boulez, another of the important composers in the period following World War II. (He is also an important conductor; from 1971 to 1976 he was director of the New York Philharmonic.) An interesting forecast of rhythmic serialization occurs in the Inn Scene from *Wozzeck,* by Webern's friend and fellow Schoenberg-student Alban Berg (page 317).

CHANCE MUSIC   *Chance Music*   The most sensational new trend in post-1950 music was chance music. (Another term is *aleatory music,* from *alea,* the Latin word for "dice.") Composers threw dice or consulted tables of random numbers to determine which instruments, which rhythms, which pitches, and how many should be introduced—or how far the dials on electronic apparatus should be twisted. Between measures X and Y of certain compositions, performers might be directed to play anything that came into their heads. Compositions were written out on separate sheets of paper, which the performers were told to throw in the air and play in whatever order they chanced to come down.

Chance music is even harder to understand than rhythmic serialization — harder to understand and harder to take. The same sort of outrage that used to be occasioned by dissonance was aroused all over again in response to chance music. But in his own way, the chance composer is groping toward a new vision of time, just as the rhythmic serialist is, although in exactly the opposite spirit. Time for the chance composer is formless, cannot be grasped or molded, lacks directionality and any sense of priority, progression, sequence, or cause and effect. Sound simply exists, whenever it happens to be experienced. One sound does not lead us to expect another. It is there for its own sake, not as part of a tune, an A B A form, a serial pattern, or any kind of time organization.

More: Chance composers are really rejecting our whole goal-directed view of time — getting up at the alarm, ten minutes for breakfast, on schedule for the bus, punch a time clock, waste time till coffee break, and so on. Rather, their vision is "timeless," like the sense of suspended time in an oriental meditation or under drugs. (This doesn't mean we have to be Zen Buddhists or take drugs to appreciate their music, any more than we have to be eighteenth-century Lutherans to appreciate the cantatas of Bach.) This radically new consciousness, a static sense of time that goes against our goal-directed culture, lies at the root of chance music.

Something of this is apparent in Riley's *In C,* with its endless brisk repetitions and its almost imperceptibly shifting image of the same original experience. *In C* leaves a good deal to chance, in fact. The score consists in its entirety of fifty-three very simple melodic fragments, written separately:

Each of the instruments — and any number can play — goes through these fragments in order, repeating them as often as the player wants to, without any prearranged coordination with the others. If we stifle our outrage and try to conceptualize this, we have to admit that the essence of the piece will not really change from one version to the next. The details, yes, but not the essential feeling. And if Riley wants the listener to concentrate on the essential feeling, rather than on details, that is his privilege as the composer.

It may not be clear why the piece *had* to be composed with random elements in order to get the effect Riley sought. Couldn't he have made up his mind and specified one particular arrangement? But however this may be, we may be prepared to admit that it makes no difference whether he left things to chance, within those certain limits, or fully specified them.

And once we have admitted that, do you see how we have admitted everything?

The Old and the New   This discussion of post-1950 music has concentrated entirely on the music of "advanced" composers, that is, those experimenting with ideas that are radical, far-out, and controversial—controversial and often pretty insane, some will say. Even our title, "The Electronic Age," would appear to elbow out conservative composers who might recoil from an electronic sound generator, as other people might shy away from a computerized memory bank or a nuclear submarine. Are there no composers in the 1970s who still work with violins and clarinets, symphonies, twelve-tone series, neoclassically oriented consonant harmonies, and even (dare we breathe the word) tunes?

There are. But in America, at least, these composers have not gained a great deal of critical recognition or prestige. This situation will strike some people as only natural, the inevitable result of "progress," while others will raise skeptical questions about the manipulation of publicity, the fickleness of public taste, and so on. The fact remains that, as compared with conservative composers of the earlier twentieth century such as Béla Bartók and Aaron Copland, these modern-day conservatives have not stirred up anything like the same interest.

In striking contrast to this, conservatism and only conservatism holds sway in Soviet Russia, which was once regarded as the seat of revolution in all areas of life. In the Marxist view, all arts including music must serve society. Only that music is allowed which interests, entertains, or uplifts the greatest number of people. "Experimentation" is out, because it interests only a small intellectual elite and might well lead to a new consciousness contrary to the established order. Rock music is out, because it is reputed to lead the young into all kinds of socially undesirable practices, from protest to outdoor sex. Russia has a strong heritage of musical nationalism dating from the nineteenth century (see page 272). What the state encourages today is watered-down nationalism, which features catchy folk songs and is supposed to build up a sense of pride in the nation or local region. There is no limit to human ingenuity, and some good music has been written under these conditions—some, but not much.

It is easy to brand this as an unhealthy situation, and not much harder to see signs of sickness in our own musical scene. It sometimes seems that we regard all music as disposable, like beer cans. Our chronic short attention span and craving for novelty make it hard for a conservative composer to get much of a hearing in America today, even assuming that he has something valid to offer. People are so anxious for the new that they cannot wait for it to sink in before going on to the next novelty. Some composers even cooperate with this attitude. Every time a chance piece is played, it's new. And disposable.

Still, after all complaints are in, it does not seem as though the old ways of making music can sustain serious composers any longer. There are some revolutions that can't be ignored, and the technological revolution of our time—for music, the electronic revolution—is apparently one of them. The value of the music of our electronic age is still an open question, and its direction or destination is another. But we must live with it; for unlike the Russians, we are really not prepared to set back the clock.

Karlheinz Stockhausen (1928–   )

GESANG DER JÜNGLINGE (SONG OF THE CHILDREN) (1956)

This is one of the early classics of electronic music. No score exists, only a master tape and its duplicates. Composed and engineered in 1955–56, when Stockhausen was only twenty-seven, *Song of the Children* was just about as revolutionary in impact as the *Fantastic Symphony*, produced by Berlioz at the same age. Since then, Stockhausen has gone on to one extraordinary new composition after another, making him without much doubt the most significant force among advanced composers today.

The piece takes its name from a hymn or canticle from the Scriptures, sung by three children of Israel who are saved by an angel of the Lord after having been thrown into a "burning fiery furnace" by King Nebuchadnezzar of Babylon (Daniel 3; but was Stockhausen also referring to the furnaces which, in his boyhood, had been used by Hitler to wipe out the Jews?) This canticle, known to Anglicans as the Benedicite, runs in part as follows:

Preiset [or sometimes *Jubelt*] *den Herrn, ihr Werke alle des Herrn;*
lobt ihn und über alles erhebt ihn in Ewigkeit. . . .

O all ye works of the Lord, bless ye the Lord:
Praise Him and magnify Him for ever. . . .

Preiset den Herrn, Sonne und Mond;
preiset den Herrn, des Himmels Sterne.

O ye Sun, and Moon, bless ye the Lord;
O ye Stars of Heaven, bless ye the Lord.

Preiset den Herrn, aller Regen und Tau;
preiset den Herrn, alle Winde.

O ye Showers, and Dew, bless ye the Lord;
O ye Winds of God, bless ye the Lord.

Preiset den Herrn, Feuer und Sommersglut;
preiset den Herrn, Kälte und starrer Winter. . . .

O ye Fire, and Heat of Summer, bless ye the Lord;
O ye Cold, and icy Winter, bless ye the Lord. . . .

Sometimes these words can be heard, but more often they are obscured. Like Debussy in *Sirens* (page 311), Stockhausen treats the voice not as a carrier of meaning but more as a source of pure sound. First he made a tape of a choirboy singing parts of the canticle and speaking other parts. Then he manipulated the tape in the studio—duplicating it, filtering it, cutting it up, running it at different speeds, and superimposing it upon itself until it sounded like a whole choir of different boys singing. From another copy of the original tape he snipped out pure vowels and also pure consonant noises. These, plus the manipulated tape and products of an electronic generator, constitute the "sound materials"—we no longer speak of notes or scales—for his piece.

The whole thing was then spliced together as a five-track stereo tape. In concert performances, the loudspeakers are strategically located at different corners of the hall; the directional sound creates an indescribable effect. Stockhausen also made a simplified two-track version for home phonograph records and binaural broadcasting. As if this were not complicated enough, pitch, rhythm, and many other musical elements were worked out according to strict serial principles, something the listener cannot actually expect to hear. It must have taken dogged patience and endless man-hours of work to put this piece together in those days, when tape and sound-producing technology was much less refined than it is today.

Yet in spite of the complexity, the piece does not sound all that involved. If we listen to it a number of times, we gradually come to hear a number of distinct sections with a sense of progression between them:

Introduction   The music begins with a dramatic gesture, as clear an announcement or summons to the listener as the beginning of any Viennese symphony. Then the superimposed voices are introduced in a kind of speedy chatter, together with the hums, bloops, whistles, and bell-like tones that seem to be characteristic of electronically synthesized sounds.

First Section   The voices come at different speeds, speaking as well as singing. Thanks to stereophonic sound, they also seem to come from different directions and distances. There are watery sounds, windy sounds, and ringing echo-chamber effects.

"Slow Movement"   After a long-held vowel note, this section begins to treat the song as a series of separate words and syllables, broken off sharply with silences between them. One passage may remind us of a night scene with crickets clicking away; it may even remind us of the weirdly beautiful pond music in *Wozzeck* (page 316). Indeed, to the extent that the sounds come together as chords in *Song of the Children,* the harmony may remind us of *Wozzeck* in general. Every once in a while, this "slow movement" is interrupted by exciting loud splashes. It concludes with a slowly broken word *"Win---ter."*

"Climax"   A long section in which the rhythm is picked up considerably by short bloops from the synthesizer. They are utterly jerky, and whether or not they are controlled by rhythmic serialization, they negate any sense of meter. The voices now tend to come as quiet sustained screams—and some not so quiet.

Thanks to the machines, the rhythm gets very fast; it is hard to follow it exactly, but the rhythmic feeling is strangely exhilarating. A final "solo" scream ends dramatically in a long low hum.

Conclusion   The music grows slower and more sustained; it definitely seems to be winding down and preparing for a cadence, though there are still a number of spasms to come. When the final cadence arrives—a rush of notes after a brief rest—it paradoxically gives all the feeling of rest that could possibly be asked for in a piece of this description. An old-fashioned "Amen" cadence would hardly fit after this particular canticle!

Stockhausen could not have devised a more effective, even brutal way of depersonalizing his singer than by cutting up the voice and subjecting it to all these scientific manipulations. Yet through all the contortions, we come to really know this boy; we may even find it easier to join in with his disconnected song of praise than with some of the more ordinary hymns produced by past composers. The Sanctus of Bach's Mass in B minor (page 140) is a magnificent piece, but are his baroque angels really speaking for us, as they chant their triumphant "Holy, Holy, Holy's" around the Throne? Brilliant and visionary in technique, impersonal and tentative in its expression of faith, the *Song of the Children* makes its own cool authentic statement for the age of technology.

Krzysztof Penderecki (1933–   )
THRENODY: TO THE VICTIMS OF HIROSHIMA (1960)

Something of the intensity and excitement of postwar developments in music is shown by their simultaneous adoption in places as different as America, Germany, Japan, and even Poland, behind the Iron Curtain. The new language for music went worldwide. In the 1950s people used to talk as though all countries in the Communist bloc followed the same policies, but this never made much sense as far as music was concerned. While Russia itself remained staunchly conservative and never let the new music in, Poland produced several interesting advanced composers. The best known is Krzysztof Penderecki.

The *Threnody* is written for a string orchestra that is sometimes divided into as many as fifty-two different parts. Penderecki is much interested in effects that can be obtained by new means of playing string instruments. Some of his special effects, and the new notation that he had to devise for them, are shown on page 374 (compare page 364). It is striking how much the strings can sound like electronic synthesizers—as though the faithful old dogs of symphonic music are striving mightly to learn new tricks.

Once again, "melody," "harmony," and "rhythm" are simply the wrong terms for talking about music of this kind. Penderecki deals in long patches of tone color, fascinating in themselves but connected to one another in relatively casual ways. The first patch consists of high, intense dissonances—real "space-age" sounds. So many simultaneous different pitches are played in part of this opening patch of texture, including quarter tones between our normal chromatic notes, that the sound approaches white noise (page 365).

Penderecki's second long patch consists of much blooping and skittering, with the strings sounding more like a shortwave radio or an electronic synthesizer than their ordinary selves. After about a minute, a pitch emerges and then dies away quietly. Patch 3 involves slow scooping sounds—like dense sirens—in the high, middle, and low registers, followed by steadier, harsher dissonant textures recalling those at the beginning of the piece. Patch 4, which is relatively short, begins with a series of definite notes that coalesce and swell up and down again into a single one, which lasts for a considerable time while wavering slightly. Patch 5 contains bloops again; perhaps here they feel like motives rather than flecks in the texture, for there is a real sense of climax about this lengthy passage. It culminates in (or, rather, explodes into) patch 6, a huge "chord" formed by all fifty-two instruments playing different pitches. They play all fifty-two of the quarter tones between C below middle C and the C♯ above it:

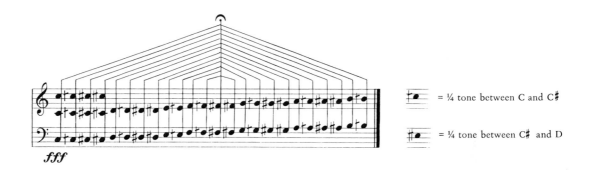

= ¼ tone between C and C♯

= ¼ tone between C♯ and D

On pages 302–305 we discussed the relativity of the concepts of consonance and dissonance. A graph was provided to help explain the idea. By now, the lines on the graph would have zoomed off the page; this wildly complex chord actually counts as a consonance, relative to the dissonances before. For on this sound the piece comes to rest in a sufficiently convincing fashion.

It is perhaps hard to see why any of the patches should go on for just the time they do rather than for a shorter or a longer time. Nonetheless, the piece has a sense of form. As a climax, patch 5 is well placed just before the end, and patch 6 makes a good conclusion, as we have just said. Patch 1 sounds like a somewhat tentative version of patch 6; it balances patch 6 and therefore makes an appropriate beginning. So this piece has a beginning, a middle, and an end, which is what musical form has always been about.

As for Penderecki's title, to inquire about that is to ask all the old questions about program music that were raised on page 226. The piece hardly seems to express the grief, pity, or rage that might be expected in a threnody (a formal song of mourning). But perhaps that is the point: our age may be beyond pity and rage, beyond any feeling, when faced with an action such as the bombing of Hiroshima. Perhaps instead Penderecki has retreated into himself, preoccupied with "hearing the unhearable," just as the H-bomb strategists on both sides of the Iron Curtain are "thinking the unthinkable" as they project casualty figures in the hundreds of millions for World War III.

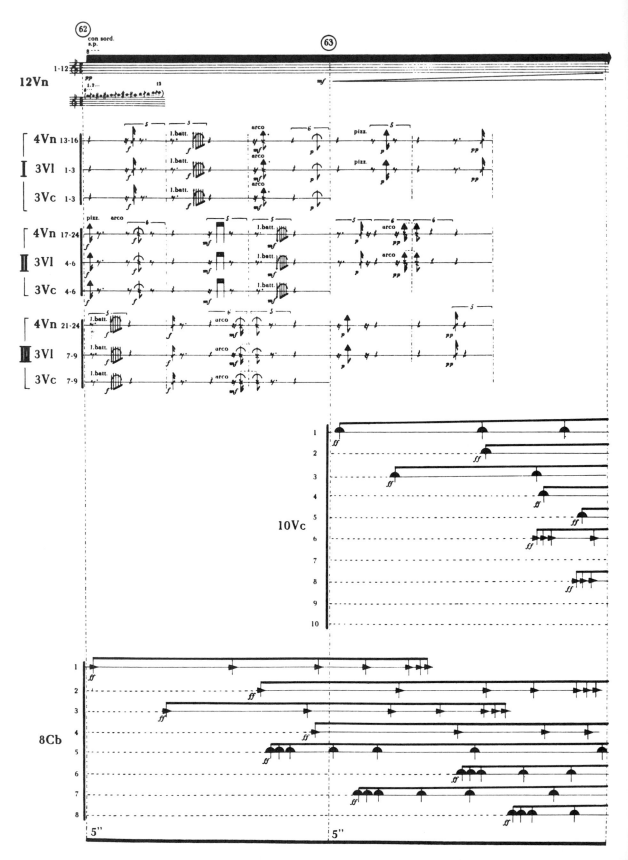

Musical Notation Today

The way people write things down depends on how they think. Systems of writing such as Egyptian picture script, or heiroglyphics, ordinary print, and punched computer input cards all reflect different styles of mental activity. Similarly with music: radically different styles call for radically different notation systems. With a little imagination, indeed, one can learn a good deal about music history simply by studying the history of musical notation as it has changed over the centuries.

For example, back on page 33 we saw that while Gregorian chant notation specified the pitches, on a four-line staff, it did nothing to specify the length of the notes, the rhythm, or the meter. For this medieval church music was free in rhythm and had no concept of meter. Furthermore, the pitch range of the monks was modest enough so that four lines, covering an octave, were usually quite enough.

Then from the baroque period to the middle of the twentieth century, musical notation remained essentially the same: pitch indicated by means of a five-line staff (or several staffs, when several instruments play) and rhythm and meter by means of whole-note, half-note, and quarter-note signs and measure lines. But after 1950, when pitch and meter often went by the board, conventional notation proved to be hopeless. Electronic composers often made no scores at all, only tapes. Other composers had to spawn a bewildering array of ad hoc notation systems, adapted to the individual composer or to each individual work.

To the left is a page of the score for Penderecki's *Threnody: To the Victims of Hiroshima.* Penderecki is still using a horizontal time scale, but instead of measures, he marks off segments of time precisely in seconds. See the bottom of the score.

Pitch is rarely notated since few exact pitches are heard in this piece. Instead Penderecki gets a great variety of new sounds by having violins and other string instruments play in thoroughly unconventional ways. For these, he had to make up a new notation, which is explained by the little table accompanying the score. (For violin terms, see page 364.) The thick line at the top is a graphic representation of the blurred, scratching-on-glass sound produced when ten violins each play notes a quarter tone apart between the high G and C. (This is spelled out on the small staff below the top.)

If you examine the cello and double-bass parts (the latter marked *Cb*, for "contrabasso"), you will see something you will probably not hear: that this seemingly disorganized music is actually highly organized. One fixed rhythm is staggered between the instruments, backward or forward. This practice is related to rhythmic serialization, widely used in the 1950s (page 367).

ABBREVIATIONS AND SYMBOLS

ordinario	ord.	lowered by ¾ tone	percussion effect: strike the upper sounding board of the violin with the nut or the finger-tips	
sul ponticello	s. p.	highest note of the instrument (indefinite pitch) ▲		
sul tasto	s. t.			
col legno	c. l.	play between bridge and tailpiece	several irregular changes of bow	⊓ V
legno battuto	l. batt.			
raised by ¼ tone		arpeggio on 4 strings behind the bridge	molto vibrato	~~~~
raised by ¾ tone		play on tailpiece (arco)	very slow vibrato with a ¼ tone frequency difference produced by sliding the finger	∿∿
lowered by ¼ tone	♭	play on bridge	very rapid not rhythmicized tremolo	

Electronic Synthesizers

The march of technology: electronic music generators of the 1950s and the 1970s. (We may reflect with a sigh that the typical instruments of our time are considerably less easy on the eyes than those of the past: compare pages 20, 99, 139.) Above is part of the RCA Electronic Synthesizer, which covers the walls of a whole room in a building in New York.

It is said that RCA pioneered this instrument in the vague hope of making union musicians obsolete, and indeed some commercial radio station "breaks" have been composed with it. During the 1950s, when it was on extended loan to Columbia and Princeton Universities, this formidable, sprawling machine had a de facto monopoly on the electronic music written in America. In an analogous way, European electronic music was centered at electronic studios located in radio stations, which are, in effect, state-controlled mass-media outlets. Stockhausen's *Song of the Children* was composed at the famous studios of Radio Cologne,

and John Cage's *Fontana Mix* at Radio Milan.

Below is an instrument of the early 1970s. Produced in several different models, the Moog Synthesizer was easily portable, easy to use, and not unduly expensive.

George Crumb (1928–   )

ANCIENT VOICES OF CHILDREN (1970)   Side 15

While Penderecki exploits new effects for string instruments *en masse*—he also employs extraordinary new mass choral effects—other composers work at the opposite extreme, inventing chamber-music sounds of equal novelty. Like Penderecki, the American composer George Crumb, who is a professor at the University of Pennsylvania, prefers not to work with electronic music. Instead he has devised new ways of playing an astonishing array of standard and non-standard instruments.

Crumb is interested in delicate, echoing, resonating sounds, and like many other composers today, he is also much interested in oriental music. Thanks to such composers, Western music has for the first time employed large groups of percussion instruments with something of the subtlety known to the Far East. Harps, mandolins, specially treated pianos, and instruments of the "chimes" type such as vibraphones and marimbas create effects reminiscent of Indonesian gamelan orchestras (page 19).

George Crumb has created his own unique new sound world—quiet, precise, vibrant, endlessly changing, a controlled musical kaleidoscope of fascinating elegance. In some other respects, his music is relatively conservative. Although his rhythms often become highly complex and although he likes to punctuate his pieces with vague, meditative silences, there is always a clear sense of direction in his music, a sense of beginning, evolving, and ending. Thus all the songs in *Ancient Voices of Children* begin with the first lines of their poems and end with the last—which might seem like a ludicrously obvious thing to say about earlier songwriters, such as Morley or Schubert or Mahler. But it no longer seems obvious today. In Stockhausen's *Song of the Children,* we have seen the text thoroughly chopped up and juggled around; the treatment of the text parallels that of the music in seeking to convey a whole new concept of temporal order.

George Crumb appears to be fascinated by the work of the great Spanish poet and playwright Federico García Lorca, who was murdered in 1936 during his country's Civil War. Poems and fragments of his poems occur again and again in Crumb's compositions. *Ancient Voices of Children* is a García Lorca song cycle (page 212). There is one main singer, a soprano, and in addition a boy soprano and seven instrumentalists: a mandolin player, a harpist, a pianist, an oboist, and three percussionists. Among them they manage some thirty different percussion instruments, including vibraphone, marimba, various gongs, cymbals, maracas, Tibetan prayer stones, and Japanese temple bells. Even the soprano and the mandolin player have to help out with the percussion, and in return the percussionists sometimes have to whisper or shout. In song No. 2, the mandolin player plays a musical saw with a violin bow. The pianist never uses a conventional piano but plays either one that is amplified with contact mikes or else a little toy piano.

1. El niño busca su voz The cycle begins with a highly imaginative and arresting vocalise (page 313), a fantastic cascade of cries, hums, warbles, musical coughs, and so on, for the soprano. A resonance effect (like an echo chamber, only more ghostly) is obtained by having her sing directionally into the piano, which is amplified and has the right pedal held down. Then she sings the first stanza of the poem, to a very "sprung" melody. The boy soprano, offstage, sings the second stanza, but his melody, though also "sprung," has a tantalizing faint air of Spanish folk song about it.

There follows an instrumental interlude, "Dances of the Ancient Earth," a solo for the oboe accompanied by oriental percussion sounds and karate shouts from the percussionists. The oboe keeps circling a few fixed notes, returning to them again and again. It may remind us of an Indian snake-charmer's pipe.

2. Me he perdido muchas veces por el mar The words of this short song are mostly whispered by the soprano through a cardboard tube, against the weird high sliding of the musical saw and the plunking of the amplified piano. Again, as in song No. 1, there is a haunting suggestion of folk-like melody at the very end.

3. ¡De dónde vienes, amor, mi niño? A famous song from the play *Yerma*. After another soprano vocalise, reminiscent of song No. 1, the three stanzas of the poem are performed in free strophic form over a steady bolero rhythm. Crumb developed this unusual notation for this passage:

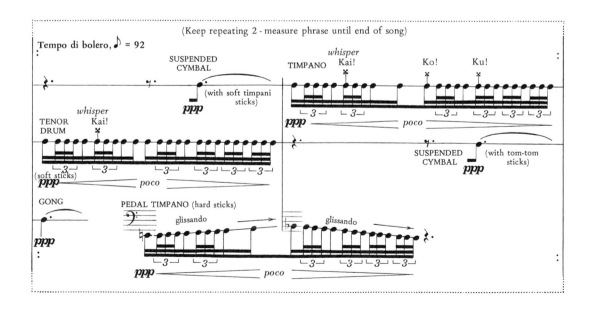

The driving bolero rhythm with its whispers or shouts, the wailing oboe, the growing stridency of the song and speech, the violent explosion at the end—this central song of the cycle is obviously the most powerful and gripping of them all.

4. Todas las tardes en Granada   The steady underlying hum sounds electronic but is, in fact, obtained by two barely audible rolls on the marimba and a harmonica chord. The soprano sings, simply and (again) with a strange folk-like air, two lines about the death of children. There is no more text in this short song.

Then, most surprisingly, the toy piano quotes six measures by Johann Sebastian Bach, from a song about the acceptance of death, *Bist du bei mir* ("If Thou abide with me"). An "in" reference, no doubt, which not everybody will get, but there is poignancy enough in the symbolism of the toy piano—a child's toy—and in its pathetic tinkly sound. It is made to sound utterly dissonant in respect to the underlying hum, and it runs down like a clockwork toy without ever reaching the expected cadence note.

Another instrumental interlude, "Ghost Dance," is a solo for mandolin. As played in a special way devised by Crumb, with a sliding glass rod, it sounds very much like a Japanese koto. The accompaniment consists only of maracas, South American gourd rattles.

5. Se ha llenado de luces mi carazón de seda   Strong bell and vibraphone sounds punctuate the final song. The meandering, circling melody of the oboe recalls "Dances of the Ancient Earth." At the very end of the piece, the boy, who has been offstage until now, is directed to walk slowly on stage, face the piano, and sing into it along with the soprano. They sing a vocalise that closely resembles the passage with which the cycle opened. Thus the piece ends with voices alone, as the whole impressive instrumental battery falls silent.

Garcia Lorca's beautiful poems tell of a child seeking his voice, but not for the purpose of speaking, of the birth and death of children, and of adults' nostalgia for their "ancient voices of children." In song No. 3 the soprano spoke for the mother and the boy soprano spoke for the unborn child. At the end of the cycle, the boy has indeed found a voice, though not for speaking but for vocalise—a gesture of human communication below, or above, the level of speech.

What with this occasional role-playing by the singers, the boy's "dramatic" entrance at the end, and the open invitation of the symmetrically placed dances ("Dances of the Ancient Earth," bolero, and "Ghost Dance"), we shall probably respond eagerly to the composer's suggestion on his score that *Ancient Voices* be performed in a theater version. Many of today's composers have experimented with "intermedia"—free-form combinations of music with dance, mime, speech, action, movies, light shows, whatever. Stockhausen has moved farther than George Crumb in this direction, but the composer who has gone farthest of all is the one we next consider, John Cage.

Ancient Voices
of Children

1. El niño busca su voz.
    (La tenía el rey de los grillos.)
    En una gota de agua
    buscaba su voz el niño.

    No la quiero para hablar;
    me haré con ella un anillo
    que llevará mi silencio
    en su dedo pequeñito. . . .

The child is seeking his voice.
(The king of crickets had it.)
In a drop of water
the child was seeking his voice.

I do not want it for speaking with;
I will make a ring with it
so that he will wear my silence
on his little finger. . . .

2. Me he perdido muchas veces por el mar
    con el oído lleno de floras recíen cortadas,
    con la lengua llena de amor y de agonía.
    Muchas veces me he perdido por el mar,
    como me pierdo en el corazón de algunos niños. . . .

I have lost myself in the sea many times
with my ear full of freshly cut flowers,
with my tongue full of love and agony.
I have lost myself in the sea many times
as I lose myself in the heart of certain children. . . .

3. ¿De dónde vienes, amor, mi niño?
    De la cresta del duro frío.
    ¿Que necesitas, amor, mi niño?
    La tibia tela de tu vestido.
    ¡Que so agiten las ramas al sol
    y salten las fuentes alrededor!
    En el patio ladra el perro,
    en los árboles canta el viento.
    Los bueyes mugen al boyero
    y la luna me riza los cabellos.

From where do you come, my love, my child?
From the ridge of hard frost.
What do you need, my love, my child?
The warm cloth of your dress.
Let the branches ruffle in the sun
and the fountains leap all around!
In the courtyard a dog barks,
in the trees the wind sings.
The oxen low to the oxherd
and the moon curls my hair.

    ¿Qué pides, niño, desde tan lejos?
    Los blancos montes que hay en tu pecho.
    ¡Que se agiten las ramas al sol
    y salten las fuentes alrededor!
    Te diré, niño mío, que sí,
    tronchada y rota soy para ti.
    ¡Cómo me duele esta cintura
    donde tendrás primera cuna!

What do you ask for, my child, from so far away?
The white mountains of your breast.
Let the branches ruffle in the sun
and the fountains leap all around!
I'll tell you, my child, yes,
I am torn and broken for you.
How painful is this waist
where you will have your first cradle!

    ¿Cuándo, mi niño, vas a venir?
    Cuándo tu carne huela a jazmín.
    ¡Que se agiten las ramas . . .

When, my child, will you come?
When your flesh smells of jasmine flowers.
Let the branches ruffle . . .

4. Todas las tardes en Granada,
    todas las tardes se muere un niño. . . .

Every afternoon in Granada,
every afternoon a child dies. . . .

5. . . . Se ha llenado de luces mi corazón de seda,
    de campanas perdidas, de lirios y de abejas,
    y yo me ire muy lejos,
    más allá de esas sierras, más allá de los mares,
    cerca de las estrellas, para perdirle a Cristo
    Señor que me devuelva mi alma antigua de niño. . . .

. . . My heart of silk is filled with lights,
with lost bells, with lilies, and with bees,
and I will go very far,
farther than those hills, farther than the seas,
close to the stars, to ask Christ the Lord
to give me back my ancient soul of a child. . . .

John Cage (1912–   )

The most radical figure of postwar music is a gentle, aging American named John Cage. Ever since the late 1930s, Cage has been asking questions that challenge all the assumptions on which traditional music rests. In words, and also in his compositions, he asks: why should music be different from the sounds of life? Why "musical" sounds, rather than noises? For that matter, why any kind of sound at all, rather than silence? Why work out music according to melodies, climaxes, twelve-tone series, and anything else that gives the impression of one thing following another in a purposeful order? *Why not leave it to chance?* Why should a piece be the same the second time it is played? Why not play pieces—any pieces—simultaneously?

If we really start to think about them, these questions are so profoundly destructive of the music we know that perhaps it is just as well that Cage has always proceeded in a mild and humorous fashion. It certainly has made it easier for people to dismiss him as a clown.

But as the years, decades, and even quarter centuries roll by, thoughtful people find it harder and harder to do this. First of all, some very arresting sounds have been produced by the "clowning." Secondly, Cage's ideas and practices, and also these sounds, have had a steady influence on other music. And not only on music: no composer since Richard Wagner has had so strong an influence on the other arts, too—on painting, sculpture, theater, movies, the dance. It is not too much to say that the course of the arts since 1950 cannot be grasped without coming to grips with Cage's aims and achievements.

Perhaps the simplest message that Cage has gotten across is that we should open our ears to every possible kind of sound and every possible conjunction of sounds. Sounds can be sung, played on instruments, heard on the streets, or created by electronic means; they can come in any combination or order, random or specified. Often, indeed, the actual sounds Cage produces are less successful than the "statement" he seems to be making *about* sounds, by means of the notions he develops for putting his pieces together.

Take *4' 33''*, one of Cage's most famous and provocative "works," which consists of four minutes and thirty-three seconds of silence (the piece has never been recorded—at least not intentionally). What Cage is saying is that silence is an entity, too, as well as sounds. When did you last really concentrate on silence? Try it. Was there *any* sound? And how would it feel to concentrate on silence for four minutes and thirty-three seconds, not three minutes or five?

Radio Music is performed by twiddling dials on eight radios according to a certain random plan, getting a mixture of talk, music, and silence, depending on what happens to be on the air at the moment. Cage may have been trying to recapture a not unfamiliar sound experience of modern life, the experience we get when we are out driving and keep punching buttons on the car radio in a random way, looking for a program we like. The sound is interrupted (again randomly) whenever the car goes under a steel bridge or passes a roaring truck. Many people would recognize the experience; few would think of it as organized music. Cage's "statement" is that music needn't be organized and that all sound experience is equally interesting, equally music.

Cage is most famous as an apostle of chance music. *Radio Music* is a sterling example. But he has also written music that involves improvisation and free choice on the part of performers (see below), intermedia pieces and music combined with actions and "happenings," electronic music—he was one of the very first to try this—and even music composed in the traditional way. He has experimented with a dazzling range of novel methods for music-making. Perhaps he is too much of a doctrinaire for his music to gain wide acceptance, but this example seems to have proved enormously fruitful for advanced composers in the postwar period.

CAGE   *ARIA* (1958)   *Side 16*

Aria is one of Cage's more conservative (!) pieces. It actually employs a score—a somewhat novel score, but one that is easy enough to grasp once the accompanying explanations have been digested (pages 384 and 385). If you detect a note of put-on as you read these directions (and as you listen to the piece), you're probably not mistaken. One thing that Cage has worked tirelessly to oppose is the solemnity of traditional music-making. Solemn or not, here is a table to show how the piece covers a range of composing techniques, from elements that are specified by the composer to improvisation, performer choice, and chance:

Voice	words	Specified by composer
	pitch, rhythm	Improvised by performer
	tone color	Chosen by performer
Accompaniment		Left to chance

Only with the words has Cage proceeded as a traditional composer would, by specifying them and specifying their order. (Since the words are nonsense, this doesn't make him all that traditional.) For pitch and rhythm, he gives neither notes nor measures but only very rough indications; these the singer follows in a general way, filling in the details according to her feeling of the moment. Here Cage is proceeding like a jazz composer, who writes out a tune with every expectation that the player will improvise around it. In tone color, which is related to what Cage calls "style of singing," the performer chooses; she can pick any ten different tone colors she likes, just so long as she sticks to them and changes from one to another as directed. (Again, this pattern of change is an element that is specified, but the piece would sound very different if someone chose dark blue = raga, black = growl, purple = Aretha Franklin, etc.) As for accompaniment, someone has to choose whether or not there is to be one. Cage goes so far as to suggest in a low-pressure way that one possible accompaniment would be an entirely different piece of his called *Fontana Mix*. And if this hint is taken, the result will be random. *Fontana Mix* itself is an electronic and *musique concrète* (page 365) piece composed according to chance procedures, procedures which we need not take the time to explain here. For however *Fontana Mix* is composed, the way it fits together with *Aria* is left entirely to chance anyhow.

A recording has been made of one version of the combination, with *Aria* performed by the brilliant singer for whom it was originally written, Cathy Berberian. Obviously, dozens of other versions could also be performed. And any version, it seems safe to say, would turn up some sounds and some conjunctions of sounds that had never occurred to you before—as certainly happens with this one.

They never occurred to Cage, either; he did not "compose" them in the traditional sense of figuring them out in his ear ahead of time. Yet without his complicated and whimsical array of chance, choice, and improvisation, these sounds would not have come into being. Some of them may strike us as arresting, others as dull and stupid—though Cage would insist that each one is exactly as valid as the others. The totality has a certain reckless cuckoodom, which can come as a breath of fresh air in the stuffy atmosphere of much concert music.

Once again, the piece is making a "statement." Perhaps it decodes like this: a woman in front of a microphone singing only in that highly artificial, singing-school style of voice production known as "contralto" is limiting her possibilities and confining our ears to a tiny (and solemn) fraction of what exists in the sound universe. She can sing in ten styles, and if she is Cathy Berberian, she can also sing in five languages. She can stomp and squeal and rattle, too. Miss Berberian as she goes through life is going to get into many utterly unpredictable situations. Let her have an accompaniment—or not, as the case may be—which sometimes allows her to be heard and sometimes drowns her out, which makes her sound sometimes important and sometimes silly, sometimes fascinating and sometimes dull. Life is unpredictable and full of surprises. Music should be, too. This is the philosophy represented by Cage and his music.

THE ARIA MAY BE SUNG IN WHOLE OR IN PART TO PROVIDE A PROGRAM OF A DETERMINED
TIME-LENGTH, ALONE OR WITH THE <u>FONTANA MIX</u> OR WITH ANY PARTS OF THE <u>CONCERT</u>.

THE NOTATION REPRESENTS TIME HORIZONTALLY, PITCH VERTICALLY, ROUGHLY SUGGESTED
RATHER THAN ACCURATELY DESCRIBED. THE MATERIAL, WHEN COMPOSED, WAS CONSID-
ERED SUFFICIENT FOR A TEN MINUTE PERFORMANCE (PAGE = 30 SECONDS); HOWEVER, A
PAGE MAY BE PERFORMED IN A LONGER OR SHORTER TIME-PERIOD.

THE VOCAL LINES ARE DRAWN IN BLACK, WITH OR WITHOUT PARALLEL DOTTED LINES,
OR IN ONE OR MORE OF 8 COLORS. THESE DIFFERENCES REPRESENT 10 STYLES
OF SINGING. ANY 10 STYLES MAY BE USED AND ANY CORRESPONDANCE BETWEEN
COLOR AND STYLE MAY BE ESTABLISHED. THE ONE USED BY MISS BERBERIAN IS: DARK
BLUE = JAZZ; RED = CONTRALTO (AND CONTRALTO LYRIC); BLACK WITH PARALLEL DOTTED
LINE = SPRECHSTIMME; BLACK = DRAMATIC; PURPLE = MARLENE DIETRICH; YELLOW =
COLORATURA (AND COLORATURA LYRIC); GREEN = FOLK; ORANGE = ORIENTAL; LIGHT BLUE
= BABY; BROWN = NASAL.

THE BLACK SQUARES ARE ANY NOISES ('UNMUSICAL' USE OF THE VOICE, AUXILIARY PERCUSSION,
MECHANICAL OR ELECTRONIC DEVICES). THE ONES CHOSEN BY MISS BERBERIAN IN THE ORDER
THEY APPEAR ARE: TSK, TSK; FOOTSTOMP; BIRD ROLL; SNAP, SNAP (FINGERS), CLAP; BARK (DOG);
PAINED INHALATION; PEACEFUL EXHALATION; HOOT OF DISDAIN; TONGUE CLICK; EXCLAMATION
OF DISGUST; OF ANGER; SCREAM (HAVING SEEN A MOUSE); UGH (AS SUGGESTING AN A-
MERICAN INDIAN); HA, HA (LAUGHTER); EXPRESSION OF SEXUAL PLEASURE.

THE TEXT EMPLOYS VOWELS AND CONSONANTS AND WORDS FROM 5 LANGUAGES:
ARMENIAN, RUSSIAN, ITALIAN, FRENCH, AND ENGLISH.

ALL ASPECTS OF A PERFORMANCE (DYNAMICS, ETC.) WHICH ARE NOT NOTATED MAY
BE FREELY DETERMINED BY THE SINGER.

FOR CATHY BERBERIAN

MILANO 1958

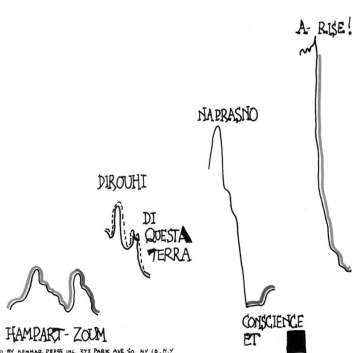

A Cage Score

John Cage is another modern composer, like Penderecki (page 375), who invents all kinds of new notations for his music. The pretty score for *Aria* counts as "conservative" in that it still holds to general ideas of high and low pitch reading up and down and time reading from left to right. But nothing is specified exactly. Instead of clefs calibrating the pitch level and measure lines marking the meter, Cage provides his own "key" in the long statement shown to the left.

Cage is also a very amusing lecturer and writer. His witty sayings have serious points behind them, or at least, points that are serious to him. Here is one to think about: "When you get right down to it, a composer is simply someone who tells other people what to do. I find this an unattractive way of getting things done. . . ."

Morton Subotnick (1933–   )

BUTTERFLIES (1974)

Among American electronic composers, one of the most impressive is Morton Subotnick, both in terms of his formidable technical expertise and his imaginative grasp of new ways of shaping time. A Californian, Subotnick has been an important musical figure in the San Francisco area and in New York. He is now at the California Institute of Arts, the big music, theater, and art school at Ventura, California, established by the estate of Walt Disney.

Butterflies was composed with The Electric Box, one of several efficient, compact electronic synthesizer systems that are now available. It consists of four related "movements" with interludes between them.

Butterfly II, which is probably the most striking of the four, begins with a hum overlaid with rapid tapping noises. They overlap in different complex meters while the hum slowly surges up and down. Listening to this first section may make us think of a whole crew of jumpy carpenters hammering away at once: a lively, urgent, humorous section.

At last only the hum remains, and a second section begins with delicate tinkling effects, somewhat reminiscent of dropping water. These gentle, irregular splotches of sound could go on forever in much the same way, we feel; we lose track of time. (Cage would like this part of *Butterflies*.) In contrast to section 1, section 2 is quiet or, rather, quietistic and almost mystical.

The dramatic third section starts with a series of hard, randomly timed bangs. They sound nervous; some people will find them almost painfully anxious. Gradually some short pitches are introduced, like the twanging of metal wires or plates (though of course all the bangs and twangs are synthesized electronically). The rhythm becomes more organized, too, until a new rattling passage builds up to an astonishing level of power. The build-up passage comes a second time, and is then cut off suddenly by the fourth section.

Section 4 is quieter, again, though it consists of fast rhythms. On page 377 we remarked on George Crumb's use of regular instruments to create the effect of "chimes" as in the Indonesian gamelan orchestra. Here in *Butterflies* similar effects are produced electronically. These little gamelan-like passages run on aimlessly, it seems. Then ultimately they run down, into a calm cadence.

The other three *Butterflies* include some of the same sounds featured in No. II, as well as many others; Subotnick seems able to produce an endless supply of fascinating sound combinations. No. I is the most quietistic, and No. IV, containing more definite pitches than the others, makes a good conclusion.

As to the title, Subotnick says that the piece is made up of three elements, which he compares to the shape of a butterfly (wing, body, wing) and also to its life cycle (larva, cocoon, butterfly). This is harder to understand than Subotnick's music, perhaps. But what we can understand is that like most composers today, he has rejected the old ways of conceiving and discussing—as well as writing—music. He is searching for new ways: and the search must go on.

Wired for Sound

This picture is also a sort of editorial on the current youth scene. The photographer has chosen his props unerringly: an electric guitar, a transistor radio, and a pair of sneakers.

One of the humorous (and sneaky) things here is the way the photograph manages to downgrade today's music artifacts to the level of footwear. But neither humor nor anything else is going to make them go away. Electric guitars and electronic organs and pianos have tended more and more to take over popular music; they are easy to mass-produce, easy to play, and capable of achieving instant power as well as a great variety of musical effects. It is not likely that the trend will be reversed. And if the "horns" of jazz slang—trumpets, trombones, and saxophones—no longer play such a large role in popular music, some unexpected newcomers owe their acceptance to electronics: flutes, violins, cellos, even harpsichords. Without electronic amplification, these instruments play too quietly to hold their own.

As for the radio and the phonograph, their effects on young and old perhaps run even deeper than those of electronic instruments. We know so much more music nowadays, music of so many different kinds: classical and popular, medieval and electronic, Japanese and Indian. Just as a child of five has seen more on TV than his grandparents saw in a lifetime, so a youngster of fifteen has heard more music. Consequently, we take our music casually, cutting it off halfway through, raising and lowering the volume, mixing up all kinds of records on the changer, and setting up "music to read by."

Music lovers of the past either played music for themselves or went to concerts. A concert was an occasion. One could hear only what was on the program—in order—and after paying one's money, one paid careful attention. Nearly everywhere today, the air seems to be saturated with music (polluted, it sometimes seems): transistors at the beach, Muzak in supermarkets, "Adventures in Sound" on jetliners. Our attitude toward music and the whole listening experience has been determined accordingly, and so has the attitude of modern composers.

Postwar Popular Music: Rock

After World War II, some of the same general tendencies that affected "classical" music also affected popular music in America. One obvious factor we have already mentioned, the increased use of electronic instruments; the Age of Rock is also the Electronic Age of popular music. Another, more profound tendency was a reaction against the complexities of prewar popular music, and a return to more basic elements. The same paradox can be discerned as in classical music: a new primitivism and new technical sophistication went inseparably together.

In popular music, this manifested itself as a rejection of those prewar favorites, the swing bands. Although a few of the big-band leaders kept going (among them the imperturbable Ellington), they did so in the face of growing apathy. As for modern jazz, this fascinating development became much too complex and private to gain wide popularity. What people seem to have wanted was, first of all, a return to *song*, to simple song instead of the essentially instrumental (and therefore intricate) art of jazz and swing. Second, they tired of the glossy "dressed up" arrangements or orchestrations of the swing bands; they preferred more natural, earthier kinds of musical accompaniment. Folk music, in the broadest, most generous definition, answered the current need.

What was chiefly involved was not actual traditional folk music, as strictly defined (see page 292), but rather music newly composed in a folk style. Many different musical genres became popular after the war, and most of them made some kind of claim on folk origins. There was "country-&-western" music, the hillbilly or cowboy style associated with the Grand Old Opry at Nashville. There was also a vogue for imitation old-style Anglo-American ballads sung in an exaggeratedly gentle fashion—numbers such as *Blowin' in the Wind* (see page 30), *Where Have All the Flowers Gone*, and *Five Hundred Miles*. (This is usually called "folk"—rather irrationally, for other genres deserve the name just as well.) The most important, from the standpoint of the future of American music, was a genre of black popular music called rhythm-&-blues.

Rhythm-&-blues of the early 1950s and beyond consists of composed blues performed in a decidedly new style. The lyrics are shouted, rather than moaned as they usually were in older blues, and the accompaniment is distinguished by an extremely heavy and regular basic beat. The intense, even violent drive of rhythm-&-blues could not be more different from the dragging gloom characteristic of the blues in earlier years.

Rhythm-&-blues was the basic influence on *rock 'n' roll*, or just rock, as the vital new musical genre soon came to be called after its inception in the mid-1950s. It has been aptly remarked that what rock took over from rhythm-&-blues was the "rhythm" and not the "blues" aspect (and it could be said even more aptly that rock took over the *beat* or *metric* aspect of rhythm-&-blues). The uninhibited shouting style was also adopted, but the words no longer had the traditional blues character nor, indeed, any particular association with black culture. And the introduction of electric guitars at this

BAND 7

RHYTHM-&-BLUES

ROCK

period gave further emphasis to the driving, violent beat.

While rhythm-&-blues was designed for black audiences, rock caught on like wildfire with a much wider segment of the American public. Here is another case of a black musical genre taken over and modified for white consumption. Just like jazz sixty years before, the new music was attacked as primitive, ugly, and dangerously sexual in its implications. Rock even had to put up with attacks from the jazz enthusiasts, who lamented its lack of rhythmic subtlety and the impersonal quality of the new instruments—the electronic instruments—as compared to the richly expressive trumpets and saxophones of the great jazzmen.

It would indeed have been foolhardy to predict that a style as crude and primitive as 1950s rock would lead to the remarkable developments of the 1960s. But, in fact, rock very soon reached a stage that was as artistic, in its own way, as anything that had been produced by the jazzmen.

The differences are interesting. Whereas jazz groups were traditionally made up of individual star performers who did not, however, compose their own basic material, the opposite was true of rock in the 1960s. Rock musicians stand out less as individuals. Their instrumental playing is more impersonal and less skilled than that of jazz players, and their singing is typically (though not invariably) group singing, in what we might call a modern type of "close harmony." On the other hand, 1960s rock groups tended to produce their own, often very interesting individual songs and lyrics. In this, perhaps, rock was harking back to a tradition from its ancestry—for lyrics had been improvised by the old blues singers, too.

The outstanding rock group, and the one that was most popular in this country during the 1960s, actually came over from England. (So firmly has American popular music taken hold abroad, that now foreigners can sometimes operate in American styles more effectively than we can ourselves.) The Beatles included two composers, George Harrison and Paul McCartney, and a composer-poet, John Lennon; for originality and talent these men can be compared only to Bob Dylan, the American poet-composer in the "folk" and "folk-rock" tradition. Musically, the Beatles borrowed from all popular genres to create their own highly individual musical numbers. They also experimented with ideas from contemporary "classical" music—with electronic and chance music, *musique concrète* (see page 365), and such instruments as the cello and the Indian sitar. On some of their 12-inch LP records, such as *Sgt. Pepper's Lonely Hearts Club Band*, the songs form a group with interconnections—thus forming, in effect, popular-song cycles (see page 212).

Poetically, the Beatles ranged at least as widely as they did in the musical sphere. Not for them the standard "moon-June-spoon" lyrics of the old popular songs, nor the unvarying world-weariness of the blues. Most welcome, perhaps, was the playfulness, fun, and sheer joy they managed to project in so many of their songs. But they could also deliver hard driving numbers reminiscent of rhythm-&-blues and haunting ballads in "folk" style. The subtlety and psychological sophistication of some of Lennon's love songs was unprecedented, not only in earlier rock, but in any popular music of any earlier time.

One striking feature of rock is not strictly musical but more sociological in nature. If there was such a thing as a distinct "youth sub-culture" during the 1950s and '60s, as some people believed, its artistic manifestation was popular music, particularly rock. Already in the 1950s, some early critics of rock linked it with teen-age rebellion, the "blackboard jungle," drugs, long hair, and of course sexual permissiveness. In the 1960s things became more explicit, as song lyrics often spoke out (in uninhibited language) against war, authority, and oppressive convention. Dylan was even more outspoken than the Beatles in this regard, while the Rolling Stones, another English group very popular in America, expressed a particularly powerful, hostile version of youthful alienation. On the other extreme, the gentle ballads of the "folk" tradition can be linked to the so-called flower-children and their concern for the tender things of life while opting out of American society.

The most exciting rock groups of the late 1960s came out of San Francisco—at the time a haven for alienated youth of the whole nation, as well as the place where huge rock concerts were first pioneered. However, few of these groups held together for as long as the Beatles or the Stones, and none of them made such a lasting impression. Some of the energy went out of the rock movement in the 1970s. Things seemed to be marking time. And this had something to do with the changing mood of American youth after the end of the Vietnam War and the arrival of economic world crisis.

It would be foolhardy (again) to try to predict the future course of popular music. Whether it will derive new energy from black sources or Britain, whether it will enter a new primitive stage or a new sophisticated one, whether it will go up or down, only one thing is certain: between the writing of this book and the reading of it, the ever-changing, ever-vital face of American pop music will have changed once again.

Popular music is always more conservative than "classical" music. But rock has already shown some signs of absorbing some of the advanced features of modern classical music, and in future years it is bound to absorb more. For what happened to music in the decades after 1950 was, in fact, the most sweeping musical revolution in nearly a thousand years. As we remarked on page 297, this revolution can make the changes which took place around 1900, and which looked drastic enough at the time, pale into insignificance. In the centuries around the year 1000, tunes as we know them came into being, as did meter and also the important notion of singing two melodies at once to make polyphony. Then after 1950, tune, melody, pitch, meter, rhythm, the idea of necessary consequence—all this was thrown into doubt. None of the changes in style that took place in between, some of which we have studied, cuts as deep as this.

Predictably, reactions to the new music ran along generational lines. People who had grown up entirely within older traditions tended to mutter darkly that music had come to an end. (At least this shows that they sensed the importance of the changes.) People born after 1950 are generally more sympathetic to the new music, more curious, more open. And well you may be: it's your music, and you will be living with it for another fifty years or more.

It is not the sum total of the music you will be hearing, of course, only one part of it. There is also music of the past, which seems to retain its vitality for years, even centuries, as each new generation comes to it. It is interesting to speculate on the reasons for this really rather amazing continuity of response to art, music, and literature of previous ages. Is it that great music of the past is somehow both of its time and above it, aloof from it? And that popular music reflects its time with such immediacy and intensity that it burns itself out? The thrust of this book has been toward an appreciation of past music—whether twenty years past or two hundred—in an effort to maintain this continuity.

Someone has said that if we do not understand the past, we are doomed to suffer its mistakes all over again. This applies to history and politics, not to art, where we have no mistakes, only successive manifestations of the human spirit. With art, if we do not understand the past, we are doomed only to living in the present.

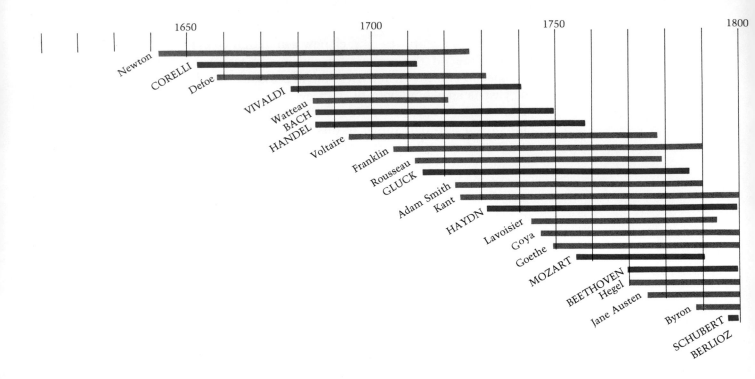

	1650			1700			1750			1800

Newton
CORELLI
Defoe
VIVALDI
Watteau
BACH
HANDEL
Voltaire
Franklin
Rousseau
GLUCK
Adam Smith
Kant
HAYDN
Lavoisier
Goya
Goethe
MOZART
BEETHOVEN
Hegel
Jane Austen
Byron
SCHUBERT
BERLIOZ

MUSICAL
Other

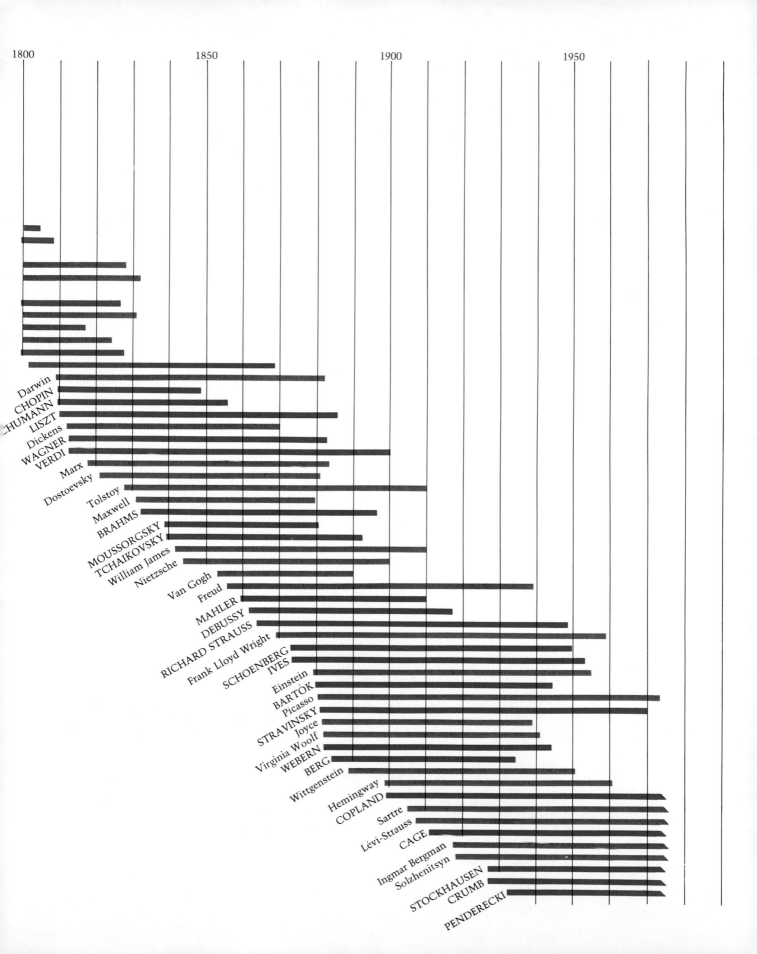

1800   1850   1900   1950

Darwin
CHOPIN
SCHUMANN
LISZT
Dickens
WAGNER
VERDI
Marx
Dostoevsky
Tolstoy
Maxwell
BRAHMS
MOUSSORGSKY
TCHAIKOVSKY
William James
Nietzsche
Van Gogh
Freud
MAHLER
DEBUSSY
RICHARD STRAUSS
Frank Lloyd Wright
SCHOENBERG
IVES
Einstein
BARTÓK
Picasso
STRAVINSKY
Joyce
Virginia Woolf
WEBERN
BERG
Wittgenstein
Hemingway
COPLAND
Sartre
Lévi-Strauss
CAGE
Ingmar Bergman
Solzhenitsyn
STOCKHAUSEN
CRUMB
PENDERECKI

Biographies

Johann Sebastian Bach

1685–1750   German baroque composer

Bach was born in the same year as Handel, 1685. The Bach family produced so many musicians over a period of two centuries that, in their part of Germany, people are reported to have said "Bach" when they meant "musician" the way we might say "Rockefeller" to mean "millionaire." From the time of his first positions, as church organist in tiny mid-German towns, Bach seems to have been headstrong and stubborn. In his first important job, as a court musician at Weimar, he got into a dispute with the Duke of Weimar about quitting and was actually jailed briefly (typically industrious, he spent the time writing his *Little Organ Book*, a collection of chorale preludes). This was followed by another court position, at Cöthen, where he wrote much of his greatest chamber music.

In 1723 Bach was appointed cantor of St. Thomas' Church and Choir School in Leipzig, one of the main towns in what is now East Germany. This was the highest musical position in the Lutheran church, but it involved onerous chores and administrative restrictions which Bach was not the man to accept willingly. At first he composed a staggering amount of music for the Leipzig churches—hundreds of sacred cantatas. But then he quarreled with the authorities and, to their annoyance, spent more of his time in city music activities. Toward the end of his life Bach prepared a few of his finest pieces for publication and made careful manuscript collections and orderings of his works.

Bach married a cousin when he was about twenty; the couple had seven children before she died in 1720. A year later he married a young musician and they had another thirteen children. Of the twenty children, ten survived infancy and two became extremely important composers of the next generation: Carl Philip Emmanuel and Johann Christian (the youngest).

Bach was always widely admired as a brilliant organist, but from his middle years on he was considered impossibly "heavy" and old-fashioned as a composer. After his death his music attracted only a few connoisseurs (who included, however, Mozart and Beethoven) until it was rediscovered by the Romantics. For many musicians and listeners today, Bach is the greatest of all composers.

Chief works: *The Well-tempered Clavier*, consisting of forty-eight preludes and fugues for harpsichord; six Brandenburg Concertos; church cantatas, *Passion According to St. Matthew*, and Mass in B minor; organ fugues and chorale preludes.

See text on page 92 and picture essay on page 104.

Béla Bartók

1881–1945   Hungarian twentieth-century composer

Bartók was born in Hungary, and it was soon evident that he was destined for a brilliant career as a pianist and composer. He wrote his first work for the piano when he was nine. Music was the avocation of his father, who was the principal of an agricultural school.

Few musicians have ever led as varied a career as Bartók. He was a prolific composer and a fine pianist. In conjunction with another important Hungarian composer, Zoltán Kodály, he undertook a large-scale investigation of Hungarian (and other) folk music, writing several standard books in the field of ethnomusicology (the scientific study of folk music and the music of non-Western cultures). Also with Kodály, he directed the Budapest Academy of Music, where the two men developed new ideas in music teaching. An outcome of this side of Bartók's career is his *Mikrokosmos*, a series of 153 graded piano pieces starting with the very easiest, which are well known to most piano students today. Bartók's compositions employ folk elements such as rhythms and melodic turns—though not actual folksongs—and he perhaps succeeded more than any other nationalist composer in making something truly individual out of such elements.

In 1940, after the outbreak of World War II, Bartók came to America, where he was not well known and there was little enthusiasm for his works. He developed leukemia, and his last years were a desperate, poverty-ridden struggle to complete the Third Piano Concerto and the Concerto for Viola and Orchestra. Ironically, his important works earned a wide audience shortly after his death.

Chief works: Six string quartets; an orchestra piece, *Music for Strings, Percussion, and Celesta*; Second Violin Concerto and Third Piano Concerto; a fascinating Sonata for Two Pianos and Percussion.

See text on page 341 and picture essay on page 347.

Ludwig van Beethoven

1770–1827   Viennese composer

It must have been a miserable childhood. Beethoven's father, a minor musician at the court of Bonn in West Germany, tried unsuccessfully to push him as an infant prodigy like Mozart. A trip to Vienna to make musical contacts (with Mozart, among others) was cut short by the death of his mother. Still in his teens, he had to take over official control of his family because of his father's alcoholism.

Unlike Mozart, Beethoven was a slow developer, but by the age of twenty-two he had made enough of an impression to receive a sort of fellowship to study with Haydn in Vienna, then the musical capital of the world. In a few years he was widely acclaimed as a magnificent and powerful virtuoso pianist, frequently playing his own compositions. Too difficult a personality to study for long with anyone, he nevertheless remained in Vienna until his death.

After the age of thirty, he became progressively deaf, a devastating loss for a musician and one that kept him from making a living in the traditional way, by performing. He was supported, however, by the Viennese aristocracy, which was awed by his uncompromising character and his extraordinarily forceful and original music.

Beethoven, then, was probably the first musician to make a career solely from composing. Already in his lifetime, he was regarded as a great genius. His character contributed to this impression; an alarmingly brusque and forceful person, he suffered deeply and seemed to live for his art alone—his domestic life was chaotic and he was well known on the streets of Vienna as an eccentric. He had an immense need to receive and to give affection, but despite various love affairs, he never married. In his late years he adopted his orphan nephew, but his attitude was so protective and his love so smothering that the boy could not stand it and actually attempted suicide. The shock of this hastened Beethoven's death. Twenty thousand attended his funeral.

Taste has changed many times since Beethoven's lifetime, but his music has always reigned supreme with audiences and critics. The incredible originality and expressive power of his work never seem to fade.

Chief works: Nine symphonies, the most famous being the *Eroica* (No. 3), the Fifth, the Seventh, and the Ninth (*Choral* Symphony); sixteen string quartets; piano sonatas, including the *Pathétique*, the *Waldstein*, the *Appassionata*, and the late-period *Hammerklavier* Sonata; opera *Fidelio*; Mass in D.

See text on pages 190 and 191 and picture essay on page 206.

Hector Berlioz

1803–1869   French romantic composer

If the deaf Beethoven was the first great composer who made his living actually as a composer, and not as an instrumentalist or conductor, Berlioz was the first who was not an instrumentalist at all. His father, a country doctor, sent him to medical school in Paris. But as Berlioz told it, he was so horrified when he entered the dissecting room, where the rats were nibbling at the scraps, that he leaped out the window and went to the Paris Conservatory of Music instead. The anecdote is typical of his emotional and utterly romantic personality.

Berlioz had two unhappy marriages, the first to the Irish Shakespearean actress Harriet Smithson; she is immortalized as the *idée fixe* in the *Fantastic Symphony*.

In spite of suffering hugely all through his life, it was a triumph of his impetuous personality that Berlioz ultimately managed to get most of his enormous compositions performed and to gain a good measure of recognition in conservative Paris. He was obliged throughout his life to support himself with musical journalism, at which he was a master; his *Memoirs* is one of the most delightful books ever written about music. He also toured extensively as a conductor of his music, especially in Germany, where he was welcomed in modernist circles.

Chief works: *Fantastic Symphony* and other program symphonies entitled *Harold in Italy* and *Romeo and Juliet*; opera *The Trojans*; oratorios *The Damnation of Faust* and *The Childhood of Christ*; a Requiem Mass.

See further details on page 240 and picture essay on page 264.

Johannes Brahms

1833–1897   German romantic composer

The son of an orchestra musician, Brahms was given piano lessons at an early age. By the time he was ten, he was studying with one of Hamburg's finest music teachers. Like most of the great composers, he was composing, as well as giving public recitals, while still in his teens. Typically, again, he early was forced to turn these talents into a means of livelihood, playing piano at dockside taverns and writing popular tunes.

A turning point in Brahms' life came at the age of twenty when he met Robert and Clara Schumann, who befriended and encouraged him and promoted his music. His style of composition was determined by his love and admiration for the Viennese "classic" composers, and it was in their city, Vienna, the city of his admired Haydn, Mozart, Beethoven, and Schubert, that he eventually settled and passed an uneventful bachelor existence, steadily turning out music. He had many close friends, especially Clara Schumann and an important violinist-composer named Joseph Joachim; he submitted his new music to them for searching criticism before releasing it. With Joachim, too, he issued a sophomoric manifesto in 1860 attacking the "modernist" music of Liszt and Wagner, and in turn he was himself attacked as a conservative.

Brahms was in his forties before his first symphony appeared, many years after its beginnings at his desk. It seems as though he hesitated to provoke comparison with Beethoven, whose symphonies constituted then, as now, a standard for the genre. Brahms went on to write three more symphonies, all harking back to forms used by Beethoven and even Bach, but thoroughly romantic in their expressive effect.

Brahms dabbled in musicology and enjoyed popular music, writing waltzes (Johann Strauss was a valued friend), delightful folksong arrangements, and the well-known *Hungarian Dances*.

Chief works: Four symphonies; much chamber music, including a fine Clarinet Quintet; piano music; songs; *A German Requiem*.

See text on page 278.

Frédéric François Chopin

1810–1849   French-Polish romantic composer

Chopin's father was a Frenchman who had emigrated to Poland and married a Polish lady. He ran a private school in Warsaw for young gentlemen, and in this atmosphere Frédéric acquired his lifelong taste for life in high society. Provided with the best teachers available, he became a remarkable pianist. A work for piano and orchestra which he published at the age of fifteen was already impressive enough to earn a rave review from Robert Schumann.

After twenty years in Warsaw, Chopin settled in Paris, where he found ready acceptance from society people and also from the literary and artistic figures of the time. He made his way as a highly fashionable piano teacher and by selling his piano music—he composed practically nothing else—to publishers. Chopin was a frail and delicate personality. Though he sometimes played in public, he really disliked the hurly-burly of concert life and preferred to perform for select audiences in great houses. The major event of his personal life was his ten-year romance with Madame Dudevant, a famous novelist and an early feminist, who wrote under the pen name George Sand. Sand sketched some scenes from their not-always-idyllic life together in one of her novels. After the affair broke up in 1847, Chopin's health declined with his spirits, and he died only a few years later at the age of thirty-nine of tuberculosis.

Chief works: Preludes, études, nocturnes, ballades, and other "miniatures" for piano.

See further details on page 230 and picture essay on page 235.

Aaron Copland

1900–   American twentieth-century composer

The son of immigrants, Copland studied in New York and then in Paris, the center of musical experiment in the 1920s. At the same time that George Gershwin was struggling to make jazz more "classical" in his Piano

Concerto, *Rhapsody in Blue,* and *An American in Paris,* Copland was working the other way around—injecting classical music with jazz in *his* Piano Concerto and *Music for the Theater.* (Copland and Gershwin both had the same piano teacher, the New York composer Rubin Goldmark.) Later Copland moved away from jazz but used other American musical sources in his compositions, such as the Shaker tune in *Appalachian Spring* and cowboy songs in the ballets *Billy the Kid* and *Rodeo.* In the 1940s he wrote some excellent movie scores—for *The Red Pony, Of Mice and Men,* and *Our Town.* After World War II, he began to work with serial techniques, but like most serial music these later compositions have not attained wide popularity. He has written an opera for high schools, *The Second Hurricane,* and a fine music-appreciation textbook, *What to Listen for in Music.* Copland keeps out of the limelight, but he has accomplished a good deal of quiet work on behalf of American composers.

Chief works: Piano Variations, Piano Fantasy; Third Symphony; ballet *Appalachian Spring* (for the dancer Martha Graham).

See further details on page 350.

Claude Debussy

1862–1918   French composer of the early twentieth century

One great composer, Debussy, was the product of a music school—the famous Paris Conservatory of Music, where he studied for ten years from the age of eleven. As a result of this training, Debussy's music was to be accepted by the musical establishment with an ease that was surprising in view of his theoretical innovations and the originality of his style. He was regarded as a radical in the composition classes, but not too radical to win the main prize (after several attempts), which earned him a three-year period of study in Rome. Later, Debussy traveled to Russia with Madame von Meck, Tchaikovsky's eccentric patron, who employed the young Frenchman to play in a trio at her home in Moscow. Debussy also visited Bayreuth, Germany, the home of the great Wagner festivals. At first fascinated by Wagner's "music dramas," Debussy eventually turned strongly against them and against most other German music as well.

Back in Paris, he settled into the city's cafe life, becoming a familiar, bearded figure in his broad-brimmed hat and flowing cape. In his early thirties he seems to have rather suddenly crystallized his musical style. It was at once very individual and very French, reflecting the influences of the French symbolist poets and the impressionist painters. One remarkable work after another was given its première, greeted with a flurry of controversy, and then generally accepted by the critics and the public.

For a short time he wrote music criticism, in which he expressed in pungent prose the anti-German attitudes that were already manifest in his music. Debussy died of cancer in Paris during World War I, actually during a bombardment of the city by his hated Germans.

Chief works: Orchestral works *Prelude to "The Afternoon of a Faun"* (a famous poem by the French symbolist poet Mallarmé), *Nocturnes, The Sea, Images, Games;* opera *Pelléas and Mélisande* (a French answer to *Tristan and Isolde*); songs; études and preludes for piano.

See further details on page 308.

George Frideric Handel

1685–1759   Anglo-German baroque composer

Handel was born in the same year as Bach, 1685. His father, an elderly and prosperous surgeon, distrusted music and wanted his son to become a lawyer. Handel actually studied law, but long before this his extraordinary musical talent had made his career a foregone conclusion. At twelve he was assistant organist at the cathedral in his hometown of Halle, composing a motet for the services every week; and by the time he was twenty he had made a sensation as an opera composer at Hamburg, the center of German opera at that time. Handel rapidly extended this success in Italy and England, where he finally settled in 1712 to become England's favorite resident composer for two generations. He wrote music for Queen Anne and Kings George I and George II, as well as for various members of the British aristocracy.

Handel was a big, vigorous man, hot-tempered but quick to make up. He ran a succession of opera companies presenting Italian opera in London—recruiting his singers in Europe, writing the music, and managing the finances—an exciting life, full of ups and downs, intrigue and activity. Ultimately Italian opera fell out of fashion, and the resourceful composer turned to writing oratorios, which were received even more enthusiastically. At the end of his life, when he had become blind, Handel still performed brilliantly on the organ and composed by dictating to a musically trained secretary. Though at times he had stood in danger of being thrown into a debtor's prison, Handel died a fairly rich man and was buried with great ceremony in Westminster Abbey.

Chief works: Oratorios *Messiah, Israel in Egypt, Saul, Semele;* twelve concerti grossi for strings; *Water Music* and *Fireworks Music.*

See picture essay on page 116 and text on page 117.

Joseph Haydn

1732–1809   Viennese composer

Haydn's career is a story of many years of hard work, steady development, and ultimate fame and fortune. He came from a musical, Austrian-village family, which sought sophisticated instruction for him. First the village schoolmaster and then a professional musician—who, though he maltreated the boy, also taught him extremely well—tutored the young Haydn. At the age of eight, he was sent to Vienna to be a choirboy in the great Cathedral of St. Stephen. After various musical jobs, he became assistant music director to Prince Esterházy and served the family faithfully for thirty years, until they retired him in 1790 with a handsome pension. His duties at the Esterházy Castle outside Vienna included performing two operas and two concerts every week.

Like Mozart, Haydn married the sister of the woman he actually loved, a mistake that might have been even more disastrous than Mozart's, for his wife was unpleasant and unkind. But Haydn soon separated from her.

After around 1765, his music slowly grew more and more popular and was widely published (it was mostly the publishers who provided the nicknames to so many of Haydn's symphonies and quartets). After he retired, he went on two triumphal tours of London, which occupied a position in the musical world like that of New York in later years. His last twelve symphonies were composed for concerts in London. Haydn scored his greatest success, however, back in Vienna with his oratorios *The Creation* and *The Seasons,* written when he was nearing seventy. At last, after producing an enormous quantity of symphonies, quartets, trios, operas, and Masses—works to which he invariably gave his best—Haydn's mind began to slip, and he could no longer compose.

Mozart, at twenty-five, was half Haydn's age when they met in 1781. Haydn readily acknowledged the younger man's greater genius and was deeply shaken when, eighteen years before his own dignified death, Mozart died ravaged by debt and illness.

Haydn was a splendid person, basically simple and modest though quite aware of his worth, but also shrewd and worldly, and generous in his reports of others.

Chief works: Symphonies, especially the twelve *London* symphonies (which include *The Surprise, The Drum-Roll, The Clock,* and *The Military*); string quartets; oratorios *The Creation* and *The Seasons.*

See text on page 170 and picture essay on page 185.

Gustav Mahler

1860–1911   Viennese late romantic composer

Mahler's early life was not a happy one. Born in Bohemia to an abusive father, five of his brothers and sisters died of diphtheria, and others ended their lives in suicide or mental illness. Mahler began to play the piano at six, and at fifteen he entered the Vienna Conservatory of Music. Later, patrons encouraged and supported him in his rapid rise as a conductor.

Mahler was one of the great conductors of his time and also a very effective musical administrator. Ultimately he came to head such organizations as the Vienna Opera, the Metropolitan Opera in New York, and the New York Philharmonic. A dedicated and uncompromising musician, his disputes with the Philharmonic's Board of Directors discouraged him profoundly and are said to have contributed to his early death. Mahler carved out time for himself to compose only in the summers, so it isn't surprising that he produced fewer pieces (though they are very long pieces) than any other important composer. Ten symphonies, the last of them unfinished, and six song cycles for voice and orchestra are all he wrote.

He married a famous Viennese beauty, Alma Schindler, who after his death went on to marry the great architect Walter Gropius and then the novelist Franz Werfel—and then wrote fascinating memoirs of her life with the composer. Despite his eminent positions, Mahler's life was clouded by psychological turmoil, and he once consulted his Viennese contemporary, Dr. Sigmund Freud.

Chief works: Ten symphonies, several with chorus, of which the best-known are the Fourth and Fifth; song cycle *The Song of the Earth* for contralto, tenor, and orchestra.

See further details on page 286.

Wolfgang Amadeus Mozart

1756–1791   Viennese composer

Mozart was the son of a distinguished composer and writer on music, court musician to the archbishop of Salzburg in Austria. Mozart's amazing musical ability was recognized early, and for ten years he toured all over

Europe as a child prodigy. He played for the young Austrian princess Marie Antoinette, who was later to be Queen of France, at the age of six and composed his first professional opera for the Italian stage at fourteen. But Mozart grew up into the sort of person for whom nothing works out right. He felt he could not tolerate the servile life of a court musician, as his father had done, and so he left Salzburg for Vienna. He fell in love with a coloratura soprano, Aloysa Weber, but she turned him down and instead he married her disorganized sister Constanze.

When he tried to make a life for himself as an independent musician in Vienna, he had a dishearteningly difficult time, even though there were moments of success and though his genius was generally recognized. Haydn, who played in an amateur string quartet with Mozart, called him quite simply the greatest composer he had ever met. Mozart died at the age of thirty-five after ten years of struggle in Vienna, heavily in debt to his Freemason lodge brothers. Constanze had a breakdown and could not supervise the funeral, and Mozart was buried in an unmarked pauper's grave.

Of all the great composers, Mozart had the most extraordinary natural genius. His Viennese contemporaries thought his music was too serious, and the romantics thought it was too light. Today Mozart is generally ranked with Bach and Beethoven as the greatest of Western composers.

Chief works: Operas *The Marriage of Figaro, Don Giovanni, The Magic Flute;* symphonies, piano concertos, string quartets and quintets; a Requiem Mass (left unfinished at his death).

See text on page 154.

Arnold Schoenberg

1874–1951   Viennese twentieth-century composer

Largely self-taught in music, Schoenberg showed great originality not only as a composer, but also as a musical theorist. Nevertheless, for much of his lifetime he was obliged to eke out an existence with rather low-level musical jobs.

As a young man Schoenberg held the somewhat messianic belief that he was destined to carry the great tradition of Bach, Beethoven, Brahms, and Wagner through its "logical" modern development. Listeners felt otherwise, and Schoenberg's revolutionary compositions of the 1900s were received with more hostility than any in the entire history of music. At the same time, they attracted the sympathetic interest of

Gustav Mahler and Richard Strauss and drew a coterie of brilliant young students to Schoenberg. A man of unusual versatility, Schoenberg wrote the literary texts for many of his compositions, painted pictures in an expressionist style, and produced very important books on musical theory.

Schoenberg's music had been growing progressively more and more atonal, but he was nearly fifty before he evolved the twelve-tone (or serial) system. For this, he was attacked even more. As a Jew, he was forced to leave Germany when the Nazis took over in 1933, and he spent his last years in Los Angeles. Schoenberg was a remarkable personality: proud, superstitious, suspicious to the point of paranoia. Of all the major composers, he was the first great teacher since Bach; among his students were Alban Berg and Anton Webern. At the end of his life he taught at UCLA.

Though his music has never won popular approval, Schoenberg is regarded by many musicians as far and away the most significant composer of the twentieth century.

Chief works: Four quartets; *Pierrot lunaire* ("Moonstruck Pierrot"), a chamber-music piece with *Sprechstimme* singer; *Erwartung* ("Anticipation"), an expressionist "monodrama" for one singer and orchestra; the unfinished opera *Moses and Aaron.*

See further discussion on page 324 and picture essay on page 329.

Franz Schubert

1797–1828   Composer of the late Viennese period

Schubert was probably the most unassuming of all the great composers. Born in Vienna, he learned music at home—there was a family string quartet—and at the choir school attached to the Imperial Court Chapel. He starting pouring out music in his middle teens: songs, sonatas, symphonies, chamber music, an opera (never performed), and a Mass. For a few years he taught at a school, alongside his father, but he preferred to struggle along in poverty without a regular job, relying on what little he could bring in from a few private lessons and from selling music to publishers. Songs, part-songs (songs for several singers), waltzes, and piano four-hand music were most in demand, and Schubert turned these out with amazing facility.

He roomed at one time with a poet, Johann Mayrhofer, who supplied him with many gloomy song poems. Fortunately, a little cult of friends and admirers attached themselves to Schubert, promoting his music and helping him as best they could; there are accounts and pictures of various convivial trips and parties of the "Schubertianer," as they called themselves. Schubert died in a typhoid fever epidemic when he was only thirty-one. Works such as his two great symphonies were never performed during his lifetime, and a great deal of his music only came to light many years after his death.

Chief works: Songs, including the song cycles *The Fair Maid of the Mill, The Winter Journey, Swan Songs; Unfinished* Symphony and Symphony in C; sonatas and chamber music, including a great string quintet.

See further details on page 207 and picture essay on page 210.

Robert Schumann

1810–1856   German romantic composer

Encouraged by his father, Robert Schumann began to study the piano when he was six. Unfortunately, his father died when the boy was in his teens and his mother disapproved of a musical career, insisting on law instead. Schumann finally persuaded her to his view and traveled to Leipzig, determined to become a piano virtuoso. He failed because of a finger paralysis which he is said to have induced in an effort to retrain his hands to a new pianistic style.

Besides his musical talent, Schumann had a great flair for literature, inherited from his father, who was a bookseller, writer, and editor. When he was only twenty-three, Schumann founded a magazine to campaign for a higher level of music; started writing regular music criticism of the highest quality, which encouraged such unknown composers as Chopin and (later) Brahms; and became a highly respected voice in the German music world. Before then, he had begun composing his highly original "miniatures" for piano—often providing them with half-programmatic titles of a literary nature such as *Carnaval, Novelettes, Butterflies,* and *Dances of the David League* (a make-believe society of young romantic spirits opposed to the Goliath of middle-class society and its conservative artistic tastes).

Schumann fell in love with Clara Wieck, the daughter of his music teacher. At sixteen, Clara was already on the way to becoming one of the great pianists of the century. Thanks to her father's fanatical opposition, the couple had to wait until she was twenty-one (minus one day) before getting married. A charming outcome of the marriage was that Schumann, whose early compositions were entirely for the piano, suddenly started to write

songs; nearly 150, including his finest examples, were composed in this "song year." He also turned to the composition of larger works, such as concertos and symphonies. Thereafter he assumed some important musical positions and did some touring with Clara, but began to develop tragic signs of insanity (probably as a result of syphilis). In 1854, tormented by voices, hallucinations, and a loss of memory, he tried to drown himself in the Rhine and was committed to an asylum. He died two years later without regaining his sanity.

Chief works: Song cycles *A Woman's Life and Love, Poet's Love;* sets of "miniatures" for piano; piano *Fantasy* (a sort of free sonata); Piano Concerto; four symphonies.

See further details on page 236.

Karlheinz Stockhausen

1928–   Present-day German composer

The end of World War II and the end of the Nazi regime meant that for the first time in a dozen years, German musicians mixed with foreigners and were exposed to the most modern trends in music, particularly the serialism of Schoenberg and Webern. Stockhausen was a student at this time—a time of amazing experiments and radical new ideas about music. Furthermore, the war had brought electronic technology to a stage where it could become a powerful tool for composers.

In 1947, Stockhausen entered Cologne's State Academy of Music to continue his study of the piano. After receiving his teacher's license *summa cum laude,* he played piano in the bars of Cologne, was an accompanist to a traveling magician, served as director of an amateur operetta theater, and held a number of nonmusical odd jobs.

Stockhausen soon assumed leadership among the brilliant international group of composers who gathered in the 1950s at the avant-garde summer music school at Darmstadt, West Germany. Director of the electronic music studio at the Cologne Radio, he has also worked with chance music, "happenings," improvisation, and ideas derived from oriental music and philosophy. Many of his recent compositions—he has composed well over fifty works to date—have emerged from sessions of a special improvisational group with which he plays, using both conventional and electronic instruments. Like many present-day composers and artists, Stockhausen is a great theorizer, explainer, and propagandist, as well as a creator; he is a very impressive writer and lecturer about music.

Chief works: *Song of the Children* for five-track stereo tape; *Moments* for soprano, four choirs, and four orchestras; *Hymns* for electronically generated sounds and *musique concrète*; *Mantra* for two pianos.

See further details on page 370.

Richard Strauss

1864–1949   German late romantic composer

Richard Strauss's father (not related to the famous Viennese Strauss family of waltz composers) was a well-known Munich orchestra player, his mother a wealthy beer heiress. Their son was a prodigy; at seventeen he saw his Symphony in D minor performed; and at the age of twenty-one he assumed the first of the many important conducting positions he was to hold in various German and Austrian towns. His earliest music was influenced by the conservative Brahms, but he turned to the style of Liszt and Wagner for his symphonic poems and operas. These were regarded as the most advanced and controversial music of the time in the years around 1900. Later he found in the poet Hugo von Hoffmannsthal a librettist with whom he produced very sophisticated operas for twenty-five years. But Strauss found it hard to move with the times after the trauma of World War I, and his later music has not gained wide recognition.

At thirty, he married the opera singer Pauline de Ahne; a scene (literally) from their continuously tempestuous private life forms the subject of his opera *Intermezzo* (Strauss had a predilection for such "autobiographical" compositions).

During most of World War II, Strauss remained in Switzerland. At first willing to accept the Nazis, he finally broke with them when they attempted to prevent him from collaborating on an opera with a Jewish author. Shortly after the worldwide observance of his eighty-fifth birthday, Strauss died at his beautiful villa in Garmisch in the Bavarian Alps.

Chief works: Symphonic poems *Don Juan, Till Eulenspiegel's Merry Pranks, Death and Transfiguration*; operas *Salome, Electra* (studies in perverse psychology), and the half-Mozartian, half-Wagnerian comedy *Der Rosenkavalier* ("The Cavalier of the Rose").

Igor Stravinsky

1882–1971   Russian international twentieth-century composer

The son of an important opera singer, Stravinsky studied law and did not turn seriously to music until he was nineteen. Then he studied with the great nationalist composer Rimsky-Korsakov, whose example served Stravinsky well in the famous (and still outstandingly popular) ballet scores he wrote for the *Ballets Russes*, a Russian ballet company centered in Paris. These brilliant, always sensational works were followed by others in a dazzling variety of styles, forms, and genres. One of the first composers, along with Debussy, to be interested in jazz, Stravinsky wrote *Piano Ragtime* in 1917 and *Ebony Concerto* for Woody Herman's swing band in 1946.

After the Russian Revolution in 1917, Stravinsky made his home in Paris, taking part in the celebrity-studded cultural life there. In 1939 he moved to Los Angeles. The end of World War II marked the start of a new, more classical, abstract, and formal style in Stravinsky's music. During the last twenty years of his life, Stravinsky had as his protégé the young American conductor and critic Robert Craft, who helped to manage his affairs, conducted and promoted his music, and introduced him to the music of Schoenberg and Webern. For a quarter of a century people had regarded Stravinsky (and he regarded himself) as the leading neoclassical composer in the French orbit, at the opposite pole from Schoenberg and the Viennese serialists. So he created yet another sensation when, in his seventies, he produced a remarkable final series of compositions employing serial technique.

Chief works: Ballet scores *Petroushka, The Rite of Spring, The Wedding, Orpheus, Agon*; the opera-oratorio *Oedipus the King*; *The Rake's Progress*, an opera in English; *Symphony of Psalms* for orchestra and chorus; *The Soldier's Tale*, an unusual chamber-music piece with narrator.

See further details on page 330 and picture essay on page 334.

Peter Ilyich Tchaikovsky

1840–1893   Russian late romantic composer

In nineteenth-century Russia, a serious musical education and a musical career were not accorded the social approval they received in Germany, France, or Italy. Many of the famous Russian composers began in other careers and only turned to music in their mature years, when driven by inner necessity. Once Tchaikovsky got started, after abandoning the civil service, he composed prolifically—six symphonies, eleven operas, symphonic poems, chamber music, songs, and some of the most famous of all ballet scores: *Swan Lake, Sleeping Beauty*, and *The Nutcracker*. Though his pieces may sometimes sound "Russian" to us, he was not a devoted nationalist like Moussorgsky and other composers of the time.

Tchaikovsky was a depressive personality who more than once attempted suicide. The son of a mine inspector, he was an extremely delicate and hypersensitive child, completely dependent on his mother for emotional support. He developed into a highly neurotic, but very charming, adult whose central fear was that his dominant homosexual bent would be discovered and exposed. In an attempt to raise himself above suspicion through marriage, he selected an unstable young musician who had attached herself to him. The marriage was a fiasco; in a matter of weeks, Tchaikovsky fled and never saw the woman again, though she pursued him, trying to extort money.

For years Tchaikovsky was subsidized by a remarkable woman, Madame von Meck, whom, by mutual agreement, he never met. Nevertheless, they daily wrote intimate letters over the thirteen years of their friendship, which was terminated, without explanation, by Madame von Meck. Tchaikovsky was crushed by her rejection. Three years later he died of cholera after carelessly (or fatalistically, or purposely?) drinking unboiled water during an epidemic.

His music has been criticized as weak in form and sentimental in expression, but this has never affected its enormous popularity with concert audiences.

Chief works: Fourth, Fifth, and Sixth (*Pathétique*) Symphonies; operas *The Queen of Spades* and *Eugene Onegin*, based on plays by the Russian romantic poet Alexander Pushkin.

Giuseppe Verdi

1813–1901   Italian romantic composer

The son of a storekeeper in a tiny village in northern Italy, Verdi had a spotty education. He played church organ and conducted the band of the neighboring little town. In those days, the center of musical life in Italy was the famous opera house La Scala (The Ladder) in Milan. After several discouraging years in that city, Verdi scored a huge success with his biblical opera *Nabucco* (*Nebuchadnezzar*) when he was twenty-nine years old. Thereafter, he composed successful operas for various opera houses in Italy and in Paris, London, St. Petersburg (now Leningrad), and even Cairo.

Many of the operas had patriotic themes; Verdi was an ardent supporter of the *Risorgimento*, or Italian liberation movement, and was made an honorary deputy in the first Italian parliament. A dour character and a tough businessman, Verdi drove hard bargains with opera impresarios, bullied his librettists, and insisted on

supervising the production of his new operas. When he had accumulated enough money, he retired to a fine country estate near his birthplace and spent his later years raising livestock and hunting.

His second marriage to the opera singer Giuseppina Strepponi, the star of *Nabucco*, who had befriended him in his youth—and was his mistress for many years—was a devoted one. When his wife died in 1897, Verdi was bereft. Disconsolate and declining, he moved into Milan's Grand Hotel; in 1901, at the age of eighty-eight, he suffered a fatal cerebral hemorrhage. By now a national institution, Verdi was mourned throughout Italy. Schools closed. Eulogies were delivered in a special session of the senate in Rome. Nearly 300,000 people saw the old man to his grave. His operas remain the most popular of all in the international repertory.

Chief works: Twenty-four operas, including *Rigoletto, La Traviata, Aïda,* and two great Shakespeare operas composed after his retirement, *Otello* and *Falstaff*; a Requiem Mass.

See further details on page 265 and picture essay on page 271.

Richard Wagner

1813–1883   German romantic composer

From his schooldays on, Wagner was a decided intellectual. His early interests, literature and music—Shakespeare and Beethoven were his idols—later expanded to include philosophy, politics, mythology, and religion. As a young man he worked as an opera conductor and started to develop his revolutionary ideal of a new kind of opera. This he finally formulated after being exiled from Germany (and from a job) as a result of his part in the revolution of 1848–1849. He wrote endless and often venomous articles and books expounding his ideas—ideas that were better known than his operas, for these were extremely difficult to stage.

Wagner's fortunes changed when he gained the support of the young, unstable, and finally mad King Ludwig II of Bavaria. Ludwig had Wagner's mature operas produced, at last. Wagner then promoted the building of a special opera house in Bayreuth, Germany, solely for his music dramas—lengthy, grandiose, slow-moving works based on myths, and characterized by high-flown poetry of his own, a powerful orchestral style, and the use of leitmotivs. To this day the opera house in Bayreuth is used only for the production of Wagner's operas.

A hypnotic personality, Wagner was able to spirit money out of many pockets and command the loyalty and affection of many distinguished men and women. He married his second wife Cosima (the daughter of the composer Franz Liszt) after breaking up her marriage to his friend, the conductor Hans von Bülow.

Half con man and half visionary, bad poet and very good musician, Wagner created a storm of controversy in his lifetime which has not entirely died down to this day. His ideas were very influential not only in music but also in other arts. Ultimately he was probably the most impressive and important of the romantic composers.

Chief works: Early operas, *Tannhäuser* and *Lohengrin*; mature operas, *Tristan and Isolde, The Mastersingers of Nuremberg, Parsifal*, and *The Nibelung's Ring*, which is a four-opera cycle consisting of *The Rhine Gold, The Valkyrie, Siegfried*, and *The Twilight of the Gods*.

See text on pages 254 and 255 and picture essays on pages 253 and 264.

Glossary of Musical Terms

The *italicized words* refer to other definitions in the glossary, which you can look up, if necessary. Page numbers refer to fuller explanations of important terms given in the text.

ABSOLUTE MUSIC: Music without extramusical associations; as opposed to *program music.*

A CAPELLA: Choral music for voices alone, without instruments

ACCELERANDO: Getting faster

ACCENT: The stressing of a note—for example, by playing it somewhat louder than the surrounding notes (*page 5*)

ACCIDENTALS: In musical notation, signs indicating that a note is to be played *sharp, flat,* or *natural*

ACCOMPANIED RECITATIVE: A type of recitative with orchestral accompaniment in addition to (sometimes in place of) the continuo; as opposed to *secco recitative* (*page 124*)

ACOUSTICS: The science of sound; also, the technology of making concert halls disseminate sound well

ADAGIO: Slow tempo

AFFETTUOSO: Gentle

AIR, AYRE: A simple song

ALEATORY MUSIC: Same as *chance music*

ALLEGRO, ALLEGRETTO: Fast; moderately fast

ALLEMANDE: A baroque dance in moderately slow duple meter (*page 118*)

ALTO, CONTRALTO: The low female voice

ANDANTE: A fairly slow tempo, but not too slow

ANDANTINO: A little faster than *andante*

ANIMATO: Animated

ANTHEM: A relatively short choral composition for the Anglican or Protestant Churches

ANTIPHONY, ANTIPHONAL: A musical style in which two or more choirs and/or instrumental groups alternate with one another

ARIA: A vocal number for solo singer and orchestra, generally in an opera, cantata, or oratorio (*page 125*)

ARIOSO: A singing style between recitative and aria

ARPEGGIO: A chord with the notes played one after another in rapid succession, instead of simultaneously (from *arpa,* Italian for harp)

ART SONG: A song consciously intended as a work of art; as opposed to a folksong or popular song

ASSAI: Very (as in *allegro assai,* etc.)

A TEMPO: At the original tempo

ATONALITY: The absence of any feeling of *tonality* (*page 304*)

AUGMENTATION: The process of increasing the time values of all the notes in a theme at one of its later appearances, thus slowing it down. The most common form of augmentation doubles the time value of all the notes

AVANT GARDE: In the most advanced style

BAGATELLE: "Trifle"; a name for a "miniature" piano piece, used by Beethoven and others

BALLAD: A song or song-poem that tells a story, in several stanzas (*page 292*)

BALLADE: A name for a "miniature" piano piece of a dramatic nature. Ballades sometimes suggest a *program* (*page 231*)

BALLETT: A type of Renaissance dance song, also called *fa-la* (*page 72*)

BAR, BARLINE: Same as *measure, measure line*

BARITONE: A type of adult male voice similar to the *bass,* but a little higher

BASS: (NB—not spelled "BASE") (1) The low adult male voice; (2) the lowest vocal or instrumental line in a piece of music

BASSO CONTINUO: See *continuo*

BASSO OSTINATO: An *ostinato* in the bass

BEAT: The regular pulse underlying most music; the lowest unit of *meter* (*page 6*)

BEBOP: A modern jazz style of the 1940s, associated with Charlie ("Bird") Parker (*page 352*)

BEL CANTO: A style of singing that brings out the sensuous beauty of the voice

BINARY FORM: A musical form having two different sections: AB form

BLUE NOTE: A note deliberately sung or played slightly off-pitch, as in the *blues*

BLUES: A type of black folk music, used in jazz, rhythm-&-blues, and other forms of American popular music (*page 355*)

BOURRÉE: A baroque dance in fast duple meter (*page 118*)

BRIDGE: (1) In sonata form, the section of music which comes between the first theme and the second group, and which makes the modulation; also called "transition" (*page 157*); (2) a separable component of the violin, cello, etc., which holds the strings up from the main body of the instrument (*page 364*)

CADENCE: The notes or chords (or the whole short passage) ending a section of music with a feeling of conclusiveness. The term "cadence" can be applied to phrases, sections of works, or complete works or movements (*page 30*)

CADENCE THEME: In sonata form, the final conclusive theme in the exposition; also called "closing theme"

CADENZA: An improvised passage for the soloist in a concerto, or sometimes in other works. Concerto cadenzas usually come near the end of the first movement (*page 188*)

CANTATA: A composition in several movements for solo voice(s), instruments, and perhaps also chorus. Depending on the text, cantatas are categorized as *secular* or *church cantatas* (*page 132*)

CANTUS FIRMUS: A melody used as a basis for certain polyphonic pieces

CANZONA: An instrumental genre of the Renaissance (*page 78*)

CHACONNE: Similar to *passacaglia*

CHAMBER MUSIC: Music played by small groups, such as a string quartet or a piano trio (*page 102*)

CHANCE MUSIC: A type of contemporary music in which certain elements, such as the order of the notes or their pitches, are not specified by the composer but are left to chance (*page 367*)

CHANSON: French for song; a genre of medieval secular vocal music (*page 56*)

CHANT: A way of reciting words to music, generally in *monophony* and generally for liturgical purposes, as in *Gregorian chant*

CHOIR: (1) A group of singers singing together, with more than one person

singing each voice part; (2) a section of the orchestra comprising instruments of a certain type, such as the *string, woodwind,* or *brass choir*

CHORALE: German for hymn; also used for a four-part *harmonization* of a German hymn, such as Bach composed in his Passions and many church cantatas (*page 133*)

CHORALE PRELUDE: An organ composition based on a chorale (hymn) tune (*page 136*)

CHORD: A grouping of pitches played and heard simultaneously (*page 36*)

CHORUS: (1) Same as *choir*; (2) the main section of a modern popular song, as opposed to the *verse* (*page 354*)

CHROMATICISM: A musical style employing all or many of the twelve notes of the *chromatic scale* much of the time (*page 305*)

CHROMATIC SCALE: The set of twelve pitches represented by all the white and black notes on the piano, within one octave (*page 24*)

CHURCH CANTATA: A *cantata* with religious words, often tied in directly to a particular church service, such as the Easter or Christmas service

CLEF: In musical notation, a sign at the beginning of the *staff* indicating the pitches of the lines and spaces. The main clefs are the *treble clef* (𝄞) and the *bass clef* (𝄢) (*page 27*)

CLOSING THEME: Same as *cadence theme*

CODA: The concluding section of a piece or a movement, after the main elements of the form have been presented. Codas are common in sonata form (*page 158*)

COLORATURA: An ornate style of singing, with many notes for each syllable of the text (*page 125*)

COMPOUND METER: A meter in which the main beats are subdivided into three, such as 6/8 (ONE two three *four* five six), 6/4, 9/8, and 12/8; as opposed to *simple meter* (*page 9*)

CON BRIO: Brilliantly, with spirit

CONCERTINO: The solo group in a baroque *concerto grosso*

CONCERTO, SOLO CONCERTO: A large composition for orchestra and solo instrument or small solo group (*page 188*)

CONCERTO GROSSO: The main baroque type of concerto, for a group of solo

instruments and a small orchestra (*page 100*)

CONCERT OVERTURE: An early nineteenth-century term for a piece resembling an opera overture—but without any following opera. Often concert overtures amount to short pieces of orchestral program music

CON MOTO: Moving, with motion

CONSONANCE: Intervals or chords that sound relatively stable and free of tension; as opposed to *dissonance* (*page 37*)

CONTINUO (BASSO CONTINUO): (1) A set of chords continuously underlying the melody in a piece of baroque music; (2) the instrument(s) playing the continuo, usually cello plus harpsichord or organ (*page 87*)

CONTRALTO, ALTO: The low female voice

COUNTERPOINT, CONTRAPUNTAL: (1) Polyphony; strictly speaking, the technique of writing polyphonic music; (2) the term "a counterpoint" is used for a melodic line that forms polyphony when played along with other lines; (3) "in counterpoint" means "forming polyphony" (*page 34*)

COUNTERSUBJECT: In a fugue, a subsidiary melodic line that appears regularly in counterpoint with the *subject* (*page 96*)

COURANTE: A baroque dance in moderately slow triple meter (*page 118*)

CRESCENDO: Getting louder

CYCLIC FORM: A large form, such as a symphony, in which certain themes come back in various different movements

DA CAPO: Literally, "from the beginning"; a direction to the performer to repeat music from the beginning of the piece at a later point

DA CAPO ARIA: An aria in ABA form, i.e., one in which the A section is sung *da capo* at the end (*page 125*)

DECIBEL: The scientific unit of loudness

DECLAMATION: The way words are set to music, in terms of rhythm, accent, etc. (*page 59*)

DESIGN: A term sometimes used to mean the form or general plan of a piece of music

DEVELOPMENT: (1) The process of expanding themes and motives into larger sections of music; (2) the second section of a sonata-form movement, which features the development process (*page 157*)

DIATONIC SCALE: The set of seven pitches represented by the white notes of the piano, within one octave (*page 23*)

DIES IRAE: "Day of wrath": a section of the *Requiem Mass*

DIMINUENDO: Getting softer

DIMINUTION: The process of reducing the time values of all the notes in a theme at one of its later appearances, thus speeding it up. The most common kind of diminution halves the time values of all the notes.

DISCORD: Sometimes used as a term for *dissonance*

DISSONANCE: Intervals or chords that sound relatively tense and unstable; in opposition to *consonance* (*page 37*)

DOMINANT: The fifth note of a diatonic scale, or the chord built on this note

DOTTED NOTE: In musical notation, a note followed by a dot has its normal duration increased by a half (*page 9*)

DOUBLE-EXPOSITION FORM: A type of *sonata form* developed for use in concertos

DOUBLE VARIATION: A *variation* in which the repeated sections of the theme are varied in different ways (*pages 189, 203*)

DOWNBEAT: A strong or accented *beat*

DUET, DUO: A composition for two singers or instrumentalists

DUPLE METER: A meter consisting of one accented beat alternating with one unaccented beat: ONE two ONE two

DYNAMICS: The volume of sound, the loudness or softness of a musical passage (*page 11*)

ELECTRONIC MUSIC: Music in which some or all of the sounds are produced by electronic generators or other apparatus

ENSEMBLE: A musical number in an opera, cantata, or oratorio that is sung by two or more people (*page 163*)

EPISODE: In a fugue, a passage that does not contain any entries of the fugue subject (*page 96*)

ESPRESSIVO: Expressively

ÉTUDE: A piece of music designed partly to aid technical study of a particular instrument (*page 224*)

EXPOSITION: The first section of a sonata-form movement (*page 157*)

EXPRESSIONISM: An early twentieth-century movement in art, music, and literature in Germany and Austria (*page 316*)

FA-LA: A type of Renaissance dance song, also called *ballett* (*page 72*)

FANTASIA: (Usually) a piece of music in a free, improvisatory form

FERMATA: A hold of indefinite length on a note; the sign for such a hold in musical notation

FIGURED BASS: A system of notating the *continuo* chords in baroque music, by means of figures; sometimes also used to mean continuo

FINALE: The last movement of a work; or the *ensemble* that concludes an act of an *opera buffa* or other opera (*page 166*)

FLAT: In musical notation, a sign indicating that the note to which it is attached is to be played a semitone lower (♭). A double flat (♭♭) is sometimes used to indicate that a note is played two semitones lower (*page 27*)

FORM: The "shape" of a piece of music (*page 40*)

FORTE, FORTISSIMO: Loud; very loud (*f, ff*)

FRENCH OVERTURE: A baroque type of overture to an opera, oratorio, or suite (*page 127*)

FREQUENCY: In acoustics, the rate of vibration in a string, a column of air, or other sound-producing body

FUGATO: A relatively short fugal passage within a piece of music

FUGUE: A composition written systematically in imitative polyphony, usually with a single main theme, the *fugue subject* (*page 95*)

GENERATOR: An electronic apparatus that produces sounds for electronic music; also called *synthesizer*

GENRE: A general category of music determined partly by the number and kind of instruments or voices involved, and partly by its form, style, or purpose. "Opera," "symphonic poem," "mass," and "sonata" are all terms for genres (*page 43*)

GIGUE, JIG: A baroque dance in a lively compound meter; often fugal in style (*page 118*)

GLISSANDO: Sliding from one note to another on an instrument such as a trombone or violin

GRAVE: Slow; the characteristic tempo of the first section of a *French overture*

GREGORIAN CHANT: The type of *chant* used in the early Roman Catholic Church (*page 54*)

GROUND BASS: An *ostinato* in the bass

HALFTONE: Same as *semitone*

HARMONIZE: To provide each note of a melody with a chord (*page 36*)

HARMONY, HARMONIC: Having to do with chords, or the "vertical" aspect of musical texture (*page 36*). The term "harmonic" is sometimes used to mean *homophonic*

HOMOPHONY, HOMOPHONIC: A musical texture that involves only one melody of real interest, combined with chords or other subsidiary sounds (*page 36*)

HYMN: A simple religious song in several stanzas, for congregational singing in church

IDÉE FIXE: The term used by Berlioz for a recurring theme used in all the movements of one of his program symphonies (*page 240*)

IMITATION, IMITATIVE COUNTERPOINT: A polyphonic musical texture in which the various melodic lines use approximately the same themes; as opposed to *non-imitative counterpoint* (*page 34*). See also *point of imitation*

IMPRESSIONISM: A French artistic movement of the late nineteenth and early twentieth centuries (*page 310*)

IMPROMPTU: A name for a "miniature" piano piece, of an improvisatory nature

INTERVAL: The distance between two pitches, measured by the number of diatonic scale notes between them (*page 24*)

INTRODUCTION: An introductory passage: in a symphony, etc., the "slow introduction" before the exposition; in an opera, the first number after the overture

INVERSION: Reading or playing a melody or a twelve-tone series upside down, i.e., playing all its upward intervals downward and vice versa (*page 102*)

JAZZ: The most important type of twentieth-century popular music (*page 353*)

K. NUMBERS: The numbers assigned to works by Mozart in the Koechel

Catalogue; used instead of opus numbers to catalogue Mozart's works

KEY: (1) A tonality, named after the main note in the tonality; (2) a lever pressed down with the finger to produce the sound on the piano, organ, etc.

KEY SIGNATURE: Sharps or flats placed at the beginning of the staffs to indicate the key, or tonality

LARGO, LARGHETTO: Very slow; somewhat less slow than largo

LEDGER LINES: Short lines above or below the staff to accommodate pitches that go higher or lower

LEGATO: Playing in a smooth, connected manner; as opposed to *staccato*

LEITMOTIV: "Leading motive" in Wagner's operas (*page 255*)

LENTO: Very slow

LIBRETTO: The complete book of words for an opera, oratorio, cantata, etc.

LIED: German for song; often used as a term for *art song* (*page 211*)

LINE: Used as a term to mean a melody, or melodic line

LUTE SONG, LUTE AIR: A solo song of the Renaissance for voice and lute accompaniment (*page 72*)

MADRIGAL: The main secular vocal form of the Renaissance (*page 70*)

MAGNIFICAT: The canticle of the Virgin Mary, often set to music for church use

MAJOR: A type of diatonic scale, characterized by the interval between the first and third notes containing four semitones (as opposed to *minor*); also applied to one type (mode) of tonality

MANUAL: A keyboard of an organ or harpsichord, usually one of two or more on a single instrument

MASS: The main Roman Catholic service; or the music written for it. The musical Mass consists of five large sections: *Kyrie, Gloria, Credo, Sanctus,* and *Agnus Dei* (*page 57*)

MAZURKA: A Polish dance in lively triple meter (*page 231*)

MEASURE (BAR): In music, the unit of *meter,* above the level of the individual *beats.* Compositions are formed of equal time divisions, called measures, made up of several beats (*page 9*)

MEASURE LINE (BARLINE): In musical notation, a vertical line through the staff(s) to mark the measures (*page 9*)

MELODY: The aspect of music having to do with the succession of pitches; also applied ("a melody") to any particular succession of pitches (*page 28*)

METER: A background of stressed and unstressed beats in a simple, regular, repeating pattern (*page 6*)

METRONOME: The mechanical or electrical device that ticks out beats at all practicable tempos

METRONOME MARK: A notation of tempo, indicating the number of notes per minute as ticked out by a metronome

MEZZO: Medium (as in *mezzo forte* or *mezzo piano* — **mf, mp**)

MEZZO-SOPRANO: "Halfway to soprano": a type of female voice between *contralto* and *soprano*

"MINIATURE": A term for a short, evocative composition for piano or for piano and voice, composed in the Romantic period (*page 225*)

MINOR: A type of diatonic scale, characterized by the interval between the first and third notes containing three semitones (as opposed to *major*); also applied to one type (mode) of tonality

MINSTREL SHOW: A type of variety show popular in nineteenth-century America, performed in blackface (*page 291*)

MINUET: A popular seventeenth- and eighteenth-century dance in moderate triple meter (*page 118*); also a movement in a sonata, symphony, etc., based on this dance (*page 173*)

MODAL HARMONY: The characteristically indefinite harmonic style of sixteenth-century music (*page 58*)

MODE: In music since the Renaissance, one of the two types of tonality: major mode or minor mode; also, in earlier times, one of several species of the diatonic scale

MODERATO: Moderate tempo

MODULATION: Changing tonality within a piece (*page 41*)

MONOPHONY: A musical texture involving a single melodic line and nothing else, as in Gregorian chant; as opposed to *polyphony*

MOTET: A sacred vocal composition (*page 67*)

MOTIVE, MOTIF: A short fragment of melody or rhythm used in constructing a long section of music (*page 31*)

MOVEMENT: A self-contained section of a larger piece, such as a symphony or concerto grosso (*page 100*)

MUSIC-DRAMA: Wagner's name for his distinctive type of opera (*page 255*)

MUSICOLOGY: The scholarly study of music history and literature

MUSIQUE CONCRÈTE: Music composed with natural sounds recorded electronically (*page 365*)

MUTE: A device put on or in an instrument to muffle the tone

NATIONALISM: A nineteenth-century movement promoting music built on national folksongs and dances, or associated with national subjects (*page 272*)

NATURAL: In musical notation, a sign indicating that a sharp or flat previously attached to a note is to be removed (♮) (*page 27*)

NEOCLASSICISM: A twentieth-century movement involving a return to the style and form of older music, particularly eighteenth-century music (*page 337*)

NOCTURNE: "Night piece": title for romantic "miniature" compositions for piano, etc.

NON-IMITATIVE COUNTERPOINT: A polyphonic musical texture in which the melodic lines are essentially different from one another; as opposed to *imitation*

NON TROPPO: Not too much (as in *allegro non troppo*)

NOTE: (1) A sound of a certain definite pitch and duration; (2) the written sign for such a sound in musical notation; (3) a key pressed with the finger on a piano or organ

OCTAVE: A pair of "duplicating" notes, eight notes apart on the diatonic scale (*page 22*)

OPERA, OPERETTA: A play set to music; an operetta is a light opera (*pages 122, 293*)

OPERA BUFFA: Italian comic opera (*page 163*)

OPERA SERIA: A term for the serious, heroic opera of the baroque period

OPUS: "Work"; opus numbers provide a means of cataloguing a composer's compositions (*see note on page 105*)

ORATORIO: Long semi-dramatic piece on a religious subject for soloists, chorus, and orchestra (*page 122*)

ORCHESTRATION: The technique of writing for various instruments to produce an effective total orchestral sound

ORGANUM: The earliest genre of medieval polyphonic music (*page 55*)

OSTINATO: A motive, phrase, or theme repeated over and over again at the same pitch level (*page 95*)

OVERTONE: In acoustics, a secondary vibration in a sound-producing body, which contributes to the tone color; also called "partial"

OVERTURE: An orchestral piece at the start of an opera, oratorio, etc. (but see *concert overture*) (*page 127*)

PART: Used as a term for (1) a section of a piece; (2) one of the *voices* in contrapuntal music; (3) the written music for a single player in an orchestra, band, etc. (as opposed to the *score*)

PARTIAL: Same as *overtone*

PASSACAGLIA: A set of variations on a short theme in the bass (*page 93*)

PASSION: A long, oratorio-like composition telling the story of Jesus's last days, according to one of the New Testament Gospels (*page 137*)

PEDAL BOARD: The keyboard of an organ that is played with the feet

PEDAL POINT: In contrapuntal writing, a bass note held for a long time

PHRASE: A section of a melody or a tune (*page 29*)

PIANO, PIANISSIMO: Soft; very soft (**p, pp**)

PIANO TRIO: An instrumental group consisting of violin, cello, and piano; or a piece composed for this group; or the three players themselves

PITCH: The quality of "highness" or "lowness" of sound; also applied ("a pitch") to any particular pitch level, such as middle C (*page 22*)

PIÙ: More (as in *più forte*)

PIZZICATO: Playing a string instrument that is normally bowed by plucking the strings with the finger

PLAINSONG: Liturgical *chant*, such as Gregorian chant

POCO: Somewhat (as in *poco adagio* or *poco forte*, somewhat slow, somewhat loud)

POINT OF IMITATION: A short passage of imitative polyphony based on a single theme, or on several used together (*page 65*)

POLONAISE: A Polish dance

POLYPHONY, POLYPHONIC: Musical texture in which two or more melodic lines are played or sung simultaneously; as opposed to *homophony* or *monophony* (*page 34*)

PRELUDE: An introductory piece, leading to another, such as a fugue or an opera (however, Chopin's Preludes were not intended to lead to anything else)

PREMIÈRE: The first performance ever of a piece of music, opera, etc.

PRESTO, PRESTISSIMO: Very fast; very fast indeed

PROGRAM MUSIC: A piece of instrumental music associated with a story or other extra-musical idea (*page 226*)

PROGRAM SYMPHONY: A symphony with a program, as written by Berlioz (*page 240*)

QUARTER TONE: Half of a *semitone*. Quarter tones are occasionally used in twentieth-century music

QUARTET: A piece for four singers or players; often used to mean *string quartet*

QUINTET: A piece for five singers or players

RAGTIME: A genre of American popular music around 1900, usually for piano, which led to *jazz* (*page 354*)

RANGE: Used in music to mean "pitch range," i.e., the total span from the lowest to the highest pitch in a piece, a part, or a passage

RECAPITULATION: The third section of a sonata-form movement (*page 158*)

RECITATIVE: A half-singing, half-reciting style of presenting words in an opera, cantata, oratorio, etc., following speech accents and speech rhythms closely (*page 123*)

REED: In certain wind instruments, a small vibrating element made of cane or metal

REQUIEM MASS, REQUIEM: The special *Mass* celebrated when someone dies

RESOLVE: To proceed from *dissonant* harmony to *consonance*

REST: A momentary silence in music; in musical notation, a sign indicating momentary silence

RETRANSITION: In sonata form, the passage leading from the end of the development section into the beginning of the recapitulation

RETROGRADE: Reading or playing a melody or twelve-tone series backward

RETROGRADE INVERSION: Reading or playing a melody or twelve-tone series backward and upside down

RHYTHM: The aspect of music having to do with the duration of the notes in time; also applied ("a rhythm") to any particular durational pattern (*page 5*)

RHYTHM-&-BLUES: A genre of black American popular music of the 1950s (*page 388*)

RHYTHMIC SERIES, RHYTHMIC SERIALIZATION: A fixed pattern of different note lengths held to throughout a piece; the technique of composing with such a series (*page 367*)

RHYTHM SECTION: The section of a jazz band concerned mainly with bringing out the meter, or the beat: the drums, piano, string bass, guitar, etc.

RICERCAR: An instrumental genre of the Renaissance (*page 78*)

RITARDANDO: Slowing down the tempo

RITENUTO: Held back in tempo

RITORNELLO: The orchestral material at the beginning of a concerto grosso, etc., which always returns later in the piece (*page 100*)

RITORNELLO FORM: A baroque musical form based on recurrences of a ritornello (*page 100*)

RONDO: A musical form consisting of one main theme or tune alternating with other themes or sections (ABACA, ABACABA, etc.) (*page 175*)

ROW: Same as *series*

RUBATO: "Robbed" time; the free treatment of meter in performance (*page 225*)

SARABANDE: A baroque dance in slow triple meter, featuring an accent on the second beat (*page 118*)

SCALE: A selection of ordered pitches which provides the pitch material for music

SCHERZO: A form developed by Beethoven from the *minuet* to use for movements in larger compositions; later sometimes used alone, as by Chopin (*page 194*)

SCORE: The full musical notation for a piece involving several or many performers

SECCO RECITATIVE: "Dry" recitative, accompanied only by continuo, i.e., bass instrument and chords on the organ or harpsichord; as opposed to *accompanied recitative* (*page 124*)

SECOND GROUP: In sonata form, the group of themes following the *bridge*

SEMITONE: The *interval* between any two successive notes of the chromatic scale; also called *halftone*

SEQUENCE: In a melody, a series of fragments identical except for their placement at successively higher or lower pitch levels (*page 30*)

SERIALISM, SERIAL: The technique of composing with a *series*, generally a twelve-tone series (but see also *rhythmic serialism*) (*page 324*)

SERIES: A fixed arrangement of pitches (or rhythms) held to throughout a serial composition (*page 324*)

SFORZATO: An especially strong accent; the mark indicating this in musical notation (**sf** or >)

SHARP: In musical notation, a sign indicating that the note which it precedes is to be played a semitone higher (♯). A double sharp (𝄪) is occasionally used to indicate that a note is played two semitones higher (*page 27*)

SIMPLE METER: A meter in which the main beats are subdivided into two, such as $\frac{4}{4}$ (ONE two *three* four), $\frac{2}{4}$, and $\frac{4}{8}$; as opposed to *compound meter*

SINGSPIEL: German for "singing play": a German comic opera with spoken dialogue interspersed with songs and other music

SLUR: In musical notation, a curved line over a certain number of notes, indicating that they are to be played smoothly, or *legato* (*page 48*)

SONATA: A chamber-music piece in several movements, typically for three main instruments plus continuo in the baroque period, and for only one or two instruments in all periods since then (*pages 112, 200*)

SONATA FORM, SONATA-ALLEGRO FORM: A form developed by the Viennese composers and used in almost all the first movements of their symphonies, sonatas, etc., as well as in some other movements (*page 157*)

SONATA-RONDO FORM: A form combining elements of sonata form and rondo

SONG CYCLE: A group of songs connected by a general idea or story, and sometimes also by musical unifying devices (*page 212*)

SONORITY: A general term for sound quality, either of a momentary chord, or of a whole piece or style

SOPRANO: The high female (or boy's) voice

SPRECHSTIMME: A vocal style developed by Schoenberg, in between singing and speaking (*page 301*)

STACCATO: Played in a detached manner; as opposed to *legato*

STAFF (or STAVE): In musical notation, the group of five horizontal lines on which music is written (*page 27*)

STANZA: In songs or ballads, one of several similar poetic units, which are usually sung to the same tune; also called *verse*

STRETTO: In a fugue, overlapping entrances of the fugue subject in several voices simultaneously (*page 113*)

STRING QUARTET: An instrumental group consisting of two violins, viola, and cello; or a piece composed for this group; or the four players themselves (*page 180*)

STROPHIC SONG: A song in several *stanzas*, with the same music sung for each stanza; as opposed to *through-composed* song (*page 211*)

STRUCTURE: A term often used to mean *form*

STURM UND DRANG ("STORM AND STRESS"): A literary and artistic movement of the late eighteenth century (*page 186*)

STYLE: The combination of qualities that make a period of art, a composer, or an individual work of art distinctive (*page 46*)

SUBDOMINANT: The fourth note of a diatonic scale, or the chord built on this note

SUBITO: Suddenly (as in *subito forte* or *subito piano*, suddenly loud, suddenly soft)

SUBJECT: The term for the principal theme of a *fugue* (*page 95*)

SUITE: A piece consisting of a series of dances (*page 118*)

SWING: A type of big-band jazz of the late 1930s and 1940s (*page 357*)

SYMPHONIC POEM: A piece of orchestral program music in one long movement (*page 248*)

SYMPHONY: A large orchestral piece in several movements (*page 171*)

SYNCOPATION: The accenting of certain beats of the meter that are ordinarily unaccented (*page 353*)

SYNTHESIZER: An electronic apparatus that generates sounds for electronic music; also called *generator*

TEMPO: The speed of music, i.e., the rate at which the accented and unaccented beats of the meter follow one another (*page 10*)

TENOR: The high adult male voice

TERNARY FORM: A three-part musical form in which the last section repeats the first: ABA form

TERRACED DYNAMICS: Two or more fixed, steady dynamic levels alternating during a piece of (baroque) music (*page 85*)

TEXTURE: The blend of the various sounds and melodic lines occurring simultaneously in a piece of music (*page 34*)

THEMATIC TRANSFORMATION: A variation-like procedure applied to short themes in the various sections of Romantic symphonic poems and other works (*page 227*)

THEME: The basic subject matter of a piece of music. A theme can be a phrase, a short motive, a full tune, etc. (*page 31*)

THEME AND VARIATIONS: A form consisting of a tune (the theme) plus a number of *variations* on it (*page 182*)

THOROUGH BASS: Same as *basso continuo* or *continuo*

THROUGH-COMPOSED (*durchkomponiert*) SONG: A song with new music for each stanza of the poem; as opposed to *strophic song* (*page 211*)

TIE: In musical notation, a curved line joining two notes of the same pitch into a continuous sound (*page 48*)

TIMBRE: Another term for *tone color*

TIME SIGNATURE: In musical notation, the numbers on the staffs at the beginning of a piece which indicate the meter (*page 9*)

TOCCATA: A piece in free form designed partly to show off the instrument and the technique of the player (usually an organist or harpsichordist)

TONALITY, TONAL: The feeling of centrality of one note (and its chord) to a passage of music; as opposed to *atonality* (*page 41*)

TONE: A sound of a certain definite pitch and duration; same as *note* (1)

TONE COLOR: The sonorous quality of a particular instrument, voice, or combination of instruments or voices (*page 11*)

TONE POEM: Same as *symphonic poem*

TONIC (noun): In *tonal* music, the central-sounding note

TRANSITION: A passage whose function is to connect one section of a piece with another

TRANSPOSE: To move a whole piece, or a section of a piece, or a twelve-tone series, from one pitch level to another

TRIAD: The "common chord" of three notes, none of them adjacent in terms of the diatonic scale

TRILL: Two adjacent notes played very rapidly in alternation

TRIO: (1) A piece for three instruments or singers; (2) the second or B section of a minuet movement, scherzo, etc. (*page 173*)

TRIO SONATA: A baroque sonata for three main instruments plus the continuo chord instrument (*page 112*)

TRIPLE METER: Meter consisting of one accented beat alternating with two unaccented beats: ONE two three ONE two three

TRIPLET: A group of three notes performed in the time normally taken by two (*page 48*)

TUNE: A simple, easily singable melody that is coherent and complete (*page 29*)

TWELVE-TONE SERIES: An ordering of all twelve notes of the chromatic scale, used in composing serial music

UPBEAT: A weak or unaccented beat leading to a *downbeat*

VARIATION: A section of music which

follows another section (the "theme") closely in certain respects—e.g., in phrase length and harmony—while varying other aspects of it (*page 182*)

VERISMO: A realistic and sensational type of late Romantic Italian opera

VERSE: (1) Another term for *stanza*; (2) the shorter, subsidiary section of a modern popular song, as opposed to the *chorus* (*page 354*)

VIVACE, VIVO: Lively

VOCALISE: Singing without words (*page 311*)

VOICE: (1) Throat sound; (2) a contrapuntal line—whether sung or played by instruments—in a polyphonic piece such as a fugue

WALTZ: A nineteenth-century dance in triple meter (*page 292*)

WHITE NOISE: The sound containing every audible frequency at the same intensity (*page 365*)

WHOLE-TONE SCALE: A scale, used sometimes by Debussy, comprising only six notes to the octave, all at the interval of the whole tone (i.e., two semitones)

WORD PAINTING: Musical illustration of the meaning of a word or a short verbal phrase (*page 59*)

Illustration Acknowledgments

Music Acknowledgments

Index

ELLINGTON, DUKE (1899–1974), 300, 310, 357, 388
Enlightenment, 152
ensemble (in opera), 163, 274
episode (in fugue), 96
étude, 224, 232
exposition, 157
  repetition of, 172
expression
  baroque, 89
  modern, 302
  Renaissance, 58f.
  romantic, 222f.
  Viennese, 151
expressionism, 314, 328, 357

fa-la, 72
figured bass, 87
finale, 166
flag, 9
flat, 26, 48
folk music, folksong, 149, 212, 231, 292, 330, 341f., 347, 378f., 389
form, 40f., 362
  baroque, 86, 102
  modern, 362
  Renaissance, 61, 79
  romantic, 225f.
  Viennese, 150f.
FOSTER, STEPHEN (1826–1864), 292, 348
fragmentation, 193, 201f.
French overture, 119, 127
French Revolution, 146, 190, 201
fret, 16, 21
Freud, Sigmund, 255, 314
fugue, 95, 103, 112f., 128, 140f.
fugue subject, 96
Fuseli, Henry, 186, 239

GABRIELI, GIOVANNI (1555–1612), 76
  canzonas, 79
  Sonata Pian' e Forte, 79
genre, 43
gigue, 118
Gilbert and Sullivan, 166, 293
GLUCK, CHRISTOPH WILLIBALD (1714–1787), 145, 336
Goethe, Johann Wolfgang von, 186, 198, 211
Good King Wenceslas, 6f.
Goya, Francisco, 197
Graham, Martha, 351
Gregorian chant, 7, 28, 33, 54f., 57, 229, 245, 375
ground bass, 84

HANDEL, GEORGE FRIDERIC (1685–1759), 117, 294
  Fireworks Music, 118f.
  Messiah, 49, 117, 127f., 141, 215
  Samson, 122f.

harmony, 36
  baroque, 87
  in Debussy, 310
  modern, 302f.
  Renaissance (modal), 58
  romantic, 222f.
harpsichord, 138f.
HARRIS, ROY (1898–   ), 277
Hartmann, Victor, 272f.
HAYDN, JOSEPH (1732–1809), 149, 156, 170, 215
  The Creation, 170
  London Symphonies, 170
  The Seasons, 170
  Sonata No. 35, 177
  Sonata No. 41, 176, 324
  Symphony No. 88, 171f., 192, 215
homophony, 36f.
  Renaissance, 60
  Viennese, 148
Houdon, Jean-Antoine, 151, 169
hurdy-gurdy, 212, 215

imitation, imitative counterpoint, 34f., 95
  Renaissance, 60
impressionism, 306, 308, 312, 357
Industrial Revolution, 152, 285
"inner form," 44, 150, 225
instruments, 11f.
intermedia, 379, 382
intervals, 24, 326
introduction (sonata form), 171
inversion, 102, 128, 324
IVES, CHARLES (1874–1954), 348f., 357
  Central Park in the Dark, 349
  General William Booth, 301
  The Unanswered Question, 349

jazz, 6, 35, 291, 299f., 350, 352f., 364, 387f.
JOSQUIN DESPREZ (ca. 1440–1521), 61, 67, 84
  "Pange lingua" Mass, 64f.

K. numbers, 105
Kafka, Franz, 315
Kandinsky, Vassily, 323
key, 41
  key signature, 48
Klee, Paul, 323

LASSUS, ORLANDE DE (1532–1594), 61
La Tour, Georges de, 215
ledger lines, 26, 48
legato, 48
leitmotiv, 255, 257, 259f., 266, 318
Lenau, Nikolaus, 250
libretto, 122

Lied, 211
life-style, 46
line (melodic), 28
LISZT, FRANZ (1811–1886), 222, 224, 230, 248, 276
  Les Préludes, 248
Lorca, Federico García, 377f.
lute ayre, lute song, 72

MACHAUT, GUILLAUME DE (ca. 1300–1377), 56
madrigal, 70, 84
MAHLER, GUSTAV (1860–1911), 29, 302, 352
  Symphony No. 4, 286f.
Mass, 33, 56, 57, 64f., 140f.
mazurka, 231f.
measure, measure line, 9, 25, 33, 60, 65
melody, 6, 28f.
  baroque, 86, 101
  modern, 300, 319, 336, 343f., 361
  Renaissance, 60f.
  romantic, 222f.
  Viennese, 149
MENDELSSOHN, FELIX (1809–1847), 230, 247
meter, 6, 9, 354 (See also "duple," "triple," "compound meter")
  Renaissance, 60
Methodism, 129, 152
metronome, metronome mark, 10
Middle Ages, 54f., 228, 253
"miniatures," 225, 230, 276
Minnesingers, 55
minstrel shows, minstrel music, 291, 353
minuet, 118, 150, 166, 173f., 182, 187
modal harmony, 58, 65
modulation, 41f.
  in sonata form, 157f.
Monet, Claude, 312f.
MONTEVERDI, CLAUDIO (1567–1643), 84, 336
MORLEY, THOMAS (1557–ca. 1603), 70
  Hard by a crystal fountain, 70
  It was a lover and his lass, 72
  madrigals and balletts, 70, 72
motet, 64, 67
motive, 31, 157
MOUSSORGSKY, MODEST (1839–1881)
  Pictures at an Exhibition, 272f., 311
movement, 100
MOZART, WOLFGANG AMADEUS (1756–1791), 154, 156, 294, 355
  Clarinet Quintet, 180f.
  Don Giovanni, 150f., 155, 162f., 238f., 250f.
  Piano Concerto in C minor, 188f., 213
  Symphony in G minor, 186f., 213
music drama, 255
musique concrète, 365, 383, 389
mute, 182